Athens

Athens

A Portrait of the City in Its Golden Age

CHRISTIAN MEIER

Translated by Robert and Rita Kimber

JOHN MURRAY
ALBEMARLE STREET   LONDON

ALSO BY CHRISTIAN MEIER
Julius Caesar

First published in Great Britain in 1999
by John Murray (Publishers) Ltd,
50 Albemarle Street, London W1X 4BD

A catalogue record for this book is available from the British Library

ISBN 0-7195-5959 6

Printed and bound in Great Britain by The University Press, Cambridge

Pour comprendre il faut aimer.

Contents

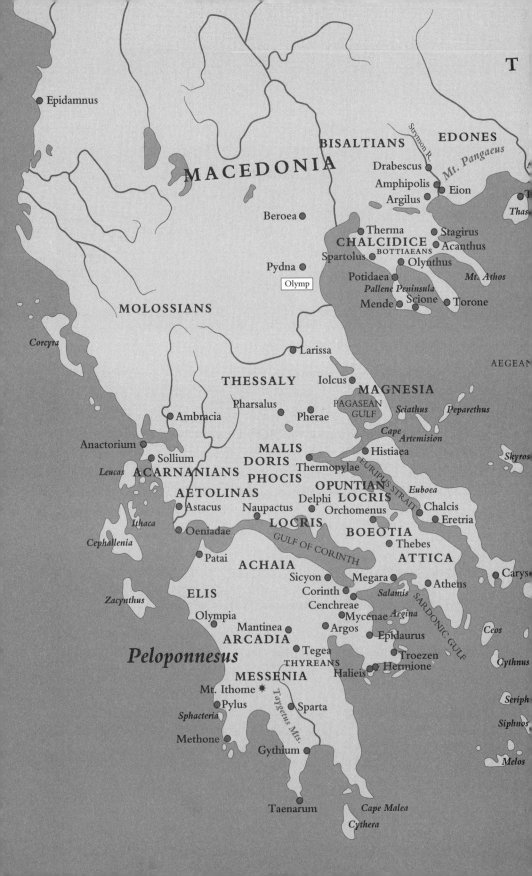

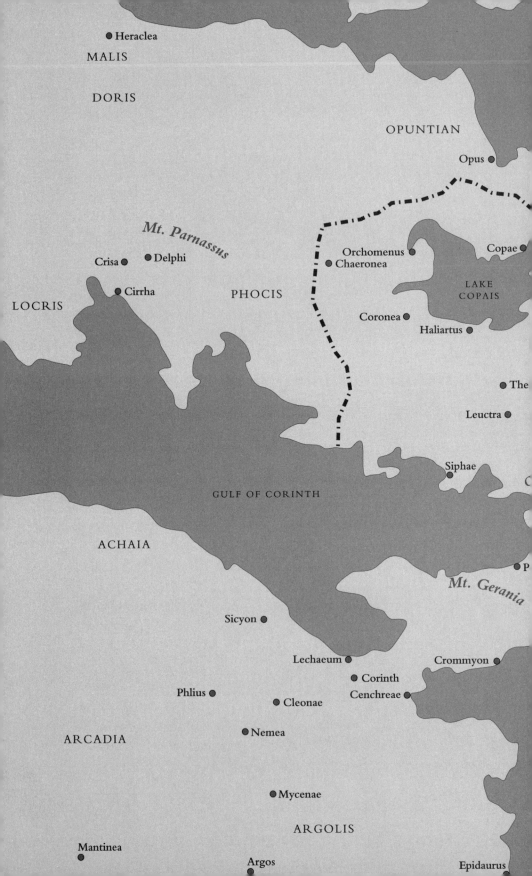

Heraclea

MALIS

DORIS

OPUNTIAN

Opus

Mt. Parnassus

Crisa   Delphi

Orchomenus   Copae

Chaeronea

LAKE
COPAIS

LOCRIS   Cirrha

PHOCIS

Coronea

Haliartus

The

Leuctra

Siphae

GULF OF CORINTH

ACHAIA

Mt. Gerania

P

Sicyon

Lechaeum   Crommyon

Corinth

Phlius   Cenchreae

Cleonae

ARCADIA

Nemea

Mycenae

ARGOLIS

Mantinea

Argos   Epidaurus

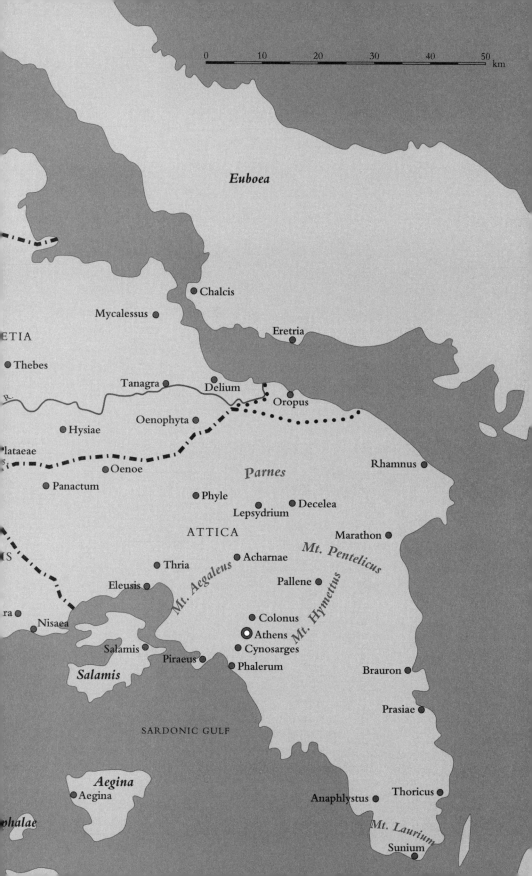

Athens

1

The Needle's Eye at Salamis: A Region Ventures into World Politics

At such times halfhearted souls take the opposite view from that of real generals. They think that by reducing their forces they can repair the damage; they resort to fragmentation, to compromising their real needs, whereas Themistocles convinced the Athenians, when Athens was threatened with ruin, to abandon their city altogether and take to the sea in order to found a new Athens there, on a different element.

—KARL MARX

Wherever in [Machiavelli's] *The Prince* we detect an honest feeling it is one of hatred and contempt for the dilettante, the bungler in political life who does things by halves, acting out half cruelties and half virtues.

—CARL SCHMITT

In the late summer of 480 B.C., most likely toward the end of September, a dramatic, heartrending scene played out on the coast of Attica. Athens' entire population, including men, women, children, and slaves, was fleeing from the approaching Persian army. Only a few people remained, mostly the old, the infirm, and a few priests. The Athenians left behind the graves of their ancestors, their shrines, homes, fields, and plantations, entrusting them to the protection of their goddess, Athena. Horses, donkeys, and dogs may have accompanied the convoy as far as the harbor, but there they, too, presumably had to be left behind. There was hardly enough room on the ships for the 100,000 or more human beings, much less their animals. The Athenians did take along the statues of some gods, at least the wooden figure of Athena, for safekeeping and probably also to invoke the goddess's assistance.

Their warships were built in such a way that there was little room for anyone beside the crew; they were not passenger vessels. At most, they could have carried a few thousand passengers across the Saronic Gulf to the Athenian-controlled island of Salamis. So the people resorted to merchant ships, fishing boats, and any other watercraft they could find. Many of the vessels had probably traveled this route before, for the only destinations besides Salamis were the nearby island of Aegina and the town of Troezen on the Peloponnesian peninsula.

This was not the first time in Greek history that an entire population had left its homeland. The citizens of the Ionian cities of Phocaea and Teos on the coast of Asia Minor had done so two generations earlier, also in flight from the Persians. But their numbers had been much smaller than those evacuating Athens, which by 480 B.C. had by far the largest population of any Greek city. Those earlier evacuees had also been much more cosmopolitan; the Phocaeans had founded numerous colonies and had trade connections as far away as the Pillars of Hercules at the Strait of Gibraltar. The Athenians, on the other hand, had been relatively stationary up to this point, and their outlook was rather narrow. The final point of difference was that the Phocaeans and the Teans had left their homes to found new cities. Greeks had done so before, but in the past it had always been only a fraction of the citizenry that left, and only when the homeland was getting too crowded.

Perhaps the Athenians, too, would have done better to look for new places to settle in the western Mediterranean, for the primary motive behind the Persian expedition was revenge against the Greek states that had so long resisted and challenged Persian imperial control. But the Athenians had decided on a different course of action. They abandoned Attica, but they did it in order to continue their war against the Persians with the help of their Greek allies. They wanted these allies to join them in a risky strategy, calculated with brilliant rationality to confound all expectations. It was, in fact, the only strategy that held out any hope for victory in this desperate situation.

The Athenians were ready to stake everything on a single card. Their flight was a daring act. As it turned out, it was not just the battle of a David against a Goliath but the greatest military campaign of the fifth century B.C., the century of Athens—and one of the boldest, most unlikely, and most momentous campaigns in world history.

The inhabitants of some of Athens' allied cities north of the Peloponnese also took flight. Some hid or barricaded themselves in the mountains; some tried to flee to the Peloponnese. But the difference was not just that between a few thousand and a hundred thousand people were leaving their homes; it was a qualitative difference between retreating from the enemy—even if done to enable the soldiers to go on fighting— and evacuating a city as part of a great, ambitiously conceived scheme, a daring, deliberate trap. In such a situation, there is a marked distinction between a city that thinks only of its own fate and one that considers that of Greece as a whole.

With this act, the Athenians embarked on a path that quickly and inevitably led them away from old traditions and involved them ever more deeply in the affairs that were bound to arise from the transformed relationship between East and West. Naturally, the Athenians always had immediate goals in mind, during those September days in 480 and in the decades that followed. What makes this period remarkable is the ingenuity with which they responded to difficult challenges.

The boats full of refugees headed for the islands and for Troezen were not the only ones to take to the sea in late September. The warships of the newly created Attic navy also set out from Piraeus in order to join Athens' allies in the narrow sound north of Salamis. The ships were triremes, ingeniously designed and highly maneuverable warships of a type that had been in use by the Greeks for some time and whose defining features were their three staggered banks of oarsmen.

While some of the departing Athenians must have mourned the loss of their homeland or been afraid of the uncertain fate that awaited them, others must have conveyed at least the impression of resolution, perhaps even of desperate courage, as the commands rang out loudly and the oars struck the water in coordinated rhythm.

Alongside one of the triremes swam a dog. It belonged to Xanthippus,

Old depiction of a trireme (fragment). Relief Lenormant. Athens, Acropolis Museum.

who was the father of Pericles and a descendent of the noble family of the Alcmaeonids. Xanthippus had been banished, but earlier that year Athens had allowed him and all other political exiles to return home. His dog swam as far as Salamis, where it collapsed, dead of exhaustion.

The vast Persian forces, traveling toward Greece by land and by sea, would soon arrive. Xerxes, the great king *(shahinshah)* of Persia, had spent years preparing for this expedition, which was to bring all of Greece under his control. But he was especially intent on punishing the Athenians. Twenty years earlier, in 500 B.C., they had assisted a rebellion of the Greeks who lived along the coast of Asia Minor and on nearby islands, and who had been Persian subjects for over a generation. A similar punitive campaign against the Athenians, undertaken ten years earlier, in 490, had failed when the Athenians defeated the Persians at Marathon. Now Xerxes determined to put the Greeks in their place and to demonstrate the full superiority of his empire. He took no chances; the campaign was expected to be a total success.

Since Greece was small as well as poor, the Persian king had begun years before to build and fill storehouses north of the Aegean Sea to ensure supplies for his army. To eliminate all risk to his navy, he had spent three years cutting a canal across the isthmus connecting the peninsula of Athos with the mainland. The canal was about 2,200 meters long and 30 meters wide, enough room for two warships to be rowed through abreast. Herodotus, our main source for this period, notes that this ambitious project was superfluous because the ships could have been hauled across the isthmus with much less effort. But that would not have been in the king's style. He wanted to leave a lasting mark on the landscape and sought to make a grand display of his empire's power.

For the same reason, Xerxes had caused two bridges of boats to be constructed across the Hellespont, between Abydos and Sestos. The bridges, one of 360 ships, the other of 340, were tied together by a network of ropes made from white flax and papyrus stems. They are said to have made a fine sight. Logs were tied across the decks of the ships and planks placed over the logs. Railings were added to keep the horses from taking fright. To the Greeks, the bridges seemed an extreme act of hubris; an attempt to subdue even the sea was bound to stir the wrath of the gods.

In the fall of 481, the Persian land army assembled near Sardis, in Lydia, a three-day march from the port city of Ephesus. The Persians must have formed a colorful camp, spread out far over the landscape. Conscripts arrived from all parts of the Persian empire, which stretched from the Aegean Sea to the Indus and from Egypt to the Caspian Sea. There probably were over 100,000 men. Meanwhile, on the coast, a fleet of over 1,200 Greek and Phoenician ships was being assembled. When scouts sent out by the Greeks were intercepted, instead of punishing them, Xerxes turned them to his own purpose. Magnanimously, he let them go, perhaps with a touch of scorn, so that they would report back home how overpowering the forces making ready for war were.

In any case, it was hard for the great king to comprehend how the few Greeks on the other side of the Aegean could have the nerve to defy him—they must have taken leave of their senses. Besides, only a minority of the Greek cities put up resistance. Many others had offered earth and water, symbols of their submission, to the envoys he had sent. And some of the city-states that wavered probably did so for appearance's sake. Only Sparta and Athens, as well as Sparta's allies on the Peloponnese and a few cities in the north and on the islands, were determined to take up arms—a total of maybe thirty city-states, most of them small and insignificant. They would be able to raise a force of some thirty thousand men at most, and had far fewer ships than the Persians.

The Persian army left Asia Minor in the spring of 480 and made its way overland, across the Dardanelles and Macedonia toward Greece. The Greeks quickly abandoned their original plan of occupying a mountain pass in northern Thessaly. Instead, a small contingent of Spartans was dispatched to the narrow pass of Thermopylae, and the main body of the Greek navy was stationed nearby, off Artemisium on the north-western coast of Euboea. The Persian land army then circled in behind the Spartans under the command of Leonidas, and after a fierce battle defeated the last Greek troops. In contrast, an engagement of the two fleets ended without victory for either side—no mean achievement for the Greeks, considering that the Persian ships outnumbered theirs by at least two to one.

After the Greeks' defeat on land, their ships hurriedly sailed south. Athens' allies headed directly for the sound between Salamis and the mainland, while the Attic ships set course for Piraeus to ready the populace to leave on a moment's notice.

Did the Athenians really think that the Persian army and navy could be stopped before it reached Attica? The Athenian leadership is said to have expected the Spartans and their Peloponnesian allies to set out for Boeotia to wage battle there. But the Spartan forces were otherwise engaged, working feverishly to build a defensive wall across the isthmus of Corinth. Sparta had fought at Thermopylae only to gain time and perhaps to put on an illusory show of strength for the benefit of the wavering communities north of the Peloponnese. In reality, however, the Spartans had long since given up on Attica. Of course, later on it may have seemed advantageous to the Athenians to pretend to have been surprised at Sparta's lack of support.

In all probability the Athenians, too, realized, even before the battle of Thermopylae, that they would have to flee. They may have reached this decision as early as June and they likely began preparations then. Arrangements had to be made with Troezen and Aegina for the arrival of so many refugees; food and water had to be brought along, and additional means of transport found. Cautious Athenians probably moved their families, cattle, and some valuables out of the country in good time.

Responsibilities were divided up, possible courses of action discussed, and old boats made seaworthy—evacuating so many people by water was no small matter. But the majority of the citizenry seems to have put off action, not wanting to suffer the misery of exile before it was necessary.

In the course of their long debates over strategy, the Athenians decided to consult the oracle of Delphi. The oracle advised the city to defend itself from behind a "wooden wall." Some citizens, especially the older ones, interpreted this to mean the Acropolis, which was surrounded by thornbushes. Others interpreted the "wooden wall" to mean the navy, and this opinion finally prevailed. The Athenians decided to evacuate their city and to fight the Persians at sea.

Themistocles, son of Neocles, is said to have put forward this motion. He was well into his forties at the time, an extraordinary man endowed with a sharp, analytical mind and a fierce independence. He possessed an astonishing clarity of vision and a passion for planning, but he did not share his thinking readily. Even so, some years earlier, in 485, he had persuaded the Athenians to build a larger fleet than had ever existed in mainland Greece. He must have convinced his fellow Athenians that he had a strategy that would work against the Persians. Not everybody was impressed by his plans; in fact, there are signs he was reviled by many Athenians. The majority, however, put their trust in him, even if in the end they did so like drowning men clutching at straws. Initially all they needed to do was vote on a motion to approve the appropriation of public funds for the navy.

Then, in 480, reality caught up with them. Heralds enjoined all to save themselves and their dear ones as best they could. The fleet sailed into port, and the crews hurried to their families. Homes and possessions were to be relinquished. Many Athenians must have been reluctant. No matter how promising Themistocles' plan had seemed, everything looked different once they had to act on it and actually abandon their property and their homes. It is normal to assume when a dangerous course has been chosen that things will not turn out quite as badly as feared. But did the Athenians hold even the slightest hope of defeating the vast Persian forces? Would it not have been better to stay home or to set out for a new place to settle permanently? Why gamble on a battle? Why put Athens' last hope, the ships it had built with such great effort, in jeopardy in a venture whose outcome appeared uncertain at best?

It is important to bear in mind how novel and strange the idea of a sea battle must have been to the Athenians. Battles were traditionally fought on land, honorably, face-to-face on solid ground, the way the Greeks had met the Persians at Marathon in 490 and, with the help of the gods, emerged victorious. Would this new, totally untested strategy succeed? Had they been right to go along with Themistocles, the peculiar man who had set everything on its head, who had planned and seen to the buildup of the fleet, and on whose advice all available men had been pressed into service on the ships for weeks and even months at a time in order to learn how to row and maneuver them? The time had come when the Athenians were to face battle on this unfamiliar element, the sea.

It is not hard to imagine what sort of speculation this situation would raise. People must have talked among themselves in the streets and as they shopped in the marketplace. Themistocles and his strategy could not have been very popular, no matter what instructions the ships' crews had been given when they landed at Piraeus.

A small scene that has come down to us by chance sheds some light on those days. A tall young nobleman, "well-built and with a head of beautiful locks," caused a stir as he and his companions strode confidently through Keramikos, the potters' quarter, and across the market toward the Acropolis. At the temple of Athena he consecrated his horse's bridle

A reconstructed trireme, finished in 1987 and christened Olympia. The battering ram can be seen in the front, and the three rows of oars are clearly visible. The rowers of the middle row are staggered in relation to the rowers of the top and bottom rows. This arrangement allowed for great oar power without the ship having to be too long. A trireme normally measured thirty-seven meters, including the battering ram. The triremes' maneuverability depended on the coordination of the rowers' movement of the oars in accordance with the mates' commands. The mates' calls or whistles must have been penetrating because the moving oars were very noisy. During peaceful travel and in favorable winds, the sails were raised. The "cheeks" mounted on the sides just behind the bow rested on a crosstimber. On both sides of the ship a beam on which the top row of oars moved was mortised into this timber. The "cheeks" acted as protection for the rowers in collisions with enemy vessels and also served as an anchor housing. The triremes rose no more than three meters above the water and had a relatively shallow draft. The uppermost oars measured about four meters.

to the goddess, picked up a shield captured in an earlier campaign, offered a prayer, and then departed for the harbor at Piraeus.

His behavior was significant because the young man was Cimon, the son of Miltiades, the victorious general in command at the Battle of Marathon. Until this day, Cimon had hardly distinguished himself politically; he was better known for his frivolous way of life. But his father had been the most influential defender of conventional warfare during the last Persian invasion in 490, and anyone uncomfortable with the idea of entrusting the entire city to ships could point to the example of Miltiades' victory at Marathon. Thus Cimon's visit to the Acropolis was a grand symbolic gesture: the scion of one of the noblest Athenian families was saying that Marathon belonged to the past. He gave up his riding tackle in exchange for the shield of a hoplite, a heavily armed foot soldier, and departed for the ships on which battles were now to be fought. By his action, the three Greek styles of battle were illustrated in rapid succession, and the goddess's blessing was invoked for the most recent one. The appealing but no longer serviceable old ways, represented by the bridle, were consecrated to her care. In exchange Athena supplied the shield Cimon would use for fighting onboard. Naval warfare entailed not just maneuvering ships but also combat on deck between heavily armed men and archers.

We know that weapons at that time were regarded not simply as tools. Certain types of arms were associated with specific peoples and with segments of society. They were seen as a man's characteristic mark, indeed, as a part of him. Helmet, shield, and spear were inseparable from the image of a Greek warrior, as shown by innumerable monuments that depict naked men with their weapons. Cimon's symbolic rejection of the old sanctioned a change that would extend beyond the military domain. The entire citizenry was entering a new phase.

As recently as Marathon, the Athenians had sent out only hoplites— men wealthy enough to supply their own arms—9,000 out of the 35,000 free male citizens. Some slaves were taken along, too, but this does not alter the fact that there was apparently no thought, or at least no possibility, of drawing on the large number of poorer citizens.

In the ten years since Marathon, much had changed. Two hundred ships had to be manned, each presumably needing 170 oarsmen (in later years that was the usual number). Add to this officers, mates, hoplites and archers. That would mean about 200 men on each ship, or a total of 40,000, more than Athens' entire citizenry (and, of course, not all men were able-bodied enough to fight). Non-citizens had to be hired, and other cities were asked to provide crews for some of the ships. In any case, all Athenians down to the least propertied had to serve. Most of the hoplites—men of rank who thought themselves above the rest—had to take places on the crowded benches of the ship's oppressive hold and lean into the oars. They had to be fully reschooled, and it could not have been easy for them to sit side by side with men of the lowest status. Instead of fighting the enemy man-to-man, they had to face backward and exert all their strength to move the ship forward. Reason and the simple demand for utility seem to have prevailed over long-standing customs. It was a triumph of the Athenians over themselves.

Herodotus later said that Themistocles transformed the Athenians into "seafaring men" *(thalassioi)*. Indeed, it soon became evident that the new kind of warfare not only represented a firm departure from the old kind but that the concerted development of naval power would transform the nature of the city.

For all the drama of Cimon's visit to the Acropolis, many other Athenian leaders made similar acts to gain the support of the populace, an effort aided by the growing pressure of time. Gradually the Athenians reconciled themselves to abandoning their city and country.

Even Athena supported this decision, for it was reported that her holy serpent had vanished from its place on the Acropolis, and the honey cake the priestess had placed there for it was found untouched. Thus, the goddess, too, by leaving the city, submitted to Themistocles' advice—perhaps with a little help from the general himself.

A minor crisis arose when some men refused to return to their oars without being given adequate pay in advance. They insisted they needed the money for their families, who now, with the men gone, would have almost nothing to live on. The members of the council of nobles are said to have used the temple's treasury and probably funds of their own in order to meet the payroll.

In this way events in Athens and Attica ultimately obeyed the dictates of one man. People began streaming toward the harbors from all directions, in small groups and large ones, forming longer and longer lines. There may have been some final arguments on the docks when, for example, someone wanted to take along more possessions than allowed. Adding to the commotion were the farewells of the men who had to board the triremes.

The entire city sailed out into the Saronic Bay, hundreds of packed ships, great and small, some moving along swiftly, some slowly, most of them in disarray. None of the passengers knew what would happen next. And because everyone was aboard a ship, there would be no witnesses to this melancholy yet impressive spectacle.

The Attic ships were not the only ones that could have been seen heading for Salamis. The fleeing Athenians were joined by an allied squadron from Troezen to the south, where other vessels had gathered. Many of the Athenians who had helped in the evacuation now had to sail to Salamis in a hurry to join the battle.

The deeper and more permanent the effect of a momentous event, the harder it is to imagine that event not having taken place (or having had a different outcome). From there it is a small step to the belief not just that the event happened but also that it had to happen. Thus, in retrospect, history loses its unpredictability.

The defeat of the Persian fleet off the coast of Salamis did not secure the Greeks' larger victory, but it was the decisive battle of the war. And the overall failure of the Persian invasion set the stage for the future history of Greece, the rise of Athens, and everything connected with it.

In this sense Greek history is unimaginable without Salamis. But military victory over the Persians was by no means assured. And it is certainly questionable whether very many Greeks believed such victory likely.

When the priestess of Delphi caught sight of the Attic envoys that had been sent to seek her advice about how to respond to the Persian threat, she chased them out of the sanctuary: "Miserable ones, what are you still doing here? Flee to the ends of the world!" It took some diplomacy and possibly a few gold pieces to produce an oracle that implied even the possibility of victory behind a "wooden wall." Perhaps these words were invented, and the oracle decided in retrospect not to object to the attribution.

Most Greeks continued to consider all opposition vain. Even in Athens, politicians who urged some kind of accommodation with the Persians were met with widespread sympathy. It seems to have taken Themistocles years to gather the necessary support for his plan. The reasons individuals, groups, or cities gave for submitting to the Persians grew increasingly persuasive with the apparent hopelessness of resistance. The Greeks were all too aware of the might at Xerxes' disposal and his readiness to use it.

Consequently, the men of Argos, of Achaea in the northern Peloponnese, and of Crete, as well as Gelon, the powerful tyrant of Syracuse, were unwilling to join the Greek cause. Some of them cited oracles. The men of Corfu devised an especially clever way out. They sent a squadron of ships but instructed the commander to stop short of Salamis and then either join the Persians or send a messenger to tell the Greeks they had been delayed by bad weather.

The warriors of Sparta, however, would not tolerate such an avoidance of duty. Most likely, the Spartans did not even try to calculate the chances of success in opposing the Persians. It was not their way to lie low in the face of danger. They were trained to stand their ground, to fall in battle rather than retreat. A Spartan warrior was expected to return from war carrying his shield or being carried on it. He had reason to fear the opinion of his fellow citizens more than the enemy. And since this attitude was at the heart of the entire community, the Spartan warriors had no choice in 480 but to fight. Furthermore, they considered themselves invincible; and their allies on the Peloponnese—no matter what they thought—had little choice but to follow their example.

Other cities north of the peninsula joined the Spartans for a variety of reasons, particularly concern for their relations with neighboring communities. For example, if one city submitted to the Persians, its rival would be inclined to join the Greek side. Domestic politics was also a factor: Cities where broad segments of the population had gained political rights feared that the Persians would reinstall the aristocracy or impose a tyrant. Adding to this was the cities' desire to preserve their independence and that of Greece west of the Aegean Sea, not to mention the shame of appearing cowardly. Where a few were determined to resist the Persians, it was hard for the others to hang back. In some cities, those who favored siding with the Greeks prevailed without debate and succeeded in turning back the Persian envoys who arrived demanding the symbolic concession of water and earth. The freedom of the Greeks was invoked, and "the shared blood, shared language, shared shrines and sacrifices, the shared way of life." For the Greeks of the Peloponnese, these were especially powerful arguments.

In such situations, motives of all kinds tend to be linked to lofty common goals. That personal and even selfish interests often hide behind the invocation of the common good by no means implies dishonesty, especially in the face of such a threat, nor are the goals themselves merely hollow words. The cause possesses powerful moral force, and anyone distancing himself from the cause becomes a traitor.

In the year 481 the cities that were readying for war—a total of about thirty—had formed an alliance, whose headquarters was located, most likely, in Sparta. All feuds and enmities between members were to be laid aside. Any Greek city submitting to the Persians without being forced to do so would have to pay a tithe to the Delphic oracle. With this provision, the alliance hoped to win Apollo over to its cause.

Scouts were sent to spy on the Persian camp at Sardis, and the allies agreed to reconvene the following year on the Corinthian isthmus to discuss a common strategy. In the meantime, the member cities urged others to join them, an effort in which they failed.

Indeed, some of the cities in the alliance defected to the Persian side as soon as it became clear that the line north of the Peloponnese could not be held. These cities must have realized before how great the odds were in favor of the Persians. Perhaps they had simply not wanted to admit their true feelings, given the prevailing mood.

And what about those cities that remained loyal to the alliance? What were their chances? They may have simply been determined to go to any lengths necessary to oppose the Persians. Or they may have been counting on luck, the help of the gods. It is difficult to believe that they imagined their combined strength sufficient to beat the Persians. Never before had thirty cities banded together to fight off an external enemy; there had, in fact, never been a need for such an alliance.

All we can say is that only a minority was determined to do battle. Even in the cities of the alliance powerful opposition must have existed. When the Persian troops moved closer, fear spread, even in Sparta. From all appearances, the fear was justified.

The historian's task is to explain the Athenians' decision to prepare for war, how they went about that preparation, and why they staked everything on one card. Midway through the decade, strong internal disagreements had led to the exiling of several aristocrats, in part because they were suspected of being on good terms with the Persians. In the end, the group that sought to emphasize Athens' political and military power won. Themistocles was the motor that drove this movement. By 483 the Athenians were ready to begin building their fleet. The necessary funds came from the profitable exploitation of newly discovered silver veins in the mines of Laurium. The decision to build triremes meant that the Athenians were preparing for war. If the Athenians had contemplated retreat into the western Mediterranean they would have built transport vessels.

The building of the navy was an almost unbelievable accomplishment. Themistocles had previously arranged for the improvement of the harbors on the Piraean peninsula, but there were no shipbuilding facilities or dockyards. Huge quantities of wood had to be found, as well as pitch and tar. There were hardly enough men with the expertise to supervise the complicated building of triremes and far too few workmen. Men and materials had to be brought from near and far, and in a great hurry. Wood may have been available in the interior of Attica, but transporting large logs by land was arduous, and the trees were of poor quality. The best wood came from Macedonia, where the forests apparently were closer to the coast or rivers than in Attica. But it seems likely that the regions north of the Aegean were already under Persian control by the time Athens was ready to build its fleet. In that case, either the Persians were unaware of what was going on or most of the wood was brought from Italy—or, perhaps from Euboea.

It is likely that Themistocles instituted freedom from taxation as an inducement to attract workmen from abroad. Laborers had to be trained to perform an enormous amount of work: building hulls, struts, oarsmen's benches, rigging, decks. It was a race against time, requiring almost unimaginable quantities of skill, physical labor, imagination, and money. Athens must have been bustling with activity during that period. This had a benefit: It left little time to reflect.

Experts in navigation had to be found to hire and train the ships' crews. The tactical superiority Athens counted on would require professionalism. Skillful maneuvering was the centerpiece of Athenian strategy. Half a generation earlier, when the Ionian Greeks were getting ready for their crucial sea battle against the Persians at Lade in 495, Dionysius, commander of the three ships Phocaea had contributed, convinced the Ionians to toil furiously for the sake of future freedom. He had the ships sail out one behind the other in two parallel lines; then one line turned and slipped between the ships of the other line, an exercise they were made to repeat over and over. This training was to teach the crews how to maneuver quickly, holding an accurate course and accelerating to ram enemy ships. The men on deck were required to wear full armor despite the heat of summer and the extreme crowding onboard. This training went on for days—until, on the seventh day, the crews rebelled in protest. The battle at Lade was lost.

The Athenians seem to have shown more enthusiasm in their preparations and were more willing to make enormous efforts. We have no reports of shipbuilding in other cities, though it may have been undertaken elsewhere on a small scale. But in most places funds for a major effort were lacking, and insufficient time was allocated to the task. The credit has to go to Themistocles and his fellow citizens for changing the balance of sea power to such an extent that the Greeks could even contemplate challenging their opponent in a naval battle.

The Athenians resolved to fight the Persians for two reasons: First was the danger that confronted the city. Its citizens had reason to expect that the Persians would not just subdue them but would destroy their city and carry many of them off to slavery. Perhaps the majority of Athenians would not have had too much to fear if the city had thrown itself at Persia's mercy. Certain Athenian exiles living at the Persian court may have sought to mediate the dispute in order to win a role in governing the city. And Xerxes might not have been averse to concessions in view of Athens' importance. But, second, although the Persians had long harbored designs to conquer Greece, it was Athens that precipitated the Persian invasion. Thus, capitulation—let alone going over to the enemy's camp—would have been especially shameful, and flight would have been no better. The Athenians were given no choice but to uphold their honor.

But the most remarkable thing about the Athenian mobilization is that Themistocles seems to have planned practically the entire war, anticipating the enemy's strategy and designing his own moves to make a Greek victory seem possible, in spite of all appearances that the Persians' might was superior. What's more, the oracle the Athenians finally brought home from Delphi spoke not only of the wooden wall but concluded with a prophetic reference to Salamis: "Divine Salamis, you will bring death to the children of women when the corn is scattered or the harvest gathered in." Whatever Themistocles had to do with the oracle, the prophecy weighed greatly in the discussions over strategy held in the first months of 480. It was also clear that if the Persians could not be turned back at Thermopylae, as seemed likely, the Greeks would have no choice but to try to intercept their navy in the waters off Salamis.

Salamis was the only place where the Persians would be unable to take full advantage of their naval superiority; the narrowness of the channel would prevent the vastly larger Persian fleet from encircling the Greek ships, as the Persians had tried to do at Artemisium. Another danger was that many of the allies would try to beat a retreat. Consequently, it was essential to engage the Persians off Salamis. If they could not be defeated here, even the mighty wall that had been built across the isthmus of Corinth would prove useless; it could be circumnavigated all too easily.

That is presumably why Themistocles had planned much earlier to confront the Persians at Salamis. The only problem was how to lure them there. But there was a logical reason for them to go to Salamis, a reason that could be neatly incorporated into the war plan. As long as the Greek navy was stationed at Salamis, it would prevent the Persians from attacking the Peloponnesian coast. And since the Persians could not wait too long before attacking, they would be eager for battle. Their other option would be to encircle the Greeks at Salamis, but that would presumably have led to battle as well.

One difficulty arose, however, and it almost caused the plan to miscarry. The Greeks quickly grew uneasy in the narrow channel off Salamis. If the Persians occupied the passages at both ends of the island, the entire Greek navy would be trapped. The Persian occupation of Attica, the subsequent burning of the Acropolis, and then the appearance of the overpowering Persian naval forces moored just a few miles off Phalerum all had a depressing effect. Some of the Greek ships fled right away. But on the other ships, too, there must have been a great desire to leave this dangerous place, and the feeling must have been expressed more and more openly as time passed.

What use were strategic arguments? Provisions were limited, and once the Greeks were surrounded there was no hope of relief, as only a few Greek warships remained outside. Besides, the Peloponnesian crews wanted to go home. What in Themistocles' scheme was held to be an advantage appeared to them as a disadvantage. Thus, apart from the Athenians, only the Megarians and the Aeginetans were willing to hold out at Salamis. Their lands would have fallen into Persian hands the moment the Greek navy fled.

A Spartan, Eurybiades, was the commander in chief. The Athenians had agreed to his appointment even though they had built most of the ships themselves. They reasoned that a Spartan was most likely to command general respect. The Athenians, with their strange ways of thinking and their bold, erratic, and demanding manner of doing things, generated anxiety if not outright distrust among their allies. Furthermore, the Aeginetans, who had contributed a large contingent to the Greek forces, had been at war with Athens only a short time before. The Athenians therefore felt they could achieve more through indirect influence than by holding the leadership position themselves. With a Spartan commander they could at least expect courage and decisiveness, and Eurybiades did in fact come around to Themistocles' view. He did, however, have to reckon with the war council.

A growing number of the council's members supported confronting the Persians on the isthmus rather than holding out at Salamis. Little is known of the council's deliberations. Accounts from that time tell of many accusations and expressions of jealousy among the Greek city-states. But in essence their version of events is credible: remaining in the narrow channel, far from the Greek land forces and with the overpowering enemy close by, became a more and more alarming proposition the longer the situation lasted. To keep the forces together, either hard discipline or faith in a strategy that ran counter to all traditional theories was necessary. And, contrary to Herodotus, the waiting lasted for many days.

As wise as Themistocles' plan was, it grew less convincing as time wore on. Even his threat to take the Athenians and their families to settle in Italy if Salamis were abondoned no longer had much effect.

It appears that Themistocles never considered the possibility that the urge to flee might become overpowering. He may have been relying on the unquestioning obedience of his forces and in doing so failed to take human feelings into account. The only possible explanation for these oversights is that he saw in this plan the only chance of winning. He must have assumed that what was so obvious to him was equally obvious to others.

Time and again, Themistocles defended his plan before the fleet's commanders, who lived in close contact with their men. Greek warfare had traditionally relied on relatively simple military strategies that everyone involved could understand. The new strategy demanded that the soldiers disregard what seemed obvious. Why should they suddenly abandon old wisdom for new? Remaining in place would not only require the Athenians to fight with their backs to the enemy but would also demand that they passively accept the will of their leaders, a trust that many were unwilling to bestow. Ultimately, the majority of the war council voted to leave Salamis. Themistocles' entire plan was abandoned.

Themistocles, however, did not waste time in taking action. He sent a messenger to Xerxes to relate the situation exactly as it was: namely, that the Greeks were planning to withdraw the following night. Apparently he wanted to let the Persian king know that he was about to lose his last opportunity to defeat the Greeks in a single great sea battle that would presumably decide the war. Once the Greek navy withdrew and dispersed, the Persians would have to conquer each city-state, one by one, an arduous and drawn-out affair.

Xerxes clearly found the report credible; it also suited his purposes. He was eager to win a quick, spectacular victory and had no doubt he would obtain it. Both he and Themistocles were intent on battle.

It is difficult to explain why the Persians did not simply block the ends

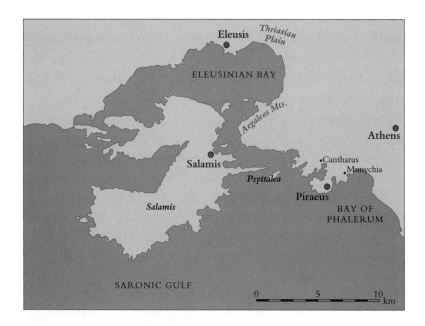

Salamis

of the channel and starve the Athenians. They did close off the western passage between Salamis and the mainland, but they rowed their ships into the eastern opening. This made sense if Xerxes counted on the Greeks trying to escape and had simply decided to attack them in the channel. Xerxes had lined up his fleet in battle formation the day before, south of the island. Thus Themistocles may have invented his ruse after the fact, and the simple truth may be that Xerxes was already determined to attack.

In all probability, Xerxes was not inclined to exercise caution anyway. What could the Greeks possibly hope to accomplish against his power? And wasn't a victory in an open battle the best kind?

So the Persian navy rowed northwest in three long lines under cover of night, though it was full moon. Then the fleet turned westward until it could array itself facing south or southwest. This maneuver was difficult and time-consuming. The crews had to function with great discipline, keeping the ships at an exact distance from one another.

The Persians worked their oars all night in preparation for a dawn attack. But when morning came, the Greeks, who had been warned in advance, were ready.

In the end, Themistocles was able to goad the Persian king into behaving exactly according to plan. What the wily Athenian had failed to achieve in the Greek war council, he managed with the help of the enemy. With almost superhuman power Themistocles remained committed to his plan until Xerxes struck.

The Battle of Salamis is described by Herodotus and in Aeschylus's play, *The Persians,* which was written a few years after the war. The sources don't reveal if the Greeks had time to make offerings to the gods. One source reports that Themistocles was forced by the troops to sacrifice three high-ranking Persian prisoners, nephews of the king. But their execution may have happened earlier. The Persians, for their part, are supposed to have sacrificed the most handsome of the Greeks they had captured. Given such an extraordinary battle, both sides seem to have felt that extreme measures were called for.

The Greek generals also ordered that the bones of legendary heroes worshipped at Aegina and Salamis be brought to them to inspire and strengthen the troops. The bones from Aegina arrived just before the start of battle.

When the Persians entered the channel they heard loud voices. "Sons of Greece, rise up and free your fatherland! Free the women and children, the seats of your ancestral gods, the graves of your forefathers! Nothing less is at stake in this battle!" This is how Aeschylus summarized the admonishments of the commanders who recited prayers while the crews spoke the refrains. All broke into loud song in honor of the gods. The rocks surrounding the channel echoed that song, as well as the commands of helmsmen and boatswains, Aeschylus reported. Music and fear accompanied the movement toward battle.

The Persian ships approached in a crescent-shaped formation. The Greek soldiers had the advantage of a good night's sleep, whereas their foes had spent all night on their oarsman's benches. The taller Persian ships also may have had some trouble with sea winds.

Still, the Greeks grew hesitant when the Persian fleet moved into action with its own loud war cries. The Greeks were just about ready to retreat when their first ship rammed a Persian one. The ensuing clash drew everyone into the action.

First the right flank of the Greek fleet, consisting mostly of Aeginetan ships, attacked. Then the fighting quickly spread to the left flank. Xerxes had positioned himself on a mountain overlooking the channel to watch the action and to see to it that his troops fought bravely. What exactly followed can only be conjectured, but it is clear that the Greeks maneuvered their fleet deftly. The Greek ships were more sturdily constructed than those of their opponents, and this may have given the Greeks an advantage in ramming. Also, the Persian ships were crowded too closely together to launch their attack effectively.

At one point, a Persian ship under the command of Queen Artemisia of Halicarnassus found itself cornered by an Attic trireme. The only means of escape the queen could see was to ram another Persian ship. This turned out to be a lucky move. The trireme she had been fleeing dropped the pursuit because its commander assumed that the queen's ship must be on his side, while Xerxes' staff thought she had rammed an enemy vessel. (The Athenians, incidentally, had promised a high reward to whoever took the queen prisoner, because they considered it "outrageous for a woman to join a war against Athens," as Herodotus wrote. She may have reminded them of the Amazons' legendary attack on their city. Xerxes, on the other hand, called Artemisia "the only man in the fleet." She is said to have told him that at sea the Persians were no more a match for the Greeks than women were for men. Since Herodotus came from Halicarnassus, we may assume that he was well informed about the queen, and he makes no secret of his admiration for her. But the number and nature of his stories about her also reflect the importance of male supremacy to the Greeks and the irritation this queen caused them.)

The Greeks sailed into the growing chaos of the Persian navy in relatively orderly formation and rammed many hostile ships onto whose decks armed crew members then advanced. The Persians lost many ships and a great number of men, many of whom could not swim. The Greeks slew them mercilessly in the water and on the beaches of Psyttalea, a small island at the mouth of the channel that a Greek detachment had seized from the Persians earlier in the battle.

By evening on that September day, whose exact date is unknown, what remained of the Persian fleet had fled into the bay of Phalerum. The Greeks were too exhausted to chase them. They, too, returned to their original position, but now they did so as victors.

Floating in the water were the remains of ships—masts, beams, planks, oars, bits of rigging, hulls—and the dead. Everything drifted back and forth. Some of it found its way out of the channel and floated along the Attic coast past Phalerum. Many a sailor may still have struggled for his life in the water. The Greek losses were not as great as those of the Persians, but they were grievous enough. Gradually quiet descended. The battle "had spent itself in the cleverly guided turmoil," to use Hölderlin's phrase from his *Hyperion*.

Xerxes soon left Attica with a small retinue. It was essential that he return home quickly lest the news of his defeat encourage rebellions. Indeed, some Persian-controlled cities in northern Greece rose up, and there seems to have been unrest even as far east as Babylon.

Concerned about interception by Greek ships, the king did not dare take the shortest route across the Aegean and had to hurry all the more out of fear that the Greeks would cut off his land route at the Hellespont. He left most of his army behind to winter in Thessaly, an allied state, and resumed fighting the following summer. In 479, the Greeks once again roundly defeated the Persians at the land battle of Plataea, spelling the true end of Xerxes' campaign. At Plataea, the Spartans demonstrated extraordinary bravery and military ability. Without the victory at Salamis, however, the Greeks could hardly have faced the Persians in 479 in such large numbers and with such unity. Had it not been for Salamis, Xerxes' army would have extended its advance into Greece to the Peloponnese in the fall of 480 and would probably have conquered or laid siege to several cities. To put it in oversimplified terms: If the Greeks had lost at Plataea, they could still have won other battles. But had they lost at Salamis they would never have repelled the Persians.

Thucydides later attested that Themistocles knew how to proceed even when everything was still unclear. Even the Spartans graciously recognized how much the victory at Salamis owed to a new factor, namely the planning and resourcefulness of one man. In the awarding of medals following the battle, they gave the usual prize for bravery to the commander in chief, Eurybiades, but they also gave Themistocles a special award for brilliance. Both honors consisted of a wreath of olive branches.

Meanwhile, the commanders of the Greek cities held a vote to decide who should receive the prize for the victory. To prevent commanders from simply voting for themselves, the panel decided to allow each man two votes. A commander could name himself first, but as they all had to cast a second vote, the majority would go to the commander who really deserved the prize. If we may trust Herodotus, even though Themistocles garnered most of these second votes, many commanders refused to accept the result, and the assembly dissolved in disagreement.

. . .

There are very few instances in history when so much was at stake in a single battle. The channel at Salamis was the eye of the needle through which world history had to pass if the decisive role was to be played not by vast, monarchically ruled empires but by a strange nation composed of small independent cities that must have seemed terribly exotic to Eastern eyes. It was a nation almost entirely without monarchs and, in many cases, one that gave a political voice to broad segments of the population. John Stuart Mill went so far as to say that Salamis was more crucial to English history than the Battle of Hastings.

It is almost impossible to imagine what would have happened if the Greeks had lost at Salamis and consequently lost the war. Modern historiographers prefer to think in terms of processes and are reluctant to admit that events may have the power to block such processes as the development of a civilization. That is not the claim here. Greek history would not have come to an end if the war had been lost. Anaximander, Heraclitus, and the great scholar Hecataeus all studied and developed their philosophies in small Greek cities under Persian rule in Asia Minor. Greek arts and architecture flourished under the Persians, and tolerant as they were, the Persians were even willing to put up with ever more powerful Greek oligarchies. And the cities west of Greece, from Syracuse to Marseilles, would surely have remained free of Persian rule.

The question here is whether without Salamis Greek culture would have taken the course it did. Would democracy have evolved without Athens' naval supremacy? Would the profound transformations that Athens experienced both domestically and in its astonishing military successes have taken place? To put it differently: What would have given rise to the evolution of historiography itself? What would have caused politics, tragedy, sophism, and classical art and architecture to develop in the ways they did? Without the challenges brought on by victory at Salamis, would there have been the incentive for such amazing growth in rational thought?

As it actually happened, all these developments were primarily due to the dynamics at work in Athens, to the changes that took place there in such breathless succession. They were due to Athens' discoveries and experiences, its successes, questionings, and sufferings; in short, to everything that happened in and to the city in the course of the fifth century. What transpired in Athens was closely linked to the political arena, which was at that time the focal point of life. As a result, Greek culture not only moved ahead at an entirely new pace but was able to realize its potential differently, more comprehensively, and more prolifically than otherwise would have been possible.

What happened in and to Athens during the fifth century B.C. was not just a new stage of development along the historical continuum, but the beginning of something fundamentally new and different. The lasting influence Greece exerted on the Roman Empire and Christian theology, on the Middle Ages and the modern era, in both direct and indirect ways, ultimately goes back to what took place in Athens during these decades.

It is of course possible that under different circumstances other cultures and peoples might have made the same discoveries for which the Greeks are famous. Antiquity could have provided different conditions from which Western history would then have taken rise. Even within the context of Greek history one could ask whether Persian domination over Greece would not have come to an end sooner or later, through rebellion perhaps, opening up new spheres of growth to the Greeks.

With appropriate qualifications, then, we can conclude that the victory at Salamis rewarded the different path the Greeks had earlier chosen for themselves. While the Eastern empires had concentrated on consolidating power on a massive scale, the Greeks, in their small and rather weak cities, had worked out special ways of living together as equals. Salamis showed that the Greeks had not only created a world of their own and achieved a distinct sense of themselves but that they could also successfully challenge the Persian empire on the military front.

Thus, small cities established themselves alongside huge empires as powerful agents in world politics. After centuries during which politics and culture were dominated by the great powers of Egypt and the Near East, the Mediterranean, which both connected and separated the Greek cities, began to assert itself. Territorial expansion has traditionally taken place across land, whereas the sea had resisted rule, conquest, or colonization. But no longer. Hand in hand with these changes went countless others, though many did not become evident for some time.

"Western" tendencies that had long lain dormant could begin to assert themselves and develop fully. With the great latitude available to them, the Greeks defined the conditions of their political life to include enormous freedom, freedom that could—as always—be used for good or ill. But much more than this was involved: From now on East and West were no longer merely points on the compass.

The greater the importance one attributes to the outcome of the battle at Salamis, the more one is led to wonder whether that outcome really depended so much on chance. Only chance can account for the fact that a man of such unique gifts appeared at the right time and in the right place to conceive and carry through a plan that determined events so dramatically. Likewise, it was only by chance that the Persians attacked when the Spartans' reputation was still high enough to put them in a leadership position and when the Athenians had already progressed to an early form of democratic rule. The Athenians' protodemocracy was a prerequisite for their politics, their military buildup, and, finally, their readiness to take the extreme step of abandoning their city and country.

But was there another quality—a "Europeanness"—already present in Athens that was a match for Persian power?

The Greeks later ascribed their victory to their own bravery. But were they really so much braver than the Persians? Herodotus didn't think so. And what use would bravery have been if the conditions of the battle had not been so favorable? The Greeks' naval tactics were obviously superior; perhaps their ship commanders were also better trained than their Phoenician and Ionian counterparts, quicker to react, better prepared to make decisions independently. Perhaps the Greek style of leadership was on the whole superior, more responsive to actual conditions than the Persian style. But would that in itself have ensured success?

There may also have been some truth in the Greek claim that the gods did not want Europe and Asia to be subject to one ruler. The expansion of the Persian empire eventually had to find its limits. The empire had been in existence for seven decades, and its kings had conquered all the empires of the Near East—Media and Babylonia, Lydia and Egypt—with amazing energy and speed, expanding northward far beyond the boundaries originally envisioned.

Never before had the Near East known an empire of such size. The Persian kings had ruled it wisely, generously, and with organizational skill. Their dynamism was still fresh, but it was bound to slow down at some point. In Greece the Persians encountered not only people and political units of a very different stamp, but they also had to contend with the sea and an inhospitable landscape.

Still, with somewhat better military leadership, the Persians might have won. Their ill-chosen strategy must be attributed at least in part to Xerxes—even if he was not as deluded as Greek sources describe him, nor as sure of his own superiority, or as blind to the capabilities of the Greeks. Chance, then, played a double role in the personal constellation of leadership: working in favor of the Greeks and to the disadvantage of the Persians.

Chance—that is, the circumstances under which different persons, groups, or even chains of events come together—can take different forms and serve different functions in history. It may have a relatively negligible effect on the overall outcome of a conflict. Murphy's Law, according to which anything that can go wrong will, must be reckoned with as well. But sometimes one side of a conflict is so much stronger than the other that it has the capacity to win even in the face of many adverse circumstances, and then there is no need to worry about chance.

For example, in his planning for the Peloponnesian War between Athens and Sparta (431–404 B.C.), Pericles could afford to ignore chance. Athens was so powerful then that victory seemed certain to him even if many unforeseen events were to intervene. Similarly, historical change, propelled by innumerable forces, can assume a kind of inevitability under which a basic course remains relatively unaffected by the multitude of chance events.

This truth can be illustrated by reference to Greece's own history. The various conflicts among aristocratic groups that were so common in ancient Greece and were so strongly determined by individual personalities brought about many superficial changes in society, but ultimately their long-term effect may have been to make possible the rise of a third force, the farmers, whose role we will take up later. And what various Greek philosophers discovered piecemeal and by chance eventually coalesced into a body of thought that exhibits a remarkable consistency. Thus, it can be concluded that the process of large-scale change within Greece was little affected by "chance."

Only when such a process is determined, either in its totality or at least in its direction and consequences, by a single event, do the particular circumstances that determined this event and its course take on enormous importance of their own. It is hard to imagine that had there been no Themistocles, someone else would have played a similar role. Given the scope of his political and military achievements, Themistocles seems uniquely qualified for the task he was set.

Even if the Greeks were in fact superior to the Persians in some ways that were not apparent to the normal thinking of the time, their superiority was not great enough to make their victory certain or even probable. In any case, there had to be someone like Themistocles who could recognize the Persians' superiority as mere appearance and, at the same time, detect the genuine though invisible advantages the Greeks derived from the balance of power.

A number of other things had to go just right as well. For even the best-laid plans cannot assure success where so much depends on factors as diverse as wind and current and coincidence, where momentary circumstances can make the strong weak and the weak strong, where so much hinges on a particular combatant attacking boldly at the very moment when his opponent has fallen prey to a brief lapse of attention. And so the battle culminates in victory for one side.

.   .   .

If the Greek victory at Salamis cannot be explained simply by reference to some secret superiority, then an understanding of the event in its world-historical significance must be sought. If, in other words, the Greek victory was not due solely to the luck of the commanders and good fortune in battle, then we must look for the structural advantages of Greek society that might have been the prerequisites for this victory.

Themistocles' shrewdness, the extent to which his strategic cunning exceeded all conventional thinking, cannot be explained away as merely the special gift of a single individual, enhanced by what "chance" contributed to his education. Contemporary sources indicate that he had no teacher in politics, but this does not mean that Themistocles was not affected in the usual manner by his nation's habits of thinking and its refinements, as well as the social positions opened up by the unique structure of the polis.

The implication here is not that the Greeks were necessarily better thinkers than others, nor that they had a genetic advantage in this area. They simply had to think differently. After all, they faced fundamentally different problems; they were confronted with different challenges, which made them think more abstractly, enabling them to push the boundaries of accepted reality. Long before Themistocles, these challenges had provoked a remarkable innovation.

When the Ionians were planning their uprising in 500 B.C., the wise historian Hecataeus proposed a strategy that involved building a fleet and using it to wage naval battle against a land power. This was, of course, beyond his fellow Greeks' comprehension. They thought in terms of individual actions on land and sea and not in terms of one comprehensive strategy. The Greeks still functioned within a paradigm they shared with the Persians—a paradigm in which the latter were infinitely superior to them.

But the experiences gained in this war certainly gave rise to lively discussion. The solution Themistocles suggested in 480 was still not self-evident to his contemporaries or he would not have had to work so long and hard to have it finally accepted. But Hecataeus's earlier proposal had prepared the way for it. His lesson was not to accept reality as it was, not merely to introduce a particular innovation, but to imagine things more freely, to turn disadvantage into strength in situations when there was no choice, and to conceive a major campaign years in advance. To this Themistocles added an essential element: the conviction of the correctness of his vision, the certain outcome of his gamble.

And then, too, there was the willingness of the Attic citizenry to let themselves be convinced by such unconventional ideas. This could be explained by saying that the Athenians seized upon—for whatever accidental reasons—Themistocles' plans. But this willingness may also have arisen from the particular frame of mind typical of the Greeks and especially of the Athenians, from their habit of listening to and following political arguments, of relying on rational solutions even if they implied risk. And above all, it may have come from Athens' newly acquired self-awareness, a result of the bold reforms that had given political voice to broad segments of the population and led to an amazing flourishing of the city. This new strength may have encouraged a certain recklessness in the Athenians and perhaps even a sense of responsibility for Greece as a whole. Later Athenians would say of themselves that their victory had been due "more to good sense than luck and more to daring than to power."

It is not known when the Athenians officially celebrated their victory, whether after their first return home from Salamis, or their second return after the battle at Plataea in the spring of 479, when they had to leave their country again because the Persian army was once more approaching Attica.

At the victory celebration, Sophocles, then fifteen years old, is said to have opened the dance, naked and anointed, with a lyre in his hands. Aeschylus had fought in the war, and Euripides was born at about the time of Salamis.

ATHENS

When the Persians destroyed the temple on the Acropolis just before the Battle of Salamis, the olive tree that had stood there was also burned. According to an old legend, Poseidon and Athena had once contended for possession of Attica. Poseidon gave a fountain as a gift. Athena gave the olive tree. The tree stood as a reminder of that story. Two days after the fire, the Athenians later related, a tall shoot had sprouted from the stump. To them, this was proof that Athens was indestructible.

2

The Late Rise of Athens

Athens came to prominence relatively late. There is little mention of the city in accounts handed down of the seventh and eighth centuries B.C., and it is therefore unlikely that Athens played an important role in that era, though even then it was mainland Greece's second largest city after Sparta in area and population.

Information about sixth-century Athens is much more abundant, though this may result in part from the interest Athens attracted in the fifth century. But even so, new forces were stirring as early as the sixth century. The reforms of Solon and Cleisthenes and the mild, beneficent tyranny of Pisistratus drew some attention to Athens then, but it was not until the end of the sixth century that conditions arose that allowed the Athenians to gather their powers in a grander style.

Athens was not involved in the seventh-century war between the cities of Chalcis and Eretria, which raged for many years and entailed the participation of allied cities from the entire Aegean region. Athens remained aloof despite its proximity to the center of hostilities: The two Euboean cities lay almost directly opposite Attica's northern coast. In the dispute with its much smaller neighbor Megara over the island of Salamis, Athens seems to have suffered several defeats before achieving a decisive victory in the sixth century. Athens was unable to fight effectively against the assaults of the small island Aegina because of an inadequate navy. Indeed, Themistocles later advocated the buildup of the navy partly on the basis of the Aeginian threat. Athens did send an army to the holy war that was fought at the beginning of the sixth century to defend Delphi against foreign claims.

But the city did not take part in the great colonizing movement that began about 750 and led to the founding of so many cities in Italy, Sicily, southern France, the northern Aegean, along the shores of the Black Sea, and elsewhere. Perhaps Athens refrained because an epidemic decimated its population around 700; archeologists have noted the dramatic increase in burials for that period. Of course, some Athenians would have joined the colonizing expeditions organized by Chalcis and Eretria as well as by Megara, but the aristocracy of Athens never undertook such ventures. Only once, toward the end of the seventh century, did an Attic contingent set out for foreign conquest. The Olympic champion Phrynon led an attack on Sigeum at the entrance to the Hellespont, the present-day Dardanelles. This effort was probably the result of his individual initiative; at any rate, the precedent was not followed.

Even the great economic, social, and political crises of the archaic period seem to have caught up with Athens relatively late. When Cylon, who had been an Olympic champion, tried to set himself up as a tyrant in the late seventh century, he failed because his opponents were able to mobilize masses of Attic farmers against him. This was at a time when Corinth, Megara, and several other cities had long been ruled by tyrants; indeed, Theagenes of Megara was Cylon's father-in-law. We may conclude from this that the world of Athens was then still in good order. After the first appearance of tyranny in Greece some three generations passed before Pisistratus was able to establish himself as absolute ruler of Athens, around 560. This delay may imply that Athens was not only relatively powerless at this time but also delayed in its internal development. This strange discrepancy between inherent potential and manifest power may explain Athens' late rise to prominence.

Geographically, Attica was situated almost precisely at the center of the region inhabited by the Greeks, an area that extended from the southern Balkan peninsula across the Aegean. Attica was approximately equidistant from the western end of the Corinthian Gulf and the Ionian cities in Asia Minor, from Corfu and from Rhodes, from the Macedonian coast and from Crete. The distance to the Sea of Marmara and Byzantium was twice as great as that to the southwestern tip of the Peloponnese.

This geographic position was of no great significance, however. Politically in that period there was only one major area of conflict: the Peloponnese. And while Athens remained a powerless city-state, it had no part in this struggle. Attica was situated alongside the most important maritime thoroughfares. The passage between Euboea and the mainland was a popular route because of its calm waters. Much of the Greek commercial trade between East and West was conducted along the Saronic Bay because sailing around Cape Malea, the southeastern tip of the Peloponnesian peninsula, was considered dangerous. A popular saying warned, "Beware of Malea." But the ships sailing these routes stopped at Attica's harbors only briefly, if at all. Goods did not accumulate there, and no trade took place—or very little. Attica imported what it needed and exported a few products. Trade in both directions increased during the sixth century, but Athens became the center of Aegean commerce only after it established itself militarily and politically as the dominant Greek power. At that point its geographical position proved to be of practical use.

Attica occupied an area of approximately 2,500 square kilometers, about the size of modern-day Luxembourg. The next largest polis, Argos, was only about half its size (1,400 square kilometers). Even cities as important as Corinth, Chios, and Samos, including their outlying territories, constituted no more than a third or a fifth the size of Attica (880, 826, and 468 square kilometers, respectively), and these were cities well above average size. Boeotia, which almost equaled Attica in territory, was made up of ten independent city-states, and on Crete there are said to have been a hundred, nearly fifty of which can be documented. Even many medium- and small-sized islands were homes to two or more. This was true of Lesbos, Rhodes, and even the tiny, mountainous Ceos. Apart from Sparta (which, including the conquered territory of Messenia, comprised a good

8,000 square kilometers), the only city-states larger than Attica were a few colonies in Sicily. The area of an average Greek polis could be traversed on foot or on a donkey in no more than a few hours. By contrast, the distance between Athens and the Attic border was in places as much as 70 kilometers, the equivalent of a long day's journey.

Athens also had many more citizens than other cities. Around 500 B.C., they probably numbered about 35,000. At that time Argos had about 15,000 citizens; Corinth, about 10,000; and many other cities, no more than a few hundred. These figures reflect, as was customary for the Greeks, only adult male citizens. Attica's total population around the year 500 was therefore about 200,000. Even the large and powerful Sparta had many fewer citizens than Attica, for only a small elite among the free landowners there, the so-called Spartiates, were granted full citizen status.

Aristotle later wrote that a city should be small enough for the voice of the herald to be heard by every citizen and for the citizens to know one another at least by sight. Athens certainly was not like this.

According to legend, the size of Athens' political realm resulted from the joining together of different communities by the mythical king Theseus. The Attic nobles were said to have taken up residence in the city at that time. Presumably the unification dates back to the Mycenaean period, when kings ruled over more extensive territories. Most of these early kingdoms, already weak and disintegrating, did not survive the invasions from the north that took place before the year 1000 B.C.

Attica alone escaped that fate, which is why the Athenians liked to claim they had always lived in their land, that they hadn't taken it by force from anybody, that they were autochthonic. During the decades of migration from the north, Attica became a refuge for many of the region's inhabitants. The early colonizing expeditions that predated the colonial period of Greece—namely, the bands of refugees from Mycenaean Greece that set out in search of new homes along the western shores of Asia Minor and founded Greek cities there around 1000 B.C.— were said to have sailed mostly from Athens. Later, Athens liked to call itself "the oldest city of Ionia," indeed, the mother city of the Ionian cities.

Although the unified political realm of Attica may well date back to

View of the Acropolis from the southwest

Mycenaean times, it did not exist in that form continuously. At least Eleusis and Tetrapolis in the plain of Marathon seem to have been independent at times. If they were in fact independent, Athens won them back in the eighth century, at the latest. But this kind of initiative on Athens' part appears to have been an isolated instance. It is difficult to say why Athenian political unity survived. Geographical position, in any case, provides no answer.

Attica's coastline was over 170 kilometers long, a potential source of trouble at a time when piracy flourished. Along the western and northern borders the country was protected by nearly impassable mountain ranges. Only a small piece of the border separating Attica from the eastern and not very menacing part of Boeotia ran across gentler hills. The land route between central Greece and the Peloponnese ran farther west through the Cithaeron mountains, and most travelers probably preferred the sea passage across the Corinthian Gulf.

In the Attic interior rose the mountains Parnes, Pentelicus (which would later supply the marble for the buildings of the Acropolis), Aegaleos, and Hymetticus, the last still forested, rich in springs, and famous for its honey. They surrounded the central plain, which was dominated by the elevation of the Acropolis, and separated it from the Eleusinian and Marathonian plains as well as the range of hills east and south of Athens that was called the Mesogeion. Several city-states could easily have coexisted in the region. In any case, the valleys separating the various mountain ranges provided direct connections from Athens to all parts of Attica.

Wine grapes, figs, and olives grew relatively well on Attic soil, as did vegetables and grains on some parts. In other areas the land could be used only for pasturing.

In the course of interior colonization, hills were terraced to provide additional arable land, but by the seventh century Attica's farms were no longer able to feed the people adequately, and increasing amounts of grain had to be imported. Beginning in the sixth century, perhaps even earlier, silver, zinc, and lead were mined near Mount Laurium in the south. The tunnels were so dismally narrow and inadequate that the slaves often had to work lying on their backs. These mines contributed significantly to the city's treasury.

Until the end of the seventh century, Athens itself was more a group of villages than a city. Only then was a sizable marketplace or *agora* laid out; public buildings were created along the west and south sides, and a system of water pipes and fountains installed. Furthermore, Athens was not the only large community in Attica. Until the middle of the fifth century about two-thirds of the population still lived in Attica's other towns and numerous villages.

The aristocracy, it seems, lived primarily in the city of Athens, along with a growing number of artisans and tradesmen, only some of whom enjoyed the rights of citizenship. In addition there must have been an increasing population of slaves. The majority of citizens made their livings from agriculture, others presumably from fishing.

Attica had a number of natural harbors, on its eastern coast and, especially, southwest of Athens. But, as far as we can tell, no improvements were made, even to the best of these—in Piraeus—until the fifth century. There was no need for deeper harbors, and the Athenians saw no reason for a major investment of labor. Ships could anchor in the shallow bay of Phalerum, and the way the coastline ran at that time, the distance to the city of Athens was only a little over four kilometers.

The varied land formations and the interplay between land and sea offered an enchanting view to anyone looking down from an elevated spot, such as the Acropolis. The almost palpable clarity of the air—what Euripides called "the sparkling ether of the sky"—lent sharpness to all the contours and enhanced the beauty of the view. Most Athenians lived in the plain, however, and were busy tending their fields, pastures, and animals, or plying their trades. Those who didn't live on the coast or weren't engaged in commerce had little to do with the sea—Attica was essentially a rural country.

Could the relatively large size of Athens and its citizenry, under the conditions of that early period, have been disadvantageous? It is certainly possible that size may have been something of a burden and a weakness. In any case, it is by no means clear what accounted for the subsequent achievements that won Athens recognition and prestige beyond other cities.

There were in those days two cities whose large size brought them power and magnified their ambition: Sparta and its rival on the Peloponnese, Argos.

The Spartans were powerful and easily provoked, qualities that caused them to adopt a foreign policy uncommonly aggressive for the time. We do not know what predisposed them to do it, but in the eighth century they crossed the steep mountain barrier of the Taygetus range and conquered Messenia. Nowhere else in Greek history of that period do we find a territorial expansion of this scale that was successful in the long run. Sparta's territory doubled with this exploit at a time when other Greek cities founded colonies far away (something Sparta did only in the highly exceptional case of Tarentum).

The conquest came at a price, however, which mounted when Messenia broke away from Sparta during the second half of the seventh century, only to be reconquered in a long, bitter, and bloody war. Because the number of Spartans with full citizenship was small and because they had subdued the indigenous populations of Laconia and Messenia, forcing them to cultivate the land, they now had to rely on extreme discipline and shrewd management to maintain their rule, both internally and externally. Jealous neighbors could easily make common cause with the subjugated population, the Helots. Several wars did break out, but finally, in the sixth century, a series of treaties involving much of the peninsula was concluded, resulting in the so-called Peloponnesian

League. Sparta had now become so powerful that it occasionally intervened in conflicts beyond the Peloponnese.

Thanks to its army, which was the best trained of its day and motivated by a strong military ethic, and to its judicious use, Sparta gained great authority. During the sixth century it was unquestionably the most highly regarded polis in Greece.

Its rival Argos, however, was never satisfied with its subordinate position to Sparta. After all, it—along with Mycenae—had been the home city of Agamemnon, the legendary commander in the war against Troy. And in the seventh century under King Phidon, Argos had held sway over much of the peninsula. Thyreatis, a territory the Spartans had wrested from the Argives, long remained a bone of contention between the two city-states. Argos usually lost in the periodic armed conflicts. But because it was relatively powerful and the natural ally of all who wanted to resist mighty Sparta in the southern part of the peninsula, Argos can be counted among those Greek cities of the archaic period that were influential beyond their own region.

One might ask why the Peloponnesian Greeks (with the exception of the Corinthians) were so territorial, forming alliances and fighting over the soil of the peninsula. Presumably this was the natural consequence of Sparta's aggressive manner in preserving its control. In any case, this territoriality sets the Peloponnesians apart from the rest of the Greeks.

All the other cities of the archaic period that were notable for citizens' achievements or influence were oriented toward the sea. These cities were centers of commerce, rapidly increasing at this time, and all kinds of seafaring activities, including piracy and plundering foreign shores. The traders, who ventured far into the western Mediterranean, soon realized the commercial and security benefits of linking their commercial outposts to Greek settlements; the next logical step was to organize colonizing expeditions to these cities. This pattern was not always followed uniformly— not in Aegina, for example—but it became the rule elsewhere.

The volume of commerce would be considered small by modern terms and even medieval standards. Most of the trade was in raw materials—often for the manufacture of arms, less in handcrafted mer chandise. Gradually foodstuffs joined the list of trade goods. Compared to agriculture, which provided a living for the majority of the Greek population and probably accounted for most personal income, trade remained economically insignificant. Still, trade was extremely important in other ways. Traditional cultural boundaries were transcended along with geographic ones, and mobility became fashionable. The centers of trade attracted open-minded individuals, adventurers, artisans, and artists, including some from the East. Wealth, experience, and all kinds of knowledge accumulated, stimulating yet larger enterprises. The material means necessary for this expansion came together along with the men needed to make use of them. The Phoenicians had been the first traders in the Aegean, but the Greeks soon rivaled them.

Cities situated at a natural meeting point of sea routes had the potential to grow into trade centers. Chalcis, for example, controlled the route from Euboea to the mainland. Because complex wind and current patterns at the narrowest point of the passage could tie up ships for extended periods, the harbor of Chalcis was a popular stopping point. Ships were waylaid there just as, in legendary times, Agamemnon had been denied favorable winds until he sacrificed his daughter Iphigenia in Aulis in accordance with an oracle. Rivalry with Chalcis seems to have spurred the neighboring city of Eretria to strive for similar prominence.

Corinth dominated the Corinthian isthmus, the land route connecting mainland Greece with the Peloponnese. Goods transported between the Saronic and the Corinthian Gulf were often unloaded there, and in later years a road—remains of which still exist—was built across the isthmus, so that entire ships, mounted on carts, could be towed from one body of water to the other. As already mentioned, sailing around the Peloponnese was both dangerous and time-consuming.

Whether out of civic necessity or thanks to the ingenuity of individual citizens, other cities likely entered the growing maritime trade in this period. In Miletus, an ancient caravan road from interior Anatolia to the coast seems already to have existed. Other cities shifted to maritime trade economies, but apparently had to make concerted efforts to attract commerce, among them Phocaea, which was a much smaller city than

Miletus but extremely active in trade; the Phocaens founded the colony of Massalia, now Marseilles, and a number of other colonies in that part of the world.

Chalcis and Eretria, both early commercial centers, were the first Greek city-states to establish colonies. Corinth followed suit quickly, and the cities in Asia Minor did so somewhat later. Once colonization was in full swing, even cities such as Megara, which had previously hardly counted as a commercial town, became active trading centers.

In the sixth century some thinkers began to devise theories that explained the world in a new and different way. This was especially true in Miletus, the most important, prosperous, and open-minded city in Asia Minor, where Thales, Anaximander, and Anaximenes developed the ideas that constitute the beginnings of Greek philosophy.

There is no indication that, apart from Sparta and Argos, any of the prominent cities of the time were involved in major wars or followed expansionist policies, except in their immediate vicinities. Nor do any of them seem to have been politically stable or well organized. On the contrary, these cities more than others seem to have been torn by severe internal feuds.

Upheavals were most frequent where the spectrum of social strata involved in the strife was particularly broad. During the sixth century, Miletus was gripped for two generations by *stásis*—that is, by radical division and violent feuds. One incident may serve as illustration. When the discontented underclass managed to seize power, they drove the wealthy families out of Miletus and let the cattle trample their children to death. When the wealthy families later forced their way back into the city, they seized as many rebels as they could, including children, covered them with tar, and set them on fire.

Corinth was the first polis in which a tyranny was established, and it is no coincidence that this form of rule was most common in the cities on the Corinthian isthmus, in Miletus, and in other commercial cities (not to mention Sicily).

Beyond the Peloponnese, it was clearly not politics or warfare but commerce and extensive maritime activity that changed some Greek cities and determined which of them would rise in importance. And it was not just power over other city-states that distinguished them. To be sure, they were superior to other cities, but their superiority was more one of rank than of influence.

The most important form of common action these enterprising cities took was the founding of colonies. Since the colonies were far away and could not be governed from a distance, they were generally set up as independent cities. The governmental form of the polis already existed when the first colonizing expeditions were sent out. *Polis* is commonly translated as "city-state," which is acceptable as long as one understands that the city was merely the focal point of an area made up of both city and countryside and that landowners were the dominant class. Furthermore, the modern sense of the word *state* is inappropriate in the context of ancient Greece.

Colonies enhanced the prestige of the mother cities by paying them tributes of respect, helping them in various ways, and facilitating their commercial ventures. From the late seventh to the sixth century, some cities, including Miletus and Phocaea, located their colonies systematically in order to dominate certain coastal sections and establish monopolies, perhaps for their mutual benefit. Naucratis, a Greek trading center in Egypt, was part of one such trade route. In this case, several cities cooperated to further their common commercial interests, but "power politics" was not their chief concern.

In this, the Greek cities differed radically from Rome, which continually increased its territory with the aim not of conquering but of maintaining and securing its position. Rome fortified what it had won by establishing colonies and regarding the area it dominated as a strategic unit over which it sought to maintain control. The Greek cities, by contrast, merely wanted their place in the world. They sat around the sea, as Plato put it, like frogs around a pond. The sea both separated and united them, a common free element that could be dominated only in a city's immediate vicinity. It is above all this position that determined the attitude of the Greeks, and all that followed from that.

From the eighth century on, none of the places that emerged as centers of the Greek world—the great sanctuaries and sites of athletic games, such as Delphi and Olympia—became focal points of power. Influential as Delphi was, its influence was primarily intellectual; cities and sacred sites were above all else places where ideas and problems were discussed.

This may explain why Athens, though located in the center of the Greek world, remained more or less isolated politically for so long, which seems counterintuitive. Usually the geographic center of a political region is occupied either by a strong, expansionist power or is subject to political pressures from the outside. It is remarkable that in ancient Greece, except on the Peloponnese, no such region developed, no region where opposing powers vied with each other, no region where a power vacuum immediately attracted outsiders or where any concentration of might made itself felt in every direction. Instead the city-states existed relatively peacefully side by side. For a long time, the reach of knowledge and trade extended further than that of politics.

Not much is written about Athens in this period precisely because Athens was not predestined by nature to become a major center of Aegean trade, nor did it make any special effort of its own to become one. Perhaps the Attic noblemen were too preoccupied with their roles in Athens itself. The most ambitious among them may have been busy with the city's affairs, and those who did engage in maritime activity seem to have been too few to convince the others even to improve the harbor.

The fact that Athens' political power was incommensurate with its size must have been connected with the difficulty the Greeks in general were experiencing in giving their energies political form.

Politically, the Greek city-states of that time were relatively weak. They had little authority, and the power they might have wielded was not consolidated. Taken as a whole, they amounted to less, not more, than the sum of their parts. Once again the only exception, Sparta, proves the rule.

This phenomenon had to do with the peculiar way in which Greek culture evolved, with the highly unusual constellations of circumstances that determined the course of Greek culture and its astonishing consequences. The character of these city-states was the result of their early history, in which power, conquest, and service to the community were of little importance.

The kings who had ruled the city-states in the archaic period were not kings in the modern sense, they were first among equals. Their importance depended largely on their person, while their institutional power and authority were minimal. The communities were too small for one family to rise far above the others and contained too little material wealth to sustain a ruling house. Above all, the monarchs failed to take advantage of the new means and energies that became available when, in the eighth century, the Greeks broke out of the old confines of the Aegean. Those who did succeed were unable to hold on to their success, and so almost everywhere in the eighth and early seventh centuries such regimes collapsed quietly and bloodlessly upon themselves. The ruling families fell back among the ranks of the other nobles, usually uneventfully.

These weak monarchies left little or no lasting impact on the city-states they ruled and instituted few policies of their own. That is why, when the aristocracies later set out to organize the city-states anew, they had no tradition of effective political government on which to model their efforts. There were no powerful public positions for the aristocrats to step into, no general expectation of superior leadership, such as existed in Rome after the fall of the monarchy there.

Some annual offices had been established under the kings to take care of certain governmental functions; later, others were added, the highest among them being the nine archons. Together with the council of nobles (and occasionally with the popular assembly in decisions about war and peace), they governed the community. Quite early on their number was relatively large, but they were given little power. This was an expression and a consequence of the city-state's lack of political centralization.

The Greek nobles were particularly concerned with retaining their autarky and self-reliance, and, on the whole, they succeeded. Sustained by the wealth of their families, they strove to be as self-reliant as possible. Not coincidentally, this impulse meshed with the desires of the polis, both then and later. Nobody wanted to depend on those over whom he had no control.

This tendency toward self-reliance is understandable in economic terms. But independence also meant limiting outside involvement in internal affairs as much as possible, even if that required resorting to arms or seeking revenge. Individuals wanted to retain their power and refused to yield it to a higher authority. Consequently, a plurality of diverse interests were in play at the highest levels of government. Curtailing them or even manipulating them in the interest of the common good was no easy task.

Self-reliance did not, however, exclude the possibility of several houses joining together in common enterprises, be they armed raids, commercial voyages, or even the founding of colonies. Such ventures might grow out of temporary alliances; any profit produced would be shared. And, of course, alliances were formed to achieve political goals.

Within the polis, too, there were cooperative projects, such as war or the building of city walls. The creation of public squares and the construction of temples, water systems, fountains, harbors, and—rarely— public buildings were also communal undertakings, though in some cases individuals acted as sponsors.

The emergence of a strong political center would have required a very different civic structure and the formation of a special governing apparatus based on the consolidation of material resources and the creation of administrative and enforcement agencies. But this could have been achieved only under a monarchy.

Thus, the ancient polis lacked an important element we take for granted today: centralization. Monarchies and, in the modern era, state governments promote and foster all kinds of goods and qualities, both tangible and intangible. They lay claim not only to taxes but to thoughts, feelings, and actions, taking them, to a certain extent, from the individual and absorbing them into the collective. This is true even if the citizenry exercises democratic control. By virtue of administration, bureaucracy, and police, centralized governments constitute a force in themselves.

Max Weber speaks of the "growing demand on the part of a society accustomed to absolute satisfaction of its needs for order and protection (police) in all areas of life." But government does not stop there. A great amount of regulation becomes necessary and is often supplied to excess. It comes into being partly to sustain and legitimize governmental power and partly as a result of increasing specialization. Ultimately, it culminates in the separation of state and society. This trend toward specialization can be resisted, but reversing it would be difficult. Political centralization does not necessarily produce a strong foreign policy.

Ancient Greece knew no such specialization in either its early or late period. It experienced no such limitation on the individual by large and impersonal forces. It had no need for regulation, much less for a separation of state and society. These differences between the ancient world and our own are so radical that the kinship we often feel for the Greeks is in many ways an obstacle to our attempts at understanding them.

There was at that time another way to create a strong political center. As happened in Rome, Sparta, and later in Athens and other cities, the aristocracy or the citizenry could have collectively identified with the polis, thus investing it with great power.

In Rome this power was concentrated in the senate and the magistrates. Because rank in the senate was linked to effort expended in the service of the *res publica*, senators increasingly adopted the state's interest as their own as they rose in influence. Powerful as individual and family ambition was, it essentially worked in favor of the republic and had to remain within well-defined and skillfully maintained limits. The result was a highly unified senate policy.

A great deal of authority was also invested in the office of the magistrates, who enjoyed much outward respect and were granted considerable responsibility. The senate needed them, and consequently it strengthened the magistrates' power while simultaneously curtailing their freedom to define their own goals. The office of the magistrates thus acquired an authority relatively independent from the individual officeholders.

The whole system functioned on the basis of a few clear and effective maxims that linked the magistrates and the senate, made both of them powerful, and were mutually enforced by them. The Romans adapted so well to this system that hardly anyone noticed how many other possible ways of life it cut off. Politics (and consequently warfare) became the central concern for the patrician members of the senate. In this sense they—

and, indirectly, the entire citizenry—were politicized. And because so much attention was focused on the republic as a whole, its political center became extremely powerful.

Crucial in all this was the fact that Rome as a political entity maintained a network of intensive foreign relations, a network that ultimately extended over the entire Mediterranean. Because Rome could draw on so many outside resources, it was able to keep adding to its military conquests in its wars and, more important, hold on to them.

Far less is known about how the Spartans related to their political structure. It is not known how strong the kings, the officials, and the aristocracy were. It is known, however, that everything, down to the last detail of daily life, was organized to promote physical and military training and to maintain a constant state of preparedness for conflict. From an early age, boys were raised in "herds" under the guidance of older youths, who instilled in them patriotism and introduced them to homosexual relations. All citizens were drilled to subordinate themselves entirely to the collective whole, which did not preclude personal contentment or pride. All of Sparta was an army camp during peacetime. And Sparta, like Rome, maintained a network of foreign holdings. Sparta's example shows that the Greeks were capable of developing the polis into a strong collective body capable of effective action. But most of the city-states considered the price of such an effort much too high. Their nobles were more inclined to pursue private interests, which they extended far into the public realm. They were reluctant to cede any measure of political control and sought to hold public offices, which they considered an honor. They were even willing to pay for this privilege, for officeholders had to meet administrative expenses themselves and were expected to make various financial contributions. The aristocrats in fact competed for public positions, and from 650 on, some of them aspired to autocracy. However, they were rather negligent in the performance of day-to-day duties and in imposing on themselves and on others the discipline necessary for acquiring, maintaining, and exercising power. Subordinating all else to the quest for power would have strained them and run counter to their emphasis on self-reliance.

These Greeks looked too far beyond the polis—their public sphere encompassed all of Greece—to become completely absorbed in the polis. They had political dealings with entities outside the city, but the values that prevailed in this larger public sphere were not of a political nature.

The leading members of Greek communities were too individualistic to feel themselves part of an abstract whole, in the Roman sense of the commonwealth. Perhaps they had this feeling at festivals, great religious celebrations, and in war. Perhaps they were occasionally joined together in outrage over miserable conditions, but this was not the rule.

Consequently, the officials, who were appointed annually, were essentially the executives of a "collective administration without a ruler," to use Max Weber's phrase. They were needed, and they had to be given authority, but it probably did not go beyond the necessary minimum. They had responsibilities, but this hardly elevated them above others of their social stratum. It is doubtful they obtained the bonuses that allowed the higher Roman magistrates to build up a relatively independent position. They were probably not expected to accomplish a great deal while in office.

Unlike the Romans, who swore allegiance to a highly defined form of government, the Greeks began in the postmonarchic period to break traditional molds and explore radical new possibilities. Whatever strengthening of discipline these new forms of government may have engendered, the danger of misuse of power remained great among the Greeks. Even the councils of noblemen failed to attain anything like the unity of the Roman senate. Without it, there was no possibility of granting public officials greater freedom of action. The Greek councils split into factions rather than acting in unanimity. It is no coincidence that, while the Romans could extend broad powers to individuals (called *dictatores*) without risking misuse of power, in Greece tyrannies frequently arose. Nor was it chance that so many bloody wars were fought among the Greeks.

Of course, the Greeks did much to strengthen their governmental structures. Creating internal peace and limiting vendettas were especially important. To this end, family disputes were submitted to arbitration by municipal organs or to judicial process. Coordination between institutions had to be established; rules on which to base decisions had to be codified. A calendar that named the years after archons was instituted. Laws were codified, and measures enacted for defense, city and harbor improvement, regulation of trade and customs, and, last but not least, for the protection of the coast against pirates and the organization of the hoplite army. Gradually, foreign policy and diplomacy—relying mostly on ties of friendship between aristocrats—became more sophisticated. Arbitration of conflicts between the cities was introduced, and certain extreme practices of warfare, such as cutting off drinking water or starving a besieged population, were prohibited. These prohibitions were largely obeyed, at least in mainland Greece. The development of cults and celebrations also figures centrally in this period.

The responsibility for all that was accomplished was shared. Much of the work must have been done by the officials and was perhaps even initiated by them, but the changes benefited them only in the sense that their responsibilities were gradually expanded and the number of public officials grew, as did the differentiation between their duties.

The broadening of their duties did not, however, lead to an accumulation of power for the officials, who enjoyed no increase in political benefits that might have raised them significantly above the rest of the citizens. Many official tasks were still taken care of by subgroups within the population. These groups maintained the census of citizens, for example, assigned rights and duties, and were responsible for military recruitment.

The officials were particularly impotent in emergencies. Wise men had to be consulted in legislative matters. Officials themselves were often involved in feud cases, and conflicts could be settled only by calling on mediators invested with special authority. Otherwise tyrannies would have sprung up more frequently and the tyrants would have found it easier to establish their power on a more permanent basis.

It is interesting to note that the Greek aristocracy largely failed to exploit the political advantages that might have derived from their role as mediators between men and the gods. The leaders of the community were responsible for performing sacrifices, but no personal prestige was associated with those tasks. If aristocratic officeholders donated altars and sacrificial animals or organized festivals, they did it to demonstrate their superiority over others but not to increase their power or influence. The priests were hardly more than executors of sacrificial rites, for which they were given respect (as well as a share of the sacrificed animals), and they performed their duties as individuals. They were not members of a priestly cast that laid claim to superior knowledge or an authority of its own. They had no monopoly on divining omens or tracing crises back to religious causes. Instead, problems of this sort were taken for elucidation to soothsayers, prophets, oracles, or, if necessary, to expiators, who often came from the East. In such cases, expertise rather than power was called for.

Consequently, life in the city-states did not promote the ambition to wield political power. The cities pursued certain foreign policies, deterring encroachments on their territories or, occasionally, conquering a nearby town. But such conquests grew out of the circumstances of the moment and were likely fueled by the ambition of individuals. The cities maintained their relationships with other cities in a similar manner. No far-reaching foreign policy developed from this situation, as might have if the city-state had cooperated more closely to form a partnership of power.

The Greek city-states of the archaic period functioned as a framework for the various activities of their aristocrats. The citizens had reason to be proud of their cities: There were times when they were willing to die for them; and citizenship in a great city carried considerable prestige.

But the true focus of the Greeks' politics—to the extent that their politics went beyond affairs immediately at hand—was on great deeds, and occasion for these deeds often arose in faraway places. Such deeds occurred primarily in the context of conflict, as in contests with all of Greece as spectator, not as policies pursued in the interest of the city.

Ironically, if the Greeks were to develop the world's first democracies, it was necessary that their leading circles not be overly concerned with power nor its disciplined application. The political form, which was to be of such consequence to the future, could arise among them only if politics was, in the beginning, of relatively minor importance. Politics could arise because the Greeks were first able to develop their culture in rich and diverse ways. But the Greeks did so in an atypical way. The first democracies in world history arose in large part because of something the Greeks lacked but also because of a wealth of abilities, talents, ideas, and philosophies they had developed in a basically apolitical public sphere.

Since each Athenian lived more or less for himself rather than thinking of the community, the city's status was of little concern. Athens' great size did not count for much in the archaic period. It may even have contributed to the inefficiency of aristocratic rule. No major defense efforts were necessary except for the protection of the long coastline. For this purpose groups of well-to-do individuals, the *naucrariae*, were each requested to supply one ship and two horsemen, the latter to watch the coast and call for reinforcements if necessary. The defeat suffered in the war against Megara seems to have had no lasting effect on the aristocrats in power.

In a Greek world where public institutions were generally not considered important, they must have been particularly marginal in Attica. We don't know how the Attic settlements outside Athens managed basic administrative tasks or how far the authority of the Attic officials and law courts reached. Perhaps these settlements were dominated by the local nobility, or they may have respected one another's domains and become involved in conflicts only when their interests collided. In any case, the impact of political and judicial power cannot have been very great, given the size of the Attic territory. Even the council of noblemen could not change this.

Most of the Attic settlements were hardly aware that they were part of Athens' domain. Their contacts were relatively minor. But this changed in the course of the great crisis that began to shake Athens around 600, as it had shaken other parts of the Greek world earlier.

It was inevitable that the great migrations of the colonial period would bring about changes in the mother country. The initial reaction in Athens to the emigration of many people was relief, but the opening up of new horizons and spheres of activity was bound to have other effects at home. Seeing the luxuries of the great Eastern cultures awakened new ambitions and material desires. As successful entrepreneurs gained wealth, living standards rose. At a time of unprecedented growth, more and more Athenians were willing to undertake daring ventures. Demands increased faster than the resources to satisfy them, and many Athenians must have lived beyond their means. Because of the risks of sea travel, enterprises abroad could bring either great gains or huge losses.

The rise and decline of families not only made for greater social differentiation but also precipitated many conflicts. In part, the changes taking place in the upper social class paralleled those among the farmers; in part, they were caused by farmers. Many of the innovations introduced at this time were also due to the influence of Eastern teachings, such as modernization in agriculture by investing in vineyards, olive trees, and livestock, all of which helped increase production over the long term. Since olive trees don't bear fruit for the first ten years, planting them had been a costly, risky proposition. Added to this were the perennial uncertainties of crop yields and animal husbandry. Often farmers could only obtain the seed for planting by borrowing capital. These problems, combined with diminished individual holdings due to the splitting of inherited land, meant that more and more farmers were no longer able to make a living on their land. In many cases indebtedness led to loss of land and ultimately of personal freedom, because the borrower and his family were subject to imprisonment if unable to repay loans.

The situation of the farmers was made even worse by the attempts of ambitious noblemen to reserve the use of public and sacred lands, such as pastures, for themselves. The nobility in general did its best to exploit the farmers, and because the courts were in the hands of the aristocracy the farmers initially had little recourse against these abuses.

But resistance formed with time, as the limit of the people's endurance was reached. Increasingly, those in desperate straits began to rebel. There were bloody battles, civil wars. Ambitious members of the aristocracy were more than willing to lead the rebels; in many cases they probably fomented the unrest themselves. From the middle of the seventh century on, this kind of situation led to the usurpation of power by individuals, or, in other words, to tyranny.

The common ground that had made it possible for people to live together was fast eroding. Reality had become more complicated, and the rules that governed social interaction were no longer obvious. Among the masses, fantasies of what might be possible were stimulated by reports from the colonies, where things were done that were nearly unthinkable in the mother country. The landless were given land, and sometimes members of the lower classes got as much as their social superiors. Such practices could not simply be imitated back at home, but they did have an alarming and provocative effect there.

The many individual injustices endured by the farmers in their relations with their creditors, primarily noblemen living in their vicinity, expanded into a broader social and political crisis. Hesiod, writing soon after Homer in the early seventh century, remarked that in poorly run cities the children no longer obeyed their parents. The authority of the older generation was apparently no longer strong enough to educate and shape the younger. Hesiod wrote that in the Iron Age, as he referred to his own time, fathers were strangers to their children and children to their fathers, and that the same held true among friends and between host and guest.

This crisis meanwhile became more acute. It could not have been resolved within the traditional system even if the aristocrats had been able to change their ways. The hierarchical structure had been too profoundly disturbed. A revolution of values loomed, and a new basis for coexistence had to be found.

This modus vivendi could not be found overnight; it took time for an alternative to the past to evolve. But in this period, overtly political and polis-oriented activities were markedly on the rise. People could no longer live alongside each other—they had to live *with* each other—and the polis as a whole was bound to become a problem. Most of what is known about this process, which occurred throughout Greece, comes from the history of Athens.

The city was the scene of an amazing series of events in the early sixth century. Because the crisis had caught up with Athens later than it did other places, the Athenians had been able to learn from what took place in other, more advanced cities. In all likelihood, no one among the Attic nobility was equipped to establish autocratic rule; some may have tried to seize power and failed; the size of the country may have made it especially hard to muster the necessary power for such a step. Whatever the case, instead of tyranny reform was given a try. That seemed the most likely way to forestall civil war.

What happened is as difficult to explain as the victory at Salamis. A man of unusual ability stepped forward, a man who stood above the confusion of the situation and saw the possibility of trying something new, something different that went beyond the solutions that immediately offered themselves. Solon was bold in his concept of a new order. He was also completely unselfish, and in this he differed from Themistocles.

Although what Solon accomplished was actually quite limited, his exploits possess an implausible fairy-tale quality. Perhaps the main reason Solon's achievements strain credibility is that the conditions of the period are so foreign to us. The course of action the Athenians took brought about only a partial solution, but it was one that opened up entirely new possibilities. This course was found not because Solon, or the Greeks in general, were particularly gifted but because a peculiar set of circumstances occurred at that time—in Athens, among the Greeks, and in the Mediterranean world in general. The time was ripe for politics to arise among the Greeks.

Around 620, a good decade after Cylon's attempt to usurp power, Dracon gave the Athenians their first written code of laws. His name is familiar primarily from the "Draconian" punishments he assigned to crimes such as larceny and vagrancy. But he also made several crucial reforms, chief among them establishing the distinction between deliberate and unintentional homicide. Someone who killed unintentionally would only be exiled, if the victim's family refused to forgive him. The majority of Dracon's legislation was replaced with new laws a generation later, but his laws concerning manslaughter remained in force for a long time.

It is impossible to classify Dracon politically. His laws show a belief in stricter regulation. They impose harsh penalties for common criminals, as well as limitations on the nobility's penchant for engaging in blood feuds. It is possible, however, that Dracon's legislation was drafted in direct response to a rapidly deteriorating social situation. Even if that were the case, the problems Dracon addressed were still relatively benign, and the conflicts that arose later were of quite a different nature and intensity. It was then that the oppressed farmers banded together, as popular anger threatened to turn into open rebellion in response to the aristocrats' refusal to introduce reforms.

In this situation Solon, son of Execestides, tried to convince his fellow citizens that their society was fundamentally flawed, that they were living in "misorder" *(dysnomia)*. Indeed, he said, they were heading toward catastrophe, but they were not helpless. He reportedly urged all parties to entrust the city to a wise man who might reestablish order.

There are no equivalents in English for the Greek words *katartister* or *euthynter*, used to describe a person given the powers Solon was given. "Arbitrator" would come closest, if the term were not so closely associated with mediation. In this case, however, mediation was at most a fortunate side effect of the reforms, because what mattered to Solon was the establishment of a new "right order," not a mere compromise between conflicting interests. (Solon considered improper the very notion that these interests could be at odds.) The best translation is the cumbersome "he who puts things right again."

Solon was ultimately elected to public office, possibly directly to the post of archon (chief magistrate), most likely in 594 (although it may have been as late as 575). When elected, he was given almost unlimited powers as well as a substantial treasury, which could have been procured only by taxes on the wealthy. He was almost certainly allowed to hire a staff and may have undertaken to build a rudimentary police force.

This marked the beginning of something entirely new in Attic history. Previous efforts to bring about a better and more just social order had been limited in scope. Now, for the first time, the entire structure of the polis underwent reform.

Nothing comparable had ever happened in world history: a profound transformation of existing conditions, initiated not by a monarch, or an aspiring monarch, but by an individual chosen by the citizenry. Solon did not relieve the citizens of their own responsibility but merely enacted what they seemed to want. In all likelihood people were willing to entrust their fate to him because their fear of violence and murder left them no choice. But whatever their motivation, they placed immense trust in Solon.

Similar attempts to restore order at the behest of the community may have been made in other cities, but what distinguishes Athens is the magnitude of both the problems and the forces mobilized to solve them.

Solon came from a noble family that claimed descent from Attic royalty. He was born around 630, traveled widely in Greece, and was in close contact with others who were concerned, as he was, with resolving the manifold difficulties that plagued the Greek poleis. Their circle is reputed to have been quite large, and their advice was in frequent demand.

The Greek nobility generally had an advantage over the farmers in education, wealth, and their connections, but they had neither a military nor a permanent police force at their disposal. At most they could hire retainers for brief periods. And because the city-states lacked political unity, there was little esprit de corps among the nobles. Consequently, members of the middle and lower strata could also acquire power, especially at moments of crisis such as a rebellion, in which case neither side could hope to win easily. If a polis were unwilling to let such a confrontation culminate in civil war or the usurpation of power by a tyrant, it had to find an impartial mediator.

In this way, a theory of politics evolved that emphasized service not to those in power but in the common interest of the polis. The large number of cities and their small size, the impossibility of monarchical rule, and the existence of a circle of relatively autonomous wise men all contributed to that development. Exactly how these elements worked together becomes clear in the context of the extraordinary path Greece followed.

The circle of wise men lent support to those who sought continued independence in the face of powerful and sometimes threatening forces. The standards and judgment the men possessed may have provided some guarantee that the person chosen "to put things right" was in fact worthy of the trust that would be placed in him. Athens' choice of Solon may have been suggested and supported by these men; his work was certainly carried out under their scrutiny.

The constant debate these men engaged in distanced them intellectually from the status quo. It was in this circle that ideas of "right order" took shape, and the effects of these intellectual deliberations are apparent in Solon's work. For however much of his political vision was original to him, it must also have been deeply rooted in the thinking of the time.

When Solon suggested the Athenians were headed for catastrophe, he was able to do so with reference to an old Greek belief: Zeus was believed to punish cities for the unjust actions of their leaders. At first, people could only imagine this punishment taking the form of bad weather or failed harvests. It was said that the oaks on the hill bore no acorns and the sea was devoid of fish to catch in evidence of Zeus's displeasure. Thus the oppressed people of Athens suffered doubly: first, from the injustice of their leaders and, second, from the punishments Zeus visited on the city. All the people could do was demand justice from the aristocracy (and suggest the alternative of a perfect, properly run city). This may have made the citizenry feel better, but it hardly provided an impetus for action; at best it expressed a resigned faith in justice.

Solon carried this thinking a step further, asserting that Zeus's punishment was more direct. Injustice, he argued, was causing the city to fall into the worst kind of servitude, one that divided it, awakened dormant hostilities, and cost many lives. The oppression, exploitation, and enslavement of so many farmers were seen as afflicting the entire city. Solon regarded the progression from servitude to civil war as inevitable and pronounced that an "unavoidable disease" was approaching the city.

But this very inevitability, Solon insisted, made it possible to act. The disease had not yet infected the majority of Athenians. The city as a whole could be saved if measures were taken in time.

These attitudes represent a major step forward in the development of the polis, and they were viewed in a theological context. Solon believed that punishment was meted out by Zeus, and the earthly events he witnessed now lent support to preexisting belief. At the same time, however, Solon separated the realm of politics from that of nature, where Zeus made the weather according to laws completely divorced from human actions. Solon's innovation was not just an analytical accomplishment, a brilliant strategy for dealing with the problems at hand, but also a feat of abstraction. No longer was everything that happened understood in reference to one's city; no longer did people naively see themselves as the center of the world (so that even bad weather was their own fault). Instead, politics was seen to have consequences in the political realm and only there.

This insight made it far easier to make important changes in the conditions under which people lived. Convincing others of the necessity for change was simplified now that certain divine punishments could be explained in purely political and social terms.

The city could now be understood as a political unit in an entirely new way. When injustice reaches a certain level, the misery of the oppressed becomes the misfortune of all. According to an old, magical belief, if a murder went unavenged the mere presence of the murderer was a stain upon the entire city and would bring on calamity. Solon now declared that in Athens not even the land was free—it suffered under the weight of mortgages—and civil war was bound to follow. Everyone was in the same boat, and these ideas had the effect of bringing everyone much closer together.

Solon directed himself particularly to those who thought the fate of the whole did not affect them. On the contrary, he said, nobody is safe from "public evil"—no gate can keep it out, evil is capable of vaulting the tallest fence. Unless it is stopped, Solon contended, evil finds everyone, even the one who hides in the remotest reaches of his own house.

In these remarks we encounter for the first time the idea that the citizens are responsible for their city. The gods, kings, and the aristocratic ruling class are not to blame if things go wrong, the collective is. Everyone may be guilty to the same degree, and nothing can be accomplished without a leader designated to "put things right again." But with the help of such a leader, a way can be found. Responsibility brought with it the possibility of action, a notion that may sound trite to the contemporary reader, but at the time it was a remarkably innovative idea. There are parallels in other cultures to the political thinking of the Greeks, especially in China, but this particular idea is found nowhere else. It represents the beginning of a specifically European way of political thinking.

Solon cut through an impenetrable tangle of misery and hopelessness that had seemed to leave only a choice between resignation and rebellion and revealed a new option: a reasonable process that could be undertaken by coordinated efforts. The city could be restored to order again, without a monarch.

Events acquire meaning in cultural contexts; the justice of what has come to pass and of what threatens to happen becomes evident to those affected. If the citizens (under Solon's guidance) warded off the "inescapable disease," they reasoned that punishment would strike only the guilty. If, however, they failed to take action (even though they were in a position to know better), they themselves would be to blame.

This view is foreshadowed in the *Odyssey* passage where Telemachus berates the people of Ithaca for putting up with the immoral behavior of Penelope's suitors. "You should be ashamed before your neighbors . . . and fear the wrath of the gods." In some way, then, attempts had been made before to place responsibility for what happened in a city as a whole on the citizens. In the absence of a monarchy or an aristocracy forceful enough to rule, this was probably only natural. Who else was there to turn to but the public itself?

Solon was distressed not only by the inner difficulties of Athens but also by its failures abroad. He was pierced "to the heart" by his home city's having given up the island of Salamis, for he valued highly the greatness and fame of Athens as "Ionia's oldest city" and felt humiliated by other Greeks who would point and say, "There goes an Athenian, one of those who lost control over Salamis." Solon urged resumption of the war against Megara. Supporting the city's government meant stronger identification with the city. This inevitably carried over into foreign relations and resulted in strengthening the city's political unity.

.   .   .

Solon's ideas were as conservative as they were visionary. He was convinced that the order he was establishing had always been right, that it had always existed in some form. He merely wanted to preserve what he saw as a timeless and enduring structure. But once such an order has been severely disturbed, any attempt to put it right again requires change, hence the new elements he introduced.

In a long poem, Solon contrasts "misorder" with *eunomia*, the "good order." He does not describe this right order, preferring instead to say simply that under it everything turns out right and that it makes everyone behave as he should. "It smooths what is rough, assuages the urge to overindulge, and cuts down presumption," he wrote. He was convinced that human affairs were like the sea, which, as long as it was not stirred up by storms, represented "the image of justice." All one had to do was remove causes of disturbance (and prevent the formation of new ones), and everything would be fine. *Eunomia* could be achieved by returning to the original right order. Proper governance was a matter of restoration, not a radical new concept. The restoration of the rights and responsibilities of the citizenry was paramount if Athens was not to devolve into a society of lords and slaves.

By combining "force with law," Solon made deep changes in Attic society. He freed mortgaged farms by decreeing the cancellation of all debts. Creditors lost their loans no matter how justified their claims had been under previous statutes. Surely not all of them deserved this as punishment for exploitation, but Solon apparently felt it important that the farmers (at least those who still lived on their land) return to the state of affairs that had prevailed before the onset of general indebtedness. One concern may have been worry, common throughout Greece, that there be enough "houses"—that is, independent farms whose owners were sufficiently wealthy to equip themselves as hoplites. In Solon's words, canceling debts "freed" the earth. Otherwise, he added, the people could not have been restrained, bloodshed would have been unavoidable, and the city would have been deserted.

Solon initiated the return of Athenians who had been legally or illegally sold into slavery elsewhere in Greece or who had fled the polis to escape their debt burden. This amnesty applied to everyone but those condemned for attempting to establish tyranny. (This exclusion may have been aimed at the surviving followers of Cylon, though all those directly involved with him had been killed.) Solon most likely turned to the affluent for the money to buy back the slaves. Whether the landholdings of returning farmers were returned to them is not known.

The relief from debt may have been necessary to preserve internal peace. What is more surprising is the decision to bring back those who had lived abroad—in some cases for many years. Perhaps there existed a solidarity among the exploited or a sense of responsibility for all who had once been Athenians; perhaps friendship and family ties played a role. But this is not a sufficient explanation. It seems likely that Solon was intent on erasing all the consequences of the great crisis—the "misorder"—and that he wanted to restore the conditions that existed prior to the crisis. It must be assumed that he considered his goals not arbitrary but predetermined— indeed, willed by the gods—and his insistence on repatriating Athenians living all over Greece supports this theory. *Eunomia* must have had this meaning for him.

Solon's policies also suggest that throughout Greece, the farmers were essential, powerful members of society. In some places they made up a major part of the infantry forces. They were therefore an integral part of the "right order" and provided Solon with another reason to conceive of this order in conservative terms, for any attempt to suppress or seize control of the farmers would have been regarded as violating tradition.

Restoration of the old conditions was clearly in the interest of the oppressed. But Solon also felt that the political order should for the most part be restored to its original conception: The aristocracy should lead, and the people, the popular assembly, should retain their previous rights. This arrangement did not preclude certain essential modifications, however. Candidacy for office, for example, was to be determined in the future by census rather than by membership in certain families. It remains an open question whether this reform significantly altered the pool of eligible candidates.

. . .

Solon also revised the census classifications. Traditionally there had been three classes: the knights (broadly equivalent to the nobility), the *zeugitae* (well-to-do farmers), and the *thetes* (peasants and laborers). After Solon's reforms, the wealthiest of the knights, the "five hundred–measures group," constituted a separate class. Members of the other classes were determined by their annual incomes, measured in increments of 300, 200, or 100 measures of corn or oil. It is not known what place merchants and artisans held in this system. The new order was obviously meant to spread civic burdens and taxes more evenly (taxes were not levied regularly but only in case of need), as well as control access to certain offices, especially those involved in the financial administration.

Solon also created the Council of Four Hundred to represent the broader base of the population. He established a people's court to decide certain legal cases and recodified all the laws, among other things setting limits on the lavishness of funerals.

His introduction of the public's right to bring criminal charges is particularly noteworthy. Previously, only the actual victim of crime could take a matter to court; now anyone had the right to do so in most cases (the exceptions being murder and manslaughter). Under Solon, if victims were put under pressure by perpetrators, others could act in their stead. With no public prosecutors, citizens themselves had to see to it that justice was done. Crimes against the community were to be handled in similar fashion by the citizenry, adding further to its growing list of civic responsibilities.

Finally, Solon's reforms included initiatives to improve Athens' economic structure. He prohibited the export of all foodstuffs except olives, so as to avert the risk of shortages or inflation. He put restrictions on the purchase of land, tried to attract craftsmen by offering them citizenship if they settled in the commonwealth, and ordered parents to arrange for their children to learn a trade if they did not have enough land to bequeath to them. In return, the children were obliged to support their parents in old age. Solon also introduced new standards for weights and measures.

Solon wrote so many laws that no building had walls large enough to hold the wooden tablets on which they were inscribed, so they were mounted on freestanding rotating panels. Every citizen had to swear obedience to the laws. To avoid being pressured into making changes, Solon left Athens for ten years of travel and study.

Although many of his laws remained in force for a long time and formed the basis of the Attic legal system, the Athenians of Solon's day don't seem to have shown much interest in his accomplishments. For them what mattered above all else was his abolishment of debts, the *seisachtheia*, or "shaking off of the burden."

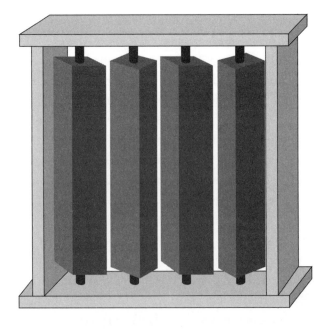

Axones. Solon's laws were carved into wooden tablets and the letters probably painted in color. To protect the wood from the elements the tablets were set up in a place that was roofed over. Because the texts were lengthy, the tablets were set up in rows on turning rods. (Axone originally meant "axle.") This picture attempts to visualize such a display of tablets.

. . .

Reform met with violent opposition. Many of the landowning class attacked Solon—they had not expected him to carry out the promises he had made—but sharp criticism came from the other side as well. A group known as the Isomoiria demanded that all the land of Attica be confiscated and redistributed evenly among the citizens. This plan seems to have originated with a few exceptionally power-hungry aristocrats but spread quickly to other segments of society, where anger at creditors and exploiters and all the illegal practices of many aristocrats was still fresh in the people's memory.

The popular demand for complete redistribution of the land was accompanied by a plea that Solon retain his extraordinary powers and become the ruler of the city. It was widely presumed that otherwise such radical changes would not survive. The great majority of the people were interested primarily in their own economic situation and reasoned that only tyrannical power could be effective against the large landowners and their friends abroad. But that was the last thing Solon wanted.

It is not easy to understand why Solon so categorically rejected the idea of ruling Athens as a tyrant. It can be deduced that he was not tempted by the personal advantages such a position would have offered—advantages that seemed to many Greeks of his time desirable beyond measure—for Solon was convinced that ill-gotten gain brought no happiness; this conviction clearly proved stronger than any temptation. What set him apart from his peers was his decision to pass up the opportunity to amass personal wealth. He was not willing to abandon his rectitude for the sake of material goods.

The noblemen, he said, were ruining the city; they were insatiable and "did not know how to enjoy pleasures in the carefree spirit of a banquet." This criticism sounds like a lecture, and it probably was delivered in that spirit. Solon shared many of the attitudes of his time but turned them upside down. Like all aristocrats, he wanted to stand out among his peers, but he did so by pursuing a unique goal: refusing to become a tyrant. It was only because he was so different from the other nobles that he was able to win the trust of the masses.

He could actually have been useful to his city as a tyrant. Tyranny was not, at that time, universally despised. Because people had little experience with a constitutional order, they did not resent the arbitrary use of power. Several of the Seven Wise Men, who were famous for their practical wisdom, had been tyrants, among them Periander of Corinth and Thrasybulus of Miletus. Pittacus of Mytilene, like Solon, had been appointed as a restorer of order but then used the authority granted him to rule as he saw fit.

The tyrants in fact remedied many ills of their cities, overseeing the development of new skills and technologies into trades, improving economic conditions, and stabilizing the economy by keeping the ambitions of their fellow aristocrats in check for many years or decades. Such a tyrant might have been quite beneficial to Athens.

But in surviving sources, including a number of Solon's poems, there is not the slightest indication that Solon considered tyranny as a means to achieve his goals. The accusations leveled at him blame him not for any lack of willingness to serve the city but for failing to close the net in which he had, with the help of God, caught the Athenians. From the standpoint of his contemporaries all that seemed to matter was Solon's fame. This attitude was completely in keeping with the spirit of the old Greek heroes, each of whom vied to surpass the others in greatness. Solon, too, was concerned with fame and honor; he, too, wanted to act toward friend and foe in the old way, loving the former and striking terror in the latter, but he also wanted to introduce new values into the contest.

There were two ideals at work here, that of manhood and that of the order of the polis. But for Solon there could be no conflict between them since his standards were based on the polis, whose order could only be right or wrong. Once the right order was established, tyranny was out of the question. Absolute power was acceptable only in a state of transition. Solon must have felt he had held that power long enough.

Solon lived at a time of fundamental change in Greek political thinking. The Greeks' efforts to find practical solutions to myriad, pressing individual problems gradually gave way to the attempt to establish a reasonable and just order for the polis as a whole. The longer the political crisis lasted, the more desperate seemed the need for generally valid principles of governance that addressed issues of property law, debt resolution, the granting of political rights, and the relationship between the aristocracy and the rest of the people.

In a situation characterized by so much conflict, it is perhaps surprising that Solon faced so little opposition. One likely explanation for the failure of a monarchy to take hold (though that would have been a more efficient form of government in the short term) is the highly tradition-bound nature of early Greek political thinking. This tendency might have been reversed if the tyrants had succeeded in effecting major changes in the way life was lived in their own city-states and beyond the borders of their immediate domains. But this was not to happen.

Consequently the idea of power remained relatively unimportant. The conviction that tyranny in itself would grow was wrong, eventually evolving into a widely accepted and influential intellectual imperative.

These newly discovered ideas—the rejection of tyranny, the administration of the polis, the responsibility of the citizens—and the fact that they gained broad acceptance all worked in the same direction. Added to this was the appearance that divine justice—in which many Greeks believed fervently, despite or because of their powerlessness—actually worked. Once the lower classes began to rebel, injustice began to be met with punishment. (If the punishments did not necessarily strike those most deserving of them, well, the same could be said of Zeus's wrath.)

For all these reasons Solon was concerned not just with rectifying economic misery or social and political tensions (which could perhaps have better been addressed with the means available to a tyrant) but also with how the polis should be constituted. Here, too, however, economic problems were much in the foreground.

Solon's bold and radical actions would hardly have been possible had he not adhered closely to the task set him and to the terms of his authority; likewise, his basic orientation toward accepted standards of what constituted the right order was essential to the acceptance of his less conventional measures. His pragmatic intellectual approach provided him a base of support comparable to that which reformers of later eras received from their monarchs and, increasingly in recent times, from the state. The importance of such an approach to a reform movement cannot be overemphasized.

At first, Solon's success was limited. While he was able to help many Athenians defuse numerous explosive situations and lay the base for future improvements of the Attic economy by profoundly altering existing conditions, he also stirred up discontent and opened up new realms of possibility in the people's imagination. Warring parties were not immediately ready to give up their claims. And though it was no longer as easy for the aristocrats to exploit the farmers, this did not restrain their excessive thirst for power. Even after Solon, the ambitions of many aristocrats continued to reach far beyond what was legally permitted. Solon's way of asserting the importance of the community as a whole may have been exemplary, but the example set was not immediately followed.

Solon was clearly confronted with a dilemma: He could not simply let the aristocracy run the city, yet the large class of farmers, though capable of rebellion, was not competent to exercise long-term, consistent political influence.

But Solon would not have viewed the dilemma in these terms. For him the aristocrats—or more accurately, the affluent—were, thanks to their wealth and education, the only ones who could lead the city. He must have assumed that once *eunomia* was established, they would once again govern justly. This is where he made his mistake.

What else could he have done? It was possible to give the common people a voice in public affairs, but this alone could never have amounted to very much, especially in Athens with its large territory to govern.

This flaw in Solon's concept limited only his immediate success, however. Indirectly, his reforms continued to have an effect because they made possible a clear distinction between the status quo and the right order. If he had become a tyrant he might have achieved more for his city in the short run, but by rejecting tyranny he reinforced his idea of civic responsibility. As a tribute to his legacy schoolchildren would learn his poems by heart for a long time to come.

In a sense Solon was the first citizen. Although he demanded more of himself than of others, he expected nothing more for himself in return, and he did not seek to be superior to the common man.

A period ensued—its exact duration depends on the date assigned to Solon's new legislation—during which dissension flared again among the aristocrats. Around 560 B.C. Pisistratus first seized tyrannical power in Athens. After being driven out, he seized it a second time a few years later, but it was not until about 547 that he established himself permanently. He died in 528 and was succeeded by his son Hippias, who was overthrown in 510.

In 566–565, shortly before the advent of tyranny, the great festival of Athena, the *panathenaea*, was instituted, probably about the same time that the first temple dedicated to the goddess was built on the Acropolis. Major communal projects could still be undertaken, it seemed, in spite of all the political infighting.

During these first decades after Solon, members of the middle and lower classes could play a role in politics only as retainers of noblemen, who were at that time not only caught up in their usual fights over mostly personal interests but had also divided into two large factions. The basic aim of both factions was to rule Athens by installing one of their leaders as tyrant. Neither side succeeded, probably because they kept each other in check. The situation changed when a third party appeared on the scene.

Pisistratus, son of Hippocrates, came from the coastal city of Brauron, about halfway up Attica's east coast. Most of his allies came from Tetrapolis, near Marathon, and many belonged to families that up to then had been of little importance in Athens. Poor peasants from the hills northeast of Athens (the "hillmen") are also specifically mentioned in historical records as being among his followers, as are some other groups who had been adversely affected by Solon's reforms.

The few extant sources on Pisistratus suggest that he was very different from his rivals: more decisive, quicker to act, willing to risk everything on a gamble. He had distinguished himself as a general in a war against Megara, and he benefited from the military honor, particularly since he liked showy appearances. He was also generous and charming in manner, qualities that won him popularity among the broader public. He must have worked to win the favor of the masses in more concrete ways, too, though it is not known if he promised redistribution of land. He was as unscrupulous as he was adept at turning every situation to his own advantage and winning allies in many circles. The story of his rise to power, especially on his first two tries, is a rather poor testimonial to the Athenians' political acumen and the quality of their institutions, but that is no reason to disbelieve it.

One day Pisistratus appeared before the popular assembly showing a wound (apparently self-inflicted) and claimed his enemies were trying to kill him. The assembly granted him a guard of fifty men armed with clubs. With their help, he soon proceeded to seize the Acropolis and install himself as tyrant of Athens.

Although he could certainly have gathered fifty men by other means, what was important about the guard was its official character. It was a visible sign of how much power the people were willing to grant this man. There is no telling, of course, who was present at this assembly; much could happen in Athens without the majority of citizens being aware of it. The element of surprise clearly played in Pisistratus's favor, because unexpected actions had the best chance of success—one just had to avoid getting into trouble afterward. But even this was not likely when one's opponents were so divided among themselves.

Solon, who was about eighty years old by this time, spoke up vigorously against Pisistratus's takeover. Several of his poems clearly refer to the takeover and the years that followed. In one poem he tries to teach the Athenians a lesson about political connections, writing that as rain falls from clouds and thunder follows lightning, so cities are ruined by powerful men. He observes that under an autocrat, the people are "plunged into servitude," and that they allow this to happen out of ignorance.

But the world of men differs from nature, and once again Solon teaches that citizens can prevent political disaster if they remain alert and act promptly. Once a ruler gains too much power it is difficult to restrain him later on. The lessons Solon wanted people to learn in his poetry were quite simple: Given proper awareness of what is taking place, the people can affect the course of events; the chain of causality can be broken.

In another poem, Solon, after sounding his warnings, expresses the bitter experience of one whose thinking is slightly ahead of his contemporaries'. Once the truth became apparent, he wrote, the people would realize how wise he had been.

A third poem deals specifically with the decision to give Pisistratus his retinue of bodyguards. Here Solon tells the Athenians that it is not the gods but they themselves who are responsible for their present plight. He reproaches them for looking only at the words of an ambitious man but paying no attention to his actions. Where their own individual interests were concerned, he said, they were shrewd and circumspect, but when it came to making communal decisions, they showed "hollow judgment."

After the assembly's decision to give Pisistratus bodyguards, Solon placed his weapons in front of his house. He was too old to make use of them himself, but he wanted to show that action ought to be taken against the usurper.

The tyranny of Pisistratus did not last long. His opponents joined together to expel him, but rivalry soon divided them again. Because they kept each other mutually in check, one of them, Megacles, got the idea that an alliance with Pisistratus could be advantageous to him. Megacles belonged to the clan of the Alcmaeonids, and was the son-in-law of Cleisthenes, the tyrant of Sicyon, and father of the Attic reformer Cleisthenes the Lawgiver. The pact was sealed with a wedding: Pisistratus married Megacles' daughter. To her father, the deal was worth the dissension it created in his own party.

Pisistratus's return to power was accomplished in a manner that Herodotus thought unworthy of the Greeks (who, after all, claimed to be smarter than the barbarians), let alone of the Athenians, who were reputed to be the most intelligent among the Greeks. The conspirators dressed a stately young woman from a village in central Attica as the goddess Athena, and Pisistratus drove into the city under her aegis. Heralds were sent ahead to proclaim that the goddess herself was bringing him back. The Athenians fell for the trick; they reportedly even bowed to the goddess, and Pisistratus took over the Acropolis a second time.

His reign did not last long this time, either. Megacles again made peace with his friends, and together they forced Pisistratus to flee. He spent ten years in exile, during which he came into possession of some silver mines in Thrace, on the northern coast of the Aegean. He leased them out and used the profits to fund his final return to Athens at the head of a conquering army.

Pisistratus could have built up a realm of his own in Thrace, as many Greek noblemen of the time did. These noblemen would conquer land or win over members of the native population who would help them found small fiefdoms. They would then bring their followers to settle the land as colonists, practice piracy with little interference, and live a princely existence. They chose this life because they were enterprising and could enjoy a freedom unknown at home; they frequently also established ties of kinship with the local kings, who appreciated the clever, crafty, and cultivated Greeks and were impressed by their methods of exploiting every opportunity. Miltiades, an uncle of the victor at Marathon, founded a small dominion of this kind on the Thracian Chersonese, at least in part to get away from the tyranny of Athens. His territory lay on the other side of the Hellespont, almost directly opposite the Attic fortress of Sigeum.

Yet such a realm was not enough for Pisistratus. He was not out for adventure—his ambition centered on Athens. He used the money from his mines to hire Thracian mercenaries, cultivated ties with noble families in other cities, and eventually put together a coalition. The leaders of Eretria on the island of Euboea granted him entry so that he could be in close contact with his Attic allies and prepare for a landing in Attica. Several cities that were beholden to him—Thebes in particular—provided him with material aid, and one of his sons added a thousand mercenaries, hired in Argos, to his forces. Lygdamis, a wealthy man from Naxos, contributed money and men. We also know that Pisistratus was later allied with the leading families of Thessaly and the king of Macedonia, relationships that may have already existed at the time of his return to Athens.

It was common in this period for noblemen to band together in order to launch private military expeditions. Some could, if they were powerful enough, call on the resources of their cities; others simply joined with their friends or contributed money. The cities gradually began to object and wanted to put an end to these practices because they did not want to be held liable for the armed exploits of their citizens. But in the middle of the sixth century, if such opposition existed at all, it was not yet strong enough to be effective. What was most unusual about Pisistratus's enterprise was that he set out to conquer a large polis, Greece's second largest after Sparta. Athens, however, had recently shown signs of weakness and seems not to have reacted at all to Pisistratus's preparations, which could hardly have gone unnoticed.

The landing at Marathon proceeded without incident. Pisistratus's followers gathered, and he had advanced two-thirds of the way toward the city before the Athenian troops confronted his forces near Athena's shrine at Pallene. Whether the Athenians were poorly equipped or ineptly led, or had evaded service for some other reason, they were unable to stop Pisistratus's private army. From this point on, his rule over Athens was solidly established.

His opponents fled or were exiled. Some families that remained were compelled to give over their sons as hostages. Lygdamis, who had meanwhile become tyrant of Naxos with Pisistratus's aid, oversaw the hostages. The citizens of Attica had to turn in their weapons. Pisistratus declared that they were to look after their domestic affairs and that he would take care of public matters from that time on.

On the whole, the reign of Pisistratus was beneficial for the Athenians, especially for the broad agricultural base of the population. The tyrant saw to it that they had relatively good legal protection against maltreatment by the aristocracy. He created, among other things, the institution of judges who traveled throughout the country to hold court in the various settlements, or *demes*. This not only saved the farmers the trip to

Athens but also prevented the intimidation they and their witnesses would have been exposed to in an urban atmosphere, which would have been quite foreign to them. They would have been at a particular disadvantage when dealing with aristocrats. Perhaps having a firsthand view of the local situation in the countryside also helped the judges reach the right decisions.

Pisistratus also took a personal interest in the economic progress of the country as a whole. He even made loans available, though probably less out of a desire to alleviate immediate need than for investment purposes. Like other tyrants, he tried to combat idleness and extravagance, and in wartime, led his mercenaries into the field. But there was only one war during his reign, the campaign to retake Sigeum. One of his sons was appointed to reign there, and the territory remained under the family's rule.

Pisistratus and his sons also initiated many public building projects. They built temples on the Acropolis and at other sites improved the water supply and constructed a new sewer system. South of the Acropolis, at a spring near the river Ilissus, an impressive "fountain house" *(enneakrounos)* was constructed, where water flowed from nine pipes.

The roads leading from Athens to the various settlements in Attica were newly surveyed and improved in many places. A nephew of Hippias donated the central milestone located at the northwest corner of the agora, a shrine dedicated to the twelve gods. Hippias's brother Hipparchus had square pillars installed at the precise midpoint between the central milestone and the settlements. The form of the pillars, each of which displayed a phallus and was surmounted by a bearded head, was new but had been inspired by the cairns formerly used to mark borders, which sometimes include huge and intimidating phallic shapes. Following this tradition, the phalli of the *hermai*, or herms, were erect. The pillars were called *hermai* in honor of Hermes, the god of the roads, trade, thievery, and education. Hipparchus had short maxims inscribed on the pillars for the edification of the farmers. If a farmer en route to the city were literate, he may have found the maxims easy to remember because reading them was accompanied by the pleasant feeling of having covered half the distance he had to travel. Similar *hermai* were later placed in front of houses and on the streets to ward off trouble.

The vase painting shows a fountain house with several pipes dispensing water. Black-figured hydria (waterjar), ca. 520 B.C. Boston, Museum of Fine Arts.

That the arts and crafts flourished is evident from the surviving artifacts—especially the beautiful Attic pottery of the time—and their wide distribution in the Mediterranean area, and also from the large number of dedicatory gifts with which artisans and craftsmen gave thanks to the gods for their success. Naturally, in such a climate, commerce also grew.

These were good years, especially for the broad population of Athens, and they were long remembered as a golden age. Athenians were able for the first time to improve their holdings and workshops enough to live well on their labor and probably even to keep slaves. With their survival needs met, they had more time to think.

Pisistratus and his sons observed the Athenian religious celebrations with great care, particularly the Panathenaea, the great festival in Athena's honor. Its magnificent procession to the Acropolis was later depicted in the frieze of the Parthenon. The Panathenaea was celebrated every fourth year with special pomp and included sports competitions in which non-Athenians, too, were invited to participate. Pisistratus also had the Homeric epics newly transcribed, compiled, and edited into definitive texts (from which all later versions are descended) and recited there. The tyrant had a special relationship to his city's goddess, and he joined with the Athenians in honoring the gods. These festivals created a sense of common purpose and provided a counterweight to the many local cults whose adherents were dominated by the aristocracy.

Pisistratus also seems to have expanded the great Dionysian festivals. The inclusion of dramatic competitions probably goes back to his time. Thespis is said to have been the first winner of this competition, around 535. Sources also mention the establishment of a library. Pisistratus and his sons attracted various poets to their court, among them Anacreon, Simonides, and Lasus. Onomacritus gathered a large collection of oracles for the tyrants. He also popularized Orphic lore, the teachings of a religious movement that claimed to date back to the mythical musician Orpheus and concerned, among other things, the creation of the world, the origin of man, and life after death.

The coins Pisistratus minted from about 525 on were also a kind of advertisement for the polis Athens. They depicted Athena on the front and her owl, the city's symbol, on the back. The inclusion of the first three letters of the city's name was quite possibly an innovation. We know of no other city before that time whose name (or part of it) was inscribed on its coins. Much earlier, in Thrace, Pisistratus had issued coins with ornaments, the so-called escutcheon coins, but those ornaments are hard to interpret. Since there was much silver in Athens, Athenian drachmas were widely used in many parts of the Mediterranean world. At first they were used less to facilitate trade within the city than to pay for foreign goods or services. As coined silver, the values in which they were issued were too large for everyday buying and selling.

Though Pisistratus had taken over the city by force, his rule, and initially that of his sons, was liberal. Since he and his sons indulged neither in great luxury nor the arbitrary use of power but instead kept the welfare of the city at heart, later sources justifiably called theirs a "political regime," that is, one appropriate to a polis. Thucydides praised their intelligence and virtue *(arete)*. Pisistratus and his sons were well aware, following the

A sculptor putting the finishing touches on a wooden herm. On the right, somewhat reduced in size, is a "citizen's cane." People liked to rest on these canes, tucking them under their arms when stopping for conversation or watching someone work. At the top is a kalos inscription, which reads: Hiparchos kalos, *or "Hipparchus is beautiful." Pottery vases often carried such inscriptions. General admiration for the beauty of adolescent boys also infected the vase painters, who often named the object of their admiration in an inscription that had nothing to do with the subject depicted. This is the case in this vase painting by Epictetus, as well as in many others. Red-figured, ca. 515 B.C. Copenhagen, Ny Carlsberg Glyptotek.*

overthrow of tyrants almost everywhere else in Greece, how difficult it could be to maintain despotic rule.

But no matter how much good they did for the city, they could not achieve one crucial thing: an identity between themselves and the commonality, the city of Athens itself. They could not do this because the city

Tetradrachma, worth four drachmas, with a picture of Athena on the front and an owl and the first three letters of the word Athens *on the back. Ca. 525* B.C.

had not yet fully formed, because the citizenry had not yet evolved into this abstract entity. The reasons for the leaders' just rule were exclusively practical. And the more assiduously they promoted the citizenry's well-being, the more they undermined the foundation of their own power. Gradually their support crumbled.

. . .

The reign became noticeably more despotic in 514, after the murder of Pisistratus's son Hipparchus by young Harmodius and his lover, Aristogiton. Hipparchus was the younger brother of Hippias, who had succeeded Pisistratus. The murder was a crime of passion. Hipparchus was in love with Harmodius, who, with Aristogiton, feared that the tyrant's son would draw the object of his affections to him by force. Honor was involved as well, for Hipparchus, angered by Harmodius's refusal, had publicly insulted his sister. A plot to uproot the tyranny was also at work—the two murderers and their accomplices had originally intended to kill Hippias, but fears that their plot had been betrayed led to a change of plan. What happened was not uncommon at that time: A ruler's despotism became truly intolerable only when it interfered severely with his subjects' personal lives.

The conspirators had, quite realistically, counted on broad support once the deed was done. But the failure of their assassination attempt resulted only in triggering a more repressive regime.

Several subsequent attempts to overthrow tyranny in Athens also failed, among them an invasion into Attica by a group of exiles who succeeded in taking Leipsydrion, a small town on the southwestern slope of Mount Parnes, three hours from Athens. The invaders, who had hoped for support from the city, may have failed because their offensive was conceived too much in the old aristocratic style.

By this time, tyranny was on the decline in Athens; the citizenry was no longer willing to tolerate it. All that was lacking was an occasion for toppling it. This was provided by Cleisthenes the Athenian, the son of Megacles and of Agarista, daughter of Cleisthenes, tyrant of Sicyon. Long before, the elder Cleisthenes, after winning the chariot race at the Olympic games, had gathered a memorable assembly of suitors for his daughter. He invited any Greek who considered himself worthy of becoming his son-in-law to come to him within sixty days, as he was planning to celebrate his daughter's wedding one year from that date. Suitors came from many cities, and Cleisthenes entertained them at his court for a full year to test their education, character, accomplishment in sports, and what was to him most important, their behavior at the nightly dinners. Megacles won the bride, but all the disappointed suitors received valuable consolation prizes.

The Athenian Cleisthenes, grandson of the tyrant, must have been an exceptionally smart man. Banished relatively young, he spent his time in exile traveling rather than nursing his resentment. Belonging to the wealthy Alcmaeonid clan probably encouraged his ambitious nature and may have contributed to his tendency to remain an outsider. Flexibility was his strength. He was a keen assessor of political realities, not just a tactician but a far-sighted strategist, and he was familiar with the latest intellectual developments.

Cleisthenes had been exiled once before, and he had constantly been plotting his return to Athens. He was convinced that this could be done only by military force—namely, with the help of a powerful ally.

Cleisthenes now collected on a good deed he had once done. Some years earlier he had been awarded the contract to rebuild the Delphic temple to Apollo, which had burned down. Delphi had been collecting money for this project throughout the Mediterranean region for years. Cleisthenes is said to have selected—and paid for—marble as the material for the columns of the facade, an act that exceeded the terms of the contract. Thanks to this generosity—and perhaps some gold—he was able to convince the Pythian oracle to advise Sparta to liberate Athens. The Spartans finally obeyed the oracle even though they were connected with Pisistratus and his heirs by ties of hospitality. The Spartans' motives were likely religious, though they may also have been displeased by the tyrants' relations with Argos.

The first contingent the Spartans sent out by sea failed in its mission, primarily because Hippias quickly called to his aid a group of Thessalonian horsemen. Hippias also ordered all the trees cleared from the plain near Phalerum so horsemen could operate freely. Angered by this defeat, Sparta next sent a larger force led by King Cleomenes. The horsemen were defeated, but Hippias and his family took refuge on the Acropolis. They could have held out there for some time, but the Spartans succeeded in capturing the tyrant's children as they were being taken to safety. At this point Hippias capitulated. He accepted the offer of unhindered departure and was given five days to pack up his movable property and leave.

The year 510 is the date given for Athens' liberation. But as time passed, the Athenians chose to dwell less and less on the actual liberation and celebrate instead the earlier exploits of Harmodius and Aristogiton, the failed "tyrant slayers" of 514. A statue depicting them was placed in the middle of the agora, and they were remembered in song. The Athenians did not relish the thought that they owed their freedom to the Spartans. One hundred years later, Thucydides traced the Athenians' fear of tyrants, which flared up at critical moments, to their recollection that they had been unable to free themselves on their own. And indeed, the memory of how their freedom was gained might well have affected the later state of mind of a people living under a form of government as risky as democracy.

Strife arose among the various aristocratic factions that revived after the tyrant was expelled, and Cleisthenes lost the 508–507 election for chief archon to a nobleman named Isagoras. But Cleisthenes reacted quickly with a bold attempt to win the common people over to his camp and mobilize them to participate in politics. His famous reorganization of the tribes of Athens *(phylae)* was probably based on earlier plans presented to him by knowledgeable advisers, for the system he instituted was not the product of improvisation; it followed a plan that had already been realized in other cities such as Corinth and Argos where broader segments of the citizenry had the right to participate regularly in politics. But the problems were of a greater magnitude in the large city-state of Athens, and the Athenian solution had wider-reaching results.

The task at hand was to reorganize the Attic citizens into new political divisions. The establishment of a new Council of Five Hundred ensured that all the citizens of Athens could make their will heard; indeed, that they, for the first time, constituted a political entity. This reorganization elevated many Athenians beyond their status of mere hoplites or followers of noblemen to that of true citizens—assuming, of course, that the will to take on such a role existed among them.

There are unmistakable signs that the Attic citizenry had undergone a change during this period. A lively interest in politics was spreading among the people. The desire to have a voice in public affairs and to take on responsibility for the polis—indeed, the insistence upon political equality—had taken root. Those who sought to attain supreme power with the help of the people could no longer enlist their support with economic promises—as usurpers had often done in the past—and then turn this political gain to their own ends. Gratitude, prestige, and influence could now be gained only by strengthening the citizenry's power rather than one's own. Cleisthenes apparently understood this.

It is hard to tell what had brought about this change in the citizens of Attica since Solon's days. But discussion of these topics presupposes a fuller understanding of the unique path the Greeks had traveled thus far. What matters for now is that the reforms would in turn forge the Attic citizenry into a force to be reckoned with.

Cleisthenes' enemies recognized the dangers to them inherent in the proposed reforms, which would largely eliminate the aristocracy's monopoly on political power. But these lords were too mired in their old ways of thinking to understand that they were rapidly becoming obsolete. We see here a pattern often reenacted in history: The adherents of the old see the dangers inherent in innovation, and even recognize the magnitude of the danger, but they are too sure of their own ways to realize that the new may be getting too strong to suppress. Their optimism may be partially justified, since the new still lacks the solidity that only comes with proven success. If they mount a counterattack, the proponents of the old alter the situation enough to put themselves clearly in the wrong. The new order passes its first hurdle.

Isagoras, Cleisthenes' rival, asked King Cleomenes of Sparta to come again to Athens, thus establishing ties of hospitality between them. The king came with a small contingent, on his own and without an official invitation, and easily took over the city. Cleisthenes fled; seven hundred of his adherents and their families were banished. Three hundred noblemen would now govern the city as a close-knit oligarchy.

Neither Isagoras nor his followers expected any major opposition to Cleomenes' takeover, and it came as a bitter surprise when the broader population rebelled against them, despite the absence of Cleisthenes and his associates. Apparently the aristocrats still thought of "the people" as subjects. Cleomenes, too, failed to make adequate preparations against a revolt, presumably for similar reasons.

When Isagoras and the lords set about dissolving the citizens' council—in all likelihood the old, rather insignificant Council of Four Hundred—it had refused to disperse, and a large mass of people gathered. Like Hippias a few years earlier, Cleomenes and his friends sought refuge on the Acropolis. But not having prepared for a siege, they could not hold out for long. Perhaps they also realized there was little hope of outside help. In any case, after two days the Spartans accepted an offer of free withdrawal under ignominious conditions—the king had to leave all of his Attic friends behind, except Isagoras, who managed to escape. The others were put in chains and later killed.

The uprising of the Attic people was as spontaneous as a popular uprising can be. Cleisthenes could not have received better proof that his reforms had been timely. These citizens were clearly ready to play their part in the new ways of political decision-making to which he would give constitutional form soon after his return.

Cleisthenes' reforms changed not just Athens but all of Greece, a fact of which Sparta was only too keenly aware. Sparta had for some time been following what was happening throughout Greece with a watchful and worried eye, and when the Spartans realized that the old ways of establishing and maintaining foreign relations had profoundly altered, they attempted on a larger scale what Isagoras had failed to do on a smaller one.

Surely Cleomenes' refusal to accept defeat was not the only reason Sparta and its allies decided to make war on Athens. The Peloponnesians' conviction that this was a necessary war can be deduced from the caution of Sparta's foreign policy—which was, incidentally, not determined solely by the kings—as well as the fact that by no means all of Sparta's allies were obliged to follow its lead automatically. The plan was to send Isagoras back to Athens, this time to establish a tyranny there. Two of Athens' neighbors, Boeotia and Chalcis, joined the Spartan campaign; meanwhile, Aeginetan ships plied the waters off the Attic coasts.

The Peloponnesian army marched into the plain of Eleusis at the same time that the Boeotians occupied the border villages of Oenoe and Hysiae and the Chalcidians began to attack Attica from the sea. But then something strange happened. When the Attic troops set out to meet the Spartans, they did not find them. The Corinthians had refused to take any further part in the action, and the second Spartan king, who also led the army, had also returned home, so that Cleomenes found himself forced to retreat.

The Athenians were consequently able to inflict major and costly defeats on the Boeotians and the Chalcidians. Of the Boeotians alone, seven hundred were taken prisoner and were later released for high ransoms. The Chalcidian noblemen were stripped of their land, which was divided among four thousand Athenians. The war against Aegina continued intermittently.

Herodotus comments that this was the time when the Athenians became strong. "The Athenians' military success is evidence of the usefulness in every respect of a political order based on the equality of the citizens." When the Athenians lived under tyranny, he adds, they did not excel over any of their neighbors in warfare. But once they threw off tyranny, they became by far the best military power. Now they were fighting for themselves. Cleisthenes' reforms also included a reorganization of the military.

Fearing that the Athenians with their new political order might emerge as an equal rival, the Spartans planned another invasion, this time hoping to restore Hippias to power. It has been suggested that they found out about the influencing—or bribing—of the oracle at Delphi and were incensed by it. But this time, the Corinthians refused to get involved from the beginning. Their envoy argued eloquently at a meeting of the allies that tyranny should never, under any circumstances, be imposed. The

Thessalians then offered Hippias the city of Iolcus and the Macedonian king offered him the city of Anthemus, but he refused both offers and withdrew to Sigeum.

Athens was obviously viewed as a troublemaker. Whether it was feared more for its power in foreign affairs or for the example it set in domestic politics is of no great importance. The two spheres could not be separated. Both within and among the city-states, it had become the custom for the different groups to live side by side in relative harmony. Many factors contributed to maintaining a balance between the aristocrats and the cities. Sparta, with its many connections on the Peloponnese and to a lesser extent beyond, saw to it that this state of affairs prevailed.

But now Sparta's old established hegemony among the city-states was being faced with a competitor. A new political center had arisen close enough to the Peloponnese to make itself felt there, yet far enough away that its influence reached other areas, such as central Greece.

The situation paralleled the Attic aristocrats' counterattack on Cleisthenes' reforms: Sparta, sensing the new power and deciding to fight it, provided Athens with a chance to prove itself; indeed, to understand, perhaps for the first time, its full capabilities. Initially, Attica's citizens must have been concerned primarily with preserving their own internal political order, but they were immediately drawn into foreign politics and war. Not long after this trial by fire they felt confident enough to support the Ionian revolt against the Persians.

It is significant that Sparta did not even hesitate to try tactics it had never used before—namely, to set up a tyranny. In its attempt to preserve the good old traditions, it resorted to means completely at odds with the generally accepted ideas of a "right order."

The Corinthians, on the other hand, may actually have felt a certain solidarity with Athens and its defense of internal freedoms, for in Corinth, too, broad segments of the population had won political rights. Corinth may have been rather pleased to see a new power emerging as a counterweight to Sparta, a shift that enhanced the significance of Corinth and probably gave the city more freedom of action. In any case, Corinth was determined that Cleomenes should not be allowed to decide what government Athens lived under. The Corinthians may initially have joined

Sparta's first campaign against Athens without understanding Sparta's intent, which was later made clear to them when Isagoras issued his first decrees on Attic ground.

So by the end of the sixth century B.C., what Solon had been unable to create finally took shape in Athens: a new political order that kept the aristocracy's selfishness and arbitrary exercise of power in check. In the new order the broad base of the citizenry predominated.

What Athens achieved was not the *eunomia* that the great lawgiver had had in mind. The name soon given to the new order was *isonomia*, or "equality of rights," which did not stand in conflict with Solon's concept but augmented it with the crucial element of equal political representation. The intent was less to grant formal rights than to bring about practical participation in public affairs. The citizens were now to take responsibility for the city not just in special situations but all the time. And this was how things were to remain.

Seen from the perspective of later history, the concept of isonomy was a preliminary step toward democracy. The two concepts overlap, but historically a clear distinction exists between them. The early isonomies did not yet imply government by the people.

Since among the Greeks significant political unity—what we would call statehood today—and equality of the citizens could be achieved only in tandem, it was only under the control of the broader population that Athens' potential power as a polis was first made manifest.

This population included the farmers and, particularly prominent among them, a group the historian Chester Starr has called the "semi-aristocrats," a kind of second-class aristocracy. These men were not really wealthy, and individually they could hardly compete with the aristocrats. But they were affluent enough to devote some time to politics, and their goal was to stand up to the aristocracy, which they did successfully as long as they maintained solidarity among themselves. Their solidarity was, in turn, a natural outgrowth of their common interest in preserving protection under the law, a voice in public affairs, and equality of political rights. This faction was also immediately drawn into foreign politics, so a common interest developed in this arena as well.

For the first time, a Greek city was able to exert political influence far beyond its borders and surrounding territories without turning into a military camp in peacetime, as Sparta had. We can only guess what would have become of the Greeks if the Persians had encountered not what was potentially Greece's most powerful polis but a political vacuum. But in view of the self-confidence and surge of new energy exhibited by Athens, and its readiness to take unusual steps such as the decision to build a navy, to abandon Attica, and, at Salamis, to risk all on an unproven strategy, the city's triumph no longer seems quite as inexplicable. Where the unity of cities was rooted in their broader populations, it was quite possible, especially for a commonwealth as large as Attica, to generate surpluses of strength and energy.

There is something seductive about political historiography. When you trace a sequence of events, it often seems that each development gives rise inevitably to the next. Reasons for what transpired at a certain time are extracted from preceding events. Partial explanations seem sufficient even for major turning points. This kind of historiography obeys "the law of narrative sequence," which is, as the writer Robert Musil said, "the most time-honored perspective for curtailing understanding."

The sequential-events approach leaves you with an illusion of understanding. The amazing and the mysterious readily disappear in it, and that in itself is an example of the falsification that Musil wrote could be brought about by "this age-old trick of epic narration, which nannies use to calm their charges."

It is true that political history can cut a narrative path through unknown territory. And following along this path, it is possible to perceive a certain order and meaning, but many questions remain unanswered.

It can be said, for instance, that the early Greek aristocracy's neglect of the polis in favor of a wider, pan-Greek public sphere may have been related to the strange dichotomy between the small scale of Greece's political entities and the vastness of the culture the Greeks shared. But inherent in this formulation is an assumption that "the Greeks," as such, existed at the outset of the story. It must first be determined how their curious culture arose among so many independent political entities, how it could arise without a political center and, for a long time, without devoting any significant attention to politics.

Among the questions that merit consideration are: Why were the Greeks unable to move beyond their tightly circumscribed political alliances? Was there resistance to the formation of larger alliances, or did certain forces that might have led to the creation of such alliances simply fail to emerge? Were the Greeks' energies differently distributed? Was there something unique about the Greeks—as opposed to other cultures—that prevented monarchy from developing?

To say that qualities specific to the Greeks account for their remarkable rise is hardly an adequate explanation. Still, the manner in which, among the Greeks, freedoms implied certain limitations must certainly be relevant to this inquiry. Likewise there may be a subtle connection between homosexuality (a topic that will be discussed in chapter 3) and the conditions from which democracy took rise. Could not the Greeks' devotion to festivals, their aversion to getting old, their unique combination of joie de vivre and melancholy also have played a part during democracy's incubation period, the little-known years between Solon and Cleisthenes? Could the almost unbelievable willingness of the wider population to be involved actively in politics—without which Cleisthenes' reforms could not have happened—be somehow related to the relationship between the sexes, or to the Greeks' desire for beauty?

To talk of such links may seem far-fetched. They clearly did not exist in any obvious way, but they may have played an indirect role in the Greeks' ability to create democracy—and much more.

The closer we approach the classical century of the Greeks and their astonishing accomplishments, the more urgently the question of the Greeks' origins presents itself. But it would be a mistake to focus only on those accomplishments. For the Greeks there must have been a particular interplay between daily life and festivities, between society and its outsiders, between myth and rite, between the hardships of life and its enjoyment. Consequently, they developed their own ways of thinking, planning, and fighting—ways that at Salamis helped make up for their weaknesses and ways that turned the smallness of their cities into an advantage. "A small city situated on a rock and in which people live according to the right order is better than foolish Nineveh," the Ionian poet Phocylides wrote, and the word here translated as "better" can also mean "stronger."

That these ways, whatever they consisted of specifically, were strengths cannot be denied, nor can the fact that Cleisthenes instituted great reforms that permanently changed the citizenry of Athens. That is why we must ask who the Greeks were and how they came into being.

3

The Greek Way

Great forests grow only once. If they are destroyed, they will never grow again.
Men and nations possess or acquire certain qualities during their youth or not
at all.

—JACOB BURCKHARDT

How was it possible for a society consisting exclusively of small city-states to revolutionize world history? History has seen a neolithic and an industrial revolution and the emergence of ancient high cultures with their great empires, but the political revolution of the Greeks ranks paramount among these world events.

If, among Eastern cultures, only one man was free and "therefore only a despot and not a free man could be a human being," as Hegel puts it, there were, by contrast, among the Greeks at least a few human beings. Though they made use of slaves and their freedom may therefore have been an "accidental, undeveloped, passing, and modest flower," the survival of this freedom could nevertheless be assured only by a political order without authoritarian powers; indeed, it required the ability of whole citizenries to govern themselves. Among the Greeks the question of who should reign arose in a new way. Previously the most that had been asked was whether one man or another should govern and whether one alone or several together. But now the question was whether all the citizens, including the poor, might govern and whether it would be possible for them to govern as citizens, without specializing in politics. In other words, should the governed themselves actively participate in politics on a regular basis?

These questions opened up new dimensions of human existence, brought on unprecedented situations, and created great new opportunities for taking action, shaping life, and thinking. The risk and uncertainty of those times gave rise at once to sadness and gaiety, to philosophy and art, as well as to much else that cannot be enumerated. And all of these developments were heavily influenced by the political.

The Greeks departed from all the rules of world history: they formed their culture not in the context of monarchical centers but in the interplay of the most varied forces; they pursued hitherto untrodden paths and were themselves enormously different from all other peoples. This cannot simply have been the result of certain inborn qualities. Rather, the Greeks evolved into what they eventually became. Their special character, like their culture, is a product of their early history.

Accordingly, the idea that the Greeks created their culture can have meaning only if we think of "the Greeks" and "Greek culture" in terms of an infinity of elements that mutually formed and transformed one another over a long period of time. Clothes may make the man, but, as Musil observed, the man in turn makes the clothes that make him.

To determine who the Greeks really were is a difficult business. The wonderfully rational, clear side of their culture that comes across in most of the evidence preserved cannot simply represent their whole being. According to Max Weber, any reference to the original character of a people is nothing more than an "admission of ignorance." To say that a people has brought certain hereditary qualities into history is to explain nothing. At best we can observe how a people, responding to environmental and historical challenges, develops one quality and neglects another. Certain kinds of action may succeed while others fail, so that preferences eventually culminate in a general attitude. We can see, in short, how certain forms of behavior, certain methods of coexistence, and certain ways of reviewing the world and the gods become accepted.

What apparently happens when a new culture arises in world history is that old traditions that had evolved, been accepted, and been taken for granted are replaced by an entirely new and comprehensive order, usually as the result of prolonged, conscious, and planned action. This step is necessarily preceded by a period during which the old order is shown to be unsatisfactory, either from an internal point of view or because of outside pressures. During this period it becomes clear that the traditional mental and intellectual habits and the ability to solve communal problems by common action are no longer adequate.

When this occurs, not only new political and religious centers become necessary, not just a new structure of society, new technologies and economic forms, but also new legitimations and rites, a new view of the world as expressed in myth, poetry, the visual arts, and architecture. In these ways the new order manifests and expresses itself and acquires permanence. This is true because the needs of the senses, among other things, go unmet during major upheavals. Those in power must finally find ways to satisfy them, ways that are as all-inclusive as the world that is being created. All this must be accomplished, of course, in addition to orchestrating the work the new culture will undertake and the wars it will wage.

Cultures such as these have appeared in world history more than once, some influenced by others, most forming independently. In Egypt, Mesopotamia, India, China, and Central America whole societies were created anew. The chaos from which these processes arose must have been perceived as golden opportunities by enterprising, strong-willed men, some of whom had perhaps already established realms elsewhere, which they then extended and made more permanent. In any case, considerable competition must have existed until powerful monarchies and priestly elites were founded and, most important, until their power became so entrenched in the thinking and imagination of the subjects that no other political order was conceivable. The only possible alternative at this point was dissolution and anarchy.

The absolutist monarchies of the modern era are the only ones in recorded history that did not permanently exclude the possibility of other political orders. These monarchies created states that were able to evolve into republics and eventually into democracies. This development clearly has its roots in Christianity and Rome as well as in classical Greece, models that were both influential in the evolution of the modern states and in the relationship they established between spiritual and worldly power.

Why did things take such a different course in Greece? How were the

Greeks able to create their culture without any significant aid from monarchs?

An important factor was the particular way in which the Greeks were forced to abandon the simple existence of their earlier history. They were confronted with challenges that could be met only by radical change from within and responded to these challenges in ways that led to highly unusual results. Of course, the special character the Greeks had developed was part of the equation, but their history might easily have developed in very different directions.

A Greek-speaking population had been living in the Aegean world since the middle of the second millennium B.C., perhaps even as early as the third millennium. It had produced the civilization we call Mycenaean, after its principal city. It is not known why this civilization collapsed after flourishing for several centuries. Possible causes include invasions by sea-faring peoples, wars among princes, devastating epidemics, and even climatic changes. Perhaps the Mycenaean rulers' ability to maintain their civilization's vigor declined at some point.

Whatever the case, Mycenaean civilization was in the end so thoroughly destroyed that nothing remained of its specific ways of life. Even its form of writing fell out of use and disappeared, except in an outpost on Cyprus, which was evidently able to resist the general decline. The population declined drastically, and many regions became only sparsely inhabited.

As little is known about the migrations that took place in the decades around 1000 B.C. as is known about the reasons for Mycenae's decline. There is no evidence that the migrations were triggered by a great Dorian invasion, to which the old principalities on Greek soil would also have fallen victim. Still, people apparently fled eastward, mostly across Attica. This refugee movement resulted in the founding of Greek cities in Asia Minor. There are also signs of several waves of migrations from the north made up of people from bordering areas, including the Dorians, who would later take possession of large portions of the Peloponnese and Boeotia, and eventually the islands of the southern Aegean.

The people who inhabited Greece from about 1000 B.C. on were enormously different from the Mycenaeans. They were a new people, a mixture of descendants of the indigenous population and others who had moved into the country. But they remembered the region's glorious past. Poets and bards kept those memories alive, constantly transforming them by weaving in new perspectives as each age passed, until finally a curious picture emerged that blended the deeds of great heroes, traces of a magnificent civilization, depictions of a relatively simple, peasantlike life, and tales about the fate of Greek seafarers. Some of these recollections have come down to us in the Homeric epics.

It is difficult to say what long-term effects these memories had, to what extent they fed the latent ambitions of later generations, and to what extent, specifically, Mycenae's heritage remained alive among the Aeolians and Ionians, as these Greeks came later to be known. We know that the bards lived on the western coast of Asia Minor. There were differences among them in dialect and in the art forms they used. Similar differences are apparent even in later periods—for example, in the features that distinguish Ionian from Dorian temples. It seems likely that each group wanted to set itself apart from other groups within Greece. The Ionians took to the seas earlier, and thus established better contacts and became generally more adaptable.

But aside from such special traits, we observe a conformity in the general patterns of life. Conditions everywhere were harsh. The need to obtain the bare necessities dominated (though gradually the ambitious began to consider a certain degree of wealth a necessity). In time the newcomers came to think of themselves as the descendants of the Homeric heroes nearly to the extent that the indigenous population did, and must consequently have adopted certain traits of the latter.

Political conditions, too, seem to have encouraged assimilation. The far-reaching ties the immigrants may have kept up faded as the immediate demands of living together in settlements alongside the original inhabitants became paramount. The more urgent these demands grew—especially in the case of communities open to the sea and therefore most directly exposed to various dangers—the more independent the settlements became. This development was primarily a function of geographical location; ethnic background played a role only insofar as the descendants of the Mycenaean Greeks tended to settle in harbor towns. Here again, things worked in Athens' favor: The emergence of civilization was concentrated primarily in the maritime cities, and the chasm between these and other places grew deeper with time.

But the independence of the small Greek settlements and settlement clusters—for which the word *cities* is rather too grand—was not yet permanently assured, nor should it be regarded as specifically Greek. The initial self-reliance of the settlements and the weakness of monarchies that we see in Homer might simply have been factors of the conditions of life there. Even the early popular assemblies described in the epic poems are no proof that the Greeks had a special inclination toward democracy. After all, we have evidence, or at least suggestions, that such popular assemblies also existed in India, Mesopotamia, and in other early civilizations.

The crucial difference between the Greeks and other ancient cultures may be that the Greeks were able to preserve many qualities of their forebears and that they abolished monarchies rather than strengthening them. In other words, their civilization seems to have come about not as the result of a break with the past and the establishing of a single central authority but rather as a fuller and ongoing development of their traditional ways. If certain breaks did occur later on, they did not affect basic values, ideals, and ways of life, to all of which the Greeks remained essentially faithful, no matter how much they may have modified them.

We also find traits in early Greece that are more or less unparalleled in other cultures. Among these are the aristocracy's peculiar desire for autarky, which is closely connected to the lack or relative weakness of kinship structures and client relationships; the private ownership not only of large herds but also of land; and the fact that everybody tended to belong to a household (family, servants, and farm), rather than a clan. This may have come about because the bands of immigrants were primarily made up of individuals rather than of whole clans, or perhaps because the Mycenaean palace organizations had not allowed the formation of clans.

In any case, a kind of individualism, a considerable self-concern on the part of heads of households, had arisen early among the Greeks. Surprisingly, it persisted and even increased as the culture developed. This, too, was probably not encouraged by any factors specific to the Greeks but by broader conditions.

Nor was the history of Greece determined by the geography of the Aegean Sea and seacoast. To be sure, that geography worked in favor of the development of small communities, which were an essential condition for the unique path Greece was to take. In many places mountain ranges reached almost to the sea, leaving open only relatively small fertile plains that were separated from each other. But this was not the case everywhere. Nothing in the landscape called for the coexistence in Boeotia of, at times, as many as ten independent, loosely connected cities. The existence of only one political entity on some islands and of several on another was less a consequence of geography than of the chance patterns of original settlement or later events and tendencies. And the geographic barrier of the lofty, steep, and wild Taygetus range did not prevent the Spartans from conquering and permanently subjugating Messenia. Likewise, the geography of the Aegean region did not preclude the formation of larger political units then, nor had it done so earlier, during the Mycenaean period, when larger principalities did in fact exist.

Geography may have played a role in discouraging the formation of powerful tribes in the mountainous interior of the peninsula. If such tribes had come into existence, Greece might have followed a pattern similar to that of Italy, where coastal cities had to expend considerable energy defending themselves against mountain tribes. Such a situation might well have given rise to larger concentrations of power and greater focus on the interior, as happened to some extent in the Peloponnese. To summarize: Geography influenced the course of Greece's development only in concert with the larger political circumstances in which the Greeks found themselves at that juncture of their history.

. . .

Three factors determined the unique course on which the Greeks set out in the eighth century B.C. First, the Aegean was a region without world-political importance or influence; second, the Greeks were able to establish close contacts with the great civilizations of the East; and third, large parts of the Mediterranean west of Greece as well as the Sea of Marmara and the Black Sea offered opportunities for trade and other activity, and it could absorb excess population.

None of the Eastern empires was interested in this area of the world—not Egypt, not the Assyrian empire, even though the latter was then extending its conquests on the Mediterranean Sea. The kingdoms of Phrygia and Lydia in Asia Minor may have eyed the region, but they represented no real danger to the Greeks, as they were oriented toward land, preoccupied with internal affairs and the defense of their eastern borders, and threatened by the Assyrians. When the Lydians finally subjugated the cities along the west coast of Asia Minor, the institution of the polis was already so well established, both there and in other places, that its further development could not be hindered. Nor did the Balkans harbor any threat. The incursion of the Cimmerians from the Caucasus, in about 675 B.C., affected the Greeks only tangentially and briefly.

Trade, however, was of major importance, making possible the second factor listed above: contact with the East. The Phoenicians, the most active seafarers on the Aegean at the time, brought not only goods but knowledge and connections to Greece. Above all, they inspired the Greeks to imitate what they were doing.

Then, too, the very nature of the Aegean region encouraged the Greeks to turn more and more to sea travel. Their lives had been oriented to the sea from the beginning. Not a single town south of Thessaly is more than sixty kilometers from the coast, and many places in the interior offer views of the sea. From the Acropolis in Athens one can see not only Salamis and Aegina but the northeastern coast of the Peloponnese as well. From Sunium one looks out not only on long stretches of coastline along the Saronic Gulf but also on a chain of islands: Ceos, Cythnos, Andros,

Tenos, Seriphus, and, on clear days, Melos. Wherever along the Aegean one looks out on the sea, land is visible beyond the water. (The view is generally clear because the trade winds carry the lower strata of air away and replace them with fresh, cooler air, which in warming up absorbs the evaporating water from the sea.) And from late March to late October the sea is almost always safely navigable.

The many islands are like pylons of an imaginary bridge linking Greece with Asia Minor. By the eighth century, Greek settlements surrounded the Aegean Sea to a much greater extent than they had in the Mycenaean period. Isolated from one another as these settlements were on land, the sea gave them easy access to one another. And the settlements depended increasingly on fishing for feeding their expanding populations.

Thus, the Greeks felt at home on the water, and the idea of following the example of the Phoenicians must have grown increasingly tempting. They, too, wanted to embark on long sea voyages, not just for the sake of trade but also in search of booty and discoveries. But first they had to build better ships. Once again, the Phoenicians served as models.

Probably as early as the ninth century, the Euboeans established a trade center where the Orontes River flows into the sea in what is today the Syrian port of Al Mina. From that time on they had access not just to commercial goods but also to knowledge, craftsmen, and experts in many fields from there as well as from Cyprus and Egypt. The influence of Eastern civilizations on the Greeks, especially during the seventh and eighth centuries, can hardly be overstressed. The Greeks were adept students, and as they gained knowledge, their desire for higher standards of living and wealth also increased significantly.

From the Phoenicians they also learned alphabetic writing, but the Greeks immediately modified the Phoenician system by changing the function of some of the letters. Unlike the Phoenicians, they wanted to write not only consonants but vowels as well, and thus they created a highly flexible system that allowed for the transcription of all spoken sounds. They may have adopted this system because they found it practical for transcribing poetry. If so, it would attest to one more amazing trait of this people, for it looks as though they meant to use this new technique primarily to give permanence to their literature. In any case, the

Iliad and the *Odyssey*—each over 15,000 lines long—were written down very early by the Greeks. This is probably the only time in history that oral works of this length were so rapidly put into written form. The transcription of the epics gives proof of a long oral tradition, a remarkable sense of form and composition, and the importance of poetry and intellectual endeavors to this people.

Once the Greeks became accustomed to extensive sea voyages, they were bound to start sailing to the West as well, in part because the West offered sources for important raw materials. The Phoenicians had preceded the Greeks westward, and the two nations shared this new sphere of influence, with the former moving in southern waters (often sailing along the African coast) and the latter following the northern route, which led by way of Corfu to southern Italy.

The exploration of the western Mediterranean was of great consequence for later Greek history. In the middle of the eighth century, the first western colonies were founded: Cyme, Syracuse, and later Naples, Tarentum, Marseilles, and many others. The increasing population pressure at home was relieved by this emigration. Full of hope and braving great danger, colonists left their homeland to make daring and arduous voyages across hundreds of miles, usually never to return. Many early expeditions failed, but better-organized ones later were more successful, and eventually large stretches of the coasts of the Mediterranean, the Marmara, and the Black Sea were dotted with Greek cities.

The eighth century must have been an incredibly exciting and rewarding time for the Greeks, a time of activity, discovery, stimulation, and rapid change. The first great temples and many shrines were built; the Olympic games, which were of ancient origin, were reorganized in 776; and, from about 750 on, many colonies were founded. The pioneering spirit that typified the times can be felt in the Homeric epics. At the same time, the first crucial decision was made to set out on the unique Greek—and European—path.

The Greeks acquired the knowledge and benefited from the highly developed material accomplishments of the great Eastern civilizations without having to pay the price that nations coming under the influence of superior powers usually have to pay. They neither had to defend themselves militarily nor submit to direct or indirect foreign rule; that is, they did not have to adapt their way of life to another's. Even as they absorbed all kinds of new ideas, the Greeks on the whole escaped political influence. They differed in this regard from their predecessors of the Mycenaean era who fell under the immediate domination of the Cretans as they developed their civilization.

None of the momentous changes overtaking Greek society at this time posed serious difficulties for the Greek colonies, where it might be expected that such changes would be felt most dramatically. If it had not been for these colonies, the ambitions of many aristocrats and the discontent of the poorer segments of the population might well have erupted within the mother country. Greece would probably have experienced the internecine struggles typical of emerging civilizations—struggles that lead to monolithic concentration of political power, to militarization, and eventually to wars of conquest and the formation of empires. Some wars of this nature were fought—among them those waged by Sparta against Messina—but so much ambition and energy was diverted to distant places that these remained the exceptions.

In short, the Greeks underwent the kind of upheaval that can lead to the emergence of a civilization but avoided the chaos that so often results in the founding of dynasties. That is why, although they went beyond their traditional horizons, they did not undergo a radical change in their way of life. They became a different people, but no one individual emerged to mold them to his own will and subject them to his rule.

New spheres of activity redefined ambitions. Entrepreneurs, not usurpers and rulers, were in demand and became the influential figures. Opportunity may make a thief of one man and a wealthy merchant of another, and in this early stage when Greek civilization was still fluid and malleable, opportunity encouraged liberality, extravagance, and the enjoyment of independent action on a grand scale. Organization and cooperation were essential, too, whether for plundering a rival colony, building a temple, or founding a new city.

Leadership was required to found a colony, and the inhabitants of colonies paid special honors to the founders of their cities after their deaths, but otherwise there was no difference in rank among the colonizing partners. They left their homes as a group of equals, even if they brought along dependent personnel employed as servants, agricultural workers, and sailors. This equal status was reflected in the equal shares of land all the colonists received.

To oversimplify somewhat, there was hardly any need to change old patterns in order to meet the new challenges. The new was created abroad, and yet it very much resembled the old.

The Greek colonists sought land of their own, as well as the opportunity to live together in small polis groups. They did not leave their homeland in order to change themselves. Whatever of these desired conditions they had lacked in the mother country, they wanted to create in their new homes. Consequently, their colonies were very similar to the city-states they had left, even in their social stratification. Locations of settlements were usually selected to recall the places the colonists had come from. As a result, many of the cities that grew on the coasts of the Mediterranean, the Propontis, and the Black Sea resembled those in the original, smaller circle of settlements around the Aegean. So as the Greeks spread out across the Mediterranean, the basic elements of their character became more entrenched.

This created a diaspora effect. Dispersed to many different coasts, the Greeks became neighbors to many different nations, and because they enjoyed a position of superiority almost everywhere, they had no need for holy scriptures or strong traditions to keep the connections among them alive or set themselves off from the neighboring barbarians. Their gods, their language, their poetry, and their way of life provided sufficient basis for communality, as did their particular self-image. The fact that men from different cities often became citizens of the same colony only increased their sense of communality. Thus, the Greek character became more and more established everywhere Greeks lived.

In the diaspora, Greek identity was based not only on language and religion but also, and perhaps more importantly, on the patterns of life: the political organization of the city-states, the layout of cities with their agoras and temples, dance, and the representation of the human form in the visual arts. The latter were primarily cultural elements. Political organization determined only the identity of individual cities, not of Greek civilization as a whole. This is an important factor, for it meant that the Greeks placed an exceptionally high value on culture. In their case, culture was not the by-product of empire building or the expression of a religious worldview. It emerged instead from the realization of many different ambitions.

The ideals of the leading citizens, the aristocracy, and therefore their very nature also became incorporated into this cultural identity. The aristocrats' undaunted individualism consisted of a desire to chart their own destinies, to pursue the same goals together with—and at times against—others of their class. They were in a good position to become relatively powerful as individuals, and they made the most of their advantage.

The aristocracy resisted any attempt at incorporation that demanded more than the observation of a few rules. It never occurred to them to subsume themselves to a larger purpose, to serve others, to move onto the new terrain of a state, where they could have expressed themselves only indirectly and would have become parts of an unsurveyable whole. In this way, the smallness of their city-states was important for the aristocracy's independence, for it meant that aristocrats, together with their equals, could constitute the polis directly and concretely. We also have to remember that although the number and density of Greek settlements spreading along the shores of the Mediterranean may look impressive on a map, each settlement involved only a few thousand men on average.

Because ownership of boats was widespread among the Greeks, the monarchs had never been able to control maritime ventures. Meanwhile, the power of the aristocrats kept growing. They were quite capable of meeting new challenges and opportunities as they arose, setting the stage for kings to step down or be forced from power.

It is difficult to draw a clear picture of the eighth-century aristocracy. The interests of the old elite must have become more differentiated as new possibilities opened up and as newcomers joined its ranks. But on the whole the aristocracy remained stable. Problems in the law of inheritance, which assigned equal shares to all sons, were kept at bay through colonization of the interior and piratical raids. Later, colonizing sea expeditions, which at first benefited primarily the sons of the elite, provided further relief.

To be sure, there was no sharp line dividing the nobility from well-to-do farmers. Given the general lack of wealth, the differences in personal property cannot have been great. The aristocracy had neither risen far enough above the farmers nor sufficiently consolidated its power to undermine the communal cohesion of the polis. Independence was presumably as much of an ideal for the farmers as for the aristocrats, and at any rate the farmers did not feel that the aristocrats, in spite of their unchallenged superiority, were fundamentally different from themselves. Still, as much as the spirit of the times encouraged many Greeks to imagine a new social order, the idea of political equality would not arise for some time.

On the whole, power was accessible to ever larger segments of the population and was not consolidated in the hands of a few individuals or institutions. No need was felt to change existing conditions. This created the political weakness of the archaic Greeks discussed earlier in this book.

Strange as it sounds, the beginnings of Greek civilization go back to the early aristocrats and those who imitated them. The customs and habits they needed they derived simply from the further development of those they already had.

Once the prerequisites for a social transformation are in place, changes only serve to strengthen them. What people think and do, and how they move and organize themselves, is prefigured in the way these activities reproduce, elaborate, and reinforce the existing conditions. This seems to be how the situation that so magnificently gave rise to the Greek aristocracy continued to affect life and shape the future, spreading into society at large as some people willingly adopted the aristocratic ideals while others were compelled to do so.

The process was kept in motion as innumerable individuals watched out for their own interests, those of small groups, or, at most, those of their city. No one knew or cared what was happening in the larger context. Even if it did occasionally occur to someone that by gaining influence over a larger territory he could consciously bring about change, such efforts did not get far.

Of course, lasting historical changes always take the form of impersonal processes. Among the Greeks, conscious planning played a minor role in changing social conditions. That is why more or less identical initial situations could result in more or less identical ways of life thousands of miles apart.

In this kind of change there are no major turning points, only continuous evolution. The overcoming of old limitations resulted in the expansion of traditional ways of life. Consequently, in spite of new ideas and the outpouring of previously unknown energies, many foundations of the old social order were preserved rather than destroyed, such as the desire for independence, the persistence of communal associations, the small size of the city-states, and access to the gods without the mediation of powerful institutions. These foundations remained part of a permanent, unchanging, essential Greek identity.

Surely the Greeks would not have become the Greeks without contact with the East. Major transformations had to take place for the "original" Greek-speaking people living around the Aegean Sea to become the Greeks we know from history. Had it not been for the East, the Greeks would not have been jolted into that burst of development they experienced in the eighth century, nor would they have had many of the essential tools they needed to continue on their new path. Alphabetic writing is just one example of such a tool. It made possible the composition of the great epics and the formulation and dissemination of all kinds of new ideas. Everyone could make use of this new medium—it was easy to learn; it could not be monopolized; and there was no institution to determine what should and should not be published. This situation opened up undreamt of possibilities, not only for the propagation of ideas but also for the construction of an entire intellectual world that called the existing order into question and laid the groundwork for further change.

. . .

What the Greeks absorbed from Asia ranged from the skills and techniques of crafts to new spheres of knowledge, new words and concepts, Eastern philosophies, and even to many of the myths, which Hesiod, Homer's younger contemporary, retold around 700 B.C. to explain the world to his fellow Greeks. Eastern notions of justice also gained ground among the Greeks because they became linked with the rising power of the middle and lower classes. Finally, there was the new standard of living and its attendant luxuries to copy from the East. But the Greeks were selective. They embraced Asian astronomy, for example, but were not interested in astrology.

The contact with Asia enabled the Greeks to rise swiftly to considerable heights of civilization while retaining their own character. We find everywhere an intermingling of elements of a fledgling culture and those of high civilization.

The Greeks may also have been indebted to the East for their continuing cohesion, because the influences reaching them from Asia encouraged not only communication and exchange among their own cities but self-confidence and the need to maintain their character. The East stimulated the Greeks in a manner that avoided the paralyzing effect that often comes from trying to emulate a distant culture.

It is safe to conclude that it was the Greeks' geographic position between Asia and the Mediterranean that set in motion the development of Greek culture. There was no power that could harness this people—or not any major part of it—to its own purpose and transform its ways of life, its art, and its concept of the world. This fact, which allowed the Greeks to seize new opportunities while maintaining their old freedoms, was not a matter of mere luck, it was the essential prerequisite that determined the path the Greeks were to take.

Today, museums, theater, books, travel, and knowledge of mythology guarantee that the word *Greek* will evoke a response in just about everyone. But what exactly was Greek culture? Even specialists in the field routinely take for granted what is so profoundly strange about the Greeks. Systematic comparisons with other cultures are difficult and unfashionable, so the question of what constitutes the special quality of Greek culture is usually ignored.

The crucial question is, how did the diverse factors of Greek culture come together and keep each other in balance and in motion, like the elements in a mobile? Individual factors considered in isolation are deceptive, because one of the first things you realize about the Greeks is how much they were given to extremes, even though this tendency is rarely mentioned in the historical record. At the same time that Hesiod cautioned against maritime travel because it was too dangerous, hundreds of ships were out on the seas pursuing trade and piracy as well as transporting settlers to the colonies. Just as the poets were proclaiming the unreliability and transience of things made by human hands, autocratic rule sprang up in many places, with rulers building massive monuments to immortalize themselves. At a time when sources indicate that every Greek was at least secretly working to establish tyranny, a broad-based movement arose demanding strict political moderation. And the very nation responsible for the discovery of politics in the true sense of the word turns out in its early period to have been politically weak and inept.

The Greeks' new energies could not be directed outward, toward the colonies, indefinitely. The awareness of new possibilities and the grand ambitions awakened by them must have affected the mother country as well. The reality of polis life may have limited those energies in some ways, but it also stimulated them and deflected them to emerging areas of enterprise, with the result that the traditional polis structure was retained but also modified.

The fundamental reality of polis life consisted of the political cohesion of the polis, the striving for autarky on the part of individuals, the great variation in land ownership, resistance to increasing the power of political offices, and certain basic ideas about equality and citizenship both within the community and in the Greek world. What evolved from the meeting of new energies and old realities was a new social form and culture, both within individual cities and in the wider public arena of all Greece. This is the real contribution of the aristocratic epoch to Greek history.

The political side of Greek civilization developed fairly directly from the broader population, but the aristocratic period provided the essential medium for all that later flourished: not just political thinking but also cultural assumptions and patterns, and, last but not least, the basic world-view. The essential conditions of Greek democracy were not just the political weakness but the cultural strengths of the aristocracy. This is what makes the social and cultural history of these centuries so important.

To be sure, the Greeks of those times, especially the aristocrats, were selfish and intent on gaining wealth and power. It was a politically eventful chapter of history, with conflicts sometimes escalating into violent civil wars. Solon's lament—that the aristocrats of his time were not satisfied with the pleasures of dining well, love, sports, and hunting, but strove after unlawful gain and indulged in exploitation—shows how powerfully this class could be dominated by material and political ambitions. But it is nevertheless true that the aristocracy took an extraordinary interest in other, nonpolitical and noneconomic spheres and developed them.

The polis as the general form of Greek life all around the Aegean could hardly have survived the momentous times after 750 if the various city-states had not respected one another's existence. There was no one to enforce this mutual respect, and it was not the result of a general agreement; it had simply become the habit.

After the Spartans' wars of conquest and other conflicts that took place up to the middle of the seventh century B.C., numerous wars were still fought, but rarely for the purpose of annexing foreign territories.

Around 650, that peculiarly Greek mode of warfare, the hoplite battle, became the typical way of fighting. Infantry marched against infantry on a flat field, with horsemen and lightly armed soldiers (primarily archers) playing a subordinate role. Whoever held the field was the winner and was entitled to the spoils. The enemy was not pursued beyond the battlefield. As a rule, one such encounter ended the entire war. Other forms of armed conflict, such as the conquest of a city by siege, become increasingly infrequent. The great raiding expeditions must also have become less common, at least in the mother country. Such wars were often fought with great brutality, despite the best efforts of the Delphic oracle to prevent the worst practices.

The significant aspect of the hoplite wars was that now not just noblemen—who had traditionally been in charge of war—but farmers as well made up the infantry. This was another sign of the emerging equality of this group of citizens, though it would be some time before their military role bore any political consequences.

It is not known how frequent wars were during the archaic period. Jacob Burckhardt assumes a "sparcity of wars." Wars were fought from time to time as contests of strength, to obtain certain stretches of land, to stop territorial encroachments, to obtain booty, or to subjugate other communities. Perhaps an irrepressible urge asserted itself to prove oneself in combat or, possibly, demonstrate the power of the polis community to the world. War was connected with other motives, not least among them the issue of city rank, for it could matter a great deal to the Greeks which of two or more city-states was the dominant.

However bloody these battles may have been, they all were essentially tournament wars. Except for minor shifts of power and territory, they changed nothing. Indeed, the emergence of the infantry battles and the consolidation of the city-states were probably just two sides of the same coin.

This kind of warfare can emerge only where conflicts are not aimed at conquest and where there is a reluctance to expend energy to hold on to conquered territory. Still, some cities might have resorted repeatedly to wars of conquest if other motives had not prevented them. Colonization offered only temporary relief from overpopulation, and the number of people seeking land must again have grown after the colonization period. Why, then, were so few attempts made to settle them on neighboring land?

It seems that conquest would have run counter to an emerging consensus based not on political morality but on the wish of the people of each polis to keep to themselves. In the case of conquest, they would have been forced to live among other people—unless they chose to kill them, expel them, or sell them as slaves. These options were considered to be the conqueror's right, though that right was by now only rarely invoked, at least in the center of the Greek world.

Communities did occasionally overcome their exclusivity and join others to form larger bodies, the so-called *synoikismoi*, some of which were actually collective settlements; others were merely associations of separate communities that remained in their original settlements. But these composite bodies remained the exception.

This exclusivity of the polis societies was the outgrowth of a particular anthropological structure. On the one hand, it stemmed from the Greek aristocrats' indomitable striving for autonomy and disinclination to form larger alliances or make long-term commitments of any kind. On the other hand, it derived from the familial structure of the polis, which reflected the aristocracy's organization. In other societies, an individual's place was defined by the strong bonds of family or clan and by the dependency inherent in clientage relationships like those in Rome; but in Greece the individual was more isolated and therefore needed the connection of the cult associations that were provided by the polis and its constituent groups. This formed the basis from which the self-sufficiency of polis societies seems to have sprung. Another contributing factor was athletic (or agonistic) competition.

If the cities had been powerful or power-hungry on a larger scale, the system would not have survived. But they never, or only rarely, were. Consequently, Greek life did not have to concern itself much with politics and was able to establish the Panhellenic public sphere that was later so important to the aristocrats.

This sphere was constituted of relationships among individuals as well as cities, regions, and settlements. The Greeks traveled and maintained friendships in other places; the aristocrats liked to marry the daughters of aristocratic families from other poleis. They met for various occasions, in the greatest numbers at Panhellenic celebrations such as the Olympic games. Much communication took place at important centers of Greek life like Miletus, Corinth, and especially Delphi; and, through friends, wandering minstrels, and traders, people got news of each other even without traveling.

In this larger arena, anybody who wanted to be important had to impress the world in some way. He might be rich or handsome; or he might have married well or organized a splendid wedding; he might have gained fame through remarkable deeds, profitable adventures, victories in sport, displays of pomp, or, later on, by aspiring to tyranny. The larger world took note of such accomplishments only if they were spectacular, and if they were of a significance broader than the person's own city. It would be of great future consequence for the Greek aristocracy that the audience before which its members wanted to shine did not represent just a single political entity.

The openness of this public sphere stood in contrast to the exclusivity of the cities. The Greeks shut themselves off from one another in their city-states and in the cities' constituent bodies or subgroups, the cult associations in which each group payed homage separately to the common gods. Nevertheless, they thought nothing of eating, celebrating, and inter-marrying with those outside their city-states. It was as though the almost impenetrable barriers they erected around their associations applied only within the poleis.

This pattern of strict isolation on the local level and accessibility to a larger common area of relative freedom was paralleled within the polis. In private households, where necessities of life were taken care of, clear hierarchies existed. This was the realm of women. At the other extreme was the city's public forum, the realm where men, considerably relieved of providing for life's needs, could interact with others like themselves.

The Greeks of that time seem to have needed their households and their cities as the basis of their lives, providing solid and secure supports, to move around freely outside of them. In these realms they consequently insisted on maintaining tradition. Changes in city organization generally came about slowly, and on a major scale only after broad segments of society had won an effective voice in politics.

The familial character of the polis was duplicated in the cities' con-stituent groups. These groups served administrative functions—such as keeping lists of citizens—but the relevance of their tasks went far beyond the administrative. Plato wrote that the gatherings of the cult associations provided relief for many ills because people had a chance to get to know each other, form friendships, and express mutual good will at the sacrificial celebrations. "Nothing is of greater benefit to the citizens of a polis than knowing each other," he wrote. These cults, then, provided a sense of belonging and solidarity, often based on the supposed descent from a common ancestor and the communal worship of the group's own gods and heroes. There were quarrels, of course, as in all families. But it is precisely because of their familial quality that these groups were able to replace other forms of social cohesion such as those provided by aristocratic families or clientage.

All this is in marked contrast to the Romans, among whom fraternal and political groups were quickly reduced to purely organizational functions. Where there was a wide network of connections based on family and clan, the family-like cohesion of such groups lost its importance. This also meant that in Rome vertical ties to the aristocracy continued to predominate, whereas among the Greeks the possibility later opened up of creating a lasting "horizontal solidarity" among the middle and lower classes.

Unlike the Romans, the Greeks rarely referred to the founders of their families. They sought to be worthy of their fathers, not their forefathers.

The same could be said of the Greek city-states. They were like isolated points, whereas Rome was always part of a wide network. The Romans, as a land power, developed a strong sense of territory and territorial domination; the Greeks, by contrast, thought primarily of the wide sea, which was impossible to rule and stretched before them like the agora amid their houses. The Persian king Cyrus wondered what kind of strange people these were who had in the middle of their cities an open area where they cheated each other. He might just as well have wondered why their cities lay around the wide sea.

Individual autonomy and the cultivation of small associations went hand in hand, particularly at the time when life really began to change for the Greeks. Confinement and a vast world complemented each other like land and sea; like winter, the time to stay home, and summer, the time to travel; or like boundaries and freedom.

These were the conditions that paved the way for the rise of democracy: a large degree of independence, a lack of clientage, the fact that dependent relationships occurred primarily within the cults and associations (which could be reformed and even dissolved), the small size and autonomy of the cities, and their respect for one another.

Another important democratizing factor was the Greeks' habit of relating to one another as equals. In the nonpolitical public arena, power counted less than rank and name; dominating others was less important than excelling. The aristocrats wanted to "perform glorious deeds and be the first among all," as Homer put it. This is also how wise Solon viewed the ideal citizen, though he focused on civic—rather than military—excellence.

The fact that violent power struggles eventually developed and many Greeks sought to become tyrants does not contradict this observation. First of all, the notion of equality is a relative one, and secondly, the history of the tyrants demonstrates the uneasiness the Greeks felt toward the exercise of power. To be sure, they wanted power, but they were unwilling to subject themselves to the self-discipline that, in Friedrich Schiller's words, is "the price of coercing others." The Greeks could not muster what historian Theodor Mommsen described as "the moral energy that can dominate the world because it knows how to discipline itself." They were not up to it as a class nor as individuals—with the exception, once again, of Sparta.

It was because status mattered more to the Greeks than power that they were able to produce their impressive and diverse culture of competition. They developed forms of competition that could generally be won nonviolently. This was true not only in sports, to which they assigned a special central place, both within the polis and at the Panhellenic games, but they also made competition a regular part of their symposia, and choruses would routinely compete at the great religious festivals.

The competition of playwrights, probably introduced in 535 at the Athenian festival of Dionysius, is a particularly prominent example. Wars had clearly agonistic aspects, with the tyrants vying to show off the splendor of their realms. Describing the great battles of the Persian Wars, Herodotus does not neglect to mention who made the most graceful combatant. The conflict over who deserved to be credited with the victory at Salamis also falls into this category. The method resorted to at that occasion—in which awards were given both for technical ability and brilliance—was the same one used to decide who was the best sculptor.

However it may have originated, the culture of competition was apparently useful for absorbing much of Greece's recently awakened energies and for stimulating new ones. Competition gave content to communal life both on the large and the small scale, and made it more intense. The strong emphasis on testing human excellence through individual contests—especially in the areas of physical, intellectual, and artistic achievement—played a large part in producing Greek culture, which had to compensate for a lack of material resources.

Other early cultures also cultivated contests in sports, singing, and debate to channel competitive energies in desirable directions. What is specifically Greek is the way that these forms of contest were preserved even as they underwent rapid and comprehensive evolution under the influences of Asia and the non-Greek Mediterranean world.

These contests almost always pitted individuals against one another (the exceptions were choral singing, tragedy, and relay races). And so the structure of the competition itself reflected Greek individualism, though the glory of victory was shared by the whole city. The Greek city-states admired the winners of the great competitions and called them beloved of the gods. Fame thus gained could even be politically useful, as shown by the example of Cylon, who tried unsuccessfully to use his Olympic victory as a stepping-stone to political power.

Thanks to this cultivation of the competitive impulse, the Greek community was able to respond easily to the challenges and opportunities of the expanding world of the Mediterranean. By the time colonization waned (as a result of the fact that suitable locations were already settled), the polis was completely shaped. But now internal problems arose, which led to new legislation and tyranny.

Understanding Greek society with modern concepts is almost impossible. In a certain sense, Greece was one unified whole. The Greeks clearly set themselves apart from the *barbarians* (which means simply "foreigners," non-Greeks whose languages were incomprehensible). Greek unity was based not just on a common language but also on a shared culture and a way of life that extended to the common design of their cities, the centrality of the agora, their sports, and their temples. From the Crimea to Africa, from Marseilles to Cyprus, the Greeks were one people. How sharply they drew the line between themselves and others is shown by the example of the Macedonians, who spoke Greek but were otherwise non-Greeks, and were not allowed to participate in the Olympic games. Except for the members of their ruling dynasty, they were not true Greeks.

The gods also figured in this sense of Greek community, even though they were worshipped in separate, usually exclusive, cults. Individuals, citizen associations, and cities prayed and offered sacrifices to them. In fact, the worshippers did not consider themselves members of a common religion. (After all, they wanted to enlist the support of the gods for themselves and against others.) In sacrificial celebrations and meals, in the encounter with death and the affirmation of life, the cult associations and the cities experienced and reaffirmed their internal solidarity. The poleis all had their own calendar of festivals, but despite all these parochial appeals to divine authority, and even if their areas of competency differed from city to city, the gods had the same names everywhere. The depictions of the gods conveyed throughout Greek poetry is quite consistent.

Here again we see the combination of provincialism and cosmopolitanism. Religious rites, particularly in the smaller cult associations, faithfully preserved a great many local beliefs, even while the poets expressed the universal essence of the gods. And the poets, who were receptive to outside influences—including those from the East—were relatively free to retell the myths as they pleased.

In time, Greek thought seized upon the gods to exemplify basic principles. The highest god, Zeus, for example, came to be associated with the demand for justice, and his name was linked to the concept of political order. Interestingly enough, even Artemis, a goddess not claimed by any ethical authority, was said in one contemporary source to take pleasure not only in "bows, hunting, shady groves, stringed instruments, and dances" but in the existence of "a city of just men." The fact that several gods worshipped by all Greeks were concerned about justice also contributed to the Greek sense of unity. Their shared understanding of what constituted law set them apart from the barbarians.

But of all the things the Greeks had in common, the most important was that they lived in politically independent city-states. Greek society was formed of both the city-states and the innumerable individuals who functioned in public arenas above the local level. However, the two levels of society were closely linked.

Society within the polis was shaped by vertical and horizontal divisions. The most prominent group was the citizenry, essentially the free, male landowners. They were clearly separate from women, non-citizens, and slaves. Those members of the citizenry that owned little or no land and earned their livings as artisans or laborers were somehow counted among the citizens, but they were of little significance, at least at first.

The separate status of women followed from the polis's organization into male associations; while the exclusion of non-citizens stemmed from the exclusivity of the citizens' associations. The distinction between slaves, whose number increased with time, and others was so clear because of the great emphasis the freemen had placed on their independent status from early on. Even wage labor was regarded with disapproval.

Similarly, clientage relationships between the powerful and the socially inferior never played much of a role among freemen. Farmers did not have to pay tribute to the aristocrats; only the tyrants levied taxes on agricultural goods, and they taxed the aristocrats as well. The dependency of the farmers on the aristocrats was temporary and not enshrined in law. (Of course, there was the creditor-debtor relationship, which was at times extremely oppressive.) One wonders why the aristocracy never tried to bind the farmers more firmly. Most likely it was because the aristocracy's desire for independence and the farmers' resistance made it impossible.

The horizontal divisions are harder to define. In terms of prestige, the "nobility" traditionally ranked above the farmers, and the farmers above small-landholders, artisans, merchants, and laborers. Broad classification based on wealth did not parallel these ranks exactly because craftsmen and merchants could equal the farmers and even the nobility in terms of wealth. For this reason it is best to use the terms upper, middle, and lower class only very broadly, as we don't know to what extent the middle class encompassed well-to-do craftsmen and merchants along with owners of medium-sized and large farms. Compared with the nobility, the middle and the lower classes were large, but once a significant number of the middle class had risen to become officials of the city, this segment of society must be regarded somewhat differently.

In the thinking of the time, the dividing lines *within* the social groups were the crucial ones. These are the ones we hear about the most. It is around them that conflicts flared up and sometimes grew into civil wars. Even though horizontal divisions persisted throughout Greek history, these boundaries could always be crossed by individuals, and eventually the middle and even the lower segments of society were able to rise to political equality.

The vertical divisions, on the other hand, were not only almost always insuperable, but they also retained their importance over time. It is thanks to them that the communal sense of the cult associations acquired such importance; in the context of the cults, the high and the low, the rich and the poor, belonged together regardless of any social gulf dividing them. The exclusivity of the cults also seems to have kept the aristocracy from increasing its power by accepting new citizens into the polis, as was often done in Rome. In Greece, only tyrants or restorers of order were able to admit newcomers to the citizenry.

To be sure, poor and socially inferior Greek citizens had little voice; they could be oppressed, exploited, and, if unable to repay their debts, sold abroad as slaves. But as long as they were freemen, they were in a privileged circle. Cult association created connections between them and the nobility, and, little as those ties often meant, they could be invoked to the benefit of the citizens. The almost familial nature of these associations explains why the conflicts that did arise among the citizens could become so explosive.

Only by taking into account both the vertical and the horizontal divisions can we get an accurate picture of the social structure in Greece. It was in the family-like associations of citizens that Greek communality manifested itself most clearly, and one important result was the strict limitation in the growth of hierarchical organizations.

At the same time, the vertical divisions fostered considerable solidarity and homogeneity, first within the aristocracy and later in wider circles. The clearer the differences between the privileged members of a cult association and those outside it, the more the members cultivated traits that emphasized their status. Members had the most in common as males, as freemen, and as citizens; in all these roles they strove to excel and to develop to a high degree what we think of as the Greek virtues: courage, circumspection, justice, and rationality. In all these qualities, Greek men thought they differed from women; consequently, they cultivated and stressed these qualities above all others. Even less affluent citizens— including the poor—idealized these qualities, although they did not necessarily share in them.

History, of course, offers other examples of societies based on male associations. The role these associations would play in the development of Greece came about because of the particular challenges to which they were exposed and were able to meet.

Homogeneity and boundaries had a unifying effect. Similarly, slaves were important not just because of the labor they performed but also because the existence of a group with a fundamentally different status reminded the more privileged Greeks of the freedom and solidarity they enjoyed. From Xenophon's later writings we learn that citizens acted as guards for one another's slaves as well as criminals.

Because there were so many differences between high and low members of society, homogeneity could exist only as long as Greek society retained its agrarian character. Landownership continued to be of great importance. In general, property ownership and full membership in the community went hand in hand. Commercial activity, including crafts, might be useful to create wealth, which was valued, but did not enjoy the same prestige. This view was a natural extension of the Greek ideal of autarky. But considering the revenues maritime enterprise generated, one might expect commercial activity to have acquired more prestige. (It may have, in fact, been more highly valued at first, but as the stability of property ownership became more desirable the more the entrepreneurs experienced the risks and vicissitudes inherent in large-scale business ventures.)

Nevertheless, trade across the sea was an attractive option. Entire cities had become rich through trade and continued to depend on it. One example is the small island of Aegina. Aegina's soil was poor, but its upper class was known for its entrepreneurial dynamics.

Sometimes mercantile considerations determined the policies of large cities. Improvements were made to harbors when colonies were founded and trading stations were established, such as the one in Naucratis, Egypt. The most important cities of the time owed their prominence at least in part to commerce and piracy (the line separating the two was quite porous). Still, in the long run, no polis was truly a commercial city. As important, indeed indispensable, as commercial revenues were, Greek traditions were stronger. Whatever mercantile activities the aristrocrats and their agents engaged in were considered secondary, at least as the years passed. Any other attitude toward commerce would have run counter to the "nonchalance in business matters" that Max Weber ascribes to such ruling elites. Aristocrats had to live according to the ideals of their class, in their own cities as well as before the broader Greek community.

The high value placed on independence also demanded that your life not be run by the demands of business. The work required to run a farm was natural; what might be required to run a commercial enterprise was not.

This attitude could prevail because the volume of commerce remained small, because manufacturing had not become highly specialized, and because material needs were not great or diverse enough to call for major exchanges of goods. One particular aspect of Greek life seems to have been of special importance in the way that commerce evolved: The cities did not shut themselves off from the countryside—they remained communities of landowners. Unlike the inhabitants of medieval European cities, the Greeks had neither the opportunity nor the inclination to make urban economic activities the basis of a value system applicable to the whole society. The specialized professions of commerce and crafts can assume a universally respected social and political position only where a differentiation between city and countryside has also taken place, for not until that happens will commerce and the crafts have a significant impact on general attitudes (unless an all-powerful monarchy, seeking the goods produced by artisans, creates a climate in which they are accorded special respect).

It is hard to say whether under different conditions impoverished farmers would have entered commerce and manufacture more quickly than they did. At any rate, the archaic nobility seem to have hesitated to do so wholeheartedly.

The sea may have been important as the connecting element among the Greeks. Seafaring activities may have played a crucial role in the first stages of their civilization and in the establishment of many high-ranking families, and all these activities may have been pursued extensively, but the maritime history is only part of the story. Greece's seafaring culture stood in a relationship of mutual dependency and influence on the agrarian character of the citizenry.

Starting in the seventh century, the Greeks began to idealize and pursue the life of leisure. This entailed extravagantly squandering time, projecting the appearance of not needing to work and other displays of luxury, as in clothing and hairstyle (by men as well as women). Such displays were not merely superfluous—they served to assert the superior social position of the upper class. The aristocrats' emphasis on activities of leisure also had the effect of slowing down the pace of life in the polis and ameliorating the turmoil that increasing trade and commerce had introduced. Culture and cultivation, in turn, made the lives of the elite as stimulating as was possible within the narrow confines of the polis.

For leisure to become the sum total of life's content for an entire class, it needs a place where it can manifest itself. Thus the public sphere expanded dramatically. But in Greece at that time, there were no palaces in which to stage public performances, for example. People had to make do with the agora, the square in the middle of the city that was already used for assemblies and courts, cult dancing and sport, festivals, sacrificial offerings, and feasts. The most important altars and temples were usually also located there. In this public forum, the affairs of the city were discussed. Singers performed here; people met one another, watched the crowd, talked, fell in love. Jacob Burckhardt describes the Greeks in the agora as "standing and wandering about, engaged in a mixture of business, conversation, and enjoyment of sweet leisure." In the larger city-states such as Athens, public gatherings took place both in the center and in some spots outside the city.

Burckhardt says that "sociability was inborn in the Greeks," that everything inclined them to socialize. Occasions at which the Greek aristocrats (and others) met, be it the construction of a building or the launching of a campaign of conquest, were part of the same public life because in each of these contexts the Greeks related to and vied with one another as participants in a common enterprise rather than as separate individuals. The public arena thus extended far beyond the political.

Whatever one's formal level of membership in the city, this membership also meant taking a direct part in communal activities, including receiving one's rightful share of sacrificial meat or wine, or of booty.

There was still competition for certain distinguished roles in communal affairs; such positions functioned as prizes or documentations of rank. It was in this environment of continual rivalry that the flexibility and freedom of the Greeks evolved.

In the *Odyssey*, the Phaeacian king, Alcinous, praises his people by saying: "We are not perfect fighters or wrestlers, but we run fast and are the best at sea, and we love feasts with music and dance. . . ." He asks his people to perform, so that his guest may tell his countrymen about them when he returns home, and Odysseus responds that there is "no more pleasant sight than when an entire people is happy and revelers listen to the singers, sitting in rows, with tables nearby laden with bread and meat and attendants mixing wine in pitchers and filling the goblets. This, it seems to me, is the most beautiful experience."

Hospitality was eventually extended by private houses. Small groups came together for symposia, in which participants met after the evening meal (usually eaten with their families) to drink wine and vie with each other in various arts, including singing. Here, on the private sphere, as in the public, incredible vitality and skill were displayed in competition.

It is interesting to see how separate the family was from the circle of friends, eating from drinking, life's necessities from its enjoyments. The room that served first for dining and then for symposia was, so to speak, temporally divided. As we have mentioned, the division also applied to the sexes: Wives and daughters were not admitted to the symposia. Only hetaerae, those women educated to provide artistic (and intellectual) entertainment as well as physical pleasure, were allowed. (They were clearly distinct from the women who satisfied the men's sexual needs.) And attractive young boys, whom wealthy hosts engaged as cupbearers, were welcome. (Several of these practices may have been borrowed from the East.)

We know that later on women were largely excluded from public life, at least in Athens and in other cities, and this was probably already the case in the archaic period. Of course, they were never simply locked up. They had their own cults. They were free to pass through the streets and public squares, and, if they belonged to noble families, probably were eager to show off their striking clothes and rich jewelry, though there were efforts to promote greater modesty. Beauty contests were also held in several places. Women of poorer circumstances shopped and sold their wares in the marketplace.

Lesbos was probably not the only place where women like Sappho, Andromeda, and Gorgo gathered young girls to introduce them to the high arts of female culture: dancing, playing, singing, dressing well, and elegant demeanor. Linked in intimate friendship to their mentors and joining them in the rites devoted to goddesses like Aphrodite, the girls perfected the grace they were expected later to display in the seclusion of their homes, and that was their pride. To Sappho, the man who enjoyed a former companion's charming laughter seemed godlike, and, she is stunned at how much she misses her friend. In Sybaris, a law was even passed stating that women were to be invited to sacrificial celebrations a year ahead so they would have time to prepare appropriate garments and adornments.

The more pronounced the separation of home and public sphere became, the more accentuated were the differences between men and women. But the sharp division between these two spheres also created the conditions that would later give rise to a special political sphere where equality ruled in spite of social disparity.

One aspect of this men's society was the open, though regulated, love for young boys and a strangely intense cultivation of beauty and style, in which young boys in particular were expected to excel. They were scrutinized by many, especially when training in sports, which they performed nude.

Clothes, hairdo, gait, and demeanor all had to be pleasing, and much effort went into perfecting them. The Ionians appeared "immortally similar and ageless forever" when they honored Apollo "with dances and song." "They seemed to be the embodiment of all grace." Homer speaks of a man who is "ugly in appearance but to whose words a god gave shape, so that everyone looks upon him with pleasure. In the assembly he speaks . . . with winning restraint and respect. . . . And when he walks through the city, people look at him as at a god."

It is not surprising that the visual arts of that time depict primarily naked youths, well trained and graceful, the *kouroi*, along with similarly graceful but modestly clad young women, the *kore*.

Symposium participants near the mixing vessel. Red-figured, ca. 480 B.C. Karlsruhe, Germany, Badisches Landesmuseum.

"She doesn't know how to raise the hem to her ankles," Sappho *writes of a* peasant girl. This, too, was an art that had to be learned. Kore from the Acropolis, ca. 520 B.C.

If the Greek aristocrats wanted to be *kaloikagathoi*, that is, beautiful and good, beauty was understood in the aesthetic meaning of the word. It was the kind of beauty Schiller calls the grace "not given by nature but achieved by the subjects themselves." This grace had, we read, great persuasive power and was apparently part of that "extracultural quality," which according to Max Weber is the qualifying factor of a ruling elite.

Greek civilization of that period consisted to an exceptional degree in improving the culture of society, primarily of the aristocrats, and special emphasis seems to have been placed on refinement in movement, sports, language, song, and perhaps love. And this could be done through competition, since what was demanded was less the perfection of subjective individuality than that of a type.

By comparison, the culture of that period produced relatively little in the material realm. Apart from city walls and a few modest temples there is hardly any impressive architecture. Not until the late archaic period were some grander public edifices built, and there are few of those. The means available would hardly have permitted anything more ambitious. As far as temples were concerned, the aim was not, after a few gigantic projects, to impress by size but by proper proportion. To be sure, there was sculpture, all kinds of minor artwork, and, most important, poetry. But even here the aim was not so much to depict concrete men—the images of gods were no exception—but to understand what man really was, to find the norm of human beauty, to create models.

An increasing taste for beauty in art went along with the ideal of leisure, especially since Greek public life was not too preoccupied with politics. Probably this taste for art sprang from the aristocrats' tendency and ability to look at things aesthetically. Sometimes economic or political issues or, more broadly, ethics predominated. But still, the Greeks regarded much in a disinterested way, from the outside, so to speak, as though it did not affect them. Their main desire seems to have been to enjoy beauty and interesting things. No restrictions of a political or ethical nature were imposed on this enjoyment, as Plato was later to point out so bitterly.

The elite did not worry much about criticisms of the aristocracy, frequently voiced even then. If adverse comment took a witty form, admiration for clever formulation outweighed annoyance at the criticism, though here, too, we are dealing with gradations. Obviously some things must have provoked anger and objection. But on the whole the elite was too lenient, undisciplined, and unconcerned to respond on more than the aesthetic level. In any case, the elite made hardly any effort to articulate a fundamental ideological justification for its ruling position or to buttress that position. Perhaps this attests to a need to see things through disinterested eyes in order not to have one's enjoyment disturbed. There may even have been a conscious intent to avoid political and ethical considerations.

At the symposia, the poetry of outsiders was enjoyed as much as that of others. Archilochus, the earliest lyric poet, was the illegitimate son of a nobleman and had to hire himself out as a mercenary. He looked at society from the outside and from a distance and was thoroughly uppity and insolent. He preferred, he said in one of his poems, a short, bow-legged officer who was bold and steady on his feet to a tall one who swaggered by, proud of his beautiful locks but "shaved below." He had no use for a warrior honor-bound to return home either with shield in hand or lying on it. After all, he said, you can always buy a new shield. And he had his doubts about much-lauded posthumous fame, for "after death no one is honored and held in high esteem by the citizens." Anyone who cared about "what people said about him" had little else to give him pleasure.

It seems likely that many mercenaries and other ordinary people felt the same way and probably said so as well, and though they were indifferent to Archilochus's wit, the aristocrats were not because his verses have been preserved. They were written down and must have been sung frequently at the aristocratic symposia in spite of the fact that Archilochus made fun of the conventions that prevailed there. All kinds of resentments—such as exist everywhere—could be put in poetic form and acquire a kind of dignity.

What the bitter, impudent, and aggressive outsiders expressed of their feelings and hatred gained resonance as it was repeated by many others. These outsiders moved among the elite but did not feel part of it and wanted to make this very clear. Perhaps the homogeneous men's associations felt secure enough to appreciate criticism. In any case, the Greeks learned to prize openness, at least within the symposia. The question of beauty versus ugliness remained secondary to the larger questions of friend versus enemy, good versus evil, but it nevertheless rose to relatively high importance.

The Homeric epics are filled with criticism of the nobility, some of it couched in stories about the gods. One of them tells about the love of Ares, the god of war, and Aphrodite, wife of Hephaestus, the god of workmen. The lame and ugly husband, constant object of the gods' ridicule, had been cuckolded, as he found out from the sun god, Helios. The wondrously skilled god now fashioned bonds that could be neither undone nor torn yet were so invisible that even gods failed to see them. Then he pretended to leave for Lemnos. Instantly Ares appeared. "Come, beloved, to bed. Let us lie down and enjoy ourselves. For Hephaestus has left the land. . . ." But as soon as they were asleep, Hephaestus tightened his net around them.

Now the workman took his revenge on the warrior. Seized by ferocious anger he called to the gods: "Come here and witness how Aphrodite, daughter of Zeus, continually disgraces me, loving hateful Ares because he is handsome and straight-legged while I was born with weak feet!" The goddesses alone stayed away out of shame.

"Irrepressible laughter rose from the gods . . ."—they were shocked. When Apollo asked who would want to lie with golden Aphrodite caught in such a net, only Hermes responded, saying, "Let me be bound by three times as many or any number of ties and all you gods and goddesses watching, still I would lie with golden Aphrodite." Poseidon was so embarrassed that he wanted to put an end to the scene as quickly as possible. He spoke on Ares' behalf, and Hephaestus set the lovers free. Aphrodite went to Paphos, where "the goddess of love was washed and anointed with the oil that gives the gods their immortal glow, and then she was dressed in lovely robes, a wonder to behold." Thus, after vengeance and humiliation have been served, what matters is beauty. The workman has triumphed over the warrior, but the triumph is artfully stripped of meaning—to the listeners' delight.

What is illustrated in this is a distance on both politics and life. The remoteness of the ruling elite, their lack of seriousness, was part of their freedom. This freedom was to find a different expression in Greek philosophy. Norbert Elias has pointed out what great difficulties we have to overcome simply to ask the right question: not "What does this mean for us?" but instead "How was it?" Greek society, in which each city saw the others as related and at the same time as different and therefore to be looked at from the outside, made it easy to gain such distance, as did the disassociation from politics and the appreciation of outsiders. Freedom brought increasing possibilities—along with difficulties for the individual.

The art, knowledge, public life, style, and social conventions a society produces and cultivates are not mere luxuries. Even beauty, however defined, is the response to a need, quite apart from the right people have to it. Beauty may be even more necessary in a society where the aesthetic is as predominant as it was among the Greeks. These are imponderable matters, but they count if a society is not to give way to resignation or break apart when great difficulties arise.

The Greeks obviously did not live on poetry and philosophy; many of them led miserable lives; they often did not have enough to eat; and many—the majority of the slaves as well as the women—who had to work for others had practically no contact with the culture of the polis. Nevertheless, culture was not the aristocracy's exclusive bailiwick even in the archaic period.

Instead culture determined the way this society expressed itself, ordered the world, defined its place in it—all this not just for the elite but also for the middle classes. Culture provided methods of acquiring knowledge and enhancing life, of distinguishing between means and ends, and of relating to the gods; it offered ways of directing and balancing needs, ways to be human.

In 431, in his famous funeral oration to the war dead as reported by Thucydides, Pericles praised Athens for all the organized activities, both private and public, "whose daily enjoyment drives away melancholy." No matter what exactly Pericles was referring to here or how much he may have idealized his city, dispelling despondency was apparently important enough that a city's accomplishments in this field were deserving of praise. Perhaps this conscious realization came only later. Still, this city's amazing concern for its citizens' morale may explain many of its institutions even in early times. It suggests that the Greeks may have had a real need for beauty, poetry, lightheartedness, as well as for wisdom.

A popular Greek anthology recounts that, when asked what was best for man, Homer said, "Not to be born, or to die early." To the next question, what was best about life, he answered, "A feast with plenty of food and drink, accompanied by a bard's song." He (or whoever made up the story) knew what he has talking about. We encounter this attitude repeatedly.

Jacob Burckhardt lists the major reasons for Greek pessimism: the cruelty—indeed, malice—of fate, the horrible envy of the gods, and the countless blatant injustices of life. He speaks of a "will to see the dark side," which must have been strong, and points out "the tragedians' inventiveness at making heroic myths increasingly monstrous," a tendency, he suggests, showing that this will must have grown stronger with the rise of Hellenic education. No wonder the Greeks regarded those who died early with some envy.

But if the horrible and frightening and everything that mocks our sense of justice, along with unrestrained hatred and revenge, were expressed (and often acted out) aesthetically by the Greeks, was this not due to the quality of Greek life itself? Was it not due to the Greeks' uniquely risky kind of life, which lacked a clearly defined political center, and the ideological underpinnings that could both strengthen this center and at the same time reassure the citizenry? Does it not seem reasonable that such conditions would give rise to both fear and the imagination, not to mention a sense for suffering?

Where the notion of divine envy—that is, the experience of the uncertainty of human fortune—was so prevalent, a theological interpretation of political rule was out of the question. But does that not mean, conversely, that such notions could—and probably were bound to—arise where rule was unable to justify itself theologically? It was exactly when "Hellenic culture" was on the rise in the fifth century, at the moment when Greece achieved unheard of successes and everything changed so fast, that unrestrained imagination and profound anxiety asserted themselves with frightening power—and had to be rationalized more and more often and thoroughly.

It was precisely against these uncertainties that the Greeks tried to protect themselves in public life, at symposia and feasts, by stressing gaiety, that correlate of sadness, which can be made to prevail at least at times or in certain areas. "In time a whole style of gaiety and mirth developed," wrote Burckhardt. Even the sports and arts for which Alcinous praised the Phaeacians should not be taken simply as pleasant entertainment but as belonging in the very center of Greek life.

On the other hand, we should not look at Greek pessimism in isolation. Are not the complaints we hear merely the reverse side of boundless expectations? Except at extreme moments, life can appear so terrible only when excessive hopes are placed on it. Is this not implicit in the Greeks' emphasis on man's "mortality"?

Their aversion to growing old, too, must have had roots in a view of life that regarded youth's vigor—including the attraction of its inherent possibilities—as the norm. Discipline and education cannot have been too oppressive. Much teaching was done in the context of play, or love. The subjects to be mastered were few, the goal of education relatively easy to achieve. Nietzsche writes that young people were probably never again treated so attentively and lovingly, so much with a view toward what would serve them best, as in the sixth and fifth centuries. The same was probably true in the seventh century. There is no trace of the modern experience Nietzsche formulates as: We suffered our youth like a long and painful illness.

According to Solon, man was at the prime of his life in his twenties. If that was so, life indeed had little left to offer once the delights of this age and the ability to enjoy them declined (though Solon's life hardly reflects this view). Once again, the complaints were the mirror image of the expectations.

What else was meant when the Greeks sang the song over and over that says man is like a leaf in the wind, the mere shadow of a shadow, meant only for the moment, like the passing day? "Earth nurtures nothing more miserable among all the things that crawl on it and have breath than man," we read in the *Odyssey*. Here again expectation speaks as much as disappointment, along with the wisdom that allows one at least to articulate what is. Whatever evidence we find in other cultures of this attitude, among the Greeks it must have had a special importance.

It seems reasonable to see all these complaints as an expression both of the high expectations and the unstable position of the Greek aristocracy at that time. They are signs of relatively unrestricted freedom, of self-reliance, and of the risks associated with those conditions.

Where the detailed regulations of Roman religion not only prescribed the rites the Romans had to perform but also set limits to their thoughts and imagination, so that their desires were centered on the normal course of things, the Greeks were conditioned to experience absolute misery and total happiness. They feared the gods greatly but also placed great hope in them. This ambivalence is at the heart of the Greek experience and it penetrated and shaped the language, especially that of tragedy.

Where the Romans paid little attention to the basic insecurity of life and to the connection between its ups and downs, the Greeks' view of the world was grounded in the awareness of change. Looking at their own fate with all its inherent risks and at that of the tyrants and the Eastern empires, they saw only change; and because there was no accepted view of history dictated by a powerful community like Rome or a governmental authority to absolve them from interpreting events and to imbue those events with a higher meaning, they felt no certainty, no matter how deceptive, that everything was taking its rightful course.

By being positively attracted to the experience of change they proved to be great realists. The outsiders, like Archilochus, contributed to this. Besides, there was no point in evading reality. Better to acknowledge one's awareness proudly. The Homeric heroes, the great models of the later Greeks, cursed war passionately and then fought again and again. Apparently the Greeks did not develop the art of self-deception very far. There were always enough of them manning a bastion of disillusionment to which those who had started out chasing after lofty goals could in the end retreat.

Two barrels, Homer tells us, are set up at Zeus's entryway. From them he dispenses ill to one and good to the next, and to a third, now some of this, now some of that. But he to whom he passes out only ill "will be disgraced, driven by insatiable voracity across the gods' earth, coming and going, honored neither by gods nor men. . . . For thus the gods have woven the fate of mortal men, that they live in sorrow."

Social psychologist Arnold Gehlen has described human beings as animals that need institutions because they lack instinct. The Greeks of that time were humans lacking in institutions. They had neither sufficiently strong primary native institutions nor authorities that could have imposed secondary artificial ones on them. That is probably why they appeared increasingly problematical to themselves (and made themselves the focus of their art), especially since the institutions they went on to create arose out of purely rational considerations, out of broad-based discussion, and so never assumed primacy over their creators. This lack of inherited institutions is the source of the Greeks' great curiosity and helps explain how they arrived at their *theoria*. Thus, the Greeks became *homines maxime humani*, as Pliny called them.

The acquisition of culture consists, among other things, of gaining control over emotions. One has to find forms for dealing with others but also find ways to deal with feelings inside: fear and joy, anger and high spirits, the desire to kill, the many moods of despair. Every culture finds it own ways. Norbert Elias may have been the first to point out and demonstrate how the formation of society and the control of feelings mutually determine each other.

Here, too, the problem presented itself to the Greeks in a special way. All that had arisen in the great changes since the eighth century—ambition, recklessness, much-bemoaned hubris in their tragedies and the struggles this gave rise to, including eventually civil war—had to be dealt with and kept in check. Though tyranny did at times contribute to a certain domestication, the decisive factor was what the Greeks achieved among themselves. Their public life was not dictated by any court; it took shape in their midst.

The energies the process of civilization sets free and simultaneously binds remained among the participants instead of being absorbed or directed by a higher authority that would, in either case, have made everything dependent on itself. What applies on the societal level—for instance, the abdication in the modern state of the right to self-defense in exchange for the promise of protection—also applies on the personal level: The individual loses (in exchange for certain advantages) what the higher powers gain. The fact that this was not the case among the Greeks worked and continued to work in favor of their self-reliance.

Mutual respect *(aidós)* became, along with justice, the basic norm of behavior. A unique kind of domestication of emotions evolved, inadequate as it may have been. Unique conditions existed for forming personality, but they offered far greater opportunities for a thorough though not exaggerated self-development and self-reliance than for a concept of the self as part of a superimposed whole.

How all this worked concretely we don't know, but we can make out at least one important strand in the process, probably the central one. Relative freedom was preserved by limiting freedom through self-control. Living together in the cramped cities urged self-control, as did the conscious separation of men and women. But what developed with time was more than that. In a kind of dialectical process the immoderate Greeks became a people of moderation. They began to adjust to norms of behavior long before they were ready to organize their poleis by formulating laws or any kind of constitution.

Metron ariston, "Moderation is best." It sounds like a banality, but it is what has come down to us of an important intellectual attitude. The Delphic oracle kept impressing on all its visitors: *Meden agan,* "Nothing in excess." *Gnothi sauton,* "Know thyself"—that is, be aware that you are human—was also the pithy formulation of a complex thought. "Plan in mortal terms" is another expression for the same idea.

On one level the Greeks' search for moderation means hardly more than striving for the middle, which is preferable to the extremes of too much and too little. Later the Greeks would trace their special quality to their geographically middle position: They combined the strong points of nations in Europe's colder regions (courage) with those of the Asian nations (intellect and artistic skill) and were thus able to lead a free and political life.

On another level, this search was for special conditions, which were thought or believed to consist of proper proportions. The culmination of this search showed tangible results only in the late archaic and the classical periods. The temples built then obey a system of proportions based on the span between two columns, with all other measurements arrived at through multiplication or division of this basic unit.

Musicians regarded the octave, the fifth, and the fourth as expressions of ideal numerical relations; and Polyclitus measured human bodies to arrive at his "canon" for depicting the male form. Hippodamus designed cities according to specific numerical relations.

The idea that measure or proportion is not only the basis of moderation but is a law embodied in material things, and that this measure can be detected, must have existed earlier. Solon assumed the existence of "invisible proportions that determine the limits of all things" and asserted that these proportions were the most difficult thing to find. His discovery of lawful processes in the polis; his concept of eunomy, which assumes that there are certain given relationships between the forces within the polis; the hunch of the early philosophers that laws govern the cosmos— all this and more demonstrates that the Greeks of that time tried to decipher the world in terms of proportional relationships and proceeded from there.

The law, the proper proportions that operated behind things, was relatively simple and abstract, like the triangle Greek mathematicians discovered, or like atoms and the vacuum, in contrast to which, according to Democritus, color and bitter or sweet taste were nothing but conventional concepts. But at the same time that this search for proportion was a Greek defense against the threat of chaos and hubris, as well as a means to establish order between each other and achieve self-control, this ability to cultivate abstract thought turned out to be the essential element of the Greeks' freedom.

The law they attempted to detect in nature and capture in their own creations contained the objectivity that lent authority to their freedom. "To say the truth and act according to nature *[physis]*, always listening to it, that is wisdom," Heraclitus wrote. And by nature he meant not just the external world, because he went on to say: "It is possible for all men to know themselves and to think rationally." It almost seems as though the Greek temples—after some exaggerations, especially on the part of tyrants—celebrated the ideal of moderation more than that of great size and were thus a manifestation of the recognition of man's mortality.

Of course, all of this discussion is based on the work and the awareness of artists and intellectuals and on the Delphic oracle. When and to what extent this kind of thinking was accepted is uncertain. Probably the insistence on moderation did not become a decisive factor until the broader segments of the population embraced it in their struggle against the aristocracy. But efforts in this direction must have started earlier.

One law the Greeks discovered was the often observed ups and downs of life, and they thought it important to spread awareness of it. Wise Pittacus of Mytilene had ladders set up in the sacred sites as a graphic illustration of the course of fate—now up, now down. Archilochus of Paros told his heart, "confused and devastated by inescapable sorrows," to recognize the rhythm that alternately raises man up and casts him down. Let the heart learn to withstand everything.

Nothing helped the Greeks as much to make their peace with suffering and misfortune as the clear recognition of an objective law at work. Suffering, which struck randomly, came to be seen as the manifestation of a great general truth. Before its law all were equal. To be sure, the Greeks, like the Near Eastern peoples, also saw misfortune as punishment for crime, even if it struck generations later. It was one means of encouraging righteous behavior, and fear must have contributed to the recognition of the law. But the Greeks also wanted to find in the workings of fate the law that made justice prevail, at least in the long run.

Recognition of a law at work offers little consolation; it does not cure pain, but it makes pain more bearable. For the rest, one has to learn self-control. That is the message of another poem by Archilochus. Once again great misfortune has struck—a boat carrying men of the city has sunk. "But, friends, the gods give us a soothing remedy against unavoidable pain, the strength to bear it. Suffering afflicts now one, now another; now it has descended on us. We are crying out under its bloody blow, another time it will strike others. Get hold of yourselves and bear it; resist women-like wailing."

Every functioning society encourages certain ways of behaving, of appearing, and of developing and discourages others. In the closeness of the cities, delicacy, witty conversation, and grace seem to have been considered appropriate. Was there a consensus that private matters and particularly private unhappiness were not to intrude too much into public life, with the result that suppressed pain and sadness were offset by cultivating a style of lightheartedness and beauty? A tendency in this direction might have predominated at least at times, along with—and indeed included in—all the contests, all the fighting, all the harshness of confrontation. Such a tendency would explain why the Greeks' art played such a big role among them and has remained so fascinating for us today.

Probably this same consensus was at work in the many divisions the Greeks set up: between home and public life; between different groups of people; between everyday life and festivals, rites and myth; between certain ancient cults and poetry. The sphere of sociability and merriment must have been similarly separated from that of aloneness and melancholy. It was possible to convey in art—as in vase paintings, for example—a picture of Greek life as uncomplicated, gay, even lighthearted. Though not self-deceiving, such a picture was only partial. Art did not always express the whole range of experience that had given rise to it.

However that may be, the Greeks must somehow have learned how to maintain internal balance, to bear up under stress, and to exert self-control. These were qualities they also needed for fighting in phalanx formation. However they may have acquired these qualities concretely—they were on their own a lot; much was left up to them. Individuals had to take responsibility because there was no higher authority to relieve them of it. Together they had to achieve what is usually provided by institutions. Thus, they must have been lonelier than people of other cultures, and they must have cultivated special abilities within and among themselves to withstand this loneliness.

It is no coincidence that the hero of one of the two great epics that formed the basis of all Greek culture and philosophy was long-suffering Odysseus, the antipode, so to speak, of Achilles, the hero of the *Iliad*. Odysseus loses all his companions and for a long time has to endure a miserable life. Though often in desperate straits, he always manages to escape, usually with the help of Athena, his guardian divinity. But between these adventures he has to learn endless patience.

Such an education was necessary for the Greek citizenries to be able to conduct civic life, as there was no single individual who would conduct it for them. This was an important factor in forming the human character that was so essential to this culture, and this is why Greek culture remains such an enigma for us, at once familiar yet also incomprehensible.

It is obvious that such a way of life had to be paid for. Among those bearing the cost were surely the slaves, the women, the exploited, and the debtors. But we should not forget that those who figured in public life— if it was as brilliant as it is depicted in art—also had to pay their price: by exerting self-control, by suppressing many emotions, and, not the least difficult, by suffering old age. We should take note, too, of the gradually increasing rate at which the foundations of this demanding culture were being used up. Burckhardt speaks of the "rapid and terrible moving ahead of the polis." It was not until the fifth century, however, that this acceleration became acute. At that time the possibilities for achieving both good and evil multiplied and the alternatives became so overwhelming that they gave rise to forces, questions, and answers of a completely new kind.

Whether or not a society possesses the memory of having overthrown tyranny by its own efforts or not has a lasting effect on it. Similarly, much depends on how a society deals with fears and demands, with enmity, the urge to dominate, jealousy, perhaps laziness; in short, with all the many anarchical elements inherent in any community. A society may expect guidance and solutions from a higher authority and become dependent on it—or it may rely on the self-restraint of equals and the self-reliance of individuals to control these elements. In other words, it does not rely on a socializing process that is ultimately imposed from above. There are few other areas in which we see so clearly how important the absence of monarchy was in the formative phase of Greek civilization.

We can see now that there was indeed a link between homosexuality and democracy, because the former was part of the tradition of the men's associations that formed the basis of the latter. The festival culture fostered by the aristocracy helped make public life so attractive that later on even middle-class citizens were willing to neglect their personal affairs to some extent to be able to participate in politics. This culture based on competition not only led to the perfection of many individual skills but also relativized aristocratic superiority: The elite might go about magnificently adorned, but in the sports arena they were as naked as the rest. Though they enjoyed the advantages of excellent training, they could still be surpassed by contestants of lower social standing.

To sum up: The ways in which the archaic Greeks mutually affected each other, their mentality, style of life, values, social organization; how they related to the rest of the world and to the gods and tried to give meaning to their lives—all this and more must have been part of one great whole. A culture as exceptional as that of Greece cannot be accounted for by this or that special feature. Only by recognizing the interrelatedness of everything can we begin to understand the Greek path toward democracy.

That such an interconnected whole could come into existence may seem amazing. But its evolution is not fundamentally different from the way cultures form in general, or, for that matter, from the way history proceeds. It is a process of alternating challenges and responses, of chance and necessity, of mutation and the stabilization of what has emerged through it.

Greek culture was unique, however, in the exceptional constellations that prevailed at its beginnings, both in the inherent character of the Greeks and in the dramatic impact that the opening up of new possibilities had on their early ways of life. The stable conditions under which their culture originated worked against the rise of strong monarchies and helped preserve many of the traditional features of Greek life in the emerging culture. One such feature was the smallness and multiplicity of the poleis. This already implied the future importance of exclusivity, mutual respect, and tournament wars, on the one hand, and on the other, the separation of household from polis, therefore contributing to the overarching, all-Greek sphere of public life. If this was the case, then the big role men's associations played in social life beyond the private house-

"Are not the beautiful boys gods, too, to us?"—Anacreon. A scene of homoerotic wooing. Homosexuality was subject to strict rules. The older man had to woo the younger one, and the youth was to react with aloofness. In Plato we read about male lovers: "They themselves admit that they are sick and not in full command of their senses" and "that they are ready to do anything they think will please the beloved." The suitor at the upper right carries a deer, proof of his valor as a hunter. This is an important motif in the homoerotic context. On the shoulder of the youth there seems to be the suggestion of a hare. The wreath in his hand may be an indication of victory in a sport. Plato wrote about the importance of homoeroticism for education: "What is to guide those who want to live well and properly later on cannot be completely conveyed either by relatives or by wealth and standing, or by anything else as well as by love." Black-figured amphora, ca. 550–540 B.C. Munich, Antikensammlungen.

hold and the strong accentuation of the agonistic were simply extensions of what already existed.

Such a theory is supported by the way these and other traits developed, as if they arose without apparent cause out of innumerable small impulses and finally culminated in one broadly based process that moved everything in one direction, co-opting apparently even chance. The Greek aristocrats simply continued to act to further their own interests, venturing beyond the polis while working internally to allay unrest. As a consequence, landed property continued to be of central importance, but so were refinement of style; the cultivation of aristocratic identity, given concrete expression in, for example, the *kouroi* and *kore*; and the manifestations of a definite type of humanity, whose image hardly changed over decades while almost everything else, including the foundations of aristocratic life, underwent substantial transformations.

The great problem of this culture lay in the area of politics. Competition, self-reliance, and style all implied relative isolation of the individual, living separately—in spite of all social activity—rather than forming connections. Nobody was eager to become deeply involved in broad social and political issues. The aristocrats ruled but without great emotional commitment. They were content to let their subjects depend on them but neglected to impose on the social consciousness a strong conviction that their own rule was proper.

The Greek aristocrats' superiority rested on their wealth, experience, and connections, as well as on their refined ways. But they were not representatives of some higher entity. They were not an estate marked by ancient wisdom and sacred selection, which could have lent them the aura of magic powers. They had not been able to—or wanted to—monopolize access to the gods.

Thus elements of equality linked the upper and lower classes and account for the cohesion of the men's associations, a cohesion based in turn on relationships within those groups. This was a fragile cohesion that had to be reinforced by setting the world of the polis off from everything that was foreign to it: everything that was potentially wild, dark, instinctual, excessive, and female. The existence of such forces made it all the more imperative to cultivate freedom, masculinity, moderation, rationality, self-control, and perhaps even gaiety (while maintaining strict order in the home).

Even though they remained dependent on the aristocracy for a long time to come, the less affluent citizens, the farmers, formed part of the community not in the form of clientage, but because they, together with others, made up the community's subgroups. They were more citizens than followers of anyone, and once they had assumed certain responsibilities, they were irreplaceable.

This also meant, however, that the citizens had to rely largely on themselves and were essentially as isolated as the aristocrats. Just as the political order of the polis had to maintain itself after Solon without outside guidance, the citizens, too, had only themselves to rely upon. They were not fitted and molded to function in a monarchy, nor dependent on the aristocracy in a way that guaranteed real security. Neither rulers nor common goals claimed their allegiance and gave meaning to their existence.

The psychic energies of this society did not converge in institutions that could take much from individuals yet also reward them so that they could, through various connections, obtain enough wealth to confront on a relatively equal footing those from whom they had gained that wealth. Instead the two groups had to deal with each other concretely and keep each other in check. There were no specialists, and each group had to cultivate more or less the same virtues.

This situation accounts for the political weaknesses and the cultural strengths of this society, without which the development toward democracy and the art forms evolving with it would have been impossible. Precisely because the Greeks had to work so hard on themselves, they became more and more problematic to themselves, with the result that art and thought kept focusing on man—the image, the nature, and the measure of man. Man became the central, dominant subject, man depicted as naked and concrete, though not in the form of specific individuals. And because man was not associated with a multiplicity of images and ideas, because the goal of depicting man was to reveal his ideal proportions and the laws that should rule public life, the polis, and man's actions—because of this the other manifestations of art, from mere ornamentation to the design of temples, were based on simple lines and laws. This interest in abstract forms was, by the way, already evident in the geometric art of Greece.

The festivals, bards, and myths, all the fantastic productions of imagination that clamored for expression in the public arena, just as the poems of the outsiders did, was all presumably just as important to the middle class and elements of the lower classes as it was to the aristocrats. Granted, they could not live on myth and poetry alone, but without them the Greeks could not have lived the way they did, evolving toward democracy and ultimately determining the beginnings of Europe, beginnings that were as archaic as they were modern.

The picture drawn here of Greek culture is inevitably flawed. It concentrates too much on the aristocracy and on its special characteristics.

It took the labor of many to support the splendid, essentially idle style of the aristocrats. Just how minimal the aristocrats' means often were is shown by Hesiod's advice to feed the cattle only half their normal ration during winter and to give just a little more to the farmhand because "the long nights help" conserve energy.

In time, growing demands and the introduction of new, more productive methods of farming gave rise to fierce competition for limited resources. Many farmers fell into debt and were exploited, and the rise and fall of many aristocratic families disrupted the old order. Aristocratic culture was expensive, and the costs added up.

The Greeks lamented how sudden the fall from wealth to poverty could be and how terrible an affliction poverty is, stripping man of honor and prestige. Poverty meant the total absence of options. Impotent criticism was aimed at the nouveaux riches, who once went about in ragged animal skins: "It is possessions that make the man," losing those, one loses one's friends; and "Wealth lets a man marry above his station."

Examples of such laments voiced at the symposia and fragments of lyrics dating from that time have survived, and although they don't tell us how prevalent the changes of fortune were, such changes were clearly not insignificant. One sign of this is the frequency of upheavals, murders, banishments, rebellions, usurpations; in short, the overall crisis for which, in Athens, Solon tried to find a solution.

All kinds of misery, sorrow, and conflict must therefore be included in any picture of Greek culture, along with all kinds of politics, injustice, and arbitrariness. These woes would have interrupted the normal course of everyday—as well as festive—life again and again, shaking the social foundations and making them unhappy. There are indications that cities were dominated by fear for whole periods, the kind of fear that often precedes a new order and is characteristic of transitional phases. By concentrating here on defining the main features of Greek aristocratic culture, all this has been left too much on the periphery.

What is important is that even the social unrest of the archaic period was shaped by the particular nature of Greek aristocratic culture, by its claims and freedoms and, specifically, by the high risks aristocrats took and the great losses their wastefulness and economic neglect caused; by their concern with magnificence and distinction rather than with power and cohesion; and, last but not least, by the fact that within the leading circle, there were no competing camps to effectively counteract excesses.

Thus, the aristocrats were relatively helpless in coping with problems they had provoked among the citizenry, especially when conflict erupted virulently. Not only did they lack the necessary abilities, they also lacked support. Anyone who wanted, like Solon, to accomplish something needed a base beyond the aristocracy, and this base had yet to form.

The Greeks faced difficulties in their attempt to impose discipline on their communities. It is much easier after profound upheavals to base the social order of a community on one will than to oblige the many to subscribe to an order that exists nowhere except within and among themselves. In the first case, the monarch is the source of all official action and makes the system function; in the second, rules and institutions have to be invented and established; they then function on their own and themselves become the source of political action. Some kind of overarching interest has to be found, some third force that stands above everybody and is not subject to any higher authority; and if this third force is to succeed in unifying the manifold concrete interests it represents, it has to be strong.

But how can the wide discrepancy between individual and general interests be dealt with? How can different factions with competing and conflicting interests be induced to make what they have in common powerful and capable of action?

This is where political thought enters, without which Greek democracy could not have arisen. The Greeks had no Greek model from which they could have learned that something like democracy was even conceivable. They had no public press, no universities. A tyrant tries to usurp a position that exists, but here the position the people were meant to occupy had to be invented first. It was not invented all at once but in stages, gradually, in a way that kept defining and clarifying the goals ahead.

The Greeks thus developed a kind of thinking and acting focused on the form of the polis. This task was no longer a matter of simply experiencing, continuing, and stabilizing their old established ways but of initiating profound changes in the polis and filling the political vacuum they faced.

The first democracies in world history had to be direct democracies. The conditions necessary for representative government or for the state to arise either as concepts or realities did not yet exist. There were hardly any suitable representatives for the people. The aristocrats who took on that role were continually tempted to found tyrannies. Consequently, the broader segments of the population had to take things into their own hands.

Those segments always constitute the majority, but seldom in history and never before the Greeks did this majority have a decisive say, let alone achieve a ruling position. Only institutional guarantees could make that possible, and they had yet to be developed.

We don't know in detail what happened in Athens during the incubation phase after Solon and before Cleisthenes. The little information we do have is concerned primarily with actions and events. Still, we can draw some conclusions from the overall course of events, from some facts we know, and from knowing the outcome of the process. Nothing comes out of the clear blue sky. Classical historians are given to forget that when it comes to important questions in their field. Yet there is much that speaks for a process leading toward democracy, and everything speaks against regarding democracy as something that needs no further explanation. So now we find ourselves confronted with the second part of the great mystery: How did Greece, after having evolved a culture without monarchs, achieve a political consolidation supported by broad segments of the population?

Greek political thought was a process that became gradually more and more inclusive. Its intellectual nucleus lay in that circle of sagacious men whose most prominent members were called the Seven Wise Men (a term actually associated with more than seven names), one of whom was Solon. But the process included this circle's interaction with and adjustment to changing reality and the masses who constituted this reality and had an increasing share in shaping it.

The fact that some people become intensely preoccupied by persistent and worsening problems is not a specifically Greek phenomenon. What is remarkable in this case is that traditional religion offered little explanation and guidance and that what it did offer was not elaborate. The intellectuals, not associated with royal courts or temples, could assume a relatively independent position in and among the cities. Consequently, their thinking did not serve special interests or increase the superiority of the ruling elite and the dependence of the ruled. These thinkers did not address only those in power but, like Solon, often made appeals to the entire citizenry. Like doctors, they were consulted by all sides, and they functioned largely in the public sphere. They could to some extent fall back on the men of Delphi, the place that attracted some of the best minds and the collection point, so to speak, of useful information that could be passed on to others.

When, for example, the citizens of Cyrene in North Africa felt a new political order was needed, the Delphic oracle advised them to send to Mantinea in Arcadia for a restorer of order. The Mantineans dispatched a man named Demonax, who, after examining the situation, proposed a program of reforms.

Of course, it happened now and then that a thinker was tempted to make common cause with those in power or to become a tyrant himself. But this was apparently not true of the wise men as a whole. The position of power was complex and unstable. Often power was useless and negotiation was called for. Knowledgeable, imaginative, and appropriate advice was expected from the wise men. In return they gained social status, fame, authority, and probably some sort of payment, as well as a sense of satisfaction—as did the Delphic oracle.

Initially, the wise men were mostly called upon to solve technical and economic problems, such as unemployment or decreasing agricultural yields. Hesiod urged farmers to concentrate on their work and not worry about what happened in the agora. Later issues were protection under the law and, especially, giving written form to (and supplementing) laws that had been passed down orally. Here the advice and proposed legislation of the wise men could coincide with the tyrants' interests. Often the laws were inspired by Near Eastern philosophy.

Gradually politics moved into the foreground. The need to find institutional ways to prevent uprisings, conflict, and civil war became more urgent. As these efforts showed success, there was a demand for more. All of Greece became a field of experimentation. What happened in one place was watched in another; similar rules required different adaptations; where some had failed others tried to do better.

But this problem-solving mode soon proved inadequate to developing an overarching model, for what was soon at stake was the entire constitution of a polis. Solon's concept of eunomy was merely one example. But no matter how varied the ideas of what should be, they all had to take account of what actually existed. To be sure, the status quo was not identical with the norm, but the active forces, the aristocracy as well as the common people, each had to be given their due. No group could be ignored, none suppressed. They kept each other in some sort of balance: Where the aristocracy was generally powerful, the masses could be so only in exceptional situations, through violence. But in this society without a state machinery the means of power were not concentrated in one place, because the Greeks kept their original order intact while developing their culture. Now was the time to find greater justification for this order.

That is why the "right order" had to be based on the status quo rather than invented anew. This principle had nothing to do with philosophy of history or with constructing a concept of society. It was based rather on the belief that *one* right order existed and that it derived from the gods. Ultimately it was this faith, not the notion that certain means produce certain ends, that inspired the political thinkers, and this faith was probably rooted in the distant past. The recognition that events obey certain laws—a recognition that supported faith—and the tendency inherent in the Greek concept of law to arrive at an all-Greek consensus worked in the same direction.

Given this context, tyranny was bound to prove unsatisfactory, though it may at times have seemed expedient. It was the exception rather than the rule, without legitimation in the past and not powerful enough to challenge the past.

But because aristocratic rule was well established since time immemorial and abuses of power were difficult to prevent, at least in problematic poleis, the political thinkers were bound to realize sooner or later that a counterbalance was needed to keep the aristocracy in check, and they looked to broader segments of the population, particularly citizens of moderate means, to fill this role.

Solon turned to those who had qualified some time ago to serve together with the aristocrats as hoplites but who had previously had no real say in political matters. Aristotle's often quoted statement that a citizen's political status corresponded to his military position does not apply in this period. Otherwise it would not have taken several generations after the introduction of the hoplite phalanges before the farmers were granted a voice in political decision-making.

These "middle" citizens were at first few in number and altogether no match for the aristocrats. They were unable to organize politically and presumably grateful just to be allowed to serve in the army, since this was regarded as much a right as a duty. Being part of the military was worth a lot in itself.

Their situation improved in time, perhaps not so much as a result of

reforms like Solon's, but definitely thanks to tyranny. The middle segments grew larger. There had probably for some time been a group of
men almost as well off as the aristocrats, the semi-aristocrats. Now this
circle expanded and formed a front together with many others in similar
circumstances. Their interests must have coincided to some extent with
those of the poorer classes, but the main question is how these groups
came to defend their interests politically and, above all, how they
achieved lasting success. For this, it was not enough to rebel.

At this point we seem to have come considerably closer to solving the
mystery. Not that the political thinkers necessarily became the champions
of the masses—there is no evidence of that. But if their suggestions were
to help reform the entire polis order—as they were expected to—then
larger segments of the citizenry had to be urged, at least in a few important cities, to share in civic responsibility.

The political thinkers had to educate the people, as Solon had, and
teach them the axioms of political judgment; they had to awaken sensitivity to the city's plight by impressing on the citizens that they collectively were responsible for the city. Irrational fears of contamination
caused by the presence of unpunished murderers worked in the same
direction and may have been deliberately encouraged to promote greater
social responsibility.

Areas of public activity had to be opened to the people, and not just in
exceptional circumstances, as when Solon was given power. It was necessary to awaken—and strengthen—the demand for political rights, for such
a demand does not arise spontaneously, at least not in the kind of situation
that prevailed then. Discontent had to be translated into political
demands, and the secondary, perennial desires for justice under the law
and for order had to be turned into primary goals.

We have some specific evidence of the transformation of values that
took place at that time. The question arose of what constituted the
essence of virtue *(pâs'areté)*. The answer varied. In Sparta it was disciplined military service for the city; in the rest of Greece, probably
wisdom and, above all, justice. All the hopes for justice harbored by the

oppressed farmers found expression in this answer, and the appeals to be moderate and assume a sensible way of life were a further effort to achieve this goal. Wisdom was called on to control emotions. Legal thinking ran along similar lines. Finally, in Aeschylus, we encounter for the first time the Platonic list of virtues: to be "just, thoughtful, brave, and of god-fearing mind."

The attempts to educate and awaken a sense of responsibility for the city are most obvious in Solon. The evolution of institutions can be followed by studying the manifold changes in the constitutions of various cities. One isolated reference suggests that Cleisthenes' reforms of the phyle system had forerunners in Ionia. And, finally, the idea of a balance of power within the city as it was to emerge between aristocracy and the people, to oversimplify somewhat, fits into the concept of isonomy.

It seems unlikely that the broader population segments could have accomplished their political rise without intellectuals, who had some education, could travel, had the time and means to gather information, and must consequently have belonged to the aristocratic class. These men must have been farsighted to bring about such amazing changes. But they must also have met with a favorable response.

Clearly the circle of wise men established for itself a position of relative intellectual independence. These men could not have withstood various expectations—perhaps even threats and temptations to take a partisan stand—as successfully as they did unless they collectively adhered to the rules on which their authority rested, and, like physicians of politics, they did just that, owing allegiance neither to individual cities nor to partisan groups.

Just as clearly they developed a special way of thinking. Anyone faced with conceiving a new order without having a base of power to fall back on has to take existing reality into account. He cannot have vested interests, whether ideological ones or personally political ones, in what he promotes. And anyone expected to establish an order that will last without his further participation has to think differently from someone in the service of an authority, such as a monarchy, that can always (and may

indeed want to) step in. He has to study interdependencies and the pre-
dictability of events more thoroughly, understand them more abstractly,
and has to figure out how to bring different forces into balance. Anyone
dealing with many comparable cities has to look past the different specific
circumstances and penetrate to the common core, to the recognition that
moderation and lawfulness are the key to everything. And if he has
to convince numerous aristocrats, as well as members of the middle class,
of the truth of his thinking, he has to learn to express his insights in
commonly accessible terms. Jacob Burckhardt calls this objective and
comparative examination of political forms "one of the dearly bought
results of Greek life and suffering."

It is hardly a coincidence that the Greek philosophers approached the
cosmos with questions and assumptions that resembled their political
thinking about the polis order. The Greek concepts of justice and of the
world dispensed with supreme authorities, whether in heaven or on
earth. Justice and the workings of the world stood above all authorities,
including the gods. If Zeus was made the guardian of justice, this meant
no more than that he guaranteed and administered it. Of the sun god
Helios, Heraclites says that he will not transgress his limits because otherwise the executors of justice will catch up with him. Order existed and
functioned by virtue of the mutual effect its constituent forces exerted on
one another. Even Zeus's responsibility for justice was subject to this
interplay of forces.

The autonomy of the order perceived in both the cosmos (*cosmos*
originally meant "order") and the polis, the absence of a monarchy, and
the independence of the late archaic period's intellectuals all led to the
establishment of a kind of third position between the contending forces, a
position that was concerned with the interests of the polis as a whole
before there was a body to defend those interests.

If political thinking began very early to include the larger population,
not just as an abstract subject but as a group that raised questions and
served as audience, that stimulated ideas and acted on them, these people
must have shared in this thinking. In this sense the history of political
thought consists increasingly of its dissemination.

The magnitude of this process is hard to grasp. It went beyond growth of knowledge and judgment, beyond an increased sense of political responsibility, and beyond heightened sensitivity and the resulting demands on the political order. The entire radius of awareness and interest must have expanded. Distance from what existed had to be gained. The more the political order was seen as adjustable, the more subject to intellectual insight the assumptions of the past must have become. Questions arose, bringing with them uncertainty, intellectual flexibility, and the ability to take risks. Most important, the citizens who were called on (and wanted) to take an active part in the community would have to change. They had to learn to look in a new way at the polis and the world in which they were to assume such an unprecedented position.

Later, after major changes had taken place, we can observe that the rise of democracy went hand in hand with a more or less radical reinterpretation of the divine myths, a reinterpretation that took place before the eyes of the people, on the stage of tragedy.

At about this time Heraclitus said, making use of a pun, that whoever wants to talk sense *(xyn nooi)* has to resort to what is common to all *(xynon)*. In this way the city resorts to laws to gain strength, because all human laws derive from *one* divine law. Sensible talk and what is common to all, the law of the city and the law of the world, are closely interconnected. This is a philosopher's way of saying what others can have at least an inkling of, for, to cite Heraclitus again, "It is possible for all men to know themselves and think rationally."

All this should not lead us to think of the Greek citizens as theoreticians. They probably spoke and thought in simple and ordinary terms, preoccupied primarily with everyday concerns. Still, the labors of their political wise men must have had some impact on their position, for the political thinking that was going on met with considerable response among the larger classes. Access to knowledge and discussion of it must have been accompanied by an increasing conviction that knowledge was important and that its dictates should be followed. This was not to remain the case indefinitely; toward the end of the fifth century B.C. things and thought became too complicated. But initially the Greek citizenries showed a remarkable capacity for participating in the thinking of the wisest men among them.

. . .

Of course, one can prefer to think, as discussed before, that the Greek democracies appeared out of the blue or were simply the product of a special Greek talent. But it is more likely that what happened had to do with real, concrete things, with needs that arose from specific circumstances, and with the basic human capacity to develop abilities to deal with those needs.

This process can be explained in purely material terms as long as one keeps in mind that reason and the ability to act according to its dictates, as well as ideas and longings, are part of human nature, and that though men act to further their own interests, socially established attitudes determine what those interests are. It is possible, consequently, for people to embrace unusual interests, goals, and identities.

Max Weber remarked that "the farmer becomes stupid only when he is forced to function in the context of an alien . . . big-state machinery or is locked into serfdom by feudal land ownership." In ancient Israel, too, intellectuals worked together with farmers, and Weber sees in this "one of the secrets that led to the rise of Yahwism." In that tradition, too, we observe the remarkable ability of a culture to turn a questioning gaze at the world—"the capacity to be amazed."

The special character of the Greeks may well have played a role in the victory at Salamis. Their bravery must have been based on discipline and esprit de corps, qualities they had to practice in the phalanges and that were of even greater significance later in the isonomies. Pressure was not just exerted by superiors but was felt more strongly from fellow warriors. Thus, the ability to cooperate must have been well established.

The expectations that placed value on certain ways of life and on order also contributed to the willingness of people to risk their lives. Mere survival was not regarded as the supreme good. Only fear argued for survival, everything else against it—glory, for example, and the attitude toward old age, not to mention the Greeks' particular way of weighing life against death. The Persian king Xerxes was amazed before the Battle of Thermopylae when he heard that some Spartans, awaiting battle, were doing gymnastics while others attended to their hair. In anticipation of mortal combat, he was told, the Spartans liked to adorn their heads, and they were so absorbed in this activity that they never even noticed the Persian spy.

For the Spartans even war and death in battle were connected with beauty. And the tendency expressed in this attitude was probably not confined to the Spartans alone.

The decision to abandon Athens may well have been encouraged by the memory of the Athenians' many colonial expeditions but also must have been made easier by the special mobility characteristic of the Greeks since their culture first took rise in the eighth century. This mobility must have occupied an important place in their cultural memory.

Granted that chance favorably affected the general and immediate conditions of the battle, the crucial factor in its outcome may still have been the Greeks' ability to make up for inferiority in numbers by the superiority inherent in their character.

The victory at Salamis made it possible for them to pursue—to excess—the opportunities their special path had opened up for them. This happened everywhere, but nowhere as splendidly as in Athens, the city that had not only made the decisive contribution to that victory but was also especially adept at exploiting it. The city had, without knowing what lay ahead, started to prepare for it decades earlier.

4

The New Founding of the
Polis Under Cleisthenes

To pledge brotherhood in this way does not mean granting or promising to each other certain services useful for obtaining concrete ends . . . but "becoming" something qualitatively different from before. Otherwise this new behavior would not be possible. The participants have to let another "soul" enter them.

—MAX WEBER

The incubation period was over. Solon's bold assertion that the citizens are responsible for the city could become reality and became so in the conduct of politics. All that was necessary was that the different insights, wishes, and ideas merge together into a political force and that institutional forms be found for that force.

One goal Solon laid the groundwork for, the economic consolidation of the middle and lower classes, was, ironically, achieved under the rule of tyranny, which Solon had abhorred. The other goal he had worked toward, eunomy—the right order to be maintained under the leadership of the aristocracy but with proper consideration of the people's rights— was not yet achieved. It could be realized only in modified form and only if broad segments of the citizenry were given an active voice in politics and, hence, the ability to look out for their own interests.

This was the conclusion the political thinkers drew from their experience with aristocratic rule and tyranny. Tyranny had tarnished the reputation of the aristocratic lords in Athens, and in some other poleis the participation of the people in politics was already institutionally guaranteed. Now in Athens, too, members of the middle class, people of somewhat lower distinction than the aristocrats, began to feel that they were basically the latter's equals, equal enough anyway to call for equality of political rights. They wanted to enter politics.

Thus, an alternative to the traditional rule of aristocrats and a political force that could support an entirely new order were taking shape. This emerging order was not yet a democracy, but it had many features of government by the people. Isonomy, the name used at the time (or a little later) to describe it, reflects its central characteristic: equality. And because what was at stake was primarily the establishment of a new relationship between the aristocracy and the larger segments of the citizenry, this name was only logical. The "middle ones" demanded to become "equals" *(homoioi)*.

The emergence of this alternative made it possible for profound institutional changes to take place, changes that had already taken place shortly before and on a smaller scale in other Greek cities. What had in previous world history been accomplished only rarely and only by monarchs, citizens were now able to do: gain control over the circumstances of their lives.

Institutions are much like medicines. Their success depends not just on their appropriateness (and correct dosage) but also on the physical condition of the body to which they are administered. New institutions can have a decisive effect only if the "body" responds to them.

Institutions can be of all kinds and, indeed, offer themselves all too readily. Once a range of possibilities exists, politicians can, in times of crisis, fall into the habit of suggesting institutions that often are quite useless. Crises that persist over longer periods come about because the forces that could support a new order formulated to remedy the existing problems and assure the success of an institution have not yet evolved.

This was probably the situation in the sixth century B.C. Attempts to solve problems institutionally, ingenious as they may have been, must often have failed. Thus, Solon thought up a very odd method indeed to avert the danger of civil war. He instituted the so-called stasis law. In case of civil war every Athenian was to join one of the sides or he would be without rights, or at least lost his citizen's rights. Solon's intent presumably was to involve neutral citizens in the conflict, so that men who did not share the outrage giving rise to the violent conflict would join the fronts. These men, he must have reasoned, would be more likely to slow down the excited and overly ambitious fighters than to add to their force. They might do this simply by taking the places of those who would otherwise have moved ahead unrestrained. Private quarrels were to be suppressed in the interest of the general public. Solon's idea was clever but not very practical. It reveals the powerlessness of a reformer faced with a problem for which he has no viable, institutional solution.

By the time Cleisthenes won the people over to his side by promising reform, the foundation for a successful resolution of the long lingering crisis was in place and needed only cementing.

As a rule, the only way oppressed classes can protest their state is to rebel, which may result, if they are lucky, in an improvement of governing practices. The modern European era differs fundamentally from this pattern. Here alternatives to past practices arose as increasingly large population segments—first the liberal middle class and later the proletariat—became involved in running the state or voicing their demands emphatically and persistently.

This way of resolving crises—the participation in regular politics of ever larger population segments—seems to characterize European history from its beginning. We see it in the medieval cities and even as early as the struggles of the estates in Rome. The first major example of it is in Athens at the time of Cleisthenes.

The members of the Attic middle class suffered no more material need than did the Third Estate at the time of the French Revolution. But the arbitrariness with which they were treated by the noble lords—the aristocrats' arrogance and insistence on special privileges—was so much at odds with their sense of self-worth that the inequality expressed by this treatment became in their eyes identical with a different abuse: injustice.

The struggle for justice seems to be at the heart of the European alternative. As Aristotle said, it is always the weaker who strive for equality and justice. And they achieve, in institutional form, their goal again and again: They win equality in the name of justice. But for this demand to be pursued effectively by the larger classes it has to be deeply rooted in the convictions of these classes. If this is the case, a power can arise that persuades others, especially ambitious politicians and intellectuals, to align themselves with it.

Such a power had formed in Athens in the period between Solon and Cleisthenes. It evolved intellectually through political thought and practically in the mentality of an entire social class. The broader classes in the poleis apparently did not stage a revolt against tyranny. Simply reinstalling an aristocratic regime made little sense to them. But if a politician like Cleisthenes proposed what seemed to them like real reform, they were ready to act. How much so is shown by their spontaneous act of taking to the streets, armed, to prevent Spartan intervention—that is, to fight for reform—even in the absence of the reformer and his associates. They wanted "things to be placed in the middle," as the Greeks liked to put it.

Most of those who did so must have been "middle" citizens, the semi-aristocrats. They also included farmers and some well-to-do tradesmen and merchants who would be the primary beneficiaries of reform, and they must have shown great commitment to maintaining the new institutions. They were not rich but could afford to take time off from their occupations. What the lower class did is unknown.

Most of the Athenians who lived at that time had grown up under tyranny. Those with some clear memory of the time before Pisistratus came to power must now have been over fifty years old. And what they remembered could not be called a well-ordered community.

Tyranny propagated no ideology. Whatever publicly hired teachers there were, if any, taught their students reading and writing. Education took place largely within the family. In the middle and upper classes the parents also relied on nannies who, we read in various places, liked to tell small children fairy tales, which probably means that they brought them up on myths. The attitudes and teachings conveyed by the mothers were probably also on the conservative side.

But the boys must have learned something about contemporary politics from their fathers and their friends, from the music and dance teachers to whom they were sent for lessons, and from older male lovers with whom boys associated—presumably in Athens as well as in other places. And they encountered politics, along with much else, in discussions at the sports arenas. A great deal of education took place through social intercourse. Protagoras was later to say that all citizens served as teachers to one another.

But what could all those preceptors the boys encountered in the public sphere say about tyranny, even if they themselves approved of it? At best they could praise the intelligence of those in power, their accomplishments, conceivably their goodwill, but this amounted to no more than an assessment of individuals, not of a system. The views conveyed referred to a concrete situation, not to an abstraction, and the assessment could easily be corrected as soon as the tyrants and their supporters appeared in a different light or were regarded from a different standpoint. All this cannot have had a strong and lasting effect in support of the regime.

Tyranny was based on the principle that the ruler took care of politics while the citizens concentrated on their own affairs. On the whole this system must have encouraged self-reliance and initiative on the part of the citizens. Then, too, the citizens could not have been unaware of the ideas evolving in political thinking. They must have heard of what was happening in other places. Therefore nothing except the lack of practical political experience kept the demand for political rights from arising.

Of course, there may have been a gap between the generations. The older men who had experienced the period before the final takeover of Pisistratus's family or knew it from stories they had been told were probably more appreciative of tyranny's benefits—unless they belonged to the aristocracy, the born rival of tyranny. Under tyranny the economic situation visibly improved; internal peace returned; security under the law appeared. The next generation, however, who were twenty to forty at the time of Cleisthenes, probably took for granted the advantage of tyranny and felt more keenly its disadvantages.

We have no reason to assume that the Greeks experienced the kind of major generational conflicts we have witnessed in recent years. History was not moving fast enough at that time, and too few issues might have rallied the young against their elders. There was no philosophy of history, nor were there outmoded ethical commands to rebel against. The young and the old lived in the same time. The adults did not know what the young had yet to learn, nor did the young think they knew what their elders would never be capable of discovering. At least this was not the case on a major scale. Old and young were too concretely involved with each other.

But we may assume that it was primarily the younger men, filled with enthusiasm and courage, unencumbered by doubt and caution, who embraced the new, supported reform, and threw their energies into Attic politics. Among the youngest to reach the age of full citizen's rights when the granting of such rights began to mean something completely new were Themistocles and Aeschylus.

Cleisthenes' reform was less a constitutional revision than a reorganization of the citizenry. It not only effected the political rise of new population segments but also transformed the polis of Athens from a political framework into a political body.

Previously a large number of people had simply been farmers, artisans, and merchants; now they became, in a meaningful way, citizens. After functioning in politics for a long time almost exclusively as liegemen of aristocrats they could now act in their own name. Before, they had been preoccupied with their domestic and economic activities and with the affairs of their neighbors, villages, towns, and citizens' subgroups; now they were also oriented toward the polis. The polis became less remote because ways were found to overcome distance, and the relative isolation that separated different regions of Attica was broken. The unity of the city was reinforced by the participation of so many citizens and became meaningful only through this citizen input.

As a result, Cleisthenes' reform was of import not just domestically but beyond Attica's borders. The size of Attica's citizenry was bound to upset the balance of the existing polis world. Sparta realized this instantly— whether because of its sensitivity as the predominant power or because of the ambitions harbored by King Cleomenes, as is shown by Sparta's efforts to derail Cleisthenes' new order. Athens' attempt to secure the support of the Persian satrap in Sardis was an understandable though not inevitable response to Sparta's policy. Never before, as far as we know, had anyone tried to draw the Persians into the politics of mainland Greece. As politics grew more intense, its horizon inevitably expanded.

The reforms were adopted in the year 507 B.C. The first attack launched by Sparta and its allies probably came in 506, and a few years later Sparta plotted to reintroduce tyranny in Athens by reinstalling Hippias, at which point Athens sent a second delegation to the satrap. Undoubtedly the Ionian revolt of 499, too, came about as a result of the unrest stimulated by Cleisthenes' reforms. Athens' example encouraged the empowerment of the broader classes and also served as an impetus for bold plans in the field of foreign policy. As a consequence, the Persians felt an invasion of Greece was overdue.

The energy released by the radical change taking place in the greatest polis in Greece made itself felt throughout the Aegean world. This energy was to serve the Greeks well in their struggle against the Persians. It was an energy supplied by men who had worked for the reforms, who felt and enjoyed their status as citizens in a new way and with new intensity, who achieved the first major military successes, and for whom—it can be said without exaggeration—a whole new world had opened up. Among these age groups a deep sense of belonging to one and the same generation must have formed.

Herodotus relates that Cleisthenes, after failing to be elected, chose "the people" as his followers. The term "the people" may have been old, but it was now conceived of in a new way. The point is that Cleisthenes did not want the citizenry to act as followers but as an independent political force. A shrewd politician, he used this new and realistic method to gain power. Instead of wooing the people economically and then using the political power gained to establish himself as a tyrant, he won greater political rights for the people in order to pursue political ends with their support.

Herodotus credits Cleisthenes with establishing the phylae, or tribes, and democracy in Athens. Even if this claim is qualified by substituting isonomy for democracy, it is still a mystery how "phyle reform" could effect such a dramatic change. This is a complicated subject, and the more aware we are of its complexity, the better we will understand it. The phrase "phyle reform" is misleading because the old subgroups within the citizenry remained unchanged. Cleisthenes did, however, add new groups and assign different functions to them.

We know of the old order that the citizens were divided into four tribes. Each of these was made up of several subdivisions, or phratries. Below them was a third level of relatively small groups, the "clans" *(gene)* and the cult associations *(orgones* and *thiasoi).* Historians have devoted much research to gain a better understanding of this system but still have nothing more than hypotheses to offer.

We have some clarity only about the general picture. Everywhere in Greece the sense of membership in the community was conveyed through these various subgroups, and everywhere the unity of the citizens could be experienced in exclusive cult associations. If this held true for Greece in general, it must have been especially important for a polis the size of Athens.

The phratries, originally brotherhoods of warriors that were later incorporated into the overall system, played an important role. A phratry probably had several hundred members. The phratries kept the lists of citizens, and anybody getting married introduced his bride to this circle, perhaps not in person, but at least by giving official notice of the marriage. If a son was born, the father carried him to the altar at which the phratry worshipped and took an oath of paternity, upon which the child was accepted into the phratry. Presumably the birth was certified as legitimate since illegitimacy was socially unacceptable.

Both of these events took place at the phratry's annual celebration of *aparturia,* at which the new husband or father was required to supply a sacrificial animal for the feast. At these same occasions young men reaching majority on turning eighteen made an offering of their hair in order to be accepted into full membership. Thus, the phratries were the scene of transition rites and were the small, concrete public sphere that played a much more crucial role in citizens' lives than the large stage of the city. Here people knew one another more or less well, and each had his own place. Those not belonging to a phratry were excluded from the community, homeless and without rights.

According to an old provision, responsibility for blood feuds, if there were no family members left, devolved on ten phratry members to be picked according to instructions by the aristocracy. Particularly in early times the protection provided by the phratry must have been valuable. Each individual was dependent on his fellows. The closeness experienced in making communal offerings (and sharing sacrificial meals) must have contributed to this mutual support. Aristotle once called the subgroups "familiar connections that go back a long time." Strong evidence suggests that the people belonging to a phratry originally lived in contiguous regions, where their altars were also located.

The recruitment of the army was organized by tribes, and rights and duties were assigned through them and probably through the phratries as well. Through this system, differences within the citizenry could be minimized by, for instance, combining groups of similar background in the same phylae, thus allowing them a certain independence while making it easier for them to feel part of the whole. Of course, tensions could also extend into these phylae.

Traditionally the aristocrats played the leading role in the tribes. The "phyle kings" came from their ranks, but they must also have donated altars and sacrificial animals. They were in charge of blood feuds and also acted on behalf of their fellow members in other respects, representing them before courts and officials at conscription time, and whenever other problems arose. Thus the non-aristocrats came to be quite dependent on them. The violent conflicts that erupted between rich and poor, especially at the time of the great crisis, probably made themselves felt in the subgroups only when they became most acute. For in the narrower context, where people knew each other, the aristocrats were perceived differently than they were when seen from the point of view of a large group with shared grievances and a readiness to rebel.

That is why the system probably functioned well as a rule. People needed this kind of mutual support as well as the experience of associating together in spite of social inequality. (There were no hereditary clientage ties to aristocratic families as there were in Rome.) The relationships among the members of the subgroups were like a net connecting the non-aristocratic citizens to the community, providing them with some access to the centers of political power.

But dependency on the aristocracy could also be felt as a hindrance, and those who valued self-reliance found it intolerable. This must have been the case particularly when large numbers reinforced this attitude in one another and wanted to be heard in politics. Consequently the ties within the subgroup began to lose their importance. However, they could be dispensed with if they were replaced with new ties. People destroy only what they can replace.

And that is exactly how Cleisthenes proceeded. He did not abolish the old system, perhaps because he felt it could still be useful to him once its effects no longer benefited the aristocracy. Or perhaps because resistance was too great, even among the masses.

Cleisthenes' new order focused on two areas. He set up self-government in the small settlement units everywhere in Attica, a self-government based on equal rights. Then he created a complex system to connect citizens from all the regions and foster cooperation among them. This system served at the same time to create awareness of the rural population's will in Athens. He set up "demes," new tribes, and a Council of Five Hundred.

A deme was normally made up of a village or small town, though sometimes several hamlets were combined in one deme. Athens was subdivided into several demes and the city of Brauron into two. This resulted in 139 local units, each including at least a hundred citizens, in most instances several hundred, and occasionally over a thousand. The deme members administered the communal property in their district, conferred about work to be done, kept the local religious cults going, and organized festivals. The demes had priests and officials and, most important, a communal council, in which members of the middle class, even in rural areas, must have had a meaningful voice and opportunity to get elected. This "grass-roots democracy" was able to connect with a neighborhood solidarity that went far back in history.

From then on the demes were also in charge of keeping lists of the citizens. To be a citizen one had to belong to a phratry. The explanation for this double registering may be that verification of family identity through membership in the old subgroups was still felt as necessary, but lists were also needed for future recruiting of soldiers. In addition, double registering was probably meant to emphasize acceptance at age eighteen into the circle of those old enough to participate in politics and to bear arms. At eighteen one was no longer merely an Athenian but a citizen in the political sense of the word. We know nothing about the specific nature of this initiation, but the majority of the Athenians then experienced their citizen status primarily in the context of these small subgroups.

Membership in the deme was hereditary. Domicile played a role only when the new order was first introduced. This may seem impractical, but apparently the sense of belonging together over generations was more important. Here, too, permanent allegiances were to develop. The citizens were asked to add the name of their deme to their personal name, presumably in place of the patronymic. The use of *citoyen* as a form of address during the French Revolution is a distant parallel.

The demes were the smallest unit in the new phyle system, which was based on a complicated system of combining and separating geographical areas. Attica was divided into three regions: the city of Athens, including its immediate surroundings to the coast; the inland area; and the rest of the coast. Ten groups of geographically connected demes were set up in each of these regions. Then Cleisthenes set up his ten phylae, each of which was made up of three deme groups, one from the city, one from the coast, and one from the inland area. Legend has it that he chose the groups by lot, but this is unlikely. The resulting numbers of phyle members would have been uneven. The deme groups were called "thirds" *(trittyes)*, reflecting their proportion within the phyle. The phylae averaged about 3,500 citizens each.

To sum up: Each phyle was to be a cross section of the different regions, every region being represented in each phyle. No phyle was to represent special local interests. Each was to consist of a tenth of Attica's citizens and be a cross section of the citizenry. Coming together primarily as citizens, the members of a phyle were to grow close and to cooperate with each other in competition against other phylae as well as in the execution of their tasks, whether in warfare or in chorus competitions between phylae. All these activities were meant to contribute to the phylae's cohesion.

For this to work, closeness had to be developed among phyle members. Each phyle, or tribe, was assigned a hero as its fictive ancestor and adopted his name. This may have been a logical step in terms of tradition, but Cleisthenes also knew its importance in the present situation. Each phyle now enjoyed the protection of one of those mighty dead whose graves had been revered for centuries in Attica because people thought special powers emanated from these heroes. The new subdivisions—and perhaps these in particular, rationally and artificially conceived as they were—were to be unified by cult practices. And in case of legal proceedings, a member could now request the support of ten of his new tribe's co-members.

Because the phyle members were also to serve together in the military, Cleisthenes transferred the function of raising an army from the old to the new system. This way soldiers served together with those they knew in other contexts and before whom they did not want to lose face. The generals commanding the troops raised by the phylae eventually became the most important officials of the polis. The demes, or *trittyes*, also seem to have formed military units, though we have concrete evidence of this only in respect to the navy. Two inscriptions mark the gathering places at the harbor for *trittyes* recruits. Of course, both the *trittyes* and the phylae had chiefs, the trittyarchs and the phylarchs. The latter were apparently civil servants, as were the generals.

But above all, the phylae were to work together politically in the Council of Five Hundred established by Cleisthenes, probably in imitation of Solon's Council of Four Hundred. This is where the citizenry was to have its most important say.

Each phyle had fifty seats in the council, with the members newly appointed every year. In the fifth century no one was allowed to serve two years in succession, and two sessions were the lifetime limit. Cleisthenes' rules were probably not so strict; if they had been, there would have been a shortage of candidates and at least one in five Athenians would have been serving on the council. But it is quite likely that Cleisthenes made sure on a more modest scale that as many citizens as possible sat on the council and that the entire membership changed every year. A later provision from Erythrae in Asia Minor stipulated that a council member could serve no more than once every four years, and Cleisthenes may have had a similar rule.

He also probably mandated that the seats were to be apportioned equally to the demes. We know this was the practice a little later. Whether council members were already chosen by lot, as they were later, or elected is unknown. But there is every indication that all parts of the country and all settlement units were meant to be represented in the council. No preference was given to the city's citizens.

The council was charged with deliberating ahead of time on issues that were to be presented to the popular assembly and with drafting decree proposals. This was an important task because the assembly could not act meaningfully without the preparatory work done by the council. But the council's major purpose was to bring the will of the entire citizenry to Athens' attention. Aristotle writes that wherever the popular assembly met only rarely, the council was the most important democratic organ.

Probably Cleisthenes also introduced the way the Council of Five Hundred functioned. Each tenth of the members, those of one tribe, was to spend one-tenth of the year in Athens. For this purpose the year was artificially divided into ten periods, or "months." The entire body met less frequently. Later on, the popular assembly met at least three times during each month, though this may not have been stipulated in the beginning. With fifty councilmen, or *prytanes*, present in Athens at all times, a maximum representation of the entire country's political interests would have been achieved. We see here, too, an additional reason for the strange composition of the phylae; namely, that all parts of the country were to be represented in Athens at all times.

In any case, Cleisthenes' reform made it possible to protest promptly against abuses of power and, in general, keep a close watch on the aristocrats' conduct of politics and performance in office. The citizenry could be called on to speak up at any time (especially if Cleisthenes had already assigned the convening of and presiding over the popular assembly to council members). Before this, the major disadvantage suffered by non-aristocrats had been that they had no leadership of their own. They met for political purposes only rarely and were often reduced to a passive role, rubber-stamping decisions in which they had no say.

Now there was one councilman for every sixty citizens; even medium-sized villages sent three or four. If the members rotated every year, this added up to an extraordinary level of contact between center and periphery. We may assume that only individuals not belonging to the old aristocratic council, the Areopagus, were eligible for membership in the Council of Five Hundred and that this new council was therefore made up not of the most influential and powerful individuals but of members of the middle class. Some aristocrats must have been council members, but even they probably felt a primary allegiance to the middle class. Because the councilmen's power did not match that of the aristocracy, they needed the support of the entire class from which they came, which meant primarily the farmers, for about two-thirds of the Attic citizens still lived outside of Athens.

Both Plato and Aristotle bore eloquent testimony to the importance for the Greek communities to maintain direct contact among the citizens. It was essential for mutual trust. Especially in a society where so much depended on individuals it was important to know with whom one was dealing. People had to be able to rely on one another. Partly because the farmers had hardly known one another before and had been restricted to the small radius of their neighborhood, they had, as Aristotle put it, developed "little talent for organization and mutual support." The tyrants used to find it advantageous to isolate their subjects from one another and to sow mistrust among them, a tactic that was apparently used often in Sicily. Although this practice was probably not widespread in Attica, the mere size of the country resulted in some isolation.

The superiority of the aristocrats had arisen largely from their connections, but now these connections counted for less. While the citizens of a phyle became acquainted with other members from all parts of the country, their neighbors from other villages made similar connections with citizens belonging to other phylae. In this way all kinds of contacts were made. Elements of the old system preserved in the new may have served to maintain existing connections and helped cement mutual relations and allegiances among the citizenry.

Thus organized and with close ties among them, the Attic citizens were less dependent on the assistance of aristocrats, who continued to wield some influence but no longer had the final say. Generally the interests of non-aristocrats could be represented by members of their own class or by men willing to serve in this capacity. Still, no matter how excellent the new organization may have been and how much sense it may have made in an emergency situation, how could it have functioned in the long run?

Year after year enough candidates had to be found for the council and for the many tasks performed by the demes. This was difficult enough, especially since councilmen often lived at some distance, sometimes a whole day's journey, from the city. Many had to spend the night there (or leave home in the night) because the sessions began at dawn. But the popular assemblies must have been well attended, or the council could not have accomplished much. The assembly had to rely primarily on men living in the city or nearby. The councilmen had to be taught to regard their office not merely as an honor but as an obligation to give their own and the people's interests a political voice and to do so regularly, over and over again.

People are willing to do all kinds of things in the first and even the second flush of excitement, but what happens later? Don't they tend to relapse into their old, accustomed ways? How can we explain, then, that the majority of Attic citizens did not gradually become reabsorbed in their own lives as farmers, artisans, or merchants, that they did not devote their primary energies to their own economic interests but continued instead to devote a major part of their time and attention to civic affairs, often at the cost of great effort?

It is not surprising that people become involved in politics when important issues are at stake, major battles are being fought, important decisions are on the docket, or when scandals stir up general interest.

But when an entire citizenry is out to win for itself a significant and respected role in political life, it cannot limit its participation to issues that affect the interest of private individuals. Its members cannot simply ask themselves whether or not any of the items on today's agenda affect them personally. Otherwise their role is restricted to a continuous alternation between frequent acclamation and occasional protest (which may have been the case with Solon's Council of Four Hundred), while the specialists—that is, mostly the aristocrats—take charge or remain in charge and retain the superiority that tends to arise from connections, experience, and regular attendance.

Since this did not happen, we must assume that the broader public's interest in politics was so great that it was unaffected by whether or not an issue touched on personal interests. In this situation, which seems so paradoxical to us, the polis must have become, as Karl Marx put it, "a truly private matter," "the true content of being a citizen" (in a context in which the private realm was left up to slaves and women). This seems like an anthropological curiosity, a puzzle.

All historical anthropology must begin with the assumption that one of man's most prominent qualities is his malleability. Humans can be very different creatures depending on the epoch, the conditions, and the kind of society in which they live.

It would not be too convincing to say that the Attic citizens' strong and persistent commitment to politics was inspired by the realization that this commitment was the only way to fight abuse of power and win a respected position in the community. How much practical effect can such a realization have? Nor would it suffice to add that mechanisms of mutual help and reinforcement are at work in societies, that strong expectations placed on one another by different members can result in everyone's acting on those expectations before they are even expressed, thus causing others to do the same until this becomes the natural way of behavior. For

if difficult expectations are to be met routinely, the needs expressed in
them must be powerful. Human beings can accomplish a great deal if
they perceive a need. But usually the welfare of individuals or their families is involved. Here, however, the focus was politics. What, then, motivated the Attic citizens?

It could only have been the special nature of their interests and their
values or, ultimately, their common identity, that inspired them. What
was apparently of prime importance was the public sphere dominated by
the aristocracy, that arena in which the leading members of the community moved in a style of relative freedom, the freedom made possible by
the clear separation of public from domestic life.

The importance and status of the "semi-aristocrats," those citizens whose
talents and ambitions destined them for a higher station, depended on
how they stood in relation to the aristocrats. In most respects they
were inferior to them and only in politics could they be equals with
them. That is why political equality, the only equality available to the
semi-aristocrats, became so important to them. Here, too, they were
individually no match for the aristocrats. But if they joined together they
could make up for their lack of power; collectively they could become
even stronger than the aristocrats.

Strange as it may seem to us, the attraction of public life and the fact
that nothing contributed as much to their status and self-esteem as politics
are apparently the reasons for the remarkable political commitment
of these men. We have to remember that the Attic citizenry was not a
bourgeoisie—that is, a class that lived in a world of its own; that placed
high value on work, personal accomplishment, and great wealth; that
had evolved special, bourgeois ways of life over centuries; that counted
among its members a great many educated people and brilliant university
graduates; and that dominated entire cities. They were not a society separate from the state, whose members were therefore private individuals
first and foremost, able to concentrate their ambitions on economic and
social activities and on a highly refined private way of life. They knew
nothing of the mediations and abstractions through which modern man

relates to the whole, or of society's segmentation, or of the specialization that creates so many different areas in which to prove one's worth and acquire prestige.

Instead the citizens of Athens were merely the moderately affluent within an essentially agrarian society (and within men's organizations that excluded other parts of society). The alternative they constituted to the traditional order was quite limited. Politics was the one and only public area in which they vied, quite concretely, with the aristocrats, and they took politics so seriously and dedicated themselves to political activity so zealously precisely because politics was the only thing they had that could replace aristocratic ideals.

The doctrine that the citizens were responsible for the city legitimized them. On the other hand, the difference between high and low was so firmly established that political equality could never be conceived of as a universal right but only as a privilege. That is why participation in politics became an end in itself. To the moderately affluent their status as citizens was more important than the advantages they might have gained in their private lives through political power. They became citizens (that is, part of the polis entity) so completely that they practically never introduced their interests as farmers, artisans, or merchants into politics.

Politics could do nothing to improve the farmers' position, and the artisans and merchants were too weak to effectively seize opportunities. Restraint in pushing private interests was the better part of wisdom for this class still in need of legitimation. Then, too, if they maintained their solidarity, which they did according to both Herodotus and Aristotle, they could hold their own against the aristocrats, who continued not only to fulfill an essential function in politics but remained powerful. Solidarity also meant that no conflicts must arise between the citizens of the city and its surroundings and those living in more distant areas. Those who could attend the popular assemblies more easily must not act to the disadvantage of the others.

These are only partial explanations, however. The decisive factor probably was that these "middle citizens" saw themselves primarily as citizens and kept the political sphere distinctly separate from the private one, whereas the aristocrats habitually and without qualms used their political position to their own advantage and that of their friends. This was exactly what needed to be combated, so the middle class defined their citizenship from the point of view of the city. They had to show and emphasize what they were collectively, what it was that justified their winning and maintaining an equal rank.

The public way in which the importance of politics was displayed—because politics did not always affect the lives of individuals in hidden ways—made it easier to devote oneself to politics. So did Athens' size and importance in the Greek world, which lent greater significance to participation in politics than would have been the case in a smaller city.

But ultimately the answer must be sought in anthropology, in the special way the Greeks were connected to one another. If the Greeks had been less self-reliant, more intimately linked together in patronage and clientage relationships, the aristocrats would probably have held on to their power by defending the interests of their followers along with their own. And if they failed to do that, their followers would have resorted to occasional protest to win certain basic rights, the way the Roman plebs did.

The Greeks wanted to live more by themselves; they did not want to be caught up in relationships. They valued the aristocracy's and, later, the farmers' autarky. Under the tyrants, however, the farmers had never been obliged to deliver levies in the form of goods or services, and their private property was never in jeopardy (except if someone had fallen into debt). They despised working for others; indeed, they despised any kind of personal dependency, an attitude that both contributed to and was made possible by colonization and slavery. This attitude was also a consequence of the fact that monarchs—those powers that "relieve" the individual of so much and make him meaningless in so many respects, teaching him to conform and become one-sided—left no significant mark on the evolving society. Thus, an ideal of personality totally different from our modern one developed, along with different abilities acquired in the process of learning to control emotion. Meanwhile, the aristocracy's superiority remained minimal, being based primarily on wealth and leisure, education and connections, appearance and manner. Add to this that the sense of a fundamental unity fostered by membership in society's various subdivisions remained unchanged.

Because the vertical link between patron and client was almost unknown among the Greeks and because they felt it to be intolerable, they had to learn to identify with the entity they formed collectively; that is, with the citizenry and the various subdivisions, especially those set up by Cleisthenes, in which they figured as nothing else but citizens. They were able and forced to develop a sense of community, a horizontal solidarity. They struck a kind of balance between the striving for self-reliance and the need to seek status through competition and participation in public life. One could not exist without the other. Any greater concentration on power would have brought with it greater obligations, hierarchy, permanent representation, a minority of specialized politicians. Democracy, however, required not just independence but also self-identification with the political entity.

Societies are what they are partly as a result of their particular ways of structuring membership and especially as a result of their collective identity. But the concept of a common identity is not restricted to the relationship with the past; it also refers, at least when we are talking about collective identity, to that among the citizens.

In Athens conformity played a strong role. It was relatively easy to be and do what was expected of a man. Pittacus, one of the Seven Wise Men, said, "It is difficult to be good," but that is not what is meant here. Instead, we are talking about what distinguishes the Greeks from others. A Greek was as a rule a landowner. He had to take care of his land, serve as a hoplite, make political judgments, be able to speak before a small group, have social skills and be skilled in sports, and have enough background in the arts to be able to participate in choral singing and dances. To be sure, different people excelled at different things, but on the whole everyone shared the same ideal and could at least come close to matching it.

Given this situation it seems only natural that people strove for and admired what was common to all, instead of the special, the unusual, the individual. That is probably why Greek statues so often tried to approximate the general and typical or, in Greek terms, to depict the citizen.

Since the first democracies in world history could arise only as direct democracies, they had to have nonspecialized citizens. To put it differently, the Greeks could become *citoyens* only because they were not bourgeois.

The collective identity of the Athenians would now be an identity based on being citizens. Neither shared economic interests nor confessional similarities, neither parties nor philosophies could create any significant sense of mutual allegiance. Nor did the Greeks need a collective nationality capable of subsuming their many individual differences. The only allegiances they recognized beyond the bonds of home, relatives, and neighbors were those to the polis and its subgroups. With minor exceptions, even the cult associations represented either sectors of the citizenry or its entirety. That is how this "most vehement form of citizenry where one is nothing but citizen," as Jacob Burckhardt put it, could come into being. It exerted such pressure to participate that, according to Democritus's later account, prominent citizens who chose to evade this pressure could become physically sick.

Burckhardt speaks of "the utter egotism of today's private person who wants to exist purely as an individual, asking of the collective whole as much protection of his person and his property as possible." Indeed, "in our present manner of relating between individual and state" there is not the slightest trace of the passion with which the "perfected individual of antiquity" wanted to be a citizen above all else. Where we today introduce our economic and other interests into politics, the citizens of Cleisthenes' era politicized their own persons.

Their devotion to politics explains why the moderately affluent were willing, if not to neglect their domestic affairs, their farms, workshops, and families, to devote less energy and attention to them. Presumably they left more up to their wives and slaves. They had no choice; politics had become for them an existential matter. Of course, some men worked hard to make money, and everybody would have enjoyed wealth. But ultimately politics was more important than acquiring material goods and luxuries. The price one would have had to pay to get them—largely absenting oneself from the common experience of the present—was high, and for many, too high.

Xenophanes of Colophon, one of the Greek wise men, complained that the cities showered the winners of athletic contests with honors but ignored the wise men. The runners and pentathlon winners contributed nothing to the city coffers, nor did they help to improve public life. He proceeded to point out in bitter words how far superior laboring in the service of the city was to the popular ideals—clearly the view of an intellectual.

If large numbers of Athenians were willing to serve the city, they were motivated not so much by a sense of obligation as by a desire to improve their own standing and to play a personal role in politics. But obligation and ambition worked toward the same end: commitment to politics. These men basically thought no differently from Solon, who also adopted the aristocratic ethic of competition, aiming to surpass all the others, though substituting new standards.

Thus, working for the communal good was in men's own interest. What they did for the polis, they did for themselves. The personal interests of the individual were inextricably linked with the communal interest of all, just as the differences among them were insignificant compared to their equality.

To fall back once more on one of Jacob Burckhardt's formulations: Life for the citizens of Athens was existence, not business. This attitude led to a clear distinction between what really mattered and what was secondary; existence resided primarily in the realm of the polis. This "citizen identity" was felt most among the middle class, though it must in some way have extended to the lower classes and to the aristocracy as well, but most aristocrats refused for some time to accept this identity.

So this anthropological curiosity begins to appear less puzzling. The strengths of the aristocratic epoch are expressed in it. They are apparent in the conditions of the small poleis with all the complicated stabilizing mechanisms of their world, their customs and their style, the all-male groups, the separation of domestic and public life, including also the particular combination of freedom and necessity, mirth and sadness in those two spheres.

We can see why the first step in Cleisthenes' radical reforms was not to give power to the popular assembly but to fundamentally reorganize society, for his primary concern was to establish a new and lasting relationship among the citizens. It also becomes clear why such an intense communal life developed. This life must have had its militant aspects, and this helps explain the Athenians' decision to fight the Persians—and their victories.

Difficult as we may find it to grasp the special nature of this citizenry that gave rise to democracy, what these people went on to do, experience, and suffer, and what they made of it all are eminently comprehensible to us. Precisely because they were so free, yet so little defined, so democratic and therefore faced with the most difficult problems, they were able in questions and answers, art and philosophy, politics, war, and the writing of history to convey in an exemplary way so much of what they lived through.

For the first time a political order had been created that was not identical with the social order; the social hierarchy that remained was no longer carried over directly into the political sphere. One factor that contributed to this was the prevalent, though artificial, separation of the domestic and public realms; another was the solidarity of the middle class. These were like two sides of the same coin, for the solidarity of equals was possible only because public life was kept so separate from domestic life (and was originally not very political). Once economic consolidation had been achieved, the problem of establishing order focused on politics.

The word introduced at that time or a little later to describe the new order was isonomy—that is, an order based on equality. It harks back to eunomy, or "right order," but replaces "right" with "equality" *(isotes)*. Equality meant equality of the citizens, and not just equality before the law—that had presumably always existed and was assured at least since Solon's time. Nor was equality as much of a problem as it later became in the modern era, when different estates were granted privileges in the name of freedom. Freedom played no special role in Greece because there was no state power to be checked (juristic means to do so were nonexistent in any case), and all that was involved was winning for the bulk of the citizenry a voice equal to that of the aristocrats.

There was no state that could be represented by a ruler. The tyrants and aristocrats merely exercised power. The polis, on the other hand, existed as a concrete entity only through its citizens. It needed not representation but an identity, which it had up to now found only under the exceptional conditions of war.

The concept of isonomy continued to have positive associations among the Greeks. It was as though the memory of the years in which it arose stayed alive. If the concept was later used to describe democracy, it then also implied democracy's ideal, the standard against which political orders have to be measured.

A connection was made between equality and law that could in the future no longer be easily ignored. What probably played a role here was that equality in the original isonomy was an equality of those who had always been considered the real citizens, the middle class, the hoplites, those who had enough to live on and could not easily be suspected, as poorer people might, of wanting to take things from others.

But the word *isonomy* also implied, unmistakably, the idea of some kind of balance. This idea probably derived from the fact that at the time the collective power of the broad-based citizenry was nearly equal to that of the aristocracy. There had been a long struggle to improve the people's position vis-à-vis the aristocracy. Now this seemed to have been accomplished. Perhaps the new order is best understood in terms of this balance, since the idea of rule by one group, let alone by the people, was still unthinkable. No one could yet imagine so far beyond existing conditions. And it was not yet possible to redefine the idea of rule enough for it to mean more than rule by a monarch or by officeholders.

Alcmaeon of Croton, one of the pre-Socratic philosophers, applied the idea of equilibrium inherent in isonomy to medicine. A balance of dry and humid, cold and warm, bitter and sweet kept the body healthy, he maintained, while imbalance in any one of these pairs caused illness.

. . .

The institutional structure of Athens was modified as a result of Cleisthenes' reforms, but there is no indication that he changed any of the offices' competencies.

The city continued to be administered by nine archons. The first archon, after whom the year during which he held office was named, was in charge of the community. He organized the city's more recently introduced festivals, such as the Panathenaea and the Great Dionysia, and was responsible for questions of family and inheritance law; that is, for the community's familial infrastructure, which had only recently assumed importance. The second archon, who inherited the king's title of basileus, attended to the old traditional festivals and the city's sacred precincts, such as the Acropolis, as the chief religious officer. He presided over the aristocratic council, which met on the Areopagus. Next came the polemarch, who was in charge of military matters, including the recruiting of armies, and who handled legal matters involving foreigners. The six remaining archons, the *thesmotetai*, were responsible specifically for the administration of justice. To become an archon it was necessary to belong to one of the top two census classes, and only members of the highest class were eligible for offices involving finances, such as the treasurership of the goddess.

A new office introduced in the wake of Cleisthenes' reforms was the board of ten elected *strategoi*, or generals, who led the phyle regiments. They probably had to meet the same census criteria as the archons. We also know that they had to be of legitimate birth and own landed property within Attica. These conditions may have applied to other offices as well.

In addition to these officials, and potentially higher in rank, was the council of the aristocrats that met on the Areopagus. It had about three hundred members, made up of former archons—that is, of the most influential aristocrats. The officials were accountable to the council and probably consulted it in important matters. If not paralyzed by internal conflict, the council could exert considerable influence on Attic politics.

Thus, the aristocracy clearly held the leading role in politics, no matter what the relationship between officials and the Areopagus happened to be. And strangely enough a barrier hard to overcome between aristocrats and non-aristocrats remained in existence for a long time, even under democracy and even long after the middle classes had won the right for their members to become archons. For generations to come the top politicians—those behind the most important initiatives, those whose voices counted the most, those who led the armies and were sent on diplomatic missions—continued to be men from the old noble families.

Apparently the advantages enjoyed by the members of this class, thanks to their education, status, appearance, their entire style, as well as to their connections, were such great advantages that they were hard to compete with. Others might acquire wealth, but neither they nor their children could quickly catch up with the aristocrats.

On the other hand, the bluntness and resoluteness of energetic agitators and rebels was no longer appropriate. In earlier days such men had been able to usurp rule and become tyrants; injustice had been so prevalent that they found followers. But by now, at least the leading members of the middle classes, sharing in public honors, knew their own worth. In spite of being potential opponents of the aristocrats, they themselves developed a sense of style. But it was only later, when aristocratic traditions began to fade, when new, efficient educational methods came into use and there was a need for energetic men, that this new elite could rise to the level of the aristocrats.

All this does not imply that members of the middle classes were unable to speak up, unable to understand, and judge what was happening or should happen in politics, nor that they were unclear about their goals. They were at a disadvantage only in stepping onto the public stage individually, and this disadvantage was probably felt less in the Council of Five Hundred—and not at all in the demes—than in the popular assembly. Perhaps we should qualify our case. Middle-class members may well have acted forcefully even at that time, but they did not penetrate into the front ranks, the only ones visible to us. We know the names of only the most prominent politicians in each generation. Overall the political influence of the middle classes derived clearly from collective power; they were heard because they were in the majority.

It was still unclear what role the popular assembly and the Council of Five Hundred should henceforth play in Athens' political order. The authority of the popular assembly obviously had to be strengthened. The council discussed all the business and formulated the proposals that came before the assembly, whose decisions could therefore no longer be as easily manipulated as before. The assembly could now discuss various subjects about which it had formerly not been consulted. But we don't know to what extent this was the case, nor who presided over the assembly.

In addition to making decisions about war and peace and about alliances, the assembly was responsible for legislation. In contested cases, it was the legislative body that had the final say. But how much actual importance it had depended on how much it was consulted. How often were bills presented for its action? How often were the assemblymen asked to deal with foreign delegations? Such things occurred occasionally, but it is not clear if they were the exception or the rule.

It may be that the aristocratic magistrates continued to decide much on their own, perhaps after consultation with the Areopagus. The Council of Five Hundred and, occasionally, the popular assembly may have demanded a voice in some matters. Perhaps the aristocrats tried, citing the authority of the Areopagus, to influence the people. Or politicians who failed to prevail in the Areopagus may have sought to get the assembly to pass regulations they favored. After all, the assembly was now the highest decision-making body.

One thing seems clear. The relationship among the political bodies cannot have been a smooth one after Cleisthenes. And it must have undergone various changes over time. At times the Council of Five Hundred may have served as effective opposition, a counterweight, against officials and the Areopagus. In any case, pushing something through against the council's expressed will was not easy. But possibly there was not that much dissension between it and the majority of aristocrats because traditional ways were still taken for granted, because the councilmen felt inferior to the aristocrats, and because for many of them the right to have a say in decisions was what mattered the most. Perhaps just being respected satisfied them. Plato says that at that time mutual respect and friendship were still the rule among the Athenians.

It may have taken the aristocrats some time to learn how to deal with the new possibilities. Many of the old leading elite may at first have watched from the sidelines. A few of the most determined opponents of the reform had been executed after Cleisthenes' departure because they had attempted to start an oligarchy. Their houses were destroyed, their property confiscated. But most must have done what members of the leading elite who are still needed generally do after a revolution: They adapted to the new situation. After all, there was much to be done.

Everything depended on how much political weight of their own the popular assembly and the council could acquire. Of course, they could no longer be easily ignored. Politicians had to learn to sway them by rhetorical means. The number of followers the powerful aristocrats had had at their command was bound to shrink, in absolute as well as in relative terms. It seems likely that some of the politicians relied more heavily on the popular assembly, as Cleisthenes had done and Themistocles would do later.

But if this was the case, could the popular assembly be anything more than the tool of aristocratic politicians? Could it see to it that its interests would prevail? Could it restrain the usual ambitious ways of the aristocrats?

Maintaining the balance of isonomy was not easy. From now on different and potentially conflicting forces, much more powerful than rivaling aristocratic camps, determined the life of the polis. This new polis experience was, by the way, reflected in a new style of depicting man in sculpture, exemplified just a few years later in Critius's statue of a boy.

During the years after Cleisthenes, Attica must in some ways have resembled a huge construction project. Realization of the reforms had to be initiated on all levels at once. The division of the country into demes cannot always have been easy. Their grouping into *trittyes*, and the *trittyes* into phylae, must have involved complicated calculations.

Perhaps Cleisthenes himself supervised the work, aided by a few prominent Athenians. Advisers from other cities may have assisted. In any case, helpers were needed from all over the country; powerful individuals had to be won over or pushed aside in various places; and all kinds of local peculiarities, desires, and differences had to be taken into account.

The demes had to draw up their first lists, elect their first officials, organize their administration. Communal property had to be identified, and festivals had to be reorganized. Representatives for the *trittyes* and the phylae had to be appointed. The citizens had to interact in new roles and—probably in many places—stand up to the influence of aristocrats.

Apparently there were disputes over who was a rightful citizen. Cleisthenes seems to have extended citizenship to a number of inhabitants, probably men who had at some previous point been considered citizens on the basis either of a Solonic law or of a tyrant's decree but whose status was (or had become) contested.

We don't know when the reorganization was completed. It is unlikely that the Athenian army was already organized into the new tribal or phyle regiments when it marched against the Boeotians and the men of Chalcis in 506, although Herodotus claims it was filled with the new spirit of citizenship. And it is doubtful whether the Council of Five Hundred was already functioning normally when Athens first decided to send envoys to the satrap of Sardis. But we can probably assume, given the Attic citizenry's high degree of mobility, that the popular assembly was well attended at that time.

Perhaps as early as the year 500 a new place, the Pnyx, was set up for it above the agora. A semicircular area there slanted slightly uphill. A retaining wall was built on the agora side, the space behind it filled in, and a speaker's platform erected. The council may have been accommodated in an existing building, and another one may have been used for feeding the *prytanes*. We don't know whether arrangements were made for them to spend the night.

We don't know either how much longer Cleisthenes, who was about sixty at the time of his reforms, lived and how much control he and his associates exercised in the following years.

But it is clear that the new order was further elaborated. The introduction of the oath that incoming councilors had to swear dates from the year 503–502. Its purpose must have been to ensure the stability of the new order. In 501–500 the first *strategoi* were elected. With these two events, the reform of the phylae and the council was completed.

In 501–500 Cleisthenes is also said to have instituted ostracism, that important device by which powerful politicians could be removed from the city for a while. Strangely, though, it was not invoked until 487. It seems unlikely that the Athenians would have created such a tool only to let it go unused. But there are many plausible reasons why it was not resorted to earlier.

According to recent dating, the miles of ceramic pipes that conducted water from springs on the mountains of Hymettus and/or Pentelicus to Athens were also built at this time. East of the Acropolis the pipes branched off to deliver water to the various fountains.

It must have taken the citizens some time to adjust to the new conditions. A whole new balance had to be struck between what was desired and what was achievable, and the mood must have fluctuated widely between hope and fear. The eagerness with which the citizens just launched into politics and took to their new role cannot always have been beneficial to business, and aristocratic politicians may have tried to turn the clock back or at least curtail the effects of the reorganization.

Foreign affairs and war deflected attention from the home scene. After defeating Chalcis, the Athenians seized the best land there from the Chalcidian aristocrats and distributed it among 4,000 Attic citizens. They demanded high ransom for the return of the prisoners of war and displayed their chains on the Acropolis wall. They used a tenth of the ransom money to donate a quadriga made of bronze to Athena. This statue was set up just inside the entry to the Acropolis.

In 506 or shortly thereafter, the Aeginetans launched a series of privateering raids, and Athens may well have reorganized the defense of its coasts or delegated this task to the demes.

The new order had an impact in many areas. The Great Dionysia festival was reorganized, at least to the extent of introducing the *choregia*:

After the archon, along with his advisers, evaluated the tragedies entered for competition, he assigned a chorus to each of the three poets whose plays had been chosen for performance, and a wealthy man, the *choregos*, was charged with financing the production, including rehearsals and costumes. Originally, individuals must have volunteered this funding, since the elite were expected to fulfill this and other pecuniary services (liturgies) to the community—with some justification, for at that time nobody in Athens paid direct taxes. Sponsoring such an event could enhance one's status, and the wealthy began to compete among themselves to fund competitions. One result of this may have been to increase the number of tragedies to be performed. A new method of financing the theater was needed because the actors were no longer paid by the tyrants as they had been previously.

The deeds of Theseus. In the center of the circle he is shown with the Minotaur, and in the surrounding band we see him in his encounters with Sinis, the bull; Sciron, the pig; Cercyon; and Procrustes. Red-figured, ca. 480 B.C. London, British Museum.

185

Soon after the overthrow of the tyrants, the recital of dithyrambs was incorporated into the Great Dionysia. These hymns in honor of Dionysus were sung by competing male choruses. In one part rather than several, they were performed with instrumental accompaniment and probably with dance movements as well. Initially, the four old tribes supplied the choruses; now ten choruses competed. We cannot tell whether they were already made up of fifty members each, nor when the distinction between boys' and men's choruses was introduced. The middle classes were eager to reach the same perfection as the aristocrats in a field as highly esteemed as music, and this may have been the underlying reason for the innovation. Probably the choruses were also meant to strengthen the cohesion of the tribes, as tribe competed against tribe to serve the city in performing "Dionysus's beautiful song."

We might ask if the Athenians really had nothing else to worry about. But this misses the point. Concern over the city's new order was to a considerable extent also a concern over the festivals. They were an important manifestation of the citizenry. How could they—after such an upheaval—be left unchanged or given over to improvisation? Then, too, the more the city demanded of its citizens, the more it needed the festivals, because the two went hand in hand. Perhaps other festivals were restructured or expanded as well, such as the Panathenaea, the festival in honor of the city's patron goddess.

As the identity of the new citizens took hold, a need arose to stress the new community's roots in the past. So it is no coincidence that depictions of the legendary King Theseus began to appear rather suddenly, at first on vases and, somewhat later, on the pediment of the Athenian treasury building in Delphi. Theseus, as he was now represented, was a strong man like Heracles and like him had earned his fame by defeating monsters. He had also been responsible for turning Attica into a unified political force, just as Cleisthenes had recently done in a kind of second founding of the city. The more strongly the Athenians experienced their unity, the more deeply it had to be anchored in the past.

Probably the decision to put a stop to the aristocrats' lavish burial practices also goes back to around the year 500. Greek funerary art came to an abrupt end just as it reached its high point; there are no more *kouroi* from this date forward. With the ending of one of the most prominent manifestations of aristocratic superiority, one further step toward equality had been made.

Soon after the expulsion of the tyrants a decree was passed to outlaw Pisistratus's sons and grandsons and to confiscate their property. This decree was displayed on the Acropolis. To prevent any possible resurgence of tyranny the councilmen had to swear to kill anyone who strove to become a tyrant or supported such ambitions. The property of any usurper was to be seized and half of it awarded to the guilty man's killer.

"Truly a great light shone in Athens when Aristogiton and Harmodius slew Hippias," Simonides of Ceos, the great lyric poet of the fifth century, wrote. The tyrant slayers apparently inspired much greater enthusiasm than Cleisthenes did.

Immediately after their liberation the Athenians set up a statue of Harmodius and Aristogiton in the agora. Made by Antenor, one of the foremost sculptors of the time, it depicted the two standing calmly next to each other. It was the first monument commemorating meritorious individuals designed to be set up in public. In the archaic period, statues served only as cult images, religious offerings, and burial figures. Here sculpture was removed from the religious context, the political having emerged as the new area of importance. Yet the statue of the tyrannicides retained some of that old religious aura. Its placement in the agora made them something like the founding heroes of Athenian freedom. When Xerxes seized Athens he ordered the statue moved to Susa. Immediately after their return to the city, the Athenians commissioned a new statue.

At symposia they sang of the two heroes' deed, praising them for having made Athens "isonomous" and portraying the assassins as liberators. The Athenians wanted to owe their new order to their own people.

But freedom, even if it had been achieved through Hippias's murder, would have meant nothing without the political structure Cleisthenes introduced in Athens. It was thanks to Cleisthenes alone that the Athenians had reason to celebrate Harmodius and Aristogiton.

We can only guess why they remembered him less. Because he did not die a martyr? Because he used Sparta's assistance to free the city? Because he was merely a politician who presented motions rather than a celebrated wise man like Solon? No statue had been erected in Solon's honor, either, but then that was not the custom at the time. (The omission was later remedied.) Still, Solon had carried out his entire reform with the help of extraordinary powers granted to him. Cleisthenes' reform was the first presented to the popular assembly for discussion and approval.

Also, some aspects of Cleisthenes' work were controversial. Historians now think that some of his subdivisions of Attica served his own and his family's interests. There are some indications to this effect, and we should not assume that Cleisthenes acted altogether selflessly. What he initiated was clearly intended to increase his power. But the means he employed brought about a restructuring of the Athenian citizenry.

His elevating the middle segments of the citizenry to political power amounted to a refounding of Athens. We might use Max Weber's term "fraternization" to describe Cleisthenes' reform, and once it was accomplished, the political part of Athens' cultural development was essentially completed.

5

The Persian Threat

We may consider it a favor of fate that names like Marathon and Salamis will live on forever in the memory of man. . . .

Fame is determined by the nature of an event, not by its moral, subjective aspect but by its objective value. Here the interest of the world spirit was at stake; all other interests, those connected with any fatherland whatsoever, were secondary.

—G. W. F. HEGEL

Athens' achievements during the second half of the sixth century were, in different ways, like those of other cities, the result of a long process that ultimately acquired a momentum of its own. From a certain point on, because of the aristocracy's weakness, the Greeks could not help but develop their political thought further and further. The demands arose for significant participation of the middle classes in politics. The process of change was practically autonomous and the forces that drove it came not from above but from those who were integrally involved in it. Eventually, a kind of intra-Greek dynamic moved other cities to form isonomies of their own. But the rise of democracy fifty years after Cleisthenes in Athens—and at first it existed only in Athens—resulted primarily from events that were in part accidental; that is, from the Greeks' encounter with the great Eastern empire.

We can detect a rhythm in the sequence of events: A phase in which the Greeks were greatly inspired and enriched by Eastern cultures was followed by one in which East and West lived alongside each other more or less separately, even after the Lydian then the Persian monarchies took possession of the Greek cities in Asia. The next period, from about 500 B.C. on, was characterized by the political and military conflicts that the Greeks called the Persian Wars. These conflicts began at the exact moment that the Greeks became ready to meet the challenge and were triggered not by the Persians but by developments taking place in the West, in Greece and especially in Athens. The refounding of the polis politicized the entire Greek world.

Sparta reacted to Cleisthenes' reforms by attempting to gain control over Athens before Athens became too powerful, and this move on Sparta's part is what motivated Athens' first mission to the Persian satrap. In other words, as soon as a competition for power arose within Greece, the Persians were drawn into Greek affairs. At the same time, the Attic example—the reforms, the politicization of the general population, and the resulting increase in Athens' power—had an impact on the Ionian Greeks, one far greater than had the founding of the earlier isonomies. As a consequence, an interchange took place across the Aegean for the first time. East and West began to collide.

Previously, the cities on the Greek mainland had maintained only loose contact. Private connections proliferated, but close political connections—and political conflicts—were rare. Now a new era of power politics was taking shape, with Athens emerging as a rival to Sparta. Sparta's alliance with various other Peloponnesian cities perhaps first developed during this period. Corinth seems to have used the opportunity to increase its influence and authority in the Peloponnesian

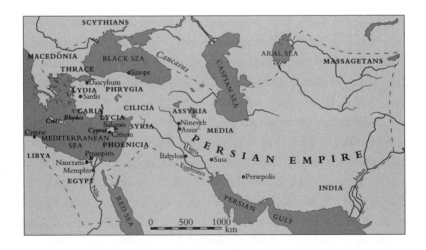

The Persian Empire

League. The balance of power was shifting as the newly fledged public interest in politics accrued importance and the citizens became involved in larger events.

In the year 500, the Persians attempted for the first time to take over an island that lay closer to the Greek peninsula than to the Asian coast. Why they waited as long as they did is uncertain—they could have made this conquest decades earlier. But Persian policy originated in Susa or Babylon, and the Aegean Sea was on the periphery of its interests; it figured merely as a natural border to Persia, which was a land power. The patchwork Greek landscape probably did not seem very inviting. But the great kings claimed dominion over the world, and not just rhetorically. Their empire was still vigorous. A few years earlier one of Persia's generals had conquered Byzantium, as well as the islands Lemnos and Imbros at the entry to the Hellespont.

The Greek city-states were organized around the seacoast, and for them the west and the east coasts of the Aegean Sea belonged together. The Persians were centered inland, but their claim on Asia Minor extended to the Aegean coast and the islands in front of it. The two realms inevitably overlapped. A real collision of interests arose only when the Greeks became restless and the citizenry of the largest polis became mobilized. This seems to have been the underlying reason for Persia's widening plans: Greece had suddenly become interesting.

We have no way of knowing whether the Athenians realized, when they sent out their first envoys, that Persian support could be obtained only if they recognized Persian overlordship—that is, offering earth and water as custom demanded. But it cannot have been merely because of Athens' inadequate awareness, its carelessness in the formulation of the mission, or its alarm at previously uncontemplated consequences that the assembly subsequently rejected the submission that their envoys had promised. The real reason may have been that the assembly believed the envoys themselves had a self-interest in fostering a connection with Persia, for as a rule individuals who already had relationships with foreign powers were chosen as envoys.

In any case, it must have soon become obvious that immediate danger of tyranny came less from within, from Sparta, than from the Persians. The Greeks were aware that the Persian satrap, who lived a day's journey from Ephesus in Sardis, might offer the former tyrant Hippias the support he would need to reassume power in Attica. The satrap, Artaphernes, stepbrother of Darius, was a highly ambitious man who might well have wanted to extend his power to the Greek mainland. Hippias would have served as a useful tool in such an attempt.

In the year 500 a fleet that was to conquer the island of Naxos for the Persian king assembled at Miletus. Naxos was known for its wealth in gold and slaves; it dominated the nearby islands, among them Andros, off the coast of Euboea, and Paros. If the Persians succeeded in their plan, they would have a foothold quite close to the Attic coast. There were already rumors that they wanted to conquer Euboea as well.

And so, the two sides of the Aegean were becoming entangled and seemed to be headed for an inevitable collision. Athens had great reason to worry.

The Persian venture failed. Naxos was warned; its inhabitants gathered in the city, where they were well provisioned. They reinforced the city walls and withstood the siege for four months, until the Persians decided the cost was too great and gave up.

But the ignominious end of that expedition was merely a prelude to the next conflict. The Persians had not mobilized without a reason. And the Greeks who had been drawn into the conflict either would not or could not pay the money they had promised to contribute. A series of events was set in motion that would culminate in the revolt of the Ionian Greeks.

The attack on Naxos had been instigated not by Persia but by Aristagoras, son of Molpagoras, tyrant of wealthy Miletus, the most prominent city on the west coast of Asia Minor. Naxos, inspired by events in Athens, had introduced equality. Some members of the aristocracy previously in power had been exiled and had fled to Miletus. Now they wanted to effect their return by military force.

Aristagoras hoped to advance his own power by helping them, but Naxos was well fortified, especially near the sea. Miletus was poorly prepared for warfare and probably could not have undertaken such an expedition without Persian support. Aristagoras therefore conceived a plan to enlarge the scope of the venture, and include the Persians. Presenting the plan to Artaphernes, the satrap of Sardis, Aristagoras played up the possible gains and promised to share in the campaign's cost. With the consent of the great king, two hundred ships and a sizable infantry force were sent out.

When the attempt failed, Aristagoras had reason to fear not only that he would have to pay his share of the cost but also that he would be removed from power. Given the situation, his only option was flight, but instead of fleeing he tried to avoid the consequences of his actions by openly rebelling against the Persians. Surprisingly, he found allies in Miletus as well as in other cities.

What Aristagoras and his allies hoped to achieve was sheer fantasy. If we believe Herodotus, and there is no reason not to, all they thought about were the gains to be made, including the possibility of rule over all of Asia. Their assessment of the Persians took into account only that the Persian weapons and way of fighting seemed to them inferior to their own. "The barbarians are poor soldiers," Aristagoras declared. "They fight with bows and short lances and enter battle dressed in pants and with turbans on their heads." Aristagoras failed to take note of the Persians' huge superiority in numbers. The rebels may also have misread the occasional expressions of dissatisfaction with Persian rule as a sign that many were ready to revolt.

Hecataeus of Miletus, a venerable scholar, geographer, ethnographer, and historian, participated in at least one discussion of the plans. He tried to impress on the others the number of countries and the great military might of the Persians. He may have made a map to illustrate his points. Aristagoras, when he set out a little later to enlist allies, had with him a bronze tablet on which a map of "the entire earth, including the seas and the rivers, was engraved."

But much as Hecataeus's map and his account of Persian resources may have impressed the Ionians—perhaps because they were so delighted at the magnitude of their potential gains—they were not swayed by the scholar's advice. He suggested to them another plan, which he thought had better chances of success: They should build ships and make themselves masters of the seas. To this end he advised them to seize the treasury of Apollo's temple at Didymus, which would be lost anyway to the Persians. Then they would at least be able to establish themselves in their own cities, from which they could secure supplies by water and launch raids on other coasts. They would be able to hold out for some time in this fashion, until other regions of the empire, in Asia Minor, Egypt, and Cyprus, decided to join their movement. Perhaps, he suggested, even Babylon might be persuaded to join. After all, the Persian empire was not so solidly built that some forceful tugging at parts of its structure couldn't shake it.

These suggestions reveal an amazing ability to consider the whole situation, to think in large dimensions, and above all to weigh the maritime possibilities. Hecataeus sketched a war plan that was based on acknowledgment of his side's military inferiority, which was considerable by traditional standards. Planning of this kind must also have figured in the early stages of Themistocles' strategic thinking.

But the Ionians saw no sense in Hecataeus's plan. Thinking along traditional lines, they wanted to make use of the military capacities they already had. They may have felt there was no time to build a navy, a task that even under the best of circumstances could not be accomplished overnight. But Aristagoras was in a hurry. The decision was left up to him, and by going along with him, the Ionians would have mighty Miletus on their side.

So the Ionians acted quickly. Their first task was to overthrow the tyrants in several cities. Persian rule was administered by the tyrants, who collected the money needed to pay the Persian tributes. The tyrants' rule was felt to be oppressive, since the Persians themselves were hardly ever seen in the Greek cities, and when they did appear were regarded as generous and tolerant. Aristagoras himself renounced his tyranny over Miletus with the intention of setting up isonomies in place of the deposed tyrannies.

The Greek fleet that had set out for Naxos was still assembled. By removing the commanders, the rebels could easily take over the ships and move on to the cities. We don't know how the Persians reacted, but they must have been aware of what was happening. Perhaps they decided to wait things out, or perhaps the size of the empire slowed their reaction time. Aristagoras meanwhile traveled to the Greek mainland to seek allies.

In Sparta he tried to win over King Cleomenes, by telling him that the Spartans would rule over Asia and describing all the treasures that could be won. When the king asked how far Susa, the Persian capital, was from the Aegean, Aristagoras answered truthfully that it was a three-month journey, whereupon Cleomenes ordered him to leave Sparta by sunset. Enterprising as he was, Cleomenes could only be horrified at such a scheme.

The Ionians met with better luck in Athens. Apparently, as Herodotus observed, it is easier to fool a crowd than one man. The matter was discussed at the popular assembly. Aristagoras used all his rhetorical powers, and the Athenians agreed to let him have twenty ships. The city of Eretria sent five ships because of a mutual defense agreement with Athens concluded over a hundred years earlier.

According to Herodotus, it was this decision of the Athenians, not the Ionian revolt against Persia, that caused the beginning of so much trouble for both Greeks and barbarians. Had the Athenians stayed out of the conflict, the Ionian revolt would have been no different from the many other uprisings that periodically occurred in the Persian empire and were always crushed. It would have been an incident without consequences for anyone beyond those immediately involved. Instead, because of the involvement of the Athenians, it turned out to be the beginning of the Persian Wars.

There is much truth in Herodotus's view, and he correctly criticizes the ill-considered way the Athenians made their decision. Yet it should be noted that conflicts would have erupted sooner or later between the mainland Greeks and the Persians, as hostilities had been brewing for some time.

As is often the case, the immediate causes of the Ionian revolt were trivial, involving personal ambition, petty grievances, and localized fear. But there was also a desire among the broader population to participate in politics, as did the citizens of Athens and Naxos. The political thinking that had developed elsewhere must have affected the mood in the Ionian cities. People wanted to get rid of the tyrants.

Some contemporary historians mention possible economic causes for the revolt. Archeologists have found no artifacts dating after about 525 B.C. in the Greek trading center of Naucratis in Egypt. This may indicate Persian interference with commerce among the Ionian cities concentrated in Egypt. Even if true, it is unlikely that the effects of such interference were still being felt a generation later.

On the whole, discontent arose more from the Greeks' rising ambitions than from a tightening of Persian rule, which had been in effect for almost five decades and followed upon decades of Lydian domination. The Greeks' discontent may have merged with their new political spirit, but the direction in which they would develop and the horizons that would constrain them were as yet undefined.

It is therefore useless to spend time searching out the rationale that made the outcome of the rebellion seem promising. Apparently emotional appeal outweighed objective analysis, and hope made up for the unlikelihood of success. As Thucydides says, men with strong desires cling dearly to foolish hopes.

Aristagoras and his friends must have supported one another. They found themselves in action before they knew what was happening. "When men wage war," Thucydides would later write, "they usually do first what should wait until later, and it is only when things turn out badly that they take refuge in rationality." Such was the case here. The ambitions of Aristagoras and his friends diminished as they began to plan and act concretely. It became clear that the immense Persian empire was an unknown quantity to the Greeks, one which they over- and underestimated by turns, and which their political thinking was not yet prepared to understand.

Hecataeus's failure to sway the Greeks with his superior knowledge is just one of many examples world history offers in which wrong decisions were reached not for lack of information but for failure to act on available information—that is, for lack of judgment. The question "What were people thinking when they did such-and-such?" is often a misguided one. World history would be considerably less eventful if the actors always calculated carefully.

The Athenians appear to have had little sense of whom they were dealing with in the Persians. They wanted to weaken or perhaps depose the satrap, though they may also have been motivated by their feelings of friendship for the Ionians, whose cities they regarded as Attic colonies. Their decision to contribute twenty ships to the rebels turned out to be one step in a long learning process. It would be interesting to know what the arguments presented at the Areopagus were. In the popular assembly much may have depended on the public mood.

Athens' stake was minuscule compared to the magnitude of the venture. A few years later, the Ionian cities would muster no fewer than 353 triremes for the decisive naval battle. It is not clear if the twenty Athenian vessels were triremes or warships of a more primitive type. Still, they cost money and were probably drawn from the coast guard fleet, exposing Athens to increased risk.

If a rebellion is to succeed, it must catch fire and attract others to its causes, for those who initiate it are usually too weak to achieve success alone. Once the initial step of rising up has been taken, the rebels seek, consciously or unconsciously, to undertake some spectacular action to drum up further support. That is probably why the Ionian Greeks decided to sail to Ephesus and march from there to Sardis, the seat of the Persian satrap. The Athenians and the Eretrians joined them. Residents of Ephesus are said to have shown the troops the way. Since the road to Sardis was well known, this can only mean that the Ephesians acted as scouts to give warning of surprise attacks.

Surprisingly, the Greeks were not met by the Persian army. It probably took them three days to reach their goal, and they were able to take Sardis. The satrap retreated to the fortified citadel with a contingent of men. Though their number was considerable, they avoided open battle. At this point, fire broke out in the city. Since many of the houses were constructed of reeds, wind quickly spread the fire to outlying quarters. The best refuge was the market, located near the river Pactol, and it was there that the population, both Persians and Lydians, gathered together in defense of their city. The conquerors departed in a hurry, however, and because there was nobody willing or able to stop them they quickly retreated to Ephesus. In all likelihood, they thought they had accomplished their goal.

Soon the Persians also assembled an army, made up primarily of cavalry, with which they overtook the retreating Greeks. In any case, a battle took place near Ephesus, which the rebel forces lost, suffering heavy casualties. They had underestimated the Persians.

According to Herodotus, the burning of Sardis began more or less accidentally when a soldier set a house on fire. The Greek command supposedly had no intention of torching the city. Indeed, as Herodotus says, its destruction by fire prevented the Greeks from looting it. In any case, Sardis in flames was like a beacon; the daring of the Ionians' exploit had a contagious effect that outweighed the fear inspired by their defeat. Persian power had proved vulnerable. Rebellion spread.

The Athenians, though, returned home. They wanted no further part in the revolt. They may have been shocked at their own rashness for joining in it at all. They thought less about what they had wanted to accomplish than about what they had witnessed; namely, Persia's might and the weakness of their own Ionian allies, as well as their lack of unity and their indecisiveness, which had kept them from challenging the Persians with all their power.

Meanwhile, the Greeks of Asia Minor established themselves as a naval force. To the north, they enlisted in their cause several cities on the Hellespont and the Sea of Marmara as well as Byzantium and Chalcedon at the entry to the Bosporus. At about this time, ships left for Caria and Cyprus, where the insurgents were also able to win allies. The entire seaboard of western and southwestern Asia Minor was temporarily released from Persian control. On Cyprus, the uprising was complicated by preexisting local enmities. Whatever the specific motives, a need for freedom sprung up among both the Greeks and the Carians during this period.

The Persian war machine took some time to gear up. It turned first on the Greeks, in part to reestablish the connection to Thrace; then it directed itself toward the Carians. A Phoenician fleet carrying a huge army landed on Cyprus, where battles were fought on land and on sea. The Ionian Greeks won the naval encounter, but the Cyprians lost the land battle. Several of their contingents had defected to the enemy before the beginning of the battle, and the island of Cyprus was lost.

Finally the focus of the war shifted to Miletus. The city was besieged by land, and Persian ships tried to cut off supply lines from the sea. The rebelling Greeks gathered once more for battle, this time near the island of Lade, just off the coast at Miletus. Chios sent 100 ships; Miletus contributed 80; Lesbos, 70; Samos, 60. The wealth that had accumulated in many of the cities on the coast of Asia Minor was once more demonstrated in this display of sea power. Formerly proud Phocaea, though, could afford only three ships. The city had lost its importance when the Persians occupied Ionia because most of its people had left to found a colony in the western Mediterranean to live in freedom. The Phocaean general Dionysius was nevertheless a man of great intelligence and independent thought. He told the war council that the navy must practice maneuvers every day. If it did, he claimed, it would be possible to defeat the Persian navy, which was almost twice as big as their own. That was assuming, of course, that the gods divided their favor evenly between the two sides. Dionysius was given command.

This was the time when the Greeks spent seven days repeating naval maneuvers, practicing turning and passing their ships—until they decided the exercises were too arduous. They returned to the island to wait, setting up tents, like a land army.

The Greeks lost the battle, which followed a few days later, in spite of valiant fighting. A significant contributing factor was that most of the Samian ships deserted the scene before the fighting began. The Persians had sent secret messages from the deposed tyrants assembled in their headquarters informing the Greek contingents that they could escape punishment for their disloyalty by refusing to take part in the battle. Only the Samians, and not all of them, responded to this appeal.

Miletus succumbed to the siege soon after. The city was looted and destroyed, its inhabitants carried off by Darius, the Great King, to Susa and then resettled in a city near the mouth of the Tigris. Part of their land was given to a neighboring Carian city, the rest kept by the Persians.

Aristagoras, the former tyrant of Miletus, had left the city years earlier. When the Persian counteroffensive began to show signs of large-scale major success, he considered the revolt lost and headed to the north of the Aegean, where he founded a colony on the coast.

Why Aristagoras chose an area within the Persian sphere of influence is inexplicable, even given the fact that he had large landholdings there. As in the past, he tried to maintain and increase his power by whatever promising means, so now he followed wherever opportunity beckoned. He acted shortsightedly, without any sense of responsibility for those he had drawn into the revolt. Or did he want to free the city from his influence? In any case, he abandoned his failed effort and immediately tried something else that worked out no better. He was quickly defeated by the tribes of the area where he wanted to settle and died in the battle.

The Ionian revolt collapsed in 494, six years after it started. In the following year, the Persian navy also subdued the islands of Chios, Lesbos, and Tenedos. On Samos, the ousted tyrant returned to power.

Herodotus reports that manhunts were carried out on all of the islands except for Samos. The victors joined hands, forming a human chain along one coast, and herded the inhabitants ahead of them. The Persians followed similar tactics on the mainland, though there it was easier to escape. The most beautiful boys were turned into eunuchs, the most beautiful girls sent to the emperor's harem. The cities, including their shrines, were burned to the ground. The Persians, presumably after taking the advice of the former tyrants and killing some of their prominent opponents, granted permission to the surviving Greeks to rebuild. The old tyrants, and perhaps a new one here and there, resumed power. But not for long.

The Persians suddenly changed policy, deposed the tyrants throughout the region, and set up isonomies instead. They found it preferable not to interfere in the Greeks' domestic affairs and saw no point in alienating the masses. Many Persians by this time had apparently become quite knowledgeable about the way the Greeks functioned. By that time the satrap had already reorganized the tribute system and introduced new procedures for settling conflicts between cities. By 480 at the latest, however, tyrants would once again be in power in many places.

The introduction of isonomies was part of a larger, broader offensive. In 492 Darius charged one of his sons-in-law, Mardonius, with establishing Persian control to the west of the empire. After reorganizing the interior affairs of the Greek cities, Mardonius crossed the Hellespont and entered Thrace with massive naval and land forces. As early as 510 B.C., the Persians had subdued a number of tribes in the area, probably including Macedonia, so various forms of Persian dominance extended as far as Mount Olympus. The Greek coastal island of Thasus, which had previously remained independent, now surrendered. The Persians' plan was to move on to the cities of the Chalcidicean peninsula, but as the navy tried to round the peninsula of Athos, a violent storm tossed most of the ships against the cliffs and wrecked them. Because the land army also sustained great losses, the expedition had to be called off.

It is not clear how far the Persians had planned to advance. Presumably their immediate goal was simply to secure the Aegean north coast. Greek cities were generally fortified, and conquering them by siege took time. Nevertheless, the Great King seems to have been determined to subjugate the Greek peninsula. Mardonius's expedition was only the first step. The era of intermittent contacts and isolated trespasses was over; the peaceful coexistence of Greeks and Persians had come to an end, at least for now.

In the burning of Sardis the great temple of Cybele was lost. The Persians used this fact to justify their later destruction of Greek shrines, among them the great temple of Didyma near Miletus. Perhaps this is the reason why the Greeks later denied responsibility for the burning of Sardis, but it seems likely that they meant for Sardis to burn. In any case, from now on each side cited justification for attacks and counterattacks. Both Persians and the Greeks held the belief, expressed as late as 415 in

Euripides' *Trojan Women*, that for each side, the destruction of their sacred shrines brought about military defeat. It was important to have the gods on one's side.

The Athenians must have followed the events in the East very attentively. Their initial experience had led them to conclude, with regret, that the Ionian movement did not amount to much. It was hard to look on helplessly as beautiful, rich cities fell, cities that they, as Athenians, imagined they had founded. And when the Persian general Mardonius turned up with his navy in the Aegean Sea, no one knew whether it would continue on to Athens.

At some point during those years, Phrynichus, the most prominent tragedian of the time, presented a play depicting the fall of Miletus at the Great Dionysia. The spectators were profoundly and lastingly disturbed by the play, responding with grief and anger. The whole city was soon in turmoil over the production, so much so that the authorities decided to impose a heavy fine on Phrynichus because he had recalled this domestic suffering. They also prohibited further performance of the play in any other theater in Attica.

This incident not only demonstrates the powerful effect theater had then but also the lengths to which the authorities went to shield the public against emotional shocks. In Athens, the people lived in close proximity to one another and were susceptible to being overcome by feeling. This was a civilized society, but danger always existed that a sudden wave of emotion might spread and be difficult to contain, or bring under control. Such emotional upheavals would have been troubling even to the aristocrats and would have interfered with their control over public life. Phrynichus had disrupted the mechanisms of deliberate forgetting, which modern psychology calls repression.

Athens' situation was already tense during those years. Around 494 the Spartans defeated the Argives, causing such heavy losses that the city of Argos was for a time militarily incapacitated. Sparta's influence in the northern Peloponnese was growing. In addition, the Athenians were still subject to maritime attacks from Aegina, quite possibly on a routine basis, and Athens was more or less powerless against them.

But we have no record of Athens' policies then. Hipparchus, son of Charmus, was elected archon for the year 496–495. He belonged to the Pisistratidae, the descendants of the former tyrant of Athens, Pisistratus, but that does not necessarily imply that his electors hoped he would improve relations with the deposed tyrant and with the Persians. We know nothing about Hipparchus's politics.

In 493–492 Themistocles became archon and urged that the harbor at Piraeus be improved. A fortified harbor was to replace the open beach at Phalerum and would accommodate both maritime trade and the Athenian navy. This plan made particular sense as a response to the repeated Aeginetan raids. To what extent Themistocles was already

Themistocles. Copy of a contemporary original, presumably the portrait, in the form of a statue, placed by Themistocles or his descendants in the temple he built in honor of Artemis Aristobulus. Ostia, Italy, Museum.

thinking of a naval war against the Persians is unknown. Nor is it known which of the three harbors was to be improved first, nor whether more than one harbor was to be worked on. It is also unclear whether fortifying the harbor's entry was the initial purpose, or whether docks and ship-building facilities were planned from the start. Was the work to be publicly financed or privately paid for in the form of tributes from wealthy private individuals? All we know for certain is that Athens improved the defense of its coast. It is likely that Athens did want to become more of a naval power.

Themistocles, son of Neocles, came from the Lycomid family, which was not a particularly distinguished lineage, but still aristocracy rather than middle class. He grew up in Phrearrhioi, a small deme in the Laurium region in southern Attica. His mother was from Athens but may not have been an ethnic Greek.

As a child he is said to have been a loner, taking little interest in the activities that absorbed his contemporaries: sports, play, and the lessons that constituted Greek education in its widest sense, with emphasis on the arts and on polite behavior. Themistocles spent as much time as possible by himself, busy with his own thoughts. He was not concerned with cultivating whatever aristocratic qualities he might lack. He did concentrate on what mattered to him, and from an early age on that seems to have been politics.

Born around 525, he grew up during Athens' last years of tyranny. He was not much more than ten when Harmodius and Aristogiton murdered Hipparchus, and he was about fifteen when Athens expelled the tyrants. Thus he grew up in a vibrant city that was in the midst of great internal transition yet sought to hold its own in the outside world. When still very young, he and his coevals were among the first to be inducted into the new subgroups of society and to become part of the reorganized citizenry. Politics must have been fascinating, particularly for a young man who was already interested in it.

Given that Themistocles was ambitious, did not get along well with his fellows, and was full of a young loner's pride, we can easily imagine him declaring that he had no interest in plucking the strings of a lute. He appears to have been an insufferable, opinionated youth of unruly temperament who vacillated from one extreme to another.

One of the leading politicians of the time, Mnesiphilus, lived in the same deme and may have introduced Themistocles to politics. Some later sources claim that Mnesiphilus actually taught Themistocles, but their accuracy is not certain. Essentially Themistocles grew up without teachers, as Thucydides attests. No one could have taught him what he learned, as what he brought to politics was something new. His close observation of politics and his first political experiences combined with his extraordinary talent and all-consuming ambition to excel. He had few scruples and was intent on just one goal, a personal one to be sure, but also one that could be rooted in a cause. So he was relatively free to choose the means of attaining his goal.

Among the best clues to his distinct, proud, and independent nature is his portrait, the oldest Greek portrait to show individual features. Other Greek aristocrats had themselves portrayed as idealized types, but Themistocles seems not to have cared for this image. He wanted to be different from everyone else in all respects, and accordingly he had his own ideas of how his portrait should look: an unmistakable, faithful depiction of the stocky, strong-willed, highly intelligent, and crafty man.

Many aristocrats adjusted themselves in one way or another to the new ways of politics and to dealing with the Council of Five Hundred and the popular assembly. Others may have hoped for a return to the old days. But all aristocrats still essentially subscribed to their traditional way of life.

It was more than a matter of mere appearances that their sons were still taught the art of elegant, gracious living, that they continued to dress in their old style, wore their hair long and fastened it with golden cicada-shaped pins. Pericles grew up having his locks curled into fanciful patterns, a fashion that would soon be considered old-fashioned.

But before this shift away from the old ways came about, the Greeks went through a strange transitional phase. During this period the last

Kouros from Sunium, ca. 590–580 B.C. Athens, National Museum.

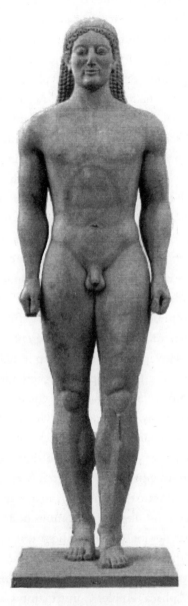

Kouros from Anavissos, Attica. The following is written on the pedestal: "Linger and mourn at the grave of dead Croesus, killed by violent Ares when fighting in the front line." Ca. 530 B.C. The fact that the youth was named Croesus like the Lydian king (died ca. 546 B.C.) suggests there were ties of hospitality between his father and the king. Athens, National Museum.

kouroi were created. These sculptures of athletic young men, often slightly larger than life, had been made according to a certain accepted model for decades. The feet pointed straight ahead, one placed slightly before the other but both carrying equal weight; the arms hung straight down; the body was erect, its position expressing discipline; the lips wore a mysterious smile probably meant to convey a sense of superiority and confidence adequate to deal with anything the relatively small Attic world might serve up. The sculptors varied this model only in minor ways.

But soon along came a new picture of man in the so-called Critius boy. Most of the body's weight rests on one leg, the other is slightly bent with the hip lowered; the body rises up in a kind of counterbalance to the legs and hips; the shoulders are not quite even, and the head is turned somewhat sideways. A new awareness of human strength is manifested here; the possibility of new human dimensions is expressed. The body is relaxed yet ready to exert effort. Instead of the smile we see seriousness. This figure, too, stands alone, but it is not as set off from its surroundings.

The Critius boy represents a major step away from a long and binding tradition. Man is seen differently: he *is* different. In the image of the Critius boy, the alternative that had opened up in political life takes visual shape. We might say that this sculpture depicts the isonomous citizen, though it expresses not so much the new equality as the freedom and mobility made possible by this equality. Greek sculpture had always aimed at giving shape to underlying sameness, at instantiating the type, but now it did so in a new way. It sought to show not simply the special quality of the isonomous citizen (as contrasted with others) but man as he appeared now, in the context of isonomy, man experiencing the impact of contradictory forces, just like the isonomous polis itself.

An especially clear demonstration of how quickly the entire style of Greece changed at that point is furnished by the example of Aegina. Shortly before the year 500, two series of pedimentary sculpture were created for the new Aphaea temple. Construction was delayed, and when the temple was finished ten to fifteen years later, the first series of statuary was mounted on the western pediment, which was the less important side, and a new one was ordered for the pediment facing east. Within this short period, the old style had become obsolete. The strictly symmetrical, late archaic composition, in which the figures stand more or less separate from one another, displaying only restrained movement, had been replaced by a living scene full of connections and overlappings. The bodies of the east pediment are much more active, caught in motion, relating to the space. And the space, which appears rather empty in the earlier west pediment group, is filled with figures. Where the dying in the earlier design smile their archaic smile, the agony of death now shows on the faces of the wounded.

Everything had begun to change and had to be seen anew and in a new context. Such change characterized the emerging political cooperation among the Greek cities. This period offered great opportunity for those who grasped the importance of the new conditions as accurately and as early as Themistocles evidently did.

Themistocles proceeded with his work in a most rational manner. Because he was not particularly affluent, he sought material wealth. Yet, not wanting to appear stingy, he spent his savings generously on well-chosen occasions, giving lavish banquets, for example, and paying for sacrificial feasts. In both attitudes, he had his own purposes in mind.

He made an effort to know as many citizens as possible by name, a political innovation. He attended to his duties conscientiously and energetically. One detail in particular stands out: When he was supervisor of the water system, he ordered a small bronze statue of a female water carrier and paid for it with the fines levied on those who were caught diverting water. This may not, however, have been a typical gesture.

It appears that he conducted himself well in the popular assembly. He was an effective and convincing speaker, even though his peremptory manner earned him his share of opponents. In any case, he knew how to make the most of the new order, an important talent because he did not initially have a large following.

In tune with the spirit of the new order, Themistocles cared about the concerns of the majority of citizens: politics, the city's well-being, and its

Critius boy. The changes from the kouroi are few but important. The weight of the body rests on the left leg. Consequently the right hip, as well as the right shoulder, is lowered somewhat, and the head is turned slightly. These few changes broke the usual strict symmetry of Greek sculpture and thus opened the way for an entirely new concept of art. The identity of the sculptor—Critius—has been deduced from the similarity between the head of this statue and that of Harmodius. Ca. 490 B.C. Athens, Acropolis Museum.

Western pediment of the Aphaea temple in Aegina, based on the reconstruction of D. Ohly. Ca. 500 B.C. Munich, Glyptothek.

stature. When these things were at stake, he spoke brilliantly and persuasively. His concern for the city's welfare generated a sense of responsibility for it, and in this way he was worlds apart from Aristagoras.

Because politics, and the politics of the city in particular, motivated him—not personal ambition or the desire to enhance his own reputation— he began almost by necessity to look ahead, to think not only about the present but also to anticipate the future. Freedom from petty selfishness or party interests made it possible to look ahead, especially in a city exposed to danger from external threats and not yet certain what to do with its newly acquired power. The skills Themistocles had acquired on his own he could therefore now apply to the polis. In particular, his outlook moved him to promote the fortification and expansion of the Piraeus harbor.

Not long after work on the improvement of the harbor was begun, Athens' internal political situation changed. An opponent to Themistocles appeared on the scene: Miltiades, son of Cimon and father of Cimon the younger. He belonged to an old and wealthy aristocratic family and was one of those lords who held small principalities on the periphery of Greece, generally north of the Aegean Sea. An uncle of Cimon's by the same name had built up the most innovative of these domains before the middle of the sixth century. It encompassed much of the Thracian Chersonese, the peninsula now called Gallipoli. The story goes that the Dolonci, the Thracian tribe who had dominated the region, asked Miltiades the elder for help against attacks by a neighboring tribe. The Dolonci were looking for the protection that would come with the presence of Greek settlers and for a strong leader with a talent for organization. Miltiades, more than ready to escape from the tyranny of the Pisistratids, accepted. Athens, too, had an interest in the region, and the Pisistratids later helped the younger Miltiades assume the powers he had inherited there.

Opposite the southern tip of the Chersonese lay the city of Sigeum, a stronghold that an Athenian aristocrat had conquered in the seventh century and that the Pisistratids had later taken over. Thus, the Athenians dominated the entry to the Hellespont on both sides. Miltiades the elder protected his dominion against invading tribes from the north by building a wall across the peninsula at its narrowest point. He and his immediate successor, Stesagoras, also tried to take over Lampsacus, on the eastern shore of the Hellespont, in order to control entry from the Sea of Marmara, though without success.

The relationship between the personal domains of Attic aristocrats and the polis of Athens is obscure and complex. The tyrannical Pisistratid family seems to have taken over Sigeum the same way it did Athens, but Athens was freed while Sigeum remained in the hands of Hippias. By contrast, rule over the Chersonese was accorded to Miltiades and his heirs from the beginning, though they sometimes needed support from the home city. Apparently an accommodating relationship between Miltiades and Athens developed on the basis of common interests. It is not clear how much the Persians' conquest of the Hellespont's eastern shore soon after 546 and their control over the Chersonese, gained shortly before 500, interfered with the interests of the Athenian lords. At any rate, the younger Miltiades, who had come to power around 520, would have liked to rid himself of the Persian overlordship. During the Ionian revolt, he apparently wrested control of the islands of Lemnos and Imbros from the Persians.

In 493, when the Persians once more took possession of the area between the Dardanelles and Byzantium, Miltiades the younger loaded his treasures onto five ships, one of which was lost while trying to escape Phoenician vessels, and returned to Athens. As a gift he gave Lemnos and Imbros, which probably no longer belonged to him, to his Athenian fellow citizens.

. . .

An unlikely thing happened next: Miltiades, a great lord, a wealthy tyrant who had lived in grand style and was used to commanding others, the son-in-law of the Thracian king, turned up in an isonomous city whose citizens were in no mood to return to tyranny. Miltiades found the city completely changed from the time he left it.

The best indication that Miltiades was able to win the Athenians' favor is that his great popularity prompted his enemies to accuse him of being a tyrant. The legal basis of the accusation is unclear, but the intention is obvious. His rivals believed him to be a major threat and were ready to try anything to get rid of him. They may also have turned against him because he was an eloquent advocate for war against the Persians. There was in Athens a faction that wanted to make peace with Persia. The court, however, declared Miltiades innocent, and soon thereafter, in the year 490–489, he was elected to office as one of the ten *strategoi*.

Miltiades seems to have conveyed to the Athenians a sense of optimism. His generosity and cosmopolitanism inspired them, bolstering their courage and self-confidence. Miltiades' reckless and carefree qualities were just what they needed at this stage. He did not interfere with their political order, and even if they had once worried that he would, they did not care at the moment. He knew the Persians and was familiar with their method of warfare, and he made the Athenians feel they had nothing to fear. This was crucial to a citizenry whose majority was ready to do whatever was required to preserve its freedom.

Whether the other politicians were really as inferior to Miltiades as the contemporary sources suggest is unclear. Themistocles must have been furious at Miltiades' great popularity, but there was nothing he could do. He, too, had boldness, but his determination to oppose the Persians lacked the infectious, charismatic quality of the grand lord's. Perhaps Themistocles was still too young, too little known, not yet sure enough of himself. In any case, Militiades' influence became the dominating force during the following months. He more than anyone else swayed the Athenians to face the Persians in open battle, and under his leadership they won.

· · ·

In 491, one year after the Persians had reclaimed the northern shore of the Aegean and reorganized their government there, the Great King sent envoys to the city-states of the Greek mainland, demanding earth and water, the tokens of submission. Most cities complied, even on Aegina, which angered and worried the Athenians. Among the cities that refused were Eretria, Sparta, and Athens.

The Spartans went so far as to push the Persian envoys into a pit. In Athens, they were thrown into a well and told they could get their earth and water there. Themistocles even insisted in the popular assembly that the Persian messengers be executed because they had the gall to defile the Greek language by using it to convey the demands of a barbarian.

The tensions that had existed at the end of the sixth century between Athens and Sparta may have eased some time before this. Now the Athenians appealed to the Spartan King Cleomenes for help against the Aeginetans, whom they feared were siding with the Persians. Sparta responded by taking twelve leading Aeginetan politicians hostage and handed them over to the Athenians. In retaliation, the Aeginetans seized a ship carrying Athenian noblemen. Athens, whose navy was rather weak, borrowed twenty ships from the Corinthians. Corinth, however, demanded a symbolic payment for the loan so that the Aeginetans could not accuse them of aiding and abetting their enemy. The Athenians also urged an Aeginetan politician to stir up trouble and establish an isonomy there. But the plans were badly coordinated, and the attempted overthrow failed, as did an Athenian land attack. Nevertheless the Attic fleet, made up of seventy mostly obsolete ships, managed to defeat the Aeginetan navy. After this, peace prevailed for some time.

In early 490, the Persians sent out another expedition. Again the army and the navy were assembled in Cilicia. The navy is said to have included six hundred triremes plus ships for transporting horses. Altogether there were around twenty-five thousand foot soldiers and a cavalry force of eight hundred riders and twelve hundred horses. If the crews of the ships are included, the expedition numbered about ninety thousand men, more than enough, the Persians must have figured, to deal with Athens, Eretria, and a few other cities. After all, most of the Greek cities had already switched over to the Persian side. The command was entrusted to two generals, Datis and Artaphernes.

On their way across the Aegean the Persians took Naxos and several other islands, where they conscripted troops and took hostages. The Persians respectfully spared the sacred island of Delos. The islands appeared prepared to submit to Persian power. Only the city of Carystus on Euboea resisted for a time.

The Eretrians against whom the Persians turned next defended themselves behind their city walls, but after six days of desperate fighting they were betrayed, and the invaders ravaged the city, including its temples. The Persians once again, as earlier in Ionia, formed a human chain to corral the inhabitants. The outcome was that many Eretrians were deported, just as the Miletians had been four years earlier. They were taken first to Susa and then resettled in Persia.

Deportation was a tactic commonly practiced by Near Eastern emperors and had been used frequently by the Assyrians. The Persians resorted to it sparingly, but could not do completely without it as a punishment for and deterrent to rebellion. The practice repeatedly followed by the Greeks when they conquered cities, of executing the men and selling the women and children as slaves, makes the Persian action appear almost humanitarian. Of course, the fact that there was plenty of room in their empire made it easier for the Persians to opt for deportation over execution, but we should not disallow the Persians' relative magnanimity, of which their kings were so proud. Still, for those subject to it, deportation was harsh—and the Eretrian deportation made clear to the Athenians just what they were risking.

The Persian troops landed a few days later near the plain of Marathon. The plan had been conceived by Hippias, who now reenacted with Persian ships what his father Pisistratus had done almost two generations earlier. He set out from Eretria and landed near Marathon to march on Athens. At Marathon there was a convenient bay where a large fleet could land safely, especially because the coast was inadequately guarded, if at all. Hippias may have hoped that many Athenians would desert to the Persian side in order to escape the fate of deportation. At any rate, Athens could be quickly reached from Marathon, especially on horseback, and landing at Phalerum, close to the city, was not advisable because the Attic army could have defended the shore there easily.

News of the landing reached Athens quickly, probably by fire signals. It came as no surprise. The following day the popular assembly met to deliberate on what to do. Whatever preparations had been made, this was the time to decide how to proceed. The hoplites most likely assembled near the city in advance, making attendance at the assembly high. Those who would have to fight the war were present, and the will of their majority—that is, the will of the middle classes—apparently made the difference. Those who would have preferred to follow an easier, more opportunistic course were either too few in number or too ashamed of their intentions. Among the politicians, Miltiades was the most vocal.

It was decided to send a messenger to Sparta as quickly as possible to report the landing and urge the Spartans to hurry—presumably they had already agreed to come. But the timing was bad. It was midsummer, and the Spartans were in the midst of celebrating the Carnean festival. An old custom forbade the army from mobilizing during the festival. Hippias must have known this and planned the date of the landing accordingly. The Athenians, however, had expected the Spartans to rise to the emergency despite the festival.

The Athenians also decided to enlist their slaves, who were promised freedom if they fought, but only a small group of slaves would have been involved, probably those who would already have been taken along by their masters to assist as carriers and servants. Some slaves may even have been skilled in the use of arms; in any case, their loyalty was beyond doubt. The members of the lowest social orders, the thetes, did not serve, except to repair the city walls—if it became necessary—and to perform guard duties.

The assembly's most important decision was that the army should provision itself and set out for Marathon to meet the Persians. The Athenians did not want to take shelter behind their walls. They feared the psychological effects of a siege as well as the possibility of treason, thinking it better to set out and bolster courage and to have the army take the initiative than to wait around. The size of the enemy force was known. With the help of the Spartans, the Athenians hoped they could defeat the enemy's infantry; the cavalry, they knew, presented more of a problem.

So the army, nine thousand or ten thousand men organized by phyle, was dispatched in great haste, probably the afternoon or early evening of the day these decisions were made, while the courier Phidippides was racing toward Sparta by way of Eleusis, Megara, and Corinth. Phidippides was among the fast runners the Greeks trained as messengers and couriers, men who could cover over a hundred kilometers a day. Phidippides is said to have reached Sparta on the second day, having run over 250 kilometers across uneven territory. According to Phidippides' own account, the god Pan stopped him along the way and asked why the Athenians had been neglecting him even though he was favorably disposed toward them. After the war the Athenians made up for their omission.

But all the hurry was in vain. The Spartans, characteristically, were not about to depart from their customs, no matter how great the danger or how much the battle's outcome depended on them. A few days later, when the moon was full and the celebration over, two thousand Spartans set out. But though they marched fast, they did not arrive until the day after the battle.

The Athenians set up camp on the southern edge of the plain of Marathon. There, from a sanctuary of Heracles on the slope of Mount Agriliki, they could survey the main road to Athens, which ran between the mountain and a marsh extending to the shore. As long as the Athenians remained there, the Persians hesitated to leave the plain, even by the other road toward Athens, which led directly west. The approach to the Greek position was narrow enough to be easily defended, making the Athenians safe from a flank attack by the Persian cavalry. The Athenians also rendered some of the territory impassable by erecting barricades of brush. In the meantime, assistance had arrived in the form of one thousand men from the closely allied Boeotian border town of Plataea, which was under Athenian protection.

But even with this Plataean reinforcement, the Athenians were reluctant to launch an attack, because once they were in the open field they would be exposed to the Persian cavalry. Unless a particularly good opportunity to strike presented itself, the Athenians thought it best not to be lured away from their advantageous spot. So they waited, thinking the Spartans would soon arrive. It must have been hard to keep up the spirit of the troops, but the enemy's reluctance to risk an attack showed that the Greek position was unassailable.

The Persian force included Ionian units, some of whose members were willing to pass information to the Athenians with a set of prearranged signals. While the Greeks were still waiting for the Spartans, word reached their camp via these signals that the Persian cavalry was gone. The Greeks were apparently unable to survey the entire plain, either because trees blocked their view or because it was dark.

According to the most plausible account we have, the Persians loaded troops, primarily cavalry, onto their ships, presumably to sail to Phalerum as quickly as possible. While the bulk of the Persian army tried to keep the Greeks occupied at Marathon, the departing troops were to take over Athens with the help of friendly inhabitants, before the Spartans arrived.

It may have been over this situation that a disagreement arose, an account of which appears in Herodotus's writings. This disagreement involved ten Athenian generals, half of whom were in favor of going into battle immediately; the others against it. The polemarch Callimachus ultimately would tip the balance in favor. There was, however, good cause to vacillate, as many felt it wiser to set out immediately for Athens to defend the city. If the Athenians risked battle at Marathon, there was the danger, quite apart from the uncertainty of the outcome, that they might return to Athens too late, after the Persian units had already landed. Miltiades' main fear was, however, that the underlying divisions among the Athenians would deepen and that their resolve and courage would collapse. At the moment, the majority still stood firm. Miltiades was convinced that as long as the gods distributed fortune equally between the two sides, the Greeks had a good chance of winning.

Callimachus let himself be convinced and cast the tie-breaking vote. It was a bold decision, probably the only correct one both militarily and politically. Miltiades' success in pushing it through may be the greatest service he performed at Marathon.

The sacrifices offered according to custom augured well. The Greeks lined up in formation. At the same time the Persian army took up its position on the plain. Then the signal was sounded, a battle song intoned, and the phalanx started down the hill in closed formation, each man with his shield in his left hand, a long spear in the right, everyone in lockstep.

The Greeks started out about 1,200 meters beyond the range of the Persian archers' arrows. When they came within range, after a good ten-minute march, they covered the last 200 meters at a run. The Greek commanders chose this tactic despite the fact that it was highly unusual and risky because it spread the Greek lines out both sideways and to the rear.

The Greeks had reinforced both wings of their battle line, massing several rows of hoplites behind one another on either side. This left the middle ranks thin, with just a few lines of men. The right flank was under the command of the Athenian polemarch; the left flank was made up of Plataeans from Boeotia.

The sight of the Persians is said to have frightened the Greeks. If correct, it must have been the unfamiliar appearance of the army that worried them. Perhaps it was the mere idea—or as Herodotus says "the name"—of the Persians that caused their reaction. The Persians fought with bow and arrow, some with short lances and scimitars. They were clothed in leather, perhaps reinforced with small metal plates, and wore turbans on their heads. The Greeks' equipment was far superior. They were protected by helmets, breastplates, leather "skirts" than hung just below the waist, and leg coverings, and they had shields, long spears, and solid swords. The Persians, though, were apparently more nimble; they were most likely well trained and were definitely brave.

After a protracted struggle, the Greeks succeeded in routing the Persians on the flanks, where they clashed against the enemy with full force, but the center line gave way. Rather than pursue the retreating enemy, the disciplined and well-commanded flanking troops instead turned to the center to fight until victory was won along the whole front.

Afterward the Greeks gathered together and advanced toward the ships. It is unclear whether the entire Persian cavalry had left for Athens. There are indications that at least some Persian cavalrymen took part in the fighting. The battle near the ships was a difficult and costly one for the Greeks. Callimachus was killed there; so was a brother of Aeschylus, who himself also fought at Marathon. It may have helped the Persians that the spit of land jutting out between the marsh and the sea, where their ships were anchored, was narrow. In any case, they were able to save almost their entire navy. The Greeks captured only seven of their ships.

The Persian infantry, however, suffered great losses. About 6,400 soldiers were said to have fallen, most of them in close combat, some because they got bogged down in swampy terrain during flight. The Greek side lost 192 men. This latter figure is most likely quite accurate, while the number of Persian casualties is more likely conjectural. Oddly, the Greek casualties amounted to exactly three percent of the Persian losses. Many men on the Greek side must also have been wounded by Persian arrows.

The Greeks may have erected a victory monument of arms as was customary, but there was not much time to celebrate. After a brief rest, the army departed for Athens, perhaps that same night. It was essential that they reach Athens before the Persians did. The men of one tribe stayed behind to guard the Persian camp. The story of the courier who ran a "marathon" to Athens and collapsed dead after announcing the victory is a later embellishment of events and almost certainly fictitious.

Some of the Persian ships stopped at an island off Marathon to pick up the captured Eretrians they had unloaded earlier, but most of the fleet sailed around Sunium toward Phalerum, following the ships already dispatched. They are said to have taken this course in response to a signal, which may have indicated that friends in Athens were prepared to deliver the city into their hands. But this account, if it is based on fact, might refer to an earlier signal that resulted in the departure of the first Persian detachment.

The army of Athenians and Plataeans did not move directly to the coast; instead it set up camp near the Cynosarges, the sanctuary of Heracles south of Athens' city walls. From there they could observe the city while remaining within a half hour's march from the shore of Phalerum. The Persians, after making an appearance and dropping anchor, departed.

This was the first time a Greek army had defeated a Persian force in open battle. The fear of being inferior to the troops of the Eastern empire was laid to rest. The phalanx of heavily armed hoplites, the basic instrument of intra-Greek warfare, had proved itself in battle. Made up of a relatively small number of equal citizens and developed for a kind of tournament combat that relegated cavalry and lightly armed soldiers to a subordinate role, the Greek phalanx was surprisingly effective against a Persian foe accustomed to victory and geared to large-scale operations.

The Greek victory at Marathon had far-reaching significance. For the first time, Greek city-states made up of equals had successfully confronted a power of continental dimensions. They had done so even without the aid of the Spartans. All that was left for the Spartans to do when they arrived was to scan the battlefield—which they did with interest—and congratulate the Athenians.

Contrary to later custom, the bodies of the dead soldiers were not taken back to Athens. Instead, they were burned at the scene of battle, and a mound about ten meters high and fifty meters in diameter was formed over the remains. Later, tablets were set up listing the names of the dead by tribe. Another mound covered the bones of the Plataeans and the slaves. Miltiades, too, received a monument, and a victory memorial of light marble, probably from Mount Pentelicus, was erected. Around 460, Miltiades' son, Cimon, ordered a monumental painting of the battle set up in the Hall of Colors *(stoa poikile)* on the north side of the agora, to commemorate his father's glory.

For decades to come the Marathon warriors were celebrated as embodying Athenian virtues. Not only brave but also honest and modest, they were citizens in the best sense of the word. Their victory would out-shine even the success at Salamis ten years later. There was nothing tech-nologically sophisticated about the victory at Marathon; it was gained the old-fashioned way, in hand-to-hand combat. Naval victories evoked thoughts about lowly oarsmen and the greatness of Athens. Marathon, by contrast, held the nostalgic charm of a beginning. No matter how great a role Miltiades had played, the success at Marathon hinged much more on the effort of all involved than was the case at Salamis.

When Miltiades asked to be awarded a garland of olive branches, opposition was immediately voiced and echoed in the popular assembly. "The day you fight the barbarians and win by yourself you can ask for honors for yourself alone," Sophanes, a distinguished soldier, is said to have replied. He may have spoken out of envy, but the positive response his words evoked in the assembly certainly indicates lofty self-esteem on the part of the Athenian citizens.

The Athenians now ran into trouble making good on their debt to Artemis of Agrotera. Before the battle, they had promised to offer the goddess a goat for every Persian slain, but now there were not enough animals available. So they decreed that five hundred goats were to be offered to the goddess annually, and they stuck to this promise for years to come. Every year they honored Artemis with a great sacrificial feast. Some of the sacrifice was also offered to Athena and other gods. For Pan they established a shrine in a cave below the Acropolis and held an annual torch race in his honor.

One year after Marathon, in 489, Miltiades asked the Athenians to outfit him with seventy fully crewed ships and money for an expedition that he said would be lucrative for them. Acting in the spirit of the old raids, whose goals could also not be publicly divulged, he did not say what he would be raiding. Such requests without specifics about the goal were fairly common at the time, and the Athenians saw no reason not to grant the proven leader's wish.

Miltiades headed for Paros to demand high punitive payments from the Parians for having joined the Persian campaign. But he met with resistance, and gave up his attempt after a siege of twenty-six days.

Upon his return to Athens, he was prosecuted for deceit. The formal accusation was raised by Xanthippus, son of Ariphron and father of

Pericles. The jury found Miltiades guilty but did not, in view of all he had done for the city, condemn him to death. It did impose a heavy financial penalty. Miltiades was already a sick man at the time of the trial and died soon after the verdict was pronounced. His son Cimon paid the fine.

Miltiades' expedition had an undoubtedly political aspect to it: The Athenians could not let pass unchallenged the desertion of the islands to the Persian side. They had to anticipate a renewed Persian campaign, and it was crucial to their interests that the Persians not be able to use these islands, so close to mainland Greece, as a base. Nevertheless Herodotus's account is unequivocal. He is convinced that the expedition against Paros was undertaken by Miltiades for the sake of personal gain and booty. In all likelihood, Miltiades was guided by both motives.

It is important at this juncture to make clear distinctions. Reading Herodotus, we get the impression that the rational element was largely lacking in political and military calculations at the time. Accounts of events suggesting supernatural influences take up an inordinate amount of space. Examples include the Athenian courier's encounter with Pan—which could be explained as a result of overexertion during his long run—and the story of Hippias setting foot on Attic soil once more when he landed at Marathon. Hippias had dreamed the night before that he was sleeping next to his mother, an omen promising that he would get "his country" back. Suddenly he sneezed. His teeth were loose, and one of them fell on the sand and disappeared. Hippias realized it was not he but only his tooth that was meant to remain on Attic soil.

Similarly, Herodotus suggests that Miltiades failed at Paros because, taking the advice of a priestess, he illegally entered a shrine to perform secret rites. When he emerged from the shrine he shuddered. The Parians later thought the priestess had wanted to betray them, but the Delphic oracle indicated that she had been instrumental in directing him toward the misfortune that had been his destiny all along.

But what actually happens and its subsequent interpretation in stories of the time are two different matters. The capacity for intellectual interpretation is perhaps bound to lag behind the capability of action—except, rarely, when the two come together at a high level, as would eventually be the case in Athens.

Consequently the stories Herodotus tells cannot be taken as direct evidence of the Athenians' mode of thinking and acting. The lengthy preparations for meeting Xerxes' campaign against Greece, which culminated in the battle at Salamis, were not the first instance of the Greeks' masterful calculations; such forethought and strategic planning was already evident earlier, in the much briefer preparations for turning back Datis and Artaphernes at Marathon. And there is no reason to assume that this kind of planning was limited to a few outstanding men; the popular assembly may have participated in it. At the same time, religious considerations and superstitions were still alive, especially in wartime and in other situations of imminent danger.

There is also the question of the relative importance of the demands of polis politics and the aristocracy's personal ambitions. The autocratic tendencies of the Greek aristocracy were never entirely suppressed. The nobility always retained some of its old self-reliance, its desire for glory unrelated to politics, and its concern with a public sphere where aesthetic concerns predominated. Aristocrats were free to engage in daring adventures and tended to succumb to the desire for personal gain and luxury. In the fifth century, the larger community often had to check aristocratic individualism in order to assert the interests of the polis.

But in the transitional phase of this period, especially around 490, the relationships between prominent individuals and the people could vary a great deal. Because Miltiades shared Athens' opposition to the Persians, he was able to serve the city in an ingenious way that won general approval. But this princely lord who had also been tyrant of the Thracian Chersonese obviously also thought of himself. As soon as the matter of common interest was taken care of, his own desires came to the fore again. His Parian campaign was the last major adventure of a great Attic nobleman. Soon after Miltiades' death, a man would appear on the scene who acquired his greatness and his power by serving Athens' political interests above all else.

. . .

The Athenians must have realized, once the immediate danger was over, that the Persians were not gone for good. They were bound to come back. The victory the Athenians had won was astounding, but for that reason they could not count on similar success in the future.

After Marathon, Athenian politics seems to have taken on a new seriousness and a new consistency. Certain changes that took place during those years are well known, even if they cannot be accurately dated. They may be connected with Marathon, but such a connection is speculative. There is clear evidence, for example, that the Athenian nobility dressed and wore their hair pinned up in the old, elegant manner as late as 490. Sometime thereafter, they changed over to the simpler, plainer style of the Spartans. This obviously did not happen overnight, and on the vase paintings of that period we find men with their hair pinned up. But the change in style may have started at about the time of the Battle of Marathon.

Somewhat earlier, *kouroi* figures ceased to be made, probably in consequence of a law to that effect. Burial monuments also became plain. Around 490 the Critius boy ushered in a new epoch in sculpture. Lastly, the whole tradition of thematic vase painting came to an end around 490. As early as 530 Athenian vase painting underwent a radical transformation, but that change was primarily of a technical nature—namely, the change from black-figured to red-figured painting. From 530 on it was possible to paint the details of a figure onto a red background instead of scratching it into a black background.

From about 520 vases show a great many erotic pictures of symposium scenes: explicit depictions of the pleasures of men who have drunk too much, including detailed drawings of various kinds of erotic encounters—intimate, voyeuristically observed scenes of men and hetaerae or courtesans, sometimes in couples and sometimes in larger groups. These pictures can be lovely and strangely charming.

We don't know if the symposia were exceptionally wild and debauched during these years, if a new, exuberant spirit delighted in portraying things

An amphora painted in the black-figured technique on one side and the red-figured technique on the other. The improvements made possible by the red-figured technique are obvious. Heracles is shown drinking and reclining on a couch, a Dionysiac drinking vessel in his left hand and a grapevine behind him. His weapons are hanging on the wall. Athena is standing on the left. In the black-figured version Hermes is there, too, and a boy in charge of the mixing bowl is seen on the right. Ca. 520 B.C. Munich, Antikensammlungen.

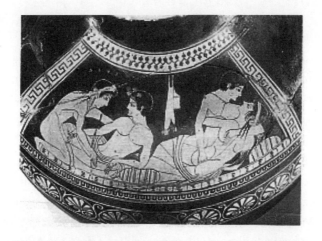

Two pairs of lovers at a symposium. Hydria, red-figured, ca. 510–500 B.C. Brussels, Musée Cinquantenaire.

previously treated with discretion or if the artists' imagination simply transposed onto the symposia what was usually not done so publicly. In any case, the vase paintings must have suited the tastes of the buyers.

Along with these pictures we find others devoted to Dionysus and his following of satyrs and maenads. As the century progresses, the dances of the celebrants become wilder, turning into madly reeling and orgiastic abandon. We see Dionysus and the maenads tearing animals to pieces and

A symposium scene. The banquet has degenerated into a drinking party. The guests have left their couches and have trouble remaining upright. One of them is being carried off, apparently passed out. But wine is still being poured. Contrary to the norm, a man plays music. This black-figured tankard, signed by both the potter and the painter, dates from the sixth century B.C. and is one of many works with highly realistic depictions of the parties that were popular at the time. Athens, National Museum.

devouring them raw. The fate of Pentheus, the king of Thebes, is also depicted. Pentheus was ripped apart by the maenads, or possibly, as later accounts have it, by his own mother and sisters because in their Dionysian frenzy they mistook him for a wild animal. Pentheus had sought to restrain the excesses of the Dionysus worshippers.

Were these vase paintings signs of exceptional licentiousness, of a somewhat artificial exuberance, or, indeed, of a kind of gallows humor that may have characterized the years between declining tyranny and the Battle of Marathon? Do they reflect a defiant withdrawal by the aristocrats into the private sphere and the world of feasting as a kind of compensation for lost power? Or do they attest to the unlimited enjoyment of new possibilities now open to middle-class circles? We know that by this time the middle class had begun to participate fully in the symposium culture.

Nietzsche points out that it was the same people who took part in the tragedies who fought in the Persian battles. The depiction of wantonness is not irreconcilable with a harsh, serious life and may in fact have formed part of it.

For the first time, in 486 B.C., comedies that included choruses approved by the archon were performed at the Great Dionysia festival. Private performances of comedies with choruses had been common for some time. Even in those early days, comedies probably satirized prominent politicians. That might have been one reason for their inclusion in the official program, which would suggest that at the same time political conflict intensified, a need arose to relieve tensions by comic means.

The change in political climate is particularly evident in 487, when an interesting alteration of the procedure for appointing archons was made. From then on, a fairly large group of men, probably one hundred, was elected—ten from each phyle—and nine archons picked by lot from among them. Most likely the pool of families that supplied the archons did not differ greatly from before. The census rules may have changed to the effect that members of the cavalry, the second of the economic classes established by Solon, were also eligible. But whereas before it was primarily the most influential candidates who obtained the nine highest positions in the city, their chances were now much reduced. Accordingly, it no longer mattered as much who held the office; the importance of the office was obviously declining.

The *strategoi*, or generals, on the other hand, may have gained by the reform. Their position improved not because of any increase in their powers—which remained what they had been—but because at least some of the *strategoi* had a better chance, thanks to their ambition, political and military skills, and personal influence, of getting elected, either within their phyle or by the assembly. In this way the power of the office was enhanced, a reform that gave it one great advantage over that of the archons—*strategoi* could be reelected, and sometimes they were, year after year. Since they also had access to the council, they had great opportunity to shape long-term policies. The position did not carry the glory of the old aristocratic positions of leadership, and therefore there was no strict limit on terms of office. There is good reason to assume that Themistocles was the moving force behind the reform; he may even have championed it.

The situation is similar with respect to punishment by ostracism, which was probably introduced or first applied at this time. Ostracism literally means "judgment by shards" because shards *(ostraka)*, the cheapest writing material, were used for voting. Ostracism could be imposed, if the assembly so chose, at a certain date midway through the Attic year (around January by our calendar). This means that the question of whether it wished to hold an ostracism vote was put to the assembly.

If the institution of ostracism goes back as far as Cleisthenes, then we can deduce that the question had been posed and rejected for at least ten years. This period includes the year when a massive faction arose against Miltiades and accused him of tyranny. If it existed then, the ostracism question had apparently become a routine agenda item to be routinely disposed of. In either case, the imposition of ostracism in 487 represented an innovation.

The regulation stated that about two months after the assembly approved ostracism, the question of who should be ostracized would be put to the people. A quorum of six thousand was required. The voting was done in the agora, and access strictly supervised. The archons and the

A symposium participant relieving his stomach, lovingly assisted by a hetaera. She has set up a basin for him, such as were normally used for washing the feet before the symposium began. The object on the wall is probably a case for a flute, suggesting that the hetaera plays music. Red-figured, ca. 490 B.C. Rome, Villa Giulia.

Council of Five Hundred, who were in charge of the voting, first had to establish the total number of persons present. Everyone present then wrote on an earthenware shard the name of the person he thought represented a danger to the community. Whoever's name topped the list was banished from the city for ten years and had to depart within ten days. He was not, however, stripped of honor or possessions and was free to return after his exile.

The institution of ostracism is the only legal means ever devised to stop the rise of a coup plotter. Usually there is no proof of a plotter's intentions until after he has achieved them, and then he is in a position to block any attempt to bring him to justice. Here, however, mere suspicion sufficed. Ostracism was imposed on anyone who was becoming, in the people's opinion, too powerful. In a sense, this institution seems to have been based on the idea of the scapegoat. For the individual affected, the

230

consequences of being ostracized were considerably less severe than those of a court's verdict (there was no threat of the death penalty, as in the case of usurpers), and this made it easier, other things being equal, to ostracize someone than to condemn him.

Ostracism played a considerable role in Attic politics between 487 and 417, and was introduced in other places as well, such as Syracuse. There, however, the votes were written on olive leaves *(petala)*, and was consequently called petalism. Whatever the inventors of ostracism may have had in mind, the decisive argument for ostracism must have been the prevention of tyranny. How else could the de facto banishment of troublesome politicians have become institutionalized?

It is unclear to what extent there was reason to fear a resurgence of tyranny, either at the time of Cleisthenes or in 487. This danger could never be entirely dismissed, and the Athenians would be repeatedly seized by fear of tyrants later in the city's history. Still, more was involved in ostracism than simply the removal of men suspected of tyrannical ambitions. If that had been the main purpose, such a procedure, which could be resorted to only at a predetermined date once a year, would hardly have been adequate.

The introduction of a mechanism for imposing an involuntary

Pottery shards with the names of Callias, son of Cratius; Hippocrates, son of Anaxileus; Themistocles, son of Neocles; and Cimon, son of Miltiades

ten-year leave from politics reflects a situation in which high expectations were placed on institutions and in which there was no reason to fear that the ostracized person's followers might organize a coup in his absence. Discussion was severely limited before the vote to ostracize was taken so as not to incite the popular assembly, and any agitating was restricted to areas outside the meeting (streets, public squares, symposia). Cheating was possible: a number of shards could be marked by the same hand.

The preventive nature of the measure implies that the level of power the people would permit an individual to attain before regarding him as dangerous was now lower. Later on, a distinction would be made between two forms of power—the one that operated within the law and accepted the fundamental equality of all citizens and the one that consisted of "wanting to have more" *(pleonexia)*, which was selfish and ran counter to the interests of the polis.

Was such a formal distinction recognized at this time? There must already have been a clear sense that certain forms of personal power were unacceptable in an isonomy, and the standards according to which such power was judged must have been strict. Could it really be expected, though, that the most powerful man would be ostracized and not his most dangerous rival? Can we assume that the power relationships, which after all were also reflected in the popular assembly, were really temporarily suspended during the ostracism vote?

Somewhat later on, the institution of ostracism came to serve mostly, if not always, to remove the second most powerful individual. Consequently it functioned to reduce competition among the politicians and became a means to strengthen the unity of Attic politics. (There is a remote resemblance here to modern electoral rules that favor the larger parties.) Yet this was not necessarily the way ostracism had to work, and at least around 487 the institution played a different role.

For one thing the popular assembly was not always well attended. The required quorum of six thousand for an ostracism vote suggests that this was an unusual meeting and that it may have been used by some who could not attend the assembly regularly as an opportunity to express their mistrust of a given politician. Consequently a politician who could generally sway the majority in his favor could not necessarily determine the outcome at such meetings. Thus, ostracism served as a corrective against politicians and political tendencies that were not popular with many citizens but that dominated everyday political life.

Power can, of course, take different forms. One historian distinguishes between "leadership on the organization plane" and "leadership on the discussion plane." And even though the goal of Cleisthenes' new order was that decisions be made within the popular assembly on the basis of discussion, argument, and rhetoric, this does not exclude the possibility that under normal conditions politicians still mobilized enough influence through alliances and personal followers to prevail over popular opinion. Up to now this had been the case, for example, in the election of the archons. To the extent that the power of these men could be seen as dangerous, they now lost out. Thus ostracism contributed to the selection of the kind of politician that Athenian politics now required.

Ostracism, then, increased the influence of the broader population. Those in leadership positions had to take the people's will into consideration if they did not want to face exile. Even the most powerful politicians were made to keep within certain limits. At the same time, the use of ostracism also indicates to what a great extent power had come to depend on a positive relationship between politicians and the popular assembly.

Of course, personal rivalries and envy must have played a role, as did conflicts over political direction, both among the leadership and the broader population. Short- and long-term effects may sometimes have coincided and sometimes conflicted. In any case, in 487, ostracism suddenly became one of the major tools used in political fights.

At first, an ostracism vote was held every year. The first victim was Hipparchus, son of Charmus, a relative of the Pisistratid family and probably Hippias's son-in-law. In 486, Megacles, son of Hippocrates, a member of the Alcmaeonid family and a nephew of Cleisthenes, was banished. In 485 it was the turn of a man named Callias, son of Cratius. One source describes these first men to be ostracized as "friends of the tyrants" but claims that this was not the case for the next victim whose name we know, Xanthippus, father of Pericles.

Perhaps Hipparchus was feared mostly because of his connection to the Pisistratids. In the case of Megacles and other members of his family against whom votes were cast in the following years, what may have been decisive was the suspicion that the Alcmaeonids had, at the battle of Marathon, given the signal that encouraged the Persians to sail toward Athens. On some pottery shards with Callias's name on them he is described as being from Medea and once caricatured in Persian attire.

But it is not clear what precisely led up to a person's being ostracized. All we can ascertain is that political debates became increasingly acrimonious and that there were regular elimination contests among politicians.

One man who was already a prominent politician in 487 emerged unscathed from the ostracism votes. According to archeological evidence, there were nearly enough votes cast against him, probably in 486, to condemn him. This man was Themistocles, who had many enemies and few supporters, who tried to work openly with the popular assembly, and who broadly identified with what he understood to be the interests of the city.

It is clear, then, that the most powerful leaders in Athens were those able to win the trust of the popular assembly and especially the middle classes. Later this cooperation between outstanding individuals and the people was the factor that made democratic politics possible. Because fierce competition could arise under these conditions, the elimination battles of the ostracism votes assumed great importance.

These battles were often connected with decisions concerning Athenian foreign policy. In the 480s there was the immediate worry about the war with Aegina, which kept flaring up, and also the connected problem of Athens' attitude toward Persia. The two were related, for Athens had reason to fear that the island would become a Persian military base—the Aeginetans had offered earth and water to the Persian envoys.

It is not clear if the improvement of the Piraean harbor was completed at this time. If it had been ongoing, continuation of the work might have come under dispute and some record of it persisted. But the most important question seems to have been whether Athens should seek some kind of accommodation with the Persians. Those who favored tyranny presumably maintained contact with Hippias (if, in fact, he was still alive). Certainly they did so with the Persian satrap. This group sought to prevent a policy of opposition and military defense and argued instead for submission. This would also have served the interests of many aristocrats.

Others opposed this position. They strove to have the city prepare for the next Persian attack, reasoning that if the Persians wanted to avenge their defeat they would arrive with a stronger military force. An Athenian army of ten thousand men was hardly up to such a challenge. Even Spartan assistance would not suffice to tip the scale in Athens' favor, especially if most other cities joined the enemy. Therefore it was essential for Athens to pursue negotiations, form alliances, and think about building up its military forces. The idea of increasing the size of the navy arose naturally from the fortification of the harbor at Piraeus.

The Persians did indeed renew their military preparations soon after Marathon. They would probably have attacked Greece again had Egypt not rebelled against their control in 486 and had Darius not died soon after that. These events caused a major delay; Xerxes, the new great king, had to consolidate his power before dealing with the Greeks, especially since a revolt broke out in Babylon around this time as well.

Some scholars today question whether the Athenians were particularly concerned about the Persians at this time. According to one source, Themistocles cited the war against Aegina as justification for the buildup of the navy as late as 483–482, though the presumably more threatening Persian rearmament was then in full swing.

In fact, the Persian threat must have loomed like a dark cloud over Attic foreign policy during these years. No matter how the Athenians tried to extricate themselves from their predicament, they can hardly have banished it from their thinking entirely. But preparing for war seems to have been difficult because they lacked unity, just as they had before Marathon. They were faced once more with the question of whether to fight or submit if the Persians invaded their territory. There were strong factions on both sides, and a protracted struggle may have taken place before the building of the navy began. Perhaps the proponents of this course gained the upper hand only when it became undeniably evident that the Persians meant business. The discovery of new silver veins at Maroneia in the Laurian mountains is also said to have been a factor.

The account according to which Themistocles used these silver deposits to finance the navy is well documented. It is possible that the funds for the construction of the two hundred ships were raised differently. We know, for example, that Cleinias, great-grandfather of Alcibiades, built a ship entirely at his expense and that he maintained a crew of two hundred men. He may have been an exception, however. Comparable contributions can hardly have been expected from most aristocrats, as quite a few were critical of Themistocles and hence opposed his plan to build up the navy. Perhaps the argument that the navy was needed against the Aeginetans was conceived to stimulate contributions from these opponents. It is also not beyond speculation that certain politicians initiated the prospecting for silver.

One way or another, sufficient funding was secured, and, finally, the building of the navy could get under way, along with all the other necessary and extensive preparations, including the hiring of craftsmen and workers from beyond Attica's borders. The first practice drills at sea and the mobilization of the entire citizenry for service in the navy followed.

At about the same time that the navy was getting under way, also in the year 483–482, Themistocles had one more elimination contest to pass, this time against a man named Aristides. Although Aristides is referred to pejoratively as "Datis's brother" on a pottery shard, he may not necessarily have opposed Athens' military preparations against the Persians. It is more likely that he objected to the building of the navy. In any case, he strongly opposed Themistocles' methods, and the conflict between the two men was in part a conflict between two totally different ways of thinking.

Aristides, son of Lysimachus, was not only a determined opponent of Themistocles, but also his exact opposite. He came from a noble family, and had supported Cleisthenes. He had been one of the ten generals at Marathon, where he took Miltiades' side and mediated between him and the generals who did not trust Miltiades' plan. During the battle Aristides' tribe fought at the center of the front line, where the Persians outnumbered the Greeks. And when the Attic army departed for Athens, he was entrusted with guarding the conquered Persian camp.

Aristides may not have been as selfless as he is depicted, but his reliability and honesty are beyond doubt. He was skilled in the arts of persuasion and argument; he gained influence by eliciting trust and, most important, earned the reputation of surpassing all others in wisdom. Later on, when it had to be determined how much according to their wealth the various cities should contribute to the Delian League, this task was assigned with general approval to Aristides, who performed it to everyone's satisfaction.

Where Themistocles was clever, wily, and perhaps somewhat deceitful, Aristides invariably acted nobly. The maneuvering of Themistocles, who planned his every move carefully and proceeded according to tactical considerations, stood in contrast to the uprightness of Aristides, who did only what he thought right in a given situation. An extremely conscientious and perhaps somewhat stodgy man, Aristides is said to have sought neither favor nor glory, in contrast to Themistocles' obvious burning ambition. Themistocles found it hard to accept his defeats and the success of others. Aristides was unperturbed by failure. He was sure of his convictions but seems never to have been unyielding and uncompromising in his advocacy of them.

The two men were of about the same age. Later in their lives, stories would be told of competitions between the two even as children and of their rivalry for the affections of the most beautiful boy in Athens. Whether or not this is true, they did find themselves in sharp opposition to each other in the second half of the 480s. This was almost inevitable given the seriousness and energy with which they both approached things. Aristides, in his righteousness, found Themistocles just as unbearable as Themistocles found him to be, with his hesitating, calm, often obstructionist manner, which appeared to Themistocles as rigidity. Each irritated the other, which seems to have made each more determined to do things his way.

It came to a point where Aristides with his great sense of duty (as shown at Marathon, where he willingly subordinated himself to Miltiades) opposed Themistocles' proposals even if he thought them useful, because he feared his opponent would otherwise become too powerful. We can only imagine Themistocles' impatience at Aristides' opposition. Everything depended on Athens' preparations for war, and this paragon of virtue, who was nonetheless plagued by political jealousy, did little but interfere. On one occasion, we are told, Aristides successfully defended a motion against determined opposition. Immediately after the vote was taken, however, his conscience stirred; he realized, or admitted to himself, that he had been wrong and withdrew his motion.

It seems that the old, traditional Greek spirit in Aristides rebelled against the utterly new ways of Themistocles, who was geared entirely to the practical and necessary; Themistocles shrugged off all convention if it interfered with his purpose.

It is not clear whether those among the population who opposed construction of the navy believed that it was still possible to meet the Persians in the conventional way, with just the phalanges of hoplites. They may also have feared that the *thetes*, members of the lowest economic class, would subsequently gain too much influence if they were employed on the ships. Whichever direction the sympathies of Aristides' supporters tended—and in case of doubt they were most likely to favor tradition—the result would have been irresolution, as was evident even in Aristides' own politics. Apparently it was difficult for a number of Athenian aristocrats to respond as the situation demanded, even in the face of danger. Instead, they directed their anger at Themistocles and his ways, which they considered "innovative," an epithet with negative connotations because innovation was regarded as a threat to the old ways. Perhaps it was Themistocles' cool and utterly rational manner, his lack of scruple, that upset them the most.

But when the assembly decided whom to ostracize, the majority sided with Themistocles, so that his rival was forced into exile. According to one account, a farmer who was voting asked his neighbor for assistance in writing Aristides' name on his shard. When Aristides—it was he the farmer approached—asked if he had done the farmer some harm, the man answered that he did not know him at all, but he was tired of all the talk about this "paragon of virtue." Perhaps his remark implies that many of the broader population were irritated by Aristides' manner.

Aristides went to Aegina. At Salamis he served Athens selflessly. He supported Themistocles, bearing no grudge for what had happened in the past. This, in view of his prestige, was a valuable tool in dealing with Attica's allies. It was under Aristides' command, for instance, that the Greeks occupied the island of Psyttalea.

Aristides' friends and supporters had little time to mourn his fate. Preparations for the war were all-consuming.

Historically, whenever the Greeks had to decide between war and peace, the proponents of war generally had a good chance of prevailing. A Greek could not be cowardly and run the risk of disgracing himself. When a clear choice existed between fighting and ignominious surrender, or when a majority or even a sizable minority strongly advocated war, there was not much the rest could do; they had to go along. Yet arguments against war must have been raised again and again, especially in view of the huge superiority of the hostile forces.

Prior to the second Persian invasion, the situation was complicated by extraordinary circumstances. This time the question was not, as at Marathon, whether to meet the enemy on the battlefield. Instead, prolonged arduous planning, preparations, and armamentation lay ahead. Above all else, the people had to accept the idea of an entirely new kind of warfare. Considering the important role the status of hoplite played in the Greek citizens' sense of self, their very identity as citizens was affected.

The Athenians nevertheless agreed to go ahead with a decisiveness that Themistocles, finally unhampered by opposition, urged upon them. Attica seemed to be in a state of emergency. The Athenians by this time fully supported building a fleet and practicing naval maneuvers, and they were unconditionally prepared—in spite of much hesitating when the time came—to give up their city and country rather than abandon the Greek cause. They were ready to stake everything they had on a sea battle, a battle they went on to win, in Thucydides' words, "more by decisiveness than luck and more by daring than power." In 481, the confederation that put an end to Athens' quarrels with Aegina was formed.

The victory at Salamis was only the first trial the Greeks passed. To be sure, Greek fears that Xerxes would seek a second battle were unfounded, even though before he departed he began, with the help of Phoenician merchant ships, to build a dam connecting the island to the mainland. But this was probably more a diversionary tactic to secure the safe departure for his forces.

The Persian navy then retreated eastward and the Persian army northward. Mardonius remained in Thessaly with the bulk of the army, while Xerxes hurried with a small contingent toward the Hellespont. Despite his haste, the journey took forty-five days because of unfavorable conditions, and upon reaching the Hellespont the Persians found their bridge of ships destroyed by a storm.

The Greeks attempted to pursue the Persian ships but were unable to catch up with them. Themistocles still wanted to sail to the Hellespont in order to cut off the Persians' escape route. As always, he was in favor of doing the job thoroughly. But Eurybiades, the Spartan commander, disagreed. He argued for letting the Persians go, figuring they would not return soon. The majority of the war council sided with him, whereupon Themistocles is said to have dispatched a messenger to tell Xerxes that it was he, Themistocles, who had dissuaded the Greeks from giving chase so that Xerxes might withdraw unhindered.

On the return journey, Themistocles demanded compensation from some of the islands that had surrendered to the Persians; some accounts claim he planned to pocket the money himself, but more likely the payments were received as a contribution toward the war effort. Ultimately, the spoils were divided. The greatest part went to the gods, primarily to Apollo of Delphi, in whose honor was fashioned the figure of a man forty-five feet tall and holding a ship's prow aloft. In addition, three Phoenician triremes were dedicated to the gods; one was placed on the isthmus in honor of Poseidon, one at Sunium, and the third on Salamis in honor of the hero Ajax.

Sometime in late fall or winter, when the Athenians were trying to reestablish a makeshift life in their devastated city, Alexander, king of Macedonia, to whom they were connected by bonds of hospitality, arrived with a message from the Persian general Mardonius. Xerxes was willing, Mardonius said, to forgive the Athenians everything. They could keep their land, adding to it as they chose, and live in freedom according to their own laws—if they were willing to become Persia's ally. Xerxes would even contribute to the rebuilding of their city. The leading naval and the greatest land power together would then subjugate the rest of Greece, and Athens would share in Persia's power by occupying a preferential position.

The Persians must have imagined this offer to be irresistible. As the head of an empire that included the most diverse peoples, including the Ionian Greeks, Xerxes found it almost incomprehensible that the Athenians would refuse. After all, they had felt his power, and Mardonius threatened that more Persian troops might be sent out against them if they declined the offer.

The Athenians, however, were outraged at the idea that they might relinquish their freedom and betray the Greeks. Never, as long as the sun traveled its present course, would they comply. When a Spartan delegation arrived with all possible speed to implore them to remain faithful to the Greeks, the Athenians found the very idea that Sparta could doubt their loyalty slanderous. Later, they maintained that their awe of Zeus had kept them from treason.

One does not muster all one's strength and risk losing one's country to win a great battle and then go on to betray the cause for the sake of which all this was done. And that cause had long since grown beyond the borders of Athens; it had become the cause of all Greece. What the Greeks had often claimed in the past as proof of their unity, they repeated again now: We share the same blood and the same language; honor the same gods and celebrate them with the same rites; even our customs are similar.

In addition, they cited the sacrilegious destruction of temples and sanctuaries at the hands of the Persian king as a cause for unity.

Great emphasis and value were placed during this period on Greek unity; a whole new sense of the difference between Greeks and barbarians arose. In the isonomy of Athens, this sense of Greek unity had especially strong emotional support (much more so than in sober Sparta). And it was to be some time before this unity began to erode.

Men like Themistocles must also have been aware that Persia was in no position to dispatch an unlimited number of new troops to Greece; after the costly defeat at Salamis, Xerxes could not mount another such campaign. The Athenians thought that the Greeks would be able to resist Mardonius's army as long as they remained united.

Alexander was sent away with the advice never again to approach the Greeks with such unthinkable suggestions. Aristides supposedly also asked the priests to curse anyone found negotiating with the Persians or defecting from the Greek confederation.

So, having been rebuffed, Xerxes gathered his forces, and the Persian army approached once more. The Persian commander, Mardonius, was intent on winning a glorious victory. On land, he thought, the Persians were clearly superior, and furthermore the naval defeat at Salamis did not prove their inferiority to the Greeks because the Persians had depended on contingents from subject nations, which, in his opinion, failed to fight valiantly. Mardonius organized a system by which beacons were to signal news of the victory to Asia by way of the Aegean islands. He paid no heed to the advice offered by his friends in Thebes, who recommended that he undermine Greek unity by sending envoys with rich presents to powerful individuals in various cities.

The Athenians hoped, indeed demanded, that the Spartans and their allies join them to meet the enemy in Boeotia. But the Spartans had no such intentions. They planned instead to defend themselves behind the wall they had almost finished building across the isthmus.

Once again, the Athenians were forced to evacuate Attica. The Persian army once again took possession of the land. Mardonius again sent an envoy to the Athenians, to Salamis, renewing his offer. One council member, Lycidas, is said to have spoken in favor of accepting, whereupon the other councilmen were so outraged that they surrounded the man and stoned him to death. Presumably, they removed from their heads the garlands they usually wore as symbols of office beforehand, as we know they did on a similar occasion. Lycidas's wife and children suffered a similar fate at the hands of the Attic women.

Meanwhile, day after day the Spartans had been putting off an Attic delegation sent out to urge them to hurry to Athens' aid. At last, a man of high repute from the neighboring city of Tegea explained to the Persians what they failed to realize; namely, that their wall could easily be circumvented by water—unless the Athenian navy prevented such a move.

With this realization, Sparta was mobilized and sent its regent, Pausanias, the guardian of one of Sparta's two kings, who was still underage, northward with an army. Several allied cities joined him. When Mardonius received news of their approach he left Attica and withdrew to Boeotia, fearing that his retreat might be cut off. Before he left, however, he devastated much of the land and property that had been left intact by the first Persian invasion.

Pausanias marched to Eleusis, where he met the Attic contingent, under Aristides' command, coming from Salamis. Both Aristides and Xanthippus had been elected generals, a gesture that seems to have been meant to make up for their earlier ostracism. It is not clear if Themistocles was reelected.

Finally, in August or September 479, the two sides, both with huge armies, met in battle in Boeotia, near Plataea. The combined Greek force, consisting of about 40,000 hoplites and over 60,000 lightly armed soldiers, was larger than any previous incarnation. Almost all the cities had sent sizable contingents. The commanders had to deal with completely new military challenges, including the problem of providing adequate food and water, which was extremely difficult because of the presence of the large Persian cavalry. There was also the difficulty of conducting a large-scale operation on a terrain so fractured by ridges and difficult to survey. It is doubtful whether Pausanias, the supreme commander, was equal to this task. In any case, the situation was much more difficult to assess than Salamis, and the Greeks were much less well prepared. The Persian force, though not as great as Herodotus claims, must at least have matched the Greeks in number, and it was accustomed to executing large-scale operations on land.

Lack of water forced the Greeks to retreat after a few days of waiting and a brief skirmish. Their army fell into such disarray that it could easily have been defeated, but the Persians, too, had lost sight of the overall situation and were only able to make limited use of their cavalry. Most important, their main force encountered the Spartans in an unfavorable spot, and in the ensuing combat Mardonius was slain and the Persians defeated; their weapons had proved inadequate for close combat, and their Greek support troops were vanquished by the Athenian contingent. Thus, the so-called Battle of Plataea was really a series of smaller encounters. The Persian survivors of the battle sought to escape toward the Hellespont. The war on the Greek mainland was over.

Meanwhile, the Greek navy left their rendezvous point on the island of Delos for Samos, whose envoys (along with others from Chios) had implored them to come, pointing out that a number of Ionian cities were prepared to rebel. The envoys appealed to their common belief in the same gods and urged the Greek navy to free these cities from Persian domination. The Persian navy, which lay at anchor off Samos, fled to the mainland out of fear that the Greeks would overwhelm them. At Mycale, where the Persian army charged with keeping Ionia calm was stationed, they pulled their ships on land and threw up a bulwark.

The Greeks are believed to have defeated this army on the day of the Battle of Plataea. After burning the Persian ships, the Greeks moved on to the Hellespont to destroy the Persian bridge, unaware that a storm had already done so.

For the moment there was no enemy left for the Greeks to fight. There was, however, the problem of the Greeks in Asia Minor who had defected from the Persians a second time. The Spartans suggested resettling them on the Greek mainland. Land and trade centers could be taken away from the cities that had sided with the Persians and given to the new settlers. As it was, the Ionians living in Asia Minor and on its coastal islands would remain free only if a Greek fleet protected them. The Spartans undoubtedly opposed such a solution. But the Athenians, who under the command of Xanthippus wanted to continue the war, argued in favor of inviting the Greek cities of Asia Minor into the confederation. That is exactly what was done, apparently with the consent of the Spartan commander, who had no time to consult officials at home.

Just how the war against the Persians was to be continued remained unclear. The Spartans had returned home. The Athenians went on to lay siege to Sestos on the Thracian Chersonese and about midway up the Hellespont.

Herodotus tells of a banquet put on by a Theban named Attaginus to which he invited fifty Persians and fifty Thebans. This took place as Mardonius and his troops were en route from Thessaly to Athens. According to the seating plan, each couch was to be occupied by a Persian and a Theban. One of the Persians, who knew Greek, said to his couchmate: "Look at these Persians enjoying dinner and look at the troops over there by the river. Soon only a few of these men will be alive." The Persian wept as he spoke. When the Theban suggested that Mardonius be told, the Persian replied: "My friend, what the gods have ordained man cannot change. Nobody who is told the truth wants to believe it. Many Persians know it very well, but we continue to obey our commanders because we cannot do otherwise. The worst suffering is to know what will happen but be impotent to prevent it."

Was, then, the Greek victory over the Persians the result of the Persian unfamiliarity with Greek terrain and waters? Or was it a consequence of the qualitative superiority of the Greeks?

The role chance and geography played cannot be ignored. Yet the Greeks evidently had a number of qualities that enabled them not only to create a culture different from all others but also one that excelled in military matters. There is much to suggest that Themistocles' kind of planning—his refusal to be cowed by the enemy's numerical superiority, his ability to devise a strategy based on the enemy's weakness, his recognition that victory was possible—was a direct product of the special bent of intelligence the Greeks were forced to develop. The same is true of the Athenians' willingness to go along with Themistocles. Quite apart from this, the Spartans, the newly powerful and self-confident Athenians, and their allies had become strong enough militarily that a Greek victory, if the gods favored both sides evenly, was not at all unlikely.

The Persians had come and gone, but nothing was settled. The fact that the Greek David had defeated the Persian Goliath was bound to have consequences. The conflict between the Greek and the Persian realms was bound to erupt again violently, this time in the east.

After the Battle of Plataea, the Greeks decided to extinguish all the sacred fires in the cities the Persians had occupied—they considered them defiled—and replace them with fires obtained from the Delphic shrine. On the advice of the oracle, an altar to Zeus the liberator was erected at Plataea, where the Plataeans were to offer sacrifices in the name of the Greeks and Olympic games were to be held every four years.

The dead were buried on the battlefield as had been done at Marathon, separated by city of origin. A tenth of the war spoils was dedicated to Delphi, where a tripod of gold' was erected on a stand formed by a three-headed snake. This memorial can still be seen in Istanbul. Inscribed on the stand were the names of the Greek cities that had taken part in the war.

6

From Devastation to Democracy:
479–461

In contrast to Greek architecture, all other architectures, whether oriental or modern, Asiatic or European, try to use mass and quantity as the language of the sublime. At Paestum, Pompeii, and Athens, however, as before all Greek architecture, we stand amazed at the modest quantities with which the Greeks could express, and delighted in expressing, the sublime.

—FRIEDRICH NIETZSCHE

At times of revolutionary transformation, people realize only gradually that the whole world around them is changing. How could the Athenians have grasped right away what their victory over the Persians meant? The event was much too great to fit quickly into their conceptions about the world.

So, without fully knowing what was happening, the Athenians found themselves on a path that led them rapidly to a complete transformation. They probably were not aware of it, but in a sense they became strangers to themselves. Without adequate preparation, without time to get used to their new role, they had become a great power. They would, in due course, prove able to deal with the problems associated with this status. They would accomplish all that was demanded of them and more. But in the process they would feel a great need to find ways of comprehending their new circumstances. Tragedy turned out to be one means for dealing with this need, leading us to wonder what role art played for the Athenians in enabling them to rise to the political demands confronting them.

When the Athenians returned to their homeland a second time in the late summer or fall of 479, most of them must have hoped or believed that they could now finally resume their normal lives.

The Persians had come and been repelled. Of course, the losses were heavy. Fathers, husbands, brothers, sons, and friends had been killed. Losses in property had to be made up for; homes, barns, public buildings, and shrines rebuilt. But the fact that they had won must have given the Athenians great satisfaction.

On the drinking vessels made in the following years are a number of pictures that show the Persian enemy in extremely degrading positions. This was completely contrary to the custom that prevailed in literary works of assigning the same rights and dignity to friend and enemy, be they Greeks or barbarians. Was the contempt a sign of the huge relief felt after the victory? Did liberation turn into a triumphant feeling of superiority? Or were the conventions of the symposia for which these vessels were made different from those found in the Homeric epics, the tragedies, and the histories of Herodotus?

The pictures are probably expressions of a passing phase of arrogance. The Greeks' relationship to the Eastern high cultures was complex. In the past the Greeks had been culturally and militarily inferior to the Lydians, not to mention the Persians. Now for the first time, after they had exposed themselves to great peril, the balance seemed to have tipped clearly in their favor. Their feelings of superiority demanded expression, especially following the excitement, worry, and state of emergency that had prevailed for years, and also because the hard work of building their navy remained unforgotten. For a long time to come, conversations, reminiscences, and dreams were dominated by the great event—its interpretation, the significance of the Greeks' victory over a world power. "Who and of what family are you? How old are you? What age were you when the Medes came?" Those were the questions, according to Xenophanes, that men asked each other sitting by the fire in the winter, drinking wine. The first incursions of the Persians in Ionia in the middle of the sixth century B.C. and the later invasion of Greece itself were dramatic enough events that Greeks reorganized their biographies around them.

The battles of Marathon, Salamis, and Plataea took their places next to the great deeds of mythical heroes. Thus, in the great *stoa poikile*, the Hall of Colors on the north end of the agora, which was donated by Peisianax of the Alcmaeonid family around 460, a painting of the Battle of Marathon was flanked by a scene from the Trojan War and one depicting the Athenians fighting the Amazons. Cimon, son of Miltiades and most likely Peisianax's brother-in-law, had commissioned them. Two of the painters are known by name: Polygnotus and Micon. The popular assembly must have approved the project and even seems to have had a say in some of its particulars.

The mythical battles between East and West—that is, between Greeks and barbarians, or, worse yet, the Amazons—seemed like earlier versions of Athens' recent struggles. Cimon had a personal reason for choosing Marathon rather than Salamis as the subject for the painting, since his

A Persian signaling his willingness to serve as a male prostitute. An accompanying inscription indicates that this humiliating depiction referred to the Persian defeat in the battle at the Eurymedon River. Red-figured pitcher. Hamburg, Museum für Kunst und Gewerbe.

father had commanded at Marathon, but the choice was perhaps logical for the Athenians as well, since only at Marathon had they won without help. And it was the hoplites who had secured the victory.

At the same time that life tried to return to normal, war continued. The confederation was still intact, and Samos, Chios, Lesbos, and some other islands had joined it. In the mother country the idea arose of punishing the Greek cities that had sided with the Persians. The Spartans, in particular, favored this course. Meanwhile, the Athenian navy, operating off the coast of Asia Minor, besieged and took the city of Sestos, which overlooked the entry to the Hellespont. Control of the Hellespont was important for access to the Black Sea, where much of the Greek and especially the Athenian grain came from. After the city was captured, some of the ropes from Xerxes' bridge of ships were found there, taken home, and placed in temples. The region's satrap, notorious for having desecrated a holy Greek shrine, was crucified with enthusiastic Greek approval.

Where all this could or should lead in the long run was probably unclear. Themistocles, of course, had very specific ideas, and the Spartans worried that they would be directly affected. Themistocles was adept at prognosticating, at seeing through surface appearances and recognizing the underlying laws any power had to obey. As for the Spartans, whatever they as individuals claimed to think and want was meaningless compared to their commitment to their common purpose. Themistocles realized that a gulf was opening up between Athens and Sparta, and that Athens had to act on this knowledge.

Because Thebes and Thessaly had joined the Persians, the Spartans proposed excluding them from the Amphictionic League, an alliance formed to ensure the Delphic oracle's independence, but Themistocles objected out of concern that this might help Sparta strengthen its role as leader on the mainland. An attempt to punish Persian sympathizers among the Greeks was also foiled. All Thebes was asked to do was hand over a few prominent men. A Spartan military expedition against Thessaly failed to accomplish its mission.

It is possible that the Spartans did not press their cause forcefully enough. Their military potential was now limited. The warrior caste of the Spartiates numbered only about eight thousand, and since the Spartans could not agree on allowing men without the required wealth to join this caste, its number kept gradually shrinking. The Spartans also had to be on constant alert against possible rebellions among the helots, an indigenous people subjugated by the Spartans. Enough ethnic cohesion remained among them to act collectively whenever opportunity presented itself.

Although the Spartans could sometimes intervene quite successfully in individual conflicts and tried to give permanence to the results of their interventions through treaties, conducting an energetic, power-based foreign policy with long-term goals was difficult for them outside the Peloponnese. Whereas the Athenians, as would later be observed, thought they benefited from operations far from their own city, the Spartans feared such activities because of the risk of losing what they already had.

Acropolis wall, seen from the agora. This wall was built of the "Persian rubble" and thus served as a permanent reminder of Xerxes' destruction of religious shrines. The bases of the columns of the old temple of Athena are clearly visible.

. . .

Soon after their return to the city, the Athenians began rebuilding their city walls, a strange priority since there was so much else to be done: prepare for winter, plant fields, and restore farms and workshops to working order. Parts of the old wall are said to have been intact, but when rebuilt the ramparts were moved outward in several directions. The population had increased, and further growth was anticipated.

It was not long, probably by late fall in 479, before a Spartan delegation appeared and asked the Athenians to stop rebuilding their walls. They urged that no cities outside the Peloponnese be fortified from then on, to prevent any returning Persian forces from entrenching themselves behind these walls. In such a situation, the Spartans suggested, the Peloponnese was large enough to offer shelter to everyone. Any counter-offensive, they argued, would be launched from there. Thucydides, who reports this, considered this argument a flimsy one but also suggests that it was not so much the Spartans as their allies who insisted on sending the delegation. Sparta's allies feared the Athenians were intent on expanding their own power.

The mention of a future Persian invasion was perhaps not as outlandish as it seems. Apparently there were plans for a common strategy under Spartan leadership, and there was even talk of raising a Panhellenic brigade. Under such conditions splitting up the forces to defend individual cities could indeed have been disadvantageous and the idea of dismantling all fortifications outside the Peloponnese reasonable. But whatever other motives were involved, the ultimate purpose of their request was to strengthen Sparta as a land power and put a check on the maritime power of Athens.

While Sparta's motives in this negotiation are clear, the ensuing developments are puzzling. Why didn't the Athenians object to interference in their affairs? Instead they decided, on Themistocles' advice, to send their own delegation to Sparta. Themistocles seems to have discussed with some of the other politicians, including Aristides, what he had in mind. He wanted to travel ahead alone and tell the Spartans that he could not negotiate with them until the other delegates arrived. These delegates, however, were not to leave Athens until the wall was high enough to protect defenders of the city. This is exactly the plan that was executed. As more and more reports of the wall-building reached Sparta, including further protests against it from Sparta's allies, Themistocles suggested that the Spartans send delegates of their own to check out the reports rather than relying on rumors. At the same time, he sent word to the Athenians to detain the Spartan delegates until the Athenian delegates returned from Sparta. In this way, the affair nearly developed into a hostage crisis.

When the two other Attic delegates—Aristides and Habronichus, son of Lysicles—finally arrived in Sparta, Themistocles declared that Athens was now well enough fortified to defend its inhabitants and that the Spartans should be aware in the future that the Athenians were quite capable of judging what was best for them and the general good. They had recognized without Spartan help the necessity of evacuating their city and fighting a naval battle at Salamis. Now they deemed it appropriate to fortify their city, and Themistocles argued that this, too, was in the interest of their fellow Greek confederates, for it was impossible to have equal weight in common councils if one city-state lacked the military preparedness of the others. Either everybody should live in open cities, including the Peloponnesians, or Sparta had to admit that Athens' fortification was justified. The wall had to be rebuilt because of the Persians, less as a protection against this enemy than as a symbol of Athens' strength among its allies.

The Spartans replied that they had only intended to offer advice. Whatever ill feeling remained between the two cities was repressed so that both delegations could return home.

But had the situation really been that serious? Was there really reason for the Athenians to expect, or at least fear, that the Spartans would dispatch an army to prevent the building of fortifications? Would the Spartans really have taken Themistocles hostage?

One hesitates to accept this view, otherwise the purpose of Themistocles' entire maneuver is unclear. It may have been devised less to deceive the Spartans than the Athenians. It is possible that the journey was undertaken to speed the building, as otherwise this laborious undertaking might

ATHENS

have been postponed indefinitely. Internal opponents of Athens' ambitious policies may have been scheming to turn the people's understandable desire for peace to their own advantage—perhaps men like the
aristocrats who we are told had wanted to conspire against isonomy
before the battle at Plataea.

Or the Athenians may have been reluctant to oppose the Spartans
openly. No matter how one looks at it, the Athenians had to consider at
least the possibility of a Spartan intervention. In Cleisthenes' day, the
Spartans had taken up arms when they felt Athens was getting too powerful. Now Sparta had reason to fear that Athens was establishing a hegemony in the Aegean, and the appeal to a future anti-Persian strategy
provided a plausible argument. It concealed Spartan jealousy, and it created a pressure on Athens not to move too far away from the solidarity of
the Greeks, or from Sparta's influence. Supposedly, the Spartans debated
declaring war against Athens in the mid-470s.

The affair of the rebuilding of the wall of Athens gives us a pretty
good picture of the situation at that time. Having jointly overcome the
danger of Persian aggression made possible a unification of the Greeks—
or, more precisely, made the continuation and strengthening of their
alliance a possibility to be seriously considered. This would have been in
the interest of Spartan politics. But the Athenians had already set out on
their own path. Others may not have known where Athens was headed,
but the Athenians' initiative was in any case alarming. Great uncertainty
arose among the city-states.

The Athenians had pursued the building of their walls with amazing
dedication. Men, women, children, non-citizens, and slaves were forced
to work on it. Nothing was sacred, no gravestone, no wall, no pillar—
everything that could be used was dragged to the wall. In all likelihood,
in the wake of the evacuation and the plundering of the country, this was
done without even the aid of ox carts.

The wall, over six kilometers long, and its speedy completion were
a remarkable feat of organization, architecture, physical exertion, and
politics. The cooperation of Themistocles and Aristides is also notable,
though after Salamis it comes as less of a surprise.

. . .

Policies initiated under Cleisthenes were now coming to fruition. As
Themistocles had declared in Sparta, Athens now no longer recognized
any authority above itself, be it Sparta or members of the alliance formed
against the Persians. But this meant that Athens' rational method of proceeding and its navy, which had led the way to victory at Salamis, took
on a rather sinister aspect in the eyes of non-Athenians. The forces that
had once functioned merely as naval support for Sparta's land army now
constituted a possible threat.

Not just the political sphere of the Greeks had doubled, but potentially the extent of their domain, which now took in all of the Aegean.
Themistocles had urged repeatedly that Athens turn its attention seaward,
saying that three things could make the city strong: the ability to defend
against attack by land, a sufficiently ample treasury, and a large navy.
Money, too, had ceased to be a problem. But where would all this lead?

In the following year, 478, the confederation, enlarged by several other
island cities, resumed its war against Persia. The Athenians and the Greeks
east of the Aegean joined in the conflict because they wanted to, but many
other communities did so out of necessity. Although the Spartans had said
the Ionians should be left to their fate, they nonetheless joined in the campaign because they did not want to be left out and, probably even more so,
because they did not want the Athenians to take charge. Thus a Greek fleet
under Pausanias's command sailed for Cyprus with the intent of ending
Persia's rule there, intimidating its supporters, and reinforcing the Greeks
who lived there. Various cities were won over to the Greek side. Then the
Greeks headed for the Bosphorus and conquered the city of Byzantium,
which had been held by a Persian garrison. The Greeks wanted to control
access to the Aegean Sea from both the north and the east.

The Spartans had been intent on maintaining the leadership of
the confederated forces, but Pausanias, with his exacting ways, arrogance,
and supposed cruelty, made himself so unpopular among the Greeks,

especially the eastern Greeks, that many of them turned to the Athenians, asking them to take over the command. Only the Peloponnesian contingents failed to join in this movement. Athens was indeed more suited for the leadership role, but the high esteem the Spartans enjoyed, regardless of actual performance, continued to give them the advantage.

Although Pausanias had been cleared of the charges raised against him, including having secret contacts with the Persians, the Spartans sent a replacement general by the name of Dorcis to accompany a small force to Byzantium the following spring. Spartan enthusiasm for the undertaking had grown lukewarm, however. When the confederate cities failed to offer Dorcis the command as a matter of course, he returned home, and the Spartans decided to have no further part in the war. They had grown tired of it, Thucydides reports, and also worried that their men would be exposed to too many temptations away from home. The refusal of the Athenians to cooperate with them may have contributed to their decision, but their main reason for withdrawing was that the enterprise was beyond their capabilities.

Negotiations to form a new alliance of various Greek cities under Athenian leadership must have begun as early as the winter of 478–477, and messengers were subsequently sent out to invite the Greek cities to a meeting on the island of Delos.

The alliance, commonly called the Delian League by modern historians, was probably formed in the spring of 477. It is unclear just who the original members were, but among them were numerous island city-states, probably including many of the small Cyclades islands and the three cities on Rhodes. Most Ionian cities on the Asian mainland also joined early, as, in all likelihood, did Byzantium and some cities on the Chalcidice. We know that the league later numbered over one hundred and eventually grew to over two hundred members, but only in a few cases do we know when they joined.

Treaties between Athens and the individual cities were signed. Oaths of perpetual loyalty were sworn and a symbolic clump of metal dropped in the sea. The alliance was to remain in force as long as the clump did not rise to the surface. Using a formula that probably went back to the conflicts between aristocratic factions in Athens, the two parties swore "to have the same friends and enemies."

An assembly of the league members was instituted and resolved to meet at least once a year on Delos to deal with all problems affecting the league. The meetings may have been held at the great festival of Apollo of Delos, which the Athenians, Ionians, and island dwellers had been celebrating together every spring for some time. Apollo of Delos was originally the league's patron deity.

The league members were obliged to supply hoplites and contribute toward the navy for common campaigns, either by sending ships whenever an operation was undertaken or by paying regular sums of money. The league's assets were to be kept on Delos, probably in Apollo's temple. The level of each city's contribution was to be set according to its revenues. This assessment was made by Aristides, who lived up to his reputation for honesty. The league's total income was considerably less than the tribute the Greek cities in Asia Minor alone had previously had to pay to the Persians. The ten treasurers *(hellenotamiai)* of the league were all Athenians.

The total annual income of the league originally came to 460 talents. A rower's wage was set at three obols, or half a drachma. With a crew of about two hundred, the cost of manning a ship was about 100 drachmas a day or 3,000 drachmas, that is, half a talent, per month. A fleet of one hundred ships, if it operated for six months, cost 300 talents in wages. Sometimes more ships were needed, so even if we take into account that some ships may have been provided without charge by league members, the amount of the tributes does not seem very high, especially since additional ships had to be built. At least some of the costs for the dockyards in Athens may have been billed to the league's treasury as well. Athon's

It was taken for granted that the Athenians would assume command, role shoulder most of the war's burden, and be compensated financially in return.

The goal of the league was to free the Greek cities in Asia Minor from Persian domination and guarantee their liberty for all time. In addition, goal the Greeks wanted revenge for all they had suffered at Persian hands. Persian rule had been oppressive before, but now the former discontent

257

was magnified by enmity and distrust, by a new consciousness of antagonism and by the Greeks' newly emerged passion for freedom. Everybody must have realized that this freedom could not be attained without Athens and that maintaining this freedom would be an ongoing problem. The open-endedness of the alliance was therefore far from being in Athens' interest alone.

The intent of the phrase "to have the same friends and enemies" was obvious as far as the enemy was concerned. It was meant to encourage acting in concert, friendship among the Greeks, and opposition to Persia. Such friendship—prescribing not just abstinence from hostilities but long-term cooperation—was something radically new for many of the Greek cities. But during this brief but momentous episode in Greek history, it was the logical course to take. Confronted with external danger, the Greeks felt so deeply united that discord and quarrels between cities could be referred to by the same term (stásis) used to describe discord among the citizenry, and were condemned with similar vehemence.

Sparta and its Peloponnesian allies surely reacted differently to this assertion of friendship. We don't know which other cities apart from Athens joined the Delian League at that time, but the ones that did ally themselves with Athens were almost exclusively city-states that had at one point or another been subjugated by or had joined the Persians. Having only recently, with great difficulty, freed themselves from foreign rule may have made it easier for them to accept the hegemony of this Greek ally whose strength they needed.

But precisely because the league did not include all the Greek cities, the vagueness of the phrase "to have the same friends and enemies" was bound to become problematic. If a city belonging to the league was attacked by an outside power, support by the allies was obviously necessary, though sometimes given reluctantly. But what if one of the allied cities decided independently to declare a non-league city its enemy?

Who had the right to define the enemy? And who would later, when the alliance expanded, decide who was a friend? The treaties Sparta signed with its allies in that period were clearer in this respect. They stated that the allies were to have the same friends and enemies as Sparta.

They were to follow the hegemonial power, no matter whom it led them against, and exceptions were made only upon request by the assembly of the allies. Apparently this arrangement went back to the regulations of the Peloponnesian League that had been in force since the late sixth century; that is, since the first conflicts with Athens. We assume that the Delian League assigned the determination of friend and enemy to the assembly from the beginning. For although the common struggle against Persia was foremost in everyone's mind at the time, it was still essential to take precautions against possible misapplications of the oath's wording.

It is unclear whether Athens' vote in the league's assembly counted for more than the others' or whether Athens was considered a partner to the assembly or a member of it. In either case, it was practically impossible for the league to do anything against Athens' will. On the contrary, with the help of many small and insignificant cities, Athens probably imposed its will on the assembly. Still, the unity of the alliance was apparently secured by invoking the clause about having common friends and enemies. Given the makeup of the leadership in Athens, it hardly occurred to anyone there how much the members of the Delian League would subsequently be drawn into Athens' intra-Greek politics.

Nor was it necessarily foreseeable that the league would gradually promote Athens' hegemony, although it seems that the balance of power was bound to shift steadily in this city's favor. Because many cities were too small to man their own warships, Athens acquired a superiority over its partners that far exceeded Sparta's over its allies. Where the contribution to common enterprises consisted of providing hoplites, the cities remained in charge of their own forces. But when they paid money, part of it always went to the leading partner. Thus the cities of the Delian League strengthened Athens' power at the cost of their own strength.

One source states that Athens' confederates turned from capable warriors into complacent farmers and businessmen. A kind of division of labor took place: Athens went to war, assimilated power, and largely determined policies while the others devoted themselves more to economic matters. This is an exaggeration, especially since the poleis had to contribute hoplites, but it is not altogether off the mark.

. . .

If we try to reconstruct the creation of the Delian League, we find one step leading logically to the next. At the beginning was Athens with the new consciousness of its potential. Its navy had served its intended purpose at Salamis, and the city was now concerned that it not be allowed to fall idle and deteriorate. The *thetes*, the lowest of the four socioeconomic classes, now saw a prospect of earning good money and playing an important role as rowers in the navy. Athens also thought of itself as the Ionians' mother city. And behind all this was the great value placed on the idea of Greek freedom and a strong sense of contrast between East and West. It would have been difficult indeed—and would have required a great self-denial—for the Athenians to keep out of the affairs the Asian Greeks were trying to draw them into. That Athens should take on the leading role was self-evident to all. Of course, the isonomous city's huge ambitions contributed to the situation. The citizens began to see their identity in their military role, and their solidarity centered increasingly on the communal fulfillment of this new role.

In spite of these factors, the course the Athenians chose and embarked upon is extraordinary. Did they really think they could take the Greek cities in Asia away from the Persians? To Themistocles' bold and calculating mind it may have seemed that the Greeks were a match for the Persian military. There was the hope that internal problems would hamper the Persians or that the situation on the western periphery of their realm would not seem important enough to cause them to assemble and dispatch an army again. The Athenians may have seen through Persia's great show of power and put great trust in what could be accomplished by their own small, yet largely battle-ready population supplemented by the combined forces of the Delian League. They may also have felt that if they wanted to be safe from future attacks, they had no choice but to make as many of their allies as possible dependent on them.

But there is a considerable difference between such strategic calculations and the willingness to accept the consequences they imply. The decision was up to the popular assembly, where the very men who would have to do the fighting voted. But they proved willing, perhaps because they felt a responsibility toward the Ionian Greeks, as well as because the promise of the power to be gained by the venture must also have appealed to them. They may also have felt they had nothing to lose.

The commitment was easier for the Athenians than for the Spartans. Where the Spartans' possibilities were severely limited, Athens could act much more freely. Many of its citizens could become professional soldiers and leave whenever necessary without endangering the civic order. For one thing there were more slaves in the city of Athens, some of whom were able to conduct the work of the absent citizens during wartime, but they were slaves who had been bought. Unlike the Spartans' slaves, they came from all parts of the world and, according to Greek experience, had little inclination and no opportunity to rebel. They shared no common interests because their individual situations differed vastly. For this reason, Athens ran less of a risk than Sparta of suffering a slave uprising during wartime.

Before the Athenians had a chance, then, to return to their old ways, a different concept of normalcy began to take shape, characterized by an ambitious foreign policy. Their new ways created the impression, which Thucydides attributes to the Corinthians, that the Athenians were inherently unable to remain peaceful or to leave others in peace.

The Athenians could hardly have realized what they were embarking upon. They could not possibly have pictured the consequences of their policies, either socially—in terms of domestic politics, the city government, philosophy, art—or in terms of world history.

It is unclear who led Athens at this time. Aristides still played a role; Themistocles' name is hardly mentioned in the surviving accounts of the era. Cimon may already have become the most influential figure; from 478–477 on he was the most prominent of the *strategoi*. He pursued his policies in close consultation with Sparta. Although the Spartans did not participate in military undertakings, they remained part of the confederation, and Cimon placed great value on remaining on good terms with them. To this extent, then, the conflict Themistocles had predicted had not yet materialized between Athens and Sparta.

. . .

The Athenians installed the new statue of the tyrannicides Harmodius and Aristogiton by Critius and Nesiotes in the agora in the year 477–476. The work must have been commissioned immediately after their return home to the destroyed city. The picture of Athens' liberators was considered an essential part of the new beginning. This new work differed from the first statue of the tyrannicides in that the two figures are not just standing next to each other but are shown at the very moment of their deed, purposefully, arms raised to strike. Depicting figures in motion now became the challenge of free-standing sculpture. The figures are meant to inspire horror, whereas all earlier depictions of horror, such as images of the Gorgons, referred to the supernatural world.

In the spring of 476, at the festival of the Great Dionysia, the first of two tragedies that would be written about the Persian Wars was performed. Its author was Phrynichus, and Themistocles acted as the *choregos*, or sponsor, of the play by meeting all production expenses. He himself recorded this fact on an inscription.

In the summer of 476, under Cimon's command, the Attic navy sailed from Byzantium to Eion at the mouth of the river Strymon. The city was Persia's most important stronghold on the northern coast of the Aegean, with huge stores of supplies. The Athenians easily defeated the Persian land army and besieged the city. When food eventually ran out and made further defense of the city impossible, Boges, the Persian commander, built a huge funeral pyre on which he burned the bodies of his wife, children, concubines, and servants, all of whom he had ordered killed. Then, after ordering all the city's gold and silver be thrown from the ramparts into the Strymon, he leaped into the fire himself. Herodotus writes that even in his time the Persians still praised Boges and did so with justice. After the city was sacked, its inhabitants were sold as slaves, and Athenians settled in it, probably along with other Greeks. Some other Persian strongholds in the area may have been taken, but there are no further reports of military engagements with the Persians during those years. They seem to have left the region of Greek settlements with minimal fighting. Only a few parts of the Chersonese had to be wrested from them by force.

The tyrannicides Harmodius and Aristogiton. Copy of the original statue by Critius and Nesiotes that was set up on the agora in 477–476 B.C. Exactly how the two figures were placed in relation to each other is subject to debate. Naples, National Museum.

For this reason Cimon was free to concentrate on other things. He conquered the island of Scyrus, supposedly because an oracle had instructed him to, but also because the piracy of its inhabitants made nearby waters unsafe. Scyrus lay along the important sea route from the Black Sea to Euboea and Athens, and so it was imperative that Athens remain in control of the seas there. Scyrus's population was sold into slavery and new settlers were brought to the island.

According to an old myth, Athens' King Theseus had been slain on Scyrus. Cimon searched painstakingly for his remains, and discovered what he believed to be Theseus's bones in a stone coffin that also contained the tip of a lance and a sword. He took them back on his admiral's ship, and the Athenians then carried them in solemn procession to a new resting place south of the agora, where they were buried. This area, the Theseum, was declared sacred, and every year Theseus was paid hero's honors in the form of offerings and games.

Ever since Cleisthenes, the Athenians had attributed their unity to this legendary founding hero. Now they could also draw upon the power that emanated from his grave. For Cimon, retrieving Theseus's bones gave him the opportunity to link his name to that of the great hero. About fifteen years later, Cimon commissioned a painting of the Battle of Marathon, which was set up in the *stoa poikile*. The picture showed Theseus rising out of the earth to aid his compatriots. It was hardly by chance that the Athenians commemorated the founding of Athens' unity and freedom then, on the eve of an epoch during which this polis would reach out far beyond its existing borders. The Athenians seem to have sought reassurance from their historical and legendary past.

As a token of gratitude for his leadership, the popular assembly granted Cimon permission to set up three herms with inscriptions. He could not make specific mention of his own name, but the deeds recorded would keep it alive. The inscriptions praised the Athenians and their generals and justified Athens' claim to leadership among the Greeks.

During these years, the Athenians were kept busy expanding the Delian League, and in the process, extending their control over the Aegean region.

They tried to get as many cities as possible along the coasts of the mainland and on the islands to join, not so much for the sake of obtaining contributions and enlarging their navy as of having a broad network of reliable allies and strongholds. Many of these cities responded to Athens' pleas and its diplomatic or economic pressure. Occasionally Athens resorted to military force, presumably when a city had earlier been a Persian ally. This was the case with Carystus on Euboea, although an agreement was reached before any battle was fought.

It was necessary for Athens to gain an overview of the entire region it sought to dominate. A network of connections had to be established with various cities and the leading aristocrats in them. Athens must have engaged in lively diplomatic activity and sent its navy to distant points. The periodic meetings of the league's assembly at Delos served at best to draw the members' disparate ambitions together as a single, coherent force. The domestic policies of many cities, of which hardly any notice had been taken in the past, and the relationships between these cities now became a matter of interest to the Athenians, who made sure they knew of any contacts between the Persians and cities belonging to the league or located on its periphery.

Many consequences arose from the fact that Athens was no longer concerned only with its own affairs. The city had been catapulted from the status of a canton to that of a hegemonic power in the Aegean, an unprecedented role in that region. Samos and Naxos, or their respective tyrants, had at times ruled over the islands in their area, but the possibility of dominating the entire Aegean had never before arisen. Initially the Athenians didn't have to do a great deal to maintain their waxing power; the Greeks' commitment to stick together against the Persians was firm. But soon enough Athens had to expand its own knowledge and connections, and do so as quickly as possible. It was no longer just one city among others. The Aegean was no longer a sea in and around which cities lived more or less independently of one another. It was a region where everything began to become interconnected.

Foreign policy within the league and beyond it now became a major concern. Although Athens restricted its diplomatic activities to the league, it could hardly hide altogether that these activities also concerned the relationship between the Delian League and the Peloponnesian League, or that the relations between these two hegemonies were affected by everything that happened within each of them.

For the time being the antagonism between Athens and Sparta remained dormant, thanks at least partly to Cimon. Caught up in the Greek ideology of freedom, Sparta was unable to react against Athens' attacks on the Persians, the development of the Delian League, nor, consequently, against many of its rival's high-handed actions once Sparta had withdrawn from the confederation. Thus the Persians continued for a while to affect Greek politics passively, but it would be a long time before there was any possibility for them to play a more active role.

As a result of the new political situation, the old institution of the Areopagus found its functions within Athens' government vastly expanded. In this council sat most of the men who were familiar with the wider world because of past travel, personal connections, family ties, and hospitality. They could therefore be sent out as envoys. In this relatively small circle, consisting of at most three hundred men, the whole complex subject of Attic foreign policy was discussed and analyzed.

The Areopagus was essential in the new Athens. Without it, the city would hardly have been able to arrive at appropriate policies or execute them. Sources call the Areopagus "the Council" while referring to the other council as "the Five Hundred." Little is known about the scope of Areopagus authority. Apart from certain legal functions its main significance may have been that the government officials were accountable to it. One source reveals that the Areopagus had to see to it that the city was governed in accordance with the laws. Officials had good reason for consulting the Areopagus on difficult issues.

But the power that the Areopagus exercised grew far more rapidly during the years after the Persian Wars than the functions assigned to it. Contemporary reports seem to indicate that the Areopagus exacted authority over the Five Hundred and the popular assembly. Its influence helped stabilize and enforce isonomous governance in Athens.

. . .

Around 470, for the first time, a city seceded from the Delian League. The citizens of Naxos apparently no longer saw any need for belonging to the group. The danger that had brought the cities together seemed to have disappeared and with it any reason for continuing to meet the obligations they had agreed to when they joined. Perhaps Naxos simply acted openly on feelings that were widespread among the city-states.

The Athenians responded by laying the city under siege. After Naxos' defeat, Athens imposed an unknown punishment. It can be assumed that the city's walls were razed, that it had to pay war reparations, and that it was barred from the league's assemblies. Perhaps it lost what would now be called "autonomy" and had to put up with Athens' interference in its internal government. In any case, Naxos later rejoined the league, but its contribution showed it no longer possessed its earlier economic resources; the punishment imposed must have been severe indeed. Remarkably, no other members defected, and the Spartans took no interest in this affair.

Soon after completion of Athens' fortification, a wall was built to protect the harbor city Piraeus against approaches by land. This time there was no need to rush, and the wall was constructed of huge, carefully hewn blocks of stone set end to end. Soon after this the great boat sheds in the naval harbors of Munychia and Zea on the south side of the peninsula were built, for it was important not to leave the wooden triremes in the water any longer than necessary. In addition, Themistocles urged Athens to build twenty ships annually, a modest program compared to the production of the late 480s, but presumably executed more carefully.

The ships being built were of a different type. Cimon favored a new naval tactic that relied more on boarding enemy vessels than on ramming them. How much tactical advantage was gained by this is debatable, but it increased the importance of the hoplites fighting onboard and diminished that of the rowers. This method of fighting may also have appealed more to Cimon because he was a general indebted to tradition and oriented more to land battles.

All this work being done in Athens attracted workmen, merchants, and men wanting to serve as oarsmen in the Attic navy. They came from all over Greece and soon, in smaller numbers, from alien countries as well. It seems possible that they were granted exemption from taxation, at least when they were few in number.

It was not long thereafter that the status of "metic" came into being. Metics were aliens who were granted permanent residence in Attica. In order to qualify for this status a person needed a sponsor to represent him before the law and register him in his deme. Metics had to pay an annual poll tax of 12 drachmas (a rower's wages for 24 days' labor; most artisans probably earned more). They were not allowed to buy real estate and had no political rights but they were under the protection of the community and its courts. Exempt from political and—except at times of great danger—military duties, they could devote themselves exclusively to work and contributed significantly to Athens' economy. Their number ultimately reached between 10,000 and 20,000, as compared to approximately 40,000 citizens.

Economic competition was spurred by artisans from different regions working side by side, and the shared expertise also led to technical advances. Shipbuilding was pursued vigorously and saw more than its share of innovation.

From time to time, replacements had to be found to do the work of the *thetes* as craftsmen, since many of them became oarsmen. Slaves were often used to fill in the gaps.

Trade must also have received a boost at about this time. Wood for shipbuilding must have been imported at this point, if not earlier, from Macedonia. Demand for other goods was also growing. By the time of Pericles, Athens had become the foremost commercial center in all of Greece, and the beginnings of that development go back to the decade of the 470s.

In order to accommodate its growing population Athens initiated a building program. In the late 460s we find mention of houses that were municipal property and in which foreigners were allowed to live. These dwellings seem to have been part of an ambitious housing project on the Piraeus peninsula, which was probably undertaken under the guidance of the architect and political theoretician Hippodamus of Miletus. The houses were probably meant primarily for rowers, but they were also used for artisans and merchants, for citizens as well as for metics.

Hippodamus had devised a new kind of city plan, later adopted in many other places, which mandated certain proportions of length and width for individual plots as well as city blocks composed of plots. Blocks were intersected by paths and combined into neighborhoods separated by wide streets. Special places were reserved for shrines and markets.

The idea of a grid of straight streets intersecting at right angles was an old one and had proved successful in many places during colonization. The number, size, and arrangement of the plots were apparently not pre-determined. Hippodamus's plan, however, seems to have aimed at creating a unified settlement; it prescribed specific proportions that created a composed whole rather than letting the city grow unplanned through accretion. There is also reason to think that the houses within a particular section all had to conform to the same type.

Hippodamus's city plan, which in theory paralleled his scheme for organizing polis society according to a tripartite principle (a plan never realized), was one of the first great attempts in the fifth century to conceive of something radically beyond what had previously existed. It is comparable to the dynamic synthesis of various elements of temple building that Ictinus achieved about a generation later in his plan for the Parthenon. Previously these elements had been combined in a more static way. The new concepts of the human figure and the polis order, which we also first observe in this decade, are comparable phenomena.

Hippodamus claimed to be an expert on all of nature. He liked to dress unconventionally, perhaps to give outward expression to his sense of being above ordinary and traditional ways. He wore simple garments of the same warm cloth both summer and winter but adorned them with expensive jewelry, and he wore his hair long and flowing. According to Aristotle he struck some as dandyish. By entrusting the Piraeus project to him, the Athenians displayed remarkable faith in the new.

. . .

Activity, a spirit of enterprise, and success characterized Athenian life at this time. These attributes were particularly evident among the urban citizens, but they also spread, with the help of the Council of the Five Hundred, to the rural population.

In the face of all the optimism, was there not also some hesitation? How did Athenians cope, for example, with the belief that the "envy of the gods" struck anyone who aimed too high? Up to now that had meant the wealthy, including kings, tyrants, and great lords. But this law might apply to a city like Athens as well. Could the gods let Athens' meteoric rise pass without response?

These and similar uncertainties seem to have been felt acutely in the city. We can conclude as much from the evidence of annual public attempts made to combat them; for example, in the tragedies performed at the annual Great Dionysia at the end of March, the festival that represented the high point of life for the entire Attic population. Presented by the poets to the assembled citizenry at a celebration organized by the community, the tragedies were unique and astonishing. Major problems of the time were worked through on the stage, mostly in material taken from myth, and presented in the sanctuary of Dionysus on the Acropolis's southern slope, away from the political arena yet in the center of Athens. There, probably around the year 500, semicircular rows of seats had been crudely hewn out of the hillside. In front of them was the orchestra, a round area for the dancing chorus, and, later, a stage. The theater could hold over ten thousand spectators; whether they could all hear what was said and sung is not known.

Every year new plays were presented. Three competing poets would each contribute three tragedies and a satyr play. The actors and chorus members rehearsed extensively and were probably exempted from military service for the purpose, quite amazing considering the importance of the military to Athens' rise. The plays were lavishly produced by ambitious *choregoi* (sponsors) and were judged by a jury selected according to carefully designed rules. During the fifth century alone, more than one thousand plays were produced (counting those that did not win), and

*Theater of Dionysus on the southern slope of the Acropolis in Athens. This site
was probably used since the beginning of the fifth century B.C., though the steps
and the seating are from a later period. The original theater must have been quite
basic; it is unclear whether the acoustics were good enough for those sitting in the
back rows to be able to understand everything.*

every year people spent three full days watching them. Even prisoners were released for the duration of the festival.

This might seem like an incredible luxury, and would be, if it had in fact been a luxury. But it was not. The theater had an urgent task to accomplish. The Greeks *needed* tragedy. In certain phases of its history, Athens presented unique challenges for dramatists, and did so in a way that changed with time. Tyrants and kings invited the Attic dramatists to put on plays at their courts. Aeschylus traveled to Sicily at least twice, and Euripides went to Macedonia toward the end of his life. In these places, their tragedies were probably appreciated above all as aesthetic master-pieces. For the Athenians, however, the plays were of existential impor-tance. The Athenians needed the tragedies no less than the council of the Areopagus or the popular assembly, especially so in the years after 480, in view of all the questions that then confronted them.

The tragedies were part of the festival dedicated to Dionysus Eleuthereus, whose cult Pisistratus had relocated from the Attic border town of Eleutheria to a spot just south of the Acropolis. Pisistratus seems to have had a special relationship to this god. The plays were probably performed in Dionysus's honor because of his singular character and per-haps also because tragedy originally evolved from the songs devoted to him. Dionysus was the god not only of wine but also of the mask, of step-ping outside oneself and identifying with others. He combined many opposites, such as life and death, chaos and order, war and peace, truth and deception, and he tended to flip from one extreme to the other.

Whatever this god and his festivals originally meant to the Athenians, once tragedy became part of the Dionysus cult, the Dionysus celebration acquired an importance within the Attic year that far surpassed its original status.

The oldest play that has survived is Aeschylus's *Persians* from the year 472. It lies in time about midway between the first dramatic competitions under the tyrants (ca. 535) and the performance in 401 of Sophocles' *Oedipus at Colonus*, the last of the tragedies that has come down to us. The genre developed more rapidly between 472 and 405 than it had during the earlier span of somewhat over sixty years. But it is obvious that it had already come a long way during those earlier decades.

The *choregos* for the 472 production was the young Pericles, son of Xanthippus, a man then in his early twenties, descended on his mother's side from the noble Alcmaeonids, the "most famous men of Athens." This is the first time he appears in the public spotlight, sitting in a seat of honor at the theater, and probably marching in the Dionysian procession.

The Persians is one of the rare instances when a Greek dramatist chose to use material from contemporary history. Of the other plays of this kind, the two best known are *The Capture of Miletus* and *Phoenissae*, both by Phrynichus. The latter play also has as its subject matter the Greek victory over the Persians, and its action also, as would be expected in a tragedy, takes place among the defeated.

The Persians opens with a chorus of the old men to whom Xerxes had entrusted his realm when he left for war. They are anxiously waiting for news, and Atossa, the queen mother, recounts an ominous dream she has had. She is about to leave to pay homage to the gods when a messenger arrives with news of the defeat at Salamis and of the king's ignominious retreat from Greece. By means of gifts and songs the spirit of the dead King Darius is conjured up. At the end of the play Xerxes himself returns and, questioned by the old men who keep wanting to hear more, reveals to them the full extent of the disastrous defeat. Xerxes has "filled Hades."

The tragedy recapitulates the events of Salamis from the Persian perspective. We hear the Greeks' war song echoing at the beginning from a mountain across the bay. The Athenians' part in winning the victory is presented proudly. The great interest Queen Atossa shows in Athens confirms the city's importance. Athens will determine whether or not Xerxes will conquer Greece. But what the Athenians themselves remembered with triumphant feelings was toned down in *The Persians* to suit the characters, who are both vanquished and in mourning. What is of lesser importance to the Greeks is enlarged on—namely, the fate of many of the fallen Persian commanders.

There is not a trace of contempt for the Persians. The chorus and Atossa are drawn with sympathy. The families of the dead are depicted with respect, even compassion. They appear not as enemies but as human beings in mourning. Praise is expressed not only for Persia's power but also for its warriors' valor. At one point, Persians and Greeks appear as relatives. In Atossa's ominous dream, Xerxes went out to bring under his yoke two beautiful sisters estranged by a quarrel. One wore a simple Greek tunic and had been allotted Greece as her fatherland; the other was robed in luxurious Persian garb, and her share was the "great world beyond." The Persian sister accepted the yoke proudly, but the Greek sister fought it so hard that the yoke broke and the king fell. The Persian was not demeaned by her obedience, but subjugation was intolerable for the Greek. Darius, finally, is shown by Aeschylus to be a well-intentioned king, a benevolent paterfamilias concerned about the heritage and wealth he has left behind.

Aeschylus's tragedy deals mainly with three issues. The first is the Persian defeat, for which there is no simple explanation. The initial supposition is that some evil spirit *(daimon)* must have been at work. Luck did not favor both contestants equally, the messenger says. Atossa and the chorus agree. Darius thinks the demon deprived Xerxes of his reason, and this apparently solves the problem. Lack of discernment is the source of all evil. Xerxes followed bad advice and overstepped his limits. He did so most obviously in trying to impose his will even on Poseidon and the sea, a point mentioned again and again. The destruction of the temples is also recalled. Zeus, it is said, meant for the Persians to fight land battles, not sea battles, and the land battles should not be fought on terrain like that of Greece, where the topography worked against the Persians. Every conceivable effort is made to make obvious the Persian king's delusion, his hubris, up to the play's end when Xerxes is shown in his full humiliation. The Greek victory is depicted as a just one, because the Persian defeat was just.

This brings us to the second issue. If the Greeks and the Persians are seen as two different societies, each with its own rights and its own dignity, did a border separate the two countries that ought to have been respected? This would have been a simple matter if the Aegean Sea were such a border. At some point in the play, Aeschylus even says that Zeus assigned all of Asia to the rule of *one* man. But the border cannot be drawn this way, because so many Greek cities were located in Asia. The real difference was that the Persians were land-oriented and the Greeks were grouped around the sea. So Aeschylus distinguishes between the land of the Greeks and that of the barbarians; between different weapons, some of them specifically Persian and others specifically Greek; between land and sea, asserting that each side will be successful only in battles waged on its assigned element. Finally, he differentiated between monarchy and freedom.

All these things, regardless of the distinction between Europe and Asia, so obviously divided the world that Xerxes upset its order just by crossing the borders of Greece. The Greeks could no more be subjugated than the sea. The status quo, which once again separated Greeks from Persians, thus received a new, solid foundation. The world order was once again the way Zeus wanted it.

The third issue, that of determining to what extent Xerxes' transgression had implicated the Persian empire, was also solved in Aeschylus's play. All too often a ruler's delusions of grandeur lead to the downfall of his realm. And so the old men of *The Persians'* chorus fear that Persia's subjects will henceforth refuse obedience, and Darius's ghost worries that the empire's end will come about sooner than expected. In Greek thinking it is precisely the illegality of a despot's power that works against the permanence of his rule.

But by introducing Darius, Xerxes' father, and by isolating the son in his deviation from the proper principles of Persian rule, Aeschylus disassociates the empire from Xerxes' story and shows that, though the Persians suffered a crushing defeat, this does not mean their time is past. Rather, the playwright affirms the empire's own god-given right to exist and to endure—as long as they respect their borders. The Persian empire is thus exempted from the theological law that links transgression to punishment. To bring off this point, Aeschylus partially falsifies actual fact by depicting Darius as an almost ideal ruler and a guarantor of proper rule.

Of course, Aeschylus's play is not a treatise. That is precisely why it is so instructive. The explanation he presents is simple, and it is impressed on the audience in the form of song, dance, and images with such insistence that it becomes almost an incantation.

Another dream Queen Atossa recounts in *The Persians* shows how the Greek victory appears improbable and contrary to all experience of power. When, in her dream, Atossa is about to offer a sacrifice to Phoenix, she sees an eagle flying toward the altar, pursued by a hawk. The hawk hacks at the eagle's head, but the eagle does not try to defend itself.

The Persians represents an important step in trying to understand the events of this war on a deeper level. It was a way of describing what had happened as being according to the gods' will and thus emotionally comprehensible. Xerxes had violated the world order, and he had to submit to the counterblow that deprived his empire of the Greek cities the Persians had once rightfully conquered. There must have been something magical in the way the restoration of the world order was celebrated on the stage. The Persians retained their place but the Greeks could suddenly coexist alongside them.

The extent of Athens' and the Delian League's plan at that time is unknown. Respect for existing borders works both ways. Darius's warning to the Persians in Aeschylus's play, that mortals should not overreach, was probably not out of place in Athens, either. The Athenians, too, were to be warned not to risk what they had by scorning their present happiness and lusting after the possessions of others. At the end of his appearance, Darius recommends: "Allow your spirits to indulge in daily joys," since wealth is of no use after death.

Around 470—the precise date is unknown—Themistocles was ostracized. Cimon was his main antagonist, and there is some suggestion that Cimon acted with Spartan approval. The very institution Themistocles may have invented—or was the first to use extensively—was now turned against him to drive him from the city that owed him so much.

At the ostracism vote, two totally different individuals confronted each other, just as happened between Themistocles and Aristides in 483–482. But it is not clear how powerful Themistocles still was at this point.

Cimon would be Athens' most important politician for many years afterward. Xanthippus disappeared from sight after his year as *strategos* in 479–478, and there are few reliable references to Aristides after his famous assessment of the Delian League members in 478–477. Sources also remain silent about Themistocles for almost a decade. In 476 he was still publicly acclaimed in Olympia, drawing attention away from the athletes. It is not known if he was elected *strategos* again, but he seems to have played almost no further part in warfare.

But this does not mean that Themistocles no longer tried to influence Attic politics. He probably continued to indulge his passion for predicting future problems and for developing political schemes. He likely continued to voice his view that Sparta would not put up indefinitely with Athens' expanding power, and he almost certainly urged preparation for a possible future conflict by joining forces with Sparta's rivals, especially Argos. He would have neglected nothing that could in the future prove of advantage to Athens.

But these thoughts opened perspectives Athens preferred to ignore at that time. The Athenians were doing fine. Why should they worry about a future conflict with Sparta? In any case, they were too busy with the Delian League, its expansion and solidification, to concern themselves with such a conflict. If they stuck with Cimon they could count on his friendly relations with Sparta. Cimon was important—indeed, indispensable—in the Athenians' present situation, both as general and as politician.

The hour for speculative planning beyond the immediate present had passed, for the time being. The gift for political calculation to which Themistocles owed his big successes, and to which Athens owed its salvation and the Greeks their freedom, proved in this new situation a handicap more than an advantage. Themistocles' gift made him a misfit in a period of general satisfaction, a nuisance at a time when everybody was trying to recover from overexertion. The fact that he was right did not help his popularity, either.

So Themistocles, about fifty years old and in full command of his powers, was quickly upstaged by the younger Cimon. He may not have understood how this came about. Now it was not Miltiades but his son who rose to the top and scored successes that incensed Themistocles and far outlasted his victories.

The two men competed on all levels. As early as the 480s, Themistocles seems to have wanted to outshine Cimon in Olympia when the latter was courting a wider public. Like a kind of newcomer, Themistocles tried to impress everyone with his exceptionally luxurious tent, his lavish hosting of guests, and his splendid appearance. High society seems not to have been impressed. In response to Cimon's sponsorship of the Theseus shrine, Themistocles dedicated a shrine to Artemis Aristoboule in the city district of Melite near where he lived. Artemis was the goddess of the waters near Salamis, and the second name, Aristoboule, refers to her good advice (it literally means "best counsel"), thanks to which Themistocles was able to lead the Greeks to victory. His picture was hung in the shrine, though it may have been placed there later. The Marathon painting in the *stoa poikile* or painted colonnade building in the agora at Athens may have been Cimon's answer. It is unlikely, however, that Aeschylus wrote *The Persians* to glorify Salamis with Themistocles in mind.

Above all else, Themistocles and Cimon stood for two entirely different kinds of aristocrat in the Athens of that time. Themistocles came from a less noble and much less wealthy family than Cimon, who belonged to one of the foremost families of the city, the Philaidids, and whose mother, Hegesipyle, was from the royal house of Thrace. Even after paying his father's high financial penalty in 489, Cimon was still very rich, having profited from his sister Elpinice's marriage to one of the wealthiest men in Athens, Callias, son of Hipponicus. Cimon thus had many connections, some of them inherited from his family. His politics seem to have been based largely on these connections, whereas Themistocles had to rely more on his own persuasive abilities.

Themistocles had by now accrued considerable wealth and used his money carefully to achieve results. Cimon, by contrast, shared what he had with others. His orchards were open to his fellow deme members. When he saw a shabbily dressed older man on the street, he asked one of his young followers to exchange clothes with him.

While Themistocles was disciplined, Cimon displayed the nonchalance of an aristocrat. He enjoyed the pleasures of life and liked women, not least among them Isodice, his wife, as Plutarch stresses for the benefit of his Greek audience. Cimon resembled Themistocles only in that neither had much interest in the arts.

Cimon was a smart, successful, and brave commander who was popular with his hoplites and rowers. He must also have been an effective politician with a good understanding of power. He did not possess the outstanding intelligence of a Themistocles, but as long as things were going well, he was extremely likeable. People found Themistocles, by contrast, increasingly irritating. Themistocles had always been a complicated man, but was accepted because his brilliance had been needed. Gradually, however, his coldness and his obsessive and audacious planning began to wear.

Frustrating and incomprehensible as it must have been to Themistocles, Cimon's much more limited brand of intelligence, which was more in tune with accepted values, now proved more convincing than his own. Part of the reason was that Cimon valued the appearance of things. He not only gave in to his senses but also trusted them. He benefited from the fact that the Athenians felt well represented by him.

Themistocles' fate has an element of tragedy about it. He had had his great moments at the center of political life in Athens. But as soon as things returned to normal and he was merely one man among others, he seems to have lost his enthusiasm and his energy. His thinking no longer appealed to the public at large or to the Areopagus, which aligned itself with Cimon. Themistocles was still a member, of course, but he had lost influence there. Both the popular assembly and the Areopagus were more inclined at that point to stick with traditional ways of thinking.

Cimon's foreign policy was relatively straighforward. He continued the war against Persia whenever the opportunity presented itself. He defended the interests of Athens and the Delian League. And he stayed on friendly terms with Sparta, in the old anti-Persia coalition, reflecting his conviction that it took two oxen to pull the Greek cart and that both had to pull under the same yoke.

Cimon's policy toward Sparta may have placed too much emphasis on preserving harmony. It certainly tried to build on the past and preserve the course of normal life (no matter how much that life kept changing), and it therefore appeared solid and respectable. But Cimon seemed unaware that the power Athens had acquired thanks to its position in the Delian League was bound to lead to rivalry and rifts with Sparta, perhaps even to open conflict. Such considerations were foreign to Cimon's way of thinking. He admired Sparta, and even named one of his sons after Sparta's mythical founder, Lacedaemon.

On the domestic front, too, harmony prevailed during the 470s. As long as everything went well, the head *strategos* was held in high esteem, both in the Areopagus and among the people. It was a period during which whatever the Areopagus proposed received the popular assembly's blessing.

The small detachment of hoplites and the many *thetes* who accompanied Cimon on his expeditions were fiercely loyal to their leader. Of course, they received their share of the spoils. This period of relative contentment would not last, however—new conflicts were looming on the domestic as well as on the international front.

The reasons for Themistocles' ostracism remain unclear. He may have been seen as a threat to Cimon. For its part, Sparta may have begun to worry because Argos was recovering its power and the citizens in the Elis region of the western Peloponnese were reorganizing their communities in imitation of the Attic model. They were obviously doing this to become more independent and powerful, but they may also have been motivated by sympathy for Athens. We know that at some point Cimon's friendliness toward Sparta began to get on the Athenians' nerves. He was often heard to declaim, "That's not how the Spartans do things!" But the date of Cimon's change of attitude is not certain.

In short, it is possible that Themistocles and his anti-Spartan policy experienced a revival around 470. The trend was not yet strong enough to prevent Cimon's move to ostracize him from succeeding, but Cimon may have felt threatened by him. Themistocles went to Argos and is said to have traveled extensively from there through the Peloponnese, probably also secretly plotting a return, possibly with the approval of friends in Athens.

Soon after 470, the Persians prepared for their first counterattack on Greece. They assembled an alarmingly large army and fleet at Pamphylia on the southern coast of Asia Minor. Now at last the Delian League would have a chance to prove how much it was still needed.

Cimon set out from Cnidus and Cape Troipium with three hundred ships to meet the Persians. The Greek city of Phaselis, where he wanted to land, initially refused to let him, but after some coercion it relented and joined the league. The Greeks met the Persians near the mouth of the Eurymedon River, and though the Persians were initially reluctant to fight, they were ultimately forced into it. It was not long, however, before many of the Persian ships retreated to shore and the protection of the army stationed there. The eagerness for combat among the Greek hoplites is said to have been so great that Cimon took the chance of landing with his smaller force. The ensuing battle was a long and costly one, but the Persians finally took flight, even abandoning their camp.

In this double battle (which occurred sometime between 469 and 466) the Greeks captured over two hundred ships and took as many as twenty thousand prisoners, whom they may have sold on the Athenian slave market. They also found valuable objects and jewelry in the Persian tents. Soon after the battle, Cimon came upon the rest of the Phoenician fleet, which had not reached the scene of battle in time, and routed it as well.

The Greek cities of Pamphylia joined the Delian League, and the Persian Wars were in essence over. The Aegean was freed from Persian domination and would remain free for many decades.

Athens was the recipient of rich booty, which is said to have helped Cimon finance the building of the south wall of the Acropolis and perhaps the initial work on two long walls that were to protect Athens' access to its harbors. Cimon also built a large colonnaded hall in Eleusis for the enactment of the mysteries. He planted trees in the agora and improved the area of the academy, about one kilometer northwest of the agora, by irrigating it and laying out shady paths.

An incident from the year 468 is worth recounting here. That year, the dramatic competition at the Dionysia aroused strong feelings. The poets—and perhaps the casts of the plays as well—began to fight among themselves. The excitement spread to the audience, and the archon feared havoc would ensue should the verdict of the jury further inflame passions. He therefore decided to abandon the customary rule of choosing the jury by lot. Instead he assigned the task of judging to Cimon and his nine co-*strategoi*, who were making the customary drink offering in the theater. The group met and awarded the prize to Sophocles. It was the first competition Sophocles won.

Meanwhile, probably in 469, a son was born to a stonemason named Sophroniscus from the deme of Alopece and his wife, Phaenarete, a midwife. The child was named Socrates.

In 467 Aeschylus produced his *Seven Against Thebes*, in which Oedipus's son Eteocles organizes the city's defense against the powerful army his brother Polynices is leading against Thebes. The boastful hubris of the attackers is evident from the embossed emblems on their shields. One after the other, the enemy is vanquished by the defenders of the city, law, and freedom. The hoplites triumph because their discipline, obedience, and courage prepare them to take on anyone, particularly arrogant opponents. When the women advise Eteocles to avoid battle because God "values success, even a coward's," he answers that no warrior will tolerate such talk.

The gravity of the situation is depicted by Aeschylus through Eteocles' short temper, which he vents on the chorus of women, whom he calls "insufferable creatures" because they wail loudly before the altars instead of raising the spirit of the surrounded army. They are shown as an internal threat more serious to the city than the enemy outside the walls. It is not clear if the poet alluded in this passage to some contemporary situation.

Whether or not it reflected the present reality, this play exhibits remarkable similarities to a trend that emerged in this period's sculpture. In the 480s sculptors started to work in the "severe style." Human figures were characterized by a curious control and restraint, a concentration on the body, and little interest in ornament. Unity became visible in the interplay of tension and relaxation between the various body parts. Previously, there had been only one basic type, the *kouroi*, that could be varied by changing the details, but now artists had a range of possibilities

Discus Thrower *by Myron. Mid-fifth century* B.C. *Copy. Rome, Thermae Museum.*

from which to choose. The figures were now so individualized that to base a new work on an existing one would be less a variation on a theme than an imitation. All the figures of this period are depicted in motion. For example, *Discus Thrower*, created by Myron around 450, captures a moment of maximum tension in which the athlete's strength is gathered in the rearward swing, as it is about to be released forward.

At the heart of the artistic freedom that developed in this period lay the desire to create a single image of man in different guises. Whether the subject were a god, a hero, or an ordinary man, what the artist sought to reveal through his work was the image of the citizen, the man who fully embodied the Greek male virtues, the man who was aware of many different human possibilities and tried with complete self-control to realize the most important of these.

Simplicity in clothing and hairstyle was part of the severe style. If Athens' leadership during that time appears "severe," the reason is the same. Here, too, within the isonomy, what mattered was the individual's self-control in consciously and freely choosing what he wanted to be. The uniformity of the arts in this period is not surprising, for the culture had not yet begun to draw distinctions between different genres in the arts and also because it was in a period of relative stasis, undisrupted by major developments or innovations.

Shortly before 465 Sparta urged the Athenians to impose the death penalty on Themistocles. He had supposedly conspired with the now discredited Pausanias to help Persia gain power over Greece. Pausanias, who had been the victorious commander at Plataea, fell out of favor because of his own arrogance and the suspicions that he was negotiating with the Persians. After not being sent to war against the Persians in 478, he went on to Byzantium on his own and stayed there until the Athenians drove him out. At that point he adopted Persian dress and a group of Persian and Egyptian bodyguards. He then settled in Troas and apparently offered the Persian king his services in subjugating the Greeks, with an aim of becoming satrap himself. The letters between him and the Persian middlemen were carried by couriers and included instructions to kill the messenger.

When the Spartans captured and finally convicted him, Pausanias fled to a sanctuary, where he was walled in and not let out again until just before he died of starvation. A letter was found among his things in which he invited Themistocles to join his scheme. Even though Themistocles did not respond to the letter, he was implicated in the plot because he failed to inform anyone of the letter, and because the two men had been friends in the past.

It didn't take long for Athens to recall alliance with Sparta against Persia, which was the basis of their present good relations, and both cities sent out agents to bring Themistocles back to Athens. The zeal and fury that his Athenian and Spartan enemies displayed were so great that Themistocles no longer felt safe in Argos. Perhaps he worried that military threats would be used against his host city. Some time later, the king of Molossia in northern Greece, who had offered him temporary refuge, was threatened with military attack.

After a harrowing flight across Corfu and northern Greece, the architect of the Greek victory at Salamis finally found asylum at the court of Artaxerxes of Persia. Themistocles had written to him in advance, claiming that though he had inflicted much harm on Xerxes, the great king's father, when his own country's safety had been at stake, he had also done things that worked to Xerxes' benefit. Such an appeal would have sounded plausible to the Persians. Pausanias, too, had won the Persian king's goodwill by rendering small services. It was crucial to the great kings that gratitude be shown for such gestures. Hardly any other virtue was esteemed as highly by them, and anyone rising to prominence in Greece had reason to think that he might, at some point, have to avail himself of that gratitude. Many Greeks had found a friendly reception at the court in Susa. Their advice was valued, and there they could not only continue to be politically active but also live safely in rather luxurious circumstances. Probably not many of them learned to speak Persian before presenting themselves to the great king, the way Themistocles did at the age of about sixty. He was given three Greek cities, symbolically representing bread, wine, and meat, but if Artaxerxes' generosity was motivated by expectations of receiving Themistocles' services against the Greeks, he was disappointed.

. . .

It is no coincidence that so much is written about prominent leaders in isonomous (and soon to become democratic) Athens. Historians speak of a Cimonian era or of Periclean Athens because these leaders determined the future course of the city, as, in a different way, Themistocles had determined events in the years preceding Salamis. But contrary to appearances, these periods represent above all phases in the history of the Attic citizenry.

Athens had no appointed or elected government, and there were no parties or other organizations for anyone to head. Nor were there formal mechanisms to guarantee a leader's position. His status depended primarily on his persuasive powers and the respect he commanded—in a certain sense, on popularity. But it worked out in such a way that one individual continued to play the leading role over extended periods. During its isonomous period—and even more so in the later democratic era—Athens needed personalities whose authority could provide guidance for the majority (or the influential minority) of citizens. That was the case, at least, until the power structure changed. Except at times of violent disagreement and great perplexity, the Athenians were psychologically willing to commit themselves to their leaders. The most extreme degree of this was reached under Pericles, when Athens was, according to Thucydides, nominally a democracy but in reality ruled entirely by its foremost citizen.

Such power could, however, only be exercised by a leader who stuck closely to a course that reflected the will of the majority. No matter how much he had himself influenced and defined this will, he always had to align himself with popular sentiment if he wanted to maintain his exalted position. Moreover, forging majorities from the variety of interests existing in a pluralistic and apolitical society was out of the question because society as such did not exist. Rather, politicians who wanted to stay in power had to identify with important issues and definite policies for which they then bore responsibility, a fact of which they were constantly reminded.

The working of this system can be explained with reference to two factors: the way a politician presented his position in speeches and proposals to the community, which then made up its own mind, and the special ability of the public to remember these speeches and proposals and not allow itself to be distracted by a multitude of other interests. However, these factors are only part of the story.

What counted even more were the people's concrete needs and their identification with their leader. They had to be able to trust a particular man to lead them well. They did not want to go back and forth from one man to another on important matters. In case of doubt, a vote on ostracism had to decide among competitors of equal power. For those who passed the test, it repeatedly reaffirmed not only their connection to, but also a certain identity with, the predominant tendencies among the people.

Cimon's complacency reflected the mood of the contemporary citizenry, which had just passed through the enormous exertion of the Persian Wars and wanted to enjoy and make the most of their successes. Only under these particular circumstances could Cimon have gotten along so well with the Areopagus of isonomous Athens.

Similarly Themistocles' reign would not have been conceivable without the citizens of his time, men who were able, with some persuasion perhaps, to judge the situation correctly and act on what they saw. Of course, what they did was necessary to preserve their city, but a great deal of intelligence and discipline are required to do what is necessary when it is inconvenient. Themistocles and the Attic citizens obviously spurred each other on.

It must be stressed, however, that the personalities that played a decisive role in Athens over many years represent only one side of Athens' history. After the Persian Wars and the city's astonishing expansion of power, the city's development was characterized more by a process of long and gradual change—for instance, in the way citizens participated in politics—than by specific situations or personalities. Where individuals did step forward, they articulated tendencies already present in the citizenry. It was probably those who were best at describing these broad popular tendencies who were needed the most. Themistocles did it in a way no one else could have, and Pericles was a genius at it. But one must not overlook the huge opportunities and challenges to which they responded.

Anyone whose agenda was not in line with the inclinations of the citizenry would eventually fail. There is no indication that those who failed were less intelligent, but it is clear that their particular ways, their connections, their methods, or their goals did not conform to the mood of the time.

Ironically, the citizenry began to change significantly at just about the time when Themistocles set out on his flight from Greece. Cimon's era was a moratorium, during which the lowest social class, the *thetes*, acquired great importance.

The *thetes* had heretofore enjoyed little respect; they had virtually no land of their own and were not affluent enough to equip themselves for military service. In the traditional view of hoplite society, they were not proper citizens, no matter what rights had been granted to them or how they used them. The existence of the middle class went back practically to the beginning of the polis, and in a narrow political sense the polis owed its existence to it. The lower class, by contrast, owed whatever importance it had to the later development of the polis—to their military pay and, later on, to the per diem allowances paid them. In return for these they rendered the city invaluable services.

The *thetes* became increasingly indispensable to the city, first when Themistocles built up the navy, and especially later, when new and more ambitious expeditions were undertaken under Cimon. It was primarily the *thetes*—along with some metics, or resident aliens—who rowed the Attic ships, and thus they shared in the spoils and vastly expanded their horizons. Their self-image as a class rose dramatically, and that meant not only that they spoke up more in the popular assembly but that the entire assembly attained new importance, as did the city of Athens as a whole. The city's great new external power was accompanied by an expansion of the circle of those who functioned as citizens.

This transition happened gradually, however. Opposition to the aristocracy, which had been an element in Cleisthenes' restructuring of the citizenry and in the creation of the Council of Five Hundred, was almost entirely absent in the early days of isonomous Athens.

Nor is there any evidence that the *thetes* were in opposition to the middle class; in fact, signs suggest the opposite. They were different, but that did not necessarily mean they had different goals. They wanted equality with the middle class, but that did not generate conflict between them. Even later on, nobody ever succeeded in pitting the primarily urban lower class against the more rural middle class.

Only one difference emerges clearly: mobility. While it was generally difficult for the farmers to participate in long military campaigns, many of the *thetes* were on extended duty. At home in Athens there was little need for their services, but on military expeditions they earned money and respect. Where the farmers hesitated to leave their lands untended, the *thetes* had few second thoughts. Where the farmers were more constrained by traditional thinking, the *thetes* were quick to decide (and do) what made sense in a given situation. They were willing to give their all to any endeavor that promised to increase the city's power.

The more self-confident and influential the *thetes* became in politics, the readier they were to support new policies. It was not simply that they imposed their will on the farmers by constituting a majority, but more likely that they were drawn into the general consensus. The balance within the popular assembly shifted somewhat, continuing a trend that probably began under Cimon. Cimon's bond with the Areopagus began to wear thin.

In 465 the island of Thasos in the north of the Aegean Sea defected from the Delian League. The island ruled several nearby sections of the mainland, as many Greek coastal islands did. But the areas on the mainland that Thasos controlled contained gold mines. That is why the city of Thasos was so rich and, thanks to its fleet, so powerful. It was also well fortified.

Athens in that period was focusing its attentions on the northern Aegean region, where, among other things, the best trees for shipbuilding grew. At the same time Athens tried to gain control of an area somewhat farther west, near the river Strymon. The Athenians wanted to establish a

colony somewhat inland from the city of Eion in a strategically advantageous spot called Enneahodoi, or Nine Ways (later the site of Amphipolis),
where several routes crossed and from which it would be possible to
dominate Mount Pangaeus, whose mines Pisistratus had previously owned
and exploited. Athens sent out ten thousand settlers, Athenians, and anyone else who wanted to go along.

The quarrel with Thasos over the trade centers and mines on the
mainland was in all likelihood deliberately initiated by Athens. And
Thasos probably defected from the league less because it no longer
wanted to belong than because it objected to Attic interference in the
northern Aegean.

The Athenian colonists succeeded in taking Enneahodoi but were
defeated in battle by the Thracian Edones, to whom the surrounding area
belonged. The Attic losses were so great that the enterprise had to be
abandoned. This was the first major defeat Athens had suffered in decades.

Thasos, however, was forced to capitulate after a long siege in 463–462.
It handed over its fleet, ceded its possessions on the mainland, and was
forced to raze its fortifications. It also agreed to pay reparations.

The herald in Aeschylus's *Agamemnon*, written a few years later, would
use the following words, which might be based partly on the experience
of the siege of Thasos, to describe the war against Troy:

> *Were I to tell you of the hard work done, the nights*
> *exposed, the huddled quarters, the foul beds—what part*
> *of day's disposal did we not cry out loud?*
> *Ashore, the horrors stayed with us and grew. We lay*
> *against the ramparts of our enemies, and from*
> *the sky, and from the ground, the meadow dews came out*
> *to soak our clothes and us, nor ever dry. And if*
> *I were to tell of wintertime, when all birds died*
>
> *. . . . .*
>
> *or summer heat, when in the lazy noon the sea*
> *fell level and asleep under a windless sky—*
> *but why live such grief over again? That time is gone*
> *for us, and gone for those who died.*

The Thasians had been secretly assured of help from Sparta. This, too, was new. For the first time the Spartans were going to take sides openly against Athens, a move that could have serious consequences.

But things never came to that point. Sparta was rocked by a heavy earthquake. Reportedly only five houses were left standing, mountain peaks toppled in the Taygetus range, and numerous fissures opened in the earth. Multitudes of helots, the Spartans' quasi-slave serf population, came from the countryside to avenge themselves on their oppressors. The city could have been rendered impotent for years if not forever, but thanks to King Archidamus's presence of mind, this did not happen. The rebels retreated to a stronghold on Mount Ithome in Messenia, from which the Spartans were unable to dislodge them. Thus the Spartan fighting forces were detained there for some time.

When Cimon returned from the successful campaign against Thasos in 463–462, he found the political scene in Athens much changed. A new group of politicians had come to the fore. It was led by Ephialtes, son of Sophonides, of whom it was said that he "lacked wealth" and was "just and incorruptible," qualities that suggest passionate political convictions in a period of fundamental change. Ephialtes and his group, which included Pericles, were of a younger generation and undoubtedly thought in more modern terms.

For one thing, they had different ideas about foreign policy. This became immediately evident when the Spartans asked Athens for help in driving the helots from their stronghold on Mount Ithome. Cimon was of course in favor, but Ephialtes stood against the idea. Sparta, Ephialtes' side argued, should not be helped but left to suffer its plight and the corresponding blow to its pride. Cimon prevailed with difficulty and was sent to assist Sparta with four thousand hoplites, but Cimon's was a Pyrrhic victory.

In 462–461, during Cimon's absence, Ephialtes and his adherents mounted an all-out political attack on the Areopagus. They pushed through a motion that deprived the council of all functions except jurisdiction over blood feuds and supervision in some religious matters. All its other functions were assigned to the Council of Five Hundred, the popular assembly, and the people's court. The aristocratic council would no longer play any political role.

Meanwhile, as the siege of the helots dragged on, the Spartans grew increasingly suspicious of the Attic troops, fearing they would join forces with the enemy. On top of it all, when they finally left Sparta, the Athenians were attacked by the Corinthians on their march home. Athens' relations with Sparta suffered lasting damage. Immediately after the troops' return, Athens terminated its alliance with Sparta against the Persians and entered into new agreements with Argos and Thessaly. Anti-Spartan feelings ran so high that Alcibiades (grandfather and namesake of the Alcibiades who became famous as a general, statesman, and associate of Socrates) was compelled to cancel a hospitality agreement with Sparta that dated back many decades. Cimon attempted to restore the powers of the Areopagus, but without success.

From then on, the only political bodies in charge of important decisions were to be a newly formed council, annually elected, of men primarily from the middle class, plus the popular assembly and the people's court. There were to be no more preliminary deliberations between the Areopagus and the popular assembly. Officials were no longer account-able to the Areopagus but directly to the people. This arrangement was bound to alter the expectations placed on the people. In short, the gov-ernment was to be run exclusively by the people—though within the context of existing institutions, laws, and oaths.

Athens had never experienced such a radical political change. The trans-formations during the time of Cleisthenes paled by comparison. The Spartans' reaction at Ithome is just one illustration of how frightening the Athenians looked to the rest of Greece after they stripped the Areopagus of power. As far as we can tell, nowhere else in Greece did a city decide to do without the political input of an advisory council made up of the most experienced and influential citizens. (If a similar situation existed anywhere else, it could only have been in insignificant towns, whose political order would have concerned only immediate neighbors.)

Athens, however, was the dominant power of the Delian League. Its influence was broad, and the rest of Greece could only watch what the city did in amazement. No one could ignore its political organization and those who determined its policies.

And now this city was under what we would now call a revolutionary government. The general assumption among those of political importance in Greece was that things would come to a bad end (even though some may have been fascinated by the experiment). Most likely, the main question people wondered about was what would happen before things returned to normal.

To understand what the Athenians themselves were thinking before the demotion of the Areopagus and, above all, afterward, we must examine how this revolutionary event came to take place.

Men like Pericles, who at the time of Salamis was still a child, along with certain ambitious older men, who for whatever reason had had practically no say up to now, saw the relationship with Sparta in a very different light from Cimon and his allies. What the latter group saw from the inside, from the political center, the former looked at from without. Cimon had proceeded step by step after the Persians' retreat, adjusting to circumstances as they evolved. The new men saw the situation as it was now. Cimon thought he had things under control, relying at least partly on his personal connections and especially on his friendship with Sparta. He felt perfectly secure. But Pericles and the other political outsiders realized the full riskiness of Athens' position. They thought more in political terms. Also, where Cimon was rather guileless, they were more clever.

The defeat at Enneahodoi had been the first time a large Athenian army was annihilated and the first time the Spartans threatened to side with a defecting city. Could this mean that the entire Delian League might be coming apart? It must have seemed evident to anyone looking at things from the outside that Athens was engaged in a risky venture. The city, which had only about 35,000 citizens (counting, according to Greek custom, only adult males), headed an alliance of many cities totaling well over 200,000 citizens. The reliability of the Delian League, which extended from one end of the Aegean Sea to the other and beyond, had now, after the defection of Naxos, come into question a second time. It had been a long time since the original purpose of the alliance, the struggle against Persia, had been invoked. Although it is true that the Persians might return, many of the allies must have been asking themselves whether it was really necessary to maintain this huge military apparatus. What if Sparta were to support the next city that decided to withdraw? The Athenians could not expect an earthquake to come to their aid every time.

So, if Cimon was accused of irresponsibility, there may have been good reasons for it. If Ephialtes argued that Athens should conserve its energies and eschew pro-Spartan policies, he could cite much to support his position. In this situation, Ephialtes saw the best chance of success in an alliance with Sparta's enemies. He and his friends may have been influenced by Themistocles' opinions.

Ephialtes and his allies may also have considered Cimon's domestic policies to be wrong. Their own ambition undoubtedly combined with their criticism of those in power and the rousing effect of political slogans to create a complex tangle of motives that it would be vain to trace in detail.

In order for the new generation to oppose Cimon, to initiate new foreign policy, and to dominate Athenian politics, they had to take on the Areopagus, whether they had originally intended to do it or not. As long as the old elite was in charge it blocked access to the popular assembly, whose majority support the usurpers had to win.

How were the upstarts able to succeed against such powerful, successful, respected, and influential men? Historians often suggest that Ephialtes relied on the *thetes* for support, who surely were an important factor in his plans. Historical sources give us some clues about how Ephialtes and his adherents accomplished this.

Ephialtes is said to have raised charges against several members of the Areopagus, accusing them among other things of taking bribes. These charges were easy to substantiate because it was still customary among the aristocrats to exchange gifts, as between guests and hosts; the line between such a custom and corruption is never very clear. At first Ephialtes may have accused only a few of the lords who really were guilty or whom he wanted to bring into disrepute. But at some point his goal must have become to discredit the Areopagus as a whole.

Pericles accused Cimon himself, claiming that Cimon could have invaded Macedonia from Thasos but had been bribed not to. Cimon was eventually declared innocent of the charges, perhaps by the Areopagus. The main purpose of Pericles' accusation may well have been to agitate in favor of expanding military activity in the northern Aegean.

Ephialtes also agitated to create general dissatisfaction with the Areopagus. He claimed, for example, that the Areopagus had acquired some of its authority improperly. They were "added on" by its members at a later date, according to Ephialtes, as though only the body's original powers, which he apparently took to be primarily the judicial functions, had validity. This was a clever strategy, because even at that time reference to tradition had popular appeal, and Ephialtes probably used this argument to counter accusations that he himself was a usurper.

Several phrases drawn from Aeschylus's tragedy *The Suppliants*, which was most likely produced in 463, supply insight into Ephialtes' conspiratorial activities. In the play prominent mention is made of the "rule of the people." This is the first time in recorded history that the word *people* is linked to the verb *to rule*. There is good reason to believe that the concept of democracy first came into use at this time. The popular assembly had long been the body of highest authority in matters of legislation and in decisions about war and peace, but initially that had not meant much. Beginning in the period of Cleisthenes, the assembly became increasingly involved in practical politics as well, but it continued to follow the recommendations of the Areopagus. It is not just by chance that well into the 460s the popular assembly is described as a "ruling" body. It was difficult to modify the idea of "ruling" (or "governing"), which had up to now been associated exclusively with holders of political office and tyrants, to such an extent that it could be applied to the people. A sense of the people as the governing body seems not yet to have existed. Initially all anybody had in mind was that the broader segments of the citizenry should in fact have equal political rights. This was what isonomy was all about. The actual governing was done by officials and the Areopagus; the Council of Five Hundred had a say in it, and the popular assembly made the final decisions, which amounted, in the thinking of the time, to a distribution of powers among the various governing bodies.

Thus, it was a considerable innovation when Ephialtes stressed government by the people. The intent of his choice is best revealed in the negative demand that followed his positive one: It was the people who were to rule, *not* the aristocracy; that is, not the Areopagus. The authority of this body was bound now to appear as paternalistic, so that it seemed essential to defend the rights of the people against the Areopagus, the institution that was supposed to act as the guardian of those rights.

Another clue is provided by some strange words, which scholars have generally failed to take seriously, Aeschylus put into the mouths of the Egyptian girls who form the chorus, the suppliants of the play's title. When they beseech the king of Argos to take them in, he declares that he cannot make the decision on his own but needs the approval of the popular assembly. Thus it seems in the play that in the legendary past a democracy existed in Argos. It is interesting to note that democracy is claimed for Argos in particular. The Egyptian girls refuse to believe—or fail to understand—the king's declaration. They insist that as king he must be able to do what he wants in Argos, but before that they address him in an odd way: They suggest that as king, he *is* the people.

Nowhere else among the Greeks do we encounter anything even vaguely resembling such an identification of an individual with the polis, an identification reminiscent of Louis XIV of France. On the contrary, the polis was so distinct from its leader that under a tyrant it appeared practically to be the ruler's property. He, not the polis, figured in political treaties. In documents, the polis appears at best alongside the ruler, not as represented by him. "What belongs to a single man is not the polis," wrote Sophocles in *Antigone*. The polis was, indeed, not a state. That abstract entity of the State was precisely the basis that had been lacking in the tyrants' claims to legitimation.

How, then, did the formulation "Aren't you the polis?" come about? Was this sentence meant to convey the chorus's Eastern view of the world, so shocking as it was to the Greek mind? Modern Egyptologists have said that the ancient Egyptians would have been most likely to translate *state* as "pharaoh." But the reason the ancient Egyptians had no word for *state* was that they had no state as such. And though the Greeks could use the word *polis* to refer to entire empires (such as the Persian), this does not imply that the king of such an empire was identified with the entire empire. It is hardly imaginable that the Greeks would ever have asked a question such as "Who is Egypt?" or "Who is the Persian Empire?" It seems Aeschylus was not satisfied with showing the strangeness of the Egyptian girls by having them assume that the king ruled the city with unlimited power like a despot; he also made them suggest that the king *was* the city and the people in their entirety.

The only way out of this confusion is to read the suppliants' question as an implied statement, as an allusion to something that might have been stated straightforwardly and emphatically about the polis of Athens; namely that "the city is all of us," meaning all of us as we stand here, the Attic people (or "demos") gathered in the popular assembly. This interpretation makes the most sense. The Attic aristocrats had never claimed to *be* the city, but surely their words and actions implied at least that they knew best what was good for it. That was, after all, the basis of the aristocratic claim to leadership. Cimon's suggestion that Cleisthenes' aristocracy should be reinstated advocated the same principle: rule by the most qualified. Perhaps the late source from which we know of Cimon's reference to Cleisthenes even retains Cimon's original phrasing, suggesting that he was responding directly to the claim that the people themselves should govern.

The people had few arguments to support their claim, except that they *were* the people. Granted, they were not as educated or as "wise" as the aristocrats, but as they pointed out, it was *their* well-being that was at stake. The aristocrats might think they knew what was best for the polis as an entity, but the people could argue that since they were the ones affected by whatever actions were taken, they should be the ones to decide on policy, and be able to decide freely. Thus the polis became the people's subject rather than the object of the aristocracy. What was called the polis was now constituted by the citizenry in its entirety, and that is exactly how the broader classes, in their new sense of entitlement, would have expressed their claim to government by the people.

The emergence of such a conflict and its subsequent propagandistic exploitation is also reflected in Aeschylus's *Suppliants* by the king's declaration that those who are to be affected by a decision must be the ones to make it. The whole development of the play suggests this. A long, somewhat agonized section is taken up by an exchange between the king and the suppliants. The Egyptian girls present their demand for asylum more and more insistently as the king writhes under the pressure of having to come to a decision.

To be sure the Greeks had encountered such dilemmas before. Here the problem is how to decide between expediency—refusing asylum because of the possibility of war if the girls were allowed to stay—and divine commands that insist on the granting of asylum. But in this tragedy the sense of *aporia*, or perplexity, is so great that it suggests an entirely new consciousness of the difficulty of decision-making. The king is unable to resolve the problem; the decision, to grant asylum, is forced on him.

By contrast, the popular vote taken after the king decides is clear in its intent. By the end of the play it turns out that the asylum seekers brought the country bad luck. The war against the girls' pursuers resulted in great losses and the fall of the king. The audience was meant to draw the conclusion that the democratic process was appropriate, but that there was no guarantee it would yield the right decision. The point was not *what* the decision would be, but *how* it was to be arrived at.

It is hard to imagine that this preoccupation with the problems of decision-making did not arise from contemporary reality. This does not mean that the play should be read as a statement of a political position, but rather that Aeschylus presented contemporary issues and experiences in the shape of drama. Behind it all, there is obviously the question of how and by whom the right decisions are to be reached and whether one person can even make decisions for others. It was no longer possible for Athenians simply to accept decisions of the Areopagus.

. . .

Cimon's reputation had long since ceased to impress the *thetes*. His reported irresponsibility presumably became worse once he thought his position was secure. His defeat in the north at Enneahodoi and the rumors (which may have been accurate) about the danger Sparta posed to Athens must have cast his alliances, his friendships, and his most cherished assumptions in a suspicious light. And with the gulf that was opening up between this leading politician and the *thetes*, many may have come to suspect that the high lords looked with contempt upon "the men from the lowest bench of oars." The mystery surrounding the deliberations of the Areopagus added to that suspicion. The *thetes* may have rebelled against these insults to their self-respect. They were convinced of the necessity of pursuing a new, more aggressive foreign policy. After all, such a policy would benefit them. The possibilities of further gains in power suggested by Pericles made that clear. Furthermore, it was flattering to the *thetes* when Ephialtes and his associates tried to win them over with arguments and otherwise took them seriously.

Events then developed a momentum of their own. The more the members of the Areopagus felt attacked, the more uncooperative they became, so that the attackers, even when their criticisms were not initially meant to be sweeping, found all their suspicions justified. Each side saw the other act exactly as feared. The Areopagus members at first refused to take the attacks seriously because they could not imagine Athens surviving politically without them, an attitude that must have further fueled their opponents' rage. But they had little choice. It was not so much that they lacked imagination as that their very existence demanded they think a certain way. They made reference to the old, time-honored tradition and charged Ephialtes with being an innovator. (Innovation in those days did not suggest improvement or alternatives but revolution and destruction.) Ultimately, Ephialtes' counterargument that the Areopagus had usurped most of its authority may have carried the day simply because he already had a greater following behind him.

The composition of the Areopagus had changed in the meantime. For some twenty-five years leading up to this period, the archons had been chosen by lot—and the longer this was the case, the greater a role chance played in the composition of the council. Over the course of time, those who became the most important politicians might have become archons anyway. Normally this expectation would have been enough, especially under favorable conditions, when the mere possibility of attaining that office enhanced a politician's power. But the situation became critical when too many ambitious men were excluded. The fact that Ephialtes and many of his friends had found themselves in this situation seems to have made the crucial difference.

Thus many factors converged, and the violent clashes between the two sides added to the crisis. It is debatable whether Ephialtes had political reason on his side. What is certain is that the new generation of Athenians prevailed. They knew about the Persian Wars only through stories and had no memory of how things had been before or how narrow the sphere of Attica's importance had been. The new class of *thetes* also came into prominence, and once empowered and roused to action they were more than ready to embrace a new aggressive policy. Out of all this developed the immense increase in power and mobility that was to characterize Athens from then on, leading to ever more successes and finally bringing forth the flowering of Athenian culture.

It was a legal revolution—legal because the popular assembly had the right to pass the resolution that deflated the Areopagus, but a revolution nevertheless because it completely and fundamentally overturned the political order. Where before there had been a splintering of power among the Areopagus, the Council of Five Hundred, and the popular assembly, there was now a true government by the people. The old Areopagus was replaced by the Five Hundred, who, though no longer subject to the former's control were nevertheless not invested with independent authority. They had to pass on to the popular assembly all the motions that had been proposed to them. Decisions were now actually made by the mass of citizens. The experienced helmsmen were no longer in command; the "man from the lowest bench of oars" was now in charge.

Stability depended on whether the cooperation between the people and their advisers, including the elected *strategoi*, worked well enough to guide politics along a proper and reasonable course. The help of the aristocrats remained indispensable for this work, but the aristocracy as a whole no longer dominated a governing organization, much less the organization in which the city-state's power was concentrated. As the farmers had done in Solon's time, now the *thetes*, the lowest social and economic class, assumed the power that had historically belonged to the aristocracy. This time there was no chance that Sparta or anyone else might intervene.

It had taken centuries after the introduction of the military phalanges in which farmers fought before those farmers were granted a regular voice in political matters. By comparison, the *thetes* were quickly granted political rights commensurate with their military functions. On the one hand, the stage for including the broader population in the political process was set (though the *thetes* had previously made little use of the political rights they already had); and on the other, the military had much greater need for the *thetes* now. Their role at Salamis would soon be forgotten, but their participation in the wars of the Delian League was essential.

Cimon was ostracized. Themistocles, the engineer of the victory over the Persians, was followed into exile by the man who had laid the foundation of Athens' power as the leader of the Delian League. Cimon, like Themistocles, had rendered the city immense services. The aristocrats who, along with Cimon, committed themselves totally to politics must have been a remarkable group. Their devotion was most unusual in the context of their times. These were the men who made it possible for Athens to bridge the gap between what it had been and what it now was, between its origins and its horizon. These men had not only filled the political vacuum that had existed in the Aegean region but they filled it with entirely novel power structures. Their policies had certainly not been bad ones, and their contribution to Athens' greatness was considerable, even if they failed to perceive some important developments and despite the fact that they based the city's relationship with Sparta on the unreliable foundation of amicable personal connections.

Ephialtes was murdered soon after the change in government. It was never discovered who killed him, but his murder can be viewed as a sign of the turmoil into which so much political upheaval had plunged Athens.

The veil that had long kept Cimon and his associates from perceiving the new reality was finally lifted. At last Athens was ready to accept the consequences of its new preeminence. Now it was a question of who would prevail: Athens or Sparta. And at this time, democracy was born.

The old concepts whose names ended in -*nomy* were joined or replaced by new ones whose suffixes were -*cracy* and -*archy*. Besides democracy they included oligarchy (which could be termed "rule of the few" only when the alternative of government by the people existed) and aristocracy. These terms expressed that there was no longer just one preordained order or law *(nomos)*, which could be well constituted *(eunomia)*, or badly constituted *(dysnomia)*, or modified by the principle of equality *(isonomy)*. Instead there were several possible political orders that differed from each other fundamentally, depending on who was in power *(kratia)*. For the first time, that which did not correspond to the old order, whether isonomous or aristocratic in nature, was not necessarily perceived as disorder or chaos but rather as an alternative order—namely, government by the people. This may not have been apparent at first to the aristocrats, and they may well have doubted that such a new order could last. But to the people it was clear, and soon others could no longer deny it.

This is how the strange, important, and uniquely Greek distinction between oligarchy and democracy came about. Because the men *were* the polis, it was crucial to know how many men actually formed the polis. Political involvement was not just a theoretical possibility but a fact. Herodotus reports that a short time later, in the debate over Athens' constitution, an argument never heard before was voiced in favor of democracy: Democracy is characterized by certain institutions, not by individuals. Institutions, it seemed, could hold the key to solving the problems of the polis.

This turned out to be an illusion, for important as the institutions were, they were soon overwhelmed by Athens' problems. The one fixed characteristic of the epoch that now began was that the very center, the foundation of the political order, had been called into question. Long-standing assumptions were quickly becoming superannuated. The Greeks had reached the limit of their ability to be fully in control of their world.

The age of *nomos*, or law, had given way to an age of *kratia*, or rule. And this affected all areas of life, politics as well as philosophy and art, internal as well as external matters.

We assign the beginning of democracy in Athens and in Greece to the year 462–461, and that beginning resulted from a negative act, the demotion of the Areopagus. But the conditions for democracy's emergence had existed for some time. Cleisthenes had laid the foundation, which in time fostered a strong sense of self-confidence and political aptitude among the citizenry. "The people" had only needed to be freed of the aristocratic council's authority to govern on their own. Only a few practical arrangements, in essence just the consequences of the change, were still lacking. Whatever Ephialtes originally intended to accomplish, he first had to help the people gain power if he were to succeed.

It was during this period that Athens began to develop the particular dynamic character that exceeded its military strength and enabled the city to win enough power to dominate the entire Greek world. Thucydides described a later phase of Athens' dynamism in words he ascribes to the Corinthians. The passage is addressed to the Spartans, whom the Corinthians compare unfavorably with the Athenians: "The Athenians are addicted to innovation, and their designs are characterized by swiftness alike in conception and execution. . . . They are adventurous beyond their power, and daring beyond their judgment, and in danger they are sanguine. . . . Their unwavering determination is matched on your side by procrastination; they are never at home, you are never away from it. . . . They are swift to follow up a success, and slow to recoil from a reverse."

The Corinthians go on to say:

> Their bodies they spend ungrudgingly in their country's cause; their intellect they jealously husband to be employed in her service. A scheme unexecuted is with them a positive loss, a successful enterprise, a comparative failure. The deficiency created by the miscarriage of an undertaking is soon filled up by fresh hopes; for they alone are enabled to call a thing hoped for a thing got, by the speed with which they act upon their resolutions. Thus they toil on in trouble and danger all the days of their life, with little opportunity for enjoying, being ever engaged in getting: their only idea of a holiday is to do what the occasion demands, and to them laborious occupation is less of a misfortune than the peace of a quiet life.

Thucydides concludes the passage with his famous remark that the Athenians were "born into the world to take no rest themselves and to give none to others."

It was precisely at the time following the fall of the Areopagus that Athens began to develop these qualities. Even if it was Ephialtes who set the process in motion and even if much of the support for the process came from the *thetes*, all Athenians were somehow involved in what was taking shape. Now, approximately one generation after the victories of Marathon, Salamis, Plataea, and Mycale, Athens was completely oriented to the new situation. The moratorium on innovation under Cimon was over. Athens was no longer content to take advantage of opportunities as they presented themselves. It began to create new ones for itself.

7

"Adventurous Beyond Their Power":
Athens at Midcentury

In love as in business, in science as in the broad jump, we have to
believe before we can succeed. Why should that not hold true for life
in general?

—ROBERT MUSIL

"Is there anything the Athenians cannot accomplish?" asks a character in
a play by the fifth-century comic poet, Eupolis, a contemporary and rival
of Aristophanes. According to Aristophanes, older Athenians used to say:
"What we decide foolishly and against all reason will in the end work out
to our advantage." He was referring to a line in one of his comedies, in
which the Athenians were shown as owing success more to luck than
cleverness, but the dictum nevertheless applies to the years after 460 B.C.
When a power is as strong as Athens was at that time, so far ahead of
others, and so quick and daring that the surprise effect alone of its actions
increases its capabilities, then such a power can afford to make quite a few
mistakes, and even its mistakes may indeed bring about desired results.

No other power could hope to equal Athens in any respect but particularly not when it came to Athens' foremost military asset, its navy.
Athenian naval superiority was based not only on money, which Athens
had to spare, but also on experience at sea. "If there is anything that
depends on a methodical approach," Pericles said, "it is sea power. Naval
prowess cannot be attained quickly and practiced on the side, as it were,
whenever one happens to be in the mood. One has to make it one's primary goal." The Athenians had been working to improve their skills at
naval warfare ever since the Persian Wars, but though short of perfection,
no one else could expect to catch up with them.

But beyond such considerations of wealth, experience, and persistence in striving toward perfection, Athens' superiority was too deeply rooted in the particular nature of the Athenian people—in their greatness, their political order, their new mentality, and their Attic identity—to be easily imitated by others.

The Greeks as a whole cared less about power than the Athenians and more about life in general, social pleasures, public appearance, and sports. They were determined to live a certain way, and the means to this end were provided by their slaves. They might work, increase their wealth, set themselves certain tasks, even strive after their city's independence and perhaps power. But they would do nothing in excess. The ambitions of the members of the Delian League were not high, and the power of the many small cities could not easily be harnessed for common action. So it was not difficult for the Greeks to make their peace with Athens' superiority.

Athens' growth, the immigrants it attracted from foreign parts, including many highly skilled and versatile men, and its position as a commercial center all worked in the city's favor.

Thucydides quotes Pericles to the effect that because of Athens' greatness goods from all over the world flowed into the city, thus allowing the Athenians to enjoy both foreign and native products. In a long passage from Hermippus, a writer of comedies, the muses tell the poet all the things Dionysus is carrying on his black ship. The reader feels himself transported to the harbor in Piraeus, where oxskins and silphium (a popular medicinal plant and drug) from Cyrene were unloaded; salted fish from the Hellespont; pigs and cheese from Syracuse; cotton and papyrus from Egypt; and frankincense from Syria. Libya supplied ivory; Rhodes, raisins and dried figs, which were believed to cause pleasant dreams; Euboea, apples and pears; Phrygia, slaves; Phoenicia, dates and almonds; Carthage, carpets and colorful pillows.

A negative perspective on Athens' character as a trading center is provided by a pamphlet claiming that all manner of effete, decadent luxury goods produced in Sicily, Italy, Cyprus, Egypt, Lydia, on the Black Sea, or in the Peloponnese found their way to Athens. The harbor in Piraeus was like a central market for Greece. In other places exotic goods could be had now and then, but in Athens everything was always available.

According to Aristophanes, fresh cucumbers, pumpkins, grapes, pears, garlands of violets, and much more were offered for sale, even in the depths of winter. Walking along the stands, he claims, one hardly knew what season it was. But this did not improve life, he said, for it tempted one to spend money foolishly. Athens, it seemed, had turned into Egypt.

The Athenians at that time incorporated many foreign words into their language and increasingly adopted foreign dress and manners. All these borrowings must have combined with Attic wit and intelligence to create a cosmopolitan atmosphere.

Pericles' remark about the virtues of Athens as a marketplace follows on his statement that Athens had also created the greatest possibilities for respite from melancholy. From this time on, Greek culture would be centered on this city. Around 460, Phidias created the first new landmark of Athens, a statue of Athena Promachos, ten meters tall. The point of her spear could be seen from far out at sea.

Because of its dynamic spirit, Athens in many ways became a foreign element in the Greek world of those days. More precisely, it was at once a foreign element and the focal point of Greek culture—a strange mixture.

A ruling power that was both outsider and mischief maker, a city given to excesses but that also set the norm would appear paradoxical. Athens must indeed have been paradoxical, and its enigmatic nature is precisely why this city attracted so much interest at the time and has continued to do so ever since.

Its prominence only added to Athens' fascination. People everywhere studied with intense interest what was happening in this city. They compared, judged from a distance, and watched to see what the consequences of events there would be.

Many developments in this period owed their inception to Athenian influence but arose in other parts of Greece. Ultimately, however, they came to fruition in Athens. Sophist thought, for example, was first explored in Abdera, on Ceos, in Chalcedon (near the Bosporus), in Elis, and Sicily, as well as other places, but its practitioners congregated in Athens. Sculptors and painters learned their art in Argos, on Thasos, or elsewhere but then often practiced it in Athens. One of the most celebrated philosophers of the time, Anaxagoras, came from Clazomenae, a city in Asia Minor, and settled in Athens, where he became Pericles' friend and teacher.

Athens was like a capital city that makes other towns look provincial by comparison. The public life of Greece as a whole was changed by the fact that Athens had moved so far beyond other cities. For Athens was not only the scene of power politics, it was also the place where Greek culture opened up entirely new dimensions. For centuries to come, Athens would remain the most important city in the eastern Mediterranean. And here we touch on what is possibly the most elusive problem presented to us by Athens and the fifth century.

There have been other highly dynamic periods in world history when states or revolutionary classes gathered together all their energies and for a time dominated or captured the countries around them or, indeed, the entire world. And of course such mobilizations of energy are, as in the case of Athens, not limited to the political, military, and technological realms but are accompanied by scientific and artistic productivity. This breadth of influence is what makes such periods remarkable.

In the fifth century, during a period of tremendous political and military activity, Athens produced great tragedies, including, around the middle of the century, Aeschylus's *Oresteia* and Sophocles' *Antigone*. The sculptors working then included Myron, who created the *Discus Thrower*, and was the designer of the *Athena Promachus* and the sculpture of the Parthenon. Some of the foremost architects of ancient Greece, such as Ictinus and Mnesicles, planned and in most cases were able to execute their great works for Athens. It was in Athens that Herodotus began his *Histories*, the first work of Western historiography. And in this same city, a radically new way of asking questions and thinking was taking shape that would culminate in Plato's philosophy. Sophist philosophy and the natural sciences were represented, too, though they flourished mostly outside of Athens.

All this was taking place largely in the public arena, before the eyes of the Attic citizens who made up the audience. It took place partly under the citizens' supervision and with their express approval. As with the construction of buildings on the Acropolis, all this activity was accompanied by their lively interest.

How was this possible? Did long-term developments in Greek art, philosophy, and wisdom follow a kind of inherent logic in order that they all reach their highest point at the same time? What role did democracy play in this flowering of poetry, the visual arts, architecture, science, and philosophy, all of which would have great impact on later times?

Of course, it would be absurd to call this art or this science "democratic." Much of it was produced under the most varied political systems. Yet democracy proved to be a competent architect, at least in the case of the Acropolis. The age of great tragedy, too, is clearly linked to Attic democracy and the audience of Attic citizens.

We must not overlook, of course, that fifth-century Athens was building on the accomplishments and qualities of all of Greece. Jacob

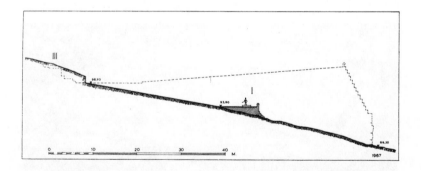

This vertical cross section shows that the Pnyx was created not by merely digging a "theater" into the hillside, but by building up the ground, modestly at first, in the fifth century B.C., with the speaker's platform on the downhill side (toward the right in the picture), and then, in the fourth century B.C., on a massive scale. At this point the semicircular arena for the assembly was created and the speaker's platform moved to the uphill side. The state of the site today reflects this latter stage.

Burckhardt asserted that there was a "great parallel" between fifth-century Athens and Renaissance Florence: In both cases, "*one* city is most eager and best able to achieve what an entire people would like to accomplish." Perhaps Athens fit this description in part because, by introducing democracy, it showed and learned for the first time that the political system as a whole was subject to choice.

The internal changes that took place in Athens in the years after 460 must have been enormous. Getting rid of the Areopagus meant the absence of established rules for dealing with complex matters. It required not just assigning new responsibilities to the Council of Five Hundred, the popular assembly, and the people's court, but it also entailed allowing uncertain new situations. Tasks the Areopagus had been carrying out instinctively, ways of doing things that must have appeared obvious after years of repeated discussion and experience, were now reexamined and debated again and again. People must have felt both more anxious and freer than ever before, a combination that offered special opportunities to those daring enough to act on them. The period was an exciting one in politics, as politics was now really taking place in the midst of the citi-

Reconstruction (after H. A. Thompson) of the Pnyx during the fifth century B.C. The view is from where the agora would have been, in the northeast. The stony ground must have been evened out, though not as smoothly as it appears here.

zenry. And it was at this time that a new place of assembly for the people, the Pnyx, was set up just above the agora.

Some citizens must have been infected by the indignant mood that prevailed among the aristocracy, for many of the noble lords found it hard to accept the Areopagus's loss of power. They could not imagine how things could go on without them. Ephialtes' murder (which was never solved) may not have been instigated by the aristocrats, but it certainly reflected the aristocracy's feelings. Years later, the aristocrats' disaffection would be revealed when several of them were suspected of conspiring with the Spartans to overthrow the Athenian democracy.

The relations between the sexes must also have undergone major changes during this period. The wives of aristocrats probably experienced enough of their husbands' superiority and benefited enough from the privileges of their station that they bore their isolation with pride. But what about middle-class women, especially the wives of the *thetes*? Their husbands were hardly superior, and apart from occasional shares in booty, they had no privileges. As long as things went well, this may not have mattered much, but when the wars began to claim many victims, and above all when the Greeks were defeated, relations between the sexes must have been affected.

The relationship to the slaves was probably less affected by all this change, although the number of slaves had increased significantly. It is unclear how the rights and responsibilities of citizens differed from those of metics, or how farmers' rights differed from those of the urban population. But in any case, these issues were not politically explosive.

Tensions arose in the process of raising and educating children in the Athens of that time. Then as before, children were brought up on fairy tales and old myths, a practice that continued well beyond children's early years. They learned little more than reading, writing, and some skills in the fine arts. The rest of education was left entirely up to the parents, and the share of teaching supplied by mothers and grandmothers must have grown larger the more the men devoted themselves to politics and war. The world the boys would eventually enter—by participating in sports and homoerotic relationships and observation of political life—was, however, completely different from that of the old myths—in its rationality, its scope, and its capacity for radical change.

The generation that entered politics during the era of Cleisthenes had by now grown old. Aeschylus was about sixty-five. Those who fought at Marathon were at least fifty. Men of forty had been barely old enough to fight at Salamis. An entire generation had reached adulthood in the years after the Persian Wars, and the world appeared to them in a completely different light. Now, too, though for reasons other than those Hesiod had in mind, people must have found that children no longer resembled their parents.

The size and ubiquity of the gulf between time-honored traditions and what was expedient must have become obvious. Armies still set out accompanied by diviners, said prayers, and made offerings before battles. But even so, the need for bold political planning was also recognized, and there was no longer any place for the gods in that planning. The coexistence of old and new was not easy to explain.

It cannot have been easy for the Athenians to reconcile what they were with what they felt they had to be. Traditional values were left further and further behind. Principles of morality no longer supplied adequate rules for politics, and it was unclear whether the new constitution, which had done away with the Areopagus, reflected the will of the gods. Now there was no routine, no sense of the resignation to fate that can so easily relieve people of the necessity to measure events and actions against generally accepted principles.

Looking back on Greek history, we wonder if the Athenians were psychologically equipped to exercise their power and occupy the hegemonic position to which it would soon lead. First of all, the Greeks had always had difficulties with exercising power—both the tasks required to maintain it and the delegation of authority to others. It remained unclear whether these tendencies could coexist in the long run with the demands of a rulership, which presupposes some kind of close connection with some of the ruled. Furthermore, the Athenians had no time to learn the skills needed to ensure the cooperation of potential allies, including the ability to exercise tolerance and strictness at the same time.

"Greek history passed so quickly," Nietzsche observed. "Never again did anyone live to such excess." And Jacob Burckhardt remarked, "It is as though nature had gathered up all her energy for centuries in order to squander it here." He speaks of a "total unleashing of forces, including the wrong ones."

After the demotion of the Areopagus, that is, after it was stripped of all effective power, changes followed each other in rapid succession. Soon after its political revolution, Athens not only canceled its alliance with Sparta and entered into a new one with Argos and Thessaly but also allied itself with Megara, which was battling Corinth, its old, more powerful rival. Corinth may have been taking advantage of Sparta's inability to act in order to expand its own power at the expense of other members of the Peloponnesian League. At issue in the dispute were only a few strips of land. Since Sparta offered no help, Megara withdrew from the league— and may at the same time have adopted a democratic constitution. The Athenians came to the Megarians' aid, occupied their harbor at Pagae on the Corinthian Gulf, and proposed building long walls connecting Megara with Nisaea, the harbor on the Saronic Bay. They then helped build the walls and provided a garrison for guarding them. Thus Megara's access to the sea was secured and the road connecting the Peloponnese with central Greece fell under Athenian control.

The building of the long walls indicates that Athens and Megara feared renewed attacks. Such attacks would have been directed not so much at Megara as at the growing influence of Athens in the mainland.

The Athenians seem to have been more at odds with the Corinthians and the Aeginetans than with the Spartans, whom the Athenians and the Argives defeated in a battle near Oenoe, south of Argos. That victory was immortalized in a mural in the *stoa poikile*.

The fighting was not restricted to Megara. The Athenians also descended on Halieis in southern Argolis, where they were beaten by Corinthian troops and allied Epidaurians, who were old foes of Argos. In a naval encounter off the island of Cecryphalea, southwest of Aegina, the Athenians prevailed, and soon after that they defeated the Aeginetans as well. Peloponnesian city-states are said to have fought on both sides, which apparently means that here, too, the Corinthians fought against the Athenians. When the Athenians subsequently landed at Aegina to lay siege to the city, three hundred Peloponnesian hoplites came to its help.

At this time, about 460–459, the rebel Messenians on Mount Ithome surrendered, on condition that they be allowed to withdraw unhindered. The Athenians offered them a place to live in Naupactus. Athens had earlier conquered Naupactus and used it to settle allies at the entry to the Corinthian Gulf.

Thus open confrontation replaced coexistence. Corinth's and Athens' old rival Aegina was bound to feel threatened by the new alliance between Athens and Argos. In any case, Athens saw greater immediate gain from the annexation of Megara than the loose community of interests connecting Athens with Corinth, which was trying to safeguard its own independence in the balance of power between Sparta and Athens.

From Pagae, Attic ships could block Corinth's harbor on the gulf. The positions at Pagae and at Naupactus gave the Athenians control over all the maritime traffic through the gulf. Corinth reacted by harassing Argos in the Argolis region. Athens in turn attacked Halieis.

The Corinthians tried to free Aegina from the Athenian blockade by invading Megarid territory. But Athens responded by conscripting men as old as fifty and as young as eighteen. The battle that ensued ended without a clear winner, but the Corinthians suffered great losses and the Athenians raised a victory column.

Eventually, Athens ran short of troops because it was simultaneously waging war in Egypt. In 460–459 it dispatched a fleet of two hundred Athenian and confederate ships to Cyprus. The intent was to rid the island entirely of Persian influence. Once there, the Greeks received a call for help from Inarus, a Libyan potentate who had started a revolt in Egypt. Sixty-five years after its subjugation by the Persians, Egypt was to be freed of Persian rule. Inarus had already caused parts of Egypt to rebel against Persia, and he had defeated a Persian army.

The Athenians apparently felt they could do more harm to the Persians in Egypt than on Cyprus. But what looked like a grand strategy ultimately, in view of limited Greek power, amounted to nothing more than a series of isolated engagements. We don't know when the

Athenians realized the futility of their campaign. Their fleet sailed up the Nile. Enemy ships were routed and Memphis was captured, with the exception of the citadel, which was successfully defended by the Persians. Large sections of lower Egypt fell into the hands of the confederates.

An inscription dating from 459, now in the Louvre, lists one year's war casualties among the tribe of Erechtheids. It contains 177 names, about five percent of the tribe, quite a high proportion. The men had fallen on Cyprus, in Egypt, Phoenicia, and Aegina, and at Halieis and Megara—six different theaters of war in one year. Phoenicia is probably counted among them because a raiding expedition had been sent there and had become involved in a sea battle off the coast. It is possible, of course, that this was not the norm, that the Erechtheids suffered exceptionally high losses that year.

In any case, the number of lives claimed by Attic warfare was high in general. Since the 470s, Athens had commemorated the dead once a year, in autumn, with a special celebration to honor the fallen soldiers. At some point the city also began to support war orphans at public expense. The year the boys reached majority, they were given hoplite equipment at a ceremony preceding the theater productions of the Dionysia.

These great military adventures typified Athens in the period after the Areopagus lost its power. The new leaders were determined to take control over both foreign and domestic politics. But the demotion of the Areopagus may also have led to a loss of competence in managing complicated foreign affairs. The men who played a key role in the Council of Five Hundred and the popular assembly would have to learn from the ground up how to do their jobs.

Another outcome of the new policies was the building, in about 459, of two long walls, one linking Athens to Piraeus, the other to Phalerum. The walls extended about 7.2 and 6.3 kilometers, respectively. Together with the walls encircling Athens and Piraeus, the city's fortifications stretched to 26 kilometers. The job of defending them was to be handled by three daily shifts of citizens who were either too young or too old for military service, along with metics and other reserve forces. Each man was responsible for about 5 meters of wall. Only the side of the triangle formed by the sea, which the fleet could defend, was left unfortified.

These long walls, which cost great amounts of money and manpower, indicate how vulnerable Athens' dominant position was. After the Persian campaign, Themistocles had suggested rebuilding the city directly on the Piraeus peninsula. Now the Athenians were fortifying an area that could accommodate the inhabitants of all of Attica, in case it became necessary to evacuate their entire country, as they had done before Salamis.

With these walls, however, the city could, in an emergency, be turned into a kind of island: unassailable by land yet able to obtain everything it needed. With its navy, control over the trade routes, and support of allies, Athens embodied the old Greek ideal of autarky. Finding themselves in such a position must have contributed considerably to the Athenians' pride. It is remarkable not just that Pericles had the idea of building these walls but also that the popular assembly went along with him. The whole system of walls must have been planned before the period when the Athenians first suggested building the long walls between Megara and Nisaea.

At the end of March 458, the Athenians witnessed the performance of one of the greatest works in world literature, the *Oresteia* by Aeschylus. Many of the spectators had come from long distances for the Dionysian festival, some leaving home in the early morning hours, others spending the night with friends in the city.

This trilogy comprised the first plays the poet had written after the demotion of the Areopagus, and demonstrates the radical nature of this event as well as the uneasiness that gripped all of Athens in its wake. In a way rarely seen in history, the three plays provided answers to the difficult questions that had arisen. The momentousness of the political change in Athens was similar in historical magnitude to Aeschylus's trilogy, which dealt with the entire history of humanity, with man's fate and the meaning of his existence. A revolution unlike any preceding it had taken place. The *Oresteia* was a masterpiece of literature that wove all these themes together in a terrifying myth and tried to make sense of it all.

The mystery of the *Oresteia* is in a sense the mystery of Athens, and the drama can serve as a key to understanding fifth-century Athens. The trilogy tells the story of the house of Atreus. The first play, *Agamemnon,* presents the king's homecoming from the Trojan War and his death at the hands of his wife, Clytemnestra. The murder is part of a generations-old vendetta. As supreme commander of the Greeks, Agamemnon had been ordered by an oracle to sacrifice his daughter Iphigenia to Artemis so that the fleet could finally obtain the winds needed to sail. By killing Agamemnon, Clytemnestra avenges Iphigenia's death. But the slaying is also revenge for her lover, Aegisthus. Agamemnon's father, Atreus, had once served a meal to Aegisthus's father, Thyesthes, that contained meat from the bodies of Thyesthes' slain older sons. This was done in retaliation for Thyestes' adulterous relationship with Atreus's wife.

The same cycle of crime and vengeance can be found in legendary Greek politics, where revenge on Troy was justified, though not the destruction of its sacred shrines. In *Agamemnon,* the old vendetta theme is taken up again and used as justification for the death of most of the

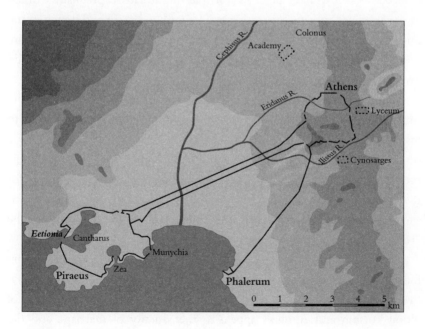

The long walls

317

warriors on their homeward journey: "Let me not plunder cities," the chorus sings, "neither be taken in turn, and face life under the power of another."

The grim logic of the vendetta also reveals the impotence of the polis, which is unable to stop the violence. The citizens experience the consequences primarily in the form of tyranny, for the unlawful rule of the queen and her lover is regarded as tyrannical in *Agamemnon* and even more so in the second play, *The Libation Bearers,* in which Orestes, Agamemnon's son, returns and plots the revenge of his father's murder. Here the extreme perversity of the law of vengeance becomes obvious. Orestes can avenge his father only by killing his mother, which Apollo of Delphi has ordered him to do under threat of severe punishment. Because there are no mortal avengers left after the matricide, the ancient and terribly feared Furies, the Erinyes, have to take on the persecution of Orestes.

The final play, *Eumenides,* presents the account of Orestes' acquittal by the court of the Areopagus, and the appeasement of the Furies by Athena. Apollo absolves Orestes of his guilt and promises to help him, but the Furies are still pursuing him. The sight of the Furies in the first performance was said to have been so horrible that it caused pregnant women in the audience to have miscarriages. The rattling breath and stench of the Furies were so nauseating that no one in the audience was able to endure their presence. Snakes poked out from their hair, and a disgusting fluid dripped from their eyes.

When Orestes travels to Athens at the end of his flight from the pursuing Erinyes, he seeks out Athena, the city's goddess. Athena listens to his story and decides that the matter is too difficult to be solved by a single individual, be it man or god, and so she appoints a court to adjudicate it, surprisingly the Areopagus. Athena convenes the Areopagus for the first time and solemnly entrusts the responsibility for Athens to its care. In her speech introducing the court, she specifically addresses the "men of Athens"—the audience.

Both sides present their case with passion and exaggeration. Apollo himself takes over Orestes' defense. The conflict is ultimately defined as that between the Furies' insistence that Orestes violated the bond of blood kinship and Apollo's appeal to the sanctity of marriage and the principles of law. The difference between men and women is also raised:

"It is not the same thing for a man of blood to die / honored with the king's staff given by the hand of god / and that by means of a woman." Apollo goes so far as to argue that a mother's only function in a child's life is to harbor the father's seed.

When the Areopagites cast their votes, Athena casts her own in Orestes' favor. Her verdict is a biased one, because she always sides with the male. After all, she herself had no mother, having sprung from her father's forehead.

The result is a tie. The majority of the mortal judges find Orestes guilty, and yet he is aquitted, thanks to the vote of a divinity. Freed, he returns to Argos. In a clear message to the audience, he speaks of the eternal gratitude his city will owe to Athens.

The Furies next vent their hatred on Athens, threatening to bring the plague and civil war down on the city. It is not Apollo but his sister who responds to them. She tries gamely to appease them, offering them a place of honor and worship just below the Acropolis. She flatters them with all the charm at her command. Three times the Furies refuse to be reconciled, but after the fourth try they give in. The play ends with songs of blessing and the Erinyes' departure to their shrine near the Areopagus, the hill where the council called the Areopagus met and from which it took its name. They have now become *"eumenides,"* well-disposed ones, rather than *erinyes*.

The Oresteian trilogy must have had a powerfully liberating effect in the way it dealt with and revealed order in the events of the recent past. The great debate in *Eumenides* touched on much that the Athenians had just experienced. Its themes all involve the struggle of the new against the old. Even the fact that it was up to a court—rather than the gods—to decide the fate of a confessed murderer was new. Orestes' acquittal was even more revolutionary. That is why the Furies lament that justice is being violated and a new kind of law introduced. They cite well-established and hallowed institutions in support of their case. Their opponents carefully avoid investing their intentions with any sign of novelty. Novelty does not win converts.

Whether or not the closeness of the vote in *Eumenides* was an allusion to the recent past, we know that Cimon had been absent from Athens, helping the Spartans, at the crucial time of the Areopagus vote. Even so, it is clear that voting and accepting the results of a vote on such a matter were extremely difficult. In this sense, too, a parallel exists between the drama and reality.

The danger from the vanquished enemies also enters into the play. Ephialtes had been murdered, and fear of civil war and treason was widespread in the city. There is no indication that reconcilation had taken place in the intervening time. It is possible that Aeschylus's *Oresteia* and the figure of Athena as shown in the play helped pave the way toward reconciliation.

Even if the *Oresteia* did address the current Athenian situation, it was in no sense a tendentious work, not even in its conclusion. Aeschylus can be cited as much in support of the Areopagus, whose role he stresses so strongly, as in support of Ephialtes. If there is anything the tragedian tried to bring about, it is the reconciliation of all parties. But this is by no means all the work is about; it is a drama with relevance for all mankind, and that is precisely why it held such interest for contemporary Athens.

It seems reasonable to assume that the questions Aeschylus tried to answer in this trilogy must have been felt by the public that watched the performance. The poet and the public must have thought alike. After all, the people of Athens were alert, wary, and constantly caught up in important decisions that conformed to no routine. The people presumed the right to understand their own actions and to fit them into the overall context of the course of events.

As Aeschylus tells it, the story of the house of Atreus in many respects parallels the historical process leading to the emergence of the polis. It shows the path that led from the time when humans were subject to blood feuds to the moment when the citizens' own political decisions and their own court determined what happened in their city-states. The path Aeschylus traces leads from the affairs of a single family, affairs that impose suffering on everyone else, to the public realm of the polis, which, remarkably, is represented by the Areopagus.

The transformation is evident even in details of the trilogy. At first, almost all of the action takes place behind the palace walls and very little in front of the gate. The chorus of old men in *Agamemnon* is able and willing to whisper only cautiously about what it knows, partly because the city is gripped by terror. The old men suspect something horrible is about to happen and are aware of the deeper connections that will bring it about. An inevitable retribution is taking place, yet they are bewildered when it happens.

"Why must this persistent fear / beat its wings so ceaselessly / and so close against my mantic heart? / Why this strain unwanted, unrepaid, thus prophetic?" Agamemnon has returned victorious. Although this should be reason for rejoicing, the mourning song of the Furies sounds in the hearts of the old men: "This whirl of drifts / that spin the stricken heart." The old men are torn between joy and foreboding. Again and again their cry of woe alternates with the hope that good may prevail.

In the second play, conspiratorial preparations are made for the murder of Clytemnestra and Aegisthus right before the spectators' eyes. The debate between mother and son that precedes the murder is carried on at the palace gate.

The third play opens in the bright light of Delphi where Orestes has sought refuge. When the scene shifts to Athens, the action there takes place in an open square. Murder has finally given way to peaceful decision-making. The citizens must act and judge for themselves. The problems are not simple, but they are out in the open. The opposing parties confront each other with all the clarity one could hope for.

At the same time, the play shows that man has no one to rely on now except himself. The citizens who have to adjudicate a quarrel between the gods cannot, like Orestes, simply follow a god's command. Athena herself has given them freedom—along with everything that freedom entails.

Presumably, Aeschylus believed in the theory of cultural evolution that was spreading at the time. People no longer adhered to the old idea of a golden age at the beginning of history, a glorious state from which humanity had subsequently descended. Instead culture was seen now as a human accomplishment—beginning from nothing, man is urged onward by need and necessity. Not unlike the Scottish social philosophers' speculative history, the Greeks' notion of cultural progress was tied primarily to a sequence of technological breakthroughs.

At the beginning of *Agamemnon*, Aeschylus himself refers to an innovation developed by the Delian League. For ten years a watchman has scanned the horizon, waiting for the beacon signal that would announce the fall of Troy. Finally the flash comes. None of the old men in the chorus believes such a thing possible, but Clytemnestra describes the passing of the signal from one point to the next in detail. Only a great power could implement such a system of signals sent across vast distances. By showing the astonishing conquest of spatial distance, Aeschylus suggests how quickly great time differences could be overcome as well. This is the theme of the *Oresteia.*

Thucydides would later reconstruct the history of the Greeks as a process leading to an increase in the size and power of the polis. In the *Oresteia*, Aeschylus traces the concomitant internal history of the polis. The trilogy starts with the polis as the helpless pawn of uncontrollable processes and ends with political will guiding events; blind force is replaced by passionate but nonviolent debate, which finally brings about reconciliation.

But the story is told with reference to a larger context, in which the entire world participates. In *Eumenides* many oppositions are introduced, between old and new, blood kinship and marital law, male and female, barbarian and Greek, wild and civilized, dark and light, and ancient gods and younger gods. Since these various forces and realms collide with each other, right cannot be told from wrong except by the rules of court procedure.

In the first two plays of the trilogy, everything is mixed up. A woman with a man's heart commits murder. Normally, civilization and wilderness are separate, and man enters the wilderness only when he hunts; even then he has to respect the fact that the unborn and the young are under Artemis's protection. In *Agamemnon*, however, men are the quarry, not the hunters; the queen is described as a "bitch" and a "she-wolf," and the killing extends to the unborn and the young. In Troy the god's sanctuaries are not just devastated, the "seed" is destroyed, too. The goal is annihilation. The whole vocabulary of the play shows how badly the world is out of kilter.

Even the gods end up on opposite sides in a conflict that involves not just the fate of individual mortals but the entire divine order. By interpreting events as determined by the gods, Aeschylus falls back on a historical belief, the myth of the succession of divine dynasties. From this myth he takes the idea of conflict between the newer, younger gods of the Zeus dynasty and the Furies, who belong to a more ancient race. But by the time the conflict develops, the supremacy of Zeus has long since been established. Zeus himself tells Apollo that Orestes must murder his mother. Apollo threatens Orestes with the wrath of the Furies, over whom he consequently must have command, if Orestes does not obey. But then Zeus does an about-face, and the gods realign themselves. This parallels the situation in Athens, where the supreme power had long since rested with the popular assembly and where the Areopagus, though it played a decisive role, was part of the isonomous order when democracy began to do away with the "rule by the best." Aeschylus does not show why Zeus changed policy so fundamentally in the midst of his rule. The only thing clear is that Zeus came to support the new.

Finally, the world-encompassing events of the play come together in Athens at Athena's shrine on the Acropolis and on the Areopagus, which stood behind the audience's back. What happens on the stage comes awfully close to a depiction of reality. Athens becomes the hub of all the action.

Because the decision concerning Orestes' fate represents an unmistakable parallel to Athens' political decision of 461, the legitimation of the one implies the legitimation of the other. The decision in 461 to divest the Areopagus of its power was not a passing delusion, a mere interruption of the proper, normal state of affairs; it had to be accepted, just like the verdict pronounced on Orestes in Aeschylus's play, a verdict that, though it barely passes and is clearly biased, is nevertheless confirmed by Athena and ushers in a new kind of law.

As *Eumenides* progresses, it shows that something else has to be accepted: the principle of moderation. Zeus alloted victory and power (*kratos*) to the "middle." The city was to be neither too uncontrolled nor too controlled. This sounds like a denial, or at least a relativization of the democracy that was advocated so strongly in *The Suppliants*. Acceptance and legitimation of a decision require reason, moderation, and the grace with which Athena softens the consequences of the decision. They require the victor's willingness to make peace. At the end of the play we are told specifically that it was Zeus Agoraeos who won, the Zeus of the marketplace and of orderly debate.

Thus the new and the old came together. Intellectually the new was integrated into the old, into the traditional view of the world and into the principles of a "right order." The old was, in return, given a place in the victorious new political system. This is a pragmatic decision, for the new needs the old—it can last only if it becomes more moderate. The play states explicitly that the right order needs a monstrous, terrible, and frightening element. This was represented by the ancient Furies—and, in the case of fifth-century B.C. Athens, the Areopagus.

The theory holds that men should not be entirely free; they have to be afraid of something. But fear by itself is useless. As we are told in *The Libation Bearers*, fear rules under a tyrant but leads only to opportunism and the worship of good fortune, which is pursued by all means available, just or unjust. To be effective, fear must be mixed with awe, with reverence for the gods, which also means respect for others. In earlier days, this reverence penetrated deeply and irresistibly into the hearts of people. It disappeared during the period of tyranny, but in Athens, on the Areopagus, it will, the goddess says, join fear and prevent injustice. Once that happens, democracy will be safe.

Aeschylus's decision to draw the gods into the action of the play makes good sense. The highest god was associated with the demand for justice, indeed with the certainty that ultimately everything on earth followed a rightful path. Zeus also stood for the idea of a right order. What was taking place when the trilogy was written was not simply a deviation from that order but the establishment of a counterorder. The ordinary, uneducated people—those meant to follow the aristocratic leadership, though with the right to a political voice—now wanted to take over leadership themselves. If this was to be accepted, the old belief that there was *one* right order could no longer hold true. Thus the authority of Zeus, too, was affected by the political revolution. The problem was no longer how different claims were to be reconciled in one order, since the aristocracy's and the people's claims to leadership were mutually exclusive. Aeschylus attempted to save Zeus's authority by suggesting that what the god really wanted was moderation—"the middle"—rather than a specific order, and that he merely insisted on a principle, which could be realized in any number of political orders.

But in the play, all the changes within the polis are to be accompanied by a new unity. In their songs of blessing at the end of the play, the Furies invoke the spirit of friendship among citizens. "Let them render grace for grace. / Let love be their common will; / let them hate with single heart. / Much wrong in the world thereby is healed." The Furies' efforts within the city will be complemented by Athena's aid in Athens' great outward achievements. The transformation in the image of friend and enemy could be described in similar terms. Internal conflict and the threat of civil war were replaced by a united front. The city's military successes were to bridge the divides those very successes had opened up when they made Ephialtes' reforms possible. The aristocrats shared in the successes, and that helped them make their peace with the new order.

Ancient Greek political "theory" was probably never as comprehensive or accurate as at this point. Both before and after, it focused primarily on internal politics and political institutions. Only during this period do we find reflections on the connection between the domestic and foreign realms. The history of politics was taking a great step forward.

Aeschylus's use of Greek legend to fit the Aeropagus's loss of power into a larger context does not necessarily imply that the past of *Agamemnon* had been overcome for good by the Athenians, or the Greeks in general. The Greeks did not tend to think in terms of historical processes. They had never before known a concept of history that took in so much of the world. They might understand certain periods of time in terms of a historical framework—Aeschylus goes quite far in this direction—but they never imagined that the connections they drew were definitive. The Greeks did not believe that the new did away with the old. The occurrences of the dark world of the past were still alive, at least as something to be contemplated. That is why the consciousness of the old had to be kept alive, and on this point popular and high culture agreed. Written literature incorporated oral tradition, the fantastic, and the vague into the theater. The formed and the as yet unformed continued to coexist. The memory of chaos was kept alive because the imagination was still given free rein and old notions were not declared out of bounds.

It may have been particularly important in newly democratic Athens to preserve everything old, including all the myths, to foster much needed unity. *Agamemnon* in particular is full of fear and confusion. All the elements are intermingled, muddled: at first, good seems to gain the upper hand, then evil does. The horror is oppressively palpable in the possible cruelty of the gods, the impenetrability of their will, and the curse sent by the "demon," for no known reason. We hear of endless misery stemming from great wealth, yet we also hear that only godless acts spell ruin, that he who respects the law will not lose happiness. To this extent justice prevails. But there are only occasional glimpses of such justice, and they are followed by passages that suggest the contrary. What is the life of mortal man like? "Alas, poor men, their destiny. When all goes well / a shadow will overthrow it. If it be unkind / one stroke of a wet sponge wipes all the picture away; / and that is by far the most unhappy thing of all."

That is why *Agamemnon* is the tragedy of all humanity, of our sorrows, fears, and vulnerability. As long as Zeus presides, the law that "He who acts must suffer" prevails. At the same time there are indications of hope, such as in the famous prayer to Zeus, which includes all the elements of a "theodicy," a defense of god's goodness in the face of evil. Zeus "taught man to think," Aeschylus writes. "He issued the law: Learn through suffering. Sorrow enters even sleep, dripping into the heart, sorrow which cannot forget suffering, and reason grows despite man's will." He who remembers Zeus and praises him as master gains understanding and insight into the totality of things. This process seems to reach its goal in *Eumenides*, where the Furies praise the Athenians as "those who love the beloved maiden Pallas Athena," thereby gaining understanding.

Similarly image and counterimage combine in *Agamemnon* to give a complete picture. The herald starts out telling about the triumph over Troy and ends up reporting how most of the victors perished on their homeward journey. The chorus sings its hymn to victory and then turns to the unhappiness the many deaths will cause. Triumph and fear, victory and disaster, happiness and guilt are all part of the whole. The idea of learning through suffering pervades the play like a desperate, ultimately triumphant hope.

How profoundly Athens must have been shaken by the city's upheavals to make necessary such a huge, all-embracing effort as the *Oresteia* to regain spiritual equilibrium. At the same time, the *Oresteia* demonstrates the Athenians' remarkably well-developed faculty of perception, their ability to mediate experience and to work things through, both in poetry and in public life.

The Athenians possessed the capacity to be amazed by the world, a capacity that Max Weber called a prerequisite of all unbiased inquiry. Clearly the Athenians had, when faced with radical change, both the ability to take into account centuries of experience and a nearly boundless imagination.

Greek tragedy from approximately 472 on reflects the human experience of the self as an autonomous being confronted with the question of what it means to be the source of all action, exposed to the delusion and sorrow that invade man's sleep and seep into his heart. Tragedy expresses what it means to know without knowing, to say the right thing without intending to, and to do what one must without being forced into it.

In responding to such experiences, tragedy fell back on the Greek myths from which it took its themes. But what it made of these myths was the accomplishment of tragedy itself in the fifth century.

In tragedy, the strange convention of alternating the lines of the chorus and the actors made it possible to present on the stage an entire world, with all its contradictions. The problems were expressed as themes taken from ancient times and usually associated with cities other than Athens. This enabled the playwright to deal with these issues at a remove from the pressure of the present.

In a city almost constantly at war, the suffering could be lamented in public. Complaints about Ares, the exchanger of men for corpses; distress over the killing; the grief felt by families; and the wrath of the embittered could all be loudly voiced. "Those who shed much blood will not escape the eye of the gods."

"The Athenians matured," Nietzsche says, "because they were challenged on all fronts." The unique advances they made were achieved in no small measure through the tragedies, which Burckhardt termed "important events involving the entire festive citizenry." Tragedy promoted advances in what we might today call the mental infrastructure.

The life of a city, after all, depends on more than a water supply and the import of food, more than a market with true weights and a reliable medium of exchange. The life of a city also depends on certain norms: customs and ethics, the existence of some basic shared principles, rules of behavior, and a language that facilitates discussion and conflict resolution. There must also be some basis for unity, or solidarity, that serves to stabilize the population in the event of a crisis.

Because developing a mental infrastructure was so important, poetry and tragedy were just as crucial politically for fifth-century Attic life as were the council and the popular assembly. There was much to be learned, and new standards to set. The entire basis of knowledge, the framework into which experience had to be fitted in order to be understood, and the set of fundamental conceptual assumptions all underwent reorganization and revisions. Much traditional knowledge came under question.

For these reasons and because so much was concentrated in the Great Dionysia celebration, work on the mental infrastructure could be done in public, with broad popular participation. The plays were presented in the context of a competition; the poets who wrote them wanted urgently to win prizes; and the jury, no matter how high its standards, could not, when deciding on awards, ignore how accessible and affecting the plays were to the spectators.

Thus poetry assumed a political function without becoming partisan. This explains some of the puzzle that the fifth century presents to us. It was precisely in art that the evolution of the Attic citizen occurred. Because everything was still so interconnected, the citizens were constantly forced to reassess the world, the gods, and justice.

Athens' problems differed from those of cultures formed under monarchy, cultures in which the meaning of the commonweal is conveyed in such a way that the population feels little sense of responsibility for it. The problems also appeared differently from those in lands under well-established aristocratic rule. Because the Greeks' path was so different, they had by now developed a long tradition of looking at the world aesthetically, from a distance. Art had flourished for a very long time, and political thought for a considerable period as well. Both played a large role at the religious celebrations and in tragedy, not just among the educated and the intellectuals but also among the people in general. The tragedians were important for all of society, just as the bards may have been earlier on, and considerably more important than even Virgil or Dante would be later on.

The subject of what we believe to be Aeschylus's last tragedies, also a trilogy, is the story of Prometheus. The only surviving play of the trilogy, *Prometheus Bound,* begins with Prometheus being chained to a rock atop a mountain in the Caucasus. We see the god Prometheus engaged in conversation and argument with his friends, foes, and others who are indifferent to his fate.

What is historically interesting is that here Aeschylus answers the question he left open in the *Oresteia,* namely, why Zeus changed his policy. The action takes place immediately after Zeus assumes supreme power. The highest god does not appear on stage in person, but the fact that he is a tyrant of the worst order is made evident by the stories told and especially through the characters who visit Prometheus, some sent by Zeus, some pursued by him, some taking opportunistic advantage of his rule. Zeus, we learn, initially wanted to do away with all of mankind in order to create a new race of people, but Prometheus prevented him from doing it.

The conflict is once again between old and new, but here it occurs on a higher level. Not just Orestes' fate is at stake but that of the new world order. Zeus is opposed not by the Furies but by Prometheus, whom Aeschylus invests with great stature. He makes him into the son of the first and oldest deity, Gaea, whom he combines with the Titaness Themis, the goddess of law, in other accounts Gaea's daughter. Prometheus thus stands for primal power and wisdom. Zeus owes his victory over Cronos to Prometheus, and Prometheus knows from his mother that Zeus can be overthrown.

Even though he is at Zeus's mercy, Prometheus possesses knowledge needed by the highest god, who has all the power. In the last two plays in the trilogy, some kind of settlement must have been reached. Zeus must have become more moderate and reasonable, and to make peace, he must have tempered his power with wisdom, lending it permanence through restraint.

This is an extraordinary development. Generally we know much about the birth of gods and their youth, but little about what follows. Once they have toppled their predecessors, they take power and proceed to rule. The Zeus of the Prometheus trilogy, however, has to change not only his policy but himself.

Apparently this was the only way a new government could be conceived after the Areopagus was deprived of its power. The difference between the Zeus of myth, who had overthrown his father, and the Zeus of philosophy, who stood for justice in the world, was felt acutely.

There were no higher authorities left to turn to, such as Zeus in the *Oresteia*. In *Prometheus Bound*, Zeus himself is a party to the conflict. Power and knowledge must be reconciled, and in order for that to happen, Zeus must be given a previous history that allows his rule to remain unchallenged in the future.

The questions that were raised when Aeschylus brought Zeus into the history of the polis in the *Oresteia* ultimately led to this point. In that context, Zeus's change of policy must have seemed accidental. But in *Prometheus Bound* it is clear that Zeus himself must have changed at some point. Whereas in the *Oresteia* everything could be resolved with the help of the highest god, *Prometheus Bound* explores what it means if Zeus, the highest authority, just like Athens' popular assembly, has no higher body to which to appeal.

This play suggests how profound an impact the introduction of the first democracy had on Athens—the reverberations reached deep into theology. During the troubled first five years after the political revolution, a new equilibrium had to be found, not just in the polis but in the heavens as well.

The problem of knowledge also enters the theory of cultural evolution propounded by Aeschylus in *Prometheus Bound*. His Prometheus is not a fire thief but someone who has given mankind many arts, including numbers, writing, and self-consciousness, for at the beginning men "looked but saw nothing, listened but heard nothing, and instead let everything flicker by, as in a dream, all their lives." They were in every respect inferior to animals until Prometheus planted "blind hope" in their hearts, so that they no longer stared dumbly at death. *Prometheus Bound* offers the oldest known theory of cultural evolution. It does not mention the ideals of mutual respect and justice, or the virtues of the polis, but perhaps Zeus made provision for them in the two lost plays of the Prometheus trilogy.

Aeschylus died in 456 or 455. He probably first entered the Great Dionysia dramatic competition in 499 and won it for the first time in 484. He won the prize twelve more times. Since he would not normally have been able to write and produce more than four plays every two years, his plays must almost always have won first place. In the 405 comedy *The Frogs*, Aristophanes has Aeschylus win the place of honor in the netherworld. Poets, he suggests, were supposed to be "useful" and "make man better," and it was the task of tragedians to educate the adult population.

Aeschylus said of the visual arts that the older works were simple in execution but deemed divine, whereas new ones were artfully crafted but looked less godlike. This statement could be applied to the tragedian's own works. Aeschylus's gravestone makes no mention of his plays and merely states that the groves of Marathon witnessed his bravery.

In 457 a law was passed in Athens that made members of the third-richest class, the *zeugitae*, eligible for the highest office, that of archon. This law primarily benefited the less affluent among those who had, since Cleisthenes, played a dominant role both in the Council of Five Hundred and in the popular assembly. The circle from among whom the archons were chosen by lot was considerably expanded, and the influence of the archon was bound to diminish as a result. For the *zeugitae* the most important aspect of the change was that it granted them symbolic equality with the upper classes.

Equality was realized in the democracy to a large extent through the positions held by the citizens; that is, through the rotation of office-holders. A later text describes that the rule of the people was achieved by having citizens take turns holding office, and it goes on to say proudly that a poor man had the same right to office as a rich one. This principle was carried out more and more often as time passed. Being in and out of office came to be quite natural, resembling the alternation of day and night, summer and winter.

This law is one of a very few from that period that we can date. Soon after 461 the Athenians began to inscribe decisions of the assembly, accounts, and documents of all kinds on stones that were displayed in public. Democracy meant among other things that the public should be able to inform itself of everything that was happening. Sometime during those years laws must also have been passed that made it financially possible for broader circles to participate in political activity. Per diem remuneration was introduced for attending the Council of Five Hundred and later for various other offices. (Payment for attending the popular assembly was not instituted until the end of the century.) Funds for these expenses were available since Athens' revenues had risen with its expanding power.

The payment of juries is probably of greatest importance in this connection. Originally justice had been administered by officials and, probably, a circle of high-ranking citizens. But from the mid-450s on this function gradually shifted to jury courts. These courts seem at first to have served mostly as councils of appeal, but with the rise in population and the rapid increase of cases, partially due to the new needs for arbitration in the Delian League, the demand for their services kept growing.

Jury courts often consisted of five hundred and occasionally a higher number of citizens. All ten tribes (phylae) were eqully represented in them, but most of the members probably lived in the city. The daily stipend was two oboli, which covered one person's living expenses. As time went on, sitting on a jury became, along with military service, one of the most important public functions the average citizen could exercise.

The large size of the juries and the selection of members by lot probably grew out of the desire to have a true cross section of the citizenry represented. But it was also a matter of involving as many citizens as possible in public life. There they could feel important, as even powerful lords had to bow to the jurors to win their sympathy. This was one of the important ways in which the rule of the people was manifested.

Pay for jury duty also played a role in the economic life of the citizens that should not be underestimated. Many citizens had served the polis as rowers in the navy for over twenty years, which forced them to neglect their ordinary occupations. Warfare and political activity practically became their profession. Their activity as jury members was a logical extension and also provided these citizens, especially the older men, with a living. Every year a list of six thousand jurors was drawn up to staff the individual courts.

At about the same time, since the Council of Five Hundred had gained so much in importance, rules governing its composition must have been drawn up. Members were now chosen by lot. No one was allowed to serve more than twice, and the entire membership changed yearly. These precautions insured that a large cross section of the citizenry was involved in previewing all matters brought before the popular assembly and in handling many administrative matters that could be settled by smaller bodies than the assembly. The intent of the regulations was to let as little power as possible accumulate in the hands of those entrusted with carrying out such tasks.

Various new offices were instituted and many of them filled with ten officials, one from each tribe. This, too, was done to involve many citizens in public administration without too much power accruing to any single individual. It may even have been a conscious principle to spread out governmental honors and tasks in order to make democracy attractive to the people and allow officeholders to feel important, all so that Athens could be governed more easily.

Soon enough, however, the actual task of governing devolved onto a few outstanding men, most of whom held the office of *strategos*, as Cimon had done earlier. Their power was even greater than before, but the difference was that they, unlike Cimon, had to work together closely with the Council of Five Hundred and the popular assembly.

We may assume that a small group of leaders, assisted by friends and perhaps by various experts, were in continual competition for decisive influence. When competition grew out of hand, ostracism could be used to decide which of two contenders was the more powerful.

One such contender during this period was Pericles. He had been instrumental in the dismantling of the Areopagus, but we have no record of what his position was at the time he became prominent.

Pericles was also credited with introducing payment for public service, a change he instituted on the advice of his teacher Damon, son of Damonides and one of the great intellectuals of the time. Damon was particularly interested in the theory of music, which he related closely to politics, because he had found that different rhythms and tonal modes affected the "ethical sense" in different ways; he therefore advocated the use of music in the education of the young.

Malicious tongues claimed that Damon advised Pericles, who was much less wealthy than Cimon, to win over the citizens by dispensing public funds. In reality, though, payment of public servants was a logical consequence of radical democracy, and nobody understood democracy better than Pericles. Damon fell victim to ostracism, probably in the 440s. We don't know if the advice he gave to Pericles had anything to do with his banishment. It is also unclear exactly when and how quickly these changes were introduced. There were still many opponents of democracy in Athens, citizens who were not reconciled to the new conditions. This may have been one reason its advocates strove to establish democracy as solidly as possible.

It is indeed amazing that democracy survived, and many must have thought it would fail. But apparently capable politicians worked for it. Successes abroad also helped; and there must have been no lack of enthusiasm or aptitude. The dynamic of the city did the rest. There was no turning back; things were vigorously moving ahead everywhere.

In the mid–450s Athens' foreign policy and military activities were dominated by the continuing war in Egypt, the siege of Aegina, and the many changes taking place on the mainland.

Thebes was trying at that time to restore its hegemony in Boeotia; it had long been unable to do so because of the pro–Persian position it had taken in 480. The Spartans, able to take more of an interest in Greek politics again now that the siege of Ithome was over, supported Thebes. Their goal was to build up positions against Athens.

When the Spartans found themselves near Athens on their return from a campaign in Boeotia in 457, Attic vessels blocked the sea route across the Corinthian Gulf, and the long walls of Megara blocked what would otherwise have been the relatively convenient land route. The Athenians apparently wanted to demonstrate their new power, but they had not considered how vulnerable they were. Rumors circulated to the effect that the aristocratic lords wanted the Spartans to enter Athens to help them overthrow democracy and stop the building of the long walls. The Spartans were near Tanagra, barely a two-day march from Athens. Their army numbered over 10,000 men.

The Athenians decided to set forth and meet them with an army of 14,000, including Argive and confederate contingents as well as some Thessalian cavalry. The banished Cimon is said to have appeared in the Athenian camp, armed and seeking permission to fight. His request was denied, but he exhorted his aristocratic friends to fight bravely in order to quiet the suspicion that they had meant to make common cause with the Spartans. They did fight bravely in the battle that followed, and hundreds of aristocratic Athenians died in combat. The battle was lost, and the

Spartans made their way home across the isthmus. Apparently they had had no intention of attacking Athens.

Two months later, the Athenians under the command of Myronides invaded Boeotia again. Now they had to contend only with the Thebans and their allies. The Athenians won a decisive battle at Oenophyta, conquered Boeotia and neighboring Phocis, and took hostages among the Opuntian Locrians. In short, they seem not only to have prevented a buildup of power on their western border but to have gained control over the entire area, in which effort they were helped by the internal divisions of the cities.

In 457–456 Aegina, too, capitulated. It surrendered its fleet, dismantled its fortifications, and agreed to pay tribute to Athens as a member of the Delian League. This was the first and only time a city that belonged to the Peloponnesian League was forced to join the Attic confederation. Athens was determined that this old rival would never recover, and it did not. The pride of Aegina's old families was broken, families that were "famous on the seas," celebrated by poets like Pindar and Bacchylides, and that had excelled in sports as well. The island was reduced to the same insignificance and poverty from which it had once risen through huge effort. It would never again build a temple like the one dedicated to Aphaea. From this time on, the Saronic Bay was dominated by Piraeus, the view from which, according to Pericles, Aegina had previously spoiled. At about the same time the long walls were completed.

This set of circumstances ushered in a strange situation. To judge by human standards, Athens was now invulnerable and could concentrate all its energies on expansion. No other power matched it on the seas. To be sure, Sparta, too, was impregnable—no one was likely to beat its army in a hoplite battle, the method of fighting still generally used in Greece. Athens could only pester Sparta by raiding its coast and showing the whole world that Sparta was too weak either to prevent Athens' attacks by sea or to come to its allies' aid. In this respect, Athens, with its options as a great sea power, was superior.

In spite of this the two sides were on the whole an even match; neither could defeat the other. The power of both was limited. Ultimately all either could do was to launch sporadic local attacks. But the Athenians exhibited a new and ambitious spirit in the way they exploited these possibilities.

It was inevitable that both powers would be drawn into affairs—internal as well as foreign—of other cities. In fact, it had been happening routinely for some time. They both had to try to keep their positions strong. This placed a heavy burden on Sparta, partly because it was a land power and partly because it had to safeguard its resources more carefully. Athens, by contrast, aggressively pursued its ambitions.

The focus of Athens' military activities within Greece was, for obvious reasons, the Gulf of Corinth. In 456 the Attic fleet under the command of Tolmides undertook the difficult journey around the Peloponnese, which offered few friendly harbors. The Athenians destroyed the Spartan dock-yards at Gytheion, ravaged some of the land, went on to capture the Corinthian colony of Chalcis in Aetolia, and attacked Sicyon. In 453, Pericles led a second expedition, setting out from Pagae. He, too, fought the Sicyonians but did not attempt to occupy the city. Since the Achaeans were on Athens' side, the Corinthian Gulf was now almost like an Athenian inland sea. Its eastern coast as well as large stretches to the north and south were occupied by the Athenians or their allies. Naupactus and Chalcis were under Athenian influence. The only action that failed was the siege of Orniadae in Acarnania.

Thus a barrier was put up between the Peloponnese and central Greece. The mainland was militarily split in two. The only territories in central Greece not under Athenian supremacy were considered politically insignificant. Sparta's power was confined to the Peloponnese. The Corinthians were isolated in their territory. They had apparently been too weak to offer Athens effective resistance. It is not clear whether Athens hoped to drive a wedge between Corinth and Sparta. But Athens had gained a foothold in the northern Peloponnese as well as in Argolis, where it had treaties with the cities of Argos, Troezen, and Hermione. At some point during those years Athens also concluded an alliance with Segesta on Sicily, though its terms are not clear.

Yet in 454 Athens suffered a severe setback in Egypt, where its soldiers had been fighting for six years. They may not have accomplished much after their initial victories, but they were determined to persevere.

Perhaps they were reluctant to admit the futility of their Egyptian expedition. The Persian king had tried unsuccessfully to bribe Sparta to mount a diversionary invasion of Attica. Finally, in 455, the Persians sent a huge contingent of naval and land forces to Egypt and defeated the rebels. The Athenians retreated to the island of Prosopitis on the Nile Delta, where the Persians blockaded them for eighteen months. Then, after draining the canal between the island and the shore, the Persians marched on the island. Only "few of the many," Thucydides writes, were able to escape by way of Cyrene. In early 454 a relief squadron of fifty Greek ships arrived but was attacked by the Phoenicians, and only a few ships survived.

The Greek fleet at that time already numbered less than its original 200 ships, and at least 80 to 100 triremes and several thousand men—Athenians, metics, and confederates—must have been lost at Prosopitis. Aggravating the pain of those losses were the dashed hopes, the humiliation of the city, and the shame of defeat, but the Athenians refused to be daunted by setbacks. They continued their political course and warfare with great determination. Pericles showed similar determination in undertaking his expedition to the Corinthian Gulf in 453.

As a precautionary measure the Athenians transferred the Delian League's treasury from Delos to Athens. The ostensible reason was the threat of the Persian fleet, but more likely the Athenians feared Delos was not safe from renegade allies; they also sought more direct access to the funds. The treasurers had always been Athenians, and the money usually went to Athens to finance shipbuilding and cover war expenses. Still, storing the money in their own city gave the Athenians a freer hand in spending it. As a rule income exceeded expenses, so a considerable sum had built up.

Starting in 454, one-sixtieth of every city's contribution to the Delian League was dedicated to Athena. Similar gifts may previously have gone to Apollo of Delos. Every year long lists of the shares paid to the goddess were compiled on stone tablets, which were then displayed in public places. Athena's treasurers were in charge of the goddess's money, and if need arose the city could borrow from those funds.

Difficulties seem to have arisen in some Ionian cities, perhaps as a result of Athens' defeat in Egypt and of Persian agitation. This was the case in Miletus, which had been rebuilt after the Persian Wars; in Erythrae; and perhaps in some of the island poleis. There is little concrete information, but we know that in Erythrae the Athenians set up a democracy and installed a new council. They also placed a garrison there, whose commander was assigned functions in the city's domestic life.

Attic politics and warfare exhibited a paradox: Athens stood against Persia as one supreme power against another, sending ships and troops to Egypt, but it also contended with other small cities within Greece, often fighting pitched battles. This was the special quality of this city: to be a great power at the same time that it was one polis among many. The city's massive expenditure of effort on its military can be explained as repeated attempts to overcome this paradox. Ultimately the strain of these efforts wore the city down.

There may have been no other military activities in the late 450s. Presumably Athens was busy trying to stabilize the Delian League. Athens had achieved what were probably its main goals in central Greece, and there was nothing more to be done there. Sicyon and Corinth could not be conquered, and Athens could not go on claiming the aid of its confederates forever. It was also difficult to make war on an enemy like Sparta that could not be conquered and was reluctant to fight.

Around 451 Argos and Sparta concluded a thirty-year peace treaty. This was reason enough for the Athenians to seek a truce with Sparta. Cimon negotiated the terms. The ten years of his banishment were over, and in fact he is said to have been recalled before the decade had elapsed on the initiative of Pericles. One source dates this to shortly after the battle of Tanagra.

Athens' interest in the truce, which stipulated the continuation of the status quo, may have had another source. Under Cimon's leadership and on his advice, the Athenians were considering renewing hostilities against Persia. They wanted to compensate for their Egyptian defeat, and probably also provide a reason for the Delian League's continued existence.

In 450 or 449 Athens relaunched the attack on Cyprus that had been given up ten years earlier when the fleet was sent on to Egypt. Once again 200 ships were dispatched—most of them Athenian but some from the confederates—along with an army since there were land battles to be fought and cities to besiege. At the request of Amyrtaeus, the Egyptian prince who had led the insurrection against the Persians and was still active in the swamps of the Nile valley, the Athenians risked sending a squadron of sixty vessels to the area. Realizing, however, that there was no chance for a major rebellion to flare up again, they did not stay long. Meanwhile the bulk of the army laid siege to Citium on the southern coast of Cyprus. Citium was the most important of the cities belonging to the Phoenicians on the island. But as the siege dragged on, provisions dwindled, and Cimon himself died, leading the Greeks to give up the blockade and withdraw. The Persian army and navy attacked them near Cyprian Salamis, but the Persians lost on land and on sea, and thus this last expedition to Cyprus yielded the Greeks at least a victory.

At this point the Athenians abandoned their plan of conquering Cyprus. In many Cypriot cities the will to overthrow the Persians had weakened, or perhaps the Persians showed more interest in the island, which was, after all, much closer to Persia than to the Aegean region. Then, too, the more sober mood in Athens may have led to a recognition of the limits of the city's power.

A delegation was sent to the great king in Susa to negotiate. No formal peace treaty was drawn up, since that would have been unacceptable to Persian honor. But an agreement was reached to maintain the status quo. The Persians promised to keep their military forces out of the Aegean Sea. No Persian fleet was to approach the sea from the north by way of the Bosporus or from Phaselis in the south. On land the Persians were to keep the distance of a three-day march or one-day ride on horseback from Greek territories. The Greek cities on and near the Asian coast remained free, but the Persian king insisted on maintaining formal authority over them, which meant they had a continuing obligation to pay tribute. In practice, however, the Persian king only rarely made use of this right, and he is also said to have granted the cities the right to belong to the Delian League. The Athenians promised to respect the same borders and, above all, desist from all military interference in Cyprus and Egypt.

The peace was negotiated in 449 by Cimon's son-in-law Callias, the richest man in Athens. He was a major landowner as well as mine owner (using the labor of hundreds of slaves he owned), and a leading priest in the celebration of the Eleusinian Mysteries, a post that also paid well. He had won three times at the Olympic games, and acted as an official host of the Spartans. He commissioned Calamis, a prominent sculptor of the time, to make a statue of Aphrodite, which he then dedicated to the Acropolis.

After his return from Persia, Callias was taken to court, probably unsuccessfully, for allegedly taking bribes. It is hard to see what he was supposed to have done wrong. The peace was long overdue. War could not win the Athenians anything beyond what they already had. The only question was what was to become of the Delian League. It had served its purpose, unless there was reason to fear that its dissolution would encourage renewed Persian attacks. But this seemed unlikely given the empire's internal weaknesses. And in an emergency the cities could always band together again. But what was now to become of Athens, of its navy and rowers, its power and dynamism? What was to become of the Athenians themselves without their confederation?

Two years before the peace of Callias, in 451, Pericles' law of citizenship was passed. The reasons for this step are difficult to understand. The law stipulated that from then on only those of Athenian descent on both sides could be Attic citizens. What counted were the parents, mother and father, not more distant ancestors. Anyone who was already a citizen retained his citizenship, including everyone born or introduced into the phratries before 451.

Before this law went into effect, all that was required for citizenship was that the father be Athenian and that the son be conceived in wedlock. Many aristocrats had married daughters from other cities, especially those of Thracian princes. This possibility was now effectively closed off to the noble lords, for they could hardly enter into marriages whose children would not be allowed to be citizens and could therefore not inherit their fathers' landed property. The law thus dealt a serious blow to the aristocrats' freedom to establish family connections, forcing them to concentrate more on Athens. But this was not necessarily the primary objective of the law, since marriages with daughters of metics and foreigners had increased dramatically among other groups of Athenians as the percentage of immigrants in the population rose.

This trend may have meant that significant numbers of Attic girls remained single. If so, this may have been one of the motives for the law, but we must assume that the law was a response to more general problems.

Strangely enough Greek political theory never concerned itself with the extreme exclusivity of the city-states. Slavery had to be justified but not the limitation of citizenship, which excluded even free inhabitants of the city—in the case of Athens, the metics. Aristotle asserted that a city should not grow beyond a certain size or the herald's voice would not reach the citizens. The people would not know each other and would therefore not know to whom they could entrust an office. When necessary, he suggested, this information could be conveyed through the associations into which the citizenry was subdivided. But apparently the fact that some inhabitants were part of the city and others were not was taken for granted and needed no further thought. To be sure, all Greeks spoke the same language, honored more or less the same gods, were part of the same civilization, and shared the same ideal self-image, a concept given visual form in the statues created by sculptors who worked from city to city. In many cases the cities were separated by no more than a day's or even a few hours' journey. And the Attic metics, to take one example, generally tried to become as much like the Athenians as possible. But all this represented just one side of the coin.

On the other side of the coin were the independence of the cities and their familial insularity. The cities could not be enlarged at will. The Greeks felt themselves to be Greek primarily in their role as citizens. This was especially true for members of the middle and lower classes, among whom a great solidarity developed, especially in Athens. Quite apart from the differences that existed between the aristocracy and ordinary people, this solidarity was based on the equality that prevailed in the men's associations. It was not the kind of equality a monarch—or a state—projects on his subjects despite the differences among them. It is no coincidence that on the Greek mainland only tyrants and restorers of order granted new citizenship to large groups. The citizenries themselves, especially the democratic ones, did not share their civil rights with other people.

This does not mean they were xenophobic. Especially in Athens the metics were able, as far as we can tell, to go about their lives freely and without arousing hostility. They were simply excluded from the homogeneity of the citizenry. It seems that democracy relied on this homogeneity to promote stability in the absence of a state, an administrative apparatus, or police. The democracy rested on the immediate and responsible behavior of its citizens toward one another. In this situation, the strong, familial bonds attributed to a fictive common descent were needed.

Granted all this, why did the Athenians impose restrictions on future eligibility for citizenship in the face of huge military demands and frequent and often large losses of life? True, rising birth rates seem to have caused a considerable rise in population during those decades, but Athens needed its men for exploits in all corners of the world.

The only likely explanation is that the Athenians feared their citizenry would lose its sense of cohesion and perhaps a certain measure of social control. It was feared that with so many wives coming from metic families, let alone foreign ones, there was no assurance that future citizens would be brought up in the customary way. Marriages of this sort might lead to major conflicts of loyalty. Pericles was rumored (in jest) to have started a major war as a favor to his mistress Aspasia. Many metics must have wished to become citizens, and the more they became integrated into society, the harder it must have been to deny them their wish. Many also acquired citizenship illegally, probably through cooperative demes or officials susceptible to bribery.

These motives may not have been openly expressed. Although they contain a kernel of truth, they may have been distorted, for example, by the anxieties of Attic fathers who feared that their daughters might not find husbands.

In any case, Pericles' law of citizenship expressed the strong need of Attic citizens to assert their difference from others. More than any other group the Athenian citizens were absorbed by politics. This distinguished them, especially from the metics. The citizens' abiding and unwavering dedication to the city and its affairs abroad, their astonishing successes, and their power gave them a sense of being special. Service to their powerful city took the form of intense political and military activity. This required an extraordinary degree of social mobility, which was possible in Athens, because it was a male-bonded society that emphasized unmediated participation in public life, a society, too, that included members of the lowest class, who may have been considered inferior from the traditional social point of view but who possessed political power and importance.

All of these factors confirmed the Athenians' sense that they were endowed with a unique character that enabled them to act in a manner commensurate with their greatness—and they were not mistaken. They were uncompromising, a trait in which they differed from all other Greeks, and of which they were openly proud. It is what they tried to express in everything, including their buildings.

The Greek philosophers emphasized the importance of developing virtue, on which, they thought, the health of the cities depended. This was to be accomplished through education of the young and also through festivals, whose function was, according to Plato, to give new strength to the participants by restoring what had become lost in daily life. According to Protagoras, the citizens also "educated" themselves in the course of conducting their affairs and maintaining relationships. From the introduction of the citizenship laws we may deduce that the Athenians were now determined to accomplish this "education" primarily within their own circle.

Beginning in 451, with the law of citizenship, we find Pericles in the foreground of Attic politics. He was entrusted with the command of important military expeditions and was repeatedly elected general. He was also the originator of the most significant political initiatives. He was not yet, as he would be after 443, the unopposed leader of the city, to whom Thucydides ascribed virtually monarchical influence within the democracy. One statesman in particular opposed Pericles. This opponent, also named Thucydides, was the son of Melesias, who had been praised by Pindar as one of the greatest wrestlers of the previous generation. Cimon was either the brother-in-law or father-in-law of this Thucydides, whom Pericles had ostracized in 443.

Unlike Cimon, Thucydides was not a great general, but he was an able politician with excellent rhetorical skills. He had numerous friends within Athens and in the other cities of the Delian League. Many aristocrats regarded him as the most capable representative of their interests and views. Thucydides tried to subvert Pericles' influence and give his supporters a stronger force in the popular assembly by having them sit together in one block at the Pnyx. Apparently he hoped the aristocrats would bolster one another's courage in taking up his causes as well as demonstrate their strength by common expressions of approval or displeasure. This strategy was probably a mistake, because the weakness of his party soon became evident, and suspicions that he was trying to manipulate the assembly worked against him. Thucydides managed to hold his own against Pericles for a number of years, though probably in a minority position.

Once asked which of them was the better wrestler, Thucydides is said to have answered: "If I wrestle him to the ground he will deny this and deny it so vigorously that he will convince even those who witnessed the fight." Thucydides may have prevailed in many instances, but as far as we can tell, all the important decisions of this period were made by Pericles.

Attic politics were dominated during the three to four years following 450 by a host of vexing problems, especially in respect to the Delian League, whose purpose had become questionable since the defeat in Egypt and whose very reason for existence collapsed with the Peace of Callias. The Athenians had the choice of acting timidly or decisively. But one thing that could not be contemplated was the dissolution of the Delian League. It provided both the income on which so many Athenians depended and the reason the citizens dedicated themselves so intently to politics and war. It was responsible for Athens' entire organization, its economic importance, its affluence, and its commerce. The city's concept of itself, its pride, its very security, which presupposed control over the navy, including replacement of ships and continuous training missions, all depended on the league's continuing existence.

The league had long since ceased to be merely an alliance but had become a realm under Athens' control, an "empire." Athens may have fulfilled its function as head of the league with some cynicism, but the loss of the league's legitimating purpose—to contain the Persians— must have had an effect on Athens. The conditions behind their all-consuming, decade-long involvement had ceased to exist, and the question of how things were to go on must have arisen. In a city like Athens this would have led to vehement dispute. There must have been at least some awareness that a fundamental change in Athens' situation could be in the offing.

Pericles' policies were initially flexible. He suggested calling a Panhellenic congress in Athens, where the form of future cooperation among the Greeks would be determined. Until then, the payment of tributes was to be suspended, and in fact no payments were recorded for the year 448. (In view of the funds already accumulated, this was of no grave consequence.) The congress would also discuss what to do about the Greek sanctuaries burned down by the Persians and about the offerings still owed to the gods for wartime promises the Greeks had made. Another pressing issue was regulation of "the seas, to ensure that all could travel them without fear and would maintain peace." Five delegations were dispatched to invite all the Greek cities on the Aegean.

At least one goal of the congress was to provide a new function for Athens' navy by assigning it responsibility for safety on Aegean waters. The restoration of the temples would benefit mostly the Athenians as well. It is unclear whether Pericles was hopeful about realizing his plans. In any event, none of them was realized. The conference never took place, largely because of Sparta's refusal to participate in it.

Within a year, however, Pericles seems to have reversed course. Tributes were collected again for the year 447, and the Delian League continued to exist. This was not all: Pericles proposed building the Parthenon and using some of the league's money for the project.

In the meantime efforts to consolidate the confederation continued. In the years after 450, *cleruchies,* or groups of Attic citizens who were granted rights to land in foreign territories, had been dispatched to various cities that were considered unreliable and deserving of punishment. These *cleruchies* ranged in size from several hundred to two thousand men, and though Athens gave them land, they were not to form towns of their own but to remain citizens of Athens. The land they settled on was only temporarily assigned to them. The *cleruchies* were to raise what they needed to live while simultaneously serving a military purpose (so that with time older men would have to be replaced with younger ones). In essence, they formed garrisons whose provisioning was taken care of by the land assigned to them. The foreign communities whose territory was assigned to the *cleruchies*—either in part or completely—remained intact; their tribute to the Delian League was reduced since they paid by supplying agricultural products that sustained the *cleruchies.* The four thousand settlers Athens had sent to Chalcis as far back as 508 had been such a *cleruchy* and accordingly did not own the land they lived on.

In midcentury, *cleruchies* were established on the islands of Naxos, Andros, and Lemnos, and a little later on Euboea as well. A colony named Brea was also established in territory belonging to the Bisalts on the northern coast of the Aegean. Its main mission was to keep the Thracians out of the area, which was rich in mines and in timber for shipbuilding. Apparently in the past several incidents of disloyalty among the islands had taken place, perhaps related to the transfer of the league's treasury from Delos to Athens. These islanders had particularly close ties to Apollo of Delos.

We have no record of the arguments the Athenians advanced in favor of maintaining the league or in justifying the renewed collection of tributes. They could have cited the role they played in the liberation of Greece, but the efficacy of this argument is questionable. They probably emphasized the importance of maintaining security in the Aegean. In any case, if there was opposition, they were not deterred by it.

The main question that divided the Athenians was what shape their

People against the idea.

relation to the Delian League should take in the future. Thucydides and his allies were strongly opposed to using the league's funds to expand the Acropolis. It was a disgrace, they argued, for Athens to act like a harlot, taking foreign money to beautify herself by building statues and temples.

Athens' aristocrats did much to keep relationships with allied cities intact. They had connections to these cities, sent delegates when asked to do so, and hosted the delegates who came to Athens from those cities. Much of the tribute money these delegates brought was contributed by the wealthy of their cities, and even if the sums were not large, the donors must have been vexed when the money was spent not on the military but on enhancing the hegemonic city. Thucydides probably made the most of such complaints, basing his thinking on the conventional concept of aristocratic relationships.

Pericles held, on the contrary, that the use of the league's money should be left up to the recipients rather than to those who paid. Since Athens provided for the protection of its allies, it could do as it wished with the surplus. He may have pointed out that Athena had long since become the league's divine protectress. The allies were each obliged to contribute a bullock and one set of hoplite's weapons to the great Panathenaea festival. The league's treasury would be kept in the Parthenon after its completion. Perhaps the temple would even represent an offering of thanks on the part of the confederation for the victory over the Persians.

The sums spent on building were always paid out by Athena's treasurers and the accounts recorded on tablets, some of which are still extant. But Pericles seems at that time to have instituted the practice of transferring surpluses in the confederate accounts directly to Athena's treasury. The money accumulated there as a reserve for future wars, but it was also tapped to finance construction.

In the speeches the historian Thucydides attributes to Pericles in later years, the statesman boldly declares that Athens was indeed exerting tyrannical powers. It might not have been right to take on such powers, but once they had been assumed they could not be relinquished without danger.

.   .   .

It is not always true, as history shows, that he who follows the most consistent policy wins. Hesitation, ambivalence, and caution, even if they run counter to the logic of things, can bring advantages in some situations. But the Athenians of that time had no desire to take the easy path. They agreed with Pericles—both with his conclusion that Athens could maintain its position only by hegemonic rule and with his policy of using Delian League funds for Athenian building projects.

Pericles placed his bet on Athens' superiority, and he did everything he could to maintain it—indeed, to flaunt it openly. His citizenship law was meant to strengthen the unity of the citizenry—and probably to alleviate many fears. He believed Athenians should be proud of their power. Thus the practice of displaying the tribute payments in public was introduced. The payments usually arrived in late March and were displayed just before the plays of the Dionysia opened. The Athenian spectators (and the delegates who had brought the money) watched as several hundred huge clay pots, each holding one talent, or about 26 kilograms of silver, were carried in. The spectators witnessed the counting before settling down to watch the play. None of Athens' power was to be hidden; all of it was to be visible. The prime intent was to remind the Athenians over and over again of the power they exercised as rulers and on which they so depended.

We may ask to what extent this attitude grew out of the social and economic conditions and to what extent it was due to the mental predisposition of the Greeks. The relationship of Athens to its allies was an unequal one, and Athens had acquired its empire practically overnight, without a concerted effort. The Greek mentality tended to place emphasis on splendor and excellence rather than on the restrained use of power, and to value autarky over the establishment of long-term cooperation with partners. It was only within the individual cities that the Greeks succeeded in building effective cooperation.

"Excellence of any kind that is beloved by the people," Goethe said, "is the rarest of all things." But this rare and winning combination has to be conceded in the case of the buildings constructed during the Periclean era. Obviously much of the credit for this must go to Pericles himself, but it must also be kept in mind that the popular assembly endorsed the projects and that public commissions approved the plans and supervised construction.

The first to be built was the Parthenon, sitting high up on the Acropolis so that it would be visible from all corners of the city, even from the harbor. It was the first temple to be constructed entirely of marble, specifically, Attic marble from Mount Pentelicus. Even the roof tiles were of marble. Eight columns stood along the ends of the buildings and seventeen on the sides, whereas other Doric temples were conventionally built with rows of six and thirteen columns.

The plan of the building was conceived by Ictinus, the leading architect of the time, and incorporated the most recent theories. Everything down to the smallest detail was carefully calculated and adhered to strict rules of proportion. The columns were unusually slender, and the appearance of cohesion was achieved by placing the columns close together and keeping the passages narrow. Almost all the vertical lines were slightly convex, the side columns narrowing from bottom to top by about seven centimeters, the corner ones, by four centimeters. The whole structure up to the entablature was so thoroughly characterized by minute curvatures or swellings that there was not a single absolutely straight line. Because of these curvatures, none of the parts were interchangeable, and each one had to be fashioned to fit its specific place. On the friezes, the size of the spaces between triglyphs for the metopes was calculated down to the millimeter.

"The architect knew the mysterious effect the tiniest variation creates," Paul Valéry wrote in appreciation of Ictinus. "Standing before a building in which mass was so sensitively lightened, a building that seemed so simple, no one was aware that the sense of happiness he felt was caused by curves and bends that were almost imperceptible yet immensely powerful. The beholder was unaware that he was responding to a combination of regularity and irregularity the architect had hidden in his work, a combination as strong as it is impossible to describe."

At one end of the unusually large interior chamber, the cella, stood

Athena Parthenos *in the cella of the Parthenon. In her right hand she carries the victory goddess Nike; in her left, she holds a shield depicting the battle with the Amazons on the outside and the writhing Acropolis snake on the inside. On the base, which is roughly human height, as can be seen in the lower right-hand corner, the creation and adorning of Pandora in the presence of the gods is shown. Pandora is the woman Zeus created in his anger after Prometheus stole the fire. Hephaestus had to fashion her of earth and water; her face was to be like that of a goddess; Aphrodite endowed her with charm; Hermes contributed cunning; and Athena taught her useful skills, such as weaving. It is puzzling why this creation of "the evil that gives pleasure to all as they embrace their own suffering" is represented here, of all places. Reconstruction from a design by N. Leipen in Toronto, based on copies and contemporary accounts.*

Phidias's twelve-meter statue of Athena, fashioned of gold and ivory over a wooden center. The cella was flanked by two rows of columns two stories high. The spaciousness of the room contrasted with the material solidity of the temple's exterior. The goddess's helmet displayed a sphinx at the center with a griffin on each side. On the front of the goddess's dress, Medusa's head was depicted, and in her right hand Athena held a statue of Nike, goddess of victory, itself measuring over one meter. A lance leaned against her left arm, and at her feet rested a shield depicting a scene of Amazons in battle. Forty talents (more than twenty hundredweights) of gold were incorporated in the statue, but in such a manner that they could be removed. Pericles observed that in case of need the gold could be melted down and used to finance the city's defense.

The pediments and the metopes were decorated with the loveliest relief scuptures, and in the interior a frieze 160 meters long ran along the outer wall of the cella, depicting the Attic citizens themselves in a Panathenaic procession.

Whether or not the procession depicts real individuals, it is obvious that the composition concentrates on the most beautiful and graceful participants, especially on the riders and their horses, which combine to present an overall picture of boundless freedom, composure, and order. It is as though the Attic citizens wanted to demonstrate that they measured up to aristocratic ideals, which were still widely accepted. That is why no hoplites were shown, and the rowers had no place in the procession anyway. It may be an exaggeration to claim that the Athenians built the Parthenon to glorify themselves, but only a minor one.

Phidias was in charge of the construction, and Pericles was most likely on the building committee. The Parthenon took nine years to build and was completed in 438. Immediately after its completion, work on the Propylaeum, the entrance to the Acropolis, was begun.

The Greek cities liked to outdo each other with their buildings and monuments. This was especially important to Athens, the city governed by its people. Art has always served the purpose of documenting a ruler's power, importance, and claim to greatness. Indeed, it aims to embody a community's identity. For the Greeks, art was, in addition, the concrete expression of proportion and harmony and thus related to truth and

Horsemen from the Parthenon frieze, 430s B.C. *The Parthenon.*

goodness. To this extent there is nothing exceptional about Pericles' building policies, though it remains remarkable that the popular assembly went along with his plans.

That Ictinus, Phidias, and the men they worked with were able to create such outstanding work in Athens is astonishing. The Parthenon was followed immediately by Mnsicles' Propylaeum and then by the Erechtheum. These works display a spirit of daring, freedom, excitement, and ambition, a desire to exceed again and again. A part of Athens is materialized in these works, something that could not have been invented or realized anywhere else, something that went on to have a profound impact on both the concept of man and his depiction in sculpture.

In 447 an expedition led by Pericles set out for the Thracian Chersonese, which had repeatedly been subject to attacks from the mainland. Just as in the sixth century B.C., aid had been requested from Athens. Pericles settled one thousand Athenian citizens in the area and built a wall across the narrowest point of the peninsula to protect the land from attacks and make passage through the Dardanelles safer.

Difficulties arose in 446. In that year the Athenians decided to intervene in western Boeotia, where some towns had come into the hands of Boeotian exiles who had had to flee from cities friendly to Athens. Athens dispatched one thousand hoplites along with confederate troops. They succeeded in taking Chaeronea and sold the town's inhabitants as slaves.

The sources report the enslavement of citizens belonging to this Greek town and many similar incidents without special comment, and it is not clear whether this was an exceptional case. In most situations the Athenians presumably executed or banished only those they considered dangerous and did not deprive the rest of the population of freedom or property. But in Chaeronea the wrath of the Athenians was apparently too great.

Though the commonality of all Greeks was often invoked, this did not keep them from selling enemies as slaves or from mounting bloody wars and performing mass executions. Slavery had always existed; human beings could be sold. A humanitarian sensibility on such matters had not yet developed. The differentiation between friend and enemy and the necessity for revenge were very much alive. It was often thought preferable to wipe the slate clean than to let potentially dangerous conditions persist. This is one aspect of the weakness characteristic of the Greeks, especially the Athenians, that prevented them from establishing stable political ties. Their political greatness was limited to the domestic arena of the city. Sparta alone excelled at weaving an extensive network of stable relations with other cities, based, of course, on mutual understanding among aristocracies.

On its return home the Attic army was set upon near Coronea by a band of refugees and exiles from various cities, men from Locris and other areas fed up with Attic domination. The Attic army was defeated near Coronea and suffered huge losses, primarily—and unusually—in the form of soldiers taken prisoner. The army had included about one-twelfth of Attica's hoplites.

What makes this incident so interesting is that the resistance against Athens did not originate in cities but among numerous individuals from different cities who had joined forces privately. The cities were apparently not prepared for such a bold step as attacking Athens. Many of them were torn by violent internal conflicts, had allied themselves with Athens or come to power through Athenian help. Or perhaps they preferred peace to open warfare. The overall Attic system of influence generally worked well enough in Boeotia, but many opponents were outside this system, and they were not willing simply to accept their fate.

The success this irregular force scored was extraordinary. Athens sought peace, and was willing to give up all of Boeotia just for the release of its prisoners of war. Boeotia promptly agreed to the terms. It would be interesting to know how the sudden consent was reached. Were the Boeotian cities now also eager for freedom? Athens was intent on the return of the prisoners, whose families may have applied pressure. But probably the most decisive fact was that Athens realized it could no longer hold on to Boeotia, except for the city of Plataea, which was allied to it by old ties of friendship. Needless to say, maintaining the Delian League had priority. What was new in this episode is Athens' realization that it had to choose between two alternatives. It could no longer afford to pursue its every goal. It had to preserve its strength.

The loss of prestige associated with relinquishing Boeotia soon brought on consequences. The island of Euboea defected from the Delian League. Pericles, leading an army, had hardly set out for the island when Megara, too, dissolved its treaty. Some Attic garrisons barely escaped from the Megarians; others fell into their hands. A Peloponnesian army was gathering and threatened to invade Attica under Spartan command. The truce between Athens and Sparta had apparently expired.

Pericles was forced to return hurriedly and came upon the Spartans near Eleusis. But no battle ensued because the Peloponnesians withdrew. Pericles had reportedly bribed the young commander, King Pleistoanax, and his top adviser not to fight. In his accounts Pericles later listed a sum of ten talents spent "on necessary expenses," and the popular assembly did not challenge the item. It is possible that peace talks between the two sides had been going on simultaneously. In any case, Pericles was able to return to Euboea and subjugate the island, which, because of its location on the route between Athens and the Black Sea, was strategically more important to Athens than any conquests in central Greece. The conditions imposed on the islanders were relatively mild; only the inhabitants

Horsemen from the Parthenon frieze, 430s B.C. Most of this section is now in London; the broken-off corner at upper left is in Athens.

of Histiaea in the north of the island were driven from their homes, replaced by Athenian *cleruchies*.

In 446 Athens and Sparta negotiated a thirty-year peace treaty. Athens had to "surrender" the Megarid ports of Nisaea and Pagae, the city of Troezen, and the region of Achaea, which meant that it had to dissolve its treaties with these places and withdraw whatever garrisons were stationed there. For the rest, Sparta and Athens agreed to respect each other's alliances. A list of the allies of both sides was appended to the treaty. Other cities were free to join whichever alliance they chose, and future conflicts were to be settled by a court of arbitration. Corinth, Sicyon, and other cities Athens had been at war with consented to the peace. It is unclear whether Athens was to concede freedom to Aegina, but it did not in fact do so, and the islanders would later raise complaints on this account. In Boeotia the old alliance under the leadership of Thebes was revived as a union of independent cities enjoying equal rights but with some central administration and the capability of mustering a common army.

After a period when Sparta had tacitly accepted the existence of the Delian League and when Athens had tried to reduce Sparta's influence, an effort was now made to cement the relationship between the two sides. From this time on, Greece was divided into two major spheres of power with a few neutral states between them.

The supporters of Ephialtes had tried to strengthen Athens' position against Sparta by taking the offensive. This attempt had failed. Except for Aegina, everything Athens had gained by military means on the Greek mainland since 460 was now lost. Athens had staked too many claims at a time when conditions were unpredictable. Athens had shed much of its blood and invested resources in vain. Now it was lucky to be able to preserve what it had before its period of expansion.

It is not clear whether Pericles should be counted among the initiators of Athens' policy of expansionist warfare. He probably played a dominant role only in continuing this policy. Otherwise he could hardly have survived its collapse without a long-term loss of prestige.

Later, when planning the strategy of the Peloponnesian War, Pericles declared that by winning a battle on land Athens would make new enemies that it would soon have to fight, and if defeated, it would lose not only the battle but also its allies, on whom its strength depended. Pericles must have realized that the city could not afford to become involved in conflicts on land and on the sea at the same time. And the sea was more crucial to Athens' strategic interest. Pericles advised against further pursuits in Boeotia in 446.

"The rule of the seas is a great thing," he stressed, and a glance at the map shows he was right. Apparently Athens had to learn this lesson for itself, by experience. In any case, it decided to consolidate its domination of the Delian League.

The Delian League had long possessed the trappings of an empire, but at this point it clearly became an empire, or, to use the Greek term, an *arche*. In the official documents we even find a reference to the "Athenians and those over whom they rule." The peace treaty with Sparta reflects this, too—it speaks not of a military alliance against Persia but of two Greek power centers facing each other.

Relations within the Delian League can be deduced from the speeches Thucydides included in his history and also from a number of inscriptions, including tribute lists and various treaties. In the speeches, what is most striking is the tyrannical power Athens exercised over its allies, something Pericles and other orators pointed at with pride. They assert that the foundations of this power were laid when Athens, at the request of its allies, assumed leadership in the war against Persia. The Athenians had kept the alliance alive for three reasons, the same three that motivate most powerful men—honor, wealth, and fear. The Athenians, like the Spartans, had only one choice, either to rule by might or to put their own position in jeopardy.

Relations within the league actually seem to have been fairly diverse. First of all, the three large islands of Lesbos, Chios, and Samos contributed their ships to the league rather than money, and in so doing apparently retained some independence. There were many variations among the obligations of other league members, one of which was the distinction between cities that had always remained faithful allies and those that had defected and been obliged to rejoin. It is interesting to note that some cities were required to pledge their allegiance to Athens alone and sometimes to the entire confederation. In some cases, overseers or *cleruchies* were sent out; in others, regular garrisons.

Many of the allied cities were so small that they could hardly have avoided becoming dependent on others in their immediate vicinity. For them, accepting the distant rule of Athens was often preferable. It is not entirely clear to what extent Athens reserved the right to interfere in a city's internal affairs. In some cities such interference was obviously possible. Others were referred to as "autonomous," a new term that indicated cities were free to determine their own form of government.

Sometimes Athens set up democracies whose leaders were beholden to it and sent members of the old oligarchies into exile. Athens initially resorted to this tactic only infrequently. In many cases, it would have been an imprudent policy. Athens preferred to come to some agreement with influential aristocratic parties rather than to impose a constitution that had little chance of success. For Athens, democracy was not a cause in itself but a means of securing Athenian dominance when the political conditions were appropriate.

Athens tried as much as possible to have contacts or "ties of hospitality" everywhere. Friends in other cities used their influence in Athens' favor and also kept Athenians informed about events taking place and plans being made in their cities. Individuals allied with Athens enjoyed its special protection. They could not, for example, be prosecuted without Athens' consent. Anyone who caused them harm was called before an Attic court. Athens also reserved the right to try cases involving exceptionally harsh sentences, such as death and exile, in its own courts. Otherwise the normal Greek judicial rules were followed. Litigation between Athenians and people from other cities came under the law of the defendant's domicile.

The allies of the Delian League soon came to be called *hypekooi*, which means both people who obey and people who are subjects. The benefits they derived from accepting Attic dominance varied. For some, safety on the seas was crucial. The unified system of coins, measures, and weights that Athens had introduced offered advantages to commerce, though loss of the right to independent coinage may have been hard to accept for some cities.

In view of all this, the cohesion of the empire was remarkable. It arose primarily from Athens' military might. The superiority of the Attic navy, to which the allies had contributed so much money, made Athens mistress of the Aegean Sea. Many coastal cities were defenseless because they had never been fortified on the side facing the water, and in some cases the Athenians had forced defecting cities or cities suspected of rebelling to tear down their fortifications. The navy or individual squadrons could appear suddenly in the most unexpected places. Even in peacetime, sixty ships seem to have spent several months a year cruising the Aegean on practice and guard missions. A signaling and communication system provided surveillance, as did the various garrisons (some with land assigned to them and some without), overseers, and "hospitality friends." No city could oppose Athens on its own, and there seems to have been practically no chance for several to band together. All rebels could hope for was that by seceding they might inspire others to do the same, but this strategy had only minimal effect.

Apart from the advantages of military power, there was inertia, which worked in favor of maintaining the dependency relationship. The league had been in existence for a whole generation when the Peace of Callias seriously called its existence into question. To be sure, the cities occasionally had had to supply hoplites, but everyone had gotten used to leaving the conduct of war up to the Athenians, who were continually on the move, in training—"not waiting around indecisively," as one source puts it—but always taking others by surprise and inspiring fear beyond their actual strength. Their mysterious ability to maintain their ruling position arose in no small part from the habits of management they had developed: they watched everything that happened closely, paid attention to the smallest detail, and did everything they undertook in a serious and concentrated manner. Thus, a clear difference and distance developed between the ruling power and those it dominated.

The words *apragmon* and *polypragmon* exemplify the essential distinction between Athenians and other Greeks. The former described those who lived quietly, following the old Greek ideals in public and private life; in other words, those who were not inclined to stir up political trouble. It characterized the Delian League members, who had by now become used to the peace and security offered by Athens. *Polypragmon*, by contrast, described the Athenians' eternal restlessness, their tendency to hatch and execute new plans.

Many of Athens' confederates would probably have loved to shake off their fetters, but they did not know how to go about liberating themselves. They may have chafed under Athenian dominance even while they envied it. They regarded Athenian power at once with fascination and abhorrence.

Pericles' speech about hatred among most cities, a hatred that he said left Athenians no choice but to hold on to their power, was most likely exaggerated. But it was correct in its conclusion, for if Athens had not exercised its power forcefully, the Delian League would certainly have collapsed. The speech was also correct in that the Athenians could hardly imagine things being different. The speech also contained an element of fear—the Athenians' fear that they might lose their power. The Athenians realized how outrageous it must have seemed from a distance that a total of about 40,000 men reigned over the entire Aegean, dominating the sea with vessels no more than 34 meters long and rising barely 3 meters out of the water. But the triremes possessed incredible oar power. Athens' authority was based on an enormous organization in whose service thousands labored almost continually as rowers, *cleruchy*, garrison soldiers, commanders, and, last but not least, hoplites.

The Athenians might not have wanted to be "plunderers of cities," but they had little choice. They either had to maintain sovereignty or themselves fall subject to attack. The element of exaggeration in Pericles' speech lay in the need to express the city's vulnerability strongly enough to justify whatever action the city undertook. For what had to be decided above all else was whether Athens should persist in its militaristic course or give up what it had, and what it had become.

Along with the fear that sometimes crept in there was a pride of almost epic proportion. In Thucydides, Pericles declares toward the end of his speech: "Remember, too, that if your country has the greatest name in all the world, it is because she has never bent before disaster; because she has expended more life and effort in war than any other city, and has won for herself a power greater than any hitherto known, the memory of which will descend to the latest posterity . . . it will be remembered that we held rule over more Hellenes than any other Hellenic state, that we carried out the greatest wars against their united or separate powers, and inhabited a city unrivaled by any other in its resources or magnitude." And he adds: "Hatred and unpopularity have become the lot of all who have aspired to rule others." He seems to be claiming that anyone who acquires many honors will also find many foes.

The startling brashness with which Athens repeatedly declared its dominance and its allies' subordination arose from this pride and from the necessity to motivate the citizenry. Neither love for truth nor a distaste for hypocrisy motivated Athens' brashness. Except to express its pride, there was really no need for Athens to deliberately confirm that it subjugated others.

It is interesting that Thucydides has Pericles foreshadow Athens' ultimate decline in this early speech by noting that nothing on earth lasts forever.

Pericles, son of Xanthippus, the victorious commander in the Battle of Mycale, and of Agariste, niece of Cleisthenes of the Alcmaeonid family, embodied the Athens of those years in a way that a community has rarely been embodied by one man. That is why he succeeded in defeating all his political enemies. Eventually, in the ostracism vote held in 443, he even rid himself of his political rival Thucydides, who may have hoped, in the wake of the debacle in central Greece, to get the better of Pericles. Instead, Thucydides was sent into exile.

We don't know how Pericles, Ephialtes, and their friends felt about democracy, or whether Pericles thought it was a fundamentally desirable and just form of government, or whether he simply saw it as a means to an end. He may have instituted the payment for public service and other such measures primarily for tactical reasons. Among the measures he initiated or expanded were the games, festival processions, and public meals.

Generally, he encouraged "pleasures that involved the muses." Thus, Pericles introduced musical contests—in singing and flute and lyre playing—into the great Panathenaea festival. For performances he had a large theater built, with many columns and a roof rising steeply on all sides and converging at the top, similar to a royal Persian tent. He may also have been responding to popular desire when he drew up the citizenship law. In any case, all of what he did contributed to his gaining solid support among the Attic demos.

The more time passed, the more Pericles identified himself with democratic Athens. He refused to take part in aristocratic feasts and symposia, which were central to the social life of his class, and it is reported that he visited no friends and only once attended a wedding, when a relative got married, and even then he left early. His incorruptibility was widely praised and no doubt accounted for his avoiding as much as possible the aristocratic custom of exchanging lavish gifts.

His face, his gait, and his manner of speech were all highly controlled. He is said to have always displayed the seriousness of a statesman and seldom laughed. His robe hung immaculately from his body, even during his most impassioned speeches. Before appearing in public he prayed that he would not utter any word inappropriate to the subject under discussion.

The description above comes from Plutarch, who wrote in the second century A.D. We cannot know how reliable his source was, but the picture he conveys is convincing even if exaggerated. Was Pericles really able to hold the entire Pnyx spellbound without gesturing freely? It is impossible to know. But it is clear that he strictly limited his appearances before the popular assembly. Plutarch notes that Pericles, like the city's courier ship, the *Salaminia*, made an appearance only when the most urgent and difficult matters required; otherwise he sent his friends in his stead. He had, of course, a group of advisers, especially on difficult legal matters.

After the ostracism of Thucydides, Plutarch goes on to tell us, Pericles led the city brilliantly. He had the ability to renew the courage of the people when they grew despondent and to calm them down when they became agitated. It was as though he was able to impose his own controlled manner on the polis.

The philosophy of Anaxagoras, who had been his teacher and whom he continued to consult, was central to Pericles' thinking. The philosopher regarded *nous*, or reason, as the central force in the universe. Pericles wanted his city to be governed by it as well. Anaxagoras's studies in the natural sciences, including anatomy and astronomy, are said to have convinced Pericles to renounce all superstition. He was a thoroughly enlightened person and ran his private estates according to modern, carefully planned, rational agricultural methods. But above all he spent his time musing over the policies of Athens, in which endeavors he may have been aided by the theories philosophers were beginning to expound. It was the period of emerging sophism.

It is not surprising that a man as powerful as Pericles was satirized in comedies. He was depicted as Zeus, as an Olympian god, and above all as a tyrant. He had the loudest voice of all the Greeks, and he thundered and spewed lightning. His private life also gave rise to comment. He had been suitably married but then parted from his wife and, with her consent, gave her in marriage to another man, a situation that gave rise to gossip about various love affairs. One story claimed that the nobleman Pyrilampes raised peacocks for the sole purpose of providing Pericles with presents for his mistresses. It was not clear what the cuckolded husbands were supposed to make of the conspicuous birds. In reality Pyrilampes was a wealthy, respected, and exceptionally handsome aristocrat who often represented his city on diplomatic missions and may have been part of the delegation to Persia that negotiated the Peace of Callias. The peacocks he raised were probably a gift from the great king, and Athenians frequently gathered to admire the flock.

Most scandalous in Pericles' private life was his friendship with Aspasia, a hetaera, or courtesan, from Miletus who also employed other women as hetaerae. According to Socrates and other witnesses, she was one of the wittiest and most intelligent women of her time. She was not without ambition, and Pericles' relationship with her—she bore him a son—was apparently permanent and close.

Many factors contributed to Pericles' extraordinary, eventually near monarchic influence. In addition to everything the ordinary Athenians, the democracy, and the city owed to his political initiatives over many years, he had many other successes and knew how to make the most of them. He possessed hard-won experience and knowledge, a gift for oratory, an outstanding intellect, excellent judgment, remarkable self-discipline, and utter incorruptibility. He placed himself without reservation in the service of the democratic polis. All of this must have given him a sizable advantage over potential rivals.

It also seems that under his influence Attic politics in the 440s became so firmly entrenched that it was not easy for others to challenge the top politician by proposing new programs, the way Ephialtes and his group had once done. Later, in the 430s, opponents did attack his weaknesses, but they could not really threaten his position. When anyone got too close for comfort, Pericles could resort to ostracism.

But there was still another reason for Pericles' supremacy: the reliability and straightforwardness of the course he steered. People felt they were in good hands and could relax with him in charge; he also relieved the popular assembly of much of its responsibility.

Attic democracy, like its forerunner isonomy, needed the authority of men such as Pericles. The Attic citizens could not decide every question completely on its own merit. They surely did make independent decisions much of the time, and there were times when politicians competed so fiercely and effectively against one another that only ostracism could decide the victors. But there were also occasions when one individual, perhaps the winner of such a contest, determined policy unhindered. Those were times of relative political peace, and it was just such a respite that seems to have existed under Pericles at a moment when it was urgently needed.

Athens underwent an intellectual revolution during those years that was closely related to politics. Pericles' policies and solutions may have been approved by the majority, and daily life may have continued as before, but the cynicism underlying the new policies could not replace all the impulses of traditional morality. Attic politicians excused Athens' politics by the time-honored method of blaming "human nature." It was later said, and believed to be divinely ordained, that people naturally strive after honor and profit and are subject to fear; it is their habit to exercise power wherever possible; and that is how it has always been.

But how was this notion of human nature to be squared with the Greeks' age-old love of fairness, justice, and decency? Should such conclusions about human nature, however accurate or reasonable, guide thinking when concrete decisions had to be made? The Athenians also wondered about the envy of the gods, who were still feared. As new situations arose rational considerations and practical politics became increasingly important. People continued to dedicate offerings to the gods and celebrate their festivals. But what did the gods have to say about what was going on on earth?

Protagoras of Abdera, who had come to Athens in the early 440s and was the first of the Sophists, reached the conclusion that it was impossible to say anything about the gods, whether they existed or not, and if they did, what they were like. They were not apparent to the senses, and the life of man was too short to speculate about their nature. Protagoras concluded that man was the measure of all things. It was man who determined what was real and unreal. The appearance of the gods and of the world thus depended on human perception and could take very different forms.

It is not known exactly when Protagoras arrived at these views. He must have expressed them first in his many lectures and in conversations carried on in the noblemen's houses he visited. Some of the lectures were public, and the conversations, though held in small groups, were not kept secret. His ideas aroused lively and widespread interest because he claimed he could teach people new skills that would make them more successful in politics, in court, and in the running of their personal affairs. The questions raised by Protagoras were much talked about, partly because they were sensational, but also because they dealt with common problems.

Faith in the gods was closely related to the old virtues of fairness, justice, and decency. In fact, it was inseparable from them, and so the more the Athenians moved away from these virtues, the more questionable the existence of the gods became. On the other hand, the centrality of man grew in importance. As more and more innovative methods were developed in all fields—from seafaring to crafts, rhetoric, sculpture, and architecture—the more everything else had to be thought through anew. Competition and consumer demand had increased. New discoveries multiplied so quickly that people dared to think beyond existing reality; all that was new and innovative became fashionable. Athens was humming with activity and ideas during this period. Entirely new realms were opening up for Athenians to explore.

Around 450 Sophocles produced *Ajax*, the earliest of his plays that has survived. The play opens after the great hero's victories have taken place and he has just committed an unforgivable, disgraceful act. Wanting to take revenge on the leaders of the Greek army because they had not awarded him with Achilles' arms, he plans to attack them at night. But Athena causes him to go mad and he sets upon a herd of captured cattle instead.

"Long, immeasurable time brings everything hidden to light and hides what is apparent. Nothing is not to be expected," the hero says in his pivotal speech. "Change is the law of the world. There is always a new winner. Winter gives way to summer; night to day; storm brings peace to the moaning sea; all-powerful sleep releases what it has bound because it cannot reign indefinitely."

These words refer to more than Ajax's plight. They fit Athens' situation at the time as well, especially when we consider that Ajax refuses to accept the consequences of his own words. He has no intention of bowing to others the way daytime, the seasons, and natural forces do. He is too proud, and he takes his own life because he cannot bear the shame he has brought upon himself. He perfectly embodies the ideal of a strong, independent, autarkic hero.

But once he is dead it becomes clear that he depends on others after all. His body has to be buried, but Agamemnon and Menelaus refuse to give permission. They are so petty as to exploit their power as commanders to get back at the dead hero, and finally the burial takes place only because Odysseus, Ajax's most determined enemy, insists. For Odysseus death means the end of all enmity. "I myself will some day be in this situation," he says. He cannot, by taking care of Ajax's funeral, ensure that he himself will be buried, for among the dead, unlike the living, there can be no mutuality. All Odysseus can do is act to uphold the common good and moral standards, with the hope that he, too, will someday benefit from communal morality. It is in the face of fate or death, when even the most powerful are powerless, that man's vulnerability, his need for human solidarity, becomes evident.

The purpose of the Greek tragedies, especially those of Sophocles, is not to explain the present. Their message goes far beyond the times in which they were written, but they did arise out of the actual world of those times and were written to be performed before the Athenian people. Sophocles must therefore have had the hopes and fears of the Athenian people in mind when he wrote about the unreliability of men and the inevitability of change. The tragedy of *Ajax* had clear implications for internal politics and also addressed Athens as a whole, with its thirst for honor, its pride in its own strength, and its autarky. The limits of all these things are the subject of the play. It was not only at funerals that human solidarity became necessary. Sophocles' point was that some rules had to be universally accepted for the sake of all men precisely because man might at any time find himself in a situation where he has to fall back on human solidarity.

The general subject of the play is man's vulnerability, his shadowlike existence, and the endless suffering of life. What did it mean that these matters were brought before the public and discussed? How were the Athenians to understand scenes such as the one where Athena shows Odysseus his enemy Ajax, ranting madly, and Odysseus turns away because the sight arouses only sadness at the miserableness of man? In the play, man, faced with the cruelty of the gods, finds himself forced in a new way to rely on himself alone.

Sophocles' *Antigone* was probably first performed in 442. It picks up the Oedipus story after the combat between his two sons, Polyneices and Eteocles, in which both are killed. Creon, the new king of Thebes, forbids anyone to bury Polyneices, who had marched against the city with foreign troops. The corpse is to be left to the dogs and birds. Eteocles, who had led the polis's defenders, is given a funeral with full honors. Antigone ignores Creon's edict and buries Polyneices, undeterred by Creon's threat that anyone disobeying his order will be punished by death.

In Creon we see a politician who takes over the leadership of his city with the best of intentions, but errs precisely by adhering too strictly to what he believes to be the city's interests. He sticks by his edict, which will, as it turns out, have dreadful consequences—the city's altars are fouled by the dead man's unburied flesh, and the offerings are polluted.

One false step is not a serious matter; people constantly make mistakes. But they have to be willing to correct them. This is precisely what Creon refuses to do. He is convinced that he is serving the city when he is in fact carrying the imperatives of friendship and enmity to unnatural extremes. He responds to his detractors by accusing them of taking enemy bribes or falling victim to an infatuation. Creon is by nature incapable of accepting advice from a woman, like Antigone, or anyone younger than he, such as his son Haemon. He insists on having his way and behaves more and more like a tyrant.

Creon embodies the dismal and overly familiar picture of a politician becoming more and more enmeshed in misguided policies. His stubbornness is reinforced by his loneliness and inability to learn; it is compounded by his supposedly enlightened views. He cannot imagine the gods caring about a corpse and claims he does not believe they would be offended, even if Zeus's own eagles were to carry bits of the corpse to his throne.

Among man's greatest accomplishments are enlightenment and reason, which the chorus praises in the famous hymn that begins: "There are many wondrous things on Earth but nothing more wondrous than man." Then follows a brief survey of everything man has achieved, ranging from agriculture and seafaring to the founding of cities and the curing of disease. For death alone there remains no remedy. The chorus continues, saying that all these accomplishments, which surpass anything that might have been expected, can be used for good or for evil. They work to the polis's benefit when man adheres to the law of the land and against it when he recklessly abandons himself to evil.

This hymn has been taken as evidence of the Greeks' belief in progress.

But progress in the political and moral sphere is not what it illustrates. In fact, the hymn is quite ambivalent about the effects of these abilities. Indeed, in the play, man's abilities are clearly limited. In the next hymn the chorus declares that mortal men do not get far in their lives unless they delude themselves. Hope is an illusion. All too often evil appears in the guise of good, either because a god deceives man's senses or because man is under the spell of a delusion. This is where the danger of courage lies, for courage is oblivious to the limits Zeus has set for mortals.

Courage is the quality often used to describe the Athenians themselves. The concept of delusion goes back to the old Greek belief in fate, but it probably plays such a big role in Greek tragedy less out of respect for tradition than because of the fears and experiences of the fifth century. The age of Greek democracy and rationally determined politics—the Periclean era—brought the notion of delusion to the forefront. The "modern" figure of the enlightened Creon contains at least a hint of similarity to Pericles. Creon is not patterned after Pericles, but his character illustrates the potential danger when a politician is tempted to elevate the laws of the polis above everything else.

The question of laws comes up repeatedly in *Antigone*. They appear in the form of Creon's arbitrary edicts, in the form of laws observed by those acting in the city's spirit, and in the form of the unwritten customs, ordained by the gods, that Antigone follows—the customs that command her to bury her brother.

Here, as in *Ajax*, we are reminded that all men are equal before death. Antigone does what she does for reasons of her own—her love for her brother is quite surprising, and she is not afraid of death because as Oedipus's daughter, she is already in deep trouble. Regardless of her reasons, she urgently wants to do the moral thing.

And she wants to do everything on her own, without help. Creon asks her if she is not ashamed to think differently than the others. But thinking differently is exactly what she has to do in her situation, and it is what the polis needs. We rarely encounter civil disobedience at that time in Greek history. This is the first recorded instance we know of, and we are immediately shown the dangers it implies. It is limited to a lonely woman in highly unusual circumstances, but the play clearly raises the question whether this woman should not be considered an example to follow. Unlike most Greek heroes, Antigone is not a rebel. She does not challenge the world. She would rather conform and obey. It is just in this one respect, when the god-given unwritten customs are to be violated, that she has to disobey.

She is exemplary not just in her action but also in her manner of suffering, in the way she meets her fate head on, without flinching. This fate, of course, has been bequeathed to her by Oedipus and the dreadful, incomprehensible guilt imposed upon him by the gods.

Aeschylus's *Oresteia* and Promethean trilogy are left far behind. The central question no longer concerns the order of the entire world, as it had after the political revolution and the creation of a completely new constitution. The dramatist's concern was no longer to elucidate divine intentions and give meaning to these innovations. Nor was it to explicate the law or to illustrate learning through suffering. Athens had found itself in the midst of a new situation rife with uncertainties, and mistakes were inevitable. Athens was beginning to experience the fact that it had limits. It saw that the delusion of greatness had negative consequences in the new political order. In *Antigone*, all pride of enlightenment is declared false, or at least put into question. Old themes reassert themselves, those of bearing suffering and remaining steadfast with the dignity of a tragic hero, the dignity of humanity in the face of divine providence, no matter how incomprehensible. This incomprehensibility had never before been felt as clearly.

Now the individual was faced with far greater tasks than before, and the tragedian recognized this fact and examined its significance. For the first time we encounter the word *autonomous*, used by Sophocles to describe Antigone. "You alone of mortals, living according to your own law *[autonomously]*, descend to Hades." It is said that she is being destroyed by a "passion obeying only its own inclination and knowledge." Antigone represents the greatness and self-reliance of the individual. These qualities are shown on the stage but arise from the experience of reality and point to a new human dilemma.

Antigone is much greater than its subject matter—however that is defined—and the situation it presents. At the same time it is clearly a commentary on the city of Athens, which at that time was violating many laws in its presumptuous boldness. This helps explain why these tragedies have remained so alive over thousands of years. They mattered not just to their authors and a small audience but to an entire society, high and low. They satisfied a strong general demand for meaning and understanding and helped people to cope with their fears, successes, and responsibility. Tragedy provided a forum for the enactment of basic paradigms that were political not only in a Greek sense but in a profoundly human and modern sense as well.

Sophocles was elected *strategos* the following year, in 441–440, perhaps on the strength of the ideas expressed in *Antigone*.

Around 440 a new contest for comedies was introduced in addition to the contest of five plays that had been held at the Great Dionysia since 486. The new contest was held at the festival of Dionysus Lenaeus, which was celebrated in midwinter, when hardly any foreigners were in Athens.

The popular assembly shortly thereafter ruled to restrict comic satire by forbidding attacks on politicians by name. Perhaps the poets had initially made too free a use of the opportunity to ridicule politicians openly. Three years later, however, the regulation was rescinded. Presumably, the Attic people would not tolerate limits on comedy.

In 444–443 the Athenians founded the colony of Thurii at the site of ancient Sybaris in southern Italy. Sybaris had once been famous for its fabulous wealth—people were said to have gathered riches as though they would live forever and spent money as though they would die tomorrow. But the city had been destroyed by Greeks from Croton in 510, and an attempt to rebuild it in the 450s failed quickly, again because of Croton's opposition. The would-be rebuilders then appealed to Athens for help. It is possible that Athens responded to the settlers' appeal because it hoped to use the colony to influence the export of high-quality Italian wood for shipbuilding. In any case, prospective settlers gathered there from all over the Aegean region, about a tenth of them Athenians. Hippodamus of Miletus, the man who had designed the expansion of Piraeus, planned the city's layout; Protagoras of Abdera wrote the constitution, which was, naturally, democratic. The seer Lampon was declared the new city's founder, and the most famous of the colonists was the historian Herodotus. The city was independent, as colonies generally were, and Athens stayed out of the conflicts that soon flared up, between Thurii and the nearby city of Tarentum.

In 443 Pericles built a second long wall to Piraeus. Socrates, about twenty-six years old at the time, was present when Pericles proposed this project, which was intended to provide extra protection for the connection between the city and its most important harbor in the event that an enemy should succeed in landing between Phalerum and Piraeus.

In 440 Athens became involved in a war with the island-city of Samos. A dispute had arisen between Miletus and Samos over possession of Priene, a city that lay between Milesian land and territories on the mainland belonging to Samos. Miletus appealed to Athens. At this time, a group of citizens in Samos wanted to overthrow the government and introduce democracy, so the Athenians decided to intervene. They dispatched a fleet, conquered Samos, and installed a garrison to support the revolutionaries, imagining that would take care of the matter. But the ousted Samians hired mercenaries with the help of the Persian satrap and recaptured the city. The depth of hatred between the parties to this conflict is shown by the fact that both sides branded their prisoners on the forehead.

At the same time Byzantium revolted and withdrew from the Delian League, and the Peloponnesian League met to discuss whether it should take advantage of the situation to attack Athens. Thucydides later suggested that Samos had seriously challenged Athens' maritime supremacy. He must have had in mind a potential coalition between Sparta and Persia. Perhaps Samos also hoped that Chios and Lesbos, the two other islands that still commanded fleets of their own, would join it in fighting the Athenians.

In the end, all the Persian satrap did for Samos was to send money. No Phoenician fleet appeared to assist Samos, as Pericles had feared, and the Peloponnesians failed to take any action, partly because the Corinthians opposed it. So Athens was free to lay siege to Samos, and after nine months it achieved its end: Samos surrendered its fleet, pulled down its

walls, handed over hostages, and agreed to pay war indemnities in install-
ments. Byzantium rejoined the Delian League.

Once more the fragility of Athens' supremacy had been demonstrated,
along with the unreliability of its peace treaties with Persia and Sparta.
The experience must also have awakened the Athenians' fear of the
hatred the subjugated people bore them.

It is in this context that we should view Pericles' pride when he
boasted of contemporary Athens' superiority over the legendary Greeks.
Athens, he said, needed only nine months to conquer one of the mightiest Greek cities, whereas it had taken Agamemnon and the heroes of old
ten years to bring about the fall of a barbarian city like Troy. The Greeks
had long believed that the greatness of the old epic heroes could never be
matched. Now Athens was favorably comparing itself to them. This sense
of invincibility was especially prevalent in Athens in those years. The
Greeks had made extraordinary political and military advances, including
the introduction of new siege techniques invented at Samos by an engineer named Artemon.

In his speech eulogizing the Athenians killed at Samos, Pericles praised
the fallen soldiers as "immortals." He also said that with the loss of the
young men in the war the city was like a year in which there had been no
spring.

8

Periclean Athens

> Conditions in Periclean Athens were such that no sensible and
> peaceful person of our day would want to live under them; he would
> be miserably unhappy in that Athens, even if he was a freeman and not
> a part of the enslaved majority. . . . And yet the Athenians of that
> period must have had a taste for life that no amount of personal secu-
> rity could compensate for.
>
> —JACOB BURCKHARDT

"Thou famous Athens, divine city; shining, violet-wreathed, song-
inspiring pillar of Greece," wrote Pindar, the great lyric poet of the first
half of the fifth century B.C. His native city, Thebes, is said to have fined
him 1,000 drachmas for praising its hated rival city. The Athenians
awarded him an honorary stipend and made him an official guest.

These lines comprise the opening of a dithyramb or hymn composed
to be sung at the festival of Dionysus. They were long remembered, and
as late as the Peloponnesian War, Aristophanes ridiculed his fellow citizens for, as he put it, swooning with pleasure every time an ambassador
from a foreign city called Athens "violet-wreathed" and "shining." The
Greek word for "shining" is suggestive of olive trees, which abounded in
Attica, but the word could also be translated as "blessed." "Violet-
wreathed" is the adjective typically applied to Aphrodite and the muses.
Pindar must have been referring to some festive custom of the Athenians
with his description.

Aristophanes, too, invoked the city's festivals in *The Clouds*. As the
chorus enters from offstage, it walks toward Pallas Athena's "shining"
dominion, the city of Athens in whose marketplace the action transpires.
The chorus describes it as a "lovely plot of land defended by brave men, the
site of the Eleusinian Mysteries celebrations, the offering of sacrifices, and

the dedication of tall temples and statues to the gods"; it conjures up the image of the holy processions of rapturous believers, the flower-adorned sacrificial animals, and the various seasonal feasts. The chorus later approaches the festival of Dionysus, which is being celebrated with dance, song, and flute playing and is, of course, the context for the production of the comedy itself.

In his great funeral speech honoring the war dead in 431, Pericles says, according to Thucydides' account: "We provide plenty of means for the mind to refresh itself following the conduct of business. We celebrate games and sacrifices all year long, and the elegance of our private establishments forms a daily source of pleasure and helps banish the spleen." (What is meant by "the elegance of our private establishments" is open to debate. The Athenians' homes cannot have been very luxurious but were probably well and tastefully furnished.)

The walls erected around Athens in 478 enclosed an area of approximately 2.5 square kilometers. Piraeus added another square kilometer. In Pericles' time over 140,000 people lived in this urban area and a few outlying suburbs and villages. The number of citizens had grown to about 40,000 men, over a third of whom—between 14,000 and 16,000—lived in the urban district. Adding family members, we arrive at a population of between 50,000 and 60,000 Athenians. If we include a conservative estimate of approximately 15,000 metics and their families, we get close to 110,000 inhabitants, which is still not counting the 30,000 to 40,000 slaves or the foreigners who, without being metics, resided in Athens for varying periods of time. In short, the city was crowded.

Unlike Piraeus, which was built according to Hippodamus's plan and where the houses were regularly spaced along straight streets and lanes, Athens' streets were crooked and winding, the way they had evolved over many generations in accordance with property lines and the nature of the terrain. The city plan for Piraeus may have prescribed standard houses, which were each about 240 square meters in area. In Athens there

was no such standardization, and houses varied greatly in size and shape. The largest ones so far uncovered by archeologists are about the size of those in Piraeus.

The houses generally did not open toward the street, though some had street-side stores or workshops, which were either enclosed within or projecting out from the building's walls. The houses faced a court-yard, onto which opened a storage room, a kitchen, often an animal shed or a workshop, occasionally a bathroom, and a room for men's gatherings, where the family may have taken its meals. The altar for the family's religious offerings was also located in the courtyard. The women's rooms and bedrooms were probably upstairs. Very little space was available for slaves. The houses stood close together or were separated only by a common wall. Most houses were small, and in many cases they were shared by several families. Athens at that time had about 6,000 houses.

The house of Callias, located in the fashionable district of Melite to the west of the agora, must have been one of the large ones. We know that it had an antechamber, because Plato's *Protagoras* recounts that Socrates spent some time waiting there when he came to see Callias. When Socrates knocked at the door he was greeted sullenly by the porter, who was annoyed at the influx of intellectual visitors stopping in to meet with Protagoras.

The courtyard was roofed over on two sides. On one side, Protagoras was walking up and down with some students, followed by a group of reverent listeners who quickly moved aside each time Protagoras and his students turned around. Against the opposite wall sat another Sophist, Hippias of Elis, whose listeners were sitting around him on benches asking questions about the stars and other celestial sights. A third Sophist, Prodicus of Ceos, held court from his bed, in a room that was originally a storage area but had been converted into a guest room by Callias because of the frequency and number of visitors. Socrates was unable to make out what Prodicus was talking about. Pillows and benches were soon moved to where Hippias had sat, so that those present could follow the discussion that had arisen between Socrates and Protagoras. There must have been enough room to accommodate many listeners.

The houses of the wealthy obviously differed considerably from those of the poor, but they were not much greater in size. Because of the restricted space in the city, the aristocrats and wealthy citizens could not express their rank or fame by living in magnificent buildings. They expressed it instead with the jewelry and clothes they wore, the number of slaves they owned, the hospitality they offered, the public events they sponsored, and, presumably, the interior decoration of their houses. Athenians had their walls embellished with paintings and probably with stuccowork.

Many people also kept animals in their houses and courtyards. They were awakened in the early morning by roosters. Chickens, donkeys, goats, pigs, and cows are mentioned in contemporary sources, as well as bedbugs, fleas, and lice.

The alleys and stairways of the city were often narrow. They were unpaved and often rocky. There were only a few wide streets, and in places we still find signs of sidewalks, some of them with grooves cut across them to prevent slipping on the smooth rock surface. Where possible, drains and gutters were installed to keep rainwater from accumulating. An underground drainage canal ran from the agora, where water collected from various directions, to the river Eridanus. Wagon tracks were cut into the main streets. The narrower streets may have been used for one-way traffic in order to avoid collisions and arguments between drivers. The noise from creaking wheels and wagons must have been deafening.

The streets and alleyways were also littered with human and animal waste. In Aristophanes' *The Wasps*, a troupe of old men, on their way before dawn to serve as jurors, is guided by children with oil lamps, but even so, the old men keep stepping into puddles and piles of feces. People habitually emptied their chamber pots on the street at night, warning possible passersby by shouting "Out of the way!" There must have been public latrines that were cleaned at regular intervals, and some courtyards had outhouses, but it is not clear how common these were—or how much they were used. In another of Aristophanes' comedies, Blepyrus, a "little man," looks for a place outdoors to relieve himself. Under the cover of darkness, he figures, "any place will do."

City magistrates, called *astynomoi*, appointed probably as early as the fifth century, were responsible for policing the city, maintaining public buildings, and keeping the streets, which were public property, clean and free of trash and garbage, especially along the paths of religious processions. They saw to it that all of the city's trash was removed to a distance of no less than ten *stadia*, or about 1,800 meters, from the city. They were also responsible for removing the bodies of people who had died on the streets. Slaves owned by the city did the actual labor. The *astynomoi* also served as building inspectors, checking that nothing was built on the public streets, that no part of a house projected beyond the legal limit, and that no stairs were built outside the front door. Front doors could only open toward the inside of the house. Otherwise walking along the streets and alleyways could have been dangerous, especially in the dark.

Some tradesmen had their workshops in separate buildings, especially those who worked with open fires or kilns or employed many slaves, such as men running metal foundries. One such was Sophocles' father, Sophilus, who fashioned swords.

The workshops and shops were connected because most manufacturers also sold the goods they made, and most tradesmen were grouped together by district. The potters lived and worked in Ceramicus, a section of the city bordering on the agora in the northwest; the tanners probably worked in Cydathen. In other sections, close to the main roads, lived the stonemasons, boxmakers, and many others. The fish mongers attracted much business. Next to bread, fish was the most commonly eaten food. People looking for work gathered on Colonus Agoraeus, the hill west of the agora.

Many vendors set up shop in the city's central marketplace, the agora. Farmers coming from the countryside of Attica, Megara, and Boeotia sold their produce at the market, though they probably also roamed the streets and alleys, calling out their wares.

The streets were busy from early morning until night, when the last participants of symposia returned home, carrying lanterns. It was mostly men who filled the streets, for the women spent most of their time at home. Occasionally they or their slaves left their houses to run errands. Unless they were able to go to the central well, they had to fetch water from fountains in various parts of the city. After the time of Solon, people were supposed to use these public fountains if they lived within 700 meters of them; if the distance was greater they were allowed to dig wells on their own property—but no deeper than about 20 meters. Great care was taken that the city have a supply of clean water. Water from cisterns and rivers was used primarily for washing.

Women went out of doors for various other reasons, such as visiting relatives or friends, tending shrines, and attending cult rituals and religious festivals.

Contrary to the custom in other Greek cities, metics and slaves in the streets of Athens did not move aside for citizens. Whereas many cities demanded respectful behavior of slaves, extracting it with cudgels if necessary, in Athens slaves differed from other Athenians neither in dress nor bearing. The city needed them desperately, as well as metics to maintain its maritime power, and so they were treated with respect. Plato was later to observe sarcastically that in a democracy even dogs, horses, and donkeys were accustomed "to keep on walking straight ahead freely and unabashedly when encountering people in the streets."

There was a great contrast between the cramped houses and streets and the spacious agora at the center of the city. It could be reached within ten or fifteen minutes from any part of Athens. The agora seems to have held a magnetic attraction for the men of the city. The market square was crowded with people by late morning. All manner of business, political and private, was settled there. People went there to hear the latest news, and, as one source puts it, everyone had some special place where he stopped regularly, whether a perfume vendor's, a barbershop, a shoemaker, or a bathhouse—usually a round building with a circle of bathtubs, head ends to the outer wall. Taverns and brothels were prevalent as well.

A citizen with leisure time would have visited one of the gymnasia, most of which were located outside the city walls, or a *palaestra* or wrestling school. Under democracy, public sports arenas were set up in addition to the private ones. In the opening of Plato's *Charmides*, Socrates says that after his return from a long tour of duty in the army he went back to visit his old haunts, among them the *palaestra* of Taureas, in the southern part of the city, where his friends immediately asked him for news about the war. He was more interested in hearing how the search for truth was going, however, and inquired if, among the boys at the wrestling schools, there was one of exceptional "intelligence or beauty, or both." His friends mentioned Charmides who, they said, was admired like the image of a god. Charmides became one of Socrates' students.

Public life was carried on in all the different places where people gathered; the people were interested in the topics of the day, in politics both foreign and domestic, in new discoveries and ideas, in festivals and tragedies, as well as in gossip about well-known figures—politicians or dandies, scholars or Sophists—including Socrates himself. The existence of these shared interests accounts for the intensity of community life in Athens.

The agora, the geographical center of everyday life, was an open, rectangular space about 100 by 200 meters and clearly marked off from the surrounding area by border stones. North of it was the old round orchestra, the former venue for dance, theater, and assemblies, and the place where in Pericles' time the chorus still danced and sang, the ostracism vote was taken, and, when conditions allowed, free grain was distributed. On one side of the agora stood the monument commemorating the tyrannicides. Along the southern edge stood Sycamore trees that Cimon had planted

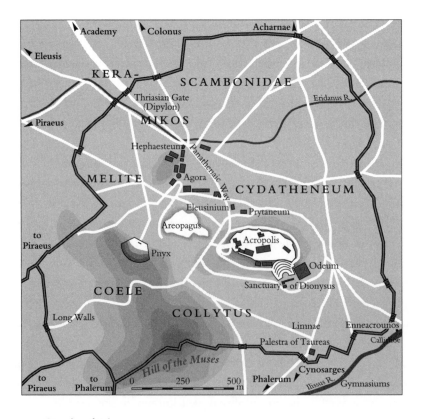

City plan of Athens

for shade. The underground storm sewer ran parallel with the agora's western edge.

Several of the major public buildings were located immediately to the north, west, and south of the agora. On the east, on the other side of the street along which the Panathenaea procession passed, were private stores, workshops, and houses until the Stoa of Attalus was built in the second century.

The most important buildings were on the western side of the agora. The meeting place of the Council of Five Hundred was located just south of the middle in an old building supported on the inside by columns. Toward the end of the fifth century a new council building was built with seats arranged in stepped semicircular rows (the old council building was then converted into an archive). The conference halls were equipped with altars and barriers behind which the public could stand and listen. Next to the council building was the *tholos*, a round building where the fifty council members who were required to attend the daily sessions at any given time stayed and ate their meals. The city's official weights and measures were also kept at the *tholos*, and an altar was placed at its center.

Just north of the council building, on the Colonus Agoraeus hill, was the Temple of Hephaestus, built in the mid-440s. The field below the

Hephaesteum, as seen from the agora. The buildings of the Council of Five Hundred were on the left, and the Stoa of Zeus Eleutherios on the right. The space in front of the temple was left open and thus dominated the western side of the agora. Built in 440s B.C.

slope where the temple stood was left open, so that the temple, built in conventional style out of Pentalian marble, dominated the entire western side of the agora. This was an unusual temple in that it was dedicated to the worship of both Hephaestus and Athena Ergane, protectress of craftsmen and artisans. Bronze statues of the two divinities, made around 420 by Alcamenes, a student of Phidias, were placed side by side in the temple's cella or central chamber. As far as we know, the Greeks erected no other shrine of similar grandeur to Hephaestus.

Hephaestus was of special significance to Athenians for two reasons. According to an old legend he attempted unsuccessfully to seduce the maiden Athena. When she brushed the semen he had spilled on her thigh onto the ground, the earth gave birth to a king named Erichthonius (or

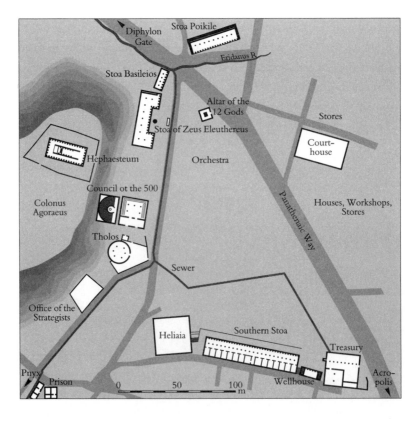

The agora with the Colonus Agoraeus

Erechtheus), who became the forefather of mortal Athenians. Though she did not give birth to the child, the goddess raised him like a mother. On the basis of this story, the Athenians worshipped Hephaestus and Athena as their progenitors. The Erechtheum, the temple that was adjacent to the Parthenon and famous for its Porch of the Maidens (caryatids), was dedicated to Athena, Poseidon, and Erechtheus, but it also included an altar to Hephaestus. The Temple of Hephaestus above the agora reminded the Athenians—and anyone else who saw it—of their autochthonous forebears and the fact that the Athenians had neither taken their land away from anyone else nor ever lost it. They were offspring of ancient Earth, like Athena and Hephaestus.

Hephaestus's shrine was also worshipped by the city's artisans. The artisans were a large and influential group, and they possessed important human knowledge and skill. According to Protagoras, Prometheus had stolen fire from Hephaestus and craft from Athena to save mankind. In the thinking of the time, artisans included both craftsmen and artists, and their continually expanding skills commanded general admiration. Members of this group were influential within the popular assembly, yet there is some indication that as a class they were looked down upon socially and politically.

In any case, the artisans, probably including metics and possibly even slaves, were wealthy enough to be able to offer sacrifices to their patron god Hephaestus in his grand temple. They also celebrated a festival of their own, the Chalceia.

Diagonally below the Hephaesteum, on the northern end of the agora's west side, was a shrine devoted to Zeus Soter, Zeus the savior in time of need, that dated back to the sixth century. Ever since the Persian Wars, Zeus had been honored as the *eleutherios*, or liberator. Around 430 a magnificent stoa was built on the site of the shrine. It was unusual in that it terminated at both ends in short, protruding wings with magnificent pediments. A statue of Zeus was placed midway between them, and a victory goddess surmounted the gables on each side. Thus the citizens were reminded at once of the autochthony and the freedom of this "freest of all cities."

Slightly to the north of this stoa was the Stoa Basileios, a relatively

*The agora during a Panathenaic procession, viewed from the Stoa of Attalus.
Athena's state robe, the* peplos, *was carried past the Areopagus on a ship that
moved on rollers. Attempt at a visualization of the scene by R. Leacroft.*

small public building housing the office of the chief archon. This was the
only one of the administrative offices that predated Cleisthenes to have
been moved closer to the agora. The other offices remained in their
original place at the foot of the northwestern slope of the Acropolis, at
the southeast corner of the new market.

The Panathenaic Way started in the northwest of Athens at the
Dipylon gate, continued diagonally across the agora, and up the hill of the
Acropolis. According to an old custom, the Athenians brought their goddess a new robe every July, the month that in their calendar ushered in
the new year. Specially chosen young girls from noble families spent nine
months weaving this robe, the design of which depicted the goddess
slaying a giant.

After a feast the night before, the Panathenaic festival began with a
race of torch bearers who ran from the academy's grove, where the
torches were lit at the altar of Eros, over three and a half kilometers to
the top of the Acropolis. The runners sprinted as fast as possible without extinguishing their torches. The winner of the race earned the privilege of lighting the fire that had been prepared on the altar of Athena
Polias.

In addition to those who had made the goddess's robe, the procession
included girls with baskets and pitchers for offerings, flute players, men
carrying branches, a contingent of hoplites, one of cavalry, a regiment
of metics, and a long train of cattle and sheep to be sacrificed on the
Acropolis. Quite a bit of filth must have accumulated, as well as blood

from over a hundred sacrificial animals. After the offering was made to the goddess, meat was passed out to various dignitaries and the rest was distributed, probably through representatives of the demes, to the citizenry as a whole. Each deme was expected to have members in the procession as a demonstration of Attica's unity. Starting in the 440s, every city in the Delian League was also required to send one bullock and one set of hoplite arms for the offering. Organizing the procession could not have been an easy task.

The festivities, which were celebrated annually, included a dance of naked young men carrying shields and lances, contests in various sports, and competitions in the performance arts. Among these events was the *apobates* race, in which fully armed warriors leapt from war chariots and ran a race across the agora. Possibly the procession stopped for a while to watch. Depictions in the Parthenon frieze indicate that horsemen may also have performed stunts there. At the Great Panathenaea, which was celebrated every fourth year, there were yet more contests, which lasted for several days. By Pericles' time, if not before, the festivities were moved outside the city walls.

At the northern end of agora was the Hall of Colors, or *stoa poikile*, and a little south of it the Altar of the Twelve Gods, a central landmark of the city since the time of the tyrants. This altar was also a place of asylum, and in this respect symbolized Athens' role as a safe haven for all who needed help. Court buildings were located both north and south of the agora. Toward the end of the century, another stoa was built at the south end. Its front was colonnaded in the usual style, but the back side of the hall housed a row of rooms, all the same size, with benches for reclining at feasts and symposia.

Continuing along Panathenaic Way from the agora's southeast corner, one came to the shrine of the Eleusinian divinities Demeter and Core (or Persephone). They were the most important gods in rural Attica and were worshipped in the city as well. Not far from this shrine were the old administrative buildings, among them the Prytaneum, seat of the chief archon and site of the sacred hearth of the city. There citizens who had performed outstanding service to the city were honored at official dinners, and winners of the Olympic games and descendents of the tyrannicides

A horseman from the Parthenon frieze, 430s B.C. The Parthenon.

were made welcome. Delegations from abroad were also entertained here. The Theseus shrine must also have been located in this part of the city.

Proceeding southwest from the agora, one passed a large building, which was probably the administrative center of the *strategoi*. A bit farther along on the left was the prison where Socrates later drank hemlock. By climbing uphill about 400 meters from the prison, one reached the Pnyx. The assemblies called there did not always attract the same large crowds— the *prytanes*, the members of the Council of Five Hundred who were in residence at Athens, would order Scythian slaves, to whom the city assigned various policing duties, to block all other exits from the agora and herd the people toward the Pnyx with a long rope dipped in red paint.

The Pnyx was large enough to accommodate about 6,000 people. The citizens sat facing the agora, and the ground was raised for the speaker's platform. Wooden benches were provided for the *prytanes*, who sat facing the people. Everyone else had to make do with bare rock, perhaps made softer by a pillow brought from home. Looking diagonally to the right, the citizens saw the Hill of Ares, or Areopagus, and to the far right lay the Acropolis, the architectural and artistic center of the city, which the

The Propylaeum by Mnesicles. Built in the 430s B.C. On the west side of the Acropolis.

Athenians started to build in 447. Its size and splendor were striking and visible from all parts of town. Even the new public buildings near the agora seemed modest by comparison.

Since about 460 Phidias's statue of Athena Promachos had stood on the Acropolis. Behind it was the wall enclosing the sanctuary of the city's protectress, Athena Polias, the ancient wooden effigy of the goddess that had, according to legend, originally fallen from the sky and that the Athenians took with them when they fled the city for the battle of Salamis. It had since been returned to the provisionally restored cella of her temple. Much on the Acropolis remained in a makeshift state until Pericles initiated his building program.

The first project in this program was the Parthenon. Immediately after its completion in 438, the magnificent Propylaeum was built. The Erechtheum was probably already planned at that time, though it was not built until after Pericles' death.

The Propylaeum, designed by Mnesicles, was not just a temple facade but an entryway to the sacred precinct of the Acropolis, with columns on three sides. Its design was a brilliant innovation, almost an anticipation of the large architectural complexes that were to be typical in the Hellenistic

The Parthenon, seen from the west. Reconstruction by G. P. Stevens.

period. The temple facade rose above four steps rather than the usual three steps, and these were interrupted by a ramp in the middle of the facade to allow the visitor to climb the grade more gradually. This ramp was flanked by rows of Ionic columns and surmounted by a magnificent coffered ceiling with golden star and flower patterns on a blue ground. At the top, the porch faced onto the Acropolis's plateau, the first sight that met both visitors and members of the Panathenaic procession, all of whom had to pass through the Propylaeum to gain access to the Acropolis. Whereas the lower section of the Propylaeum was designed with Ionic columns, above they were Doric and the facade resembled that of a Doric temple. The juxtaposition of Doric columns on the building's outside and Ionic ones on the inside was a daring innovation. Taken as a whole, the Propylaeum was of a magnitude hitherto unimaginable, especially given the fact that it led to a vast hall on the northern end, which would later serve as a picture gallery. A similar hall was originally planned for the south end as well.

The Propylaeum was probably built by a combination of citizens, metics, and slaves. No distinction was made between these workers from different classes, though in the case of slaves the wages went to their owners; the type of work done had no effect on an individual's status.

390

Detailed records were kept on the building of the Erechtheum. We know, for example, that one column required 350 workdays: 50 for the accurate rounding of the column; 90 for cutting angles for the fluted grooves; 100 for rounding the grooves; and another 110 for the final shaping with fine chisels and for polishing.

In the fifth century, the Acropolis when viewed from the Propylaeum looked very different than it does today. To the right one saw the wall that enclosed the shrine of Artemis Brauronia, which had been established, like the Eleusinian shrine, to link one of Attica's important divinities to Athens. The wall continued on to surround the Parthenon precinct, so that that temple itself was only partially visible. Even after entering the Parthenon's sacred ground, one still had to climb a tall stairway to reach the level of the temple. The steps were covered with offerings to the goddess.

The two other temples whose ruins are still found on the Acropolis, the temple of Athena Nike and the Erechtheum, were not built until the time of the Peloponnesian War. Nike commemorated the victory over the Dorians attained in the ancient past, which the Athenians hoped to repeat in the present. The Erechtheum incorporated three structures on four different levels, and contained several shrines deserving of this most venerable spot on the Acropolis, the site of the ancient Mycenaean royal palace and burial ground of those mythical rulers. This was where Athena and Poseidon had contended for possession of the city, the goddess planting an olive tree and the god opening a salt spring with his trident. The olive tree had eventually sprouted again, after being burned down during the Persian Wars, and in the meantime had grown back to full size. The Erechtheum was also the home of the snake that, according to legend, was a reembodiment of King Erichthonius, who had been born out of the earth. The snake, which had disappeared at the Persians' approach in 480, was the guardian appointed by Athena to look out for the city's well-being. Erechtheus, another legendary king, was also honored with a shrine here, and it was his name that gave rise to the popular name of the temple, the Erechtheum. He has sometimes been confused with Erichthonius and even with Poseidon, who was also honored here, as was the grave of the mythical king Cecrops, Erechtheus's son. Altars

The group of Athena and Marsyas by Myron. Ca. 450 B.C. Reconstruction in Braunschweig, Germany.

were also dedicated to Hephaestus and to the wooden statue of Athena Polias, which was presumably brought there after the old temple of Athena burned down in 405. It was this statue for which each year Athena's new robe, the *peplos*, was made.

The multiplicity of cults observed was matched by the complexity of the temple's structure, which had to conform to the site's uneven topography. Whatever unity it lacked was made up for by clever use of perspective, and above all by the variety of forms, the frieze, the capitals, the exquisite embellishments of the door frames, and through what has been called "the loveliest miracle of this building," the Porch of the Maidens with its six statues of young girls serving as supporting columns.

All over the Acropolis and especially along the walls of the sanctuaries there were inscriptions and statuary, some of the latter the work of the best artists. Among the statues were, for example, Phidias's *Athena Lemnia*, a present to the goddess from the Attic *cleruchy* on the island of

Lemnos, and Myron's statue of Athena and Marsyas, depicting Athena beating the satyr as he tried to pick up the flute the goddess had thrown away. (Athena herself invented the flute, but seeing in the mirror how ugly her puffed out cheeks looked while playing it, she wanted to get rid of the instrument. In another version of the story, she hated flute music because the forest god Silenus liked it.)

A path called the *peripatos* ran around the Acropolis, which had additional shrines in the back, just below the level from which the rocks rose steeply. The path led to the mountain's caves, where there were shrines as the one dedicated to Aphrodite and Eros, the main fertility divinities, and the one the Athenians had established to honor Pan after the Battle of Marathon. In the southeast, the path skirted the Dionysus theater and ran above the odeon built by Pericles.

"Yesterday I went down to Piraeus with Glaucon, the son of Ariston," Socrates wrote, "to worship the goddess and to see how the people would celebrate her festival, which they were doing now for the first time." This is how Socrates begins his story in the first book of Plato's *Republic*. Socrates was already on his way home from Piraeus when Polemarchus, son of Cephalus, sent a servant after him to ask him to wait. It turns out that on this evening a torch race was taking place. It was to be a relay race, with the contestants riding on horseback—and this was something new.

The festival, which was first celebrated in 429, honored the Thracian goddess Bendis, who was related to Artemis. This cult had been introduced to honor the Thracian king Sitalces, with whom Athens had formed an alliance. Thrace was of strategic importance to Athens, and this cult served the colony of Thracian merchants in Piraeus. Zeus was believed to have approved the new cult in the oracle of Dodona. The procession consisted of two parts: one, composed of Athenians, who approached from the Prytaneum in Athens, and another, made up of Thracians who started from Piraeus. According to Socrates both were beautiful to watch.

There were many reasons to travel the seven kilometers to Piraeus. Piraeus was the site of the large commercial port of Cantharus, where ships from all over the world docked, foreigners did business, and the

The Erechtheum, seen from the northwest. In front of it, the olive tree Athena gave the city.

most varied merchandise was available. There were also the naval ports of Zea and Munychia, where the city's proud navy could be admired in the water or in the boat sheds. These two ports had moorings for 82 and 196 vessels, respectively. The rest of the triremes were moored in the southern bay of Cantharus. The harbors were fortified. Fathers could show their sons the naval might of the city that was their home. Passing the graves along the roads leading out of the city, the fathers may also have taught their sons some Attic history. Outside the Dipylon gate, for instance, where the main road to Piraeus branched off, were the graves of

Athenians killed in war. In the 430s, Attic funereal art developed new styles of depicting humans in sculpture, though this was probably not of great interest to young boys.

An especially exciting sight was a fleet as it prepared to sail. Aristophanes describes Piraeus as being noisy and full of soldiers and rowers, crowds gathered around the ships' commanders, or *trierarchs*, who were also responsible for outfitting their vessels. In one place, wages were being paid; in another, artisans were putting last-minute touches on the *palladia*, small images of Pallas Athena holding shield and lance, that were mounted as talismans on the ships' prows. The marketplace was a sea of activities: grain dealers weighed grain; animal skins were filled with wine and water; leather straps for the rowers were sold, as were baskets, garlic, olives, nets full of onions and anchovies, as well as wreaths that were hung on the ships' sterns or worn by the rowers to bring good luck. Oarsmen examined their calluses, and flute-playing girls offered

Reconstruction of the harbor of Munychia, with piers, fortified wall, boat sheds, and some triremes. Phalerum harbor and Mount Hymettus are in the background. The drawing of the boat sheds is based on archeological findings. This picture attempts to reproduce the harbor as it was in the fourth century B.C., but it probably did not look significantly different in the fifth century. Drawing by J. F. Coates.

themselves. The wharf throbbed as new oar blades were sawed out, and the harbor's pilings groaned. Oars were mounted on ships, some of which were already leaving on practice runs, so that the air was filled with loud boatswains' whistles and shouts of the stroke setting the rowers' pace.

Athens and its harbors were fascinating places. The excitement was not confined to political and military events, nor to new philosophical innovations or discoveries. It pervaded everything, as festivals and everyday routine alternated throughout the year.

It is almost impossible to enumerate all the festivals that were held. In winter and spring many celebrations were held in honor of Dionysus, among them the rural Dionysia celebrated by the demes. There were the ancient fertility rites devoted to Demeter and the Thesmophoria, celebrated by women only. Again and again there were processions, sacrificial offerings and the accompanying distributions of meat, dances, choral singing, torch races, wild Dionysian revels, phallic parades, and, of course, plays.

One of the strangest celebrations, mentioned in Aristophanes' *Clouds*, was that of the Eleusinian Mysteries, celebrated in September. The *archon basileus*, or chief religious officer of the polis, was in charge of the Mysteries, though they were organized mostly by two old aristocratic families, at least one of which originally came from Eleusis. Those interested in participating prepared themselves months earlier by going through certain initiation rites, and now they registered by paying a considerable fee. They then went to the shore to cleanse themselves, atoned for sins with offerings, and spent a day fasting at home. Most of the participants had probably been introduced to the Mysteries by a priest. Men and women, freemen and slaves, even Greeks from outside of Attica could be initiated, as long as they were not defiled by having committed crimes.

A procession of thousands set out from the holy gate in Ceramicus for Eleusis, twenty-one kilometers away. They carried sacred objects that had been brought to Athens from the distant sanctuary a few days earlier. The marchers sang and played the flute, shouting out *"Iacche!"* an invocation of the deity Iacchus, over and over again.

The actual Mysteries began toward evening in the Telesterion of

Eleusis, the hall of initiation. This building, the largest covered structure in existence at the time, measured 50 by 50 meters, with the ceiling resting on 42 columns. The rear of the building was constructed on the edge of a steep dropoff, but each of the three accessible sides had two doors. Inside, all around the walls, were banks of eight steps, which offered standing room for about five thousand people. The entire building was dark, except for a little moonlight coming through a small opening in the ceiling (the celebration took place four days after full moon) and the glow of the fire burning on the shrine in the middle of the Telesterion.

There are reports of initiates "going astray, of painful marching, endless and restless wandering in the darkness" and of suffering the "horrors of the underworld" before one finally emerged into "the places of light, the blissful realms," sometime near dawn when the sunlight penetrated through the opening in the roof. The priest announced that the goddess had given birth to the holy son. The celebrants partook of a drink made of barley meal, water, and mint. A mysterious rite followed that involved grinding grains of barley. To a smaller group of initiates participating in the Mysteries for the second time, "the great, miraculous, and most perfect . . . mystery of the place" was revealed: a sheaf of grain was cut in silence.

The rites were secret, but a few writers, especially the Christians in later times, disregarded this rule, so that we have at least some idea of the events that took place. The myth of Demeter, the goddess of Eleusis, was reenacted. According to the myth, she had chosen this place to give mankind her two most valuable gifts: the fruits of the field, to provide a basis for civilized life, and the Mysteries, as a guarantee of "hope for a better life" after death. The celebration was related to the myth in which Demeter won back her daughter Persephone from Hades, who had abducted her to the Underworld. Demeter had forced the gods to return Persephone to her by temporarily preventing grain from growing, but as a compromise Persephone had to spend three months of the year in the Underworld. This alternation of life and death, darkness and light, sowing and harvesting was somehow enacted by the initiates in the Mysteries.

The Mysteries were believed to bring the initiates bliss in their present lives and to promise a better life after death. The priests were said to have "shown that death was not evil but good," but we will never know exactly how they did this. It remains the secret of all those who fasted, cleansed themselves, and gave themselves over to exhaustion, fright, and the excitement of the proceedings.

Mysteries were celebrated in other places as well, arising from the beliefs of certain cults and the various needs people felt. But the Eleusinian Mysteries were apparently the most important. The crowds they attracted were so large that the Telesterion, which was probably first built under Pisistratus in the fifth century, twice had to be rebuilt on a larger scale. Some of the attraction was no doubt due to the draw of the city of Athens, though this ought not minimize the seriousness of the rite's participants, their isolation, their need for consolation, or the hopes they felt. The appeal of the Mysteries, which from the fifth century on inspired so many people to undertake this often long and difficult journey, is remarkable.

Other sacred sites in Attica aroused much less interest, even important ones such as the temple of Artemis in Brauron and of Nemesis in Rhamnus. The splendid temple of Athena on the Sunium promontory may or may not have received many pilgrims, but it was at least seen frequently by the sailors of Athens' fleet—it was the first sight of home on their return.

Some critics, including a few aristocrats, said that no city celebrated as much as Athens. By contrast, the Corinthians claimed that Athenians knew no pleasure except in laboring to achieve their goals. These are not necessarily contradictory statements. The Athenians' festivals were not just times of relaxation or special events looked forward to in the course of the year, as festivals were in other cities. Rather, they were part of the spirit of movement that pervaded this city, its eagerness for new experiences and adventure, an expression of its greatness and supreme political power.

festivals represented

. . .

"Our love is for beauty and propriety without ostentation, and for intellectual pursuits but without being soft," said Pericles of the Athenians in his famed funeral oration. By "without ostentation" he presumably meant that no material luxury was involved, that the beautiful and proper were manifested more in form than in content. For in Athens, as he went on to say, wealth was regarded more as an opportunity to accomplish deeds than as a means for bragging.

The words *beautiful* and *proper* are translations of one Greek word, which includes both meanings. Perhaps this linking of two qualities is typical of all periods when a society justifies the beauty and splendor of its public life by emphasizing that it is not concerned only with aesthetics but also seeks to realize other ideals.

In the case of Athens the old ideal of beauty was closely tied to a striving for harmony and knowledge. What mattered was not so much beautification but the very structure of life in the city, its standards and its concept of order. It is not surprising to learn that a number of artists of that period also wrote theoretical treatises.

Polycletus of Argos took many measurements of the human body and averaged his findings in an attempt to derive proper proportions and symmetry. He made use of mathematical theories and combined theory with his empirical data. Beauty, he concluded, came about through minute variations in mathematical proportions. This insight, which he formulated in his *Canon*, is realized most completely in his statue *The Spear Bearer*, which depicts the legendary Achilles but also stands for the ideal citizen and political equality. The Greek painter Zeuxis also believed that beauty is not found in one single human body, "because nature does not produce anything by making all its parts perfect." When he was asked to decorate Hera's temple in Croton, Zeuxis agreed only on the condition that the most beautiful maidens be made available as models. By a public resolution all beautiful girls were called together. Zeuxis chose five of them to derive from them the image of perfect beauty. The same technique of combining many mathematical proportions with minute deviations is also what made the Parthenon and the Propylaeum such outstanding architectural monuments.

Among the impulses that led the Greeks to look for answers in beauty was the recognition that laws underlie all natural phenomena. But the Greeks also wanted an ideal image of themselves, the gods, and the heroes of ancient times. All this came together in the Parthenon, on whose pediments the birth of the city's goddess and her contest with Poseidon for possession of Athens were depicted. The metopes of the frieze showed the Greeks battling the Trojans and all kinds of monsters; on Athena's shield the Greeks fought the Amazons. These scenes also depicted what was happening on the home front as Athens fought against the barbarians and struggled to gain security and protect its civilization. The Ionic frieze of the cella portrayed the citizenry itself in the Panathenaea festival procession.

By taking up the rich heritage of the Greeks and elevating it to new heights, Athens became, in Pericles' words, the school of Greece. He proudly pointed out that Athens had developed its political system on its own, not learned it from others, and that it was a model for others—as if Athens' very political order had grown from native soil.

We have two related accounts of Periclean Athens. One is Pericles' funeral oration of 431 as reported by Thucydides. The other is a pamphlet by an unknown author usually referred to as Pseudoxenophon because the pamphlet was found together with Xenophon's works. It was written sometime in the 420s.

Pseudoxenophon's *On the Constitution of Athens* is an attempt by an opponent of democracy to show other Greeks that Athens' constitution, though basically bad, did promote the lower classes' interests. This assessment applied not just to the constitution in the narrow sense of the word but to the entire system of the city, from the way public offices were filled to the makeup of the navy's crews, from the politics of the Delian League to the organization of festivals and sacrifices, and from the building of sports arenas to that of bathhouses.

From this pamphlet one gets the impression that in the rest of Greece

The Spear Bearer *by Polycletus. A bronze reconstruction by G. Roemer based on the best Roman copies. University of Munich.*

the ideal of *eunomia*, or government dominated by the aristocracy, was still largely accepted—to such an extent, in fact, that other Greeks could not understand why the Athenians were so stupid as not to trust in the integrity and wisdom of the aristocrats. To counter this view the author states simply that the people of Athens were concerned primarily with their own advantage and thus preferred to listen to uneducated and common men, as long as such men were on their side. He concluded that the only choice was either to abolish democracy altogether or to leave it alone. The introduction of minor improvements would accomplish nothing.

Pseudoxenophon thus knew that the interests of the aristocracy (to the extent that it adhered to the old order) and those of the people were mutually exclusive. He favored an aristocratic government but was fully aware that, to the common people, the aristocrats seemed to favor their own class and therefore acted in conflict with the people's aims. The common man might be ignorant and rude, but he was not stupid. He knew exactly what was good for him.

Unlike the pamphleteer, Pericles did not speak of conflicts or party interests in Athens. He regarded the city as a unified whole. When he mentioned democracy he pointed out that it was a political order embracing all, not the rule of some over the rest. Though he referred to many institutions and customs, he was primarily concerned with one thing: defining the special quality of the Athenians, which characterized both the fallen soldiers and the living. He sought to explain the miracle of Athens by the character of its citizens.

Where Pseudoxenophon examined Athens in isolation, Pericles presented it as a foil to other cities, primarily Sparta. Thucydides reports Pericles' speech as if it were addressed also to posterity. Athens is made to appear as a unified whole in the wider context of the Greek world.

For Pericles, freedom and the mutual trust deriving from this freedom were of central importance. Education had to be liberal; training for military service could not be a strict, lifelong process but happened almost incidentally and as needed. People submitted to laws and obeyed public officials of their own free will. They regarded others with tolerance. Foreigners were allowed to see and learn whatever they wanted, even when it would have been more prudent to withhold information. The Athenians relied more on their own mental powers than on deception or precautionary measures. In addition, Pericles said, they were blessed with a "cheerful attitude" and the ability to recognize dangers clearly without letting themselves be discouraged by them. All of these traits were supposedly shared by the high and the low alike.

Where Pericles does mention differences, he refers to the remarkable fact that in Athens even the poor enjoyed respect, and poverty did not prevent anyone from serving the polis and being recognized for this service.

Pericles claimed that in Athens everybody tended to his own business but was still able to make political judgments, and nowhere does he suggest that such judgments might be based on partisan interests. Where Pseudoxenophon attributes cleverness to the common people only where their own advantage is concerned, Pericles is intent on showing that their judgment is just as sound as that of the aristocrats, a situation he suggests is particularly Athenian. Every individual's judgment was supposedly based on what was best for the city as a whole. For in Athens alone among the Greek cities, Pericles continues, anyone who failed to participate in politics was considered to be not a peaceful citizen but a useless one. This fact accounted for the widespread political awareness and judgment in Athens.

Pericles at last arrives at the remarkable conclusion that in Athens every man was autarkic—or "able to show himself the rightful lord and owner of his own person, and do this, moreover, with exceptional grace and exceptional versatility." The city's might was proof of this.

Not only did specialization go hand in hand in Athens with a talent for doing many things, but the common people embodied the aristocratic ideals of grace and autarky. In this same period Herodotus wrote that it was impossible for any man or country to be autarkic, even for a king. But Thucydides referred to autarky in a different sense—namely, the ability to deal effectively with the demands one confronted. The concept of autarky had shifted from possession of adequate land and people to possession of adequate abilities. Thus Pericles could assert that Athens was the most autarkic city in war and peace, even though its territory did not supply it with everything it needed, because the city was prepared to deal with any eventuality and could obtain everything it needed. It is in this sense that he now applied the notion of autarky to individuals. They lived up to almost anything demanded of them, including duties as members of the popular assembly or the council, as officeholders, soldiers, rowers, as singers in the chorus, as judges of speeches, buildings, plays, and festivals, and as people carrying out their everyday obligations. There is a faint echo here of the Corinthians' characterization of the Athenians as jealously husbanding their intellect to be employed in Athens' service.

The word *grace*, too, was probably used by Pericles in a new sense to describe the relative effortlessness and elegance with which so much in this superior and affluent city was accomplished, for only if he intended the word this way would it have made sense for Pericles to cite the city's might as proof of his claim.

Whatever the Athenians may have lacked in grace their artists and artisans compensated for in their depiction of the city and the citizenry in the Parthenon's frieze. The scene is an aristocratic one, with horseback riders in the foreground; no hoplites are depicted, though all the details of the building had been planned with input from the popular assembly and the committees appointed by it. In Pericles' last speech, shortly before his death, Thucydides reports him as saying that the Athenians had grown up with an ethic worthy of the city's greatness. In another context Pericles claimed that people were most likely to submit to rulers who were like the Athenians. All this suggests that the Attic citizenry was in essence an aristocracy. It may have lacked aristocratic style but not the aristocratic ideal of style. It may not have had the aristocrats' poise and nonchalance, but it adopted their freedom and their lofty standards.

Pericles is said to have given his famous funeral oration some time before the terrible plague struck Athens, and Thucydides probably did not compose his version of it until after Athens' final defeat in the Peloponnesian War. The speech as we have inherited it combines elements contributed by a great statesman and elements provided by a great historian; it is impossible to separate the two voices. Thucydides apparently felt that Pericles' funeral oration was meant as a legacy to Athens. As a document, it obviously is worlds apart from the pamphlet of Pseudoxenophon.

We cannot simply say, however, that Pericles was right and Pseu-doxenophon wrong. In some places their pronouncements amount to almost the same thing, and in others they complement each other. It is only to be expected that Pericles, in keeping with the occasion, would present an idealized picture. Thus he never mentions the tyrannical power that Athens, which he calls the freest of all Greek cities, exercised over others, even though he mentions it repeatedly on other occasions. Because Thucydides places his description of the Great Plague of 430 B.C. right after Pericles' speech—and because of the events of Athens' later history—the city at the time of the funeral oration comes to seem like a sky bathed in gorgeous colors, just before a storm.

Pericles should not be criticized for expressing attitudes that were taken for granted at the time in Greece. The might of his city was an accepted fact. Athens' particular qualities were so valuable because they had brought about the city's prominence and helped maintain it. The city was far ahead of its potential rivals in myriad ways.

Pericles did overlook a few things: The Attic qualities he praised did not, in fact, arise in the distant past or grow from the soil along with the Athenians. Nor were those qualities the natural consequence of democratic freedom. They were both cause and result of Athens' specific situation, and as such they grew more pronounced over several decades. In this sense, Pericles' claims should be taken seriously, but with the caveat that they were valid only under a set of specific and highly favorable circumstances—circumstances that would not prevail in Athens much longer. Athens' might was not just the result of those specifically Attic qualities but also of the necessary condition for these qualities to flourish.

Athenians felt a strong pressure to conform, which minimized the negative consequences of freedom. There was pressure to take part in politics as well as to engage in the mutual "education" Protagoras spoke of, the moral training that Athenians provided for one another. Protagoras believed Athens' citizens would even devote themselves to teaching each other to play the flute, if they were convinced that this was important for the polis.

The Athenians may have been so involved in the events of their city that it seemed only natural to them to make relatively restrained use of their freedom. The foundations of their societal life, their thinking, and their beliefs were shaken repeatedly, not because their culture was declining but because new opportunities had become available. The Athenians faced painful questions, too, but they had magnificent tragedies to help them deal with them. Innovations were taking place not just in sculpture and architecture but also in science, Sophism, and historiography—Herodotus was giving public lectures at the time. Questions were asked, old beliefs were overturned, and answers were arrived at, the effects of which would be felt for thousands of years. But even at that time the Athenians were aware of being the center of an entire world.

Probably nowhere else have the small events of everyday life been so intimately linked to the large ones of the city and of world politics as in Periclean Athens. The same topics were discussed at the symposia, in the marketplace, in the outlying gymnasia, *palastrae,* and in houses where the most recent discoveries were passed on. Where else could a philosopher like Socrates and his disciples become the central subjects of a play watched by the whole city the way they did in Aristophanes' *Clouds*? (Though to be sure, this comedy was not as popular as his other plays.)

The Athenians were sometimes accused, as audience members, of always demanding something new. They were said to be addicted to the innovative and to disdain the habitual. As one joke from *The Clouds* would have it, anyone who had been away for three months would not recognize the city upon returning. If it is true, as some evidence suggests, that during this era sports and physical fitness were pursued less energetically than before, this shift of interest was the result of a greater involvement in the city's intellectual life.

Around the middle of the fifth century there arose in Greece an awareness of human ability distantly related to the modern belief in progress. There was a sense that *techneior*—the ability to solve the most varied problems through craft, knowledge, and application of properly understood methods—had already advanced significantly. Artists believed they had reached the ultimate potentials of their art. Physicians were in the process of confidently inventing a new science. The author of *On Ancient Medical Practice*, published at that time, suggested that the insights of previous times be incorporated into their process of raising medical science to perfection, which they expected to accomplish in the not too distant future. Thinkers were busy drafting entire new social orders. The Sophists claimed they could teach their students to achieve anything they wanted in business as well as politics; even how to turn a weak case into a strong one in court.

People began to believe there was no such thing as chance; chance was merely the excuse used by those who had miscalculated. Pericles thought that even the coming conflict between Athens and Sparta could be planned out in advance.

The most memorable expression of this confidence in human ability is found in the famous choral hymn in Sophocles' *Antigone*, where the chorus asserts repeatedly that man possesses methods and knowledge surpassing all previous expectations. This confidence went hand in hand with the realization that culture was the product of human activity and with a theory of cultural evolution that reconstructed the entire process from the dawn of human civilization up to the emergence of the polis. This process could be traced even further, as it was implicitly in Aeschylus's *Oresteia*, to the rise of democracy. But as aware as the Greeks may have been that their culture was the product of cultural evolution, they were still unable to take the next step and see history itself as an ongoing process. It is this uniquely Athenian sense of progress and human abilities that underlies the musician Timotheus's proud, extraordinary proclamation toward the end of the century: "I do not sing old songs; my own are much better. Young Zeus is in charge now; Cronos is dethroned."

The Greeks felt free to assert that they had reached a high point of human achievement. The sculptors said that if anyone were to sculpt in an old-fashioned manner he would be subjected to ridicule. The philosophers thought similarly, that the ideas of their predecessors were outmoded. And yet one of the most popular Sophists, Hippias of Elis, stated that he thought more highly of the older generations than of his own because the former "took precautions against the envy of the living and feared the wrath of the dead." The Greeks were unable to break through the barrier that, until the modern era, blocked the awareness that people are children of their time.

It is difficult, especially when contemplating history, to recognize that what appears natural and obvious to us because it has already happened is in fact something special, an exception in world history. Ever since the eighteenth century, history has been understood as a huge process of transformation affecting more or less all aspects of life. Statesmen and nations may at times wield great power and events of radical consequence may occur, but the evolution of technology, science, society, of the entire fabric of life including religion and mentality goes on regardless. "Events and human beings all serve this evolution," wrote de Toqueville. "Where are we headed?" he asked. "No one can say, for we have no basis for comparison."

It took decades—by now centuries—of experience for de Tocqueville's insight to evolve, an insight rooted in what the Third Estate itself experienced in revolutionary France. The improvement in the Third Estate's situation was so vast that this class could equate itself with humanity as a whole, in whose name it was advancing. Since that time, the recognition of history as a process has been inescapable despite any changes in direction.

For the Greeks, however, the world as a whole seemed to remain unchanged. Most of their experience confirmed this perception, and anything to the contrary appeared to be an aberration. Innovations, developments, and other new elements they encountered—and there were quite a few in the fields of technology, seafaring, and commerce alone—they understood as isolated discoveries, improvements, or indicators of great human potential, but no more.

Even the social order remained largely unchanged in spite of all the theoretical thinking about it. It was never even suggested, for example, that slavery might or should be abolished. The political form of the polis was sacred to everyone. Unlike Athens, Greece as a whole remained utterly faithful to the old. Thus the Greeks never crossed that threshold that has kept all cultures up to the modern era from seeing the world as history and history in turn as a huge, all-encompassing process of change.

Change is always threatening, because it poses a threat to any form of rule. That is why the pre-classical high cultures tried to explain away all change by subsuming it into periodic cycles that always led back to what had been before, therefore ultimately guaranteeing that the whole would remain the same. That is why, for example, a monarch's reign or the history of a dynasty was presented as analogous to the year's seasons, sometimes with ritual celebrations alluding to the seasonal changes.

Where government was the business of all the citizens, as in Greek democracy, the danger inherent in change was acutely felt. Democracy was based on people's involvement in politics; decisions were made by them. Processes like the powerful forces at work in Aeschylus's *Agamemnon* and *The Libation Bearers* were frightening to them. The Greeks wanted to have things under control. It was important to them to be able to predict the course of the world, a need that grew out of their old belief that the universe was based on laws. The rise and fall of dynasties, wealthy individuals, and cities were part of the lawfulness of the universe; retribution eventually came to those guilty of wrongdoing. But despite such minor changes, the consistent rule of laws presupposed a world that remained the same.

The Greeks had no experience with such future-oriented ideologies as would emerge in the modern era. They lacked the rigid social patterns—centuries old and enforced by religious belief and societal discipline—characteristic of later Europe. They had always preserved a certain degree of equality among themselves, and they did not have to overcome entrenched respect for powerful institutions. When political changes favoring the broader segments of the population were felt to be desirable, as they were from the sixth century B.C. on, these changes could be brought about quite quickly. After all, it was the majority that determined the decisions of the popular assembly. It was not necessary to think very far ahead since the time that elapsed between the conception and realization of an idea was typically short. All expectation was focused on immediate goals; there was no need to hope for far-reaching processes of transformation.

Some Sophists went so far as to claim that all human beings—freemen and slaves, Greeks and barbarians—were alike, but this was a radical, marginal idea, and never served as the starting point for further thinking. It was never an idea that had practical or political consequences.

The idea of historical process could be applied by the Greeks only to a reconstruction of their past. The theory of cultural evolution extended no further than the formation of the polis. Thucydides limited himself to tracing the changing relationships among political powers within Greek history. Zeus was given a biographical history but only for the purpose of lending permanence to his rule, ensuring its future stability.

In the literary genre that they came to call "history" the Greeks consequently included only accounts of deeds and events. By the standards of the modern era, the Greeks' concept of human advancement was limited. This should not, however, be taken as evidence of a lack of progressive thinking. The Greeks' strength was their awareness of human beings' enormous potential for action and of what that action can accomplish.

What the Greeks noticed was how much individuals could accomplish—though it might take many of them—not where a tendency led or ought to lead in the future. If change was needed, the possibility for change always existed, as when the entire citizenry benefited from exposure to tragedy and music. But the Greeks did not recognize the possibility—let alone the desirability—of transforming one's nature, the personal and societal renewal that would characterize Christianity.

We might say that the Greeks were more intent on being than becoming. Part of the reason was that the experience of accomplishment was so limited to the small population of experts in the various fields that no general sense of accomplishment developed among the people. Like the Greeks in general, the experts were too independent to be absorbed into (and thus to influence) a larger context, such as state or church.

Nor did the Greeks' political and social concepts take on a temporal meaning as they did in the modern era, when such concepts became strongly associated with expectations that could be realized only in the future. Instead the Greeks politicized their concepts. Freedom, equality, justice, and the "right order" were regarded either as already existing in the present or as goals requiring immediate political action. With the Greeks, everything focused on the present. That is why technical knowledge was so central to their sense of human capacities. The Sophists were bragging about their technical rhetorical skills when they advertised their ability to turn a weak case into a strong one. The fifth century's advances in weapons and siege technology also contributed to this attitude. The famous choral hymn of Sophocles even suggested that man could make either beneficial or pernicious use of his new technical capabilities. (Incidentally, the same is true, and to a considerably greater degree, of modern technological progress, though this negative possibility runs counter to the very concept of progress.)

The successes Athens achieved, the victories it won, its position of supremacy, and its general affluence and good fortune must all have been important reminders to the Athenians of the breadth of human ability. Athens' "wealth of experience," its open-mindedness, and its flexibility allowed it to keep developing new techniques and methods that were by no means restricted to the navy.

"Just as newer technical skills are bound to prevail over older ones, here the new will prevail," or so the Corinthians are said to have told the Spartans, referring to Athens. It was the city where most innovations arose or were brought, where there was the greatest demand for them, and where the expectations of their success always exceeded the limits of experience. Eventually Athens claimed, in a way almost insulting to others, to have invented just about everything; even the method of sowing grain was supposed to have been passed on from Eleusis.

Phidias's monumental gold-and-ivory statue of Athena Parthenos, goddess of the city and of the Delian League, was an especially dramatic expression of this consciousness of ability. Phidias incidentally went on to make an even larger statue, the twelve-meter-tall seated figure of Zeus, set up in Elis on the Olympic plain where the Olympic games were held. Its aspect was awe-inspiring; people were afraid Zeus would rise and cause the building to collapse. To satisfy the laws of *agon* or opposition and conflict, a similarly impressive image of Hera had to be created for the goddess's temple in Argos.

One might ask why this extreme consciousness of their abilities did not arise among Greeks before the fifth century. There were, after all, many major and brilliant technical achievements dating back to the archaic period. But such achievements had to become more common and perhaps develop a certain momentum before they could be experienced in such a conscious way.

Another contributing factor was that the citizens learned, after having existed for a long time in an unquestioningly accepted world, to gain control over the conditions of their lives. This happened when democracy was introduced and again when the order of the city became the subject of deliberate decisions. It is surely no coincidence that so shortly after fundamental political alternatives were developed it became possible to do more in art than vary traditional techniques in minor ways. The whole human figure was freely reinvented. The Athenian sculptor Myron, in particular, explored these possibilities in new ways, most prominently in his *Discus Thrower*. The painter Zeuxis was said to have broken new ground and produced ever stranger pictures each time he set to work. The exquisitely detailed and innovative design of the Parthenon, too, demonstrates a new ability to conceive of the temple as a whole. Similar things could be said of the Propylaeum and the plan—never executed—that Ictinus, the architect of the Parthenon, designed for the Telesterion in Eleusis.

Thus we see that Pericles' assertion that the Athenians were autarkic people, adept at accomplishing most things with skill and grace, was part of the prevailing consciousness of human ability. This consciousness, seen in its proper context, was the basis of remarkable self-confidence. This self-confidence in turn was rooted at least partly in the political order of the city and helped the city overcome many difficulties.

According to Pericles, Athens' political order was called rule of the people, *demokratia*, "because we pay attention not to a few but to the majority of our citizens." In personal disputes, each citizen had the same rights and privileges as any other, and no distinction was made between the high- and low-born. Only the individual's virtue, *arete*, was considered. Lowliness of station did not keep poor men from performing useful services for the city.

This notion of virtue came about through a strange shifting of attitudes. Supposedly equality applied to political relationships among citizens in a democracy. But citizens were on equal footing only in a certain sense: According to Pericles, it was above all the aristocratic ideal of virtue that served as the standard of value in the political realm. Political virtue might consist of deeds proving one's noble manliness or of service to the city.

Thus *arete* was democratized or, rather, politicized. It was conceived exclusively in terms of the needs of the polis, and a new aristocracy was created in which there was room for the common people as well as the nobles and aristocrats. As the city became the focal point of increasingly large-scale activity, it also developed into an entity existing beyond its citizens. The Greeks always proclaimed that it was the citizens alone who constituted the city, but in the case of Athens, the city had an independent existence—it made demands on its citizens and rewarded them.

Democracy as it took shape under Pericles was intended to be a government by the people. It went as far in that direction as was possible within the narrow confines of the polis. Periclean democracy was so different from our modern democracies it is reasonable to ask whether ours deserve to be called by the same name.

Athenian democracy followed two fundamental principles: First, all decisions were to be made as openly as possible and on the basis of public discussion, with the deliberating bodies being as large as feasible. Second, as many citizens as possible were to take part in the political process and also hold office. Organized groups of aristocrats were thus prevented from using their influence in the appointment of public officials. In general, political manipulation by small groups was not to be tolerated.

To achieve this, it was determined that the popular assembly should meet at least three times in each of the ten months of the Greek year. In order for the assembly to be able to make informed decisions, preliminary discussion of the issues were held in a small forum, the Council of Five Hundred. But to prevent this body from accumulating power of its own, its composition changed every year. Beginning in Pericles' time at the latest, there was a rule that no one could serve on the council for two years in succession or more than twice in his lifetime. The council members were selected by lot. To make it possible for less affluent men to sit in the council, the councilmen were paid a daily allowance—an arrange-ment that would have been unthinkable earlier, when political duties were assumed only by those who could afford it.

Council members were not intended to have the kind of power that results from long terms in office, collaboration with others, experience, and connections. They were to provide a service for the popular assembly, not to tell it what to do. The council was simply a group of individuals randomly selected from among the population at large. Each tribe, or phyle, contributed fifty councilmen as prescribed by Cleisthenes, and within the tribe the seats were apportioned equally to the different demes.

The number of proposals submitted by the Council of Five Hundred (the *probouleumata*) was large because the people were to decide everything, major matters as well as less important ones. For this reason, procedure allowed the popular assembly to pass noncontroversial recommendations without discussion. It was always possible to demand a debate, but on the whole the goal was for the sessions to concentrate on just a few issues. This was where there might have been room for manipulation, but considering the makeup of the council it is doubtful that much use was made of this opportunity.

Any citizen with a clean record had the right to submit proposals that the council was then obliged to consider and pass on to the popular assembly in the form of a bill. When an issue was up for discussion in the popular assembly, amendments to the bills presented by the council could be proposed.

All Attic citizens had a right to speak in the assembly, and they were proud of this fact. As Euripides wrote, "Freedom is proclaimed every time the herald calls 'Who has some useful suggestion for the polis?' Those who speak up are treated with great respect, and those who do not want to speak remain silent. Where could more equal right be found in a polis?" In Plato's *Protagoras*, Socrates confirms that carpenters, smiths, shoemakers, merchants, and shipowners, rich and poor, aristocrats and ordinary men took the floor. The term *isegory*, meaning the equal right to speak and present proposals, was sometimes used synonymously with isonomy. At times, we are told, citizens over fifty years old were called on first, but we don't know how long this practice was followed. In the 420s there are reports of conservatives expressing the wish that those without beards would once again keep silent on the Pnyx.

For important decisions—matters involving legal procedures against individuals, war and peace, or ostracism—at least six thousand citizens were supposed to attend the assembly; at regular sessions there were probably fewer, and the number no doubt fluctuated considerably. In the absence of modern sound technology it must have been difficult, even with the help of well-trained heralds, to conduct the meetings. Quiet and discipline were essential, and Athens maintained a police detachment of Scythian archers whose duties included the enforcement of these conditions.

In Plato's *Protagoras*, Socrates notes that architects were consulted on matters of building and shipbuilders on naval questions. If someone the assembled citizens did not regard as an expert tried to give advice on such matters, he was greeted with ridicule, no matter how handsome, rich, or aristocratic he was, and the uproar would not subside until the archers, acting on magistrates' orders, pulled the offender off the speaker's platform or expelled him from the meeting. On political issues, however, anyone was entitled to speak.

The council met daily except on holidays, usually in the council hall next to the agora, but occasionally, when naval problems were on the agenda, in Piraeus or rarely in other locations. It met indoors, though almost always with the doors to the agora open.

One of the council's tasks was to direct and check on all activities of the Attic officials. The responsibility for getting tasks done lay primarily with the council, and the councilmen would render an account of what was accomplished under their guidance at the conclusion of their term.

The preliminary work for the meetings was done by the prytanes, the fifty council members who were in residence and on twenty-four-hour duty in Athens at the time. These fifty councilmen worked, lived, and took their meals in common during their month of service as *prytanes*. The chairmanship rotated daily, nobody being allowed to be chairman more than once during the prytany. The chairman conducted the council session as well as the meeting of the popular assembly, if there was one that day. On the day he was in charge, he was also entrusted with the key to the sacred shrines where the treasures and the documents of the city were kept with the municipal seal.

Care was taken that public officials, like the council, did not acquire too much power. One way to ensure this—apart from the control exercised by the council—was to select most public officials by lot, the same way the archons had been selected as early as 487. Anyone could enter the pool of candidates for most offices, but no one could hold any one office more than once. Those who drew the winning tickets were then tested by the council in what was called a *docimasy*. But the test had nothing to do with competance; the applicants were asked about their citizenship status, who their parents and grandparents were, if they practiced the rites of certain cults that were important for citizenship, if they owned family burial plots, and whether they treated their parents well and had performed their duties in the military and as taxpayers. In short, an applicant was required to be a model citizen.

Generally ten men were appointed to each office or committee, one from each tribe. These individuals were then collectively responsible for fulfilling their tasks and therefore had to check up on one another.

In the so-called main popular assembly, held ten times annually, once during each of the ten Greek months, people were asked to vote on whether the officials were performing their duties properly. Any official who did not pass this test was suspended and had to appear before the people's court. He would be reinstated only if the court acquitted him. Quite apart from this, charges could always be brought against any official who was suspected of a serious offense, such as trying to subvert the constitution, treason, accepting bribes, or deceiving the people.

There is little detailed information about the Attic constitution before the fourth century. Control over officials may have tightened by then, but it seems reasonable to assume that some form of public oversight over officials existed during the fifth century, though it may have been more in the hands of the council than the assembly. The officials did have to give an account of their activities at the end of the year.

Few positions were held by elected officials. Elections were held annually, after the sixth prytany—that is, in or after February, on a date that was determined to be especially propitious. The aim of the elections was to find the best candidates, and there were few restrictions. Elected positions could be held year after year. The most important elected office was that of the *strategoi*, the ten generals who were chosen from the ten tribes' slates of candidates. If a tribe had no suitable candidate, or if it seemed desirable for some other reason, two generals could be elected from the same tribe. The generals no longer functioned as commanders of their own tribe's military contingents, so this posed no threat to their command.

The office of *strategos* was considered highly desirable, and since the time of Themistocles it was often held by leading politicians. Cimon and Pericles both served as generals several times, Pericles holding the office without interruption from 443 until he died. The *strategoi* were entitled to command Athens' armies and fleets either singly or together with fellow commanders, and the office also gave them access to the council and the *prytanes*. They could influence the council's agenda and speed up the consideration of proposals. The *strategoi* could also convene the popular assembly to discuss military matters such as armament and the conduct of war, as well as foreign policy. Still, it would be a mistake to think that the power of a man like Pericles derived from this office. Being a *strategos* was the expression rather than the source of such power, though to be sure, it was also one of the prime instruments for exercising power. The *strategoi* were required to own land in Attica and their children had to be legitimate. Their conduct of duties was subject to special scrutiny by the council, by the popular assembly, and, if the situation called for it, by the people's courts. Shipbuilding supervisors and architects were also elected, as were the officials in charge of public fountains and the water conduits.

The composition of the people's courts was randomly determined, like that of the Council of Five Hundred. The juries of the various courts were selected annually by lot from a list of 6,000 citizens. The courts varied in size, consisting sometimes of 201, sometimes 401, most commonly 501 members, and on occasion greater multiples of 100 (an odd number of members was preserved, presumably to avoid ties). In one instance all 6,000 candidates had to serve. Like the Council of Five Hundred, the juries were representative of the various groups composing the citizenry—which accounts for their large size—and they came in equal numbers from all the tribes.

The jury members had to swear to follow the laws as well as the decrees of the council and the assembly. They were not allowed to base their decisions on personal feelings, notions of fairness, or unwritten rules of justice, and they cast their votes without discussion among themselves. Their role during the proceedings was a passive one. It was up to the contesting parties to explain the circumstances and applicable laws and to propose a verdict. All the jury could do was to cast secret yes or no votes on the question of guilt and on the proposed sentence.

Thus the questions before the jury were simple, no matter how complicated the case. There was no such thing as jurisprudence, which is in fact the only major intellectual discipline that was developed into a science first by the Romans, not the ancient Greeks. The Greek juries merely had to apply positive law.

In many situations—even in murder cases—only the victims or their families had the right to take the offender to court. But there was also a broadly defined right to public accusation, which every Athenian was entitled to use. Its function was similar to that of a modern public prosecutor. To encourage people to bring public accusations, rewards were offered: two-thirds to three-quarters of the convicted individual's property would be awarded to the initiator of the proceedings. As a consequence of this rule, a number of people became professional informers, or sycophants. They may have served a useful function, but they were detested, and not only by those they harmed. To try to prevent frivolous accusations a rule was passed stipulating that if less than a fifth of the jurors declared the accused guilty, the person who had brought him before the court would be fined and forbidden to raise similar accusations in the future.

The courts were terribly overburdened with cases, many of them having to do with the affairs of the Delian League. Partisanship was also a problem. The courts constantly had to deal with questions of the officials' reliability, accountability, and performance of duties, as well as with the constitutionality of bills presented to the popular assembly. Their proceedings therefore often touched on politics. Many political conflicts, major and minor, were carried on in court, and citizens were often urged to lodge complaints against individuals for improper performance of official duties. Legal fees and fines provided the money for the jury's pay. It may have been justified to ask if the judges were not, as Pseudoxenophon thought, influenced more by the interests of the common people than by the demands of justice. Suspicions were repeatedly voiced that rich men were accused and found guilty simply because they were rich.

There is too little information to offer an accurate assessment of the Athenian legal system. The purpose of the courts was to save the popular assembly time by assigning juries to decide whether or not an official was fulfilling his duties. The courts had more time to deliberate, and as a consequence of the legal proceedings and the oath taken by the jurors, justice was believed more likely to prevail. The very existence of such a mechanism of legal review may have acted as a deterrent to fraud.

In terms of their composition, the courts were similar to the popular assembly. Their mandate was to proceed in strict adherence to the interests of the city, which often meant the interests of the populace and of the assembly. This was especially so where politics and the conduct of office were concerned. Naturally, the services an accused person had performed for the people and the polis and his attitude toward them were taken into account. In cases of doubt, this might carry more weight than the legality of his behavior. It could happen, however, as it did during the Peloponnesian War and even earlier, that a *strategos* was condemned to exile or death for sheer lack of success in military campaigns.

The demos of Athens was a suspicious and demanding master, and both these qualities found expression in the people's courts. We must remember that the separation of powers was an unknown concept to the Greeks. Rule by the people was most fully realized in the institution of the people's courts; indeed, it became effective only through the courts. That is why jurors were the only public functionaries who were not held accountable for their decisions.

According to Jacob Burckhardt, the individual citizen was required to be "judge and magistrate for his own protection against injustice" because the Greeks never advocated equality of civil rights as a counterbalance to political inequality. Under democracy, however, the socially inferior could win over his superior in court.

Civil disobedience, as presented in Sophocles' *Antigone*, must have been especially problematic for the Athenians. It speaks for Greek democracy that Sophocles won a prize for this particular play. The free expression of opinion was a different matter from civil disobedience.

The writers of comedy were free to subject the governing populace, Lord Demos, to biting satire. The tragedians and even many politicians also expressed themselves freely and with candor, and it was apparently considered important that they do so. People wanted to know what was really going on, wanted to make informed decisions, and for this it was necessary to hear all arguments, pro and con. Aristophanes says of a character who dares to speak up against his fellow citizens that he is "sticking his neck out for the city." This may in part be comic exaggeration, but it also points out the obvious fact that it takes courage to voice dissent.

It is not surprising that, in spite of all the dangers and restrictions elected officials faced, capable men were always found for offices such as that of the *strategoi*. In the final analysis it was worth exposing oneself to considerable risk in order to work for the city and hope for the personal glory this service might bring. We must keep in mind that the ancient Greeks, given the greater vicissitudes of their lives, had different standards of safety from ours, a different concept of risk, and different views of honor, life, and death.

There is no doubt that the citizens of Attica lived up to the demands their political order imposed on them. They did so with astonishing success and were to this extent autarkic. Every citizen was expected not just to have the necessary know-how to occupy any office, but to have it on the first try. The first time a man faced the difficult task of conducting a council meeting or a session of the assembly he was doing it without previous training or experience; after having done it once, he had at best one more chance, the following year. Beyond that there was no further opportunity. Even the council clerks, who were responsible for taking minutes of the sessions, writing down the decisions of the council and the assembly, and entering them in the archives, were appointed for the period of just one prytany, which was one Greek month or somewhat longer than one modern month. The principle behind all this was that everybody should be interchangeable. Clearly some people did a better job than others, and those who performed especially poorly could be removed or penalized, whereas good work was often rewarded with honors.

The people govern, Euripides declares, by one person succeeding the other. Aristotle later called the rotation of roles between those who govern and those who are governed the essential characteristic of democracy. In commenting on the council, the prytany, and the people's courts, Karl Reinhardt remarks that at least theoretically "the sovereign citizenry was of a substance that showed the same quality and mixture in any random sample as the body had as a whole."

Undoubtedly a circle of citizens from different classes formed over time who were particularly interested in politics and who were most likely to hold elective offices. But this circle was relatively large for the size of the population: it must have numbered in the thousands.

The execution of many offices may have been facilitated by the availability of secretaries, but there are indications that they also were not allowed to hold the same position for any length of time, probably no longer than a year or two. Consequently they gained only secretarial expertise without specialized knowledge, ensuring that they, too, had as little influence as possible.

The tasks to be performed must have been clearly defined. The "job descriptions" were probably formulated in such a way that anyone could run for the offices. In some cases, the pool of candidates could be limited, such as for the office of treasurer, which was available only to the highest property class. In spite of this restriction, we should not underestimate the degree of intelligence, ability to learn skills, and readiness to accept responsibility of the average Attic citizen.

The existence of a citizenry made up of individuals who were used to doing as much as possible themselves was crucial to Athens' organization of democratic government. The government did not express the will of a state; it was not dominated by an organizational structure serving the interests of a monarch or a national entity; nor was it a bureaucracy intent on self-perpetuation.

For example, no such thing as a unified fiscal system existed. There was, of course, the polis treasury, which may have existed in rudimentary form as far back as the aristocratic period. The treasury collected money from the lease of public land, from mines, harbor duties imposed in Piraeus (amounting to one-fiftieth the value of the goods carried), the head tax of the metics, and revenue from the sale of the skins of sacrificial animals. Most of the money was spent on various remunerations for public service, and some on hiring personnel and the purchase and basic needs of publicly owned slaves, among them the police force.

The Athenians had access to several temple treasuries in addition to the treasury of the Delian League. The temple treasuries, whose income derived from donations, gifts, assessment of penalties, harvests from land owned by the temples, and the sale of skins from sacrificial animals, belonged to the temples, but they were administered by municipal officials, and the city could borrow money from them at low interest rates (one to two percent during the Peloponnesian War). They served primarily as reserve funds, and the money in them was left untouched as much as possible.

This was especially true of Athena's treasury on the Acropolis, which also received one-sixtieth of the dues paid to the Delian League. Surplus funds of the league were deposited there, mostly for safekeeping, but the money could be used, for example, for the building of the Parthenon and the Propylaeum. The treasuries of the other gods were eventually consolidated into one, probably in 435–434.

A number of factors affected the use of funds from these treasuries for payments. The council and the popular assembly were entitled, depending on the size of the accounts, to draw on various treasuries for necessary expenses. They could even dip into the Delian League's treasury. Sometimes the debts owed by the city to the temple treasuries grew large and the polis was forced to try to pay the money back. At such times it passed resolutions making it more difficult to approve expensive projects. When financial affairs got badly out of hand—for example, when a large number of debts could not be collected—a fiscal reorganization was mandated or sometimes an investigating committee appointed.

The financial obligations of the polis fluctuated widely from year to year; everything depended on the appropriations needed for warfare. Assuming that the daily wages for one trireme were 100 drachmas, which added up to 3 talents semiannually, maintaining a fleet of 150 ships for half a year would have cost about 450 talents—a sum greater than all the annual fees normally paid by the members of the league in the 430s. Sometimes more than 150 ships were needed, and infantry troops had to be paid as well. Waging war on such a massive scale was extremely expensive. It was beyond what Sparta could afford, but Sparta had little choice but to keep up with Athens' military spending.

In other years it was possible for Athens to put aside considerable savings. We read that a fleet of about sixty ships was plying the Aegean Sea; the annual expense for wages during those years would have amounted to about 180 talents, less than half the contributions to the Delian League.

The siege of the city Potidaea at the beginning of the Peloponnesian War lasted more than two years and cost over 2,000 talents, more than what was spent on the Parthenon and the Propylaeum combined. Around 422, Athens could count on annual revenues of about 2,000 talents, but now the debts the city owed to the temple treasuries amounted to 5,600 talents plus interest on loans granted for periods of up to seven years. Clearly, the city could not rely exclusively on its own treasury, from which money flowed out as fast as it came in. The polis desperately needed the temple treasuries as well.

Athena's treasurers were selected annually by lot from the ten tribes, and similar arrangements probably applied to the consolidated treasury of the other gods, though the administrators of the Delian League's funds may have been elected officials. In addition to the treasurers, ten *apodects* were responsible for receiving various payments, including the contributions to the league, and for assigning them to individual accounts. Ten *poletes* handled the leasing of public property. They did not themselves collect rents, custom duties, and taxes but delegated that chore to lessees. And finally, ten *practores* were responsible for collecting fines and debts not paid on time. The large number of offices involved in the city's fiscal administration paralleled the way citizen activity extended to all official functions. The leasing of property, the delivery of lease money to the *apodects*, and the annual money transfer from the temple treasuries took place in the presence of the Council of Five Hundred. The administrators of the polis treasury had to give the council a financial report once during each of the year's ten months. In all these ways, the citizenry respected what belonged to the gods yet at the same time made use of it.

In Athens, as in all other Greek city-states that could afford it, no taxes were levied on harvests; this would have been considered tyrannical. Only a small percentage was claimed for the goddess of Eleusis, a six-hundredth of the earnings from barley and one twelve-hundredth of those from wheat. These contributions were collected by the demes. In an emergency it was possible to impose a property tax on members of the three most highly assessed classes, but requests for this levy could only be made after having been approved in the popular assembly with at least 6,000 voters present. Basically, this tax was unconstitutional, and it could be resorted to only in exceptional situations and under stringent requirements.

It was expected, however, that the wealthy would, through liturgies or personal sponsorship commitments, pay for things like the outfitting of ships, the production of plays, the choruses, and the torch races. At first they did so on a purely voluntary basis; later the financing seems to have become compulsory, and organized in a more planned manner.

The total number of functionaries was relatively large. Historians estimate that there were about 700, including the archons and *strategoi*; market overseers; and officials responsible for grain supplies, municipal streets, rural roads, shipyards, arsenals, water conduits, and fountains. In addition, there were thirty treasurers, accountants, and other officials concerned with various aspects of the city's finances. Still more officials had the task of preparing the fiscal accountability reports. Special committees could be elected to office for special tasks. An additional 700 functionaries normally worked for the Delian League.

If we also count the Council of Five Hundred and the 6,000 jurors, a total of close to 8,000 citizens were performing official functions for the city of Athens every year. Add to this those who participated in the political process on a fairly regular basis, and the number rises to about 9,000. This represents as much as a quarter of the citizenry. We may realistically assume that about 8,000 of the 9,000 came from the urban area, which had a population of 15,000 to 16,000 citizens. (This figure includes some nearby villages and assumes that the number of citizens increased between the Persian and the Peloponnesian Wars.) Thus half of all those eligible for it were engaged in some political or administrative activity.

Beyond these forms of service to the state were the various religious tasks that had to be performed by citizens. Also, many individuals took part in the choruses, the plays, and the dithyramb singing, all of which constituted a kind of public service.

Finally, the duties of the city's 139 demes had to be attended to. These included the functions of the headmen, or *demarchs*, and tasks associated with running the frequent assemblies, where property matters, cults, and above all the right of members to citizenship were dealt with. There was plenty to do in the demes, especially for those who lived in the countryside and found it hard to travel to the city regularly.

None of this reckoning takes account of the thousands who were absent from the city for considerable periods as rowers and hoplites, or those who served in *cleruchies* or garrisons and helped maintain, directly or indirectly, Athens' supremacy in the Delian League. The *cleruchies* must have included members of the rural population, and among the rowers and perhaps even the garrison soldiers there must have been quite a few metics.

It is difficult to imagine the amount of energy the Athenians expended performing these various tasks. In all this activity, it sometimes happened that matters did not get the attention they needed. Pseudoxenophon reports that people often waited a full year without getting a response from the council and assembly. "How could they deal with all the business when, first of all, they have more festivals than any other Greek city (during which it is not convenient to take care of polis matters); and second, they have to deal with more private and public complaints and accountability reports than all other people taken together. And the council has to deal with matters of war, collecting money, legislation, municipal issues and those involving the allies; it has to receive tributes, and oversee the shipyards and the temples. . . ."

Since all the officials, councilmen, and jurors received daily allowances, this kind of government and administration not only demanded a lot in human effort but also came at considerable financial expense, even though the sums paid to the individuals were relatively small—less than the daily wages paid to the craftsmen employed in building the Erechtheum. The craftsmen received one drachma per day; a juror's pay was two oboli, or a third of a drachma, and increased to three in the mid-420s. The allowances for the councilmen and officials may have been somewhat higher. Pseudoxenophon's assertion that the less affluent Attic citizens were interested in politics primarily because of the income they could generate by holding office is therefore questionable at best. It may be that political activity was more pleasant than other kinds of work, but on the whole people must have been motivated more by the honor and social rank political office bestowed, than by the financial rewards. The moral obligation to do one's part must also have played a role. The remuneration hardly made up for the loss of earnings from regular work.

The relationship between political life and work is an ambiguous one. The jurors were probably primarily older men, and their services were not needed all the time. Attendance at the assembly, for which there was no remuneration, could be combined relatively easily with practicing a trade, and many offices may have required only a few days' work on a monthly or occasional basis. Council membership, on the other hand, took up a lot of time during the one-year term. In any case, a large proportion of the citizens must have been available for political activity for many years, quite apart from military and naval campaigns.

Some artisans may have run their workshops with the help of slaves. These artisans had to be flexible, as did the rowers, who were not necessarily called on every year. They were paid three oboli a day only for days they actually served and had to make a living some other way the rest of the time. Even so, Pericles remarked that poor citizens were to blame if they failed to improve their lot.

The enormous civic obligations of citizens go a long way toward explaining Athens' dependence on the metics and why this group had such a good chance for advancement and enjoyed general respect. This was also true of slaves who were skilled at a trade; they often worked independently, paying their masters about one obol a day for the privilege. If they did well, they could buy their freedom.

The Athenian social and political order grew from the Greeks' conviction that the citizenry constituted the polis. Citizens sought to participate in public life and occupy public offices, so the number of offices had to increase. Since appointment to office was not to be subject to the influence of powerful individuals, people were chosen by lot. Nobody was to be ineligible for lack of means, and therefore daily allowances were instituted. The citizens themselves wanted to determine what was going to happen, so everything had to go through the council and the popular assembly.

The equation of the democratic citizenry with the city was possible only with the sharp differentiation between public and private life. Democracy always requires a certain homogeneity of its citizens; even more so in ancient Greece, where there was no state structure, and especially in Athens, whose foreign policies could have become disastrous had they not been backed by the great unity of the citizens.

Thus the concept of the polis as standing above its citizens arose largely from the fact that the citizens really did approach their various public functions with the polis's rather than their own private interests in mind. To be sure, they thought of themselves when making political decisions, but they did so as citizens and officials, not with the intent of benefiting themselves, their houses, professions, or their workshops, all of which they considered to lie outside the political realm.

The economic problems the polis dealt with were restricted to basic necessities. Above all, the city had to be provided with grain, which was obtained both from surrounding areas such as Euboea and from distant places like Egypt and the Black Sea region. As Attica's population grew, the task of importing grain grew increasingly urgent.

Whatever social welfare Athens provided arose primarily from the waging of war, which made it necessary to look after war orphans. Military success at times made it possible to distribute grain donated by foreign leaders in gratitude for, or expectation of, military assistance. Other social policies were related to democracy. Payments to the old men who made up the majority of jurors may well have constituted a kind of welfare for the elderly.

Although a great deal of the business of the Attic democracy could be taken care of by randomly appointed, more or less interchangeable individuals, some things could not. Difficult questions of domestic and, especially, foreign policy could not be dealt with in this anonymous manner. Here there was room and need for the abilities of special individuals. The further democracy developed, the more this was the case.

Thucydides characterized Periclean Athens by saying it was "a democracy in name but one that in reality was ruled by its most prominent leader." This situation was atypical, however, a passing phase in the history of Athens and its democracy. Pericles was not only a brilliant orator and statesman, but he had also played a major if not decisive role in broadening democracy. It might even be argued that the extreme democratization he introduced (including the establishment of public sports arenas and the elaboration of the festivals) were an extremely clever way of serving Pericles' own interests by enhancing his popularity and thus removing obstacles to his policies.

Pericles was, of course, not the only outstanding political figure. There were a number of other prominent men in the popular assembly, excellent orators and politicians, and it was not uncommon for violent conflicts to arise among them. The opportunity to resolve bitter rivalry through ostracism presented itself only once a year. It was also possible for citizens to accuse their rivals of endangering the constitution or of treason. In addition an "accusation of illegality" could be invoked against any law or bill and, if substantiated, could result in heavy fines or even the death penalty for the sponsors. But we don't know how commonly citizens resorted to these means. These did not, in any case, prevent Attic politics from becoming turbulent and unpredictable.

The citizenry was not divided into major opposing camps or parties. The history of Attica in the fifth century records no efforts to do so, except for Thudycides' one failed attempt to have his supporters sit together in a block. Organized influence in the popular assembly could at most help tip the scale in situations where proponents and opponents were about evenly balanced. Most issues were decided on the basis of factual arguments and the orators' prestige and rhetorical power.

Party-type divisions did sometimes exist among prominent politicians, as between Pericles and Thucydides, and, earlier, between Cimon and Ephialtes, but these were rivalries largely based on personal, not theoretical, differences. Allegiances in the popular assembly were fairly weak. The majority sometimes vacillated from one side to the other, and on many specific issues it was difficult to reach consensus.

But the potentially powerful influence individual personalities could exert on the popular assembly was an inherent part of Attic democracy, as was the frequent reliance on elimination contests. If someone emerged as a front-runner after prevailing repeatedly over others or perhaps surviving several attempts at ostracism, his authority was generally assured, at least for some time.

This was never more the case than with Pericles, who was so capable of working within the framework of radical democracy. He played his part with complete consistency: though blessed with the aristocratic advantages, he exactingly rejected all aspects of the old aristocracy that did not fit into democracy. He did not permit himself even the slightest deviations from what he had determined was the proper course. He allowed himself liberties only in the company he kept. He associated with some of the best minds of his time, and he had a long-term conjugal relationship with the courtesan Aspasia.

Pericles gained control over democratic Athens by identifying completely with it. He could raise the spirits of the Athenians when they began to lose courage and keep them in check when they threatened to get carried away. But the identification worked both ways. Pericles

character

modeled himself on democratic Athens. To see Athens achieve its full potential was the purpose of Pericles' cultural policies. The music, the festivals, the buildings, and everything that Pericles promoted was meant not only to refresh the Athenians' spirit but also to turn Athens into the democratic aristocracy he described in his legendary oration for those who had fallen during the Peloponnesian War. And this, despite all his successes, is also the weak spot of his policies. Pericles wanted to make it possible for the greatest and most advanced aspirations to be realized, but the people were not always able to share his ambitions.

Another major issue stood in the foreground: Athens' foreign policy, specifically the politics of the Delian League, the policy toward Sparta, and the consolidation of Athens' power. Athens' policies required the presence of Athenian officials, delegates, garrisons, and fleets throughout the league's area. The maintenance of its empire and the building and preservation of democracy were the two areas in which Periclean Athens had to prove itself.

Pericles was a man of extraordinary judgment, imagination, far-sightedness, inner independence, and intellectual discipline. Perhaps the conditions that prevailed in fifth-century Athens offered a man with his qualities special opportunities to develop, display, and strengthen them. But Pericles' success nevertheless relied greatly on his personal achievement. An inner affinity existed between the man and the city, and Periclean Athens was the result of this affinity.

Once again Pseudoxenophon is only partly correct: Pericles' policies did indeed represent the interests of the common people, but by no means theirs alone. We could also counter Thucydides by saying that although Athens was ruled by Pericles, it was a true democracy because of this very fact.

The *thetes* played a central role in Athenian democracy, but the homogeneity of the Attic citizenry extended far beyond them.

In *Eumenides*, Aeschylus quite realistically invokes the citizenry's unity against outside forces. But while many aristocrats took part willingly in the city's wars and politics, some others withdrew or tried unsuccessfully to make their peace with democracy. These oligarchs may have voiced their dissent, but their views didn't spread much beyond their clubs and symposia. The young aristocrats and sons of other well-to-do families who were followers of the Sophists would later have a larger impact, but that impact was not yet felt.

The aristocrats and wealthy citizens contributed a great deal of money to the polis in the form of liturgies. These contributions, which were made in the absence of direct taxation, grew out of the Greek view that honor—in this case, a prominent position in the polis—should come at a price. For although the aristocrats were no longer necessarily in leadership positions, they did very well in this economically flourishing city. The liturgies both repaid the polis for their success and added to their personal honor.

Two-thirds of the citizenry lived outside the city district of Athens. While rural citizens were often unable to attend the popular assembly, their representatives made up two-thirds of the council and of the *prytanes*. The primarily urban turnout at the popular assembly would on occasion reject bills presented by the council, and city members could always outvote rural ones in important committees, but it is unlikely that this happened too often. In any case, there is little evidence that urban and rural camps formed and clashed. The farmers helped carry out the policies of the league; they fought as hoplites in Athens' wars and surely shared in their city's pride, in the successes of its foreign policy, and probably also in the attendant material gains; they were represented among the settlers of Athenian colonies and *cleruchies*; and they must have regarded Athens' democracy as their own.

As Athens developed, some interesting contradictions arose. At certain critical moments the urban *thetes* became politically more influential than the farmers. They must have absorbed more of the charm, wit, and cleverness characteristic of city dwellers. But by and large the old social hierarchy remained in place—artisans and merchants, not to mention day laborers, enjoyed less prestige than farmers.

During this period, we find reference to a law that made it a punishable offense to denigrate citizens or their wives for engaging in business in the marketplace, implying that mercantilism was looked down upon. In comedies, affluent politicians are constantly ridiculed as small merchants. Around the time of Pericles a new term to describe tradesmen gained currency, *banausos*, derived from *baunos*, meaning "furnace" or "forge." Xenophon hypothesized that *banausos* activities weakened the body because they were performed sitting down and in the shade, sometimes all day long and near an open fire. The soul was also adversely affected, and, Xenophon says, these workers had no time to assist friends or the city.

Old prejudices based on social class continued even though the artisans' works, their art, and their abilities were often greatly admired, and even though all citizens were equal in the popular assembly. Reinforcing these attitudes is the fact that the artisans did work that was also performed by metics and slaves. The law mentioned above and the construction of the great Hephaestus temple near the agora represent efforts to combat these persisting prejudices.

This continuation of social prejudices is not surprising. We find it in many societies and epochs. The low esteem in which a class is held does not necessarily improve when that class makes gains in political power. On the contrary, things can get worse because that class is blamed for receiving what it does not deserve. The idea of general equality is still a long way off.

The hoplites continued to enjoy greater respect than the rowers, in spite of the navy's crucial importance. It was the victors of Marathon, not those of Salamis, who were commemorated. In the Parthenon frieze and many similar pictures the horseback riders are prominently shown in the foreground. The *thetes* might have reacted to these prejudices by rebelling, but despite their numerical superiority and their importance as rowers they seem to have accepted their place in society with relative humility. Our knowledge of the political and military undertakings of Athens suggests that the various segments of the Attic population worked together quite well during the Periclean era.

Where the farmers may have been inclined to passivity and hesitation, the *thetes* were more enterprising and perhaps had a better grasp of Attica's imperial and cultural politics. But that did not place them in conflict with the farmers (or the aristocrats who led the opposition against Pericles). Although many minor differences and conflicts may have emerged, as long as times were good the sense of unity of all who enjoyed the distinction of being Athenians prevailed.

When Pericles replaced the old distinctions with new ones based on the degree of commitment to the city, he set up new standards that transformed the entire Attic citizenry into a kind of aristocracy. This new order may have been only temporary, but it lasted long enough to create a picture of Athens that impressed itself so strongly on the world that no alternative to its democracy would take form for a long time to come.

It is difficult to comprehend that this Athens was entirely a men's community. Whatever women knew about politics or anything else that was happening, about the tragedies and comedies and the many festivals, they knew only from hearsay. They caught only occasional glimpses of the new public buildings and they were affected hardly at all by the changes that were occurring at an accelerating pace. They may have been proud of their city and highly esteemed by its citizens, but their lives were severely restricted.

9

The Eve of the Peloponnesian War
to the Peace of Nicias

Among primitive peoples, goals are determined mostly by emotion; among the advanced, by reason. The difference, however, is not attributable solely to the primitive or advanced nature of a society but rather to the circumstances and institutions of cultures. This difference, therefore, does not apply in all cases, but it does in the majority of them. In short, even the most advanced nations can be seized by passionate hatred toward each other.

—CARL VON CLAUSEWITZ

With the signing of the thirty-year peace treaty with Sparta and its allies in 446 B.C., Athens had realized its goals. The Persian danger had long since faded away, and the two major Greek powers now recognized and accepted each other and their spheres of influence.

The Spartans would henceforth have to share power over Greece with Athens. They did not suffer any direct loss; the Peloponnese remained under their control. But now the Aegean Sea was subject to Athens' political influence. In this respect the Spartans found their overall position much weakened.

Greece now consisted of a land power, a sea power, and a few neutral states. The time when Greece was a collection of independently existing city-states was gone for good. The two spheres of power did not overlap. Athens' failed attempt to extend its supremacy to the Corinthian Gulf had clearly revealed its limits. Athens could not hold the area militarily, and the political support it initially thought it could count on soon collapsed, without very much effort on Sparta's part.

Attica continued to be relatively vulnerable to Spartan invasions. A mere forty kilometers separated the city of Athens from the territory of

Megara, which was an ally of Sparta. But thanks to its long walls the city could not easily be taken by land. And because the Athenians dominated the sea (and the vulnerable coasts of the Spartan Peloponnese were long) their position would, in an actual contest, be superior to that of Sparta.

The troubles with Samos and the defection of Byzantium in 440 had given Athens a taste of the dangers to which its empire continued to be exposed. Such dangers could emanate from within the Delian League as well as from Persia or Sparta. Athens had thus far been resilient enough to meet the challenges that faced it, but the Athenians could not be sure that would always be the case. Its relationship to the league was burdened with an alarming mortgage. Sparta was bound sooner or later to respond to Athens' provocations by trying to extend its own sphere of influence.

Machiavelli observed that "men never complain when they are forced to do what they are accustomed to doing. . . . That is why it is always easier to maintain a regime, which has over time extinguished opposition, than it is to establish a new one, which for many reasons can easily be overthrown." There are several reasons why this age-old truth remains valid. When a regime persists over time, the subjects get used to it, as do the rulers themselves. Habits are established and become entrenched. If things go well for a long time, an inner security can grow that relieves all the nervous tension aroused by the possibility of disruption.

Because of this persistence of established patterns, it was not easy for Athens and Sparta to establish a balance. One impediment was the fact that most of Athens' allies did not consider Sparta an enemy. Sparta continued to enjoy considerable sympathy in the parts of Greece dominated by aristocrats. After Persia ceased to be a threat, Sparta became the Delian League's opponent almost by default, without ever having engaged in any hostility against Athens' allies.

Thucydides, who had been following politics closely since about 440 when he was in his early twenties, saw the situation in different terms. For him what counted were money and the number of troops each city possessed, a measure that verified the superiority of Athens. He took into account Athens' financial resources, which allowed it to pay for and expand its navy; its wealth of experience; its prowess as a naval power; and the overall military capabilities on which it could call. The Athenians' "strength of soul," which Pericles makes so much of in Thucydides' account of the funeral oration, is conspicuously absent in the historian's own list of Athens' assets. The might of Athens, Thucydides concluded, was still on the rise. That was why the Spartans feared Athens and would eventually have to opt for war.

In Thucydides' view too, then, there was no such thing as a balance or a stable relationship between the old and the new power. He perceived Athens' superior military resources as the essential factor. If we look at the situation from the point of view of established habit and the automatic advantage of the status quo, Sparta emerges as the stronger of the two.

Thucydides studied the history of his time and the relative power of the participants more intensively than anyone else and consequently could judge them better. In addition he was on the side of the vanquished, and thus was one of those great historians who analyzed and wrote about events that ran counter to their own allegiances. He had to reexamine his own predictions to understand what had happened. He came to remarkable insights in this process, but there are no guarantees that his theses were necessarily correct. One important question he failed to address is how Sparta's fear of the Athenian threat was translated into action.

At roughly the same time, Thucydides' predecessor, Herodotus, the "father of history," wrote: "Know above all that human affairs are determined by a wheel of fortune; as it spins, luck changes." He put these words in the mouth of the defeated king of the Lydians, Croesus, who also says of himself, in clear allusion to Aeschylus's *Oresteia*, that he has been taught by bitter suffering.

Not many years earlier, the chorus in Sophocles' *Antigone*, which dwelt on human accomplishments in its first hymn, sang in the second: "Near time, far future, and the past, one law controls them all: any greatness in human life brings doom." Of course, everyone hopes this will not be the case in his own life, but "though phantom hope helps many, it also fools many if they give in to their frivolous desires." Then the chorus cites the then-famous saying: "Ill fortune appears good to those whose senses are deluded by a god."

Where Herodotus described only the result of the wheel of fortune's work, Sophocles revealed the mechanism behind it: *ate*, or delusion, the force that made Creon persist in his misguidedness—as did certain contemporary politicians, and perhaps even the Athenians themselves, whose expectations and hopes tended to range far beyond existing reality. Politicians, too, were not above behaving like tyrants from time to time, convinced that they knew better than the people.

In the early and mid-430s Athens adhered strictly to the terms of the peace treaty with Sparta. But meanwhile, it strengthened its position on the northern coast of the Aegean. After two unsuccessful attempts to establish a colony there, the Athenians finally accomplished this goal in 437. They defeated the Edones and founded the city of Amphipolis in a spot surrounded on three sides by the river Strymon, about 20 kilometers inland, at the intersection of the most important roads of the country. Amphipolis was an Attic colony, but only a small portion of the settlers were Athenians; most probably came from the Chalcidice.

By establishing Amphipolis, Athens ensured availability of the high-quality wood from this region that it needed for shipbuilding as well as access to the mines Athens owned there. Access to these resources was crucial because the Macedonian king, Perdiccas, whose sphere of influence reached quite close to Amphipolis on the western side, was hardly a reliable ally.

In the same year Pericles mounted a spectacular naval expedition to the Black Sea. The purpose may have been to strengthen political ties—a major part of Athens' imported grain came from that region—but the main motive was most likely to display Athens' might and distract the attention of his countrymen. It is not clear how far north Pericles pushed; the extant accounts mention only that he expelled the tyrant of Sinope, a city on the northern coast of Asia Minor, and sent six hundred Attic settlers to take over his possessions.

At any given time, thousands of Athenians were temporarily or permanently settled and granted land all over the Aegean, and now they were on the Black Sea. One cannot help but wonder how Athens managed to spare so many people for this purpose. The main reason for posting so many large groups of citizen soldiers in various places must have been to secure Athens' domain.

Given the treaties with Persia and Sparta, Athens could expand its empire in only two directions. To the north there was little to conquer apart from Thrace, and Athens was unlikely to be able to establish strongholds along the Black Sea. It is, in fact, surprising that the city had not already run into trouble with Persia when it took over Sinope.

Nor did the west offer many opportunities, even though Athens still had a few allies near the mouth of the Corinthian Gulf. It still had an alliance with Segesta, as well as with Rhegium on the straits of Messina and Leontini to the northwest of Syracuse. Small squadrons of the Attic navy made appearances in that region and are said to have sailed as far as Naples.

In 434–433, however, Athens entered into an alliance with the island of Corcyra (Corfu), an event that would have considerable ramifications in the Peloponnesian Wars.

All that is known about domestic events in Athens during these years is that the construction of the Parthenon was finished in 438 and that the large gold-and-ivory statue of Athena was inaugurated in the same year. While work on the temple's friezes continued, construction of the Propylaeum was begun. The city was in all likelihood busier than ever and the political agenda so full that the council and the assembly could hardly keep up with it. The time and effort invested in safeguarding democracy must have continued to be considerable.

But this restless city was unlikely to have been content simply with continuing the routine of ordinary life, without great projects and great ventures. The apparent attainment of all Athens' goals must have brought to the surface all manner of unsatisfied desires. The kind of dynamic

Athens had developed simply could not give way to the enjoyment of peace and rest.

In the 430s an important generational shift took place. By this time, the bulk of the citizenry was made up of men born after the Battle of Marathon. If a citizen had experienced the evacuation of Attica and the Battle of Marathon at all, he had likely done so as a child. The majority of citizens had grown up in a period without danger, during years of easy successes, unimagined gains of power, and an almost unlimited sense of what was possible. Naturally, they had tended to take all this for granted.

Pericles was about sixty at this time. He and his contemporaries, the fathers of democracy, had been the leading political figures for a quarter century; they were dominant if not oppressive forces. Younger men may have felt the urge to rebel against them.

Some sources mention a number of trials in which charges were brought against enlightened men. The seer Diopeithes is said to have made a motion to prosecute anyone who did not believe in "the divine." The philosopher Anaxagoras escaped court proceedings (or, according to other accounts, sentencing) by fleeing the city. Protagoras and others were reportedly tried and, in some instances, convicted. Aspasia, Pericles' consort, was accused of godlessness and barely escaped standing trial, thanks to Pericles' influence. The reliability of these accounts is highly questionable, however. We know for sure only that the sculptor Phidias ran into serious difficulties and stood trial for embezzlement of ivory or gold intended for the statue of Athena, but he was able to leave Athens.

Over all, peace prevailed during this period. Maintaining the empire was more important than expanding it, and consequently careful politics was more important to the city than energetic action or military victories. Thoughtfulness, caution, and negotiation were valued above all, and the vulnerability of the city's position was felt strongly, regardless of how much the Athenians reassured themselves of their military superiority over Sparta.

Once this insecurity had gained a foothold, all new views, questions, and assertions voiced in Athens and all the strange characters who were around must have begun to look suspicious. People sought peace and security, but what they encountered instead was the nervousness and excitement associated with innovation. Pericles was part of that spirit.

It is difficult to make clear pronouncements about Athens' mood: the available sources are ambiguous, and it is difficult to quantify intangibles such as fear, mood shifts, anxieties, and the atmosphere of mistrust. Suffice it to say that all of these emotions would have been heightened by the general feeling that war lay ahead.

During the 430s, the prewar years, the intellectual movement we now call Sophism began. It may not have emerged in Athens, but it became increasingly centered there.

Originally the word *sophist* was used to describe a learned man, a poet or one knowledgeable about religion or other matters. The Sophists undoubtedly wanted to be considered wise and often were experts in all kinds of subjects. Jacob Burckhardt speaks of the "wealth of knowledge with which the Sophists benefited contemporary Greece." But the use they made of their knowledge gave the word a new and different slant. The teachers called Sophists passed on what they knew in many different places but always for a considerable fee. Along with their knowledge they offered to teach methods that supposedly assured success in just about anything.

Hippias of Elis and Gorgias of Leontini in Sicily are said to have told their audiences that they could deliver the answer to any question extemporaneously. They performed at the Panhellenic games, and their listeners were so impressed that the two were invited to lecture in many places, even in Sparta. Whenever Elis needed an ambassador it chose Hippias for the task. Hippias made all his own clothing and was said, in this sense, to be autarkic. His mnemonic skills were so great that he could repeat fifty names in the same order after hearing them just once. Gorgias, too, came to Athens, as an envoy of his city, in 427.

The great self-confidence that characterized these men was one of the sources of the entire period's sense of mastery. Societies and cultures sometimes reach a point when circumstances create such rich opportunities for their most gifted members that they come to place great trust in the powers of intellectual inquiry and think almost any problem solvable. In such cases, openness is the rule rather than limitation; discoveries are expected rather than merely hoped for. This is the kind of situation that seems to have existed at that time in Greece.

We know about the Sophists almost exclusively through Plato, who casts them in an unfavorable light. His teacher, Socrates, is depicted in the dialogues as being doubtful about their conviction that virtue can be taught. Their pride elicited Socrates' ironic contempt, and he has nothing but scorn for their acceptance of fees in exchange for their wisdom. In Plato's account of Hippias's visit to Athens during the Peloponnesian War, the Sophist brags that he has earned over two and a half talents in Sicily in very little time and that he could make more money than "any two Sophists taken together." "That is certainly a great and impressive proof of your wisdom, Hippias," Socrates responds. "It shows how far today's men surpass the old sages," an allusion to the many philosophers who sacrificed their material wealth to pursue scientific inquiry.

What the Sophists had in common was their beliefs, their demeanor, and their ability to make money and inspire their audiences. In other respects they differed widely from one another. Protagoras, for example, the oldest among them, disassociated himself from Hippias, who drilled his students in arithmetic, astronomy, surveying, music, ancient history, mnemonics, and much else. Protagoras himself taught only skills of use in domestic affairs and political dealings: "how to best advance, in word and deed, matters concerning the polis." He also placed himself in the tradition of Greek literature beginning with Homer but claimed that he was free of the fear that had caused his predecessors to disguise their insights in poetic form.

In his famous *Myth* Protagoras tells how Prometheus introduced men to technical skills, which Prometheus had stolen from Hephaestus and Athena. But despite these advances men were still at the mercy of wild animals, because to overcome their predators men had to be able to live together in cities, a skill that could not be stolen for them but had to be granted freely by Zeus. This ability consisted of justice and *aidós*, or respect, both for the gods and one another. These qualities, in contrast to technical skills, had to be given to all, after which everyone could have a voice in politics: carpenters, smiths, shoemakers, merchants, and ship-owners, the rich and the poor, the noble and the lowly.

This, then, was the political virtue that humanity had learned long ago, passed along in primitive form, and democracy had taken to its logical conclusion by extending political rights to all. It was this virtue Protagoras was now able to teach—in exchange for money—to students from well-to-do families. It is typical of Protagoras that, as we see in the Platonic dialogue that bears his name, he used the terms political virtue *(areté)*, political skill *(téchne)*, and political science *(epistéme)* interchange-ably. To him, the word *political* meant "for the betterment of the city," and everything he taught supposedly served the city's interests. Knowl-edge and practical skill improved the citizens by making them better able to further the city's well-being. It must have been in this spirit that Protagoras drafted the democratic constitution of the newly founded out-post of Thurii.

Many other Sophists probably had similar hopes. But in practice the knowledge and especially the rhetorical skills they taught were used by their students primarily to realize personal goals and ambitions. This was not the Sophists' fault—the teachers were only exploiting the intellectual advances being made at that time.

In the heated intellectual discussions of those years new questions were constantly being raised and answered. New information in all fields was absorbed, expanded on, and shared. Everywhere accepted conceptual limits to reality were being broken through.

The Sophists' rules were strict. Any opinion, no matter how subjec-tive, had to be supported by evidence. On this basis, Protagoras was forced to conclude that he did not know whether the gods existed or not. One could learn the various opinions expressed about a particular propo-sition but not whether it was actually true. The Sophists seem never to have delved deeply enough into things to come up with opinions they actually considered to be the truth. The influence the Sophists had may have been partly due to the variety, interchangeability, and continual evolution of their opinions.

It is not surprising that in these discussions, which drew on so many different fields of knowledge, that traditional beliefs came into question. As the claims of the intellect grew, it was easy to start doubting if the gods existed at all. "Do you think there are gods in the heavens?" Euripides writes. "No! There is no such thing, unless someone is determined foolishly to stick with the old fairy tales." He continued: "Think for yourselves; don't just take my word for it. The tyrants kill many people and steal everything they have; they break their oaths and devastate cities. Yet in spite of all this they prosper beyond those who live in peace and decency. I know of small, god-fearing towns that have to obey larger, godless ones, forced into submission by the latter's greater number of lances."

As the existence of the gods came into doubt, those who claimed to know the divine will lost their authority. Addressing the "manufacturers of oracles," Euripides wrote in 432–431: "Why are you sitting on your seers' seats and swearing you are telling us the will of the gods? Anyone pretending to know anything about the gods knows only one thing: how to fool people with words."

Once the gods cease to be sacrosanct, so do the customs and laws that derive their ultimate justification from the gods. Critias later said that the gods were invented so that people, thinking the gods were watching them, would obey the laws. As any traveler would have known, different nations obeyed very different customs and laws. Any traveler was struck by this. Herodotus tells the story of how the Persian king Darius once asked some Greeks who happened to be at his court how much they would have to be paid to be willing to eat the dead bodies of their fathers. The Greeks reacted in revulsion at the very suggestion. Then he asked some guests from India, whose custom it was to eat the flesh of the dead, whether they would burn their fathers' bodies. The Indians, too, were horrified at the thought, and Herodotus concluded that custom, or *nomos*, was king everywhere, as Pindar had put it before him. Custom had to be respected. Socrates would teach the same thing.

During the time of the Sophists the conclusion was reached that *nomos* was nothing more than convention; even the long-established differences between Greeks and barbarians, and those between freemen and slaves, were now seen in this light. People began to ask if it was not possible to invent better systems. They found that ultimately all laws and customs were arbitrary. From this uncertainty arose the need to seek principles that were immutable, not influenced by man and the chance elements of his existence. In the 420s we find first mention of the contrast between *nomos* and *physis*, or nature. *Physis* represented the immutable, that which is ordained by nature and has to be the way it is. Of course, even this distinction was subject to interpretation: one could conclude from nature, for example, that all men are equal, or one could conclude that the stronger has the natural right to dominate the weaker, like the lion among the weaker animals.

The Sophists' ideas were fascinating to the Greeks but also evoked disapproval. Crowds listened to their lectures enthusiastically, but others turned away horrified. The Sophists were said to corrupt the young, and as time passed they were blamed for undermining the old virtues. Jacob Burckhardt expresses doubt "that men like the Sophists were able to *bring about* such a change of mind among the wider public; the change had taken place long before, and all the Sophists did was to provide the formulas to describe it." In other words, the analysts are not to blame for what they analyze; their questions should not be divorced from the context in which they arose. The Sophists found themselves at an increasing intellectual distance from existing reality, yet this fact would have had no further consequences were a group of Athenians not already aware of the many new possibilities that lay open to them. A separation between those educated in the new manner and the rest of society was in the making.

This intellectual shift was much more profound than the one following the Persian Wars, which grew out of the upheavals caused by the demotion of the Areopagus. In the 450s, the emerging contradictions and possibilities could still be subsumed under comprehensive conceptions like that of the *Oresteia*. But in the 440s everything was in flux, and the outlook of the period emphasized relativity and ambiguity, rather than stability and fixity.

The soldier, historian, and essayist Xenophon recorded a dialogue, presumably fictitious, that took place in the 430s between Pericles and his young ward Alcibiades. The boy innocently asks the older man to tell him what law is. The answer is simple, he is told: Law is "what the assembled people have written down after careful consideration, which tells us what to do and not to do." Alcibiades then asks whether that means to do the good or the bad and is told: "The good, of course, my boy." When Alcibiades asks how this applies to oligarchies and tyrannies, Pericles calmly explains that whatever the authorities decide is called law.

Next Alcibiades, versed in Sophist argumentation, approaches the subject from a different angle and asks for a definition of "force" and "illegality." "Are they not merely terms that enable the strong to bend the weak to their will," he asks, "without having to persuade them?" Pericles assents, and Alcibiades concludes that laws issued by tyrants are consequently illegal. Pericles backtracks and declares that what tyrants—and oligarchies—decree without the consent of the citizens is not law. Alcibiades then voices his last question: "Does this not mean that laws decreed by the common people, who constitute the government, restricting the rights of property owners without their consent belong to the category of force rather than of law?" Pericles has no choice but to admit defeat. He remarks that in his youth he and his friends had raised similar questions and that Alcibiades was clearly ready to do so.

What had once been considered a great accomplishment—the basing of the entire legal system on deliberation and resolutions—now appeared in a different, more negative light. The great enthusiasm at the heart of democracy began to wane. From the distance of intellectual scrutiny, democracy was merely one kind of constitution among others.

Such discussions were, of course, carried on primarily in small groups and among the young, and they were in many ways academic. But in the Athens of those years such debates inevitably filtered down in oversimplified form to the streets and public squares.

The instability of the situation in Greece became fully evident in 434–433, when a delegation from Corcyra (Corfu) arrived in Athens and asked for the city's support in a war against Corinth. Neutral cities were free to join whichever alliance they liked. What made this case tricky was that, by acceding to the request, Athens ran the risk of getting involved in a war against Corinth, and that constituted a breach of the thirty-year peace agreement. The Corinthians, who had also sent envoys to Athens, emphasized this point.

At first glance, the conflict between Corinth and Corcyra was of no concern to Athens. It had to do with Epidamnus, later called Durazzo, a city located almost 200 kilometers north of Corcyra in what is now Albania. Epidamnus was a colony founded jointly by Corinth and Corcyra. Its democratic government was supported by Corinth. Corcyra, after initial hesitation, had sided with the exiled aristocrats (and some local tribes who were allied with them). What was suspicious in this was the extent to which Corinth, along with several allies, had become involved in the conflict. It had built a considerable fleet in a short time and obviously was intent on becoming the prevailing power on the western coast of Greece.

The Corcyrians pointed out that their island was in a strategic location. It was from Corcyra that Greek ships set sail for Italy and Sicily. If the western Greeks were going to become involved in the conflicts of the mainland, it would matter a great deal in whose hands Corcyra lay. Because of its geographical location the island had become extremely prosperous; it had a large navy, second only to that of Athens in Greece. (It may have needed a large fleet to protect its routes to the Adriatic Sea.) Powerful as Corcyra was, it had never sought allies.

Now the Corcyrians declared that a war between the Athenians and the Peloponnesians was inevitable. Athens could therefore not afford to pass up the chance of allying itself with such an important power.

The popular assembly was initially inclined to side with the Corinthians, but at a second meeting it decided in favor of an alliance with Corcyra, because of the likelihood of war with the Peloponnesians. This had presumably been Pericles' argument, and it was he who persuaded the assembly to change its mind. But since the Athenians did not want to break the thirty-year peace, they did not sign a normal alliance *(symmachia)* but a pact of mutual defense *(epimachia)*, which obliged them to come to Corcyra's aid only if the island was in danger of immediate attack. The Corcyrians were to help if Athens was in similar danger.

Athens first sent out ten ships and soon after, another twenty, with instructions not to interfere unless the Corinthians were about to land on Corcyra itself.

The Athenian squadron was unable to prevent the Corinthians from winning the naval battle that ensued, even when it finally did join in the fighting, but it was able to deprive the Corinthians of the fruits of their victory. The Athenians could have rejected Corcyra's plea for help, but that would have meant not only depriving themselves of a powerful ally but also allowing a considerable increase of power for Corinth. It was fairly clear that sooner or later the western coast of Greece would be drawn into the growing sphere of political conflict. With the balance of power as precarious as it was, anything that could tip it one way or the other had to be seriously considered. Any nervousness on the part of the Athenians arose from the difficulty of maintaining their ruling position and perhaps from the change in Corinthian military policy that was beginning to become evident fifteen years after the conclusion of the thirty-year peace treaty.

Corinth's massive military buildup could not be explained solely by its involvement in the problems that had arisen in Epidamnus. Something in Corinth had changed. The polis was attempting, as it had once before in the early 450s, to increase its territory. Its period of restraint, having lasted almost twenty years, was over. The Corinthians now realized, perhaps because a new generation had reached adulthood, that they could not simply let matters take their course. According to Thucydides, the Corinthians told the Spartans somewhat later on that one cannot cling to the old ways when dealing with an innovative city like Athens. Thus, for diverse reasons, Athens' example seems to have caught on. Where Sparta vacillated, Corinth, along with several allies on the Peloponnese and the western coast of Greece, wanted to expand its power and once again be taken seriously in the political arena.

Having foiled Corinthian ambitions at Corcyra, the Athenians feared, according to Thucydides, that the Corinthians would try to retaliate. Athens' suspicions centered particularly on the Corinthian colony of

Potidaea, located in the northern Aegean Sea on the isthmus of Pallene jutting out from the Chalcidice. Potidaea was a member of the Delian League, but at the same time had close ties to its mother city, which it honored at festivals and other occasions, as all colonies generally did. In addition, Corinth sent a high-ranking magistrate to Potidaea every year. Corinth maintained particularly close relationships with all its colonies except for emancipated, mighty, and headstrong Corcyra.

In the spring of 432, out of concern that Potidaea would defect from the Delian League, Athens demanded that the colony pull down its fortifications facing Pallene, the side from which the Athenians could attack; that it deliver hostages into Athenian keeping; and that it dismiss the Corinthian magistrate and refuse to accept others in the future.

Athens' fear was hardly unfounded, not just because of Corinthian ambitions but because the Macedonian king, Perdiccas, was encouraging the Greek cities of the region to rebel against Athens. In 432 Athens was already preparing to send out an army against Perdiccas. Now its army was additionally charged with imposing the Athenian demands on Potidaea. The colonial city barred its gates. It dispatched delegates to try to dissuade the Athenians, and it also tried to obtain Sparta's promise to invade Attica in case of an Athenian siege. Corinth sent two thousand volunteer troops to Potidaea's aid. Eventually, when negotiations in Athens failed and the Spartans agreed to support Potidaea in case of siege, Potidaea and other cities in the Chalcidice revolted against the Delian League.

The Corinthians used the ensuing siege, which dragged on and cost Athens a great deal of money, as grounds to ask Sparta to declare war on Athens. Athens had broken its treaties, they said, and the treaty partners should not tolerate this.

Other signers of the peace treaty added further complaints. Aegina accused Athens of not having granted it the autonomy promised in the treaty, and Megara claimed its citizens had been forbidden to engage in commerce in Attica or any of the cities belonging to the Delian League. This was true, and had been a punishment imposed for Megara's supposedly having sheltered runaway Athenian slaves and having built on sacred land and contested land. It is hard to tell how much this restriction hurt

Megara economically, but it was in any case a serious affront to Megara, and also to Sparta. Later, when the Athenians grew tired of the war, reproaches were often and angrily leveled at Pericles for instituting this policy toward Megara, which was apparently meant as a provocation.

The Spartans found themselves confronted with the question of war or peace. This was not the first time it had come up since the signing of the peace treaty, but now it was posed more urgently than before.

When the Spartan assembly discussed the Corinthians' request, the majority of the orators spoke in favor. According to Aristophanes, it was primarily the prominent members who were for the war; the assembly as a whole was more evenly divided. Sthenelaidas, the assembly's moderator, advocated war and resorted to a trick. The usual practice was to judge the majority opinion of the assembly by the respective loudness of the yeas and nays rather than by counting votes. So Sthenelaidas claimed he had not heard enough of a difference between the two sides to indicate a clear winner. He asked the Spartans to move to one side or the other according to their vote. With this method of tallying the yea side grew considerably larger, because the danger of appearing cowardly loomed too large.

The Spartans then asked the oracle of Delphi if they were likely to win a war. The god supposedly answered: "Victory will belong to those who pursue the war with all their might, and I myself will help if I am called, or even if I am not called." Another assembly meeting was held, in which the majority voted in favor of declaring war. The Corinthians in the meantime conferred with many of the delegates and, in their final speech at the allied Congress, urged the Spartans to declare war:

"Wise men certainly choose a quiet life so long as they are not being attacked; but brave men, when an attack is made on them, will reject peace and go to war, though they will be perfectly ready to come to terms in the course of war. In fact, they will neither become overconfident because of their successes in war, nor, because of the charms and blessings of peace, will they put up with acts of aggression."

This rhetoric was convincing, although Sparta's king Archidamus had reservations on the grounds that though war could be started by one side, it took two sides to make peace. An Attic delegation that happened to be in Sparta asked that the dispute be resolved by a court of arbitration, as the peace of 446 stipulated, but hardly anyone in Sparta except Archidamus was ready to do this.

War did not break out right away. The immediate actions taken were to cancel the peace treaty of 446 and to prepare for war in case the Athenians were not willing to meet certain demands. Contrary to what is often said, war was not at that time the normal state of affairs but the exception. However aggressively a small conflict between two cities was handled, convincing reasons had to be found to justify a large war that threatened to involve practically all of Greece; the public had to be prepared for the idea of such a war. Thucydides writes that the prime reason for the delay—almost a year passed before war actually broke out—was the Peloponnesians' inadequate military preparedness, but there is no indication that the Spartans used the time to remedy this lack.

The first demand presented to the Athenians by Sparta was of a purportedly religious nature: "to end the curse of the goddess." Two centuries earlier the followers of the Athenian usurper Cylon had been murdered when they sought refuge in Athena's temple. Sparta now asked that the descendants of those murderers be banished because the blood guilt of their forebears still clung to them. This demand was apparently motivated by the fact that the descendants of the guilty men included Pericles, whose mother belonged to one of the accused families. The Spartans claimed that the Athenians had made similar demands on Sparta in the past, though in the Spartan case the original offense to the god dated back only a few decades.

After this standoff, the Spartans sent another group of envoys with new ultimatums calling for the withdrawal of military forces from Potidaea, the granting of independence to Aegina, and the annulment of the Megarian decree—the last of these demands being the most important. If the Athenians gave in on this point, the Spartans claimed, war could be avoided. Thucydides, who reports these negotiations in a somewhat confusing manner, says that the Spartans also presented one last and even more consequential demand, which was that all Greek cities under Athenian domination be granted autonomy. Meanwhile the Athenians, still under the impression that peace could be preserved if they agreed to cancel the Megarian decree, discussed the matter in the assembly. Several speakers argued in favor of doing so, but Pericles' insistence on a refusal prevailed. Again Athens answered Sparta with demands that mirrored Sparta's own, including a request that Sparta's allies also be granted autonomy.

The negotiators apparently intended to leave room for bargaining when they presented their maximum demands. It seems that minor concessions could have saved the peace, and such a course was favored by many, both in Athens and in Sparta.

But according to Thucydides, the arguments of speakers and envoys, the events, accusations, and discussions of those months did not really matter much. "For in my opinion," he writes, "the truest cause of the war, which was, of course, least apparent in the speeches, was the growth of Athens' power and the fear it inspired in the Spartans, forcing them to start the war."

The distinction between the precipitating event and the deeper cause of a war has long and justly been recognized as one of the great discoveries of the historian's science. But in specific cases, such as this one, some interpretation is needed to avoid leaving the impression that there was no chance for political action or that war was inevitable.

The physicians of Thucydides' time began to use an old word, *prophasis*, in a new sense. The term now came to refer to that which became evident in the search for the causes of an illness. What became evident could be anything from the triggering event to the deeper cause. In the process of diagnosis, the physician sought to get as close to this cause as possible. As Thucydides interpreted the term, *prophasis* was the diagnostic method with the greatest potential of leading to the "truest cause" of an illness.

Thucydides was strongly influenced by medical science, though the center of medical study was in his day not Athens but the island of Cos, where Hippocrates taught. Much of what impressed Thucydides about medical procedure was simply the ideal of scrupulous exactitude, or *akríbeia*. This concept seems to have been derived from carpenters' jargon but was ironically adopted by physicians and, indeed, by those at the highest levels of society. The elite liked to claim *akríbeia* for themselves, contrasting it with the "lawlessness" of the demos, which, in their opinion, often overlooked irregularities, failed to follow the law rigorously, and was often profligate. But in applying *akríbeia* to science, the physicians came to serve as the model.

Thucydides shared with the physicians an interest in understanding human nature, though he approached it from the point of view of politics. He found that man's actions derived from three basic motives: fear, a desire for honor, and striving after personal advantage. Because of this insight into human nature, his historical work is timeless, and remains useful to anyone interested in politics. Knowing human nature also made it possible for Thucydides to make political predictions, the same way physicians made medical prognoses.

Of course, conditions vary from situation to situation. The Spartans were very different from the Athenians; life in the fifth century differed from that of ancient times; and, most important, people did not act the same way during war as they did in peacetime. As Thucydides wrote, "In peacetime and under favorable conditions the spirit of the polis and of individuals improves because they are not forced into making impossible choices." A major war, on the other hand, does involve such choices, and during such times the primal motives of men become more apparent than usual.

The negotiations themselves were not without interest, however, and Thucydides described them in detail. But ultimately what mattered more were the power plays by one side that aroused such fear in the other that it *had* to initiate war. It was no longer a matter of words and personalities; these were the real cause of the war.

Thucydides believed that the essential determining factors of the Peloponnesian War were the conditions in Greece that allowed Athens to become so powerful and Sparta's history of hegemonic power. Everything else was incidental.

This kind of thinking is an example of Thucydides' nomological knowledge, or knowledge of the prevailing laws and customs of his culture. It represented a major intellectual advance and was Thucydides' basic frame of reference for everything he experienced and learned. In positing that human nature was responsible for the course of history, he took a considerable epistemological step, bringing his intensive reflection to a close approximation of an empirical approach.

By asking what nature *(physis)* was, Thucydides and the physicians reflected their time's quest for truth. The philosopher Democritus's assertion that the perceptions of color and taste were merely conventions and that "only atoms and emptiness really exist" represented a delving beneath the surface to underlying reality. On a basic level, Thucydides' project, his search for the "truest cause" of the Peloponnesian War, was the same as the philosopher's.

Examined in view of the many possible mitigating factors, Thucydides' thesis is quite convincing. Its underlying reasoning, however, gives rise to some doubt. Even if we grant that it was likely that the Spartans would at some point decide on war, the immediate reason could just as well have been a reduction rather than a gain in Athens' power. A threat to Athens' hegemony, brought about perhaps by the defection of powerful cities like Samos, would have turned it into a target. On a more general level, we must not forget that a major power's assessment of its opponent's military potential does not necessarily reflect reality but is often exaggerated out of insecurity. The decisive factors, then, were the tension between Athens and Sparta; the dissatisfaction with existing conditions felt by the Greek city-states; the ambition of cities like Corinth to get into power politics, seriously aggravating tensions between the major powers; and the likelihood of rash and ill-considered reactions.

Pericles had come to the conclusion in the early 440s that the power of Attica had reached its limits and it was time to scale back Athens' ambitions. His policies seem not to have aimed at war at all, and he may have hoped that the peace would last the thirty years stipulated in the treaty. He was not particularly peace loving, but he knew how much effort, suffering, and risk were connected with war. "Anyone who has a choice and lives well would be foolish to start a war," Thucydides reports him saying.

But Pericles also knew that peace can never be relied on; and he hardly needed the reminder of the Spartans' deliberations at the time of Samos's revolt. The determination with which the Corinthians expanded their influence on the western coast of Greece may have been the final signal to convince him an armed conflict was unavoidable in the near future. The treaty with Corcyra supports this view, as do the decision to attack Potidaea and the restrictions on Megarian trade, which was a response to such a minor infraction that it was clearly meant as a challenge to Sparta. Apparently Pericles thought that since war was imminent it was best to bring it about quickly.

The Spartans, for their part, may not have feared Athens' growing might all that much. They may rather have been angered by its audacity. Since Sparta had taken hardly any military part in Greek affairs for almost fifty years, the impression might gradually have arisen among other states that this old power could no longer be counted on. The Corinthians had already threatened that if no help was forthcoming from Sparta it would look for other allies. The leading Spartans may have been quite eager to reverse this impression by agreeing to the Corinthians' and others' demand to declare war.

The fact that no understanding was reached in spite of all the opportunities is once again attributable to Pericles. He declared before the assembly in Athens that the Spartans' position on the Megarian decree was an insult. They had presented it not in the form of a request but of a command. For Athens to give an inch would be tantamount to submission. The decree was not some minor matter, it had broad significance. Athens' policies and its very freedom were at stake. Athens, Pericles said, should be willing to bring the matter before a court of arbitration and would not start a war, but would respond with force if others did. He concluded: "We have to realize that war is a necessity." The popular assembly of Attica rejected Sparta's demand.

How much Pericles was influenced by theories current at the time is unclear. One such theory held that two evenly matched powers had to battle each other to see who would be preeminent. But there is no suggestion that Pericles thought in these terms. He was more given to sober calculation, based on what he considered to be his city's needs.

. . .

The two sides differed widely in their war plans and expectations. In Thucydides' account the Corinthians voice their intentions in vague terms, whereas Pericles presents highly specific information. Nothing at all is said about the Spartans' thinking.

In trying to convince the Spartans to declare war, the Corinthians argued that the Peloponnesians surpassed the Athenians in numbers, courage, and dedication. The only thing they lacked was a large navy, but a fleet could be built with loans from the Olympic and Delphic temples, and the offer of higher wages would induce Athens' foreign mercenaries to man the new ships. The Corinthians said Athens' power could be bought with money and its technology learned, whereas the natural virtues the Peloponnesians possessed were nontransferable. They acknowledged that it would also be necessary to win Athens' allies over to their side. All of Greece was supposedly convinced that the Athenians would not be able to hold out for more than one or two years, at most three, if the Spartans invaded their land.

Pericles, on the other hand, explained to the assembly that the Athenians would have to abandon all their outlying land and retreat within their long walls. They should not, he cautioned, let themselves be drawn into any land battles. For if they won, the enemy would only reappear with a new, equally large force. And if they lost, their allies would use this as an excuse to defect. That was why Attica was to concentrate all its warring activities on the sea, where its navy was unchallenged master and where no one could hinder any of its operations. The Attic navy would be ordered to attack and plunder the Peloponnese from all sides and set up bases along its coasts, from which it could launch raids at any time. Pericles insisted that this strategy would wear down the Spartans and their allies and make them surrender.

Pericles urgently advised Athenians not to waste energy and resources trying to win new territory while they were at war. The Athenians were to concentrate on keeping what they had.

It is not clear whether Pericles expected the war to last long. In any case, he was confident that Athens' resources were formidable.

Unlike the Corinthians, he mentioned only concrete, tangible assets: Six thousand talents of silver lay stored on the Acropolis (the amount had previously risen as high as 9,700 talents, but some of the money had been spent on the public buildings and the siege of Potidaea); there were also other precious metals given as offerings or seized from the Persians and sacrificial vessels worth at least 500 talents. In an extreme emergency the 40 talents of pure gold in the statue of Athena could be melted down. The Delian League supposedly contributed 600 talents annually, but this seems an inflated estimate; normally, at that time, the dues paid were more in the neighborhood of 400 talents. Finally, Athens had 300 triremes; 13,000 hoplites; and 1,200 cavalry horses, a number considered exceptional at that time. The troops also included archers, the soldiers stationed in garrisons, and the 16,000 older men and youths who guarded the walls.

Thucydides praises Pericles' foresight. Athens' resources were indeed, as Pericles knew and later history would show, so massive that Athens could easily have defeated the Peloponnesians. In war, Pericles had said, the outcome is determined primarily by two things: the use of reason and an abundance of money. Pericles' war plan was a great example of the human ability to calculate. He knew that war brings many reversals, and in the Peloponnesian War, apparently almost anything could happen without seriously affecting Athens' prospects. To this extent even chance was included in his calculations. Of course, Athens' huge military and economic superiority over its rivals was the crucial factor.

In its attempt to calculate and anticipate an entire war, Pericles' plan is reminiscent of Themistocles' plan for Salamis. Thucydides does not credit Themistocles, as he does Pericles, with "foreknowledge," a term that implies accurate assessment of what lies ahead. Instead he calls Themistocles "the best guesser of what lay ahead." Apparently Thucydides felt that a step forward had been taken in the intervening time, from instinctive to well-founded anticipation of events. He probably underestimated Themistocles' use of reason but did justice to the scale of Pericles' calculations. For although Themistocles had to deal with only one campaign, the superiority of the enemy was overwhelming. Both leaders executed superb planning, which in both cases included giving up Attica, although only in the first instance did Athens have to be abandoned. But in the end, Themistocles' plan worked out and Pericles' did not.

In the final analysis, Pericles' war plan contained a deep inner contradiction. It was conceived in terms of the "state," rather than in terms of the polis's citizenry. The modern concept of a state should generally be avoided in discussions of ancient Greece because it is anachronistic, but here we encounter something like a *raison d'état*: thinking guided by the needs of power politics as played by the political entity of Athens. Policy was not determined, as it is in a modern state, by a governmental body acting in strict adherence to tradition and bureaucratic rules, but by the de facto monarchy of one man. Pericles had analyzed the political needs of his city in depth and was determined to make them the guiding principles of his thinking and actions. In his mind, the polis of Athens assumed a character that went far beyond the totality of the citizens. The polis took precedent over them in almost the same way the states of the early modern era took precedent over society.

Pericles could plan his city's policies as he did—in a way never to be repeated in history—because for over ten years his position of power was firmly established, and he no longer had to fight for control. He came to identify himself with his polis—he was the creator of Athens' democracy, the initiator of many of the steps that transformed the Delian League into an empire, the shaper of the city from the Parthenon to the agora, and the organizer of festivals. The tendency of Attic democracy to rely on one leading individual worked in his favor.

Thucydides remarks bitterly that the failure of the war plan was caused primarily by the politicians who succeeded Pericles. They pursued their own interests, vying with each other for supremacy instead of working together for the city's well-being. By acting in this way they left the polis at the mercy of the people's whims. Pericles, too, had feared above all else the mistakes the Athenians themselves would make.

If we simply accept Thucydides' version, we avoid the question of whether this internal fighting was destined to arise, given the structure of Attic democracy. In the absence of one relatively undisputed leader, demagoguery was inevitable and ostracism proceedings were bound to begin. Pericles himself, in the early days of his rise, must have considered other things besides the well-being of the city, namely, his own career. Anyone whose position of leadership is precarious will find it difficult to pursue policies aimed at long-term goals.

Though Pericles had often explained that what counted above all else was to control the seas, the people, once they were no longer under his influence, were hard-pressed to believe that it made sense to let the enemy destroy the plantations, vineyards, fields, and houses of the mightiest polis of Greece. They wanted to fight the Spartans openly, as honor had prescribed for centuries. It was hard for the people to accept that there were to be no great victories, only a policy of slow attrition. Pericles' strategy went against the prevalent psychology of war. It might have been technically correct, but it was so abstract that many found it difficult to comprehend. The politicians who succeeded Pericles, men who yet had to win the people's favor, could not continue to support such an unpopular war plan.

Furthermore, Pericles' strategy ran counter to the Attic temperament. The Athenians were renowned for taking the initiative and acting boldly. If they had resorted to evacuation in the past, as during the Persian Wars, it was for only a brief time, under the pressure of an overwhelming military threat—and in order to be able to deliver one great counterblow.

The weak point of Pericles' war plan, then, was in the area of domestic politics. His death soon after the outbreak of war deprived Athens of perhaps the most important condition for the success of his plan—his own presence and prestige.

It is, of course, precisely the nontraditional, un-Athenian aspect of Pericles' war plan that attests to his flexibility and open-mindedness, his ability to pursue paths divergent from custom so as best to serve the demands of the situation. The problem was that most Athenians were unable to think the same way.

But there was another weakness in the war plan, which was soon to become evident. The war very quickly drew other parts of Greece into its vortex, and it aroused such strong passions that it could not easily be brought under control and ended. Pericles' strategy of attrition was conceived from the standpoint of peace. As he predicted, it resulted in much misery, devastation, and shortages, but once people found themselves at war, they inevitably became filled with the thirst for revenge. They resolved to persist until victory.

Many internal conflicts arose during wartime. Before, under the civilized conditions that had evolved over the years, Athenians had been content with constitutional forms of power. But now, in many quarters, the hope of assuming total power sprang up—whether as a small ruling clique, an oligarchy, or as the most influential group within a democracy. These factional claims to power often had outside support. Foreign and internal politics became intertwined, and, increasingly as the war continued, ambitious citizens used the situation to achieve their personal ends.

Civilization can be, as Freud observed, a thin veneer that is easily broken. In the case of Greece at the beginning of the Peloponnesian War, the long period of relative peace may have magnified the crisis that arose. Most Greek peace treaties were made for a term of thirty years; in other words, each generation was thought to have the right to a war. Given the sudden change of circumstances brought about by Athens' supremacy and its carefully maintained balance of power with Sparta, however, no wars had been fought for a long time, other than the conflicts over the confederacy and Athens' imperialism. Might there not have been some need to make up for missed opportunity?

Whatever the case, we must conclude that, despite all of Pericles' foresight and the fact that he even took unforeseeable events into account, he started this war with many illusions. Athens' impressive financial resources were probably used up much more quickly than he had anticipated. As Pseudoxenophon shows, certain of Athens' structural problems were already apparent in the 420s, and it was possible for individuals to gain political power in excess of what the constitution intended for them to have.

By attributing everything that happens in his history to the doings of specific personalities, Thucydides severely limited the scope of what he could have achieved; his History of Individuals falls below the structural demands of his work. This failing could be attributed to his relative lack of interest in domestic politics, but there is also a biographical factor: Thucydides was strongly and lastingly affected by the time and place in which he grew up, which makes his work especially interesting as an indicator of what Athens was like in those years. Despite continuous reflection and acute observation over the first two decades of the twenty-seven-year war, he never abandoned his view that the war plan had been sound, a view he defends almost belligerently at two important moments in his work. We need to look to his biography to explain why he clung so tenaciously to this position.

Thucydides, son of Olorus, must have been born in 460 to an old family belonging to the Attic aristocracy and closely related to the family of Cimon. His grandmother was the daughter of a Thracian prince. Thucydides inherited large gold mines near Amphipolis, probably from his grandmother, and became one of the most powerful men of that region.

By 424–423 he had been elected a *strategos* but soon thereafter was exiled because of a failed military enterprise, though he had not been responsible for it. He was not able to return to Athens until 404.

Thucydides wrote his history of the war with an accurate knowledge of both sides and a strong desire to be objective, and it is unquestionably one of the outstanding historical works ever written. He examined politics and warfare using the tools of historiography. Especially impressive is his continual comparison of the expectations and calculations of the actors to the actual course of events. This approach grew out of his great interest in examining the possibilities various plans and actions opened up—and, consequently, in the unexpected turn of events that could foil any plan. The range of reflection he attributes to his speakers is so broad as to be almost inexhaustible. The speeches are presented in a highly concise style that Karl Reinhardt has called an "artfully serious" and "muscular style." His reflections always attempt to penetrate to the "truest causes" of the speakers' underlying claims and intentions, and they are presented in a magnificent Greek that captivates the reader.

The question for subsequent historians is to what extent Thucydides identified not only with Athens' leading statesman but also, rather more problematically, with his own city, that grand, arrogant, demanding, beautiful, and selfish community of men who stirred up trouble wherever they roamed.

There is no doubt that Pericles made a lasting impression on the young Thucydides, who observed his political activities with utter fascination. It is from Pericles that Thucydides learned the potential magnitude of human endeavor. In the pairing of Pericles with Thucydides, an outstanding talent for action met with an equally outstanding talent for interpreting events.

Commentators have spoken of Thucydides' "optimism." This word has too many ironic associations to be accurate, but it is true that Thucydides fully shared the Greek and, above all, Athenian sense of being able to achieve almost anything.

Thucydides strongly defended Pericles' war plan. He also refused to blame the war on Athens' leading statesman, reasoning that if the war had to be fought one way or the other, it did not matter when and how it started. This thinking allowed him to deliberately downplay the importance of the Megarian decree, which had played such a large role in the events leading to the outbreak of war.

There may have also been an implicit apologetic tendency in Thucydides' theory of the basic drives behind human action. According to him, "human nature" explains Athens' politics—the strange, unprecedented, indeed, sometimes scandalous laws that dictated its actions, including its hated tyranny over its "confederates." The Attic delegates in Sparta declared that Athens had to rule by force or else expose itself to danger; its only choice was to be either hammer or anvil. As Thucydides has it, it was only consistent with human nature that the Athenians refused to let go of what had been handed to them; they acted "in obedience to the three mightiest factors: honor, fear, and the desire for personal advantage." After all, it was a universal rule that the weak are kept down by the strong.

This argument relieves Athens of considerable responsibility for acts committed in furtherance of its ruling position. Athens' hegemony arose from historical processes; everything else, including Athens' decision to perpetuate its rule over the confederates of the Delian League even after the Persian threat was removed, is explained by reference to natural laws and human nature.

We wonder to what extent Thucydides developed his views and explanations precisely because they prevented moral questions from arising. It seems best to try to understand the harshness of his observations, the emotional frigidity he imposes on himself, as well as his strict adherence to facts not just from his own point of view but from that of his native city. Writing as a kind of archetypical Athenian citizen, he reduces all the issues the politicians grappled with to questions of power, making open mention of moral considerations only when they turn up as the source of tactical errors.

Sometimes we get a glimpse of his awareness of more profound concerns, such as those existing in the realm of tragedy. The lavish praise of Athens contained in Pericles' funeral oration is followed in Thucydides directly by a description of the plague, just as a speech in a Greek play is usually followed by a response. And before recounting how the Athenians set out on their Sicilian expedition, Thucydides makes the full cynicism behind their policies evident in a dialogue between the army's commanders and the council of the island of Melos.

Taken together the Attic delegates' reference to all-powerful human nature and the Athenians' obeisance to this concept in maintaining their hegemony epitomize the city's politics of that period. Anybody else would act the same way given their position, Thucydides' delegates say, even the Spartans. The Athenians claim they are trying, to the best of their ability, to act fairly. With this line of argument, politics ceases to be deliberate action and is reduced to the playing of a role.

We find the same thought expressed shortly before the outbreak of war in Euripides' *Heracleidae*, when King Eurystheus declares, after having devised "torment after torment" for Heracles and mercilessly persecuting the hero's sons, that Hera has unleashed this fury in him and that even Heracles' own mother would have done the same had she been in his place. By contrast, it is impossible to imagine Sophocles' Antigone declaring she was related to her brother only by chance or that she would have preferred not to do what she did. Nor can we think of Creon, let alone Oedipus, distancing himself from his role. But now such assertions were possible. We have to add here the caveat that attributing human motivation to divine interference is quite common throughout the literature of ancient Greece. But this never relieves men of responsibility for what they do.

We have touched here on a theme Euripides returns to repeatedly and one that clearly preoccupied Athens. The citizens had adjusted relatively well—probably too well—to their ruling position. But in the short period of their rise they had not had the chance to develop the moral standards usually associated with a great power. Consider by contrast the many false starts, disappointed hopes, successes, mistakes, and failures that ancient Rome or England, for example, passed through as they grew into empires. A similar process must have accompanied the emergence of coexistence among European states.

For a nation to rise, might is crucial, but not sufficient. The exercise of power must conform to certain rules, which reflect specific moral standards—even if these standards favor the strong over the weak, reward them for injustice, or depart from the standards that apply to private individuals. With such standards, a quasi-objective understanding of political conditions develops, which helps maintain stability.

Not so in Athens. There had been no time for such developments. The reigning morality was still the old one, derived from the aristocratic world and modified by the interests and views of the middle classes. The reality, however, was largely new. Its essence, Athens' supremacy, could not really be justified under the moral code. Whatever justifications of Athens' political role were offered, they amounted to nothing more than arguments hurriedly tailored to fit the case. The Athenians were lacking both the actual experience and the established rules, which when gradually worked out over generations of trial and error made evident the rights and responsibilities of a major power.

The Athenians may have hit on the human nature argument as a justification for their activities as early as the 430s. But it is possible that Athenians really thought this way, not because, as is often said, they had been corrupted by the Sophists, but because their world had grown too quickly. Among the justifications advanced by the Athenians at that time was one Thucydides did not even consider worth mentioning—namely, that they had to look out for the weak and persecuted. This motive evoked Athens' role as the savior of Greece, and it is the central theme of Euripides' *Heracleidae*. Once again, as in Aeschylus's *Suppliants* of 463, refugees—in this case the sons of Heracles—are seeking asylum. This time, too, the pursuers represent a danger not to be ignored—they are prepared to go to war over the issue. But in this instance the question is not whether to give the suppliants sanctuary in Athens in obedience to religious commands or to turn them away for the sake of the city's safety. The pursuers offer an alliance if Athens will hand over the refugees, a highly tempting offer in view of their large army. The offer is reminiscent of the one Corcyra presented a few years before this drama was first produced.

But the Athenians are swayed neither by expedience nor by danger. Without any hesitation they decide to protect the children of Heracles from persecution. They do so not just to obey Zeus and because of family ties, but above all because the king fears the disgrace that would otherwise mark him if people believed his city was not free. This freedom is invoked several times in the play. Athens, then, could not afford to let its freedom be limited in any way.

Euripides touches on another aspect of the problem: This notion of freedom is not the same one Pericles attributes to Athens in his funeral speech, the freedom that characterizes the city's domestic affairs and lies at the heart of democracy. Rather, it is freedom of action in international dealings. This freedom, though, is another consequence of might, for no political entity can act freely in foreign affairs if it does not have the power to enforce its policies.

An ideological tension is present here between the inner freedom and autarky that guaranteed Athens' independence, on the one hand, and the tyrannical power that permitted Athens freedom of action on the other.

Thucydides writes that no effort was spared "where the highest priorities—freedom and rule over others—were at stake." Freedom and rule are not imagined as opposites but are meant to complement each other. Tyranny was viewed at the time with ambivalence: it was condemned, but it also found praise because of the advantages it offered to the one who exercises it. In his plays, Euripides repeatedly raised the question of what made man free, for freedom seemed to be limited on every side. Men were prisoners to fate or to money, or they were constrained by popular will or written law. This reluctant awareness of the limits of freedom implies an understanding of what freedom could be. The political possibilities of freedom were greater in Athens than anywhere else at that time. The high value the Athenians placed on freedom is indicated by the construction of an exceptionally lavish stoa, located next to the agora and dedicated to "Zeus the Liberator," beginning in 430. It was in the same spirit that Pericles declared that revoking the Megarian decree in obedience to Sparta's demand was the equivalent of "servitude."

It is interesting that Euripides associates the exercise of freedom so closely with the role of protector. But this, too, was in essence only a reflection of Athens' status as a superpower and the difference between it and the other city-states, to whom it offered protection but over whom it insisted on asserting its supremacy.

In trying to stress the unprecedented magnitude of the war, Thucydides cites the unheard-of level of power and financial resources and the fact that almost all Greek cities were involved, on one side or the other. He describes the length of the war and the enormous amount of suffering that accompanied it. But he also gives accounts of a number of apparently unrelated natural disasters. He reports that earthquakes of extraordinary force shook wide regions of the earth; solar eclipses occurred with greater frequency than ever before; withering drought and famine affected many places; and, above all, the plague descended on Athens. The following line from Shakespeare's *Julius Caesar* comes to mind: "When beggars die, there are no comets seen; The heavens themselves blaze forth the death of princes." Machiavelli commented on such phenomena as well: "I don't know why it is so, but both old and recent examples show that in no town or country have events of consequence ever happened that had not been predicted by seers, prophecies, miracles, or other supernatural signs." Thucydides, too, mentions such predictions in his history.

Before the outbreak of war, in early March of 431, the Thebans, allies of
Sparta, launched a surprise attack on Plataea, which had joined the
Athenian side. But a small advance force, let into the city late at night by
conspirators, was overpowered and forced to surrender. The main army,
which approached the city the next morning, was induced to withdraw by the threat that the prisoners would otherwise be killed. But the
Thebans had hardly left the country before the one hundred and eighty
men were nevertheless put to death. The Athenians had sent a messenger
urging the Plataeans to refrain from drastic actions, but the messenger
arrived too late. The Thebans' breach of the peace treaty unleashed the
war. It is not known whether there was an official declaration of war.
Thucydides merely writes that after this incident both sides made ready
for war.

Of the tragedies produced at the end of March in 431, only one has survived, Euripides' *Medea*. The daughter of the king of Colchis (a non-
Greek country on the Black Sea, south of the Caucasus) has been
abandoned by her husband, Jason. Medea had once helped Jason obtain
the Golden Fleece, but in doing so she deceived her own father. As the
play opens, Jason wants to marry the king of Corinth's daughter. Medea
and her two children are ordered to leave the country. The wronged
Medea plots her revenge.

The history of Greece and Greek tragedy are full of men who wreak
vengeance for the sake of honor, sometimes at great cost to themselves.
But Medea, a woman from a barbarian country, far exceeds them in their
zeal. She kills not only her husband's future wife and father-in-law but
her own children as well.

The fact that she loves her children is immaterial. Only after she has
set her plans in motion and administered the poison to the bride and the
father does Medea realize what she is about to do to her children. For a
brief moment she is overcome with horror and resolves to give up her
plan. But then she imagines the jeers of her enemies and realizes she

cannot abandon her children to them. Her enemies cannot be allowed to kill them; she will have to do it herself. It is widely believed that Euripides added infanticide to the original myth, in which Medea does not even consider killing her children.

Once again, it would appear at first glance that the law of vengeance had taken on a perverse quality, as in the case of Orestes, who is forced to kill his mother to avenge his father. But this time there is no divine command that has to be satisfied; Medea's act is voluntary. Above all, it is not a question of enacting justice but one of satisfying an individual's monstrous need for redress. To be sure, she is a barbarian, a woman who has yet to be taught Greek custom, law, and proper attitude; someone who— as Jason tells her reproachfully—ought to be grateful to have been transplanted from the land of barbarians to the world of Greek civilization; a woman, too, who pursues her personal ends with a ruthlessness that brings to mind Athens itself.

The tragedy was finished by the middle of the year 432. Rehearsals began in the summer preceding the year of production. At that time Sparta had already decided on war, and it was becoming clear in Athens that the assembly would reject the Spartan demands. At the very time the Athenians were watching the tragedy, final preparations were in progress for the war to which *Medea* could almost have served as motto.

At the end of the play Medea flees to Athens, where King Aegeus offers her refuge. The closing words of the chorus are: "Many things are determined by Zeus on Olympus, and many wishes are unexpectedly granted by the gods. But many things we expect to happen do not come to pass, for the gods contrive to bring about what we did not expect."

Euphronius, whose name is now almost unknown, took the first prize at the Great Dionysia that year; Sophocles placed second, and Euripides came in last. However, no other Greek tragedy has had such a lasting impact on world literature.

The participants of the war included, on the Spartan side, all the Peloponnesian city-states except Argos and Achaea: Megara, Boeotia, Locris, Phocis, Ambracia, Leucas, and Anactorium. Fighting on the

Athenian side were Chios, Lesbos, Plataea, the Messenians in Naupactus, most Acarnanians, Corcyra, and Zacynthus. Also supporting the Athenians were subjugated cities in various parts of the Aegean Sea, including all the islands except for Melos and Thera.

According to Thucydides most Greeks sympathized with the Spartans, because they "posed as the liberators of Hellas. . . . So great was the hatred of Athens among most of them that they joined the Spartans either because they wanted to shake off Athenian rule or out of fear of being subjected to it."

The Spartans and their allies assembled two-thirds of their troops on the Corinthian isthmus and marched against Attica. They moved slowly, supposedly because King Archidamus, who commanded the army, was still hoping to avoid war. He sent one more herald to Athens, but the Athenians refused to receive him because the assembly had passed a resolution, on Pericles' advice, not to negotiate if the enemy was poised for military action. The herald was therefore escorted out of the city and kept from making any contact with his supporters. "This day marks the beginning of a great misfortune for Greece," the herald is said to have exclaimed as he returned across the border.

The Athenians thus had time to evacuate women, children, and some of their belongings from the Attic countryside. The cattle were taken to Euboea and other islands. There must have been well over 100,000 people who had to find a place to live between the long walls of the city; some could stay with friends or relatives, but most had to construct some kind of shelter in vacant places or in the precincts of various religious shrines. Some camped next to the walls or in Piraeus.

It was almost as though they had been forced to emigrate from their country. The new life in the city was difficult. No matter how well the rationale behind the new strategy may have been understood, it offered little comfort to those whose circumstances were so miserable. Motivated partly by the wish to provide a better place for some of their rural compatriots but also out of old enmity, the Athenians expelled the Aeginetans from their island and settled some of their own people there.

Archidamus moved his army to Acharnae, ten kilometers north of Athens, and set up camp. He thought the Athenians would come out and meet him in battle. Many of the young men in the city were impatient to do just this, and the Acharnians demanded it. Their settlement was relatively large with 3,000 hoplites of its own, representing as much as a seventh of Attica's entire levy. Under such circumstances, Pericles had a hard time maintaining his policy of nonaggression. At times he even prevented the popular assembly from meeting. All he was willing to do was send out cavalry to keep the fields outside the city gates safe from enemy raids.

Without a battle to fight, the Spartans and their allies concentrated on mowing down the grain that had just ripened and otherwise laying the land to waste. Soon afterward they withdrew.

The Attic navy had meanwhile sailed around the Peloponnese, landed in various places, and begun ravaging them. The Athenians won over the island of Cephallenia at the entry to the Corinthian Gulf. Pericles himself led an army of 13,000 hoplites, including 3,000 metics, in an invasion of Megarian territory. In the north, Athens concluded a treaty with the powerful Thracian king Sitalces, whose help was sought against the Macedonians and whose son was granted Athenian citizenship. Soon after this, games in honor of the Thracian moon goddess Bendis were instituted in Piraeus.

In the fall of 431 the Athenians held their first celebration since the outbreak of the war honoring the men killed in battle. It was on this occasion that Pericles delivered his funeral oration.

In his speech, praise for the city is followed by praise for the dead. In conclusion, Pericles offers words of consolation to the bereaved families and encourages those who are able to have more children. This would not only help them overcome their sadness but would also be a twofold benefit to the city: keeping it from becoming deserted and adding to its security. The latter end would be achieved not so much because the sons would later serve as soldiers but because the assembly's sense of responsibility would be strengthened. "It is impossible for men to reach fair and just decisions unless all share in danger equally as fathers," Pericles continues.

The celebrations in honor of the war dead lasted three days. First the remains of the dead were laid on a large platform, where the families could place objects to be buried with them. On the third day the bodies were put into great cypress coffins, one for each tribe, and driven to a cemetery in Ceramicus. An empty one was taken along for the missing in action. Anyone was allowed to follow behind, citizens, foreigners, even female relatives. After the grave was filled with earth, the speech in honor of the dead was delivered. Afterward all wailed in mourning for those they had lost, and then they went home. The names of the dead were later engraved in stone in lists organized by tribes. Thus in death a true equality prevailed, whereas in life Athenian equality was in fact limited.

In the spring of 430, after the Peloponnesians and their allies had once more invaded Attica, "the disease," as Thucydides called the plague, broke out there. The exact medical nature of the epidemic is unclear. Thucydides, who was infected himself, described the symptoms in detail. The illness began with a burning feeling in the head, inflammation of the eyes, and irritation and bleeding inside the mouth. Then it moved to the chest and stomach and caused cramps, coughing, vomiting, and diarrhea. If death did not occur then—seven to nine days after onset—the disease attacked the intestines, genitals, and limbs. Many lost their eyesight and memory.

The skin of the body became reddish, covered all over with rashes and ulcers. The stricken felt terribly hot and suffered from thirst, insomnia, and anxiety. Perhaps worst of all was the depression that usually accompanied the illness and made patients give up hope. The disease attacked indiscriminately, taking the strong and the weak alike.

As no one was familiar with the illness, the physicians had no cures to offer. The danger of contagion was considered extremely high and reduced the willingness of healthy people to take care of the sick. Only those who felt it shameful to place personal safety above concern for others tended to the infirm, and among these the number of fatalities was correspondingly large.

The cramped conditions of the city made things even worse. Those who had left their homes in the countryside and were living in miserable shelters suffered more than the rest. Corpses lay everywhere; dying people underwent convulsions in the streets; the half dead crowded around the fountains, desperate for water. Even the sanctuaries were full of dead bodies, although this violated all rules. Survivors began to grow indifferent. Families buried their dead wherever they could. If someone built a funeral pyre, others might place the corpses of their own relatives on it and light the fire before the person returned. People also threw corpses on pyres that were already burning and ran off as quickly as possible.

People began to lose all restraint. Everybody did what he pleased without regard to law or custom; after all, who knew if one was going to live for more than a few days? Respect for the gods was lost since both the devout and the nonbelievers suffered and died. No one expected to live long enough to be brought to justice for crimes committed during the plague.

For two years, 430 and 429, the plague wreaked havoc. It abated briefly but flared up again in the winter of 427–426 and lasted for another year. More than four thousand hoplites and three hundred knights died, according to Thucydides. The number of other fatalities, he stated, was beyond calculation. It must have been close to twenty thousand. Nothing else during the Peloponnesian War hit Athens as hard or weakened its might and its economy as drastically. The Athenians were so discouraged that they sent a delegation to Sparta to initiate peace talks, but without success.

The people's anger was directed at Pericles. He was tried in court, stripped of his office as *strategos*, and fined heavily, probably early in 429. But the city did not take long to change its mind, as, in Thucydides' words, "the masses are apt to do." The citizens reappointed him *strategos* for the year 429–428. But he was no longer able to do much for Athens. The preceding few months had taken a heavy toll on him. Not only had he suffered political defeat, but he had lost his two sons to the plague. In order to have any heirs at all, he pushed through the temporary repeal of the law of citizenship of 451 he himself had proposed, so that his son by Aspasia could become an Attic citizen. The repeal may have also been intended to replenish the ranks of citizens in general. Soon after, in the fall of 429, Pericles died at the age of about sixty-five. In all likelihood, he did not die of the plague because he was sick for several weeks, while those who died of the plague perished more quickly.

Pericles, whose name is associated with democracy and with an era of his city's history, was not the creator of "Periclean Athens" in the same sense that Themistocles had been the creator of the Attic navy or Cleisthenes that of the new phyles. The demotion of the Areopagus, which marked the beginning of Athenian democracy, had been accomplished with Pericles' help but not on his initiative. He is credited with extending government by the people through instituting payment for public service, increasing the number of official jobs, and instituting the selection of officeholders by lottery. It is not clear to what extent the transformation of the Delian League into an Athenian empire was already under way when Pericles began to exert a significant influence on Attic policies.

But from the early 440s on, Pericles was the undisputed leader of Athens. He put his stamp on the city to such an extent that the term "Periclean Athens" is fully justified. It was due to Pericles that the city kept the Delian League alive despite the Peace of Callias and the failure of efforts to win new legitimation for the league's continued existence. Athens not only kept the league alive but extended its realm and invested a great deal of energy in its service. Pericles' influence encouraged the Attic citizens to devote much of their lives to their com-

Pericles, thought to be part of a statue placed near the Propylaeum on the Acropolis. The statue was probably a nude, carrying a lance in the left hand. The helmet indicates Pericles' status as a strategos. The face reveals no individual traits. The statue was meant to meet the expectations much of the public had of how a leading politician should be portrayed. Copy made after a contemporary work. London, British Museum.

munity, which was therefore increasingly a democratic one. Pericles also gave the Acropolis the shape that was to distinguish it through the ages by building the Parthenon.

Athens could have instead followed the path advocated by Thucydides, son of Melesias (and not the historian), and maintained its rule cautiously, making minor concessions here and there. But that would not have resolved the question of what purpose the league still served.

Whatever his reservations, Pericles stated clearly the direction things should take: Athens was totally committed to maintaining the league and took all necessary steps to do so. But because Athens' hegemony over the league was exercised by a democracy, this commitment had to be publicly acknowledged, and the entire community had to be willing to fight for it.

Pericles' strength consisted primarily in his ability to detect and articu-

The Acropolis, seen from the west

late the goals of his city. It appears that most of the middle classes and especially the lower ones identified with these goals. It would have been unimaginable to give up the city's power, the revenues that power brought to the city, and the navy (whose vessels lost their seaworthiness if kept out of the water too long). How could the entire city, at the height of its power, after thirty years of determined political effort, return to a quiescent cantonal existence? Consequently it was crucial, as Pericles says in Thucydides' account, that the Athenians fearlessly acknowledge what they had won, and he sought to bring about the necessary conditions for this to happen. Enactment of the law of citizenship was one way of furthering this goal.

There was no example for Pericles to follow because no Greek city had ever found itself in such a position. The past offered no guidance. Pericles invented a new kind of politics. His convictions were gradually reinforced by the results they produced in shaping Athens and its political life.

It might be suggested that Pericles fell victim to the dynamic he had done so much to set in motion. But Periclean Athens could not have lasted forever. It owed its existence to exceptional circumstances, specifically, the conditions created by Pericles in the 440s and 430s, the tasks and opportunities that had arisen during the war against the Persians, and the extraordinary circumstances under which it was able to pit itself, with the scant resources of a Greek polis, against the Eastern empire.

The culture that had produced democracy had also prepared the way for the development of philosophical reflection, the concept of man, and the idea of proportion. A spirit of critical inquiry lay behind these remarkable achievements. And the creations, ideas, and values that Periclean Athens generated still speak to us powerfully.

It must be borne in mind that much of what Pericles attempted and accomplished during his reign was considered audacious and reckless in many quarters. But in spite of all the justified and sharp criticism his contemporaries in Athens and beyond leveled at him, Pericles could hardly have realized the fragility of the course he was pursuing with such determination. He could at most be accused of adhering to his highly rational mode and applying maxims from the world of the old epics and the old Greek aristocracy to a situation that was totally new. "To be hated and unpopular in the present has always been the fate of those who consider themselves worthy of ruling over others. He who experiences the greatest animosity is on the right path," Thucydides reports him to have said, as if the hatred of others were a criterion of proper action.

This was a profoundly Greek sentiment, and the Greeks never abandoned it, partly because they knew, like Herodotus, that human affairs followed a circular course. Fame was the way to break out of the circle and make possible a brilliant future. Apparently Pericles thought similarly when doubts assailed him about what lay in store for Athens as a city.

Greek culture was strongly marked by aristocratic standards, even the democratic polis of Athens. The role Pericles assigned to Athens—politically and militarily—followed these standards and was consequently highly ambitious. But the city played its part so well that it ended up becoming not only the "School of Greece" but the school of all Europe.

One wonders if there is some deeper significance to the fact that of the three great statesmen who led Athens in the fifth century, only one died in full honor. This was the uncomplicated Cimon, who trusted his senses and, though defending Athens' interests vigorously, was sympathetic to Panhellenic ideas and maintained friendships in Sparta. By contrast, Themistocles ended his life in exile and Pericles was removed from office, to be restored to it only when he was already close to death.

It seems likely that Sophocles' tragedy *Oedipus Rex* was first performed soon after Pericles' death. At the beginning of the play a devastating plague is ravaging Thebes. Many of the details are reminiscent of the plague in Athens, but in this case even plants and animals are afflicted. A vengeful god is punishing the city and its land. Oedipus sends for the oracle at Delphi and is told that the city is suffering from a "defilement" because the murder of King Laius has not been avenged. Until the murderer is punished, there is no hope of relief. After cursing the murderer and those witnesses who have failed to shed light on the deed, Oedipus launches an inquiry.

He discovers that the man he himself killed many years ago at the crossing of three roads was his father, and that Jocasta, the woman he married shortly thereafter, and who has borne his children, is also his mother.

Oedipus had acted within the law when he slew the man who attacked him. And his marriage to the queen was a well-deserved reward for having rid the country of a monster, the Sphinx. The reason he did not recognize his own parents is that he had been taken from his family shortly after birth and raised by other parents.

But great as his accomplishments were, Oedipus had acted blindly. Now that he sees the truth, he blinds himself. It never occurs to him to try to exculpate himself, to say that he had no way of knowing what he was doing. He accepts his fate and is prepared to go into exile, just as he had vowed to demand of the murderer.

Oedipus Rex is the tragedy of a man honored for the great services he has rendered the city. His fellow citizens, whom he addresses as "children," look to him with admiration. He is intelligent, enlightened, and truthful; his only flaw is his ignorance of the fact that he himself is the cause of his city's misfortunes.

The priest in Sophocles' play had earlier warned: "Let us not have to remember of your reign that it raised us up only to plunge us down again." When Tiresias tells Oedipus during the investigation that Oedipus himself is the man he is seeking, the king refuses to believe him. He accuses his brother-in-law, Creon, of having set Tiresias against him. He suspects a conspiracy and considers executing Creon, as a tyrant would his enemies. Creon reminds him of the ideal of democracy and says that he only wants an equal share of power. Oedipus, who has earlier declared that he acts with the well-being of the polis in mind, claims that his rule is necessary. "Not if your rule is unjust," Creon rejoins.

A little later Jocasta upbraids Oedipus for having become the slave of his moods, taking counsel from anyone who happens to be near. She denies the possibility of what Pericles was so proud, the use of foresight to direct events; instead, she believes, man's life is ruled by chance.

In its memorable hymn in the middle of the tragedy, the chorus praises the unwritten laws, "For God is great in them and grows not old. . . . Insolence breeds the tyrant." There follows a passage reminiscent of the contest between Pericles and Thucydides; the chorus asserts that such "wrestling" benefits the city. It prays that high ambition may never cease.

But, it warns, "If a man walks with haughtiness / of hand or word and gives no heed / to Justice and the shrines of Gods / despises—may an evil doom / smite him for his ill-starred pride of heart!" If injustice triumphs, it asks, echoing the attitudes of many Athenians during the plague, "why should I honor the gods in the dance?" Nowhere else in Greek literature is the claim of tragedy so exalted and its meaning questioned so profoundly as in this hymn.

If *Oedipus Rex* was indeed modeled after Pericles, the message of the tragedy is that the great and intelligent man who ruled like a despot offended the order of the world without knowing it. He did as much harm as good. Sophocles did not state this directly—it was not something tragedy could say—but there are plenty of hints to this effect and many listeners must have understood the play in this sense. It must have made people think of Athens and of Pericles. The play would then, despite all the respect implicit in it for Pericles and Athens, have been an expression of profound concern.

About a year after Pericles' death and the performance of *Oedipus Rex*, in Attic in the year 428–427, a son was born to one of the most distinguished families of Athens. The father was Ariston, the mother, Perictione, and the child was named Plato. After Ariston's death, his mother married Pyrilampes, the aforementioned wealthy friend of Pericles who both served as an envoy and gained fame in Athens for the peacocks he raised.

The war between the Athenians and the Peloponnesians continued with no major changes for six years, until the spring of 425. Both sides repeatedly launched sallies into enemy territory without being able to engage the opponent in battle. The damage inflicted was generally not very serious and neither side seems to have known what to do to break the impasse.

It was only on the periphery that more ambitious military operations were undertaken, primarily by the Athenians. In western Greece, where Corinth had some colonies and garrisons, there lived several warlike mountain tribes that the Athenians wanted to enlist as allies and into whose local hostilities they became drawn. Athens was quite successful in these efforts, though the plan devised by its general, Demosthenes, of invading central Greece from the west with the aid of local allies did not work out.

Most important, the Athenians succeeded, with some difficulty, in maintaining an alliance with Corcyra, which was itself in the grip of civil war. The democratic forces there were more powerful than the elite, and they also received more energetic support from Athens than the oligarchs did from Sparta.

Corcyra was especially important to the Athenians because it could serve as a way station to Sicily, in whose affairs they wanted to interfere, though with only a small force. Athens' Sicilian allies were at war with Syracuse, and the Athenians' primary motive was to keep Syracuse from gaining further power. But Athens was probably also eager to draw Syracuse into battles, because the city was on friendly terms with the Corinthians and might support them militarily. If that happened, the Peloponnesian naval forces would finally have overcome their inferiority to the Athenians'. After a short time, however, the Sicilian Greeks settled their differences and stayed out of the Greek war.

Sparta tried repeatedly to win Persia's support and dispatched several delegations. At one point the Athenians intercepted a Persian envoy and learned that the great king was puzzled by the message from the Spartans. Apparently the Spartans had requested money from him but were reluctant to say what they were willing to do in return. The only possible offer they could have made was to recognize and further his rule over the Greek cities in Asia Minor. But that would have blatantly contradicted Sparta's claim to be the liberator of Greece.

Plans put forth by the Corinthians to build up a navy of their own with money borrowed from Delphi and Olympia were never realized, if they were ever seriously pursued.

On the whole, it was possible to keep the Delian League intact. The cities in the Chalcidice that had defected had to be given up for the time being, but Potidaea surrendered after a siege of more than two years. Only one other Athenian ally rebelled, in 428, Mytilene on Lesbos, which was the most important polis on the island. After Athens' victory over Samos, Mytilene and Chios were the last truly autonomous confederates, supplying their own ships instead of paying tribute. The Athenians learned of Mytilene's intentions before the rebellious polis had finished its preparations; the harbor and city were not yet sufficiently fortified, nor had the troops from sympathetic city-states arrived to aid in the uprising. Even the support Sparta had promised did not come in time, so the Athenians were able to subdue the city easily.

The Spartan fleet, under way for Mytilene, turned back when it heard the city had fallen, despite the urgings of the Lesbian and Ionian sailors that the commander keep his course with the hope of surprising the Athenians and thereby turning the course of the revolt. Thucydides reports that the same men next suggested that the Spartans should take Cyme or some other Ionian city and stir up a revolt there, cutting Athens off from an important source of revenue. If it sent a fleet out to quell the revolt, the effort would cost them additional money. This suggestion was not without merit, but the Spartan commander, Aleidas, was most interested in returning to the safety of the Peloponnesian coast. Sparta was still far from feeling comfortable on the wide-open sea.

The war dragged on indecisively. The Athenians mounted some attacks into Megarian territories, and the Spartans besieged and captured Plataea. Pericles had once declared that the Spartans, though successful in battles, lacked the stamina for a major, prolonged war, but it now turned out that the Athenians, too, found such a war difficult to endure. It might have been easier for them if they had taken the offensive: their strategy of attrition, in any case, was bearing little fruit.

But neither side was prepared to engage in full-scale war until the spring of 425. Both sides lacked the strategies and, probably, the imagination for it. The Spartans continued their annual springtime raids on Attica, never remaining there longer than forty days. They took the harvest, destroyed vineyards and houses, and cut down fig and olive trees, but it is not known how thorough they were in their destruction. Their small, roaming troops of soldiers were constantly subject to counterattack from Attic cavalry.

The Athenians had several strongholds in the Attic countryside, which offered some protection to the surrounding areas, especially in the south, where the mines continued to operate throughout the war. The Spartans penetrated into this area only once. After the Spartans left, the Athenians always resumed possession of the land, and they probably planted the fields anew. It is unknown how much reciprocal damage the Athenians caused on the Peloponnese peninsula.

The Spartans once planned a second, summer attack on Attica, but they could raise barely any troops. The men were busy working their own land, and the number of Spartiates—Spartans with full citizen rights—who could have spared the time probably did not exceed 3,000 or 4,000. The Spartans generally included in their military campaigns the *perioeci*, literally "dwellers around," a class of people who lived freely in communities of their own but had no political rights, but apparently even they could not be called on indefinitely. And there was the constant danger of helot uprisings.

Theoretically, the Athenians had more forces at their disposal, but they seem not to have made full use of them. The plague had reduced their numbers somewhat, but more important was the fact that their resources were being used up faster than anticipated. In 428–427 Athens had to impose a three-percent property tax, which brought in 200 talents. From this time onward they also sent out ships regularly to collect the confederates' dues for the coming year. The loans the treasurer of the Delian League had taken from the temple treasuries since the beginning of the war already came to about 7,000 talents, interest included, by the year 422, a thousand talents more than Pericles had proudly declared the city's treasury contained. It should be mentioned, though, that the Athenians still had 1,000 talents set aside, to be touched only if a foreign fleet threatened Athens.

By 425–424 the dues of the cities belonging to the Delian League had to be raised. They were increased over 300 percent. Even if we take into consideration that the dues had up to now been based on Aristides' assessments and were therefore relatively low, the new rates still represented a significant burden, which was borne primarily by the well-to-do; the middle class and the poor were hardly in a position to contribute much.

.   .   .

In spite of both sides' difficulties mustering troops and funds, the war, once begun, developed a dynamic of its own even during the first six years. It drew the opposing sides—and an ever growing number of participants—more and more into its orbit.

The combatants came to rely heavily on new types of combat units. Battles fought by hoplites became increasingly rare. With the larger scale of warfare what mattered most were speed of troop movements, blockage of the enemy's approach, control of larger territories, and, sometimes, the devastation of entire regions. To meet these new realities and to provide a distinguished function for young gentlemen of the city's noble families, the Athenians created a division of 1,200 cavalry troops. They also kept a standing force of thousands of lightly armed soldiers, among them 1,600 Thracian archers.

The cavalry were not of much use in a close battle against a phalanx, and their activities were limited by their lack of saddles or stirrups. But the cavalry could interfere with the formation of the phalanx, attack

The agora of Athens, seen from the south. The Hephaesteum is at the left.

from the flank, and intervene when a line began to give way or retreated. Then they could assist either defensively by protecting the soldiers of their own side or offensively, helping seal the victory. The cavalry could move fast, an important asset both in defending the coast and in making incursions into enemy territory. Soon after 425, the Spartans were forced by the Athenians' methods to build up a cavalry force of their own, even though this was in complete opposition to their ideas of proper warfare.

The new lightly armed troops could, similarly, be used in varied ways. Considerable advances were made in siege tactics during this period. Extraordinary amounts of labor were invested in sieges, and the technique continuously evolved. For the siege of Plataea in 429–428, the Spartans and their allies worked day and night for seventy days building a huge mound of earth up against Plataea's city wall. The Plataeans responded by raising the height of their wall, digging a tunnel beneath it and the mound, and carting off the lower layers of earth. When the enemy brought battering rams to the walls, the Plataeans caught some of them in lassoes and broke off the front ends of others with heavy beams dropped from poles extending beyond the walls. The Spartans responded by moving huge piles of wood between the mound and the wall and setting them on fire with the help of sulphur and pitch. It was the biggest fire ever set by human hands, but a heavy rain thwarted this attempt as well. The Peloponnesians contented themselves with cutting the city off from its surroundings. After their provisions ran out, the Plataeans capitulated. The Spartans killed most of the men and sold the women as slaves.

Not many years later, in 423, the besiegers of Delium would use a new device. They hollowed out long tree trunks like flutes, placed bellows at one end and bowls filled with hot coals at the other. The coals were then fanned to flame to set the city's wooden palisades on fire.

Above all else, the cruelty of the war was escalating. The debate on Mytilene, reported in detail by Thucydides, is a prime example. It also gives us some insight into the conflicts within Attica's popular assembly of those days: When the Mytilenians surrendered, the assembly decided to execute not only those who had actively opposed Athens but the city's entire adult male population, and to sell the women and children as slaves. The measure had been proposed by Cleon, son of Cleaenetus, who was the man most trusted by the common people at the time and was known to favor violent means. A trireme was dispatched, charged with executing the decree. But the next day many in the assembly regretted the decision, and the outvoted politicians were able to call another meeting to overturn it.

Cleon subjected those gathered to a tirade, passed down to us in one of the speeches of Thucydides' *History*. Their softheartedness, Cleon said, rendered them utterly gullible; they looked at things from a merely aesthetic point of view and seemed to confuse the popular assembly with the theater. The citizenry, he ranted, was like a childish and fickle audience, always demanding something new and anticipating the dialogue so as to applaud the punch lines before they could be uttered. They let themselves be duped by these orators, he said, who acted out of self-interest or had been bribed. They did not behave like citizens discussing the welfare of their city.

Cleon followed this upbraiding with a presentation of his own conviction that anyone choosing to revolt must know that treason is punishable by death. He argued that the Athenians either had to exercise their rule with utter ruthlessness or else give up ruling altogether.

We know nothing of the speaker who answered him except his name, Diodotus, son of Eucrates. He objected to Cleon's method of intimidating listeners with insinuations and called instead for real orators and objective, nonslanderous debate.

Regarding the case at hand, Diodotus argued that if the Athenians executed not only the ringleaders of the Mytilene revolt but the entire population, they would lose many potential allies. The common people of Mytilene had only joined the revolt under pressure of force and had handed the city over to the Athenians as soon as they had weapons.

The assembly was nearly equally divided, but by a narrow margin ultimately voted against killing all the Mytilenians. A second ship was dispatched one day after the first. The Mytilenian delegation that had traveled to Athens supplied the crew with plenty of wine and flour and promised rewards if they arrived before the first ship. Half of the crew ate while the other half rowed, and the men took turns sleeping. There was no headwind, and the first ship had been in no particular hurry, so the second ship managed to land on Lesbos just as the Attic commander was ordering the execution and too late to halt it.

The entire upper class of the city, more than 1,000 men, was put to death as Cleon had decreed. It is hard to imagine how it was done, and it could not have been very easy. Diodotus had argued that the fate of the Mytilenians should be determined dispassionately, but at least to this degree Cleon had his way.

It is doubtful that Cleon's decree served to strengthen Attic rule. But it clearly demonstrated that brute violence—quite apart from the acts of war—was in the ascendancy, even though a far greater slaughter had just barely been avoided in Mytilene.

The spiral of violence reached particular heights in the civil war of Corcyra. One of the leaders of the common people in Corcyra had wanted to extend the treaty with Athens so that the two city-states would officially have the same friends and enemies. Corinthian sympathizers responded by killing him and about sixty of his followers. In the struggle that ensued, the people's party eventually triumphed after it had enlisted the mass of slaves by promising them freedom. Even the women took part, hurling bricks and entering the fray "contrary to their nature," as a commentator notes. The Peloponnesians and Athenians were drawn into the war in support of the oligarchs and the democrats, respectively. An agreement brokered by an Attic commander did not hold, and the conflict ended in a horrible massacre.

The defenders of democracy locked some of their foes into a sanctuary, which the latter had entered as suppliants. Some of them were induced to come out, given mock trials, and put to death; many of the others "killed each other there in the temple, some hanged themselves on the trees, or others found various other means of committing suicide," Thucydides writes. For seven days, as long as the Attic squadron was present, the democrats murdered anybody they suspected of being an enemy; in the process some debtors also seized the opportunity to rid themselves of their creditors. Fathers slew their sons, and many victims were pulled away from the gods' altars or killed where they stood; others were walled up in the temple of Dionysus and left to die.

Thucydides follows this description with the famous passage known as "The Pathology of War." These events, he writes, caused great consternation because they were the first to demonstrate such profound hatred, but afterward such incidents were to occur quite often. Throughout Greece, democratic leaders called the Athenians to their aid, and oligarchs called upon the Spartans. In peacetime such appeals would likely have been ignored, but now each side in regional struggles requested and received outside help.

"The sufferings which revolution brought upon the cities," Thucydides writes, "were many and terrible, such as have occurred and always will occur, as long as the nature of mankind remains the same. . . . In peace and prosperity states and individuals have nobler sentiments, because they do not find themselves suddenly confronted with imperious necessities; but war takes away the easy supply of daily wants, and so proves a rough master who brings most men's characters to a level with their fortunes." Men lose their reserves, Thucydides continues, no matter how great the strength they have built up in the past is depleted. Men become the helpless victims of circumstance, completely dominated by the events taking place. This mood spread through Greece like another plague. What took place in one polis was imitated in the next; indeed, it was carried out with greater malice, more intrigue, and a stronger desire for retaliation.

Thucydides records that the very meaning of words changed: "Reckless audacity came to be considered courage; prudent hesitation became cowardice; and moderation was held to be a cloak for unmanliness. The extremist was considered trustworthy."

Politicians formed factions, one side supposedly fighting for democracy, the other for the aristocracy. In reality, the polis, whose well-being the orators claimed to serve, was the prize each side tried to wrest from the other. The factions formed "not for mutual benefit and to obey the laws but in violation of the laws and to increase personal power and property."

Even blood ties were subordinated to the demands of the factions, which now determined all political action. All energies were concentrated on helping these political groups attain power, which Thucydides writes was "sought out of lust for it and out of ambition." In their passionate commitment to the factions, people no longer looked beyond the immediate future; everyone was intent on attaining a momentary advantage. Trust was supplanted by suspicion, decency by deceit, and the thirst for power made coexistence increasingly difficult. Those appealing to the lower instincts usually won the upper hand.

The Peloponnesian War shook the very foundations from which the communal life of the cities had grown. The lament, often voiced in the past, that man was like a leaf in the wind, buffeted about by Zeus, acquired a new meaning. Since the old days, customs and conviction, the acceptance of lawfulness, and the functioning of institutions had inhibited man but also allowed him to rise above the illusions and temptations of the moment. Now this store of moral values was running low—as were many other supplies.

In some cities such warring factions never arose; in others the drift to anarchy was successfully fought. When the city of Megara, for example, readmitted exiled aristocrats, it had them swear *mè mnesikakeîn*—"I will not remember past injustice." Of course, this oath was promptly forgotten as soon as some of the oath-takers were back in office.

The civil war in Corcyra came to an end in 425, when the democratic leaders tricked most of their opponents into surrendering under false terms and then locked them into a building, from which they were taken in groups of ten and forced to run a gauntlet to the place of execution. When the rest refused to come out, the roof was torn off, and the unfortunates within were bombarded with bricks and arrows. Those not killed by the barrage did anything they could to kill themselves as quickly as possible. Some stuck arrows in their throats, others hanged themselves with strips of bedding or clothing. The next morning the victors loaded the corpses on wagons and drove them out of the city. The second Athenian squadron, which had been present while all this was taking place, left the harbor and headed for Sicily.

After Pericles' death the policies of Athens seem to have been determined primarily by Cleon, who was about fifty years old at that time. His principal opponent was a man his age or slightly older, Nicias, son of Niceratus. Both men, as well as the other less well known politicians, tried at first to continue the war along Pericles' plans.

Nicias was very wealthy; his property was estimated at 100 talents. He owned 1,000 slaves who worked as miners and whom he rented out in the mining region of Laurion. This alone brought him an annual income of $8^1/_2$ talents. Whether he also operated mines on his own is unknown. Cleon was the owner of a large tannery and manufactured leather goods with the labor of his slaves. Neither man belonged to the old Attic aristocracy.

Nicias tried to imitate Pericles' style in appearance and demeanor, but he was a different kind of man from the statesman who had guided Athens during its greatness. Though he cultivated an image quite different from Pericles' superior and relaxed one, he admired Pericles' "statesmanlike" quality and tried, rather ineffectively, to imitate that. Like Pericles, he, too, avoided social gatherings and parties. A conscientious man, Nicias took his duties seriously. He put in long days as a holder of public office and would almost certainly have drawn attention to how hard he worked compared to Pericles.

Nicias's conscientiousness extended to his way of life, in which honor played a conspicuous role. He adhered strictly to traditional customs and laws. He served repeatedly as *choregos*, producing plays at the Great Dionysia and outdoing everyone else in the magnificence displayed. Above all he was devout, making daily offerings, and he employed a soothsayer on whose advice he relied heavily. He took all omens seriously and seems to have been fearfully superstitious. Pericles' enlightenment was totally foreign to him.

An extremely reserved and shy man, he was not popular. The prestige he enjoyed among the masses seems to have been based on the general conviction that he was trustworthy and reliable, and the well-to-do regarded him as the defender of their interests. But Nicias's scrupulous

Temple of Athena Nike, on a Mycenaean bulwark on the southwestern spur of the Acropolis. Erected in the years 427–424 B.C.

loyalty, which made him respect not just the laws but democracy as well, apparently prevented him from taking positions opposed to the majority of the demos. Doubtless he was also motivated by tactical considerations.

From 427–426 on, Nicias was repeatedly elected *strategos*. He was an experienced and effective commander, but it was said that he hesitated and lost where he could have won victories. He was confident only in situations that could be easily surveyed and in which he had sufficient forces at his command. Unusual situations unnerved him. Fortunately for him, he did not have to deal with real difficulties until 415, on the Sicilian expedition, where the results were catastrophic.

Cleon was in many ways the exact opposite of the upright, honorable Nicias. He was a man of strong, imperious, and unrestrained character. Unlike Nicias, whose timid caution expressed feelings of inadequacy in the face of Athens' huge problems, Cleon seems to have felt quite free and determined to run the city as he saw fit, with energy and without much scruple. Danger did not faze him, he liked to say, and he earned the reputation of being a boaster. He was willing to try almost anything, and identified with Athens' strength as well as with its tyrannical side.

He had even pitted himself against Pericles in earlier days. In a comedy by Hermippus, probably performed in the first year of the war, Pericles is called the "king of the satyrs," a leader who likes to make speeches but is reluctant to go to war. If even the smallest knife is sharpened, Pericles winces, as if "bitten by fiery Cleon." Cleon thus seems to have excoriated Pericles' reluctance to engage in land battles.

When he decided to enter political life, Cleon is said to have cut off his friendships, as they would have interfered with his new duties. His friendship, indeed, his love, belonged to the people. He seems to have stressed this much more than Pericles and in a different way.

Little is known about Cleon's education, but he often acted crudely and expressed his scorn for education in general, both the traditional aristocratic kind and the new rhetorical cleverness. He was the first person to shout, curse, and gesticulate wildly in the popular assembly. In all likelihood, Pericles also made use of his hands when speaking. Like any other orator, he must have spoken as loudly as he could, or people could not have heard him in the assembly. He must sometimes have been carried away by passion. But Cleon apparently crossed borders that Pericles and his contemporaries still respected. And he probably did so deliberately; he wanted to make common cause with the masses.

For all his crudeness, Cleon accomplished a great deal for Athens. He, too, was conscientious, though not in the same way as Nicias. He carefully monitored those in his command, and may even have spied on them, and he was quick to suspect conspiracy. He pitilessly took to court anyone who failed to do the work assigned to him. He was full of Athenian enthusiasm and his boundless energy seems to have made him indispensable.

The Athenian people were especially demanding of their generals. Paches, who had engineered the victory at Lesbos, is said to have pulled out his sword and killed himself when the people's court demanded he explain an episode of misconduct. In 424, two admirals involved in the Sicily campaign were exiled and one was fined for having accepted bribes. Thucydides remarks, "So great was the Athenians' confidence that they accomplished not only the possible but the almost impossible as well, whether their resources were plentiful or scarce. The source of their confidence was that most of their undertakings had succeeded beyond expectation, which in turn greatly increased their expectations."

Such zeal could be acted on in different ways. Cleon's essential characteristic was the iron will with which he pursued his goals, recklessly, thoughtlessly, and regardless of cost. This was precisely what seems to have impressed the Athenians about him, though some disliked his boastfulness. It turned out that Cleon could achieve much that others lacked the courage to try. Ruthlessness often has this effect if the people are unaccustomed to it. The greatest problem is that such success is not proof of actual ability.

In January of 425, when Aristophanes was probably about twenty-five, his comedy *The Acharnians* was produced. It was one of his first plays and is the oldest that has survived. The farmer Dicaeopolis is sitting in the popular assembly, listening to various delegations deliver false reports of battlefield victories. Dicaeopolis observes that all the delegates were really interested in was eating well and receiving travel expenses. Suddenly, the assembly ends without any discussion about peace—which Dicaeopolis earnestly yearns for—having taken place. To make things worse, Dicaeopolis's garlic bag is stolen by a group of mercenaries.

Dicaeopolis then goes off and concludes a separate peace of his own, which will entail thirty years of wine deliveries from Sparta. (The Greek word for treaty was also used for the distribution of wine, which was customary at the signing of peace treaties.) The chorus, a group of elderly charcoal-burners from Acharnae, want to stone him to death. They despise him even more than Cleon, for to sneak out of the city to negotiate with the enemy is worse to them than pushing through a misguided policy. The only way the defector is allowed to speak to them is to actually put his head on the block. He is able to convince the Acharnians not to kill him and to accept the peace. The war, it turns out, was caused by a ridiculous incident in which a drunken Athenian had abducted a prostitute from Megara. In retaliation the Megarians stole two Athenian girls, who were, unfortunately, employed by Aspasia. Pericles punished Megara by issuing the Megarian decree, and from there things took their inevitable course. By taking offense, Dicaeopolis says, Sparta reacted no differently than Athens would have under the same circumstances.

Having won the debate, Dicaeopolis sets up a private market where the Megarians and the Boeotians can finally trade their long-embargoed goods. While Dicaeopolis gets ready to go to the celebratory feast, the general, Lamachus, is called to the front. The two men take turns speaking. Lamachus orders his pack, while Dicaeopolis requests a food basket; Lamachus demands bread and onions (the soldier's diet), while Dicaeopolis asks for freshwater fish; the general requisitions "salt meat, even if it is rancid"; the farmer, having concluded peace, orders fresh meat for cooking. At the end of the play, one drags himself home, gravely wounded and supported by two soldiers, while the other, tipsy and well fed, walks home leaning on two girls and looking forward to the pleasures of bed.

Was this political propaganda, delivered in comic form? The comedy clearly satirizes Cleon, who had earlier publicly attacked Aristophanes for making fun of the polis and offending the demos and had summoned him before the council. In the play, the politicians, ambitious bureaucrats, and hypocrites are all raked over the coals, and the rationale of the war is questioned.

But if the point of propaganda is to indoctrinate and keep people from forming their own judgment, Aristophanes aimed at the exact opposite. He offered the spectators a chance to look at themselves in a mirror and to recognize their powerless dependence on politicians. The spectators are made to recognize their self-induced indoctrination and to see in themselves either the Acharnians' stupid enthusiasm for war or Dicaeopolis's longing for peace—or both at once. Aristophanes offers the spectators a chance to achieve self-knowledge by laughing at themselves. This comedy offered no advice for action, but it may well have had an indirect effect, encouraging criticism and informed decision, which this democracy urgently needed.

The previous year, in his lost comedy *The Babylonians*, Aristophanes depicted Athens' allies as mill slaves who complained about their miserable lot. This was what had sparked Cleon's wrath. Now Aristophanes' chorus speaks directly to the audience about Aristophanes, claiming that he had really done the Athenians a service by teaching them not to be fooled by their allies and showing them the true nature of democratic rule in these cities. This can perhaps be most logically understood as suggesting that the governments of these allies were democracies only in appearance and that the Athenians had let themselves be taken in by appearance, and therefore had exposed themselves to danger. Such an interpretation would be in keeping with Aristophanes' decision to have the "slaves" complain and at the same time flatter their master. Thus the Athenians also stood accused of being dupes.

Aristophanes' chorus declares proudly that his openness and courage in speaking the truth was one of the conditions for Athens' victory. For as they tell it, word of Aristophanes' fame had reached the Persian great king, who asked the Spartan envoys which of the two warring parties had the greater navy and which had been criticized by Aristophanes. The answer in both cases was obviously the Athenians, and the great king concluded that "those who have such a man as advisor must be the ablest people and they will win."

Far-fetched as this may sound, it should not be dismissed as mere comic buffoonery. The kind of candor Aristophanes displayed was a condition of democracy. It is no wonder that Cleon was furious. Aristophanes' satire not only exceeded Cleon's sense of humor (if he had one), it also seemed to weaken his iron will and undermine his attempt to mobilize the various forces. And that is exactly why this comedy was needed. Where Cleon's opponents had little chance of prevailing in the popular assembly, the poet could have an effect.

It is not clear to what extent the Acharnians in the play reflected the mood of the citizenry at the time of performance. We may assume that after six years of war, repeated devastation of their land, uncertainty, and evacuation the people were longing for peace. At the same time, like the Acharnians, they badly wanted revenge on the Spartans for what had been done to them. Was public opinion likely to favor peace? For the time being at least, the peace concluded by Dicaeopolis, a man of "proper, political, citizen-minded attitudes," had merely been a dream.

. . .

In the summer of 425 the war heated up again. The Attic fleet, sailing along the western coast of the Peloponnese on its way to Corcyra and Sicily, was forced by adverse winds to touch land in the harbor of Pylos in Messenia. It is not known if Demosthenes, son of Alcisthenes, planned it this way or if it happened by chance. He conceived the idea of occupying and fortifying the town, which had been deserted since the helot uprising of 464, reinhabiting it with Messenians who had moved to Naupactus, and inciting the Messenians who had remained in their homeland to revolt against their Spartan overlords. Judging by the Spartan response, the plan was an excellent one.

The Spartan forces that had just invaded Attica were recalled after fifteen days because their commanders considered it essential to drive the Athenians out of Pylos. They prepared to blockade the port and, after the Attic fleet had left for Corcyra, intended to cut off access by sea. For this purpose they occupied the long, narrow, uninhabited island of Sphacteria, which was situated in front of the harbor. They planned to bar the relatively narrow passage between it and the mainland with ships, but they never got that far. The Attic fleet hurried back, secured the harbor, and defeated the Peloponnesian forces. The Spartans had failed to take Pylos, and now the roles were reserved. The Athenians surrounded Sphacteria, where 420 Spartan hoplites were stationed, along with the helots who accompanied them as servants. All Spartan attempts to rescue them failed, and the most the Spartans could do was try to slip through the blockade with small boats, swimmers, or divers to keep the hoplites supplied with food.

From an overall perspective, 420 hoplites, including about 150 Spartiates, would seem to be a small number, but in view of the much diminished number of Spartan citizens, their importance was great. The Spartans could not bear the thought of losing them. They sent officials to investigate the situation personally, and when they heard that freeing the men on the island was out of the question, the Spartans said they wanted peace.

This incident is revealing. All it took for Sparta to feel pressured into giving up the "great war" was Athens' occupation of a strategically located harbor in Sparta's territory, a panic reaction by the Spartans, and the threat of death to 420 hoplites. Pericles' war plan seemed to be correct after all. Sparta's disappointment over the negligible successes of the preceding six years of war surely played a part in its decision, but it is still amazing that the fate of so few men swayed such a major power.

A truce was concluded. All the Spartan ships were handed over to the Athenians for the duration of the truce. In return, the men trapped on the island were to be supplied with fixed amounts of food. In the meantime a Spartan delegation was to negotiate in Athens. The delegation offered peace and an alliance—indeed, friendship—and demanded only one thing: that the men on Sphacteria be freed.

But the Athenians would not budge. The more fortune smiled on them, it seemed, the more they wanted. Thucydides makes no mention of any serious consideration of the Spartan proposal. He writes that Cleon, especially, urged the Athenians to respond by demanding that the men on the island surrender and be brought to Athens. Spartans were to return to Athens all the territories Athens had relinquished in the peace of 446, including the harbors of Megara and Troezen and the region of Achaea. Only then would the Spartans get their men back and could a treaty be concluded, the duration of which was yet to be discussed. When the Spartans asked to discuss the matter in a small group, the assembly, acting on Cleon's motion, denied the request angrily. The Spartans returned home, having failed in their mission.

The war resumed. The Athenians kept the Spartan ships under some pretext contrary to the terms of the truce. But their blockade of Sphacteria proved difficult because the blockaders themselves ran short of water and grain. They had hoped the Spartans would give in quickly, but food was regularly smuggled in to the men on the island. The Attic commanders feared they would have to break off the blockade.

In Athens, meanwhile, anger at Cleon mounted. He tried to assuage public opinion by claiming the commanders' fears were unfounded, whereupon the popular assembly commissioned him to go to Pylos himself to find out how things stood. He, in turn, made a counterproposal that a new contingent, with Nicias as commander, be dispatched to storm the island. Cleon claimed he could accomplish the task easily if he were a general, but that year he was not one. It must have been a dramatic scene, with proposals and counterproposals coming in rapid succession. Finally, Cleon's plan was accepted. Nicias offered him his command, and the assembly urged Cleon to accept it. His opponents did not object, figuring the Spartans might take him prisoner or, better yet, do away with him.

Cleon was lucky. Before he arrived, fire had broken out on the island, burning down the trees and undergrowth that acted as a shield. Demosthenes had already prepared for an attack and, with the reinforcement of Cleon's troops, now executed it. The landing succeeded. The Athenian force was far superior, thanks especially to its contingent of lightly armed soldiers. These troops were able to fight from a distance, shooting arrows and hurling rocks, spears, or whatever they found at hand at the Spartan hoplites, who were arranged in a classical phalanx. The Athenians caused a near panic among the Spartans, who found themselves enveloped by dust and smoke raised by the fire. They nevertheless fought on bravely, as the Spartans had done for centuries, until they were attacked from the rear. The battle went against all accepted rules and the Athenians used unscrupulous methods. It was as though a mob had been let loose on the aristocracy. Cleon's ruthlessness was a major factor in winning this victory.

When the Athenians had the Spartans surrounded, Demosthenes and Cleon called an end to the fighting. They wanted to take the enemy alive. Talks were held, and heralds went back and forth between the Spartan commanders on the mainland and the men on the island. At last, the commanders asked the men on the island to decide their fate themselves but to avoid doing anything dishonorable. The men decided on a course of action that went entirely against their tradition: They surrendered. There were 292 hoplites, among them 120 Spartiates.

All of Greece was astonished. No one had expected anything like this from the Spartans. One of the troops justified the decision by pointing out the irregularities of the battle, a battle they could not have won no matter how brave they were.

On Cleon's advice, the prisoners were put in chains in Athens. The Athenians threatened to kill them if the Peloponnesians invaded Attica again. The Athenians continued to occupy Pylos, and the Spartans, fearing a renewed helot revolt, sent several delegations asking to have the prisoners released for the sake of peace.

The following year, in 424, the Athenians occupied the island of Cythera, just south of the Peloponnese. The Spartan mainland now lay open to Athenian attack. The Spartans responded by organizing archery troops and a contingent of 400 cavalry. They saw themselves, as Thucydides wrote, "surrounded on all sides by a quick-moving war, against which they had no means to defend themselves."

Sea power had won out over land power; modern democracy had prevailed over the ancient aristocratic order. The chances for peace were excellent—if only the Athenians wanted it.

But they, too, found themselves overwhelmed by the newness of the situation; they did not know how to take advantage of their victory. They needed Pericles. Nicias probably would have been ready to accept peace, but he was unable to assert himself against Cleon. Aristophanes and Thucydides both emphasize the extraordinary control Cleon exerted over the Attic people at that time.

But it may be that Cleon's influence derived precisely from the fact that he accommodated the wishes of the Attic demos. The determining role he played might not have been due solely to his personality; likewise the power of Themistocles, Cimon, and Pericles had had other roots. But this does not free Cleon of responsibility. As Diodotus, who had challenged Cleon in the assembly, put it, orators and politicians were supposed to be able to analyze and predict things better than their listeners in the council and the popular assembly.

But the underlying affinity between Cleon and the city explains the opportunities that opened up to a politician of his stamp and ambitions. He was able to build on the old tendency of the Athenians to always want more and to set higher goals. In the last decade of Pericles' life—and, later, under the pressure imposed by his war plan—this tendency had been repressed, but only with great effort.

Periclean Athens of the 430s and the early 420s was marked by a deep, inherent contradiction. Athens tried to enshrine permanently an order that depended on movement, expansion, and success. The rival, who had been feared for so long, lay defeated. And it had been Cleon who had won this success with his uncompromising and unscrupulous ways. He had achieved the impossible as the Athenian character demanded, but he had done so in an ignoble fashion. The times when ignoble behavior was unacceptable to the popular assembly had passed. Cleon's brashness may in fact have held a certain fascination for the majority.

Cleon had the jurors' pay raised by half a drachma, probably in 425, from two to three oboli. Aristophanes cites this move as an example of Cleon's cleverness. The jurors' allowances were paid with money collected as legal fees and fines, and Cleon was famous for indicting as many opponents as he could, *strategoi* and others, thus increasing court revenues. "You deprive yourself of your own pay if you don't find the accused guilty," the chorus shouts at the jurors in Aristophanes' *The Wasps*. Aristophanes' broadside suggests that Cleon wanted to devote more money to the court system while other politicians argued for building more battleships. In view of how expensive life had become, increasing the wages of the judges was not an unreasonable decision.

In January of 424, during the winter following the victory at Pylos and one year after *The Acharnians*, Aristophanes' play *The Knights* was produced. It remains one of the most scathing political satires ever to reach the stage.

Two slaves of Lord Demos, Nicias and Demosthenes, suffer under the control of another, "the Paphlagonian," who has newly been made the overseer and has Lord Demos completely under his thumb. This overseer, a leather monger, clearly represents Cleon, whose father was a tanner. "Since that fellow has established himself here, beatings are our daily bread," the two slaves complain. The only way to improve their lot is to find a competitor to supplant the Paphlagonian as Lord Demos's overseer. The man they turn to is Agoracritus, a sausage seller who is a rather coarse individual. He refuses at first, but the knights, the young aristocrats who form the chorus, talk him into accepting. He hesitates initially, worrying that he is a common man, a peddler without any education. He is literate, but only barely. His literacy could work against him, he is told, because governing is not for people of character and education. One has to be mean-spirited and ignorant to be suited for such a job. "You have a loud voice," the chorus tells him. "You are a knave and a huckster; in short, you have all it takes to lead the polis."

Much of the play is taken up by the contest between the Cleon figure and the sausage seller. They attack each other verbally, but most of all they try as hard as they can to outdo each other in currying favor with Lord Demos. They offer him everything, from cheap fish to freshly killed rabbits, and from pillows to soften the stone seats on the Pnyx to world dominion. Lord Demos clearly represents both the petit bourgeois and the people as a whole.

The Paphilagonian always sets the terms of the wager in these contests. After all, he possesses all the power. The sausage peddler is forced to outdo him with presents and promises.

The play levels one criminal charge after another against the most powerful politician of Athens. He takes bribes, helps himself to public funds (and his character admits it: "Yes, I steal, but only for the good of the polis"), he lies, slanders, and accuses people falsely. If anyone questions his authority he immediately accuses that person of treason and threatens to denounce the critic to the Council of Five Hundred. He truly identifies with the polis, for whatever harms him also harms it, and he is vigilant as a watchdog. The victory at Pylos has made him vainer than ever, even though he is but a slave and has merely cashed in on the labor of others. Above all, he cynically deceives and defrauds Lord Demos, using all his cunning to make the master dependent on him.

Demos himself appears as an old, conceited fool, all the more so for declaring that he knows exactly what is going on. He claims to be glad that his champion steals from him because in the end he will get everything back from the fool. Here the satire reaches its climax: Demos is not just putting up with his servant's evil doings but derives malicious pleasure from them. Demos is variously called King of Greece, Sole Ruler of the Earth, Tyrant, and Lord of the Entire World.

In the end Demos is given renewed youth by the sausage peddler. Demos is once again his old self, like the Athenians at the time of Marathon. The sausage peddler will now ride herd on him. The oarsmen of the triremes are once more to be paid their salary in full upon landing, something that had apparently not been happening for some time. No one is to evade military duty anymore. Young men will go hunting again rather than influence decisions in the popular assembly, a reference to the fact that young men were beginning to dominate there. Demos is revitalized both personally and through the restored order; miraculously, the rogue and huckster has become a statesman in the best sense. In retrospect his disgusting competition with Cleon turns out to have been a clever game that served the good, and did not bring victory to the worst scoundrel. This ending may have been necessary because otherwise everything that preceded it would have been too provocative, not only to Cleon but to the demos as well. Or it may have expressed the author's hope—which alone made his devastating criticism possible—that the miserable state of the city would lead to a new beginning. The play, on that reading, would express not so much hatred for Cleon as love for the city and faith in its renewal.

In spite of all its exaggerations, we can probably take the play as an indication that, in 424, the victory at Pylos swelled the head not only of Cleon but of the people as well. Athenian hegemony over all Greece seemed almost within grasp. The old arrogance had been revived, perhaps all the more strongly because of the suffering of the past years.

Once again, however, the fact that Aristophanes was awarded first prize for this comedy speaks well for Attic democracy, even if the jury supposedly based its decision primarily on aesthetic factors.

In the winter of 425–424 the Athenians suspected that the people of Chios, the last independent member of the Delian League, were on the verge of revolting and forced them to tear down their newly erected city walls. In 424, they took Nisaea, the harbor of Megara. With the help of the democratic contingent there they almost succeeded in taking the city itself but were foiled by the intervention of a Spartan general, Brasidas, son of Tellis, who was near Corinth at the time and came to the Megarians' aid.

Brasidas was one of a small group of young Spartan officers who strongly disagreed with their city's policies and conduct in the war. They were dissatisfied with the caution and timid restraint of the Spartan leadership and its tendency to give in too quickly. They must have been well aware of the limitations of the old-fashioned Spartan army and felt that if the old ways no longer worked, new ones should be found.

In this respect they followed Athens' example. They were independent, open-minded, and determined to win. Any doubts arising from the old Spartan traditions that might have stood in their way meant nothing to them in view of their city's situation. So, before Athens knew what was happening, it was confronted with Brasidas, and later others—an entirely new generation and a very dangerous enemy. Unlike Cleon, these generals really knew how to wage war. They also displayed remarkable skills as politicians and statesmen, which were rooted partly in old Spartan tradition and partly in their ability to recognize the new situation and act according to it. They assessed their own strengths soberly and realistically. In addition to all these qualities they had a wide-ranging understanding of warfare that Sparta had lacked up to now. Athens had assumed that a land power could not act forcefully far from its base. Brasidas proved this assumption wrong.

We first meet Brasidas in Thucydides in the early phase of the war, in the winter of 429–428, when he attempted a daring exploit as the commander of a squadron in the Corinthian Gulf that had been forced to retreat from the Athenians. Brasidas ordered his crews to pick up their oars, tholes, and cushions and march to Nisaea, where they pulled the Megarian fleet of forty ships into the water with the intent of launching a surprise attack on Piraeus, which lay "unguarded and open, as was natural given Athens' superiority on the seas." They might very well have succeeded, but they lost their courage, and made do with pillaging Salamis. Nowhere did they encounter any guards. Athens nearly dissolved into panic when it received news of the attack by flare signals. The enemy was feared to have landed on the mainland already, and in Piraeus people expected the ships to appear any minute. From this time onward, the harbor was guarded more carefully.

Now Brasidas planned to hit Athens in the one part of its empire that was vulnerable to attack by a land army: the northern coast of the Aegean. Both the Macedonian king, Perdiccas, and the cities on the Chalcidice that had defected from the Delian League feared reprisals from the Athenians, now that they were regaining strength. Jointly, they were willing to finance the Spartans' campaign. Sparta sent 700 helots—glad to get them off the Peloponnese, since it still feared an uprising—and recruited an additional 1,000 mercenaries. With this force Brasidas marched across Thessaly, which was an Athenian ally, so quickly that he nearly avoided detection. In little time he convinced a number of cities to defect from Athens.

It is doubtful that his small army would have been able to conquer many cities in battle or by siege; all Brasidas could do was to threaten to destroy their land, but in most cases the cities surrendered voluntarily. We know that some cities were afraid of him, but what seems to have carried more weight was that he took seriously Sparta's stated goal in this war.

Brasidas stressed that he had come to liberate the Greeks from Athens. The Spartan citizens, he said, had solemnly sworn to grant autonomy to those who allied themselves with them. He refused to interfere in the internal affairs of the cities. He would neither support any one individual or group, nor subjugate the majority to a minority, nor a minority to the collective whole. He wanted to differ favorably from the Athenians in every respect and was ready to accept new cities into the Spartan alliance regardless of their political systems. They had nothing to lose and their autonomy to gain. Brasidas did insist that each and every one of them had the obligation to contribute to the liberation of all.

It is not clear whether the majorities in all the cities that opened their gates to Brasidas were really willing to rebel against Athens, but it seems certain that they were not unalterably opposed to the idea. Apparently no major internal divisions existed in these cities, and Brasidas did everything he could to preserve their internal peace, displaying a rare generosity of outlook.

The widespread trust Brasidas earned in many places was extraordinary. He must have had great powers of persuasion and a charismatic personality. Certainly he was convinced of his mission to an astonishing degree. People believed that he was without guile. "It is more disgraceful to gain one's end by deceit that pretends to be morality," Thucydides quotes him as saying, "than by open violence. Straightforward aggression has a certain justification in the strength that is given us by fortune, but the other form of attack comes simply from the treacherous devices of an evil mind." Of course, Brasidas also benefited from the reputation Sparta still enjoyed. People believed they could rely on its solemn oaths. All these factors combined to make his call for liberty inspirational.

In the fall of 424 the Athenians decided to launch an attack on Boeotia. Exiles from that country had raised Athens' hopes that democratic forces in some Boeotian cities would side with the Athenians. Demosthenes was to lead an attack from the Corinthian Gulf while a large army would invade the country's northern coast.

Boeotia was informed of the plan in advance, however, so the attack failed. The Athenians did succeed in seizing and fortifying the temple at Delium, but they could not hold it, and in the battle that followed they were routed. The Theban troops, under the command of Pagondas, son of Aeolades, employed, for the first time on record, a new tactic that later became famous. It consisted of a unique formation where the right flank was twenty-five rows deep and thus extremely strong. The Athenians, about equal in numbers to the Thebans, fought in a uniform line of eight rows along the entire front. The Boeotians lost fewer than 500 hoplites; the Athenians over 1,000, as well as lightly armed soldiers and much of the supply personnel.

One of the hoplites was Socrates. Alcibiades, who was serving in the cavalry at the time, saw him during the retreat. In Plato's *Symposium*, Alcibiades describes the scene: "He was walking with the same 'lofty strut and sideways glance' that he goes about with here in Athens. His 'sideways glance' was just as unconcerned whether he was looking at his own friends or at the enemy, and you could see from half a mile away that if you tackle him you'd get as good as you gave—with the result that he and Laches both got clean away. For you're generally pretty safe if that's the way you look when you're in action; it's the man whose idea it is to get away that the other goes for."

In the winter of 424–423, Brasidas delivered a great diplomatic blow against Athens. He talked the men of Amphipolis into coming over to the Spartan side. By this action he not only disrupted the delivery of wood to Athens for shipbuilding but also gained the means to build a fleet of his own and, eventually, make possible further expeditions into the east, since the city dominated the only access to the land route leading there. In addition, the Delian League lost a major financial contributor.

The Attic army, which was sent out to save the city for Athens, arrived too late. Its general was the historian Thucydides, who was either exiled because of his mission's failure—though it was not his fault—or, who, anticipating such a verdict, decided not to return. He does not give us a full account.

At this point the Attic allies in the region outdid each other in their eagerness to join Brasidas. They read weakness in Athens' defeat at Delium. Brasidas wanted to make the most of his victory and asked Sparta for reinforcements. He began building a fleet before hearing their response. Things finally seemed to be going in Sparta's favor.

But the Spartans refused his request—partly out of envy, partly because they still hoped to get back the men taken prisoner on the island (some of whom belonged to the most influential families). The Spartans had become apprehensive of the entire war. They must have felt that it undermined their way of life, and they wanted to end it with as little further investment as possible.

In the spring of 423 the Athenians, too, were ready for an armistice, and a one-year truce was concluded. Nicias participated in the negotiations. The Athenians planned to use the time to prepare for fighting against Brasidas, and the Spartans hoped to make peace in the strength of his successes. Both sides were to keep the territories they held as of the signing of the armistice.

Brasidas received news of the armistice from a delegation consisting of one Athenian and one Spartan. He had just won over the city of Scione on Pallene, probably two days after the treaty's date, and he refused to give up his new conquest. The Athenians were particularly upset at the defection of Scione because the Pallene peninsula was similar to an island—the Athenians commanded the narrow isthmus in Potidaea—and the loss of the city did not bode well for the rulers of the sea. On Cleon's suggestion, the popular assembly responded to Brasidas's refusal by voting to destroy Scione and kill all its citizens. The decree could not be acted on at the time since the Athenians were unable to take the city back, but they sent out an army, claiming the armistice had been broken. They laid siege to Scione, and in 421, after the Peace of Nicias had gone into effect, they carried out the decree and killed all the men.

Despite this the armistice lasted its year, but when the terms ran out in the spring of 422, war flared up once more. Cleon was acting general now, a sign that Aristophanes' *Knights* had done no serious damage to his reputation. He was intent on retaking Amphipolis and the other northern cities. These efforts met with some success, but at Amphipolis he demonstrated such poor strategic judgment that Brasidas was able, despite commanding a much smaller force, to defeat him decisively. The Athenians fled in disarray. Six hundred of them were killed, compared with only seven casualties on the other side. Cleon himself was slain in the retreat.

Brasidas, too, was mortally wounded. The people of Amphipolis gave him a hero's funeral, burying him in their city, in the place that later became the agora. They instituted games and made annual sacrifices in his honor and named him founder of the city. In Scione he had been crowned with a golden wreath as the liberator of Greece and decorated with strips of wool and the first spring flowers like an Olympic champion. In life and death he received the highest honors. Brasidas combined the old Greek virtues with great open-mindedness and a modern outlook, and he emerged for a rare and brief moment during this terrible war as a true advocate of Greek freedom. Equally adept as a politician and as a soldier, he knew how to turn the desire for freedom into military advantage.

"Three things are necessary to succeed in warfare," he said before the battle of Amphipolis. "One must want to fight; one must be able to feel shame; and one must obey one's commanders." Apparently he irritated the Spartans because of his generosity and absolute fair-mindedness. In any case, after his death they violated the agreements he had made during his brief, successful campaign, and they sent overseers to the cities whose allegiance he had won by promising that the Spartans would not interfere in their affairs.

With Cleon dead, there was nothing left to block peace. Prolonged negotiations took place and the treaty was ready to be signed in the spring of 421. Both sides were to restore the territories they had conquered during the war, with the exception that Athens could keep Nisaea. The peace was fixed for a term of fifty years. A special rule applied to the cities north of the Aegean that had defected from the Delian League. Their tributes were to be paid not at the rates set in 425 but according to Aristides' original, lower assessment. In addition, the cities were to be autonomous; they owed allegiance neither to Sparta nor to Athens unless they chose to rejoin the Delian League. If they paid tribute, Athens was not allowed to use military force against them. Seventeen men from each city were to take binding oaths, and the oaths were to be renewed annually. Tablets with the oath inscribed on them were to be set up in Olympia, Delphi, and on the Corinthian isthmus, as well as in Athens and Sparta.

Four of Sparta's allies voted against the treaty, but according to the rules (or custom) of the Peloponnesian League the majority determined the outcome, and the majority was clearly in favor of peace. Which side would first relinquish its conquests was to be decided by lot. It turned out to be Sparta, and the plan for peace was foiled immediately. The Spartan commander in Amphipolis resisted giving up his territory, and then, when he was finally ready to withdraw, the citizens of Amphipolis refused to open their gates to the Athenians.

In view of this refusal to go along with the treaty, the Spartans concluded an agreement of mutual defense with Athens, also for a period of fifty years. Anyone attacking either of the two parties would be considered the enemy of the other as well, and peace could be restored only with the consent of both of them. The Athenians further promised to assist the Spartans in case of a helot revolt. Sparta was worried also that it would once again be drawn into war with Argos because their thirty-year peace agreement was due to expire in 421 or 420.

Around 421 the Athenians began construction of the Erechtheum, and the temple to Athena Nike was probably completed sometime in the 420s.

Aristophanes' *The Peace* was staged at the festival of the Great Dionysia of 421, most likely just before the signing of the treaty. In the comedy, the grape grower Trygaeus is flying to heaven on a huge dung beetle to bring back the goddess of peace. But he finds only Hermes there. All the other gods have left Olympus, angered by the Greeks' lust for war. The god of war has hidden peace in a cave and is preparing to crush several cities in a giant mortar, but neither of the two pestles, named Cleon and Brasidas, can be found.

Again in this play, Aristophanes stresses Pericles' responsibility for the war. The explanation here is not that Pericles wanted to avenge Aspasia's kidnapped hetaerae but that domestic policies have landed him in trouble, and he hopes war will extricate him. The weapons smiths and manufacturers of feathered helmet crests, spears, and trumpets are all angry about the peace. Nobody is interested in purchasing their wares. The helmet crest feathers are of no use even as feather dusters. Trygaeus tries to use his breastplate as a chamber pot but it does not work. By contrast, the Attic farmers of the chorus claim they will become twenty years younger once the noise of war stops and they are relieved of the nuisance of military drills.

The peace was named after Nicias, the main negotiator on the Athenian side. His Spartan counterpart was King Pleistoanax. Both men took a strong personal interest in bringing about peace, and they won the consent of their respective populations, probably because for a short time the domestic situation in each of their cities worked in their favor.

For Thucydides, the six years and ten months before open hostilities broke out again could themselves only be described as a time of war.

10

The Long Road to Collapse

Ancient Greece had no interest whatsoever in compromise. It pursued
everything to the point of self-destruction. The Greeks saw glory in
the fall of states, cities, and kings. Such a mentality is totally foreign to
our own.

—JACOB BURCKHARDT

Whether or not there is meaning in history is a question for philosophers.
But it could not even be asked until there was such a thing as history;
namely, the notion that the countless actions and events that occur in this
world constitute a process that may or may not be directed toward some
kind of goal. It was not until modern Europe that this idea emerged.

But the conviction that there is meaning in the actions and events
brought about by or experienced by a particular political entity—a
dynasty perhaps, or an empire—goes back to earliest times. People have
always wondered whether and how they deserve what is happening to
them. Whatever their fate, they feel it is designed specifically for them.
The Israelites, for example, went so far as to see the expansion of the
Assyrian Empire as an expression of Yahweh's wrath and a punishment
for having worshipped false gods.

Everyone knew, even in ancient times, that events are greatly affected
by chance and the interplay of various forces. No battle or complex
diplomatic mission could otherwise have been understood in retrospect.
But most people belonging to Eastern cultures did not think long-term
processes could be comprehended in this way. Therefore, in the official
accounts of what had transpired, the people themselves or their kings
were typically assigned the leading roles in events.

The Greeks were the first people to attempt to understand, reconstruct, and describe changes that took place over generations as a succession of events resulting from the interaction of numerous individuals and affected by random conditions.

Herodotus, who is called the father of history, was the first to do this, and throughout his work we can still see traces of the old ways of interpreting events. He places an inordinate amount of responsibility on individuals. One of the best examples is his description of a battle between the Greeks of Cyrene in northern Africa and the Egyptians. Herodotus refers to this event twice, first in the story of King Apries, whose defeat is recounted in the old style, with no detail at all, and the phrase "for he was not to escape disaster in the end." When he writes about Cyrene, by contrast, Herodotus mentions only military factors, explaining that the Egyptians had never previously fought against the Greeks and therefore underestimated them.

In Herodotus's view, the gods did, from time to time, have a hand in things. He believed, for example, that even the Persian Wars ultimately had some meaning: they confirmed the rule that no single man, no monarch, nor any empire should become too powerful. All that he, or the Greeks, could see was that their fortunes kept going up and down and that "human affairs moved in cycles." In individual situations—say at the rise or decline of a dynasty—they were aware that a comprehensible process might be taking place, but it was always just one of many such processes that defied explanation.

The distance with which Herodotus contemplated his subject was derived from the tradition of Greek science or, more precisely, from Ionian "history"—at the time, the word merely meant learning by inquiry and by the questioning of witnesses. This was the concept of history that prevailed in the world of the Greek polis, in which no city could consider itself the center of the world. The distance this attitude afforded allowed one to observe the movement of the masses and the chains of events that followed from their interactions.

The Greeks' ability to look at the world in this distanced way made it possible for them to see their own community as just one among many. Thus it never even occurred to the city-states until the fifth century to write down their own actions and events. They did not see themselves as having a history and certainly not as belonging to history.

Thucydides had a completely different outlook. He paid no attention to non-Greeks unless they affected events in Greece. Following contemporary theories of cultural evolution, he constructed a "prehistory" of rapid growth in the fifth century, including expansion of trade, security, wealth, and power. Next, he described the fifty-year period between the Persian and the Peloponnesian Wars as the history of Athens' rise to power, which inevitably led up to war. He suggests that in the process a high point of human capabilities was reached, personified by Attica's leading statesman, Pericles.

In Thucydides' telling, Athens moved to center stage. Thucydides felt something larger had to be at work to give the Peloponnesian Wars meaning—something that reached far back and had not come about by chance.

In any case, Thucydides' organization of his history was an accurate reflection of the power of his city, its place in the center of the Greek world, and the striving of its citizens to maintain this position. One may question Thucydides' conclusion, based exclusively on the contemplation of Greek history, that the Peloponnesian War was "the most devastating shock ever experienced by the Greeks and many barbarians, indeed, practically by humanity as a whole." But even so, it can hardly be disputed that Thucydides was correct in his overall view of Greek history up to 431.

In reality, the Peloponnesian War represented the culmination of more than just the Greeks' power and military potential. It was also their attempt to preserve the polis as a political entity. It was the beginning of the end of a process that had taken centuries to develop.

The Greeks had been able to assert themselves against the empire of the Persians. But they could do so only because one city at a very propitious moment in its history had the foresight, the means, and the will necessary for one decisive encounter, the battle at Salamis.

Because this victory led to the liberation of the Ionian Greeks, military success could be permanently assured and extended only if Athens became a major power and eventually assumed supremacy over large parts of Greece. It did so as quickly as possible, but without preparing itself for the role. As a result most of the city-states lost their independence.

A certain inevitability accompanied this process, not just in Athens' expansion of its power but also in the development of radical democracy and the politicization and mobilization of its citizenry, which in the decades after Salamis reached proportions unmatched even in "permanent" revolutions. The remarkable innovations of that era and the situation they gave rise to challenged the Greeks to see the entire world in rational terms. Old assumptions were increasingly discarded and were replaced by a spirit of critical inquiry. Pericles' claim that Athens' fame would last forever turned out to be true, if for a different reason than the one Thucydides presented. Athens is remembered not for its military victories or for its influence over Greece but for its extraordinary innovations in confronting the most fundamental challenges of world history.

It must also be said, however, that Athens had become its own worst enemy. Grandly as it dealt with its problems, it had long since overextended itself. As Sophocles reluctantly suggested, Athens was in basically the same situation as Oedipus. Athens, like that legendary king, did not know its own true identity, which was that of a small city, a canton, no matter how much it claimed to be a supreme power.

There is some justification in interpreting Athens' fate during the Peloponnesian War in terms of tragedy. This view repeatedly creeps into Thucydides' work. Naturally, the historian works with different concepts from those of the tragedian, but in the case of Athens, even historical concepts produced results that might best be explained by reference to tragedy.

The Peace of Nicias was never destined to last. The very fact that it stipulated peace for a term longer than the usual generation—fifty rather than thirty years—indicated that it was a utopian undertaking that ignored the realities. The major signatories sought peace eagerly because they felt they were in great danger. They wanted to achieve the impossible by simply asserting it was so. The less able they were to comply with the terms of the treaty, the more determined they were to conclude the peace.

The Attic war goals as originally defined by Pericles had been attained almost in full. The small advantages granted the defector cities in the northern Aegean did not really curtail Athens' supremacy, nor did the fact that Athens had to cede Plataea.

Sparta, on the other hand, had proven itself unable to inflict much damage on Athens. The success Brasidas had achieved was more or less disclaimed by his city. Sparta did not even manage to emerge with its supremacy within the Peloponnesian League intact. The treaty called for approval of the peace by the majority of the cities in the league, but Corinth and several others refused to recognize it, and the allied Boeotians agreed only to several ten-day armistices with Athens. Consequently, Sparta was unable to fully meet the conditions of the peace. The exchange of the Spartan prisoners from Amphipolis proceeded without incident, but the Spartans charged with returning the city of Amphipolis to Athens were unable or unwilling to do so. This aroused suspicion among the Athenians, who were probably also aware that a faction in Sparta was already urging resumption of the war. In turn, the Athenians delayed their withdrawal from Pylos.

What resulted was not so much peace as uncertainty, not order but a power vacuum. Sparta's weakness made the situation particularly difficult for many of its allies, who were at the mercy of the Athenians if the old leader of the Peloponnesian League no longer functioned as a counterbalance. Boeotia and Megara were in immediate danger, especially since internal conflicts between the democratic and the oligarchic parties seemed likely to shift the balance in favor of Athens. The Corinthians complained because they did not get back the lost cities they had founded in western Greece.

The treaty took exclusive account of Sparta's interests without tending to its allies. Only certain circles had been in favor of peace. This was briefly true of Athens as well. Those for peace had succeeded by capitalizing on the people's war weariness. Internal conditions in both cities were too unstable for the peace that was achieved to be reliable. The less satisfied everyone was with the peace, the less Greece could settle down. The combative energies had not yet spent themselves, in spite of the horrors that had already taken place. Consequently, resistance to accepting the new state of affairs was especially strong.

In this unstable situation Sparta's allies who felt disappointed and vulnerable looked for new alliances, and a period of busy diplomatic activity set in. For a while Argos was the focus of Athenian interest. The Spartans had already tried to extend their thirty-year peace treaty with Argos, but demanded that Sparta relinquish the region of Thyreatis, long an object of contention, and Sparta could not accede to that demand without losing the last remnants of its prestige.

Argos was a large city by Greek standards. It probably had about fifteen thousand male citizens and occupied a sizable territory in Argolis on the Peloponnese peninsula. It was an obvious ally for anyone wanting to inflict damage on Sparta, and it had functioned as such for Athens in the 460s and 450s. Themistocles had maintained close relations with Argos. The two cities were also on friendly terms because they both had democratic constitutions.

But the Argives' politics had been motivated by their long-standing enmity for Sparta. They hoped to hand the Spartans a decisive defeat and at the same time take the town of Thyreatis on the Sparta-Argos border away from them. Their plan was to accomplish this by the traditional method, in an open hoplite battle. But they had tried and failed at this consistently since the beginning of the century. After each defeat they signed peace for thirty years. It was as though, generation after generation, the sons of those who had last suffered defeat lived with the sole goal of paying back the Spartans.

In the 490s the Argive force had suffered such heavy losses at the hands of the Spartans that even the members of a class of non-citizens that previously held only minimal rights were drafted. When the next generation grew powerful enough, however, they were once again excluded. In the 450s no major battle took place: In the battle at Tanagra between the Athenians and Spartans in 457, only a thousand Argives had taken part. Argos refrained otherwise from military action and, around 450, was the first of the Athenian allies to sign a new peace treaty with Sparta.

The Corinthians were the first to attempt to conclude a treaty with Argos. Then a group of Spartans working to undermine the peace with Athens made a similar attempt, hoping that Sparta would be willing to resume war if hostility from Argos were no longer a deterrent. This group was also responsible for a new treaty with Boeotia, even though that country was still engaged in war with Athens.

The Athenians grew impatient with Sparta in this atmosphere of hectic activity and uncertainty. Among them a young man had come to prominence who was highly respected because of his ancestry. Alcibiades, son of Clinias, had opposed the peace with Sparta all along and now set in motion a plan to forge an alliance between the Athenians and Argos. Nicias worked against these developments with all the power at his disposal, but after his attempt to convince Sparta to rescind its alliance with Boeotia had failed, the popular assembly approved—in anger, Thucydides reports—an alliance not only with Argos but with Mantinea and Elis as well. These were the three states in the Peloponnese that were more or less open enemies of Sparta. The alliance was to last for a hundred years, but the situation it created was highly confusing. Athens continued to be officially allied with Sparta. Corinth observed its treaty obligations with Argos but did not join the newly created alliance. It did maintain an agreement of mutual defense with Elis, Argos, and Mantinea, but it tended from now on to look more to Sparta. That was how things stood in the year 420.

In 419 Alcibiades, now a *strategos*, moved with a small force through the territories of Athens' allies on the Peloponnese and made arrangements to solidify ties and perhaps to strengthen allied military capabilities. He also wanted the city of Patras to build long walls to the sea, but the Corinthians and others managed to prevent this. Argos meanwhile wanted to take action against Epidaurus, a Sparta-allied city which it regarded as a Corinthian outpost and which also occupied an important position on the way to Athens.

In 418 Sparta sent its entire army out against Argos. The Spartans were joined by troops from Corinth, Megara, Boeotia, and other allies. The combined force was described as "the most splendid Greek army" ever assembled. The Spartans were confident of victory over Argos, but the Argives, too, thought their chances of success were excellent. The conflict was delayed when a group of Argives who maintained friendships in Sparta and were visiting there took it upon themselves to arrange a four-month truce. There were many who objected to the truce on both sides, since both had been optimistic about the outcome, and soon after the four months elapsed, the two armies of allied forces met in the territory of Mantinea. Thucydides called it the greatest battle that had taken place among Hellenic states in a very long time. The forces of the Athenian allies suffered a heavy defeat. Together with the Aeginetans they lost two hundred men, including both their generals. After the battle, Argos and Sparta made peace once again, this time for fifty years.

The men who negotiated the peace on the Argive side hoped to topple the Argive democrats from power. Aided by Sparta, they succeeded in their plans in the spring of 417, but their success was short-lived. The people rose up, killed some of the oligarchs, and drove the others out of the city. Argos once again sought an alliance with Athens and, with the support of Alcibiades, the building of the long walls to the sea was undertaken for the city's defense. Everyone was compelled to help in the project, freemen and slaves, and even women. Stonecutters and masons were brought in from Athens. But in the fall, before the walls were quite finished, the Spartans attacked and destroyed the work. Argos itself remained democratic.

This complicated story demonstrates one thing: The Spartans' behavior after concluding peace with Athens thoroughly undermined the power relationships among and often within the cities of the Peloponnese and central Greece. In the resulting struggle for power, diverse forces resorted to daring, more or less rash, and often extremely shortsighted tactics in the interest of both self-defense and self-advancement.

What Thucydides said about the treaties held for domestic politics in general: People kept their promises only as long as it suited their purpose. Everyone was out for himself without regard for existing rules. Though necessary for the realization of immediate needs, oaths, treaties, and alliances were nothing but empty formalities with no meaning beyond the moment. The less meaningful they were, the longer the terms for which they were made tended to be, as though in conscious mockery of reality.

Ultimately, though, an earlier order reasserted itself on the Peloponnesian side. The hegemony of Sparta reemerged and the city regained its former power. The factional fighting subsided significantly the moment the city returned to its former policies. It was unclear what to do about the peace, which Athens had officially broken, but which neither side had ever properly observed.

The mere fact that a political entity has a democratic government is no guarantee that it will develop rational policies. If successful policies are in fact arrived at, this may not be the result of the political institutions but of fortuitous economic and international conditions.

That had undoubtedly been the case in fifth-century Athens. The city's situation had been improving almost without interruption for many years. The conditions made it possible for able politicians to rise to the top. Athens had the good fortune of having in Pericles a leader with enough imagination and authority to discipline the city and guide it when outward expansion was no longer possible.

After Mantinea, the city faced tasks of a different kind. If peace was to be preserved, it was essential that trust again develop, primarily between Athens and Sparta. Trust exists when people feel secure and powerful. But with this Athens already had a problem because security depends on reliability of government, and Athens could not count on a stable government. It was also important that the city not allow itself to become suspicious at the slightest provocation and react hastily. Instability and disturbances required cautious yet forceful management so that Athens' full power and resources could be expanded for an emergency.

The upright Nicias had done much for the city but shied away from any exceptionally demanding task. Such a man had little chance of gaining the authority needed for waging this kind of politics. Even more important, the Athenian people could not be expected to go along with the policies that would be necessary to build such trust. Their demands were great, and their expectation of success extreme. The fears they may have felt concerning the security of their empire were so ingrained in their mentality that instead of inspiring caution such fears encouraged the display and expansion of power. Pericles had taught the Athenians not to hide their power but to show it openly. This difficult situation was complicated by the fact that Athens' policies were determined by the mass of ordinary people. There is plenty of evidence that the Attic people knew how to act responsibly. But now problems arose for which the Athenians were thoroughly unprepared.

Athenian democracy had lost most of its ability to react creatively to unexpected challenges; it seems to have entered a period of what might be called "pathological learning," in which what they had learned in the past interfered with further learning. The people had reached the point where, instead of preserving what they had and working toward peace, they opted to continue on a path that offered only the illusion of further advance.

Thucydides reports Diodotus as saying in the debate about Mytilene that no resistance is possible "when human nature is passionately intent on a certain action." This holds true, Thucydides continues, not only for individuals but for entire cities as well, especially if, as in Athens, the greatest prizes are at stake—freedom and sovereignty.

A passage in Plato suggests how ill-prepared the leadership of Attica was for the new situation. In the *Laches*, which takes place shortly before 415, the sons of Aristides and of Thucydides, son of Melesias, remark that though their fathers were great politicians they passed along none of their skills because they neglected their sons during adolescence. The two young men have a strong sense of their own inadequacy and are determined to treat their own sons differently. They reveal the helplessness of a generation whose education has proven inadequate and who consequently lack the ability to learn. The young disparage their elders. There is an element of irony in the two young men's intention to have their sons trained, first of all, in the art of fencing. Plato also brings Nicias, who was anything but a visionary, in on the conversation.

There was no past experience to fall back on in dealing with what lay ahead, and there were no clear principles to guide one's actions. Even someone endowed with exceptional clarity of vision and with excellent judgment would have been inadequate to the task. It would have taken the divining powers of a seer to gain insight into all that was taking place. Nobody in Athens had this ability, especially not Nicias. He turned for inspiration to old models, such as Cimon's cooperation with Sparta, which served well after 480 but was of little help after 421.

It must have been this inadequacy that lay at the root of Athens' political failure. But as the upper classes tend to do, they blamed it on others, on the fact that, for example, tradesmen were now active in politics, people like the tanner's son Cleon, and the lampmaker and rising politician Hyperbolus. These were men of lesser birth, less inhibited, and less well educated than politicians tended to be under the old, aristocratic standards. But they probably had been trained to work hard from early youth. That is why, though at a disadvantage in many respects, they had one great advantage over the aristocrats: their strong and ruthless will to achieve their goals.

The other group that is often blamed for the disastrous policies Athens followed in the ensuing years, the Sophists, were natural scapegoats. They were trying to remedy intellectual shortcomings; the extent to which they failed to do this at the important moments is open to debate. Another individual who was concerned with proper education but was equally unable to guide policies was Socrates.

Consequently, the boundless self-confidence of men like Cleon, their audacity and willingness to resort to the appeal of the city's greatness carried the day. Hyperbolus, who was preparing to take over Cleon's role, had already proposed a naval expedition to Carthage and agitated against the Peace of Nicias. His policy seems to have been to flatter the demos and above all to paint Athens' position and its powers in the most positive light, as is easy to do after a long history of accomplishment. Nicias had little chance against such men. To be sure, he had supporters among the people, and he was by no means inferior to Hyperbolus. But he would not likely have been able to maintain a policy for the long tern against the opposition of Hyperbolus and later Alcibiades.

Alcibiades was the aristocratic version of Cleon and Hyperbolus. He was by no means a "better" man than they. On the contrary, he was truly immoral. But he was much smarter, better educated, and far more charming and clever. He was capable of applying more sophisticated methods than they were. What they labored to achieve came to him without effort. His thinking and his goals were of an entirely different nature.

Alcibiades was born around 450. His great-grandfather, Clinias, had come to prominence as a relatively young man in 480, when he equipped a trireme at his own expense in order to fight the Persians. Alcibiades' father was killed in 447 at Coronea. On his mother's side he was descended from the Alcmaeonids, "the most famous men of Athens." After his father's death, Alcibiades was raised by Pericles, his uncle.

Alcibiades was an exceptionally handsome and strong man with extraordinary charm. He had trained in sports, studied with the Sophists, and at various times joined the circle around Socrates, who made it a point to converse extensively with the gifted and attractive young man. Stories that Alcibiades loved Socrates as a teacher and was affected by his words are not necessarily untrue, despite Alcibiades' divergence from his teachings. He was probably deeply engaged in these lessons.

The trouble was that Alcibiades was equally engaged in many other things. He found much that interested him and became completely captivated by all the intellectual currents of the time. This meant that he pursued everything he did as if it were an intellectual sport rather than striving to develop concrete, useful, and rational judgment. Even so, he acquired spectacular knowledge and developed the ability to analyze problems brilliantly; he also devised grand political schemes and was an outstanding military strategist.

In the late 430s, the brightest members of his generation began to appear wherever in the city the Sophists were staying and continue the conversations they heard there among themselves and with the most intelligent men of the city in palaces, at symposia, and in the agora. They learned the art of argumentation, and how to look at things from more than one angle. This kind of intellectual freedom is typical of societies for whom an entire new world has suddenly opened up and whose previously held notions have been abandoned. These young Athenians had become aware of their own—and others'—subjectivity and were learning to fight with intellectual weapons the same way they did with those made of steel. They took an active part in the variety of intellectual experiments that were going on. Simple truths that went back to the archaic period and had held for so long no longer applied. Nor did the new ones that the generations of Cleisthenes, Themistocles, Cimon, and Pericles had evolved: the belief in isonomy, democracy, defense of the city, and the unquestioning assumption of serving its greatness. These newer truths had arisen in response to the needs of the polis and ultimately served to promote and defend its ruling position. In the past it had been possible not only to refer to the past but to point to the requirements of the present.

But now everything had to be rethought, and nothing could be taken for granted. Laws and conventions lost their authority. It was once again possible to doubt whether democracy was the best form of government. A plausible case could be made for oligarchy or other kinds of political order. There were even arguments suggesting that outstanding individuals were meant by nature to rule over the others the way the lion was the king of the animal world. Nature seemed to be the only solid realm that could serve as guidance.

The new generation enjoyed the new freedom, insights, and forms of expression that arose not only in the symposia but also in the courts, and they gained through their association with all this. What was prized was not so much genuine insight and judgment as intellectual engagement and competition in any chosen arena. Alcibiades was one of the most popular members of this exuberant youth culture, full of high spirits and mischief. It was hard for people to get angry at his behavior. With his quick intellect, open-mindedness, and charm he must have taken first place in debates again and again. Plato depicts him cornering Pericles with questions about democracy and law.

A deep gulf seems to have opened up at that time between the generations, at least within the upper social class. Most of the older men found that the younger generation was already living in a different world, and they shared little in common.

Alcibiades, more than any of his peers, was subject to an overwhelming need to be noticed. The attention his beauty and charisma elicited was not enough to satisfy him. He cultivated a slight speech defect by consciously—and charmingly—lisping, a trait often picked up in the comedies of the day. He was known for his long, purple robes trailing along the ground, which he sometimes wore like a woman. Mounted on his hoplite shield was a small figure of Eros equipped with Zeus's thunderbolt instead of the usual bow and arrow. Once he spent the exorbitant sum of 7,000 drachmas (which could have bought him forty slaves) for a huge, beautiful dog but then cut off the animal's tail. When friends asked him why he had done it, he replied that he wanted to get people to talk about him even more.

The incredible lavishness of the productions he staged as *choregos* and the many love affairs he had hardly stand out in the overall picture of this man. What he was most famous for, outside the political arena, were his racehorses. At the Olympics of 416, he entered seven quadrigas. No private individual had ever done anything of the sort. His teams took first, second, and fourth place. The fame of his horses had spread all over Greece even before the event, and major cities of the Delian League, eager to have a share in the glory, perhaps for political reasons, contributed to the magnificence of his presence at the games. Ephesus presented him with a beautiful Persian tent twice the size of the one that housed the official Athenian delegation. Chios sent feed for the horses and animals for the sacrifices and the feasts. Lesbos supplied the wine.

On other occasions Alcibiades seems to have acted with deliberate perverseness and indifference to the results of his actions. In 416, for example, he petitioned the popular assembly to have all the men of the city of Melos killed and the women and children sold as slaves. Then he bought one of the women himself, fell in love with her, and had a child by her. An anonymous author of the time wrote that if such a thing happened on the stage, the Athenians would be outraged, but when it happened in reality, especially when Alcibiades acted this way, they accepted it without as much as a murmur. So, too, when Alcibiades locked up one of the most renowned painters of the day, Agatharchus, and did not let him go until he had finished a series of paintings for him. Alcibiades' fabulously wealthy brother-in-law, Callias, declared before the popular assembly that if he should die childless his money was to go to the polis; his motivation was the fear that Alcibiades, whose expenses far exceeded his income, might kill him.

Alcibiades thought he could do in public what he'd done in private life, things that others would consider impossible. His boundless ambitions were directed primarily at politics, and he wanted his success to be spectacular. He had in his favor not only his family background, rhetorical gifts, intelligence, and winning personality but also a moral callousness lacked by Nicias and his other competitors. This enabled him to fight effectively, with great determination and few scruples, for whatever he set his mind on. His dubious judgment was not of grave consequence given the instability of the situation. The fact that his plans failed on occasion does not ever seem to have discouraged him.

Alcibiades was a spoiled man with a high opinion of himself; he was vain, willful, and always ready to take offense, as is typical of those who treat others with disdain and condescension. All these qualities he displayed both in private and in politics, where they went hand in hand with his genius.

The explanation for his turning against the Peace of Nicias was simply that the Spartans and Nicias had negotiated it without him. He had been passed over because of his youth, despite having revived his family's old hospitality ties with Sparta. So, because he felt he was not being taken seriously enough, he agitated against the peace treaty and later argued for the treaty with Argos. He may have been merely testing his powers and seeking to beat the mighty demagogue Hyperbolus at his own game. In any case, he had success in Athens and achieved much of what he wanted in the Peloponnese, though in the end almost all of it came to nothing.

Thucydides recounts a speech Alcibiades gave saying that there is nothing wrong with a man being proud of himself and refusing to settle for being one among many. Where his uncle Pericles had exercised restraint, Alcibiades asserted that the victories of his horses were proof of Athens' greatness and demonstration to all of Greece that the city had not been crippled by the war as had been generally assumed. In a vein similar to that of Pericles, he boasted of the splendor that others may envy today but would bring glory in the future. The essential difference between Pericles and Alcibiades is that the former had Athens in mind whereas the latter was thinking only of himself.

According to Thucydides, Alcibiades described the path the city should take as follows: "We are in no position to exercise our rule sparingly; since we have risen to this position of power, we have to attack some and keep others from asserting themselves. For there is the danger that we ourselves will be subjugated if we don't subjugate others."

The city, he implied, cannot live in lethargic peace and become absorbed in itself, lest its knowledge and abilities grow obsolete. It must always move ahead. This was the spirit in which Alcibiades acted, at a time when the city was paralyzed with indecision. Some of his efforts benefited the city while others hurt it. The city itself, as Aristotle put it later, "loved and hated him, but could not free itself from him."

Alcibiades was not so powerful that he could dominate the popular assembly, however. He was only one of three top politicians who vied for the people's favor. A strange incident is recorded in the year 417. Hyperbolus, who was another of the three, requested an ostracism vote, expecting that either Nicias or better yet Alcibiades, his immediate rival, would be forced to absent himself for ten years. But his two rivals combined forces and asked their friends and followers to vote against Hyperbolus himself.

It is not clear how big each man's personal following was or what kind of men belonged to them. These followings may have consisted only of immediate friends and others closely allied with one or another of the politicians, or they may have been assembled from proponents of a certain policy.

Clearly there were individual politicians who enjoyed broad-based sympathy and who shared certain basic assumptions with many voters (if only as a matter of temperament), but at the same time there was a great mental openness and a readiness to be swayed—depending on the question under consideration, the arguments presented, and other appeals.

. . .

In the year 417 Alcibiades was once again *strategos*. He set out for Argos with twenty ships and arrested three hundred Argives he suspected of being friends of Sparta. They were deported to islands under Athens' rule, probably in the Cyclades.

In the same year the Athenians tried to force the island of Melos to join the Delian League. The island had been a member in the past, but had since disassociated itself and was officially neutral in spite of its fundamental sympathy toward Sparta, the state from which its original settlers had come. The presence of this neutral state in the middle of the Aegean Sea caused great resentment in Athens, so they sent out a contingent of nearly three thousands troops. The generals ordered the city to submit without resisting. They sent envoys to negotiate, but the Melians would not allow them to make their case before the people. Instead they were received by a small group of magistrates and influential citizens.

Thucydides represents the ensuing dialogue as having been a blatant expression of cynical power politics. The Athenians began by saying they would not discuss whether their demand was right or wrong. The Athenians stated they would start out with what both sides knew was the truth—namely, that right plays a role only in confrontations between powers of equal strength. In all other situations the strong do whatever they can and the weak suffer what they must. It was a simple matter of expediency, the Athenian spokesmen concluded. Athens found it advantageous to incorporate Melos into its realm, and it would be to the advantage of both sides if the city was saved; that is, if it accepted its fate without putting up a fight. The Athenians had an answer to any argument the Melians presented against this arrangement. The islanders could not understand why they could not be Athens' allies without being their subjects. They were told that if the Athenians consented to friendships, it would be a sign of weakness on the part of Athens. Rather, Athens cultivated the hatred of others because it proved the city's strength. Athens could not afford to have an independent island in the Aegean Sea.

When the Melians said they hoped the gods would support them in the rightful defense of their island, the Athenians replied that the gods viewed Athens' ambitions as just as valid. Laws of nature dictated that anyone could rule over whatever realm he could lay claim to. The Athenians pointed out that if the Melians ever found themselves in the position of power, they would do the same.

The Athenians also called the Melians' request for help from Sparta unrealistic, and in this they were quite correct. They claimed, with Melos as well as Sparta in mind, that expediency was inextricably linked with concern for safety. Taking a stand for justice and the good was dangerous, and Sparta was not likely to take upon itself the perils inherent in military confrontation.

Finally, the Athenians argued that the Melians should not resist out of their own sense of honor because it would only result in disaster. It was no disgrace to submit to the greatest city of Greece. Athens would leave the island to the Melians as long as they agreed to Athens' demands.

The Melians refused, unwilling to deprive their city, which had existed for seven hundred years, of its freedom. They trusted in the help of the gods and of the Spartans. The ensuing siege lasted several months. It did not succeed in its aim until the spring of 415. The subsequent punishment proposed by Alcibiades, approved by the popular assembly, and then visited on the Melians has already been described. This outcome was no different from that of many other cases, but Thucydides portrays this episode differently, making a bitter mockery of everything the Melians had lived by in their proper Greek fashion.

The superpower possessed no justification other than that Melos's capitulation was Athens' will. Athens was strong, but not strong enough to tolerate the neutrality of a small island of 161 square kilometers and a population of perhaps 1,500 men. The hatred of other states that Pericles had once regretfully accepted as part of political power, Athens now considered essential and desirable. The city believed it acted in accordance with nature, with the laws that prevailed among men and even gods. Euripides had once cited the injustice in the world as an argument against the existence of gods. The Attic envoys in Melos made the gods witnesses to and accomplices of their injustice. No trace is left of the awareness that power—if it is to last—needs boundaries, as Aeschylus had shown in *Prometheus Bound*. Modifying their goals was out of the question for the

Athenians. People of other cities may not always have adhered to the customary morality, either, but they showed at least outward respect for it; Athens now prided itself on openly proclaiming its unscrupulous disregard. This attitude was nothing other than Pericles' overt demonstration of power taken to its logical extreme.

In the winter of 416–415 Athens was also deliberating whether it should come to its Sicilian allies' aid. Segesta was at war with Selinus, and its envoys to Athens suggested their city would finance an Attic expedition to Sicily, for which plenty of money was available. But when Athens agreed to such an expedition, Segesta's appeal was only a pretext; in reality, Athens' aim was to conquer the island. The moving force behind the idea seems once again to have been Alcibiades.

Thucydides merely states that most Athenians had no idea how big Sicily was—it would take a transport ship close to eight days to sail around it. Another source, however, reports that the Athenians were so excited by the prospects of this invasion that men gathered in the palaestras to sketch the contours of the island. Both reports are probably correct, since knowing the shape of an island doesn't imply an appreciation of its size. People supposedly marked the harbors and cities on the southern coast of the island, which faces Africa, for Alcibiades also cast a covetous eye on the old Phoenician colony of Carthage, which is now in Tunisia. In the feverish excitement that gripped the city such ambitions seem to have made sense. The citizenry of Syracuse, the largest and wealthiest city of Sicily, at that time probably consisted of 20,000 to 25,000 men.

Athens decided first to send a delegation to see whether the Segestaeans could fulfill their promises of financing. The delegates returned with sixty talents in bullion silver, enough to man sixty ships for a month, but they had let themselves be fooled about the city's wealth. They had failed to notice, for example, that they were eating off the same magnificent gold and silver dishes at each of the various houses where they were invited. Some of them were even borrowed from neighboring cities. Their hosts seem to have entertained them well and put them in the best of moods, with the result that the guests were willing to be convinced by the Segestaeans' seductive speeches. The Athenians decided to send out sixty ships and appointed as commanders Alcibiades, Nicias, and the old, plainspoken but experienced general Lamachus, son of Xenophanes, who was a favorite target of ridicule in the comedies because he was poor enough to seek reimbursement for his expenses on military campaigns. The Athenian force's mandate was to help Segesta against the Selinuntines, to repopulate to whatever extent possible the city of Leontini, which the Syracusans had destroyed, "and otherwise to do whatever they deemed to be in Athens' best interest."

Four days later, a second meeting of the assembly was called to discuss preparations for the expedition. Nicias, who considered the venture a great mistake and had been appointed against his will to lead it, tried to get the Athenians to reconsider their decision. Peace in the mother country was far from secure, he told them, and it was unwise to splinter one's forces. If anything went wrong, the old enemies would instantly reassert themselves, and even if victory was achieved, it would be impossible to hold on to the island. Why mount this whole expedition? he asked, and concluded with a scathing attack on Alcibiades and the young men who supported him.

Few of the orators who spoke after him took Nicias's side. Alcibiades defended himself tenaciously against the attacks. According to Thucydides, it was on this occasion that he declared there was nothing wrong with not wanting to be one among equals. Besides, he said, the power of the Sicilians should not be overestimated. From what he had heard, they had far fewer hoplites than they claimed and were unable to fight as a united force in defense of their country. He suggested it would be possible to win many allies on the island in the fight against Syracuse, the dominant city on the east coast. In Thucydides' rendering of the speech, Alcibiades then spoke of the necessity that Athens remain true to its tradition and continue to expand its claims.

There was no reason to fear the Peloponnesians, the logic held. The expedition would demonstrate Attic power and intimidate them. Once again, as so often before, Athens would display its strength in a surprise move. If the Sicilian Greeks could be won over he predicted Athens could achieve supremacy over all of Greece. Their mastery of the seas would allow the Athenians to decide at will whether and how long they wanted to stay in Sicily. According to Alcibiades, the Athenians were free to do as they chose.

Alcibiades called for intergenerational unity. Where Nicias had denigrated Alcibiades and the young men who supported him as reckless, Alcibiades himself invoked the far more upbeat and appealing idea of a united front, "understanding that neither youth nor old age can do anything without the other, but that levity, sobriety, and deliberate judgment are strongest when united." We have indications that this notice of working together and the uniting of the different parts of the city was popular at that time. Especially in a democracy, Alcibiades declared, various groups had to work in combination with one another.

But whom did Alcibiades have in mind when he spoke of "levity, sobriety, and deliberate judgment"? The phrase "deliberate judgment," which implies a serious, rigid, and meticulous mentality, characterized Nicias but could also have described the upper social class or the older

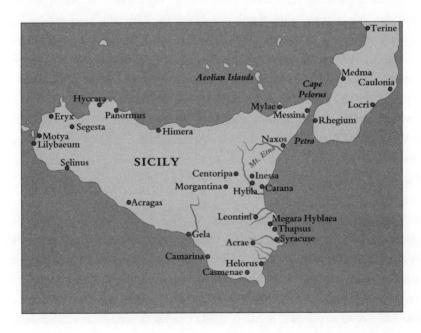

Sicily

generation. The word for levity could also be translated as common or simple: it was aimed at the lower classes but not at youth—unless Alcibiades used the term ironically in the sense of "the small" or "the young." It may have been this combination—indeed, coalition—of highly educated aristocrats and "the people" that played such an important role when Alcibiades beat men like Cleon and Hyperbolus at their own game.

In Euripides' *Suppliants*, produced a short time before, Theseus praises all the things "god" has given to mankind, saying that those who complain about not having enough are misguided. But men believe themselves to be wiser than the gods and strive after more. Theseus accuses Adrastus, the king of Argos, of giving in to ambitious young men who perpetuate the war unjustly and impose suffering on the people so that they can gain personal glory. Theseus's mother counters that cities grow through struggle and that those who live peacefully in obscurity are not well respected. Theseus retorts that neither the rich represented by the young, who favored war, nor the poor benefit a country but that it is those in the middle that serve the cause of democracy. Thucydides, by contrast, mentions this third group only for the sake of completeness.

A division thus existed not only between the upper and lower classes but also between young and old. The schism between the generations escalated into a conflict in Athens, and the younger, educated members of the upper class, who did not necessarily believe in democracy, carried the day precisely because Athens was ruled by a demos that tended to overestimate rather than underestimate the potential of the city. Nevertheless, Alcibiades' call for the different elements working together would become a reality.

After Alcibiades and the Sicilian envoys who were pleading for help swayed the Athenians, Nicias made one final attempt to dissuade the people from the Sicilian venture. He spoke respectfully of the strength of enemies they would be dealing with and the size and kind of investment that would be required. He pointed out that there were many big cities in Sicily, all independent of each other and none of them in a situation where major groups were thinking of revolt. The Sicilians had large land and naval forces and an outstanding cavalry. In addition the island was far away, and in winter a messenger might easily take four months to reach Athens.

Not only would many ships and soldiers and a great deal of money be needed, but wheat and roasted barley would have to be sent along, as well as bakers. Nothing could be left to chance. Even if the Athenian force were superior, it would have a hard time gaining the victory. Nicias was willing to abdicate his command to anyone who saw the situation more optimistically.

But when a crowd has its mind set on something, counterarguments only strengthen its resolve. The people now felt sure they knew how to win. Thucydides described that all the citizens without exception were seized by a passionate desire to undertake the expedition. The older ones were convinced that Athens would conquer their enemies; the younger ones longed for adventure, confident they would return home again; and the lower classes, which supplied the ordinary soldiers, expected they would both earn good money in this undertaking and gain enough clout to guarantee them per diem payment from then on. The eagerness of the majority to embark on the venture was so overwhelming that many who did not agree kept silent out of fear that to vote against it would appear unpatriotic.

Nicias was asked to state in concrete figures what he would need. He asked for one hundred triremes, numerous transport vessels, at least five thousand hoplites, as well as archers and slingers. Additional contingents were to be supplied by the allies.

The popular assembly granted the commander unlimited authority in both financial and strategic matters. The city that had just completed its recovery from the plague and years of continuous warfare prepared once again for armed conflict. In the years since the last war, a new generation of young men had grown up, and money had once again accumulated.

As these deliberations were taking place, in the spring of 415, Euripides' Trojan trilogy was performed at the Great Dionysia. Rehearsals must have started in the summer of 416 and the text completed sometime earlier.

According to legend, before the birth of her son Paris, Queen Hecuba dreams that she has brought forth a firebrand who will set Troy aflame. Therefore, when the baby is born it is abandoned. Raised by shepherds, Paris grows into a strong and handsome young man and returns to the city to take part in a contest, which he wins. The first play of the trilogy—in which Paris judges the goddesses and carries Helen away—is lost, as is the second one, which takes places in the Greek camp before Troy. Only the last one, *The Trojan Women,* has been preserved.

As *The Trojan Women* begins the city has fallen and its sacred shrines have been polluted with the blood of the slain. Poseidon and Athena decide to punish the Greeks for this transgression. Zeus will pursue them with bad weather and thunderstorms on their homeward journey, and Poseidon will stir up the seas. The victors are destined for death. "The fools who destroy cities and desecrate temples and tombs, the sacred places of the dead, will finally meet their own end, the gods decree." In the meantime, Greeks are busy dividing and carrying off their spoils.

After the two gods exit, the scene shifts to the camp of the Trojan women captives, where everyone gathers around Hecuba, the old queen who has lost her husband, her children, her home, and her position, and whom Odysseus will soon carry away into slavery. The women are parceled out to the victors; and one of Hecuba's daughters is sacrificed at the grave of Achilles. Cassandra, who is assigned to Agamemnon, predicts that Troy, in its moment of agony, will turn out to be more fortunate than the Greeks. As Andromache, the wife of Hector, bids farewell to her home, she learns that her young son is to be thrown from the city's towers. For a short while Hecuba finds some solace in the belief that the treacherous Helen will be punished by death. The chorus conjures up the life of the city, the temples, the sacrifices, the happy choral songs, the nocturnal celebrations of the gods who have abandoned Troy to its fate.

In this play Euripides shows the Athenians the suffering and senselessness of war. He clearly alludes to their plans for the Sicilian invasion. The allusion is made even clearer as the Trojan women discuss where they might end up. They don't want to go to Sparta; Athens would be acceptable, or Thessaly, southern Italy, or Sicily. Sicily is called the land of Aetna, belonging to Hephaestus, for the Greeks thought that under Mount Aetna lay the workshop of the blacksmith god, whom they honored as their primeval ancestor. The women also mention that Phoenicia—that is, the Phoenician colony of Carthage—lies opposite the island.

The play contains scathing parodies of the new customs and conditions. Helen declares that she bears no responsibility for the war. She blames Paris; Hecuba, who gave birth to him; Hera, who set the war in motion; and Zeus, who was willing to do her bidding. She also presents a new version of Paris's choice. According to Helen, both Hera and Athena offered him power over Greece if he chose them, but he chose Helen instead, for she was the reward offered by Aphrodite. Thus Helen suggests that he freed the Greeks from Asian rule, and they should in fact be grateful to Helen.

Later in the play, a herald gives the command for setting fire to the city, "so that, once Ilium's walls have sunk into the dust, we may sail happily homeward." Little does he know what the journey has in store for the Greeks. Was Euripides trying to make his audience reflect on what might lie ahead of them? The tragedy has a tone of pessimism and despair; it seems certain that the play stayed alive in the memory of many and especially of those who were soon to sail with the fleet.

One morning, when the city was preparing for the Sicilian expedition, it was discovered that the faces of the herms, which had been placed throughout the city to protect streets and houses, had almost all been mutilated during the night. This was clearly not a spontaneous act of vandalism on the part of a few drunks, since such a coordinated action could hardly have been undertaken on the spur of the moment. It seemed to the Athenians to be the result of organized planning and possibly an attempt to have the expedition canceled. The news of the defilement broke in an atmosphere already fraught with anxiety, and it was immediately taken as a bad omen. Accusations were hurled recklessly.

The council and the assembly met in emergency session. Large rewards were offered for information of any kind leading to the arrest of the vandals. An investigation of the crime was initiated. Anyone with knowledge of other religious profanations was urged to report them. Amnesty was offered to people who confessed that they had been involved with profane acts, and in this way information was gathered— some true, some false—but nothing was learned concerning the herms. Some other damage to divine icons came to light, which had been committed under the influence of alcohol. Most important, it was learned that travesties of the Eleusinian Mysteries had been conducted at private parties attended by Alcibiades. The Eleusinian goddesses had been profaned.

Alcibiades' enemies reacted with alarm and claimed that forces were at work trying to bring about the fall of democracy. They cited past deviations from tradition and the extravagance and wantonness of the rich young aristocrats as proof of the danger posed by Alcibiades. Androcles, who is otherwise practically unknown, figures most prominently among Alcibiades' enemies.

Alcibiades later appeared before the court and asked for a prompt trial. He could not, he said, serve as general in such an important campaign while under serious allegations. This was not necessarily proof of complete innocence. The accounts of his participation in the travesty of the Mysteries may well have been true, but he would also have known that the soldiers and oarsmen would stand up for him. Several hundred men from Argos and Mantinea who were to join the expedition declared they were doing so only because of him. Chances for his acquittal were therefore good. His enemies recognized this and announced they would not delay the army's departure—the case could be taken up later, after his return.

The expedition set out in June or July. Many of the allies as well as the ships carrying supplies had been ordered to Corcyra, where they were to be joined by the others for the crossing to Italy. The flotilla included thirty grain ships that also carried bakers, ships with stonemasons, and ones carrying siege equipment.

The day the fleet actually left, everyone in Athens, citizens and foreigners alike, rose early; at dawn people streamed to Piraeus from every direction. Members of the procession came to see off sons, fathers, relatives, or friends; others came to witness the spectacle of this splendid armada setting out on an expedition more ambitious than anything the Greeks had ever planned before.

The citizens charged with outfitting individual ships had spared no expense on their vessels. They were also responsible for paying the rowers of the top bench and offering an extra allowance to the rest of the crew. The city paid each sailor one drachma per day, which was more than usual, perhaps twice the normal rate. Each outfitter tried to raise his ship's speed of travel, though it is not clear how—whether through improved technology or the use of drills and practice runs.

It might seem that the magnificent display of power and wealth, intended to be seen and heard about by all Greeks, mattered more than the military preparations. But the field army was also excellently equipped. It was claimed by some that this was the Greek navy's longest journey from home, which is not quite true; they had gone farther for the Egyptian expedition. But it is true that Athens' boldness had never been greater.

When the ships were loaded and manned, the blast of a trumpet calling for silence traveled over the harbor and far beyond. The prayers usually recited individually for each ship before putting out to sea were in this case recited by the herald for all of them together. On all the ships wine was poured into big bowls, and the commanders and hoplites offered libations in silver and gold cups. Everyone joined in a hymn praising the gods and asking their blessing. Then the ships departed, leaving the harbor in a long line, to row as fast as possible to Aegina. From there they continued quickly around the Peloponnese to Corcyra, where the rest of the fleet of allies was gathering.

The mood at the moment of departure was perhaps a bit more sober than the one that prevailed when the Athenians had voted in favor of the expedition. Now they thought of the dangers that lay ahead. But the magnificence of their force restored the crowd's confidence. Some Athenians in their eighties may have remembered the time when the fleet left for Salamis. But how things had changed! The city was now a powerful one with vastly improved harbors and an imposing navy, as the carefully planned expedition testified. And this time there was no need for the Athenians to flee.

The news of the Athenians' impending expedition was not taken seriously at first in Syracuse. It seemed so unlikely that they would venture such a difficult campaign. As a result, the preparations for defense were only halfhearted.

But apparently the Athenians had not prepared adequately, either. Along the Italian coast they had to ask one Greek city after another if they could land there. If they were lucky, they were granted permission to drop anchor off the coast and replenish their water supplies. Not until they reached Rhegium, on the way to Messina, were they given access to a market, but the city refused to open its gates to them. While camping there, they found out that they would not receive much money from Segesta, the city that had promised to support the expedition.

The generals differed widely from each other in their plans. Nicias was in favor of minimal engagement. He wanted to convince and if necessary coerce Selinus to make peace with Segesta and then, after Athens had shown its might and trustworthiness, return home. Alcibiades asked if such results would justify all the money and work Athens had invested. He wanted to find allies and take on both Selinus and Syracuse. There is no mention of further plans. Lamachus, for his part, was eager to head for Syracuse and engage in battle immediately, before the enemy was ready. But the immediate problem was to find a place to establish a base of operations. This they did in Naxos and Catana, north of Syracuse. But while they were there a ship caught up with the fleet and delivered a recall order for Alcibiades. He, along with a few other Athenians in the army, was asked to return to the city at once to face charges of profaning the gods.

The investigation had continued during all the time the fleet was under way, though still without results. As it dragged on, an atmosphere of suspicion flourished. More and more people felt compelled to incriminate others. Anybody accused was apprehended, including, we are told, "many honorable men denounced by mean people." The city was seized by a hysterical fear of revolution that Thucydides said was typical of countries unable to free themselves from despotism. Over a hundred men were under suspicion when one man, Andocides by name, decided to speak up, confessing his own guilt and claiming the promised immunity from prosecution. Whether or not his testimony was true remains uncertain to this day. Thucydides doubts it, but the Athenians were relieved to have gotten to the bottom of the matter. Those cleared were released; those convicted were sentenced and executed; those who fled were condemned to death in absentia, with public rewards offered for their murder. The property of those found guilty was confiscated and auctioned off, and, in line with that period's passion for documentation, the lists of the prices were hewn in stone tablets and publicly displayed. Most of the tablets have survived.

It is possible that the mutilation of the herms was an act inspired by oligarchic forces, but this does not mean it was carefully premeditated. Doubts about the viability of democracy were circulating freely at the time and would soon be translated into action. To many groups, this may have seemed an opportune moment to spread uncertainty in the city and in this way call off the Sicilian expedition at the last minute. Such an elaborate scheme would explain the extent of the mutilations, which after all does imply some planning was done in advance. It would also explain why everything was kept so secret, for the oligarchic circles were well versed in secrecy. Whoever was behind it probably never anticipated that the action would have such different results, especially not that many men would lose their lives, property, and homeland. But this oversight was not atypical of the oligarchic circles, either. In all likelihood, they had not thought that far ahead.

The suspicion of the democrats that a coup was in the making may therefore not have been far-fetched. But their anxiety expressed primarily the profound doubts the Attic demos had about itself. The Athenians must have worried that they had taken on more than they could handle. The army and the navy were far away, and once winter came, news from the western front would take months to arrive. In such a state of uncertainty and difficulty, a leader was needed who could be trusted. Many vied for the popular assembly's favor, cajoling Lord Demos and following the old pattern of telling the people only what they wanted to hear.

In this atmosphere it was easy to slander a man who, though he may have been beloved by the people, also caused them discomfort. Alcibiades was a man in whom the people recognized themselves and who embodied their determination and courage. But he also made them afraid. The fact that the citizens now dared press charges against Alcibiades is evidence not only of the Attic leaders' pettiness in pursuit of their self-interest but also of the determination of the demos. It is immaterial whether there was actually a connection between Alcibiades and many of the other hundred accused. He—like many others—may well have toyed with the idea of joining the oligarchic movement. That he was involved in defacing the herms is unlikely, however. There were many reasons for Andocides to implicate him, and the authorities were glad to have an opportunity to get rid of him.

Thucydides is probably correct in locating the great irrationality of the proceedings in the fact that the man most capable of bringing the Sicilian venture to a successful conclusion could now no longer lead it. But we should not overlook the role the structural weakness of Attic democracy played here. The Athens created by Pericles had grown, in the course of the intervening twenty-some years, beyond the abilities of his nephew. This was not so much because Alcibiades lacked the brilliance of his uncle but because he lacked authority. It is no wonder that in his early adulthood Alcibiades felt superior, since the older generation had failed to keep up and, having grown accustomed to easy and fortuitous conditions, was no longer capable of learning.

Intellectual ability and political power no longer went hand in hand. As much as men like Alcibiades were needed, they also became intolerable. Though they were able to get their way in individual cases, the power of the democracy was splintered among various demagogues, and the people were pulled in many different directions. The demands imposed on them by the great war and the burdens of empire had long been beyond their strength.

. . .

The *Salaminia*, one of the two courier boats that Athens maintained for transporting envoys and for other special missions, was charged with carrying Alcibiades along with the other accused men back to Athens. It had to make frequent stops along the way, as did all the other ships, and in Thurii Alcibiades managed to escape his guards.

The Athenians condemned him to death in absentia. They decreed that all priests and priestesses were to curse him, but one priestess, Theano, the daughter of Menon, refused to follow the order, saying she had become a priestess in order to pray, not to curse people. This is the earliest incidence of actual civil disobedience we know of in Athens. Antigone's action, after all, took place only on the stage. It is noteworthy that in both cases it was a woman who refused to act against her conscience.

Alcibiades was able to cross over to Cyllene on Elis in a small boat, and after some negotiations conducted by his friends, he proceeded to Sparta. This marks the beginning of the war's final chapter.

It is reported that when he got news in the winter of 415–414 of the death sentence imposed on him, Alcibiades said, "Well, then we will show them that we are still alive." He also wanted to demonstrate to the Athenians that his exceptional talents could have led them to victory. With the death sentence upon him, he proved his abilities by placing himself in the service of the Spartans.

He told the Spartan leadership that the Athenians had planned to take over Sicily and then go on to Italy and Carthage in order, ultimately, to conquer the Peloponnese and extend their rule over all of Greece. He said he believed that the Athenians had a good chance of succeeding unless Sparta sent help to Syracuse. He suggested that an experienced and effective general be sent and that the ships be rowed by men who could also serve as hoplites, to lessen the transport problem.

Alcibiades went on to advise the Spartans to wage war openly and effectively against Athens at home. This was necessary so that the Syracusans would not feel that they were carrying on the struggle against

Athens all by themselves. Intermittent invasions of Attica were not enough. Instead the Spartans should seize, fortify, and occupy a strategic spot, Decelea, which was situated on an elevation four hours north of Athens and visible from the city. This would allow the Spartans to survey the roads in Attica constantly. Athens would lose its revenues from the countryside and the workshops outside the city, as well as from the Laurian silver mines. Furthermore, Athens' allies would be more reluctant to pay their tributes if they saw that Sparta was really committed to fighting with all its might.

In his speech, as related by Thucydides, Alcibiades also justified his previous anti-Spartan politics. He reminded the Spartans that they had, after all, helped his personal enemy to power by negotiating peace with Nicias. Consequently, he argued, he could not be blamed for having harmed them in the past. And nobody in Sparta should criticize him for taking the side of the people, he suggested, since Athens was a democracy. He and his family had always attempted to exercise a moderating influence. Of course, he conceded, they had known that democracy was an acknowledged folly.

To those who were upset by Alcibiades' willingness to join the enemies of his father city, he replied that love for one's country was ill placed if that country behaved unjustly and contrary to the law. It was better, he said, to exert oneself as a worthy citizen in safety. His present efforts were an attempt to gain a new homeland to replace the one he'd lost.

In Greece, exiled individuals, usually aristocrats, often tried to force their return home with the help of foreign cities, a fact that could be cited as parallel to Alcibiades' situation. But Alcibiades' case nevertheless remains unique. He was not an ordinary person seeking an ordinary city's help to force his way back to an ordinary country. Such an incident would have involved a hundred or perhaps a thousand people. Here an individual wanted—for personal reasons and to satisfy his desire for recognition and revenge—to help turn a war against his own country, a war that meanwhile affected the entire Mediterranean world.

His actions are often interpreted as an expression of exaggerated individualism or even egomania. But whatever the interpretation, Alcibiades' treason reveals that he had grown beyond the polis. He was indeed a harbinger foretelling the end of the polis world. There were others, too: The very manner in which his city reigned over its allies and its subject cities showed little respect for the independence of the polis as an independent political unit. Athens was often more concerned about its own friends in other cities than about the cities themselves. That is what transformed its sovereignty over the Delian League into an empire, even if only for a short time.

For their part, the Spartans, who had initially planned merely to dispatch a delegation to Syracuse, now appointed a general: Gylippus, son of Cleandrides, and a man not unlike Brasidas. They gave him a few ships and some troops, and he received additional support as well, primarily from the Corinthians.

At the end of March 414, Aristophanes' *The Birds* was first presented in Athens. The play opens with two Attic citizens having decided to move away from their city. They acknowledge that it is a great city, open to anyone willing to spend all his money on litigation, but they are fed up with it. They are looking for a place where they can live in peace. A showy, cuckoolike bird, the hoopoe, appears. Because he has a good view of the surroundings, he makes various suggestions, but they reject his advice. They have resolved that they do not want to live by the sea—the *Salaminia*, the courier ship that recalled and apprehended Alcibiades, might appear and pick them up. Life in the country is too provincial. But why not live up in the air with the birds? They decide to establish a bird city, observing that the birds have completely ignored their political potential. After all, they occupy a key location between the heavens and earth and are in a position to control communication between the gods and humans. If they put their minds to it they could become a world power. Thus Cloudcuckooland is founded.

Immediately various stock characters turn up: The poet beggar, the prophet, the geometrician, the supervisor, and the dealer in decrees appear and are unceremoniously sent packing. "Ornithomania" breaks out among humans; everyone wants to sprout wings. The humans win their battle with the gods, thanks to some good advice from Prometheus.

In the end, Zeus cedes the rule of the world to one of the two founders, Pisthetaerus, whose name means "persuasive friend." He is also given as his bride Zeus's daughter Basileia, whose name, built on the word *basis* or *king*, makes her the embodiment in maiden form of the kingdom or tyranny.

In Karl Reinhardt's words, "The spirit of daring activity typical of Attica celebrates its loftiest triumph" in *The Birds*. The play depicts the Athenians as unchangeable. Even those who want to leave the city and its doings behind for good find themselves forming their own empire and ultimately turning into God. Since this is a comedy, the spectators are left laughing, but the play makes a serious comment on the Athenian character that was surely reflected upon by those who saw it. It depicts a community without any dark sides—no informers or sycophants—that nevertheless manages to reign over the world. This masterpiece excels especially in its lyrical passages, but critical and irreverent as it was, *The Birds* was given only second prize. The winner of the competition was a play by a comic poet named Ameipsias, who is hardly remembered at all.

After Alcibiades' departure, the Athenian fleet in Sicily first sailed along the island's northern coast to Segesta, which had promised to underwrite the campaign. Thirty talents is all the Athenians received there, though they obtained another 120 from the sale of prisoners they had taken when seizing a town at war with Segesta.

In the winter of 415–414, Athens began its operation against Syracuse. The troops had already frittered away time that could have been turned to good use, but now Nicias proceeded with great skill. Because of their lack of cavalry the Athenians had many difficulties to overcome. Above all, they would have to cut the city off on the land side. North of the city was a high plateau, at least part of which the Athenians encircled with fortified walls. In addition a stronghold had to be established south of the bay, in the "great harbor," so as to be able to control access to the port.

In spite of all these obstacles the Athenians were successful enough in their assault for the Syracusans to initiate peace talks in the spring of 414. But just one day before the popular assembly of Syracuse was to meet to

An actor in costume and mask, perhaps from Aristophanes' The Birds. *From a mixing vessel, ca. late fifth century* B.C. *Los Angeles, California, J. Paul Getty Museum.*

vote on the negotiations, the new Spartan general Gylippus arrived, and the city was filled with new courage.

Gylippus, like Brasidas ten years earlier, was able to succeed at what had previously been Athens' forte, namely, to conduct war imaginatively and energetically. He was unhampered by outmoded tradition and responded freely to the demands of the situation, deploying his forces in completely new ways.

With the help of the Syracusans, Gylippus was able to turn the tide. Receiving support from all over the country, he assembled an army that was far too large for the Athenians to take on. Now they were the ones taken by surprise, and, apparently spoiled by a long and almost unfailing history of military success, they no longer possessed their old adaptability.

It was not only in strategic and tactical matters that Athens' enemies began to excel over the Athenians at that time, but in technical innovation as well. The technique of naval tactics is a good example. According to Attic thinking, confirmed by many successes, a prow-to-prow encounter was always to be avoided. The proper mode of attack was to ram an enemy ship from the side. To achieve this, the Athenians had developed in the days of the Ionian revolt their famous tactic of slipping through the line of enemy ships and then, in a skillful maneuver, attacking them as they turned around.

Athenian ships were constructed with this tactic in mind. The bow was not built to be sturdy because it was the protruding battering ram that was to deliver the thrust. But precisely this feature turned out to be a weakness once the Corinthians seized on the idea of strengthening the bow of their ships and attacking the Athenians head on. For this purpose the Corinthians and Syracusans reinforced the cheeks of their triremes, and this new design proved highly successful.

By the fall of 414, the position of the Athenians had deteriorated so much that Nicias decided to send an account of the facts to the popular assembly. He acknowledged the assembly's habit of wanting to hear only pleasant news and becoming angry later on when the expected success failed to materialize. For this reason he thought it better now to let them know the truth. The Athenians' land forces surrounding Syracuse found themselves in a siege situation, and incredible as it might sound, even their naval forces were in danger. Because they had to be on constant alert, they could not pull their ships on shore, and the vessels became water-logged. Provisions were also running short. Battle losses and defections were slowly but steadily decimating the Athenian forces. Many soldiers, particularly the mercenaries, were going over to the enemy, and others simply disappeared. Some rowers had successfully offered their captains captured slaves to serve in their stead, undermining the fleet. It was common knowledge that the crews could keep up their peak performance for only a short time and that it was just a few top oarsmen who really moved the ships ahead and kept the stroke rhythm the rest followed. Now that all of Sicily stood united and another army was expected to arrive from the Peloponnese, Nicias informed the assembly that the Athenian army should either be recalled or receive significant reinforcement.

The Athenians decided to send out another sixty ships and a few thousand hoplites, along with a considerable sum of money. In order to pay for all this, they introduced a new system of taxation. Instead of collecting the old contributions from the Delian League, they levied a five-percent import and export tax at all the ports of the empire.

The new army left in the spring of 413. In the meantime, the Spartans had invaded Attica for the first time since the peace treaty and, following Alcibiades' advice, fortified the plateau of Decelea just fourteen miles outside of Athens. Demosthenes, the commander of the new Athenian army, was eager for action. He may have realized that time was working against Athens. Perhaps he went to Sicily with the intention of making one supreme effort to win and, if it failed, of giving up the enterprise, which must have appeared increasingly futile in view of the Spartan occupation in Attica. Demosthenes was ready to put things to the test. With little hesitation, he tried to capture the plateau north of Syracuse. After an unsuccessful nighttime attack, in which the Athenians suffered great losses, he immediately advocated breaking off the entire campaign. Demoralization and sickness spread among the troops.

But Nicias refused to go along with Demosthenes. He was apparently more optimistic, because he had heard that Syracuse was also tiring of the war. In reality he was most worried about returning home to face the judgment of the popular assembly in Athens, where those who could properly assess the situation had little influence and the people listened to whomever could sway them with "clever speeches."

Nicias admitted that, if necessary, he would rather die in battle than be subjected to disgrace and unjust accusations in Athens. This is understandable, though perhaps he should have worried less about his personal fate and been more concerned instead about the fate of what had been entrusted to him as general: tens of thousands of men, including the entirety of Athens' youth, as well as the entire fleet.

Nicias subsequently asserted that he was powerless as commander because it was not in the nature of Athenians to obey authority. Thucydides praises Nicias in a later obituary passage, which in itself is very unusual in his work, as "having been guided all his life by what is taken for virtue." The praise is justified, but it leaves out a great deal.

Nicias was simply not up to the job imposed on him. The city's decision-making body was no longer functioning rationally and military bungling was common.

Finally, after further reinforcements had reached Syracuse from the Peloponnese, Nicias gave up his opposition. The command to depart was given, and on the night we can reconstruct to have been August 27, the Athenians were about to leave secretly under cover of darkness. They were waiting for the signal to lift anchor when the full moon was hidden by an eclipse. Most of the soldiers were frightened, and Nicias himself tended, as Thucydides observes, to abide too much by signs and omens. The soothsayers advised the commanders not to do anything until three times nine days had elapsed. Solar eclipses no longer caused great concern by that time because they had been explained, but lunar eclipses remained mysterious because it was not understood that they were caused by the earth's movement between the sun's light and the moon.

The land battles that followed brought defeat after defeat, as did the naval engagements. In the Attic camp, disappointment turned into anger at the senselessness of the whole enterprise. When the Syracusans blocked the exit of the great harbor—for they were intent now not just on defeating the enemy but on its annihilation—the Athenians tried to get their entire force out of the harbor all at once. Disregarding the usual pre-cautions, they loaded the ships full with hoplites, slingers, and archers. They constructed grappling irons with which to pull enemy ships close in order to board them. But the Syracusans, having seen their preparations and heard reports of this tactic, covered the bows of their ships and part of the decks with skins, which offered no grip to human hands. A violent struggle ensued. For a long time it remained unclear who was winning—until the Athenians finally turned toward shore in retreat. Their fleet was still strong enough for Demosthenes to suggest another escape attempt, but the crews refused to get back on board. They demanded to retreat by land.

If they had set out promptly, they might have reached safety rela-tively unharmed, for the victors were celebrating their success. But the

Athenians postponed their retreat too long, and the Syracusans again blocked their way.

The Athenian departure presented a pitiful sight. They were leaving almost their entire navy behind, proof that all of Athens' great hopes had ended in failure. The very act of breaking camp meant misery and suffering. The dead lay about unburied; the men had neither strength nor courage to deal with them properly. The Athenians had not even asked the victorious enemy for permission to collect the bodies of their fallen and drowned soldiers. Worst of all were the sick and wounded, who begged the departing troops to take them along. Many dragged themselves along as far as they could before succumbing to exhaustion. At last they fell behind, shouting accusations, begging for help, and wailing while their comrades, tentmates, friends, and relatives went off dejectedly, themselves overcome by feelings of helplessness and self-disgust. They resembled a procession of refugees abandoning a sacked city, and a sizable one at that, since the army still comprised about 40,000 men. The servants who ordinarily accompanied the cavalry and hoplites had long since left, so that everyone had to carry his own equipment, along with whatever rations remained. Food had become scarce, and despondency reigned. The troops remembered the splendor of their departure from Athens, the prayers and happy paeans that had accompanied it. Now they would be lucky to make it back home.

They did not get very far. Both retreating armies, first that of Demosthenes, then that of Nicias, were decimated by the enemy. Both generals were taken prisoner and executed by the Syracusans, though this was done over Gylippus's objections. Captured Athenians were immediately sold as slaves; some Sicilian soldiers had already sold captives they had taken. Later, it was said, many Athenian slaves could be found all over Sicily, though quite a few escaped. The number of official prisoners of war was thus relatively low, amounting to only about 7,000, who were confined in quarries near Syracuse, crowded together in deplorable conditions. Many became ill, according to one account, "because they were forced by the lack of space to do everything in the same place; and, because the dead were also piled up there . . . the stench was unbearable.

In addition, they were tormented by hunger and thirst." After seventy days all of the prisoners except the Athenian citizens and their Sicilian and Italian allies were sold into slavery. What became of those who remained is unknown. Many must have perished where they were; others were secretly removed, some to be sold.

In a peculiar footnote to this episode some captives as well as fleeing soldiers owed their lives to Euripides. The poet was popular in Sicily, and Athenians who could sing passages from his plays—and apparently quite a few could—were often treated as welcome guests and helped or freed. When they were home again they expressed their gratitude to the poet. But the fortunate were few in number.

Thucydides' observation that the failure of the Sicilian expedition did not result primarily from "a mistake in assessing the power against which it was launched" should be taken in the context in which he presented it. Athens had in fact had sufficient forces, Thucydides reminds the reader. After all, it almost managed to defeat Syracuse. If Thucydides' account may be believed, it is probable that the turn in Spartan policy that led to the defeat of the Athenians was brought about by Alcibiades. His alliance with the Spartans directly resulted from the machinations of demagogic elements in Athens. Their interference deprived him of the chance to bring the expedition he had planned to a prompt and successful conclusion.

Of course, the Athenians had, even after Alcibiades' departure in 414, created an important precondition for what followed. They had attacked Sparta's coast in order to support Argos. This was an open violation of the Peace of Nicias, not the first, to be sure—in 418 they had participated in the Battle of Mantinea—but the Spartans considered this the first serious breach.

But what would the Athenians have done had they won in Syracuse? What purpose would victory have served? Would they have attacked Carthage next, or the Peloponnese? And how could they have stayed on in Syracuse, in Sicily? The expedition has been described as "pure madness." It was the madness of a democracy possessed of such incredible powers that it could not easily return to a state of normalcy. It was a democracy that only a man of Pericles' stature could guide successfully. Alcibiades was quite correct when he called continual forward motion the city's dominant law.

The Athenians refused at first to believe reports of the magnitude of their defeat. Then their wrath turned against the orators who had argued in favor of the expedition, even though the decision had been reached collectively. They also blamed the soothsayers, who had encouraged their hopes. They felt not only grief but great fear. Most of the able-bodied young men were dead; few triremes remained in the dockyards; neither money nor crews to row ships were left. The Athenians feared that their Peloponnesian enemies, joined now by the Sicilian Greeks, might attack on land and water simultaneously.

Attica was for all practical purposes no longer their own. The Spartans and their allies took turns manning Decelea, where they held almost unchallenged sway. Athens' cavalry was in poor shape, many horses being injured and others worn out from constant use and frequent traveling on hard ground. The city's walls had to be guarded day and night. Almost all the sheep and draft animals had been lost. Supplies from nearby Euboea could reach Athens only by sea, by a long route around Sunium. Twenty thousand slaves, mostly skilled workers, had gradually defected to the enemy.

But the Athenians refused to give up. According to Thucydides, they possessed a "will to succeed which . . . would have earlier seemed incredible." Their strength and daring far exceeded all the reasonable expectations of the rest of the Greeks. The Athenians were ready to submit to a rigid regime and great hardship to hold on to what they had. This determination may not have been shared equally by all, however. The wealthier circles, where, according to Thucydides, the greatest losses were suffered in difficult times, were particularly beset by doubt. We don't know how free the dissenters were to express their opposition in public. For among the broad masses the cause of democracy had become closely linked to the war. They feared defeat would bring the end of democracy.

It may be wrong to search for reasons why the war was allowed to drag on. Looking back from our perspective we wonder how the Athenians could possibly have continued fighting. Why didn't the total disaster of the Sicilian expedition, embarked on with such high hopes, lead to a reassessment of Athens' possibilities?

It is probably true that the Athenians overestimated their strength when they thought they could still win the war and maintain or regain their supremacy. Their misjudgment may have arisen from the assumption that they were still facing the same Spartans they had known for decades and against whom they had generally fought successfully during the first ten years of the war. They may still have been convinced of their superiority, not just in resources but in initiative and inventiveness. In the past they had always come up with new solutions when their problems seemed to exceed their strength. But even if they had wanted peace, they could not immediately lay down their arms. They first had to negotiate. And they could not negotiate from a position of total defenselessness. Consequently, measures had to be taken, and the implementation of such measures implied a decision to continue the war.

Things might have taken a different turn only if the Spartans had immediately presented a peace offer advantageous to the Athenians. As far as we can tell they did nothing of the sort. They had no reason to.

The Athenians therefore decided to impose extreme austerity, build a new fleet, and do everything within their power to preserve the loyalty of their confederates. In order to prevent the popular assembly from passing rash and injudicious decrees, they established a new body of ten *probouloi* or "pre-advisors." Only older men were eligible for this office and they had to be elected. The names of only two are known. One was Hagnon, son of Nicias (but not the Nicias who had been a general). Hagnon had been *strategos* in 440, 431, and 430 and had founded Amphipolis in 437. The other was Sophocles, who was by then in his nineties. The exact relationship between the *probouloi* and the Council of Five Hundred is unclear, but the pre-advisors were most likely expected to exercise an authority similar to that held earlier by the Areopagus.

The Spartans meanwhile had reached the point where they were determined to bring the war to a victorious end and disinclined to show mercy for Athens. They had had ample reasons for deciding on war in 431, but now they also had come to realize that Athens was a much stronger and more resilient enemy than they had thought.

Thucydides writes that in the winter of 413–412 all the Greeks were burning to join the war. The end of the war seemed in sight, Sparta's allies were newly motivated, and many who had not previously taken sides were now eager to be counted among the victors. The Spartans were counting on the arrival of troops from Sicily. They already saw their old hegemony over all of Greece restored.

Many of the cities tied to Athens were finally ready to defect—most important, Chios, the last of the Athenian confederates that still had a navy of its own. Every city eager to disassociate itself from Athens worked to persuade others to do the same. But these cities anxiously waited for the Spartans to come to their aid, for Athens still inspired great fear. Sparta ordered a fleet of one hundred ships to be built, and different cities were told how many triremes they were to supply.

Soon thereafter, in 412, the Spartan fleet appeared off Ionia and began to move freely around the Aegean Sea, as previously only the Athenians had done. Sparta could now attack Attic territories on the eastern shore of the Aegean, whereas even Brasidas had previously been able to accomplish this only in the north.

In view of the possibility that the Attic empire might be collapsing, Persia once again appeared on the scene. The Delian League had originally been formed to keep Persia out of Greece. Upon his accession Darius II had renewed the Peace of Callias in 424–423, but in 414 the Athenians had broken it—as they had the Peace of Nicias—by recklessly supporting a revolt in Caria. They wanted to gain additional allies there and had given little thought to the possible consequences.

Now the great king once again demanded tributes from the Greek cities in Asia Minor, tributes Athens had prevented him from collecting. His governors, led by Tissaphernes, the satrap of Sardis, entered into talks with the Spartans about a possible alliance, with the condition that they recognize Persia's domination of its old Greek subjects.

The Spartan commanders signed three treaties with Persia in the years 412 and 411. The first one stated that "all land and all cities in possession of the King or at some earlier time in possession of the King's forefathers are to belong to the King." The second treaty leaves open the question of the Persians' claims to possession and merely states that the Spartans agree to refrain from attacking these cities and from demanding tribute from them. The third treaty again recognizes the Persians' claims to its former possessions but limits these claims to land and cities in Asia. Without this clause Persian dominion could, because of many Greeks' voluntary submission in the years 481–480, have extended as far as Boeotia.

The Persian satrap Tissaphernes agreed in return to subsidize the crews of Sparta's and its allies' fleet. The Persians were clearly unwilling to take an active part in the fighting. Only occasionally was a small Persian contingent dispatched to assist Sparta. Persia promised repeatedly to send a Phoenician fleet of nearly one hundred and fifty vessels, and in fact moved such a fleet to Pamphylia, closer to the action. It never joined the fighting, even though Tissaphernes kept announcing its imminent arrival.

These negotiations brought to an end the great unity of the Greeks that had emerged during the Persian Wars. The Spartans' promise of liberation was now limited to the Greek mainland and the islands (not counting those considered part of Asia). They were now willing to sacrifice much more for money and for victory over Athens. The times when they were prepared to offer peace for the sake of a few hostages were past. Now they had other means at their disposal and made deliberate use of them.

There is no evidence of protests from Ionia. Such protests could have come only from cities that had already renounced Athens or were about to do so, and these cities were by now more afraid of a reassumption of Attic power than of Persian rule. Persian domination might cost them considerable money, but Attic dominion could lead to loss of life, banishment, and revolution.

This reentry of Persia into the Greek world throws an interesting light on Athens' power. It would seem that the city's means were exhausted after the disaster of the Sicilian expedition, or at least that Athens' enemies—Sparta, Corinth, Sicyon, Boeotia, the Sicilians, the cities north of the Aegean and those in the east that had been part of the Delian League and recently defected or were contemplating defection—would have been strong enough to deal with a much weakened Athens. The anti-Athenian forces had plenty of men and would soon possess ships as well, but they lacked the means to keep them in service. The Athenians, by contrast, quickly built a new fleet and began to operate with several squadrons. This could not have been easy for them, for they had reached the limits of their financial resources, but the city still had more determination and willingness to fight the war than its opponents. Repeated levies of property taxes presumably provided the needed funds.

When Chios defected the Athenians decided to fall back on the iron reserve of one thousand talents they had set aside at the beginning of the war. They knew they could not count on the rest of their confederates to remain loyal, and soon afterward Erythrae, Clazomenae, Miletus, Libedus, and Lesbos went over to the enemy. The Athenians were able to recover Lesbos quickly, and Clazomenae, too, was reconquered. Athenian forces landed in Chios, laid waste to large areas, and surrounded the city. They also began a siege of Miletus. But they lost Cnidus, Rhodes, Phocaea, and other places.

The Athenians' most important base in Ionia was Samos. A revolution ushering in democracy had just taken place there, with the support of Athens. The new government had executed and exiled many aristocrats, as was usual in such situations, and the democrats also confiscated the aristocrats' property and divided it among themselves. They forbade ordinary people to marry aristocrats. Those members of the nobility allowed to stay in the country were to be segregated from the population. The atrocities committed by the democrats strengthened their unity, and this unity was to be preserved at all cost. Athens, convinced that the Samians could now be counted on as a reliable ally, was willing to give the city back its autonomy.

The Attic fleet, which was gradually enlarged, could not achieve all of Athens' goals, but it was strong enough to limit the Spartans' freedom of movement considerably. The two sides held each other in balance.

Sparta was nevertheless able to score successes from time to time, especially in the north, along the Propontis, a region that was crucial as a shipping route for grain from the Black Sea area to Athens. In the spring of 411 the Spartans succeeded in winning Abydos and Lampsacus over to their side—after approaching them by land rather than by sea. The Athenians were able to retake only Lampsacus, which was not fortified. They placed a large garrison in Sestos, opposite Abydos, in order to secure the Hellespont. In the summer of 411, however, Byzantium, Chalcedon, and Cyzicus revolted; the Athenians were able to recover only Cyzicus.

Alcibiades had served the Spartan fleet as an adviser since the beginning of its offensive in Ionia. He had been of great assistance to the Spartans, in part thanks to his old family connections there, and had participated in a battle.

His situation was not an easy one, however. There were those in Sparta who did not like him, among them King Agis, whose wife he had seduced. Others were distrustful of him. Suspicions arose easily concerning this restless and clever man, who was constantly involved in scheming and negotiating, and in the process had developed a close relationship with the Persian satrap Tissaphernes.

It is possible Alcibiades began to fear for his safety, or that he finally saw a chance to achieve his most prized goal. Whatever the motive, he entered into a secret communication with the Attic commanders in Samos. He wanted to return to his home city, to fight for it and advance its cause.

This does not imply that Alcibiades felt any remorse for his efforts on Sparta's behalf. He had demonstrated his military prowess, and his achievements filled him with pride. It seemed to him that now he could accomplish something even greater by saving his native city after having brought it to its knees. His vigorous support of Sparta may have been motivated by the secondary aim of forcing Athens to reaccept him. The urge to prove himself anew and the desire to be of use to Athens may once again have pointed in one and the same direction.

Perhaps Alcibiades felt Athens needed a new Pericles, and that he should fill that role. How better to acquire the authority of a Pericles than by helping win the war at this crucial moment? But this presumed that he would be given the opportunity.

Alcibiades was capable of fitting in wherever he went. As one source put it: "He parties in Ionia more wildly than the Ionians, trains and does calisthenics in Thebes, in Thessaly outdoes the Aleuadae, a prominent family in working the horses and driving chariots, displays more strength and simplicity than the Spartiates, and, in Thrace, drinks more unmixed wine than the natives."

Alcibiades knew that if he could lead his city out of its desperate straits, he would earn fame not only as an outstanding and shrewd adviser but also as a statesman. In this position he could have identified with his city completely.

Alcibiades' distinctive brand of individualism was the combined result of growing up freely among many different influences, including Sophism and the element of aristocratic self-reliance. Alcibiades represented a revival of the concentration of the Panhellenic public sphere, which had been pushed into the background in Athens during the period between Cleisthenes and Pericles in favor of a greater concentration on the interests of the city itself.

The story of Alcibiades' recall and his betrayal of Athens took place at a moment when his ambitions were extremely high and the demos as incapable as ever of living up to them. He may have believed that the gulf that had opened up between them could be closed again. But it was not to be.

Alcibiades informed the Attic commanders of Samos that he was on good terms with the Persian satrap Tissaphernes. Alcibiades said he was in a position to create ties of friendship between Athens and the satrap and even with the great king. The only condition was that Athens change its form of government: the Persians were reluctant to trust a democracy. Alcibiades was willing to return to Athens if an oligarchy was in charge there instead of the democratic government and the "rabble" who had driven him out.

Alcibiades was in fact a welcome guest at the court of Tissaphernes. He had explained to the satrap that it was not in Persia's interest for one Greek power to dominate both on land and on the seas. It would be to the Great King's advantage to play one Greek power off against the other; by doing so, the king could achieve much without sending out an army of his own. Besides, Sparta's stated aim of liberating all the Greeks made it much harder for Sparta to relinquish Asia Minor.

The treaties between Sparta and Tissaphernes were binding only for the commanders and not the city as a whole, so Alcibiades advised the Persians to be sparing in their payments to Sparta. To this extent Alcibiades' suggestions were in line with Persia's Athenian interests. But it seems unlikely that the Persians would have been willing to do anything more to be of service to the Athenians.

However, Attica's powerful fleet admirals and the wealthy triarchs— those chosen from Athens' wealthiest few hundred men to equip triremes and to command them—saw in Alcibiades' overtures grounds for new hope. They were delighted to have Alcibiades reenter the picture and eagerly grasped the opportunity to work toward a change in government. It was they and others like them who carried the heaviest financial burden of the war—why should they not assume the political power as well?

For the first time since Cleisthenes there was a movement in Athens to make the constitution more oligarchic. In past years, an oligarchy could only have been established with the help of the democrats. Now this paradox seemed possible, because of the desperate state the city found itself in.

In any case the Athenian officers in Samos came together with the aim of amending the constitution. They swore allegiance to one another, and a conspiracy was formed. Only one of the generals, Phrynichus, son of Stratonides, spoke up in opposition. He could not imagine the Persian king making common cause with the Athenians, and he did not think that a revolution would benefit the city. Above all, he objected to the plan of the conspirators to establish oligarchies in Athens' subject cities as well. Popular allegiance to Athens in these cities was the direct result of Athenian support for democracy. Nowhere, Phrynichus argued, did the upper class have any interest in the Delian League, and in this he was certainly correct.

The plan to foment revolution in the democratic subject cities is revealing of the scheme's rashness and the conspirators' determination to do anything whatsoever to lead Athens to victory. They unwisely assumed that the elite factions in other cities shared their point of view.

Phrynichus was an intelligent observer and a good tactician. He had shown this recently when he insisted on giving up the siege of Miletus because he, unlike Nicias, was unwilling to expose his troops to unreasonable danger, even if it meant evoking the assembly's disapproval. His foresight enabled him to move the wounded and the siege equipment to safety.

Phrynichus came from a modest background. He was said to have once been a shepherd, and made himself a name by bringing various changes before the people's court. His activities earned him many enemies. As responsibly as he had acted at Miletus, he did not shy away from intrigue and was even ready to betray the Attic army if it would bring him personal advantage. Since he was an enemy of Alcibiades, he later joined the oligarchs when they turned against his rival. Now, however, he opposed them unsuccessfully.

The conspirators in Samos spoke to their troops in veiled terms of the necessity of a change. Morale was improved by promises that the Persians would soon pay generous wages. Some men traveled to Athens to lay the groundwork there.

Thucydides describes what happened in Athens in the summer of 411 almost as if it were a political morality play. The spokesman of the conspirators in Samos, Pisandros of Acharnae, and the other envoys told the popular assembly that a chance for victory had improved because

Alcibiades' return would make possible a treaty with Persia. The only condition was that the Athenian democracy would no longer be able to function as it had. Cautious as they were in their choice of words, the conspirators nevertheless felt bold enough to say as much publicly.

When the assembly responded with profound indignation, Pisandros called every opposition speaker back to the tribune and asked if he knew of any other way to save the city. When they all responded in the negative, he repeated after every speaker that there was no alternative but "to conduct the affairs of the polis more rationally and to reduce the number of public offices." It was crucial to winning the great king's trust and bringing back Alcibiades. What the Athenians had to concentrate on now, he argued, was saving the city, not the constitution. The status quo could always be restored once the crisis had passed.

For the time being, however, nothing was decided except to dispatch Pisandros and some other envoys to speak with Alcibiades and Tissaphernes. Before they left they consulted with various *hetaeriae* in the city, secret societies whose members had sworn to support each other in legal cases and the candidacy for public office. These associations were probably little more than social clubs, but on occasion the help of fellow members was needed. The overall influence of these *hetaeriae* had been quite limited, but they were of major importance to individuals who were threatened legally or had specific political ambitions. Since the members came from the city's elite, they were obvious supporters of the oligarchic movement. Pisandros asked them to collaborate to overthrow the democratic government.

They must all have realized that they could not simply seize political power the way it had once been done in Athens and was still often done in other Greek cities. The change in government had to take legal form, following a period of massive intimidation and terror.

The talks with Tissaphernes were inconclusive. The satrap, on the advice of Alcibiades, set terms the Athenians could not agree to, no matter how eager they were to cooperate. They felt betrayed and began to lose faith in Alcibiades. But they continued to prepare for the fall of democracy.

Meanwhile in Athens the *hetaeriae* had arranged the murder of

Androcles, a popular democrat. Rumors circulated that the daily allowances paid for public service were to be abolished and that participation in political decision-making was to be limited to the five thousand wealthiest and most influential citizens. This was the version put out by the plotters. In reality a much smaller group was planning to assume power.

The popular assembly and the Council of Five Hundred were put under great pressure. They continued to attend to business in accordance with the constitution, which was still in effect, but the entire agenda was determined by the oligarchs. Their supporters were the only ones allowed to address the assembly. Others no longer dared to, perhaps out of fear. The democratic forces may have overestimated the number of conspirators, whose self-assurance and the general deference they commanded suggested great power. In fact, their cleverness—and utter unscrupulousness—cloaked their small numbers. Those who spoke out against the oligarchs were quietly disposed of, and no attempt was made to investigate even the most flagrant political killings. Fear gripped the city, and it became impossible to trust one's own neighbors.

In this way a relatively small number of men succeeded in intimidating the whole city. After Pisandros's return, the popular assembly appointed a commission charged with devising proposals on how best to govern the city. The meeting at which it was directed to report back to the assembly was held not at the Pnyx but at the temple to Poseidon at Colonus, an hour and a half's distance from the city. The place offered only limited space, and broad participation was probably further discouraged by the fact that it was surrounded by armed men.

The ten-member commission made a motion that any Athenian be allowed to propose any measure whatsoever and that anyone accusing him of illegality be punished by death. Once this motion was passed, all safeguards of democracy were gone.

Next the new council resolved that the old tenure of office and payment for public service be terminated and that five men be elected and charged with picking one hundred men, each of whom would in turn pick three more. This body of four hundred was given full authority to govern as it judged best and was to assemble a list of five thousand individuals it could call into session at will.

The Four Hundred included the conspirators and their close friends. Thucydides mentions some of them by name, singling out Antiphon, son of Sophilus, as the architect of the plan. Thucydides praises Antiphon's intelligence and talent, even his "virtue." What he does not mention is that the plotter's leader, Pisandros, was among those who had capitalized on the desecration of the herms in 415.

This new council took over the council building with the help of soldiers and a following of one hundred and twenty young men. The Council of Five Hundred who were meeting inside were asked to leave the building. They were informed they would be paid through the end of their year of service, of which a few weeks remained. They were handed the money outside the door, in the agora, and left. In the weeks that followed a few men were assassinated, and others were imprisoned or exiled. Numerous changes were made in the existing constitution, but those banished under democracy were not called back because this would have brought the return of Alcibiades. A delegation was sent to Sparta to explore the possibility of peace.

But the attempt to gain the support of the army at Samos for the new constitution failed. The oarsmen were outraged at the idea of losing their political rights. They immediately set about planning a democratic takeover of the city and deposed the generals in charge, along with some of the triarchs. Among the new generals they elected was Thrasybulus, son of Lycus, a firm believer in democracy. The crews declared the fleet to be independent and claimed to be acting henceforth on behalf of the majority of the citizenry.

In a "popular assembly" of their own, they proceeded to declare Alcibiades exempt from punishment and to permit his return. The exiled leader came to Samos and, following a speech in which he cited the injustice done to him, was elected commander. The sailors wanted to sail to Athens immediately and had to be dissuaded by Alcibiades. Such a move would have meant sacrificing Athens' position in Ionia. The same scene repeated itself when envoys from the Four Hundred arrived in Samos and rekindled the sailors' wrath.

In Athens, news of these events revived opposition against the new regime. People were also turning against the Four Hundred, which had begun to exercise their rule despotically, yet had accomplished little. Above all, they had no success in their attempts to save the polis. The peace talks with Spartans had come to nought. According to Thucydides, the oligarchs found it much easier to cooperate in taking over power than in preserving unity once they were in power.

One of the oligarchs, Theramenes, son of Hagnon, became disaffected and began to speak against the others. He argued that the Four Hundred should not continue to hold exclusive power. Instead, five thousand men should be appointed, as proposed, and take part in governing. He may have suggested that the Four Hundred should in the future be selected on a rotating basis from the duly constituted Five Thousand.

It was further proposed that only those able to equip themselves as hoplites and serve in the army be considered true citizens of the polis. This idea reflected the opinion that the hoplites carried most of the city's burdens while the *thetes*—the oarsmen—were for all practical purposes supported by public funds.

It remains a mystery how these ideas were intended to be combined with the role the navy was playing at that time. The *thetes* were not to be excluded from the popular assembly but were no longer eligible for some offices, as well as the council and presumably the people's court. Thucydides thought Theramenes' proposal represented a fair balance of the interests of the few and the many. It was the first time in his lifetime, he wrote, that Athens had a good constitution.

But before this constitution could be adopted a great tumult arose over the fortification of Eetionia, the peninsula that protected the entrance to the great harbor of Piraeus on the west side. A wall already protected the peninsula to the west and south; now the peninsula's east side was to be fortified as well, so that a kind of citadel would be formed. The Four Hundred wanted this work to be done by a contingent of hoplites. Theramenes, who had been one of the leaders of the coup but came to oppose the rule of the Four Hundred, asserted that the Four Hundred intended to place a garrison there to assist the Spartans in entering Piraeus. He suspected them—quite correctly according to Thucydides—of wanting to hand Athens over to the enemy.

The oligarchs' original intentions were to retain power in the city in

ATHENS

any way possible, or at least to maintain Athens' independence. But now, since the Spartans had rejected their peace overtures and their own regime was threatened by Theramenes' machinations, they had reason to fear the people's retribution. Staying in power by Sparta's grace seemed the best alternative still open to them.

Theramenes' suspicions were reinforced by the appearance of a Spartan fleet in the Saronic Bay. Its mission was supposedly to press Euboea to defect, but the most direct route to Euboea would not have called for the ships' passing near Aegina and Piraeus.

Whatever the case, the hoplites in Eetionia mutinied and took prisoner the general appointed by the Four Hundred to oversee the work. Theramenes pretended to act as mediator but in fact gladly permitted the fortification to be dismantled. Then the hoplites held council in the Dionysus theater at Munychia, marched up to the city, and demanded that a date be set for the popular assembly to meet.

At this meeting the Four Hundred were deposed and their power transferred to the Five Thousand. It was also decreed that in the future no one was to be paid for holding public office. The laws were to be reformulated and written down. The constitution of the Four Hundred had lasted about four months. It is unknown how long this new constitution survived.

Theramenes was one of the most controversial men of his time. Many intellectuals admired his notions of a moderate constitution. But he was also sharply criticized for changing sides so often, and he was nicknamed "Cothurnus," from the word for boots worn by actors that fitted either foot.

He had first distinguished himself in Athens' democracy, then joined the forces plotting to topple it, but left them when it became obvious they wanted to introduce and maintain a strictly oligarchic regime. (Alternatively, he may have left when it became clear that the plotters were so unpopular that their rule could not last long.) Later, in 404, he was once again among those who brought democracy down, and he again disassociated himself from his co-conspirators when their arbitrariness became unbearable. He was undoubtedly driven by ambition and was not always scrupulous when his own interests were at stake. He was not on principle opposed to violence and did not object to the murder of political opponents any more than most politicians at that time. But he knew that force could be used only within certain limits and for specific purposes. A highly educated man, having studied under the Sophist Prodicus, he showed great creativity in his approach to constitutional questions.

Theramenes' biography should be regarded as emblematic of his time and situation. He recognized that democracy was incapable of solving the problems that confronted it, and he tried wherever possible to deal with difficulties by improving governmental institutions. But the oligarchs were far less capable of establishing permanent and rational rule than the democrats. In both camps, he recognized this failure and refused to participate in the oligarchic regime. His principled refusal did not succeed, and the second time he paid with his life.

Theramenes possessed many attributes in common with Phrynichus, the general who opposed the oligarchic coup at its inception in Samos. Both pursued responsible and rational policies, including warfare, each in his own way and according to his own concept of a proper constitution. If they felt in danger they were unconstrained by conscience or concern for others and would do whatever was needed to save themselves. That men of unusual ability reacted in this way was part of their self-reliance, their independence, and their disregard for convention, which made them capable of almost anything.

During the days when the Four Hundred were being overthrown, Euboea fell into the hands of the Spartans. This was a great blow for Athens, for a large part of the city's grain and other necessities came from that region. The Athenians had also evacuated some of their cattle there, and now they were lost.

Democracy was restored to Athens in 410, in a somewhat modified form made necessary by the extreme deprivation of that era. According to a motion put forth by Demophantus, anyone henceforth involved in toppling democracy or holding office after its fall was to be regarded as

Athens' enemy and declared an outlaw. All Athenians had to swear, in the context of their tribes and demes, to fight and, if possible, kill anyone guilty of the crime.

The Four Hundred and their collaborators were prosecuted; many of them had to pay large fines; others forfeited their civil rights; a few were sentenced to death.

Shortly before the Four Hundred assumed power, in January of 411, Aristophanes' *Lysistrata* was first presented. It is the play of his most often produced today. It shows the women from Greek cities that were at war with each other joining together and swearing to refrain from sexual relations with their husbands and lovers in order to force them finally to make peace. The chorus of women says:

> All the long time the war has lasted, we have endured in modest silence all you men did; we never allowed ourselves to open our lips. We were far from satisfied, for we knew how things were going; often in our homes we would hear you discussing, upside down and inside out, some important turn of affairs. Then with sad hearts, but smiling lips, we would ask you: Well, in today's Assembly did they vote Peace?—But, "Mind your own business!" the husband would growl, "Hold your tongue, do!" And I would say no more . . . but presently I would come to know you had arrived at some fresh decision more fatally foolish than ever. "Ah! my dear man," I would say, "what madness next!" But he would only look at me askance and say: "Just weave your web, do; else your cheeks will smart for hours. War is men's business!"

The play is above all a superb comedy, but these words must also reflect the state of relations between the sexes. Could the women, so many of whose husbands, fathers, sons, and brothers had been away in the army, if not killed in battle, really go on believing in the political wisdom of the men? Wisdom was so obviously lacking, at least if it was to be judged by success. The women were bound to rebel.

Insecurity can often lead to foolhardy decisions, especially if it is accompanied by false hope or exaggerated self-confidence. This seems to have been precisely what happened here. Contrary to the opinion once expressed by Pericles, it made no difference that those making the decisions might have to send their own children off to war. Euripides had said in his *Suppliants* that when deciding on war nobody thought of his own death but only of that of others. Otherwise war would not be so lightly embarked on.

Starting in the fall of 411, the fighting took place mostly in the Propontis area, and Athens was able to score some victories. The Spartans, poorly provisioned and with morale in their ranks alarmingly low, received some aid from an unexpected quarter. Pharnabazus, the satrap responsible for northern Asia Minor and resident in Dascylion, was freer with money than Tissaphernes, the satrap of Sardis, and he offered the Spartans aid if they would help wrest the Greek cities of Asia Minor from Athens' control. The Spartans gladly accepted Pharnabazus's offer. Then, too, they had the additional motive of wanting to cut off supplies that were reaching Athens from the Black Sea. The flow of supplies to Athens by sea had frustrated the attempts of King Agis, who was in command of Spartan forces at Decelea, to do Athens any significant harm.

But the Athenians defeated the Spartans at Cynossema in the fall of 411, and in the spring of 410 Alcibiades managed to inflict a decisive defeat on the Spartan fleet near Cyzicus, capturing almost all the enemy vessels. "Timbers [ships] gone, Mindarus [the general] killed, the men starving. We don't know what to do," read the message sent back to Sparta. The Athenians failed to retake Byzantium and Chalcedon, but they built a fort opposite Byzantium, with the intention of demanding tariffs from all ships passing through the Bosporus.

The Spartans proposed peace. Their offer would allow each side to keep the territories it now held, except that Athens would have to withdraw from Pylos, and Sparta from Decelea. However, Cleophon, a lyre-maker by trade and a demagogue in the style of Cleon, was at the height of his popularity and convinced the majority in the Athenian assembly to reject the offer. He demanded that the Spartans return all the cities that had belonged to the Delian League, which was of course out of the question. The people put their faith in Alcibiades.

Cleophon also initiated the payment of an allowance of two oboli per day to poor citizens. This may reflect the fact that the city's revenues had improved somewhat as a result of the victory of Cyzicus. In 409 work on the Erechtheum was resumed. The fleet, however, continued to depend largely on tributes and contributions to the war effort, imposed in its area of operations, and on booty.

As of 411 the Athenians were again the masters of the sea. The building of a new Peloponnesian fleet, financed by Persia, progressed only slowly. But Athens lacked the resources to besiege cities, let alone break up the front of all those that had turned against them.

In the winter of 410–409 Athens lost Pylos, and in the summer of 409 the Megarians recaptured Nisaea. At the same time Corcyra canceled its treaty of alliance; the island had once more fallen into the hands of the oligarchs.

On the other hand, the Syracusan troops, who had demonstrated special bravery and tactical imagination in fighting with the Peloponnesian navy, were called home. They were needed there to fight against the Carthaginians. This, too, was a result of the great war. Greek influence had diminished in Sicily, and Athens maintained friendly relations with Carthage. In the winter of 409–408 Alcibiades took Byzantium, and in the summer of 408 the Athenians won back Thasos, which had defected when the Athenians attempted to install on oligarchy there.

At this point Alcibiades interrupted his military activities. He wanted to return to Athens, as did his troops. Even before his return he was elected *strategos*. A large crowd gathered at Piraeus in June 408 to welcome him. But not feeling safe, he did not leave his ship until he spotted his relatives and friends. Under their protection he went to the city, followed by a large crowd. Before the council and the popular assembly he protested against the old charge brought against him of having desecrated the Eleusinian Mysteries. Nobody contradicted his account of the incident, so strong was his support among the crowd. He was elected commander in chief with unlimited powers. As compensation for his confiscated property he was given an honorary reward.

He stayed in Athens for four months, probably the time it took for his ships to be repaired. In September, under his protection, the solemn procession to Eleusis once again followed the sacred land route, instead of the sea route that celebrants had been taking since 413 out of fear of the Spartans.

In this period the Athenians built a balustrade around the small platform formed by the projection of the Acropolis on which the Nike temple stood. The reliefs, done in the "rich style," depicted Nike erecting trophies in the presence of Athena and leading cattle to the sacrifice. In one of these reliefs she is shown removing her sandals before entering the sanctuary. These images celebrated Athens' victory and at the same time paid homage to the goddess who had granted it.

Around 410, Euripides produced his *Phoenician Women*, which deals with the strife between Oedipus's sons. Much of the play can be read as an indictment of the unrestrained lust for power, of the "immoderate ambition" that had gripped Athens. The mother, trying to reconcile her two sons, cites the equality inherent in natural phenomena, such as the alternation of day and night. Among men, she maintains, equality fosters loyalty among friends, among cities, and among allies. Her speech reads like a program for reforming the Delian League and accepting one's place in a democracy.

Her son Eteocles has other ideas, however. He believes power to be the highest deity. He had earlier promised to share power with his brother democratically by taking turns at rule, but now he refuses to step down and give his brother his turn. "I'll never relinquish power to him. If one is going to act unjustly, it is best to do so in the name of power; in everything else it is best to respect god's laws."

In his *Orestes*, presented in 408, Euripides seems to take issue with Aeschylus's *Oresteia*, to which he alludes in many places. The ending of the myth is completely recast. Orestes appears shortly after killing his

Representation of Athena Nike removing her sandals. From the balustrade of the sacred precinct of the Nike Temple. Ca. 410 B.C.

mother. Having been pursued for days by the vengeful Furies, he has taken leave of his senses and enjoys only occasional moments of rational awareness. The men of Argos are about to pronounce judgment on him and on his sister Electra. Just as things look most ominous, a last chance for salvation suddenly presents itself. Menelaus, Orestes' uncle, has just sailed into port. When Orestes hears the news, he suddenly recovers his ability to act, and his uncle, a hero, announces his willingness to help. But when the time comes to speak up before the assembly, he remains silent.

Without his troops, the uncle is apparently helpless. Orestes is condemned to death along with his sister. He escapes being stoned only by promising that he and his sister will kill themselves that very day.

But the suicides never take place. Pylades, Orestes' friend, reasons that since the two will have to die anyway, they should first kill Helen, the wife of Menelaus, who bore responsibility for the Trojan War. If they carry out the deed, they will gain immortal fame. An elaborate plot is hatched. Menelaus's daughter is taken hostage, and Orestes threatens to kill her. Orestes announces that he will set the palace on fire to die along with others. Finally Apollo intervenes as *deus ex machina* and sets things right.

The play must have appeared profoundly relevant. There is cowardly Menelaus, whose words are impressive but empty and who is nothing but an opportunist hoping to ascend the throne. Tyndareus, Orestes' grandfather, is almost unbelievably petty and heartless. He appears primarily to tell Orestes how to behave and urges him to obey the law. He is secretly intent on seeing his grandson cruelly punished. His motive is not to avenge his daughter, Clytemnestra, however; he cared for her as little as he did for her sister, Helen. He merely wants things to take their proper course, a desire he voices with the cold logic of an accountant.

Orestes himself, whom Euripides draws with some sympathy, considers the crime he plans to commit a just punishment of Menelaus and therefore heroic. This is an utter perversion of the old ideals. Orestes says occasionally that he wants to be worthy of his father and states that one must bear the fate assigned by the gods. But this is merely hollow talk; his words bear no relation to his deeds. In response to his grandfather's criticism, he claims that he acted in the interest of all of Greece by punishing the faithlessness of women and the murder of husbands. He then turns on the old man and accuses him of being the cause of the trouble, having sired Clytemnestra. Finally he blames the god whose oracle commanded him to avenge his father. Orestes claims he was innocent, because he was merely following orders.

Euripides had expressed similar criticisms in other plays. People no longer assume personal responsibility for their actions, he claimed; they insist they can't help what they do. The assembly did the same, after all, often punishing others for what it itself had decreed. And so did those accused of crimes who, in a climate of incrimination and counterincrimination, projected their guilt on others.

But *Orestes* goes far beyond Euripides' other plays. From beginning to end the play depicts a perversion of values. Its subject is not fate, whose meaning may be obscure but is never doubted, but rather the inescapable consequences of human shortcomings. Injustice, demagogy, and the desire for retribution will inevitably triumph, aided by a healthy dose of opportunism. Characters cling to old but corrupted ideals, sometimes out of cowardice, sometimes out of stupidity, sometimes out of passion. In the end a god has to set everything right again. Helen is transported to heaven. Her beauty, we learn, was meant by the gods to trigger the war so that the accumulated evils of humanity would be wiped off the earth. Orestes is dispatched to Athens, where he will be acquitted.

Several of Euripides' plays before 408 reflect the shocking failure of Athens' leadership, which had at first evoked such high expectations. The leaders were corrupt, dishonorable, incompetent, vain, and selfish. It is obvious in Aeschylus's *Oresteia* and many other early Greek plays that the tragedians tried to deal with the problems the citizenry faced. In the late Euripides we see just as clearly that tragedy was no longer able to exercise its great, central, ordering function. The relationship between the playwright and his public was presumably still close, but now all the tragedian could do was analyze and express how senseless and unjust everything had become. As a consequence, the public's enjoyment must have been purely aesthetic.

Soon after Alcibiades returned to Ionia in the fall of 408, the military situation changed profoundly. Seeing the Athenian successes, the Persians decided to support the Spartans more vigorously. Two crucial changes in the Persian and Spartan military leadership would also have lasting consequences. On Queen Parysatis's urging, her son Cyrus, about seventeen at the time, was given supreme command of the coast and appointed satrap of Lydia. In 407 the Spartans made Lysander, a man of great ability, general of their military forces. Lysander formed a close friendship with

Cyrus, who was so eager to please Lysander that from that time on plenty of Persian money was available to Sparta.

Lysander was one of those modern Spartans characterized by great decisiveness and prudence. He was highly ingenious at organizing and deploying all the forces at his command to great effect. He was uniquely disciplined and averse to debauchery and luxury of any kind. He was cold and calculating, and scorned no means that seemed to advance his purpose, including flattery and arm twisting, bribery, cheating, and resorting to perjury as well as brute force. In short, he subordinated everything to the end he strove for—namely, Sparta's victory and the expansion of his own power.

He was a brilliant politician, a clever diplomat, and a gifted strategist. Much about him—his abilities, extreme ambition, and arrogance—is reminiscent of Alcibiades. The big difference is that he was much more disciplined, patient, and single-minded, as well as craftier.

In his first year of command Lysander avoided all actual combat and concentrated on building up and training the navy. Only once, at Notion, did he engage in a battle, and that was started by the Athenians when Alcibiades' substitute decided, against Alcibiades' explicit instructions, to taunt him. The Athenians thought the enemy was unprepared because most of its ships were on dry land. But the Spartans moved their ships into the water with great speed and went on to defeat the Attic fleet.

This victory had the unexpected result that the Athenians, after celebrating Alcibiades and granting him exceptional powers, suddenly removed him from office. His mistake was to fail to live up to their expectations. He was certainly guilty of an error of judgment—he had left the fleet in the charge of an irresponsible individual, who happened to be a drinking companion of his.

Lysander went on to call together the most powerful men from various Greek cities in Asia Minor, promising them his aid if they would introduce oligarchic governments in their cities and cooperate with one another. In this way he strengthened his support in the region.

But the conservatives in Sparta detested Lysander and consequently insisted with special vehemence that he relinquish his command after a year, following the usual custom. His successor, Callicratidas, ruled more in the old Spartan mold. He was an aristocrat and an effective leader, but he did not get along as well with Cyrus, who treated him disdainfully. Cyrus was most intent on Lysander returning to his command as soon as possible. Meanwhile Lysander had returned to Cyrus the unspent Persian money so that Callicratidas would not get it. The advantages he had gained for Sparta were not to be used by anyone else.

Despite the forces arrayed against him, Callicratidas achieved a triumph by blockading Conon, the top Athenian commander, in the harbor of Mytilene. At this time, in the summer of 406, the Athenians decided once more to build a large fleet. They melted down objects offered to the gods, issued new gold coins, and obliged the citizens, including many knights, to man the oars. A long-standing shortage of manpower had forced the authorities to relax the Periclean law on citizenship, and even those of Athenian stock on only one side were allowed to become citizens. Slaves were hired with the promise of future freedom. They also enjoyed somewhat restricted civil rights.

The Athenians were able to equip 110 ships, though not all of them of the most modern type, and the crews were not especially well trained. Still, Athens succeeded in winning a battle against the Spartans off the Arginusian islands, between Lesbos and the mainland. The Peloponnesians lost 70 ships and the Athenians only 25. But the weather was so inclement that the Athenians were unable to rescue many of their shipwrecked crews and lost about two thousand men.

Understandably, the joy in Athens over the victory was marred by the losses. But disappointment gave way to anger. The popular assembly removed the generals from office. Two of them, suspecting trouble, did not even return to Athens. The remaining six were thrown in prison and charged before the assembly with capital crimes. Some tried to divert attention from themselves. As a triarch Theramenes had been charged, along with others, to rescue the shipwrecked crews while the commanders were off pursuing the enemy fleet. The storm had prevented him from setting out on the rescue mission, and at his trial he was eager to clear himself by shifting the blame to the generals.

The generals were permitted to speak before the assembly but were not given the time allotted to them by law. Even so, they were able, by calling on the testimony of the helmsmen, to convince the majority in the assembly of their innocence. But those most intent on seeing them convicted would not give up and made a motion to delay the vote because of darkness. The council in the meantime was to prepare a verdict.

By chance, it was at this time that the feast of the Apaturia was being celebrated. The phratry members gathered together a large crowd of mourners (not just those who had lost a family member or friend but others merely for effect), who could be seen wandering around the streets in black garb and with shaven heads.

When the assembly met, the council, acting on the motion of a man named Callixenus, recommended voting immediately on whether the defendants were guilty or not, since both the prosecution and the defense speeches had already been made. If a majority found them guilty, the commanders were to be sentenced to death and their property confiscated, a tenth of it to be dedicated to Athena.

A few courageous men, among them a cousin of Alcibiades named Euryptolemus, son of Pisianax, protested sharply and demanded that Callixenus be tried for making a motion in violation of the rules. This would have meant that the vote had to be postponed until the court had decided the procedural question. Euryptolemus argued that each of the accused had the right to a separate trial, but the generals had been indicted together. They had not been given adequate opportunity to defend themselves. In addition, if the vote proceeded as proposed the principle of secret ballot would be violated, since the ballots for guilty and innocent were to be placed in separate boxes, making it obvious how people voted.

The speech was greeted by a clamor of protest. The protesters insisted it was outrageous to try to prevent the people from deciding whatever they wanted. To loud cheering, a man named Lyciscus moved that Euryptolemus and those siding with him be included in the verdict against the generals unless they withdrew their request.

When some of the *prytanes* who presided over the assembly refused to allow such an unlawful vote, Callixenus spoke up once more and demanded that they, too, be included in the proceedings against Euryptolemus. The *prytanes*—with the exception of Socrates—let themselves be intimidated. Socrates declared he would not do anything contrary to the law.

In the end, the generals, including Pericles' sole remaining son, were condemned to death. The city dissolved into a frenzy. Democracy was degenerating into anarchy. Theramenes' behavior was particularly reprehensible. He is said not only to have initiated the charges against the generals but also to have urged as many citizens as possible to wear mourning clothes, even if they were not personally affected by the calamity. Whatever his motives—to curry favor with the people or to avoid being victimized by the popular wrath—his actions were inexcusable.

Socrates, son of Sophroniscus, was the only one to remain steadfast. He had been a well-known figure in Athens since at least the early 420s, in part because of his notorious ugliness. The portraits of him that remain are stylized but the face is unmistakably homely. The sources of the time suggest that he looked like a satyr and in no way resembled the traditional ideals of beauty. He dressed simply and was known to move about barefoot, even on ice, as when he served as a hoplite in the winter siege of Potidaea. He enjoyed being with people and usually could be found at the wrestling schools, the gymnasia, along the banks of the Ilissus, or in the agora. He evoked interest everywhere, especially because he was generally surrounded by a small crowd of acolytes, many of them belonging to the highest circles of Attic society. He fascinated them, and the contrast between him and them must have been striking. His ability to draw people extended to artisans and the plain folk as well. He talked with them about their work, and sought their opinions about morality, politics, and the issues of the day.

Socrates does not seem to have spent much time plying his trade (he was a stonecutter like his father) but was nevertheless counted among the third—not the lowest—census class. He would hardly have qualified for such a lowly designation if the financial assistance he received from his aristocratic friends were also considered.

Most of what we know about Socrates comes from the accounts of his pupil Plato and to a lesser extent from Xenophon. The two writers draw very different pictures. Xenophon dwells mostly on Socrates' many practical insights and suggestions (he probably ignored a lot of what was of less interest to him). Plato focuses on the theoretical, and it is difficult to separate the Socratic from the Platonic elements of the dialogues.

It seems clear that Socrates first turned his attention to the philosophy of nature but soon found it of little interest to him. He was primarily concerned with man, like the Sophists, although this starting point was the only thing he had in common with them.

The Sophists, having discovered the relativity and subjectivity of all knowledge, sought absolute truth in nature—or what they defined as nature—a realm that existed independently of human consciousness. Socrates' questions, by contrast, focused entirely on consciousness, on what ordinary people said and thought, and what lay beyond their opinions.

The Sophists found applications for their knowledge that allowed them to teach their students many different skills. They pursued their inquiries only up to a certain point, at which they turned to the practical aspects of their teachings. Socrates, by contrast, would continue questioning.

Socrates may also have dispensed practical advice, but what is more important is that he felt no need to escape *aporia*, the state of remaining in doubt. He could not rest until he reached the ultimate truth, a goal in which, of course, he never succeeded.

If Socrates felt superior to others, it was because he was aware that he might never be able to find answers to the questions he raised. Alone among his fellow citizens, he knew just how little he knew. He surely did not intend this insight to be the end of his quest, but it was apparently as far as he was able to go. He encountered this unknowability again and again, and—unlike the Sophists—kept asking the same questions. This is what made him so unique in Athens.

His purpose was elusive. He refused to focus on practical applications of his knowledge. He developed a much-feared dialectic, which we know from Plato's accounts of it. Socrates' method was greatly admired by his listeners but evoked irritation in those subjected to his questions. Socrates' use of irony in the dialogues is famous. He would approach others, especially clever Sophists, with humble respect, and ask his questions with admiring naïveté. Frequently, he would agree with what they

Socrates. Copy of the oldest portrait known to us, which was made two or three decades after the philosopher's death. Ca. 380–370 B.C. Naples, National Museum.

said, but in his assent and admiration there would always remain a hint of doubt that would, finally, reveal the hollowness of their reasoning.

One puzzle in particular preoccupied Socrates: How was it possible for the artisans and artists of his time to have developed such impressive knowledge and master the technical aspects of their trade so perfectly while similar competence was lacking in the political realm?

Socrates' approach was in a sense more democratic than that of the Sophists, who sought to help people attain their goals and become more powerful. Socrates was, by contrast, interested primarily in ordinary people. Like them, he accepted the validity of traditional morality. But as a result of his questioning he came to the conclusion that the people who determined the city's policies in the assembly were insufficiently prepared for this task. They were not even able to answer simple questions about justice.

Socrates made it a point to take part in political life. He fulfilled his civic and military duties scrupulously and did everything the official religion demanded of an Athenian. Indeed, he adhered to the laws with special strictness because he recognized how important it was to follow them, whether they were just or unjust, for the sake of the polis. He possessed the determination to act on this conviction even in the hardest of situations. But adherence to the law did not relieve him—or his fellow citizens—of the need to arrive at an understanding of justice.

For all his greatness, Socrates could not make an effective speech, but instead merely conducted conversations. Rather than develop a philosophical system or produce a great work, he entangled himself in complex paradoxes. Where others searched for answers, promulgated laws, sought to change the political order, or reinterpreted the world, he recognized that a much more fundamental approach was needed: Man had to learn first that he knew nothing.

His insight into his own lack of ultimate knowledge in no way discouraged Socrates. He regarded it as his duty to keep asking questions, and an inner voice urged him to devote his life to the young people of Attica by involving them in his investigations. Solon declared that his spirit *(thymos)* had told him to convey his insight to the Athenian people. But for Socrates it was a *daimonion*, a deity who serves as a messenger between men and the gods, who spoke.

In 407–406 Euripides died in Macedonia, where he had moved in 408. At the *proagon* (the gathering at which the plays to be performed were introduced) preceding the Great Dionysia of 406, Sophocles and the actors appeared in dark mourning garments, and the audience wept. The plays Euripides had worked on before his death were performed soon afterward. The last to be produced was the *Bacchae*, the most troubling of his tragedies.

In the play the god Dionysus, son of Zeus, arrives in his native Thebes. His mother was Semele, the daughter of Cadmus, the city's founder. Years earlier, when she claimed that Zeus himself had impregnated her, the people of Thebes chose not to believe her. When she was killed, the infant Dionysus was delivered by lightning.

When the play opens, all the women of the city are enthralled by this stranger, who looks unusual but is not recognizable as a god. Together, they roam through the woods, thyrsus in hand and clad in fawnskins. Under Dionysus's spell, the people are seized with the urge to make merry and dance.

The young king, Pentheus, tries to restore order by resorting to enlightened reason. His appeals have no effect, however. In desperation, he decides to summon the army, but his grandfather, Cadmus, and the prophet Tiresias prevail upon him to try diplomacy instead. Convinced that the city is in grave danger and that the rationality of male society is at stake, Pentheus vows to take drastic action.

He orders the stranger to be put in chains. Suddenly, an earthquake shakes the building where Dionysus is being held, and as it goes up in flames, he frees himself. Supernatural forces are obviously at work. No one knew the stranger was a god, though they submitted to him implicitly by abandoning themselves to the Dionysian frenzy.

The king succumbs to the stranger in a different way, by letting himself be drawn into conversation. He eventually accepts the god's advice, and lets himself be dressed up to masquerade as a woman so he can go among the frenzied women on the mountain without having them kill him. He means merely to spy on their doings. But Dionysus knows that the women will find him out, which they do. In their frenzy they tear Pentheus to pieces. His own mother returns to the city with her son's head speared on her thyrsus. In her delusion, she imagines she has killed a lion.

Dionysus is a terrible god. He is profoundly cruel and will do anything to achieve his ends. (Of course, such behavior was not foreign to the Greek gods.) The fate that Dionysus imposed on Pentheus was particularly brutal: Pentheus descended into madness, then was not even accorded the status of a hero who has failed tragically; instead he was made to appear ridiculous. Dionysus acted with calculating deceit, enjoying his victim's misery. He destroyed the king utterly, urged on by the chorus of the Bacchae, whose commentaries reflect his depraved satisfaction at the extent of his powers.

The *Bacchae* is not only a painful spectacle to observe but a depressing one as well. Those who ought to be able to save the city either join in the madness immediately or are drawn into it by trying to fight it. Madness reigns supreme—until the intoxication wears off and the disastrous consequences are visible to all.

Is the play meant to depict the recent history of Athens, the intoxication of its male citizens, who no longer act rationally but instead behave like the Bacchae of the play? And what about those who try to confront the madness? They, too, have no choice in the end but to play the female role and perish in doing so. There are times, according to Robert Musil, when the only choice in life is between howling with the wolves and giving in to neurosis. Does Euripides mean to say that war is this kind of intoxication? And does the Dionysus of Euripides' *Bacchae* represent the war? And what of the theater itself—has it been reduced to absurdity?

The play raises these and many other questions, and we can only conjecture for answers. At the beginning of the war, monstrous Medea gave way to her thirst for revenge and killed her own children. Now, with the end of the war in sight, a god's insistence on vengeance is shown to turn everything to chaos by means of a madness for which there is no cure. The only hope is that it will pass eventually so that the other side of Dionysus can manifest again. This other side is the power of wine, for which Dionysus is also responsible, and which brings peace and reconciliation.

In 406 Sophocles died at about ninety years of age. In 401, his grandson staged the old master's last tragedy, *Oedipus at Colonus,* in which the exiled hero seeks peace shortly before his death in the groves of the Eumenides at Colonus, Sophocles' native deme, near Athens. King Theseus generously offers Oedipus refuge in Attica despite his past. A divinity calls Oedipus home with claps of thunder and finally with the words: "Oedipus! Why do you delay? It is time to go!" According to an oracle, the grave of Oedipus will be a source of blessings for Athens.

This play, more than *Oedipus Rex*, written twenty years earlier, suggests that the protagonist was the victim of his fate rather than the deliberate perpetrator of a crime. No explanation is offered as to why the divinities imposed this fate on him, but the hero is now, to quote Goethe, "transformed into a relative of the gods, deserving, as a protective spirit, of sacrificial ceremonies."

It has been said that Euripides sought the meaning of events, but was unable to arrive at an answer. It might be more accurate to say he knew he would find no answer. As far as the gods are concerned, he was faced with the following alternatives: either they exist and therefore what happens is just or we must doubt their existence. We also find in Euripides a considerable increase in tolerance for the evil men can do and still be permitted to live—to the point where Heracles can go on living after he has killed his children. In the glaring light of Euripides' insight, all honor and everything heroic break apart. Even a hero's life is now petty and shabby.

The plays of Sophocles and Euripides expressed not only differences in these poets' personalities and mentalities but great differences between their generations.

In January 405, the Athenians watched Aristophanes' *The Frogs*, in which the patron god of theater descends to the netherworld in order to bring back his favorite playwright, Euripides. There he is drawn into a dispute between Euripides and Aeschylus, who occupies the seat of honor reserved in Hades for the best tragedian. Euripides declares that the honor should belong to him. Sophocles also joins the fray. In the ensuing contest it is revealed that Athens desperately needs at least one of the tragedians to help it through this trying period. Even though Dionysus personally prefers Euripides, the final decision is in favor of Aeschylus. The verdict is clear: what the city needs are the good, old-fashioned Athenian virtues. There is only one problem, however: those virtues no longer exist.

The chorus of the frogs makes an open plea for the elite, which in the course of the events of 411 had been deprived of its special privileges. The Athenians, the chorus declares, deal with their best citizens the way they do with money. Instead of the silver coins of old they now use cheap copper ones.

The Athenians were unable to capitalize on the favorable position they had achieved as a result of the victory at Arginusae because there was no general capable enough to lead and because they were running out of strength. The only thing the citizenry still found easy was to refuse an offer of peace. The Spartans had once more suggested ending the war. The Athenians declined, but since they were no longer able to win in regular fighting, they resorted to barbarism. They decided, for example, to chop off the right hands of all prisoners of war, presumably because some earlier captives had later been discovered back in combat. But this explanation can hardly justify such a decree.

It seems senseless for men to sacrifice themselves or be sacrificed in a war that is unwinnable. Indeed, if there had been a possibility of peace, then it would have been inexcusable to ignore it. And yet there was a certain logic to the course the Athenians followed. As they saw it, all they could do under the circumstances was continue the hostilities. They could not admit that all the suffering, sacrifice, and devastation had been in vain, and they badly wanted retribution. Furthermore, the citizenry had grown so unused to normal life that they were vulnerable to all delusion. At this point, anyone who dangled some hope in front of the assembly was bound to win more popularity than the skeptics. To rehearse the consequences of the lost war would have been cruel.

Expectations for victory and continued hegemony still seem to have been as high as ever. The process of "pathological learning" had to run its course. It would not have been easy to establish peace in any case because the conflict between the two sides had become so extreme that only the unconditional surrender of one side—which would have meant Athens—could have been discussed. It was this extreme division, not just the fact that Athens was ruled by a radical democracy, that made peace seem so difficult a goal to reach.

In the end Lysander, who had resumed the command of the Spartan navy although he was not formally appointed to the position, was able to capture almost the entire Attic fleet at Aegospotami, with little actual fighting. He tricked the Athenians into believing that he wanted to avoid battle. Alcibiades, who was living nearby, recognized the danger and warned the Attic commanders, but they rebuffed his counsel, saying they were in command now, not he.

After his victory Lysander called a meeting of the Spartan allies to discuss what should be done with the prisoners of war. As Xenophon recounts: "Many accusations were voiced against the Athenians concerning the illegalities they were already guilty of and others they would probably have committed if they had achieved victory at sea. . . . After capturing two triremes, one from Corinth, the other from Andros, the Athenians had thrown the crews overboard. It was the Athenian commander Philocles who had given the order. Many other Athenian misdeeds were cited, and then the victors decided to kill all the prisoners who were Athenians except for Adeimantus, who had been the only one in the Athenian popular assembly to object to the proposal of chopping off the hands of prisoners. He was, by the way, later accused by some of having betrayed the fleet."

Attic sea power had been practically annihilated. Athens' desperation is made clear in a treaty it concluded at that time with the city of Samos. The treaty gave the Samosans the Attic citizenship they had been asking for, and the city was allowed to retain its independence. Samos had been seeking recognition as an equal.

In the winter of 405–404 Athens was cut off from the sea. One hundred and fifty Peloponnesian ships blockaded Piraeus. The Athenians soon began to go hungry, but in the popular assembly Cleophon still prevailed. He never considered that Athens might be forced to capitulate. He apparently thought the city should follow its course to the bitter end, and he seems to have had the majority of the assembly on his side. The sources report widespread fear that the enemy would make Athens pay for transgressions. Perhaps the Athenians wanted to delay as long as possible the kind of suffering they had imposed on others. In any case, reason had long since ceased to function. Finally, a trumped-up charge was brought against Cleophon for evading military service. The court had the good sense to condemn him to death.

Cleophon was the last in a series of leaders, starting with Cleon, who possessed the ability to exert great influence over people. They did this by flattering the masses, lowering themselves to their level, and advocating aggressive foreign policies based on an exaggerated assessment of the city's potential. Moderating forces could prevail, but this was rare, since the extremists did not hesitate to resort to any means, including show trials, to achieve their ends.

In the spring of 404 Athens finally dispatched a delegation to negotiate peace. Agis, the Spartan king, who greeted the delegation outside Athens' gates, told them to travel on to Sparta to talk with the officials there. Somewhat later, the delegates were met on the road by Spartan messengers who demanded to know what their mission was. When they answered that Athens wanted to make peace, but only on the condition that it retain Piraeus and the long walls, the Spartans told them to return home. If they really wanted peace, the Spartans said, they should come with more acceptable proposals, such as an unconditional surrender.

When the news reached Athens that the delegation had failed in its mission, a mood of depression descended on the city. To dismantle the walls was unthinkable. When a man by the name of Archestratus had proposed such a move some weeks earlier, he had been arrested, and the assembly decreed that henceforth such proposals were not permissible.

Theramenes volunteered to speak to Lysander to find out whether the Spartans wanted the long walls razed only for security reasons, or in order to enslave the Athenians. His offer was accepted, and he spent three months with Lysander. Theramenes' real purpose had been to kill time until Athens' food supplies were exhausted. When he returned to Athens, Theramenes reported that Lysander wanted him to travel to Sparta and negotiate directly with the Spartan leadership. With pressure building on Athens, Theramenes was finally granted unlimited powers to reach a peace settlement.

The Spartan government was also ready to discuss peace. It had convened a general meeting at which the Corinthians, Thebans, and others demanded the complete destruction of Athens. Sparta rejected this idea on the grounds that Athens had once done the country an enormous service during a period of crisis. Such a city, Sparta argued, must not be enslaved. The conditions finally agreed on were that the Athenians demolish the long walls and the fortifications of Piraeus and surrender all but twelve of their ships. They also had to permit exiled Athenians to return to the city. Furthermore, Athens lost the freedom of conducting an independent foreign policy; it had to promise to keep the same friends

Hall of the Kore in the Erechtheum

and enemies as the Spartans and to follow Sparta's military leadership. Athens had no choice but to accept these conditions. The enemy fleet, commanded by Lysander, entered Piraeus, the exiles returned, and people began to tear down the walls enthusiastically to the accompaniment of flute music. The Athenians believed a new age of freedom was beginning for Greece.

. . .

Athens' rise bears an intimate connection to its fall. The city had risen to such heights of power thanks to its extraordinary good fortune, and the rise happened very rapidly. Power accrued in this way is unlikely to last. Athens' dominance depended on the conviction shared with Sparta that Persia must be kept out of the Aegean region. The moment Sparta was seriously prepared to let the Persians once again play a role in the region's affairs—that is, as soon as Persian money began to flow into Greece— Athens' supremacy was in trouble. Athens itself was to blame for the fact that things came to such a pass. Athens' decline was the result of the city's unrestrained striving for power, a striving that grew out of the volatile nature of its hegemony. Athens' might on the seas had led inevitably to radical democracy because the importance of the *thetes* as oarsmen could be maintained only by such a democracy. Yet the city could no longer function democratically once it succumbed to the temptation of irresponsible policies. In this sense events followed the circular pattern Herodotus had detected in history. Athens' great adventure ended in 404.

But the adventure lasted long enough to transform the literature and general outlook of all the Greeks so thoroughly as to have a significant effect on world history. Were it not for Athens, Greek culture would have been a charming flower blossoming west of the Persian empire: lovely, puzzling, and strange with its small, weak city-states organized into cults and men's associations. We cannot be certain that its remarkable art, its public life, its ideal of humanity, and its freedom would be known to us today.

Isonomies had occasionally arisen before the appearance of the Persians, as had independent political thought and a philosophy that made use of abstract reasoning to investigate basic universal principles. But the essential element had been lacking. Athens supplied what had been missing: democracy, the free choice of a constitution, and an empire.

These achievements came with a heavy cost. The city was in a state of constant tension. People feared that the foundation of life would crumble and disappear. This led to the remarkable innovations we still have today:

the tragedies, the historical writing, sculpture, architecture, and Greek philosophy.

Athenians were willing to tolerate the shedding of blood and the commission of crimes, but they retained a spirit of critical judgment. Out of a confused and unstable world, a philosophy evolved that posed a fundamental question—What is justice?—and thereby opened up entirely new dimensions of thought.

Xenophon writes that when news of the navy's final defeat at Aegospotami reached Piraeus in the late evening, the sound of wailing traveled from group to group, starting at the harbor and moving between the long walls to the city. Nobody could sleep that night. People cried out laments for the dead, and even more for their own fate. Athenians realized they could expect to suffer the same atrocities they had imposed on the Spartan settlers of Melos after that city had been taken by siege, or the misery they had inflicted on the people of Scione, Torone, Aegina, and many other Greeks.

The war had consumed vast resources; the Athenians had lived prodigally and, toward the end, they drifted from crisis to crisis as if intoxicated. They had plundered and destroyed on a massive scale, but they also had achieved things that would transform the history of human civilization. The great century of Athens was over, but the city lived on and indeed remained the most important city of the Greeks. It had simply ceased to be a major political power.

Postscript

The classical world is very close,
is fully in us,
the cultural circle
is not yet completed.

—GOTTFRIED BENN

This book is about the history of a city, over a period of only four generations. Because the city in question is Athens of the late sixth and fifth centuries B.C., it has been necessary to discuss at some length the years that led up to this period. For what took place in Athens in that time had roots much further back. Athens had to pass through certain crucial stages in order to make possible its unprecedented contribution to world history: the formation of a civilization in which neither monarchy nor religion played an influential part and found political expression in small cities rather than big empires. These developments brought about the rise of democracy, which itself created many formerly unknown difficulties and an entirely new spirit of freedom.

The aim of this book has been twofold: first, to paint a picture of Athens and its history and thereby to understand better what happened there; and second, to perform an experiment in historiography.

I wanted to write history as if it were a literary project, a book that contained in as concrete and comprehensive a form as possible the complete record of scholarly research on the subject. At the same time, I felt it was crucial to make the text accessible to the reader; indeed, the reader's interest had to be kept alive and satisfied so that he or she would want to go on reading about the subject.

The history of an epoch has to include more than just events and their interconnection or structures and their history. The historian must not neglect the contemporaries who made and experienced this history, the important personalities and ordinary folk, their way of thinking and the challenges they encountered. In the case of Athens in the age of Pericles, it was the response to these challenges that brought into existence tragedy, new forms of sculpture and architecture (the planning of which was, down to the last details, voted on in the popular assembly), as well as revolutionary developments in the celebration of festivals, in language, and indeed in the art of living itself.

We should not leave the history of Athens abruptly in the year 404, when the city's great century came to an end. A few further remarks are in order.

The reader might assume that in the wake of everything that had happened, especially after 415, democracy would have lost much of its appeal in Athens. But that was not the case. Surprisingly, democracy was invigorated by the city's defeat. In this the Athenians showed a remarkable degree of political sense.

It was not just the legacy of the city's great past that contributed to this reassertion of democracy. Crucially, the regime that was established immediately after democracy's collapse turned out to be a particularly despotic oligarchy. Thirty men were appointed by the people and charged with putting in writing "the laws of the fathers" that were to govern the future administration of the polis. But the Thirty proceeded to choose a council and officials of their own liking and to set themselves up as absolute rulers. Conspicuous among them was Critias, who had been a pupil of the Sophists as well as of Socrates.

The Thirty asked Sparta to supply an occupation force, and with the help of this force they put to death a great number of people: men who had been popular with the masses whose opposition they feared, as well as personal enemies and wealthy individuals whose property could be seized. Fifteen hundred men, both citizens and metics, are said to have been killed. Others went into exile voluntarily or were banished. Blameless citizens were required to assist in arresting fellow citizens so that they would become accomplices to the crimes. Socrates alone refused to cooperate.

When it was decreed that each of these accomplices was to pick a metic, kill him, and confiscate his property in order to pay for the occupation force, Theramenes objected. He was murdered.

Finally, the democrats came together under Thrasybulus, who had earlier, in 411, proven himself a reliable democrat at Samos. They occupied Piraeus and defeated the force sent by the Thirty. Critias fell in the battle as did Charmides, another friend and pupil of Socrates and one of the ten men who governed Piraeus. The Spartan king mediated a settlement of the hostilities. Remarkably, the terms of this reconciliation declared an amnesty. The Athenians decided only to prosecute the Thirty, the ten of Piraeus, and the actual executioners, and even these individuals could avoid prosecution if they were able to justify their actions. The city had had its fill of violence. It had proved its internal unity and was able to continue on in a new (and modified) form of democracy.

In 399 Socrates was put on trial. He was charged with failing to believe in the city's gods, with having introduced new gods, and with corrupting the young. The first two accusations were obviously unfounded. For one thing, the polytheistic religion of the time allowed for a great deal of latitude. What mattered was that the religious duties in honor of the gods be performed, and Socrates had observed these duties meticulously. That he kept referring to new gods can in no way be interpreted as a lack of piety; after all, it was part of polytheism that occasionally homage was paid to new gods. The only restriction was that the new cult not appear as a threat to the city.

But herein lay the problem. Socrates' activities were perceived as dangerous. His citing of new gods was actually part of the activity his accusers regarded as corrupting to youth. It is not clear why action was brought against him at that particular point, however. Socrates had been acting in the same way for decades. A few of the tyrannical Thirty and some of their closest collaborators—Critias and Charmides, and probably others as well—had been his pupils. There was a circle of families among whom the Thirty played a special role and who were also friendly with Socrates. This fact no doubt had something to do with the prosecution, but those in power were also annoyed in general at the trend of Sophistry, and since the Sophists were not Athenians and charges could not be brought against them, Socrates may simply have been accused because he was, in the authorities' mind, the "last Sophist" they could get their hands on.

The court declared him guilty by a vote of 281 to 220. Ordinarily the verdict was followed by consideration of the appropriate punishment. The prosecutor argued for the death sentence. Socrates declared that his activities were of such importance to Athens that he should be rewarded with the highest honor the city normally offered to its most deserving citizens; namely, that he be permitted to live at public expense at the Prytaneum. This suggestion seems to have added to the confusion and anger of the jurors. According to Attic law they had to vote for one of the two proposals, and thus Socrates was condemned to death by a majority of 361 over 140 votes.

The trial of Socrates is clearly a blot in the history of the newly founded Attic democracy, and it is probably best understood as an over-reaction of the restored democracy. The time when irreverence could be appreciated was over. Tolerance, however, was still alive, for Plato was allowed to open his school in the groves of the Academy, where ideas obviously contrary to democracy were discussed. Attic democracy settled down; the schisms of the past were healed enough that life was possible again.

Plato gives an account of Socrates' defense and his last days in the *Apology*: It would have been easy for Socrates to escape from prison before his death sentence was carried out, but he did not want to escape. To the friends who wanted to help him get away he explained his decision by declaring that death might very well be desirable. He is even said to have asked them to sacrifice a cock to Asclepius, the god of healing, as thanks for delivery from the painful disease of life. But he also said that the laws of Athens deserved to be obeyed by him. Athens was a free city, and he could have freely left it. But since he had chosen to stay after seeing what the laws prescribed he had an obligation to obey them. After all, he responded, they were the laws that had brought him into the world, because it was by them that his father had married his mother and fathered him. He had been raised according to these laws and had become who he was thanks to them. Thus he had no right now to evade them. When the time came, he drank the cup with the precisely measured amount of hemlock, then wandered back and forth as he had been told to do, until his legs grew heavy and he departed from life.

In the *Seventh Letter*, which, if not authentic Platonic text, was nevertheless composed with the most accurate biographical information available, Plato wrote that after all he had experienced during the preceding years in Athens, his head was reeling. Plato was barely thirty years old at the time of Socrates' death, the city was in turmoil, and he could not go on living any other way than by continuing to ask the questions of his teacher Socrates, eventually creating that philosophy which, if measured by the force it has continued to exert, we must regard as the most significant legacy of fifth-century Athens.

Bibliographical Notes

The question of how the Greek civilization came into being has occupied me for thirty years, and it continues to do so. The book is based throughout on my own research, but I have made grateful use of the work of others. I cannot acknowledge this debt in detail here because it would take up too much room, but I should mention at least the following books from which I have quoted repeatedly: Jacob Burckhardt's *Griechische Kulturgeschichte* and Karl Reinhardt's *Tradition und Geist* (Göttingen, 1960) and *Vermächtnis der Antike* (Göttingen, 1963).

Difficulties arise repeatedly in historical research on the ancient world because original sources are so scarce and because we cannot always take what they say at face value. Future research will undoubtedly be able to elucidate some details.

I have used no footnotes in this book. The most important and detailed sources are the histories of Herodotus, Thucydides, and, toward the end, Xenophon. The section on the early history of Greece draws on the *Iliad* and the *Odyssey*, Hesiod's *Works and Days*, and passages of early Greek lyric poetry collected in *Anthologia Lyrica Graeca*. Important for the interpretation of these poems are Hermann Fränkel's *Dichtung und Philosophie des frühen Griechentums* (Munich, 1962) and the fragments of the pre-Socratic philosophers. For the biographies of Solon, Themistocles, Cimon, Pericles, Nicias, Alcibiades, and Lysander the essential source to Plutarch's *Lives of the Noble Greeks*. The plays of Aeschylus, Sophocles,

Euripides, and Aristophanes are another source I have drawn on heavily for the history of the fifth century. G. F. Hill's *Sources for Greek History between the Persian and Peloponnesian Wars*, 2nd ed. (Oxford, 1951) is a selection of contemporary source materials and of later historical writing, especially that of Diodorus. For inscriptions the reader may consult the Greek texts in R. Meiggs and D. Lewis's *A Selection of Greek Historical Inscriptions to the End of the Fifth Century B.C.* (Oxford, 1969) and K. Brodersen, W. Günther, and H. Schmitt's *Historische griechische Inschriften in Übersetzung*, volume I (Darmstadt, 1992). Other information was provided by the examination of coins, architecture, and sculptures, as well as by many archeological findings.

For more detailed information I refer the reader to the following works: E. Will, *Le Monde Grec et l'Orient: Le V siècle, 510–403* (Paris, 1972) and the *Cambridge Ancient History* volumes 3: 1, 2, and 3; 4; and 5 (1982, 1988, 1991, and 1992). The notes in H. Bengtson's *Griechische Geschichte* (most recent edition: Munich, 1977) give references to the political history—in the narrow sense of the word. *Die athenische Demokratic* the same title by J. Bleicken (Paderborn, 1985) is of similar help with respect to Athenian democracy. Original sources, except for recently discovered inscriptions, are listed in great detail in G. Busolt's *Griechische Geschichte*, 2nd edition (Gotha, 1893–1904).

For the history of Greek religion, I refer the reader to W. Burkert's *Griechische Religion der archaischen und klassischen Epoche* (Stuttgart, Berlin et al., 1977). L. B. Zaidman and P. Schmitt Pantel's *La Religion Grecque* (Paris, 1989) is a recent, brief, and interesting treatment of this subject.

On classical economics, M. Finley's *Ancient Economy* should be consulted; on literature, A. Lesky's *Geschichte der griechischen Literatur*, 3d ed. (Bern, 1971), and *Die tragische Dichtung der Hellenen* by the same author (3d ed., Göttingen, 1972); and on architecture, G. Gruben's *Die Tempel der Griechen* (Munich, 1976). On the history of Greek mentality, especially during the early period, G. Murray's *Das frühe Griechenland* (Munich, 1982) is useful, though the political aspects of the subject are not given proper weight. Another book on this topic has recently been published, P. Schmitt Pantel's *La Cité au banquet. Histoire des repas publics dans les cités grecques* (Paris, 1992).

In conclusion I should like to mention a few works of my own, not because they are of special importance but because they contain some background (and because they are not listed anywhere else). They are: *Die Entstehung des Politischen bei den Griechen* (Frankfurt, 1980), which examines themes that are continued, in collaboration with P. Veyne, in *Kannten die Griechen die Demokratie?* (Berlin, 1988); *Die Welt der Geschichte und die Provinz des Historikers* (Berlin, 1989); *Politik und Anmut* (Berlin, 1985); *Die politische Kunst der Tragödie* (Munich, 1988); and "Die Rolle des Krieges im klassischen Athen" in *Historische Zeitschrift* 251 (1990), reprinted in a collection of my essays entitled *Gehegte Gewalt* (Frankfurt, 1994).

My project was greatly aided by a year spent at the Wissenschaftskolleg in Berlin and by a grant from the Stiftung Volkswagenwerk, which allowed me to take a year's leave from my duties at Freistaat Bayern. I am very grateful for this support.

I should like to express special thanks to those who contributed to this book in person. The encouragement I received from Hans Jonas was invaluable, and the conversations with Luca Giuliani, Tonio Hölscher, and Paul Zanker were extremely helpful in thinking through various aspects of this book. (However, these individuals bear absolutely no responsibility for whatever mistakes, misinterpretations, or omissions may be found.) Suggestions made by Franziska Meier and Katja Schneider, as well as by Wolf Jobst Siedler, Sr. and Jr., helped improve the final text of the manuscript; Annette Hupfloher assisted me in finding appropriate illustrations; and, finally, Lilian Utz-Schimkus worked on the project with much dedication and patience.

Chronology of Events

ATHENS

462–461	Demotion of the Areopagus
461	Cimon ostracized
459 (?)	Expedition to Cyprus and Egypt
458	Aeschylus's *Oresteia*
457	*Zeugitae* become eligible for archonship
454	Treasury of Delian League transferred to Athens
451	Five-year peace treaty between Athens and Sparta
451–450	Pericles' law of citizenship proclaimed
450	Expedition to Cyprus. Death of Cimon
449 (?)	Peace of Callias
447	Battle of Coronea
	Construction of the Parthenon begun
446–445	Thirty-year peace treaty between Athens and Sparta signed
443	Thucydides ostracized
441–440	Revolt of Samos
437–436	Founding of Amphipolis
433	Treaty between Athens and Corcyra signed
432	Revolt of Potidaea
431	Beginning of the Peloponnesian War
430	Outbreak of the plague in Athens
	Fall of Potidaea
429	Death of Pericles
428	Revolt of Mytilene
427	First expedition to Sicily
425	Landing at Pylos; capture of Sphacteria
424	Brasidas's march to the north; Battle of Delium
421	Peace of Nicias
418	Battle of Mantinea
415	Departure for Sicily
413	Occupation of Decelea by the Spartans
411	Overthrow of democracy in Athens
410	Alcibiades' victory at Cyzicus
	Restoration of democracy in Athens
407	Alcibiades' return to Athens

Index